BEST Solution
Guaranteed •••

NCERT
EXEMPLAR
Problems - Solutions

Physics 11th

Author
Mukesh Kumar

ARIHANT PRAKASHAN (Series), MEERUT

卐 **Administrative & Production Offices**

Regd. Office

'Ramchhaya' 4577/15, Agarwal Road, Darya Ganj, New Delhi -110002
Tele: 011- 47630600, 43518550

卐 **Head Office**

Kalindi, TP Nagar, Meerut (UP) - 250002
Tel: 0121-7156203, 7156204

卐 **Sales & Support Offices**

Agra, Ahmedabad, Bengaluru, Bareilly, Chennai, Delhi, Guwahati, Hyderabad, Jaipur, Jhansi, Kolkata, Lucknow, Nagpur & Pune.

卐 **PRICE.** ₹225.00

卐 **PO No. :** TXT-59-T071684-6-26

Published by Arihant Publications (India) Ltd.

For further information about the books published by Arihant, log on to www.arihantbooks.com or e-mail at info@arihantbooks.com

Follow us on   

PREFACE

NCERT Exemplar Problems published by NCERT aim to provide students with a wide range of quality problems in various formats like Multiple Choice Questions, Multiple Choice Questions (More than One Option), Very Short Answer Questions, Short Answer Questions, and Long Answer Questions, catering to varying difficulty levels.

Exemplar Problems are crucial for both school and board exams, as well as competitive exams like engineering and medical entrances. Practicing Exemplar Problems equips students to tackle the challenging problems effectively.

This book, **NCERT Exemplar Problems-Solutions Physics 11th**, provides accurate and detailed solutions to all questions in the **NCERT Exemplar Physics** book. Each solution includes explanatory notes and authentic explanations to help students understand concepts and enhance their analytical abilities.

Key features

- **Thinking Process** Alongside solutions, this section guides students on how to approach problems, addressing potential areas of confusion.
- Also included **Concept Insight** understanding necessary concepts required to solve the questions.
- **Mistake Alert** ! Highlights such points where students may commit mistakes.
- **Notes** Highlight special points which can be of added value.

I hope this book proves to be a valuable resource, aiding students in their academic journey and leading them to great success.

Author

CONTENTS

Chapter 01

Units and Measurements

Multiple Choice Questions (MCQs)

Q.1 The number of significant figures in 0.06900 is

(a) 5 (b) 4 (c) 2 (d) 3

Thinking Process If the number is less than 1, the zero(s) on the right of decimal point and before the first non-zero digit are not significant.

Ans. ***(b)*** In $\underline{0}.\underline{0}6900$, the underlined zeros are not significant. Hence, number of significant figures are four (6900).

Q.2 The sum of the numbers 436.32, 227.2 and 0.301 in appropriate significant figures is

(a) 663.821 (b) 664

(c) 663.8 (d) 663.82

Ans. ***(c)*** The sum of the numbers can be calculated as 663.821 arithmetically. The number with least decimal places is 227.2 is correct to only one decimal place. The final result should, therefore be rounded off to one decimal place *i.e.,* 663.8.

Mistake Alert ! *In calculating the sum, we should not confuse with the number of decimal places and significant figures. The result should retain the least number of decimal places.*

Q.3 The mass and volume of a body are 4.237 g and 2.5 cm^3, respectively. The density of the material of the body in correct significant figures is

(a) 1.6048 g cm^{-3} (b) 1.69 g cm^{-3}

(c) 1.7 g cm^{-3} (d) 1.695 g cm^{-3}

Thinking Process In multiplication or division, the final result should retain as many significant figures as are there in the original number with the least significant figures.

Ans. ***(c)*** Density should be reported to two significant figures, because the final result should retain least significant figures among operated values.

$$\text{Density} = \frac{4.237\text{g}}{2.5\ \text{cm}^3} = 1.6948$$

As rounding off the number, we get density = 1.7 g cm^{-3}

Q.4 The numbers 2.745 and 2.735 on rounding off to 3 significant figures will give

(a) 2.75 and 2.74 (b) 2.74 and 2.73
(c) 2.75 and 2.73 (d) 2.74 and 2.74

Ans. ***(d)*** Rounding off 2.745 to 3 significant figures it would be 2.74. Rounding off 2.735 to 3 significant figures it would be 2.74.

Note If a digit to be dropped is 5 followed by zero, the preceding digit remains unchanged if it is even and is increased by one if it is odd.

Q.5 The length and breadth of a rectangular sheet are 16.2 cm and 10.1 cm, respectively. The area of the sheet in appropriate significant figures and error is

(a) $164 \pm 3\ \text{cm}^2$ (b) $163.62 \pm 2.6\ \text{cm}^2$
(c) $163.6 \pm 2.6\ \text{cm}^2$ (d) $163.62 \pm 3\ \text{cm}^2$

Thinking Process If Δx is error in a physical quantity, then relative error is calculated as $\frac{\Delta x}{x}$.

Ans. ***(a)*** Given, Length $l = (16.2 \pm 0.1)$ cm

Breadth $b = (10.1 \pm 0.1)$ cm

Area of the sheet $A = l \times b$

$$= (16.2\ \text{cm}) \times (10.1\ \text{cm}) = 163.62\ \text{cm}^2$$

Rounding off to three significant digits, area $A = 164\ \text{cm}^2$

Now, $$\frac{\Delta A}{A} = \frac{\Delta l}{l} + \frac{\Delta b}{b} = \frac{0.1}{16.2} + \frac{0.1}{10.1}$$

$$= \frac{1.01 + 1.62}{16.2 \times 10.1} = \frac{2.63}{163.62}$$

$$\Rightarrow \quad \Delta A = A \times \frac{2.63}{163.62} = 163.62 \times \frac{2.63}{163.62} = 2.63\ \text{cm}^2$$

$$\Delta A = 3\ \text{cm}^2 \quad \text{[By rounding off to one significant figure]}$$

$$\therefore \quad \text{Area, } A = A \pm \Delta A = (164 \pm 3)\ \text{cm}^2.$$

Q.6 Which of the following pairs of physical quantities does not have same dimensional formula?

(a) Work and torque
(b) Angular momentum and Planck's constant
(c) Tension and surface tension
(d) Impulse and linear momentum

Ans. ***(c)*** (a) Work = force × distance $= [\text{MLT}^{-2}][\text{L}] = [\text{ML}^2\text{T}^{-2}]$

Torque = force × distance $= [\text{MLT}^{-2}][\text{L}] = [\text{ML}^2\text{T}^{-2}]$

(b) Angular momentum $= mvr = [\text{M}][\text{LT}^{-1}][\text{L}] = [\text{ML}^2\text{T}^{-1}]$

Planck's constant $$\frac{\text{Energy}}{\text{Frequency}} = \frac{E}{\nu} = \frac{[\text{ML}^2\text{T}^{-2}]}{[\text{T}^{-1}]} = [\text{ML}^2\text{T}^{-1}]$$

(c) Tension = Force = $ma = [M][LT^{-2}] = [MLT^{-2}]$

Surface tension = $\dfrac{\text{Force}}{\text{Length}} = \dfrac{[MLT^{-2}]}{[L]} = [ML^0T^{-2}]$

(d) Impulse = Force × Time = $[MLT^{-2}][T] = [MLT^{-1}]$

Momentum = Mass × Velocity = $[M][LT^{-1}] = [MLT^{-1}]$

Mistake Alert ! *One should not be confused with the similar term tension in both the physical quantities-surface tension and tension. Dimensional formulae for both of them is not the same.*

Q.7 Measure of two quantities along with the precision of respective measuring instrument is

$A = 2.5\ \text{ms}^{-1} \pm 0.5\ \text{ms}^{-1}$, $B = 0.10\ \text{s} \pm 0.01\ \text{s}$. The value of AB will be

(a) (0.25 ± 0.08) m
(b) (0.25 ± 0.5) m
(c) (0.25 ± 0.05) m
(d) (0.25 ± 0.135) m

Ans. ***(a)*** Given, $A = 2.5\ \text{ms}^{-1} \pm 0.5\ \text{ms}^{-1}$, $B = 0.10\ \text{s} \pm 0.01\ \text{s}$

$$x = AB = (2.5)(0.10) = 0.25\ \text{m}$$

$$\frac{\Delta x}{x} = \frac{\Delta A}{A} + \frac{\Delta B}{B} = \frac{0.5}{2.5} + \frac{0.01}{0.10} = \frac{0.05 + 0.025}{0.25} = \frac{0.075}{0.25} = 0.3$$

$$\Delta x = 0.3 \times 0.25 = 0.075\ \text{m} = 0.08\ \text{m},$$

rounded off to two significant figures, The value of AB is (0.25 ± 0.08) m.

Q.8 You measure two quantities as $A = 1.0\ \text{m} \pm 0.2\ \text{m}$, $B = 2.0\ \text{m} \pm 0.2\ \text{m}$. We should report correct value for $\sqrt{AB}$ as

(a) 1.4 m ± 0.4 m
(b) 1.41 m ± 0.15 m
(c) 1.4 m ± 0.3 m
(d) 1.4 m ± 0.2 m

Ans. ***(d)*** Given, $A = 1.0\ \text{m} \pm 0.2\ \text{m}$, $B = 2.0\ \text{m} \pm 0.2\ \text{m}$

Let, $Y = \sqrt{AB} = \sqrt{(1.0)(2.0)} = 1.414\ \text{m}$

Rounding off to two significant digit $Y = 1.4$ m

$$\frac{\Delta Y}{Y} = \frac{1}{2}\left[\frac{\Delta A}{A} + \frac{\Delta B}{B}\right] = \frac{1}{2}\left[\frac{0.2}{1.0} + \frac{0.2}{2.0}\right] = \frac{0.6}{2 \times 2.0}$$

$$\Rightarrow \quad \Delta Y = \frac{0.6Y}{2 \times 2.0} = \frac{0.6 \times 1.4}{2 \times 2.0} = 0.21$$

Rounding off to one significant digit $\Delta Y = 0.2$ m

[As error is given in one significant figure]

Thus, correct value for $\sqrt{AB} = Y \pm \Delta Y = 1.4 \pm 0.2$m

Q.9 Which of the following measurement is most precise?

(a) 5.00 mm
(b) 5.00 cm
(c) 5.00 m
(d) 5.00 km

Ans. ***(a)*** All given measurements are correct upto two decimal places. As here 5.00 mm has the smallest unit and the error in 5.00 mm is least (commonly taken as 0.01 mm if not specified), hence, 5.00 mm is most precise.

Mistake Alert ! *In solving these type of questions, we should be careful about the units although their magnitude is same.*

Q.10 The mean length of an object is 5 cm. Which of the following measurements is most accurate?

(a) 4.9 cm (b) 4.805 cm (c) 5.25 cm (d) 5.4 cm

Ans. ***(a)*** Given length $l = 5$ cm

Now, checking the errors with each options one by one, we get

$$\Delta l_1 = 5 - 4.9 = 0.1 \text{ cm}$$
$$\Delta l_2 = 5 - 4.805 = 0.195 \text{ cm}$$
$$\Delta l_3 = 5.25 - 5 = 0.25 \text{ cm}$$
$$\Delta l_4 = 5.4 - 5 = 0.4 \text{ cm}$$

Error Δl_1 is least.

Hence, 4.9 cm is most accurate, because it is nearest to the measured value.

Q.11 Young's modulus of steel is 1.9×10^{11} N / m^2. When expressed in CGS units of dyne/cm^2, it will be equal to

($1\text{N} = 10^5$ dyne, $1 \text{ m}^2 = 10^4 \text{ cm}^2$)

(a) 1.9×10^{10} (b) 1.9×10^{11} (c) 1.9×10^{12} (d) 1.9×10^{13}

Ans. ***(c)*** Given, Young's modulus $Y = 1.9 \times 10^{11}$ N /m^2

$$1\text{N} = 10^5 \text{ dyne}$$

and $$1\text{m} = 100 \text{ cm}$$

$\therefore$ $$Y = 1.9 \times 10^{11} \left(\frac{10^5 \text{ dyne}}{10^4 \text{ cm}^2}\right) \quad [\because 1\text{m} = 100 \text{ cm}]$$

$$= 1.9 \times 10^{16-4} \text{ dyne/cm}^2$$

$$Y = 1.9 \times 10^{12} \text{ dyne/cm}^2$$

Mistake Alert ! *While we are going through units conversion, we should keep in mind that the proper relation between units are mentioned.*

Q.12 If momentum (p), area (A) and time (T) are taken to be fundamental quantities, then energy has the dimensional formula

(a) $[\text{pA}^{-1}\text{T}^1]$ (b) $[\text{p}^2\text{AT}]$ (c) $[\text{p A}^{-1/2}\text{T}]$ (d) $[\text{pA}^{1/2} \text{ T}^{-1}]$

Ans. ***(d)*** Given, fundamental quantities are momentum (p), area (A) and time (T).

We can write energy E as

$$E \propto p^a A^b T^c$$

$$E = kp^a A^b T^c \quad \dots\text{(i)}$$

where k is dimensionless constant of proportionality.

Now, equating dimensions on both sides of Eq. (i) we get

Dimensions of $E = [E] = [\text{ML}^2\text{T}^{-2}]$ and $[p] = [\text{MLT}^{-1}]$

$$[\text{A}] = [\text{L}^2]$$
$$[\text{T}] = [\text{T}]$$
$$[\text{E}] = [\text{K}][\text{p}]^a[\text{A}]^b[\text{T}]^c$$

Putting all the dimensions, we get

$$[ML^2T^{-2}] = K[MLT^{-1}]^a[L^2]^b[T]^c$$

$$[ML^2T^{-2}] = K[M]^a[L]^{a+2b}[T]^{-a+c}$$

By principle of homogeneity of dimensions,

$$a = 1 \quad \text{...(ii)}$$

$$a + 2b = 2 \quad \text{(iii)}$$

$$-a + c = -2 \quad \text{(iv)}$$

$$\Rightarrow \quad 2b + 1 = 2 \Rightarrow b = \frac{1}{2}$$

Now solving Eqs. (ii), (iii) and (iv), we get

$$-a + c = -2$$

$$\Rightarrow \quad -1 + c = -2$$

$$\Rightarrow \quad c = -1$$

Hence, $E = KpA^{\frac{1}{2}}T^{-1}$

$$E = [pA^{1/2}T^{-1}]$$

Multiple Choice Questions (More Than One Options)

Q.13 On the basis of dimensions, decide which of the following relations for the displacement of a particle undergoing simple harmonic motion is not correct?

(a) $y = a\sin 2\pi\, t/T$ (b) $y = a\sin vt$

(c) $y = \frac{a}{T}\sin\left(\frac{t}{a}\right)$ (d) $y = a\sqrt{2}\left(\sin\frac{2\pi t}{T} - \cos\frac{2\pi t}{T}\right)$

Thinking Process We know that angle is dimensionless. Here, a is displacement and y is also displacement, hence they are having same dimensions.

Ans. ***(b, c)*** The argument of trigonometric functions (sin, cos etc) should be dimensionless. Y is displacement and according to the principle of homogeneity of dimensions LHS and RHS should be same. Looking into option (a) we get,

$$[y] = [L], [a] = [L]$$

$$\left[\frac{2\pi t}{T}\right] = \frac{[T]}{[T]} = [T^0]$$

For option (b), $[vt] = [v][t] = [LT^{-1}][T] = [L]$

For option (c), $\left[\frac{a}{T}\right] = \frac{[a]}{[T]} = \frac{[L]}{[T]} = [LT^{-1}]$

$$\left[\frac{t}{a}\right] = [L^{-1}T]$$

$$\therefore \quad [\text{LHS}] \neq [\text{RHS}]$$

Hence, (c) is not the correct option.

In (b), the trigonometric function should be dimensionless, but it is not.

So, option (b) is also not correct.

Q.14 If P, Q, R are physical quantities, having different dimensions, which of the following combinations can never be a meaningful quantity?

(a) $(P-Q)/R$ (b) $PQ-R$ (c) PQ/R (d) $(PR-Q^2)/R$
(e) $(R+Q)/P$

Thinking Process We should keep in mind that two physical quantities can be added or subtracted only if they have the same dimensions.

Ans. ***(a, e)*** In this question, it is given that P, Q and R are having different dimensions, hence they cannot be added or subtracted, so we can say that (a) and (e) are not meaningful. We cannot comment about the dimension of product of these quantities, hence (b), (c) and (d) may be meaningful.

Note Since, it is given that all the quantities are dimensionally different, so we can not add or subtract them individually but their products may be added or subtracted.

Q.15 Photon is quantum of radiation with energy $E = h\nu$, where ν is frequency and h is Planck's constant. The dimensions of h are the same as that of

(a) linear impulse (b) angular impulse
(c) linear momentum (d) angular momentum

Ans. ***(b, d)*** We know that energy of radiation, $E = h\nu$

$$[h] = \frac{[E]}{[\nu]} = \frac{[ML^2T^{-2}]}{[T^{-1}]} = [ML^2T^{-1}]$$

Dimension of linear impulse = Dimension of momentum = $[MLT^{-1}]$

As we know that linear impulse $J = \Delta P$

$\Rightarrow$ Angular impulse = $\tau dt = \Delta L$ = Change in angular momentum

Hence, dimension of angular impulse

= Dimension of angular momentum

$= [ML^2T^{-1}]$.

This is similar to the dimension of Planck's constant h.

Q. 16 If Planck's constant (h) and speed of light in vacuum (c) are taken as two fundamental quantities, which one of the following can, in addition, be taken to express length, mass and time in terms of the three chosen fundamental quantities?

(a) Mass of electron (m_e) (b) Universal gravitational constant (G)
(c) Charge of electron (e) (d) Mass of proton (m_p)

Ans. ***(a, b, d)*** We know that dimension of $h = [h] = [ML^2T^{-1}]$

$$[c] = [LT^{-1}],\ [m_e] = M$$

$$[G] = [M^{-1}L^3T^{-2}]$$

$$[e] = [AT],\ [m_p] = [M]$$

$$\left[\frac{hc}{G}\right] = \frac{[ML^2T^{-1}][LT^{-1}]}{[M^{-1}L^3T^{-2}]} = [M^2]$$

$$M = \sqrt{\frac{hc}{G}}$$

Similarly, $\dfrac{h}{c} = \dfrac{[ML^2 T^{-1}]}{[LT^{-1}]} = [ML]$

Hence $L = \dfrac{h}{cM} = \dfrac{h}{c}\sqrt{\dfrac{G}{hc}} = \dfrac{\sqrt{Gh}}{c^{3/2}}$

As we know $c = LT^{-1}$

$\Rightarrow$ $[T] = \dfrac{[L]}{[C]} = \dfrac{\sqrt{Gh}}{c^{3/2}c} = \dfrac{\sqrt{Gh}}{c^{5/2}}$

Hence, (a), (b) or (d) any can be used to express L, M and T in terms of three chosen fundamental quantities

Alternate Method

Energy of a photon $E = h\nu$

$$[h] = \frac{[ML^2T^{-2}]}{[T^{-1}]} = [ML^2T^{-1}]$$

$$[c] = [LT^{-1}]$$

$$[G] = [M^{-1}L^3T^{-2}]$$

For mass, let $m = c^a h^b G^c$

Where, a, b and c are exponents of c, h and G respectively,

$$[ML^0T^0] = [LT^{-1}]^a [ML^2T^{-1}]^b [M^{-1}L^3T^{-2}]^c$$

Using the principle of homogeneity of dimensions

$$b - c = 1 \quad \ldots\text{(i)}$$

$$a + 2b + 3c = 0 \quad \ldots\text{(ii)}$$

$$-a - b - 2c = 0 \quad \ldots\text{(iii)}$$

Solving, we get a, b and c as $\dfrac{1}{2}, \dfrac{1}{2}, \dfrac{-1}{2}$ respectively

Hence, $m = c^{1/2}\, h^{1/2}\, G^{\frac{-1}{2}}$

$$m = \sqrt{\frac{ch}{G}}$$

Similarly, for length, $L = \dfrac{\sqrt{hG}}{c^{3/2}}$ and for time, $T = \dfrac{\sqrt{hG}}{c^{5/2}}$

Mass can be expressed by m_e and m_p

Q.17 Which of the following ratios express pressure?

(a) Force/Area

(b) Energy/Volume

(c) Energy/Area

(d) Force/Volume

Thinking Process While solving this type of questions, we should first write an expression and try to express it in terms of quantities given in the option.

Ans. ***(a, b)*** We know that pressure $= \dfrac{\text{Force}}{\text{Area}}$

$$\text{Pressure} = \frac{\text{Force} \times \text{Distance}}{\text{Area} \times \text{Distance}} = \frac{\text{Work}}{\text{Volume}} = \frac{\text{Energy}}{\text{Volume}}$$

Mistake Alert ! *Here, we should keep it in mind that above values are not exactly equal but are equivalent with respect to their units.*

Or Dimensions of pressure $= [ML^{-1}T^{-2}]$

(a) Dimensions of $\dfrac{\text{Force}}{\text{Area}} = \left[\dfrac{MLT^{-2}}{L^2}\right] = [ML^{-1}T^{-2}]$

(b) Dimensions of $\dfrac{\text{Energy}}{\text{Volume}} = \left[\dfrac{ML^2T^{-2}}{L^3}\right] = [ML^{-1}T^{-2}]$

(c) Dimensions of $\dfrac{\text{Energy}}{\text{Area}} = \left[\dfrac{ML^2T^{-2}}{L^2}\right] = [ML^0T^{-2}]$

(d) Dimensions of $\dfrac{\text{Force}}{\text{Volume}} = \left[\dfrac{MLT^{-2}}{L^3}\right] = [ML^{-2}T^{-2}]$

Q.18 Which of the following are not a unit of time?

(a) Second
(b) Parsec
(c) Year
(d) Light year

Ans. ***(b, d)*** We know that 1 light year $= 9.46 \times 10^{11}$ m

= distance that light travels in 1 year with speed 3×10^8 m/s.

1 parsec $= 3.08 \times 10^{16}$ m = 3.26 light year

= Distance at which average radius of earth's orbit subtends an angle of 1 parsecond

Hence, only second and year represent time.

Very Short Answer Type Questions

Q.19 Why do we have different units for the same physical quantity?

Ans. The value of any given physical quantity may vary over a wide range depending upon its size. Therefore, different units of same physical quantity are required.

e.g. The length of a pen can be easily measured in cm, the height of a tree can be measured in metres, the distance between two cities can be measured in kilometres and distance between two heavenly bodies can be measured in light year.

Q.20 The radius of atom is of the order of 1 Å and radius of nucleus is of the order of fermi. How many magnitudes higher is the volume of atom as compared to the volume of nucleus?

Ans. Radius of atom $R_A \approx 1\text{Å} = 10^{-10}$ m

Radius of nucleus, $R_N \approx 1\,\text{fermi} = 10^{-15}$ m

Volume of atom $= V_A = \dfrac{4}{3}\pi R_A^3$

Volume of nucleus $V_N = \dfrac{4}{3}\pi R_N^3$

$$\frac{V_A}{V_N} = \frac{\frac{4}{3}\pi R_A^3}{\frac{4}{3}\pi R_N^3} = \left(\frac{R_A}{R_N}\right)^3 = \left(\frac{10^{-10}}{10^{-15}}\right)^3 = 10^{15}$$

Note In these type of questions, always convert the values in same unit.

Q.21 Name the device used for measuring the mass of atoms and molecules.

Ans. A mass spectrograph is used for measuring the mass of atoms and molecules.

Q.22 Express unified atomic mass unit in kg.

Ans. One atomic mass unit is defined as the mass of $\frac{1}{12}^{th}$ of a $_6C^{12}$ atom.

Mass of one mole of $_6C^{12}$ atom = 12 g

Number of atoms in one mole = Avogadro's number

$$= 6.023 \times 10^{23}$$

$\therefore$ Mass of one $_6C^{12}$ atom $= \frac{12}{6.023 \times 10^{23}}$ g

Now $1 \text{ amu} = \frac{1}{12} \times \text{mass of one } _6C^{12} \text{ atom}$

$$\therefore \quad 1 \text{ amu} = \left(\frac{1}{12} \times \frac{12}{6.023 \times 10^{23}}\right) \text{g} = 1.67 \times 10^{-24} \text{ g}$$

$$= 1.67 \times 10^{-27} \text{ kg} \qquad [\because 1 \text{ g} = 10^{-3} \text{ kg}]$$

Q.23 A function $f(\theta)$ is defined as $f(\theta) = 1 - \theta + \frac{\theta^2}{2!} - \frac{\theta^3}{3!} + \frac{\theta^4}{4!} + \ldots$

Why is it necessary for $f(\theta)$ to be a dimensionless quantity?

Ans. Since, the 1st term in the RHS is a constant and all the other terms are summed with it so all of the terms should be dimensionless. By principle of homogeneity as RHS is dimensionless, therefore, LHS should also be dimensionless.

Q.24 Why length, mass and time are chosen as base quantities in mechanics?

Ans. Length, mass and time are chosen as base quantities in mechanics because

(i) Length, mass and time cannot be derived from one another, that is these quantities are independent.

(ii) All other quantities in mechanics can be expressed in terms of length, mass and time.

Short Answer Type Questions

Q.25 (a) The earth-moon distance is about 60 earth radius. What will be the diameter of the earth (approximately in degrees) as seen from the moon?

(b) Moon is seen to be of $(1/2)^\circ$ diameter from the earth. What must be the relative size compared to the earth?

(c) From parallax measurement, the sun is found to be at a distance of about 400 times the earth-moon distance. Estimate the ratio of sun-earth diameters.

Thinking Process To solve this question, we have to treat radius of earth as an arc as seen from the moon.

Ans. (a) Angle subtended at distance r due to an arc of length l is

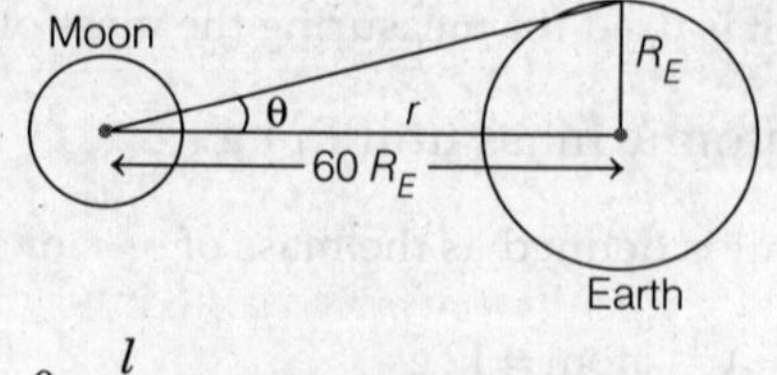

$$\theta = \frac{l}{r}$$

Given, $l = R_E;\ r = 60\,R_E$

$$\theta = \frac{R_E}{60\,R_E} = \frac{1}{60}\,\text{rad} = \frac{1}{60} \times \frac{180}{\pi}\ \text{degree}$$

$$= \frac{3}{\pi} \approx 1°$$

Hence, angle subtended by diameter of the earth = $2\theta = 2°$.

(b) Given that moon is seen as $\left(\frac{1}{2}\right)°$ diameter and earth is seen as 2° diameter.

Hence, $$\frac{\text{Diameter of earth}}{\text{Diameter of moon}} = \frac{(2/\pi)\ \text{rad}}{\left(\frac{1}{2\pi}\right)\ \text{rad}} = 4$$

Therefore, the size of the moon is approximately $\frac{1}{4}$th the size of the earth.

(c) From parallax measurement given that sun is at a distance of about 400 times the earth-moon distance, hence, $\frac{r_{sun}}{r_{moon}} = 400$

[Suppose, here r stands for distance and D for diameter]

sun and moon both appear to be of the same angular diameter as seen from the earth.

$$\therefore \quad \frac{D_{sun}}{r_{sun}} = \frac{D_{moon}}{r_{moon}}$$

$$\therefore \quad \frac{D_{sun}}{D_{moon}} = 400$$

But $$\frac{D_{earth}}{D_{moon}} = 4$$

$$\therefore \quad \frac{D_{sun}}{D_{earth}} = 100$$

Q.26 Which of the following time measuring devices is most precise?

(a) A wall clock (b) A stop watch

(c) A digital watch (d) An atomic clock

Given reason for your answer.

Ans. The least counts of a wall clock, a stop watch, a digital watch and an atomic clock are 1 s, 10^{-1} s, 10^{-2} s and 10^{-13} s, respectively. So, an atomic clock is the most precise.

Q.27 **The distance of a galaxy is of the order of 10^{25} m. Calculate the order of magnitude of time taken by light to reach us from the galaxy.**

Ans. Given, distance of the galaxy = 10^{25} m

Speed of light = 3×10^8 m/s

Hence, time taken by light to reach us from galaxy is,

$$t = \frac{\text{Distance}}{\text{Speed}} = \frac{10^{25}}{3 \times 10^8} \approx \frac{1}{3} \times 10^{17} = \frac{10}{3} \times 10^{16} = 3.33 \times 10^{16} \text{ s}$$

Q.28 **The vernier scale of a travelling microscope has 50 divisions which coincide with 49 main scale divisions. If each main scale division is 0.5 mm, calculate the minimum inaccuracy in the measurement of distance.**

Thinking Process Inaccuracy will be measured by difference of 1MSD and 1VSD, where MSD = (main scale division) and VSD = (vernier scale division).

Ans. By question, it is given that $50\,\text{VSD} = 49\,\text{MSD}$

$$\therefore \quad 1\,\text{VSD} = \frac{49}{50}\,\text{MSD}$$

$$\text{Minimum inaccuracy} = 1\,\text{MSD} - 1\,\text{VSD}$$

$$= 1\,\text{MSD} - \frac{49}{50}\,\text{MSD} = \frac{1}{50}\,\text{MSD}$$

Given, $1\,\text{MSD} = 0.5\text{ mm}$

Hence, minimum inaccuracy $= \frac{1}{50} \times 0.5\text{ mm} = \frac{1}{100} = 0.01\text{ mm}$

Q.29 **During a total solar eclipse the moon almost entirely covers the sphere of the sun. Write the relation between the distances and sizes of the sun and moon.**

Thinking Process Solid angle $= \dfrac{\text{Area of patch of spherical surface}}{(\text{Radius})^2}$

Ans. Consider the diagram given below

R_{me} = Distance of moon from earth

R_{se} = Distance of sun from earth

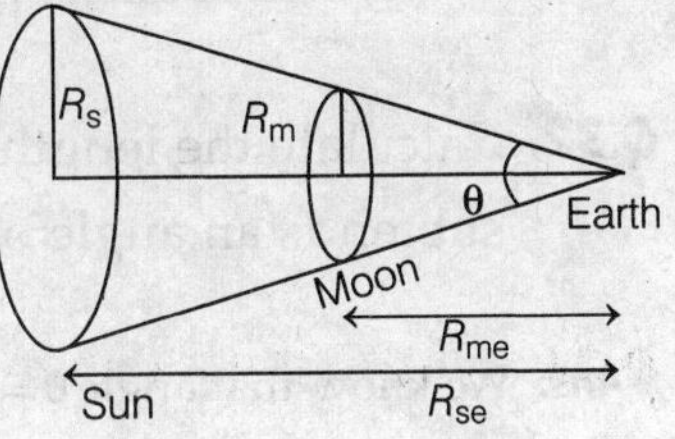

Let angle made by sun and moon is θ. So, we can write

$$\theta = \frac{A_{sun}}{R_{se}^2} = \frac{A_{moon}}{R_{me}^2}$$

Here, A_{sun} = Area of the sun

A_{moon} = Area of the moon

$$\Rightarrow \quad \theta = \frac{\pi R_s^2}{R_{se}^2} = \frac{\pi R_m^2}{R_{me}^2}$$

$$\Rightarrow \quad \left(\frac{R_s}{R_{se}}\right)^2 = \left(\frac{R_m}{R_{me}}\right)^2$$

$$\Rightarrow \quad \frac{R_s}{R_{se}} = \frac{R_m}{R_{me}}$$

$$\Rightarrow \quad \frac{R_s}{R_m} = \frac{R_{se}}{R_{me}}$$

[Here, radius of sun and moon represents their sizes respectively]

Q.30 If the unit of force is 100 N, unit of length is 10 m and unit of time is 100 s, what is the unit of mass in this system of units?

Thinking Process First write dimensions of each quantity and then relate them.

Ans. Dimension of force $(F) = [MLT^{-2}] = 100$ N

$$\text{Length } (L) = [L] = 10 \text{ m}$$

$$\text{Time } (t) = [T] = 100 \text{ s}$$

$$M = ?$$

$$[M] = \left[\frac{FT^2}{L}\right] = \frac{100 \times 100 \times 100}{10} = 10^5 \text{ kg.}$$

Q.31 Give an example of

(a) a physical quantity which has a unit but no dimensions

(b) a physical quantity which has neither unit nor dimensions

(c) a constant which has a unit

(d) a constant which has no unit

Ans. (a) Plane angle $\theta = \frac{L}{r}$ radian

its unit is radian but has no dimensions [other e.g. mole]

(b) Strain $= \frac{\Delta L}{L} = \frac{\text{Change in length}}{\text{length}}$

It has neither unit nor dimensions [other e.g. specific gravity]

(c) Gravitational constant $(G) = 6.67 \times 10^{-11} \text{N - m}^2/\text{kg}^2$

[other e.g. acceleration due to gravity]

(d) Reynold's number is a constant which has no unit.

[other e.g. Avogadro number]

Q.32 Calculate the length of the arc of a circle of radius 31.0 cm which subtends an angle of $\frac{\pi}{6}$ at the centre.

Ans. We know that angle $\theta = \frac{l}{r}$ radian

$$\frac{\pi}{6} = \frac{l}{31} \text{cm}$$

Hence,

$$\text{length} = l = 31 \times \frac{\pi}{6} \text{ cm}$$

$$= \frac{31 \times 3.14}{6} \text{ cm} = 16.22 \text{ cm}$$

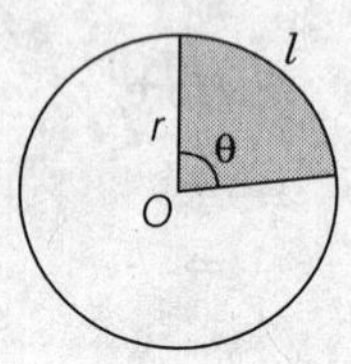

Rounding off to three significant figures it would be 16.2 cm.

Q.33 Calculate the solid angle subtended by the periphery of an area of 1cm^2 at a point situated symmetrically at a distance of 5 cm from the area.

Ans. Given, area $= 1 \text{cm}^2$, $r = 5 \text{cm}$

We know that, solid angle $\Omega = \dfrac{\text{Area of patch of spherical surface}}{(\text{Distance})^2}$

$$= \frac{1 \text{ cm}^2}{(5 \text{ cm})^2} = \frac{1}{25} = 4 \times 10^{-2} \text{ steradian}$$

Mistake Alert! *We should not confuse, solid angle with plane angle,* $\theta = \dfrac{l}{r}$ *radian.*

Q.34 The displacement of a progressive wave is represented by $y = A \sin(\omega t - kx)$, where x is distance and t is time. Write the dimensional formula of (i) ω and (ii) k.

Thinking Process In solving these type of questions, we should apply principle of homogeneity of dimensions.

Ans. Now, by the principle of homogeneity, *i.e.*, dimensions of LHS and RHS should be equal, hence $[\text{LHS}] = [\text{RHS}] \Rightarrow [\text{L}] = [A] = \text{L}$

As $\omega t - kx$ should be dimensionless, $\omega t = [\text{M}^0\text{L}^0\text{T}^0]$

$\Rightarrow$ $\omega = [\text{T}^{-1}]$ and $kx = [\text{M}^0\text{L}^0\text{T}^0] \Rightarrow K = [\text{L}^{-1}]$

Q.35 Time for 20 oscillations of a pendulum is measured as $t_1 = 39.6$ s; $t_2 = 39.9$ s and $t_3 = 39.5$ s. What is the precision in the measurements? What is the accuracy of the measurement?

Thinking Process We will apply formula for mean value, absolute error as well as mean absolute error.

Ans. Given, $t_1 = 39.6 \text{ s}, t_2 = 39.9 \text{ s}$ and $t_3 = 39.5 \text{ s}$

Least count of measuring instrument = 0.1 s

[As measurements have only one decimal place]

Precision in the measurement = Least count of the measuring instrument = 0.1 s

Mean value of time for 20 oscillations is given by

$$t = \frac{t_1 + t_2 + t_3}{3} = \frac{39.6 + 39.9 + 39.5}{3}$$

$$= \frac{119.0}{3} = 39.66 = 39.7 \text{ sec} \quad \text{[After rounding off to one decimal place]}$$

Absolute errors in the measurements

$$\Delta t_1 = t - t_1 = 39.7 - 39.6 = 0.1 \text{ s}$$

$$\Delta t_2 = t - t_2 = 39.7 - 39.9 = -0.2 \text{ s}$$

$$\Delta t_3 = t - t_3 = 39.7 - 39.5 = 0.2 \text{ s}$$

$$\text{Mean absolute error} = \frac{|\Delta t_1| + |\Delta t_2| + |\Delta t_3|}{3} = \frac{0.1 + 0.2 + 0.2}{3}$$

$$= \frac{0.5}{3} = 0.17 \approx 0.2 \quad \text{[rounding off upto one decimal place]}$$

$\therefore$ Accuracy of measurement $= \pm 0.2$ s

Long Answer Type Questions

Q.36 A new system of units is proposed in which unit of mass is α kg, unit of length β m and unit of time γ s. How much will 5J measure in this new system?

Thinking Process For solving this question, we will apply the formula for a system of unit, nu = constant.

Ans. We know that dimension of energy $=[ML^2T^{-2}]$

Let M_1, L_1, T_1 and M_2, L_2, T_2 are units of mass, length and time in given two systems.

$$\therefore \quad M_1 = 1\,\text{kg}, L_1 = 1\,\text{m}, T_1 = 1\,\text{s}$$

$$M_2 = \alpha\,\text{kg}, L_2 = \beta\,\text{m}, T_2 = \gamma\,\text{s}$$

The dimensions of a physical quantity remains the same, whatever be the system of units of its measurement *i.e.*, $n_1 u_1 = n_2 u_2$

$$\Rightarrow \quad n_2 = n_1 \frac{u_1}{u_2} = n_1 \frac{[M_1 L_1^2 T_1^{-2}]}{[M_2 L_2^2 T_2^{-2}]} = 5\left[\frac{M_1}{M_2}\right] \times \left[\frac{L_1}{L_2}\right]^2 \times \left[\frac{T_1}{T_2}\right]^{-2}$$

$$= 5\left[\frac{1}{\alpha}\right] \times \left[\frac{1}{\beta}\right]^2 \times \left[\frac{1}{\gamma}\right]^{-2} = 5 \times \frac{1}{\alpha} \times \frac{1}{\beta^2} \times \frac{1}{\gamma^{-2}}$$

$$n_2 = \frac{5\gamma^2}{\alpha\beta^2}$$

Thus, new unit of energy will be $\frac{\gamma^2}{\alpha\beta^2}$.

Q.37 The volume of a liquid flowing out per second of a pipe of length l and radius r is written by a student as $V = \frac{\pi}{8} \frac{pr^4}{\eta l}$ where p is the pressure difference between the two ends of the pipe and η is coefficent of viscosity of the liquid having dimensional formula $[ML^{-1}T^{-1}]$. Check whether the equation is dimensionally correct.

Thinking Process If dimensions of LHS of an equation is equal to dimensions of RHS, then equation is said to be dimensionally correct.

Ans. The volume of a liquid flowing out per second of a pipe is given by $V = \frac{\pi}{8} \frac{pr^4}{\eta l}$

$$\text{Dimension of LHS i.e. } V = \frac{\text{Dimension of volume}}{\text{Dimension of time}} = \frac{[L^3]}{[T]} = [L^3T^{-1}]$$

[$\because$ V is the volume of liquid flowing out per second]

Now, Dimension of $p = [ML^{-1}T^{-2}]$

Dimension of $\eta = [ML^{-1}T^{-1}]$

Dimension of $l = [L]$

Dimension of $r = [L]$

$$\text{Now, Dimension of RHS} = \frac{[ML^{-1}T^{-2}][L^4]}{[ML^{-1}T^{-1}][L]} = [L^3T^{-1}]$$

As dimensions of LHS is equal to the dimensions of RHS.

Therefore, equation is correct dimensionally.

Q.38 A physical quantity X is related to four measurable quantities a, b, c and d as follows $X = a^2 b^3 c^{5/2} d^{-2}$. The percentage error in the measurement of a, b, c and d are 1%, 2%, 3% and 4%, respectively. What is the percentage error in quantity X? If the value of X calculated on the basis of the above relation is 2.763, to what value should you round off the result?

Thinking Process We will apply the formula for percentage error in quantity x, as $\frac{\Delta x}{x} \times 100$.

Ans. Given, physical quantity is $X = a^2 b^3 c^{5/2} d^{-2}$

Maximum percentage error in X is

$$\frac{\Delta X}{X} \times 100 = \pm\left[2\left(\frac{\Delta a}{a} \times 100\right) + 3\left(\frac{\Delta b}{b} \times 100\right) + \frac{5}{2}\left(\frac{\Delta c}{c} \times 100\right) + 2\left(\frac{\Delta d}{d} \times 100\right)\right]$$

$$= \pm\left[2(1) + 3(2) + \frac{5}{2}(3) + 2(4)\right]\%$$

$$= \pm\left[2 + 6 + \frac{15}{2} + 8\right] = \pm\ 23.5\%$$

$\therefore$ Percentage error in quantity $X = \pm\ 23.5\%$

Mean absolute error in $X = \pm\ 0.235 = \pm\ 0.24$

[rounding-off upto two significant digits]

The calculated value of x should be round-off upto two significant digits.

$\therefore$ $X = 2.8$

Q.39 In the expression $P = El^2 m^{-5} G^{-2}$, E, m, l and G denote energy, mass, angular momentum and gravitational constant, respectively. Show that P is a dimensionless quantity.

Thinking Process A dimensionless quantity will have dimensional formula as $[M^0 L^0 T^0]$.

Ans. Given, expression is $P = EL^2 m^{-5} G^{-2}$

where E is energy $[E] = [ML^2T^{-2}]$ $[\because E = Fx]$

m is mass $[m] = [M]$

L is angular momentum $[L] = [ML^2T^{-1}]$ $[\because L = mvr]$

G is gravitational constant $[G] = [M^{-1}L^3T^{-2}]$ $\left[\because G = \frac{Fr^2}{m_1 m_2}\right]$

Substituting dimensions of each term in the given expression,

$$[P] = [ML^2T^{-2}] \times [ML^2T^{-1}]^2 \times [M]^{-5} \times [M^{-1}L^3T^{-2}]^{-2}$$

$$= [ML^2T^{-2}][M^{-2}T^{-1}]^2[M^{-5}][M^{-1}L^3T^{-2}]^{-2}$$

$$[P] = [M^0L^0T^0]$$

Therefore, P is a dimensionless quantity.

Q.40 If velocity of light c, Planck's constant h and gravitational constant G are taken as fundamental quantities, then express mass, length and time in terms of dimensions of these quantities.

Thinking Process In this problem, we have to apply principle of homogeneity of dimensions that is LHS and RHS of an equation will have same dimensions.

Ans. We know that, dimensions of $(h) = [ML^2T^{-1}]$

Dimensions of $(c) = [LT^{-1}]$

Dimensions of gravitational constant $(G) = [M^{-1}L^3T^{-2}]$

(i) Let $m \propto c^x h^y G^z \Rightarrow m = kc^x h^y G^z$ ...(i)

where, k is a dimensionless constant of proportionality.

Substituting dimensions of each term in Eq. (i), we get

$$[ML^0T^0] = [LT^{-1}]^x \times [ML^2T^{-1}]^y [M^{-1}L^3T^{-2}]^z$$
$$= [M^{y-z} L^{x+2y+3z} T^{-x-y-2z}]$$

Comparing powers of same terms on both sides, we get

$$y - z = 1 \quad \text{...(ii)}$$
$$x + 2y + 3z = 0 \quad \text{...(iii)}$$
$$-x - y - 2z = 0 \quad \text{...(iv)}$$

Adding Eqs. (ii), (iii) and (iv), we get

$$2y = 1 \Rightarrow y = \frac{1}{2}$$

Substituting value of y in Eq. (ii), we get

$$z = -\frac{1}{2}$$

From Eq. (iv) $x = -y - 2z$

Substituting values of y and z, we get

$$x = -\frac{1}{2} - 2\left(-\frac{1}{2}\right) = \frac{1}{2}$$

Putting values of x, y and z in Eq. (i), we get

$$m = kc^{1/2}h^{1/2}G^{-1/2} \Rightarrow m = k\sqrt{\frac{ch}{G}}$$

(ii) Let $L \propto c^x h^y G^z \Rightarrow L = kc^x h^y G^z$ ...(v)

where, k is a dimensionless constant.

Substituting dimensions of each term in Eq. (v), we get

$$[M^0 LT^0] = [LT^{-1}]^x \times [ML^2T^{-1}]^y \times [M^{-1}L^3T^{-2}]^z$$
$$= [M^{y-z} L^{x+2y+3z} T^{-x-y-2z}]$$

On comparing powers of same terms, we get

$$y - z = 0 \quad \text{...(vi)}$$
$$x + 2y + 3z = 1 \quad \text{...(vii)}$$
$$-x - y - 2z = 0 \quad \text{...(viii)}$$

Adding Eqs. (vi), (vii) and (viii), we get

$$2y = 1 \Rightarrow y = \frac{1}{2}$$

Substituting value of y in Eq. (vi), we get

$$z = \frac{1}{2}$$

From Eq. (viii), $x = -y - 2z$

Substituting values of y and z, we get

$$x = -\frac{1}{2} - 2\left(\frac{1}{2}\right) = -\frac{3}{2}$$

Putting values of x, y and z in Eq. (v), we get

$$L = kc^{-3/2}h^{1/2}G^{1/2}$$

$$L = k\sqrt{\frac{hG}{c^3}}$$

(iii) Let $T \propto c^x h^y G^z \quad \Rightarrow \quad T = kc^x h^y G^z$ ...(ix)

where, k is a dimensionless constant.

Substituting dimensions of each term in Eq. (ix), we get

$$[M^0L^0T] = [LT^{-1}]^x \times [ML^2T^{-1}]^y \times [M^{-1}L^3T^{-2}]^z$$
$$= [M^{y-z}L^{x+2y+3z}T^{-x-y-2z}]$$

On comparing powers of same terms, we get

$$y - z = 0 \quad \text{...(x)}$$
$$x + 2y + 3z = 0 \quad \text{...(xi)}$$
$$-x - y - 2z = 1 \quad \text{...(xii)}$$

Adding Eqs. (x), (xi) and (xii), we get

$$2y = 1 \Rightarrow y = \frac{1}{2}$$

Substituting value of y in Eq. (x), we get

$$z = y = \frac{1}{2}$$

From Eq. (xii), $\quad x = -y - 2z - 1$

Substituting values of y and z, we get

$$x = -\frac{1}{2} - 2\left(\frac{1}{2}\right) - 1 = -\frac{5}{2}$$

Putting values of x, y and z in Eq. (ix), we get

$$T = kc^{-5/2}h^{1/2}G^{1/2} = k\sqrt{\frac{hG}{C^5}}$$

Alternate Method

(a) $\frac{hc}{G} = \frac{[ML^2T^{-1}LT^{-1}]}{[M^{-1}L^3T^{-2}]} = [M]^2 \Rightarrow M = \sqrt{\frac{hc}{G}}$

(b) $\frac{hG}{c^3} = \frac{[ML^2T^{-1}][M^{-1}L^3T^{-2}]}{[L^3T^{-3}]} = [L]^2 \Rightarrow L = \sqrt{\frac{hG}{c^3}}$

(c) $c = [LT^{-1}] \Rightarrow T = \frac{[L]}{[C]} = \sqrt{\frac{hG}{c^3}} \times \frac{1}{c} = \sqrt{\frac{hG}{c^5}} \Rightarrow T = k\sqrt{\frac{hG}{c^5}}$

Q.41 An artificial satellite is revolving around a planet of mass M and radius R, in a circular orbit of radius r. From Kepler's third law about the period of a satellite around a common central body, square of the period of revolution T is proportional to the cube of the radius of the orbit r. Show using dimensional analysis, that $T = \frac{k}{R}\sqrt{\frac{r^3}{g}}$, where k is a dimensionless constant and g is acceleration due to gravity.

- **Concept Insight** In this problem, we will use the concept of Kepler's third law, $T^2 \propto r^3$, which says that the square of time period (T^2) of a satellite revolving around a planet is proportional to cube of the radius of the orbit (r^3).

Ans. By Kepler's third law, $T^2 \propto r^3 \Rightarrow T = kr^{3/2}$

We know that T is also a function of R and g.

$$\Rightarrow \qquad T \propto R^a g^b r^{3/2}$$

$$\text{Let} \qquad T = kr^{3/2} R^a g^b \qquad \ldots\text{(i)}$$

where, k is a dimensionless constant of proportionality.

Substituting the dimensions of each term in Eq. (i), we get

$$[M^0 L^0 T] = k[L]^{3/2}[L]^a[LT^{-2}]^b$$
$$= k\,[L^{a+b+3/2}\,T^{-2b}]$$

On comparing the powers of same terms, we get

$$a + b + 3/2 = 0 \qquad \ldots\text{(ii)}$$

$$-2b = 1 \Rightarrow b = -1/2 \qquad \ldots\text{(iii)}$$

From Eq. (ii), we get

$$a - 1/2 + 3/2 = 0 \quad \Rightarrow \quad a = -1$$

Substituting the values of a and b in Eq. (i), we get

$$T = kr^{3/2} R^{-1} g^{-1/2}$$

$$\Rightarrow \qquad T = \frac{k}{R}\sqrt{\frac{r^3}{g}}$$

Mistake Alert ! *When we are applying formulae, we should be careful about r (radius of orbit) and R (radius of planet).*

Q.42 In an experiment to estimate the size of a molecule of oleic acid 1 mL of oleic acid is dissolved in 19 mL of alcohol. Then 1 mL of this solution is diluted to 20 mL by adding alcohol. Now, 1 drop of this diluted solution is placed on water in a shallow trough. The solution spreads over the surface of water forming one molecule thick layer. Now, lycopodium powder is sprinkled evenly over the film and its diameter is measured. Knowing the volume of the drop and area of the film we can calculate the thickness of the film which will give us the size of oleic acid molecule.

Read the passage carefully and answer the following questions

(a) Why do we dissolve oleic acid in alcohol?

(b) What is the role of lycopodium powder?

(c) What would be the volume of oleic acid in each mL of solution prepared?

(d) How will you calculate the volume of n drops of this solution of oleic acid?

(e) What will be the volume of oleic acid in one drop of this solution?

Ans. (a) Oleic acid does not dissolve in water but, it is dissolved in alcohol.

(b) Lycopodium powder spreads over the entire surface of water when it is sprinkled evenly.

When a drop of prepared solution is dropped in water, oleic acid does not dissolve in water. Instead it spreads on the water surface, pushing the lycopodium powder away to clear a circular area where the drop falls. We can therefore, measure the area over which oleic acid spreads.

(c) In each mL of solution prepared volume of oleic acid $= \frac{1}{20}$ mL $\times \frac{1}{20} = \frac{1}{400}$ mL

(d) Volume of n drops of this solution of oleic acid can be calculated by means of a burette and measuring cylinder and measuring the number of drops.

(e) If n drops of the solution make 1 mL, the volume of oleic acid in one drop will be $\frac{1}{(400)n}$ mL.

***Q.43** (a) How many astronomical units (AU) make 1 parsec?

(b) Consider a sunlike star at a distance of 2 parsecs. When it is seen through a telescope with 100 magnification, what should be the angular size of the star? Sun appears to be (1/2)° from the earth. Due to atmospheric fluctuations, eye cannot resolve objects smaller than 1 arc minute.

(c) Mars has approximately half of the earth's diameter. When it is closest to the earth it is at about 1/2 AU from the earth. Calculate what size it will appear when seen through the same telescope.

Ans. (a) By definition,

1 parsec = Distance at which 1 AU long arc subtends an angle of 1 s.

$$\therefore \quad 1 \text{ parsec} = \left(\frac{1\text{AU}}{1\text{arc sec}}\right)$$

$$1 \text{ deg} = 3600 \text{ arc sec}$$

$$\therefore \quad 1 \text{ parsec} = \frac{\pi}{3600 \times 180} \text{ rad}$$

$$\therefore \quad 1 \text{ parsec} = \frac{3600 \times 180}{\pi} \text{ AU} = 206265 \text{ AU} \approx 2 \times 10^5 \text{ AU}$$

(b) Sun's diameter is $\left(\frac{1}{2}\right)^\circ$ at 1 AU.

Therefore, at 2 parsec, star is $\frac{1/4}{2 \times 10^5}$ degree in diameter $= \frac{1}{8} \times 10^{-5}$ degree

$$= \frac{60}{8} \times 10^{-5} \text{ arcmin}$$

$$= 7.5 \times 10^{-5} \text{ arcmin}$$

With 100 magnification, it should look 7.5×10^{-3} arcmin. However, due to atmospheric fluctuations, it will still look about 1 arcmin. It cannot be magnified using telescope.

(c) Given that

$$\frac{D_{mars}}{D_{earth}} = \frac{1}{2} \quad \text{...(i)}$$

where D represents diameter.

Note (*) *Topics related to these question have been removed from latest NCERT.*

From answer 25(c)

we know that, $\frac{D_{earth}}{D_{sun}} = \frac{1}{100}$

$\therefore \quad \frac{D_{mars}}{D_{sun}} = \frac{1}{2} \times \frac{1}{100}$ [from Eq. (i)]

At 1 AU sun's diameter $= \left(\frac{1}{2}\right)^{\circ}$

$\therefore$ mars' diameter $= \frac{1}{2} \times \frac{1}{200} = \frac{1}{400}$

At $\frac{1}{2}$ AU, mars' diameter $= \frac{1}{400} \times 2^{\circ} = \left(\frac{1}{200}\right)^{\circ}$

With 100 magnification, mars' diameter $= \frac{1}{200} \times 100^{\circ} = \left(\frac{1}{2}\right)^{\circ} = 30'$

This is larger than resolution limit due to atmospheric fluctuations. Hence, it looks magnified.

Q.44 Einstein's mass-energy relation emerging out of his famous theory of relativity relates mass (m) to energy (E) as $E = mc^2$, where c is speed of light in vacuum. At the nuclear level, the magnitudes of energy are very small. The energy at nuclear level is usually measured in MeV, where $1\text{MeV} = 1.6 \times 10^{-13}$J; the masses are measured in unified atomic mass unit (u) where, $1\text{u} = 1.67 \times 10^{-27}$ kg.

(a) Show that the energy equivalent of 1u is 931.5 MeV.

(b) A student writes the relation as 1u = 931.5 MeV. The teacher points out that the relation is dimensionally incorrect. Write the correct relation.

- **Concept Insight** In this problem, we will use the concept of Einstein's mass-energy relation. $E = mc^2$, to calculate the energy equivalent of the given mass.

Ans. (a) We know that $1 \text{ amu} = 1\text{u} = 1.67 \times 10^{-27}\text{kg}$

Applying $E = mc^2$

$$\text{Energy} = E = (1.67 \times 10^{-27})(3 \times 10^8)^2 \text{ J}$$

$$\Rightarrow \quad E = 15.03 \times 10^{-11} \text{ J}$$

$$= \frac{15.03 \times 10^{-11}\text{J}}{1.6 \times 10^{-19}} = 9.3937 \times 10^8 \text{ eV}$$

$$= 939 \text{ MeV}$$

which is nearly equal to 931.5 MeV

(b) The dimensionally correct relation is

$$1 \text{ amu} \times c^2 = 1\text{u} \times c^2 = 931.5 \text{ MeV}$$

Chapter

02

Motion in a Straight Line

Multiple Choice Questions (MCQs)

Q.1 Among the four graph shown in the figure, there is only one graph for which average velocity over the time interval $(0, T)$ can vanish for a suitably chosen T. Which one is it?

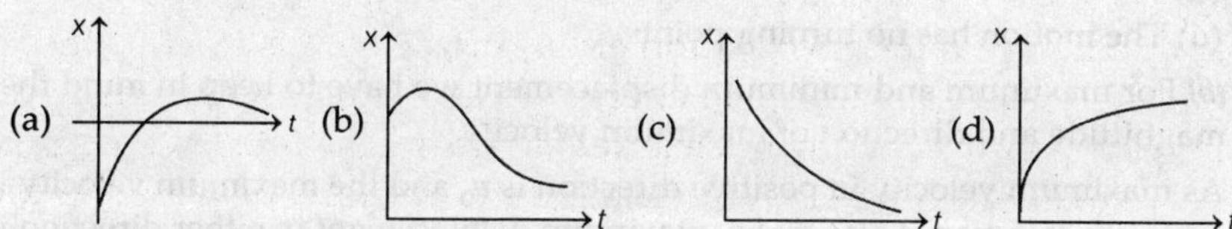

Thinking Process In this problem, we have to locate the graph which is having same displacement for two timings. When there are two timings for same displacement the corresponding velocities will be in opposite directions.

$$\text{Average velocity} = \frac{\text{Total displacement}}{\text{Time taken}}$$

Ans. *(b)* In graph (b) for one value of displacement there are two different points of time. Hence, for one time, the average velocity is positive and for other time it is negative.

As there are opposite velocities in the interval 0 to T hence, average velocity can vanish in (b). This can be seen in the figure given below

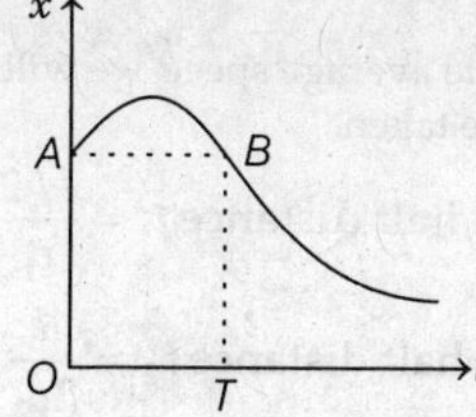

Here, $OA = BT$ (same displacement) for two different points of time.

Alternate Method

At point A and B displacement from origin is same so, net displacement in time T is zero.

Q.2 A lift is coming from 8th floor and is just about to reach 4th floor. Taking ground floor as origin and positive direction upwards for all quantities, which one of the following is correct?

(a) $x < 0, v < 0, a > 0$
(b) $x > 0, v < 0, a < 0$
(c) $x > 0, v < 0, a > 0$
(d) $x > 0, v > 0, a < 0$

Ans. *(a)* As upward direction is taken as positive, so displacement and velocity are in negative direction therefore $x < 0$ and $v < 0$

We know that due to downward motion displacement will be negative. When the lift reaches 4th floor is about to stop hence, motion is retarding in nature hence, $x < 0; a > 0$.

This can be shown on the adjacent graph.

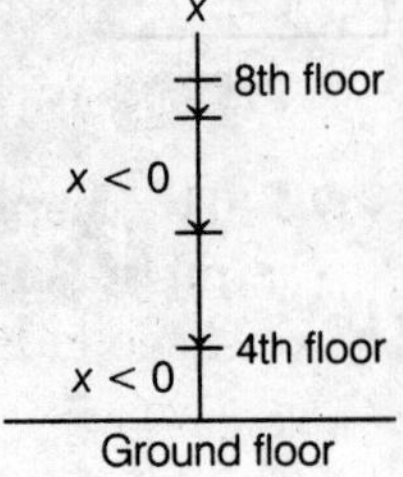

Q.3 In one dimensional motion, instantaneous speed v satisfies $0 \le v < v_0$.

(a) The displacement in time T must always take non-negative values.
(b) The displacement x in time T satisfies $-v_0 T < x < v_0 T$.
(c) The acceleration is always a non-negative number.
(d) The motion has no turning points.

Ans. *(b)* For maximum and minimum displacement we have to keep in mind the magnitude and direction of maximum velocity.

As maximum velocity in positive direction is v_0 and the maximum velocity in opposite direction is also v_0. So, maximum displacement in either direction is $v_0 T$.

Hence, $-v_0 T < x < v_0 T$.

Note We should not be confused with direction of velocities i.e. in one direction it is taken as positive and in another direction is taken as negative.

Q.4 A vehicle travels half the distance l with speed v_1 and the other half with speed v_2, then its average speed is

(a) $\dfrac{v_1 + v_2}{2}$
(b) $\dfrac{2v_1 + v_2}{v_1 + v_2}$
(c) $\dfrac{2v_1 v_2}{v_1 + v_2}$
(d) $\dfrac{L(v_1 + v_2)}{v_1 v_2}$

Thinking Process To calculate average speed we will calculate total distance covered and will divide by total time taken.

Ans. *(c)* Time taken to travel first half distance $t_1 = \dfrac{l/2}{v_1} = \dfrac{l}{2v_1}$

Time taken to travel second half distance $t_2 = \dfrac{l}{2v_2}$

$$\text{Total time} = t_1 + t_2$$

$$= \frac{l}{2v_1} + \frac{l}{2v_2} = \frac{l}{2}\left[\frac{1}{v_1} + \frac{1}{v_2}\right]$$

We know that, V_{av} = Average speed $= \frac{\text{total distance}}{\text{total time}}$

$$= \frac{l}{\frac{l}{2}\left[\frac{1}{v_1} + \frac{1}{v_2}\right]} = \frac{2v_1v_2}{v_1 + v_2}$$

Note We should not confuse with distance and displacement. Distance ≥ displacement.

Q.5 The displacement of a particle is given by $x = (t-2)^2$ where x is in metre and t in second. The distance covered by the particle in first 4 seconds is

(a) 4 m (b) 8 m (c) 12 m (d) 16 m

Thinking Process In such type of problems we have to see whether the motion is accelerating or retarding. During retarding journey particle will stop in between.

Ans. *(b)* Given, $x = (t-2)^2$

Velocity, $v = \frac{dx}{dt} = \frac{d}{dt}(t-2)^2 = 2(t-2)$ m/s

Acceleration, $a = \frac{dv}{dt} = \frac{d}{dt}[2(t-2)]$

$= 2[1-0] = 2\ \text{m/s}^2$

When, $t = 0$; $v = -4$ m/s

$t = 2$s; $v = 0$ m/s

$t = 4$s; $v = 4$ m/s

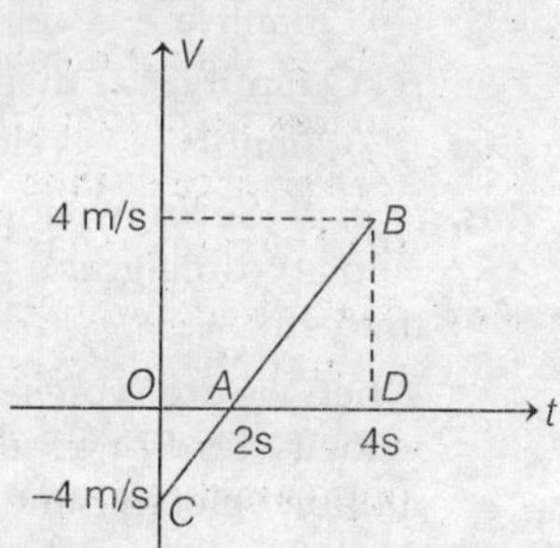

v-t graph is shown in adjacent diagram.

Distance travelled = area of the graph = area OAC + area ABD

$$= \frac{4 \times 2}{2} + \frac{1}{2} \times 2 \times 4 = 8\ \text{m}$$

Q.6 At a metro station, a girl walks up a stationary escalator in time t_1. If she remains stationary on the escalator, then the escalator take her up in time t_2. The time taken by her to walk up on the moving escalator will be

(a) $(t_1 + t_2)/2$ (b) $t_1t_2/(t_2 - t_1)$ (c) $t_1t_2/(t_2 + t_1)$ (d) $t_1 - t_2$

Ans. *(c)* In this question, we have to find net velocity with respect to the Earth that will be equal to velocity of the girl plus velocity of escalator.

Let displacement is L, then

velocity of girl $v_g = \frac{L}{t_1}$ [when escalator is at rest]

velocity of escalator $v_e = \frac{L}{t_2}$ [when girl is at rest]

Net velocity of the girl and the escalator $= v_g + v_e = \frac{L}{t_1} + \frac{L}{t_2}$

If t is total time taken in covering distance L, then

$$\frac{L}{t} = \frac{L}{t_1} + \frac{L}{t_2} \Rightarrow t = \frac{t_1t_2}{t_1 + t_2}$$

Multiple Choice Questions (More Than One Options)

Q.7 The variation of quantity A with quantity B, plotted in figure describes the motion of a particle in a straight line.

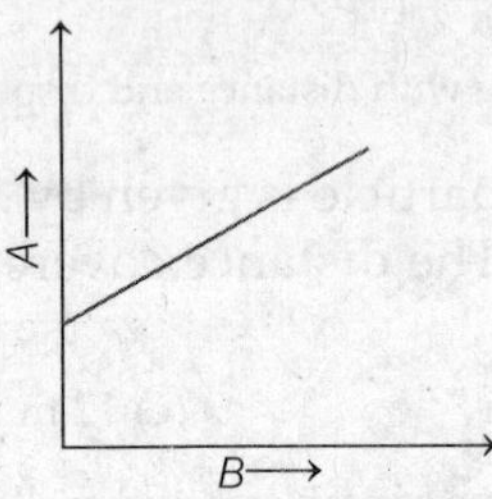

(a) Quantity B may represent time

(b) Quantity A is velocity if motion is uniform

(c) Quantity A is displacement if motion is uniform

(d) Quantity A is velocity if motion is uniformly accelerated

Ans. *(a, c, d)* We know slope of displacement-time graph gives velocity and slope of velocity-time graph gives acceleration. When slope is constant motion will be uniform.

When we are representing motion by a graph it may be displacement-time, velocity-time or acceleration-time hence, B may represent time. For uniform motion velocity-time graph should be a straight line parallel to time axis. So option (b) is not correct. For uniform motion velocity is constant hence, slope will be positive. Hence quantity A is displacement. For uniformly accelerated motion slope will be positive and A will represent velocity.

Q.8 A graph of x *versus* t is shown in figure. Choose correct alternatives given below.

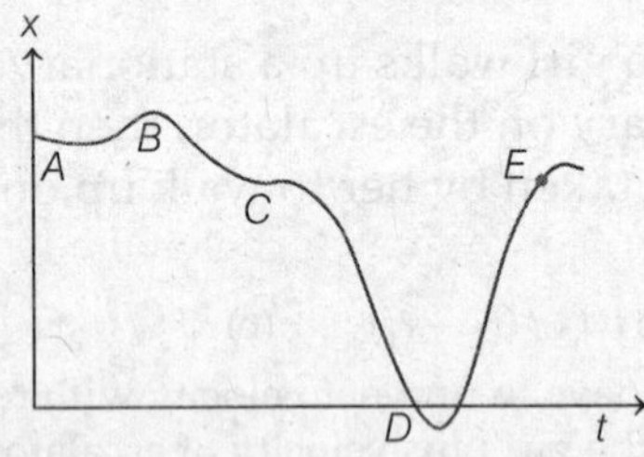

(a) The particle was released from rest at $t = 0$.

(b) At B, the acceleration $a > 0$.

(c) At C, the velocity and the acceleration vanish.

(d) Average velocity for the motion between A and D is positive.

(e) The speed at D exceeds that at E.

Thinking Process In this problem, we must keep in mind that velocity $= \dfrac{dx}{dt}$ (Slope of $x - t$ graph)

Ans. ***(a, c, e)*** At point A, $\frac{dx}{dt} = 0$, hence the particle is either at rest or its instantaneous velocity is zero.

At point B, the slope of the curve is parallel to time axis and hence, $\frac{dx}{dt} = 0$ and since the point B is a maxima, so $\frac{d^2x}{dt^2} < 0$ and hence, $a < 0$.

At point C, both the 1st and the 2nd derivatives of x are zero since it is a point of inflexion and so both acceleration and velocity vanishes.

The average velocity between A and D is negative since the net displacement is negative.

The slope at point D is steeper than that of point E even though they are in the opposite direction and so the speed at D is greater than at E.

Q.9 For the one-dimensional motion, described by $x = t - \sin t$

(a) $x(t) > 0$ for all $t > 0$

(b) $v(t) > 0$ for all $t > 0$

(c) $a(t) > 0$ for all $t > 0$

(d) $v(t)$ lies between 0 and 2

Ans. ***(a, d)*** Given, $x = t - \sin t$

$$\text{velocity } v = \frac{dx}{dt} = \frac{d}{dt}[t - \sin t] = 1 - \cos t$$

$$\text{Acceleration } a = \frac{dv}{dt} = \frac{d}{dt}[1 - \cos t] = \sin t$$

As acceleration $a > 0$ for all $t > 0$

Hence, $x(t) > 0$ for all $t > 0$ i.e. option (a)

Now, Velocity $v = 1 - \cos t$

When, $\cos t = 1$, velocity $v = 0$

$$v_{max} = 1 - (\cos t)_{min} = 1 - (-1) = 2$$

$$v_{min} = 1 - (\cos t)_{max} = 1 - 1 = 0$$

[As maximum and minimum value of $\cos\theta$ is +1 and −1]

Hence, v lies between 0 and 2. i.e. option (d).

$$\text{Acceleration } a = \frac{dv}{dt} = +\sin t$$

When $t = 0$; $x = 0$, $v = 0$ and $a = 0$

When $t = \frac{\pi}{2}$; $x = \frac{\pi}{2}, v > 0, a > 0$

When $t = \pi$; $x = \pi, v > 0$, $a = 0$

When $t = 2\pi$; $x = 2\pi, v = 0$, $a = 0$

Note (i) When sinusoidal function is involved in an expression we should be careful about sine and cosine functions.

(ii) We should be very careful when calculating maximum and minimum value of velocity because it involves inverse relation with $\cos t$ in the given expression.

Q.10 A spring with one end attached to a mass and the other to a rigid support is stretched and released.

(a) Magnitude of acceleration, when just released, is maximum

(b) Magnitude of acceleration, when at equilibrium position, is maximum

(c) Speed is maximum, when mass is at equilibrium position

(d) Magnitude of displacement is always maximum, whenever speed is minimum

Ans. *(a, c)* When spring is stretched by x, restoring force will be $F = -kx$

Potential energy of the stretched spring = $\text{PE} = \frac{1}{2}kx^2$

As restoring force is central hence when particle is released it will execute SHM about equilibrium position.

Acceleration will be $a = \frac{F}{m} = \frac{-kx}{m}$ i.e. $a \propto -x$

At equilibrium position, $x = 0 \Rightarrow a = 0$

Hence, when just released $x = x_{\text{max}}$

Hence, acceleration is maximum. Thus option (a) is correct.

At equilibrium whole PE will be converted to KE. Hence, KE will be maximum and speed will be maximum.

Q.11 A ball is bouncing elastically with a speed 1 m/s between walls of a railway compartment of size 10 m in a direction perpendicular to walls. The train is moving at a constant velocity of 10 m/s parallel to the direction of motion of the ball. As seen from the ground,

(a) the direction of motion of the ball changes every 10 seconds.

(b) speed of ball changes every 10 seconds.

(c) average speed of ball over any 20 interval is fixed.

(d) the acceleration of ball is the same as from the train.

Ans. *(b, c, d)* In this problem, we have to keep in mind the frame of the observer. Here we must be clear that we are considering the motion from the ground. The velocity of train (10 m/s) is greater than speed of ball (1 m/s).

The speed of the ball before collision with side of train is 10 + 1 = 11 m/s.

Speed after collision with side of train = 10 − 1 = 9 m/s.

As speed is changing after travelling 10 m and speed of ball is 1 m/s hence, time duration of the changing speed is 10 seconds.

Since, the collision of the ball is perfectly elastic so, there is no dissipation of energy hence, total momentum and kinetic energy are conserved.

Since, the train is moving with constant velocity hence, it will act as inertial frame of reference as that of Earth and acceleration will be same in both frames.

We should not confuse with non-inertial and inertial frame of reference. A frame of reference that is not accelerating will be inertial.

Very Short Answer Type Questions

Q.12 Refer to the graph in figure. Match the following.

Graph		Characteristics
(a)	(i)	has $v > 0$ and $a < 0$ throughout
(b)	(ii)	has $x > 0$ throughout and has a point with $v = 0$ and a point with $a = 0$
(c)	(iii)	has a point with zero displacement for $t > 0$
(d)	(iv)	has $v < 0$ and $a > 0$

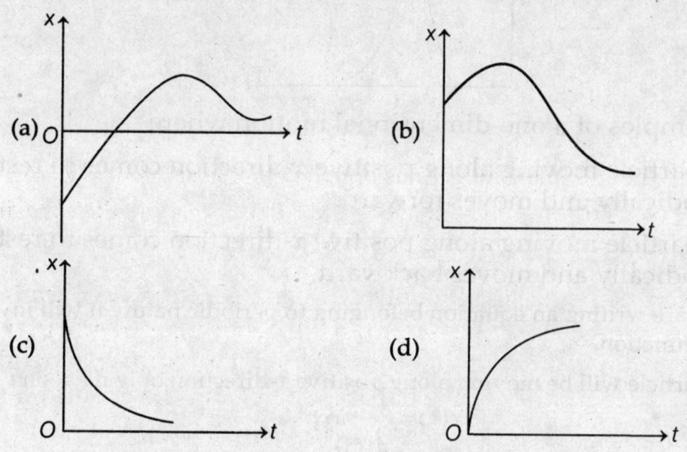

Ans. We have to analyse slope of each curve i.e. $\frac{dx}{dt}$. For peak points $\frac{dx}{dt}$ will be zero as x is maximum at peak points.

For graph (a), there is a point for which displacement is zero. So, a matches with (iii)

In graph (b), x is positive (> 0) throughout and at the point of maximum, $v = \frac{dx}{dt} = 0.$

Since, at point of curvature changes so $a = 0$, hence b matches with (ii)

In graph (c), slope $v = \frac{dx}{dt}$ is negative hence, velocity will be negative and slope is increasing, so $a > 0$.

So matches with (iv)

In graph (d), as slope $v = \frac{dx}{dt}$ is positive hence, $v > 0$ and as slope is decreasing, so $a < 0$.

Hence, d matches with (i).

Q.13 A uniformly moving cricket ball is turned back by hitting it with a bat for a very short time interval. Show the variation of its acceleration with time (Take acceleration in the backward direction as positive).

Ans. If gravity effect is neglected then ball moving uniformly and turned back with same speed when a bat hits it. Acceleration of the ball is zero just before it strikes the bat. When the ball strikes the bat, it gets accelerated due to the applied impulsive force by the bat.

The variation of acceleration with time is shown in graph

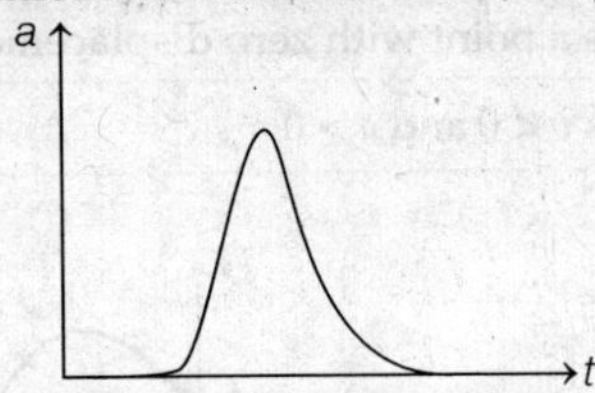

Q.14 Give examples of a one-dimensional motion where

(a) the particle moving along positive x-direction comes to rest periodically and moves forward.

(b) the particle moving along positive x-direction comes to rest periodically and moves backward.

Ans. When we are writing an equation belonging to periodic nature it will involve sine or cosine function.

(a) The particle will be moving along positive x-direction only if $t > \sin t$

Hence, $$x(t) = t - \sin t$$

$$\text{Velocity } v(t) = \frac{dx(1)}{dt} = 1 - \cos t$$

$$\text{Acceleration } a(t) = \frac{dv}{dt} = \sin t$$

When $t = 0;\ x(t) = 0$

When $t = \pi;\ x(t) = \pi > 0$

When $t = 2\pi;\ x(t) = 2\pi > 0$

(b) Equation can be represented by

$$x(t) = \sin t$$

$$v = \frac{d}{dt}x(t) = \cos t$$

As displacement and velocity is involving $\sin t$ and $\cos t$ hence, these equations represent periodic motion.

As at $t = 0,\ x = 0,\ v > 0$

at $t = \frac{\pi}{2};\ x > 0,\ v = 0$

Q.15 Give example of a motion where $x > 0,\ v < 0,\ a > 0$ at a particular instant.

Ans. Let the motion is represented by

$$x(t) = A + Be^{-\gamma t} \quad \text{...(i)}$$

Let $A > B$ and $\gamma > 0$

Now, velocity $x(t) = \frac{dx}{dt} = -B\gamma e^{-\gamma t}$

Acceleration $a(t) = \frac{dx}{dt} = B\gamma^2 e^{-\gamma t}$

Suppose we are considering any instant t, then from Eq. (i), we can say that

$$x(t) > 0; v(t) < 0 \text{ and } a > 0$$

Q.16 An object falling through a fluid is observed to have acceleration given by $a = g - bv$ where g = gravitational acceleration and b is constant. After a long time of release, it is observed to fall with constant speed. What must be the value of constant speed?

Ans. When speed becomes constant, acceleration

$$a = \frac{dv}{dt} = 0$$

Given acceleration $a = g - bv$

where, g = gravitational acceleration

Clearly, from above equation as speed increases acceleration will decrease. At a certain speed say v_0, acceleration will be zero and speed will remain constant.

Hence, $a = g - bv_0 = 0$

$\Rightarrow$ $v_0 = g / b$

Alternate Method

Here, $a = g - bv$

When an object falls with constant speed v_c its acceleration becomes zero.

$\therefore$ $g - bv_c = 0$

or $v_c = \frac{g}{b}$

Short Answer Type Questions

Q.17 A ball is dropped and its displacement *versus* time graph is as shown (Displacement x from ground and all quantities are positive upwards).

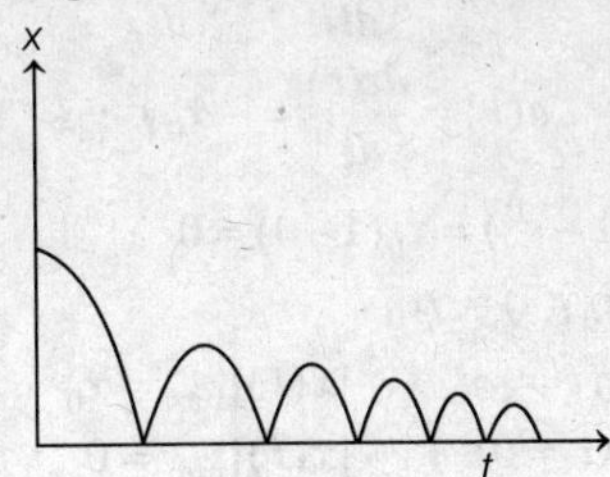

(a) Plot qualitatively velocity *versus* time graph

(b) Plot qualitatively acceleration *versus* time graph

Thinking Process To calculate velocity we will find slope $\frac{dx}{dt}$ from displacement-time curve and to find acceleration we will find slope $\frac{dv}{dt}$ from velocity-time curve.

Ans. It is clear from the graph that displacement x is positive throughout. Ball is dropped from a height and its velocity increases in downward direction due to gravity pull. In this condition v is negative but acceleration of the ball is equal to acceleration due to gravity i.e. $a = -g$.

When ball rebounds in upward direction its velocity is positive but acceleration is $a = -g$.

(a) The velocity-time graph of the ball is shown in Fig. (i). Keeping in mind that after striking earth direction of velocity changes.

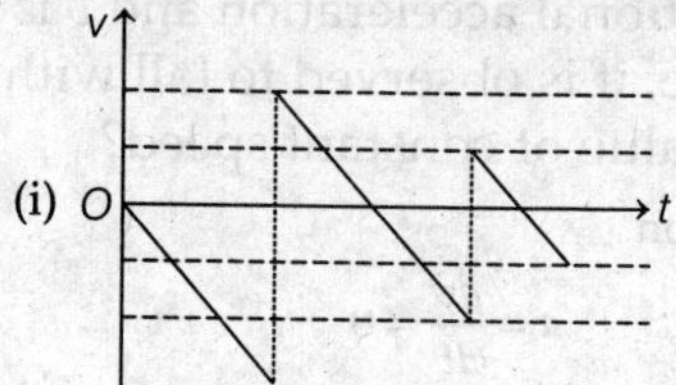

(b) The acceleration-time graph of the ball is shown in Fig. (ii).

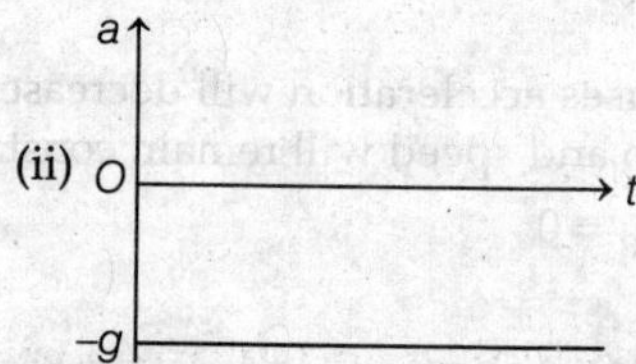

Q.18 A particle executes the motion described by $x(t) = x_0(1 - e^{-\gamma t})$; $t \geq 0$, $x_0 > 0$.

(a) Where does the particle start and with what velocity?

(b) Find maximum and minimum values of $x(t)$, $v(t)$, $a(t)$. Show that $x(t)$ and $a(t)$ increase with time and $v(t)$ decreases with time.

Thinking Process First we have to calculate velocity and acceleration and then we can determine the maximum or minimum value accordingly.

Ans. Given,
$$x(t) = x_0(1 - e^{-\gamma t})$$
$$v(t) = \frac{dx(t)}{dt} = x_0 \frac{d}{dt}[1 - e^{-\gamma t}] = x_0 \gamma e^{-\gamma t}$$
$$a(t) = \frac{dv(t)}{dt} = -x_0 \gamma^2 e^{-\gamma t}$$

(a) When $t = 0$; $x(t) = x_0(1 - e^0) = x_0(1 - 1) = 0$
$$v(t = 0) = x_0 \gamma e^0 = x_0 \gamma(1) = \gamma x_0$$

(b) $x(t)$ is maximum when $t = \infty$; $[x(t)]_{max} = x_0$

$x(t)$ is minimum when $t = 0$; $[x(t)]_{min} = 0$

$v(t)$ is maximum when $t = 0$; $v(0) = x_0 \gamma$

$v(t)$ is minimum when $t = \infty$; $v(\infty) = 0$

$a(t)$ is maximum when $t = \infty$; $a(\infty) = 0$

$a(t)$ is minimum when $t = 0$; $a(0) = -x_0 \gamma^2$

Mistake Alert ! *We should be careful about nature of variation of the curve and maximum and minimum value will be decided accordingly.*

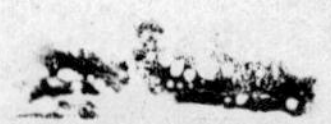

Q.19 A bird is tossing (flying to and fro) between two cars moving towards each other on a straight road. One car has a speed of 18 km/h while the other has the speed of 27 km/h. The bird starts moving from first car towards the other and is moving with the speed of 36 km/h and when the two cars were separated by 36 km. What is the total distance covered by the bird? What is the total displacement of the bird?

- **Concept Insight** In this problem we have to use the concept of relative velocity. It will be subtracted for velocities in same direction and added for velocities in opposite directions.

Ans. Given, Speed of first car = 18 km/h

Speed of second car = 27 km/h

Speed of bird = 36 kmh^{-1}

$\therefore$ Relative speed of each car w.r.t. each other

$= 18 + 27 = 45$ km/h

Initial distance between the cars = 36 km

$\therefore$ Time of meeting the cars $(t) = \dfrac{\text{Distance between the cars}}{\text{Relative speed of cars}} = \dfrac{36}{45} = \dfrac{4}{5}\text{ h} = 0.8\text{ h}$

$\therefore$ Distance covered by the bird $= v_b \times t = 36 \times 0.8 = 28.8$ km

Displacement of bird = Speed of first car $\times$ 0.8 h $= 18 \times 0.8 = 14.4$ km.

Q.20 A man runs across the rooftop of a tall building and jumps horizontally with the hope of landing on the roof of the next building which is at a lower height than the first. If his speed is 9 m/s, the (horizontal) distance between the two buildings is 10 m and the height difference is 9 m, will be able to land on the next building? (Take $g = 10\text{ m/s}^2$)

Thinking Process When the man runs on the rooftop the velocity will be horizontal. Then, acceleration will be vertically downward taken as g and then equations of kinematics will be applied.

Ans. Given, horizontal speed of the man $(u_x) = 9$ m/s

Horizontal distance between the two buildings = 10 m

Height difference between the two buildings = 9 m

Vertical speed of man $v_y = 0$

and $g = 10\text{ m/s}^2$

Let the man jumps from point A and land on the roof of the next building at point B.

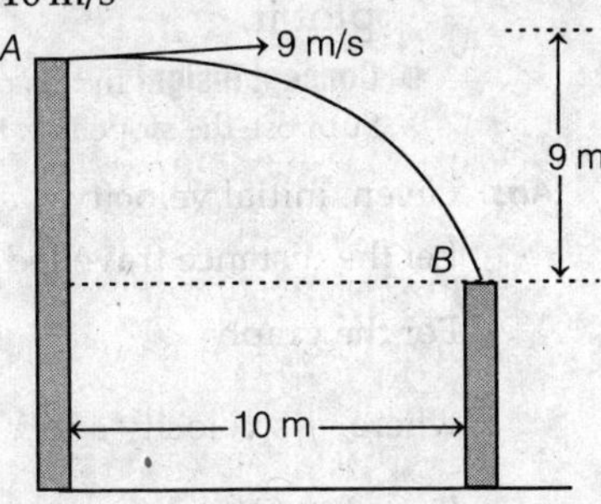

Taking motion in vertical direction,

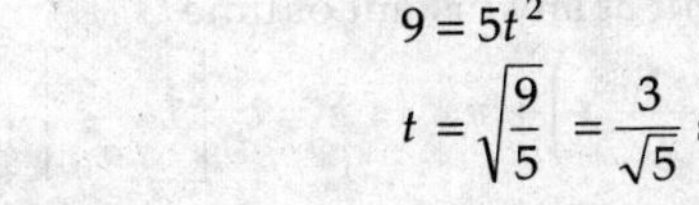

$$y = u_y t + \frac{1}{2} g t^2$$

$$9 = 0 \times t + \frac{1}{2} \times 10 \times t^2$$

$$9 = 5t^2$$

or $$t = \sqrt{\frac{9}{5}} = \frac{3}{\sqrt{5}}\text{ s}$$

$\therefore$ Horizontal distance travelled $= u_x \times t = 9 \times \frac{3}{\sqrt{5}} = \frac{27}{\sqrt{5}} \approx 12$ m

As horizontal distance travelled by the man is greater than 10 m, therefore, he will land on the next building.

Q.21 A ball is dropped from a building of height 45 m. Simultaneously another ball is thrown up with a speed 40 m/s. Calculate the relative speed of the balls as a function of time.

Thinking Process In this problem as ball is dropped, initial velocity will be taken as zero. We will apply equations involving one dimensional motion.

Ans. For the ball dropped from the building, $u_1 = 0$, $u_2 = 40$ m/s

Velocity of the dropped ball after time t, (in downward direction)

$$v_1 = u_1 + gt$$

$$v_1 = gt$$

For the ball thrown up, $u_2 = 40$ m/s

Velocity of the ball after time t (in upward direction)

$$v_2 = u_2 - gt = (40 - gt)$$

$\therefore$Relative velocity of one ball w.r.t. another ball

$$= v_1 + v_2 \quad \text{[As they are in opposite direction]}$$

$$= gt + (40 - gt) = 40 \text{ms}^{-1}$$

Mistake Alert ! *When we are applying equations for rectilinear motion we should carefully put up the signs for the physical quantities.*

Q.22 The velocity- displacement graph of a particle is shown in figure.

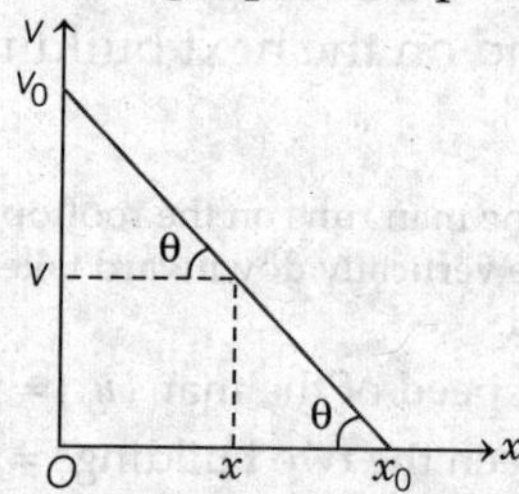

(a) Write the relation between v and x.

(b) Obtain the relation between acceleration and displacement and plot it.

Concept Insight In this problems we will use the concept of equation of a straight line. Suppose the slope is m then equation will come out to be $y = mx + c$.

Ans. Given, initial velocity $= v_0$

Let the distance travelled in time $t = x$.

For the graph
$$\tan\theta = \frac{v_0}{x_0} = \frac{v_0 - v}{x} \quad \text{...(i)}$$

where, v is velocity and x is displacement at any instant of time t.

From Eq. (i)
$$v_0 - v = \frac{v_0}{x_0} x \Rightarrow v = \left(\frac{-v_0}{x_0} x\right) + v_0 \Rightarrow v = v_0\left[1 - \frac{x}{x_0}\right]$$

We know that

$$\text{Acceleration } a = \frac{dv}{dt} = \left(\frac{-v_0}{x_0}\right)\frac{dx}{dt} + 0$$

$$\Rightarrow \quad a = \left(\frac{-v_0}{x_0}\right)(v) \Rightarrow a = \left(\frac{-v_0}{x_0}\right)\left(\frac{-v_0}{x_0}x + v_0\right)$$

$$a = \left(\frac{{v_0}^2}{{x_0}^2}\right)x - \frac{{v_0}^2}{x_0}$$

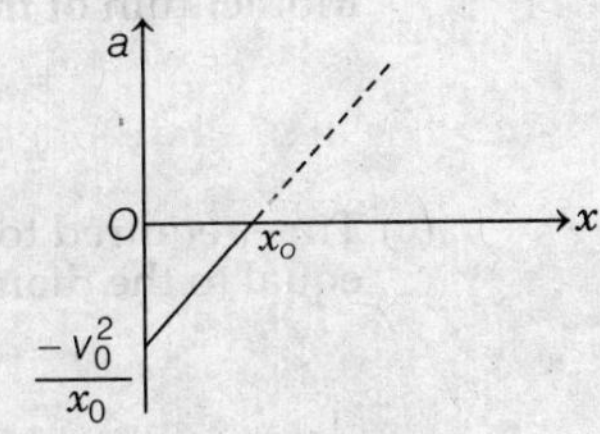

Which is required relation between acceleration and displacement.

Compare it with $y = mx + c$

Here, $m = \frac{v_0^2}{x_0}, c = -\frac{v_0^2}{x_0}$

Slope is positive and intercept is negative.

Long Answer Type Questions

Q.23 It is a common observation that rain clouds can be at about a kilometer altitude above the ground.

(a) If a rain drop falls from such a height freely under gravity, what will be its speed? Also calculate in km/h ($g = 10\text{ m/s}^2$).

(b) A typical rain drop is about 4 mm diameter. Momentum is mass × speed in magnitude. Estimate its momentum when it hits ground.

(c) Estimate the time required to flatten the drop.

(d) Rate of change of momentum is force. Estimate how much force such a drop would exert on you.

(e) Estimate the order of magnitude force on umbrella. Typical lateral separation between two rain drops is 5 cm.

(Assume that umbrella is circular and has a diameter of 1 m and cloth is not pierced through.)

Thinking Process In this problem equation of motion and Newton's second law that is $F_{ext} = \frac{dp}{dt}$ will be used, where dp is change in momentum over time dt.

Ans. Given, height (h) = 1 km = 1000 m

$g = 10\text{ m/s}^2$

(a) Velocity attained by the rain drop in freely falling through a height h.

$$v^2 - u^2 = 2gh \qquad [\text{as } u = 0]$$

$$v = \sqrt{2gh} = \sqrt{2 \times 10 \times 1000} = 100\sqrt{2}\text{ m/s}$$

$$= 100\sqrt{2} \times \frac{60 \times 60}{1000} = 360\sqrt{2}\text{ km/h}$$

$$\approx 509\text{ km/h}$$

(b) Diameter of the drop (d) $= 2r = 4\,\text{mm}$

$\therefore$ Radius of the drop $(r) = 2\,\text{mm} = 2 \times 10^{-3}$ m

Mass of a rain drop $(m) = V \times \rho = \left(\frac{4}{3}\pi r^3\right)\rho$

$= \frac{4}{3} \times \frac{22}{7} \times (2 \times 10^{-3})^3 \times 10^3$ $\quad$ [$\because$ Density of water $= 10^3$ kg/m^3]

$\approx 3.4 \times 10^{-5}$ kg

Momentum of the rain drop $(p) = mv$

$= 3.4 \times 10^{-5} \times 100\sqrt{2} = 4.7 \times 10^{-3}$ kg-m/s

$\approx 5 \times 10^{-3}$ kg-m/s

(c) Time required to flatten the drop = time taken by the drop to travel the distance equal to the diameter of the drop near the ground

$$t = \frac{d}{v} = \frac{4 \times 10^{-3}}{100\sqrt{2}} = 0.028 \times 10^{-3}\ \text{s} = 2.8 \times 10^{-5}\ \text{s} \approx 28\,\mu\text{s}$$

(d) Force exerted by a rain drop

$$F = \frac{\text{Change in momentum}}{\text{Time}} = \frac{p - 0}{t} = \frac{4.7 \times 10^{-3}}{2.8 \times 10^{-5}} \approx 168\ \text{N}$$

(e) Radius of the umbrella $(R) = \frac{1}{2}$ m

$\therefore$ Area of the umbrella $(A) = \pi R^2 = \frac{22}{7} \times \left(\frac{1}{2}\right)^2 = \frac{22}{28} = \frac{11}{14} \approx 0.8\,\text{m}^2$

Number of drops striking the umbrella simultaneously with average separation of 5 cm $(= 5 \times 10^{-2}$ m)

$$= \frac{0.8}{(5 \times 10^{-2})^2} = 320$$

$\therefore$ Net force exerted on umbrella $= 320 \times 168 = 53760\ \text{N} \approx 54000\ \text{N}$

Note In practice, the velocity of the drops decreases due to air friction.

Q.24 A motor car moving at a speed of 72 km/h cannot come to a stop in less than 3.0 s while for a truck this time interval is 5.0 s. On a highway, the car is behind the truck both moving at 72 km/h. The truck gives a signal that it is going to stop at emergency. At what distance the car should be from the truck so that it does not bump onto (collide with) the truck. Human response time is 0.5 s.

- **Concept Insight** This is to illustrate why vehicles carry the message on the rear side "Keep safe distance".

Ans. In this problem equations related to one dimensional motion will be applied. For acceleration, positive sign will be used and for retardation negative sign will be used.

Given, speed of car as well as truck = 72 km/h

$$= 72 \times \frac{5}{18}\ \text{m/s} = 20\ \text{m/s}$$

Retarded motion for truck $\quad v = u + a_t t$

$$0 = 20 + a_t \times 5 \quad \text{or} \quad a_t = -4\ \text{m/s}^2$$

Retarded motion for the car $v = u + a_c t$

$$0 = 20 + a_c \times 3$$

or $$a_c = -\frac{20}{3}\ \text{m/s}^2$$

Let car be at a distance x from truck, when truck gives the signal and t be the time taken to cover this distance.

As human response time is 0.5 s, therefore,

Velocity of car after time t,

$$v_c = u - at = 20 - \left(\frac{20}{3}\right)(t - 0.5)$$

Velocity of truck after time t,

$$v_t = 20 - 4t$$

To avoid the car bump onto the truck,

$$v_c = v_t$$

$$20 - \frac{20}{3}(t - 0.5) = 20 - 4t$$

$$4t = \frac{20}{3}(t - 0.5)$$

$$t = \frac{5}{3}(t - 0.5)$$

$$3t = 5t - 2.5$$

$\Rightarrow$ $$t = \frac{2.5}{2} = \frac{5}{4}\ \text{s}$$

Distance travelled by the truck in time t,

$$s_t = u_t t + \frac{1}{2}a_t t^2 = 20 \times \frac{5}{4} + \frac{1}{2} \times (-4) \times \left(\frac{5}{4}\right)^2 = 21.875\ \text{m}$$

Distance travelled by car in time t = Distance travelled by car in 0.5 s (without retardation) + Distance travelled by car in $(t - 0.5)$ s (with retardation)

$$s_c = (20 \times 0.5) + 20\left(\frac{5}{4} - 0.5\right) - \frac{1}{2}\left(\frac{20}{3}\right)\left(\frac{5}{4} - 0.5\right)^2$$

$$= 23.125\ \text{m}$$

$\therefore$ $$s_c - s_t = 23.125 - 21.875 = 1.25\ \text{m}$$

Therefore, to avoid the bump onto the truck, the car must maintain a distance from the truck more than 1.25 m.

Q.25 A monkey climbs up a slippery pole for 3 seconds and subsequently slips for 3 seconds. Its velocity at time t is given by $v(t) = 2t(3 - t);\ 0 < t < 3$ and $v(t) = -(t - 3)(6 - t)$ for $3 < t < 6$ s in m/s. It repeats this cycle till it reaches the height of 20 m.

(a) At what time is its velocity maximum?

(b) At what time is its average velocity maximum?

(c) At what time is its acceleration maximum in magnitude?

(d) How many cycles (counting fractions) are required to reach the top?

Ans. It this problem to calculate maximum velocity we will use $\frac{dv}{dt} = 0$,then the time corresponding to maximum velocity will be obtained.

Given velocity $$v(t) = 2t\,(3 - t) = 6t - 2t^2 \quad ...(i)$$

(a) For maximum velocity $\frac{dv(t)}{dt} = 0$

$$\Rightarrow \frac{d}{dt}(6t - 2t^2) = 0 \Rightarrow 6 - 4t = 0$$

$$\Rightarrow t = \frac{6}{4} = \frac{3}{2}\text{s} = 1.5\,\text{s}$$

(b) From Eq. (i) $v = 6t - 2t^2 \Rightarrow \frac{ds}{dt} = 6t - 2t^2$

$$\Rightarrow ds = (6t - 2t^2)\,dt$$

where, s is displacement

$\therefore$ Distance travelled in time interval 0 to 3s.

$$s = \int_0^3 (6t - 2t^2)\,dt = \left[\frac{6t^2}{2} - \frac{2t^3}{3}\right]_0^3 = \left[3t^2 - \frac{2}{3}t^3\right]_0^3$$

$$= 3 \times 9 - \frac{2}{3} \times 3 \times 3 \times 3 = 27 - 18 = 9\,\text{m}.$$

$$\text{Average velocity} = \frac{\text{Distance travelled}}{\text{Time}} = \frac{9}{3} = 3\,\text{m/s}$$

Given, $v = 6t - 2t^2 \Rightarrow 3 = 6t - 2t^2$

$$\Rightarrow 2t^2 - 6t - 3 = 0$$

$$\Rightarrow t = \frac{6 \pm \sqrt{6^2 - 4 \times 2 \times 3}}{2 \times 2} = \frac{6 \pm \sqrt{36 - 24}}{4} = \frac{6 \pm \sqrt{12}}{4} = \frac{3 \pm \sqrt{3}}{2}$$

$$\therefore t = \frac{3 + \sqrt{3}}{2}$$

$$\therefore t = 2.375 \text{ or } 0.635$$

So, the average velocity is maximum during 2.375 s and 0.635 s.

(c) In a periodic motion when velocity is zero acceleration will be maximum putting $v = 0$ in Eq. (i)

$$0 = 6t - 2t^2$$

$$\Rightarrow 0 = t\,(6 - 2t) = t \times 2\,(3 - t) = 0$$

$$\Rightarrow t = 0 \text{ or } 3\text{s}$$

(d) Distance covered in 0 to 3s = 9 m

$$\text{Distance covered in 3 to 6s} = \int_3^6 (18 - 9t + t^2)\,dt$$

$$= \left(18t - \frac{9t^2}{2} + \frac{t^3}{3}\right)_3^6 = 18 \times 6 - \frac{9}{2} \times 6^2 + \frac{6^3}{3} - \left(18 \times 3 - \frac{9 \times 3^2}{2} + \frac{3^3}{3}\right)$$

$$= 108 - 9 \times 18 + \frac{6^3}{3} - 18 \times 3 + \frac{9}{2} \times 9 - \frac{27}{3}$$

$$= 108 - 18 \times 9 + \frac{216}{3} - 54 + 4.5 \times 9 - 9 = -4.5\,\text{m}$$

$\therefore$ Total distance travelled in one cycle $= s_1 + s_2 = 9 - 4.5 = 4.5$ m

Total distance covered in second cycle $= 4.5 + 9 - 4.5 = 9$ m.

Total distance covered in third cycle $= 9 + 9 - 4.5 = 13.5$ m

Remaining distance $= 20 - 13.5 = 6.5$ m

So, monkey will reach top in fourth cycle because it will reach top before slipping.

Q.26 A man is standing on top of a building 100m high. He throws two balls vertically, one at $t = 0$ and after a time interval (less than 2 seconds). The later ball is thrown at a velocity of half the first. The vertical gap between first and second ball is $+15$ m at $t = 2$s. The gap is found to remain constant. Calculate the velocity with which the balls were thrown and the exact time interval between their throw.

Thinking Process In this question equation of kinematics will be applied with proper sign and to calculate time interval we will take difference of displacements.

Ans. Let the speeds of the two balls (1and 2) be v_1 and v_2 where

if $v_1 = 2v, v_2 = v$

if y_1 and y_2 and the distance covered by the balls 1 and 2, respectively before the 1st ball comes to rest, then

$$y_1 = \frac{v_1^2}{2g} = \frac{4v^2}{2g} \text{ and } y_2 = \frac{v_2^2}{2g} = \frac{v^2}{2g} \qquad [v^2 - u^2 = 2gh]$$

Since, $$y_1 - y_2 = 15\text{m}, \frac{4v^2}{2g} - \frac{v^2}{2g} = 15\text{m} \text{ or } \frac{3v^2}{2g} = 15\text{m}$$

or $$v^2 = \sqrt{5 \times (2 \times 10)}$$

or $$v = 10 \text{ m/s}$$

Clearly, $v_1 = 20$ m/s and $v_2 = 10$ m/s

as $$y_1 = \frac{v_1^2}{2g} = \frac{(20)^2}{2 \times 10} = 20\text{m},$$

$\therefore$ $$y_2 = y_1 - 15\text{m} = 5\text{m}$$

If t_2 is the time taken by the ball 2 to cover a distance of 5m then

$$y_2 = v_2 t - \frac{1}{2} g t_2^2$$

$$5 = 10t_2 - 5t_2^2 \text{ or } t_2^2 - 2t_2 + 1 = 0,$$

where $$(t_2 - 1)^2 = 0 \text{ or } t_2 = 1\text{s}$$

Since t_1 (time taken by ball 1 to cover distance of 20m) is 2s, time interval between the two throws

$$= t_1 - t_2 = 2\text{s} - 1\text{s} = 1\text{s}$$

Mistake Alert! *We should be very careful, when we are applying the equation of rectilinear motion.*

Chapter

03 Motion in a Plane

Multiple Choice Questions (MCQs)

Q.1 The angle between $\mathbf{A} = \hat{\mathbf{i}} + \hat{\mathbf{j}}$ and $\mathbf{B} = \hat{\mathbf{i}} - \hat{\mathbf{j}}$ is

(a) 45°
(b) 90°
(c) – 45°
(d) 180°

Thinking Process To solve such type of questions, we have to use the formula for dot product or cross product.

Ans. ***(b)*** Given,

$$\mathbf{A} = \hat{\mathbf{i}} + \hat{\mathbf{j}}$$
$$\mathbf{B} = \hat{\mathbf{i}} - \hat{\mathbf{j}}$$

We know that,

$$\mathbf{A} \cdot \mathbf{B} = |\mathbf{A}||\mathbf{B}|\cos\theta$$

$$\Rightarrow \quad (\hat{\mathbf{i}} + \hat{\mathbf{j}}) \cdot (\hat{\mathbf{i}} - \hat{\mathbf{j}}) = (\sqrt{1+1})(\sqrt{1+1})\cos\theta$$

where, θ is the angle between **A** and **B**

$$\Rightarrow \quad \cos\theta = \frac{1-1}{2} = \frac{0}{2} = 0$$

$$\Rightarrow \quad \theta = 90°$$

Q.2 Which one of the following statements is true?

(a) A scalar quantity is the one that is conserved in a process.
(b) A scalar quantity is the one that can never take negative values.
(c) A scalar quantity is the one that does not vary from one point to another in space.
(d) A scalar quantity has the same value for observers with different orientation of the axes.

Ans. ***(d)***

(a) This statement is false as kinetic energy is not conserved during inelastic collision.
(b) Temperature can have negative value, so this statement is false.
(c) In space gravitational potential energy varies from one point to another, so this statement is false.
(d) A scalar quantity is independent of direction and hence has the same value for observers with different orientations of the axes. Therefore this statement is true.

Q.3 Figure shows the orientation of two vectors **u** and **v** in the XY-plane. If $\mathbf{u} = a\hat{\mathbf{i}} + b\hat{\mathbf{j}}$ and $\mathbf{v} = p\hat{\mathbf{i}} + q\hat{\mathbf{j}}$, which of the following is correct?

(a) a and p are positive while b and q are negative.
(b) a, p and b are positive while q is negative.
(c) a, q and b are positive while p is negative.
(d) a, b, p and q are all positive.

Thinking Process In this question, according to the diagram, we have to decide the components of a given vector.

Ans. *(b)* Clearly from the diagram, $\mathbf{u} = a\hat{\mathbf{i}} + b\hat{\mathbf{j}}$

As **u** is in the first quadrant, hence both components a and b will be positive.

For $\mathbf{v} = p\hat{\mathbf{i}} + q\hat{\mathbf{j}}$, as it is in positive x-direction and located downward, hence x-component p will be positive and y-component q will be negative.

Q.4 The component of a vector **r** along X-axis will have maximum value, if

(a) **r** is along positive Y-axis
(b) **r** is along positive X-axis
(c) **r** makes an angle of 45° with the X-axis
(d) **r** is along negative Y-axis

Ans. *(b)* Let **r** makes an angle θ with positive X-axis component of **r** along X-axis

$$r_x = |\mathbf{r}| \cos \theta$$

$$(r_x)_{\text{maximum}} = |\mathbf{r}| (\cos \theta)_{\text{maximum}}$$

$$= |\mathbf{r}| \cos 0° = |\mathbf{r}| \quad [\because \cos \theta \text{ is maximum of } \theta = 0°]$$

As $\theta = 0°$, so **r** is along positive X-axis.

Q.5 The horizontal range of a projectile fired at an angle of 15° is 50 m. If it is fired with the same speed at an angle of 45°, its range will be

(a) 60 m (b) 71 m (c) 100 m (d) 141 m

Ans. *(c)* Given, $\theta = 15°$ and $R = 50$ m

We know that,

$$\text{Range } R = \frac{u^2 \sin 2\theta}{g}$$

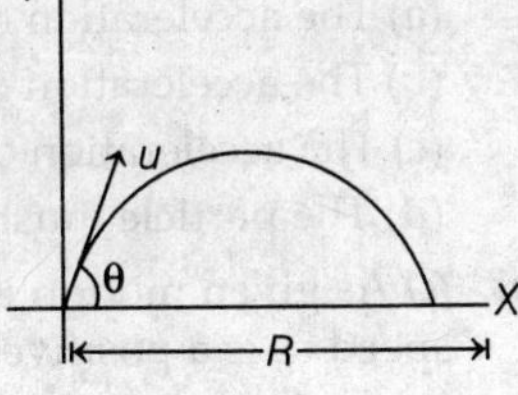

Putting all the given values in the formula, we get

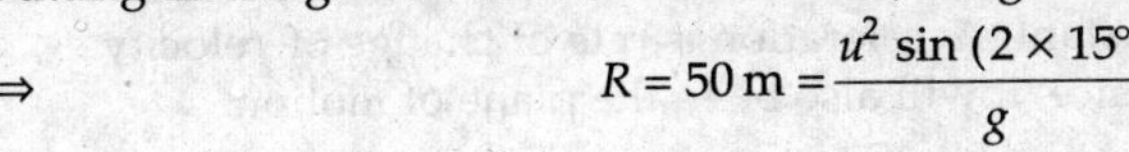

$$\Rightarrow \quad R = 50 \text{ m} = \frac{u^2 \sin (2 \times 15°)}{g}$$

$$\Rightarrow \quad 50 = \frac{u^2}{2g} \Rightarrow 100 = \frac{u^2}{g} \quad \text{...(i)}$$

Now, $\theta = 45°$, so new range,

$$R' = \frac{u^2 \sin 90°}{g} = \frac{u^2}{g} = 100 \text{ m} \quad \text{[From, Eq. (i)] } [\because \sin 90° = 1]$$

Q.6 Consider the quantities, pressure, power, energy, impulse, gravitational potential, electrical charge, temperature, area. Out of these, the only vector quantities are

(a) impulse, pressure and area
(b) impulse and area
(c) area and gravitational potential
(d) impulse and pressure

Ans. ***(b)*** We know that, impulse, $J = F \cdot \Delta t = \Delta p$, where F is force, Δt is time duration and Δp is change in momentum. As Δp is a vector quantity, hence impulse is also a vector quantity. Sometimes area can also be treated as vector, having direction perpendicular to area.

Q.7 In a two dimensional motion, instantaneous speed v_0 is a positive constant. Then, which of the following are necessarily true?

(a) The average velocity is not zero at any time.
(b) Average acceleration must always vanish.
(c) Displacements in equal time intervals are equal.
(d) Equal path lengths are traversed in equal intervals.

Thinking Process As speed is a scalar quantity, hence it will be related with path length (scalar quantity) only.

Ans. ***(d)*** We know that,

$$\text{speed, } v_0 = \frac{\text{total distance travelled}}{\text{time taken}}$$

Hence, total distance travelled = path length = (speed) × time taken

Mistake Alert! *We should be very careful with the fact that speed is related with total distance covered not with displacement.*

Q.8 In a two dimensional motion, instantaneous speed v_0 is a positive constant. Then, which of the following are necessarily true?

(a) The acceleration of the particle is zero.
(b) The acceleration of the particle is bounded.
(c) The acceleration of the particle is necessarily in the plane of motion.
(d) The particle must be undergoing a uniform circular motion.

Ans. ***(c)*** As given motion is two dimensional motion and given that instantaneous speed v_0 is a positive constant. Acceleration is rate of change of velocity (instantaneous speed) hence, it will also be in the plane of motion.

Q.9 Three vectors **A**, **B** and **C** add upto zero. Find which is false.

(a) $(\mathbf{A} \times \mathbf{B}) \times \mathbf{C}$ is not zero unless **B**, **C** are parallel.
(b) $(\mathbf{A} \times \mathbf{B}) \cdot \mathbf{C}$ is not zero unless **B**, **C** are parallel.
(c) If **A**, **B**, **C** define a plane, $(\mathbf{A} \times \mathbf{B}) \times \mathbf{C}$ is in that plane.
(d) $(\mathbf{A} \times \mathbf{B}) \cdot \mathbf{C} = |\mathbf{A}|\,|\mathbf{B}|\,|\mathbf{C}| \rightarrow \mathbf{C}^2 = \mathbf{A}^2 + \mathbf{B}^2$.

Ans. It is given that $\mathbf{A}+\mathbf{B}+\mathbf{C}=0$.

(a) Now, $(\mathbf{A}\times\mathbf{B})\times\mathbf{C}=(|A||B|\sin\theta|c|\sin\phi)\hat{\mathbf{n}}$

where θ is the angle between **A** and **B** and ϕ is the angle between the vector $(\mathbf{A}\times\mathbf{B})$ and $\mathbf{C}$. This can only be zero if **B** is parallel to **C** because only then $\phi=0$ and hence $\sin\phi=0$.

$\therefore$ option (a) is true.

(b) Since, **A**, **B** and **C** lie in the same plane, so whatever be the orientation of **B** and **C**, the vectors $(\mathbf{A}\times\mathbf{B})$ and **C** will always be perpendicular to each other.

$\therefore$ option (b) is false.

(c) **A**, **B** and **C** defines a plane.

Now, $(\mathbf{A}\times\mathbf{B})$ is a vector perpendicular to the plane containing **A**, **B** and **C** and $(\mathbf{A}\times\mathbf{B})\times\mathbf{C}$ is perpendicular to the plane containing $(\mathbf{A}\times\mathbf{B})$ and **C**, which again lies in the plane containing the vectors **A**, **B** and **C**.

$\therefore$ option (c) is true

(d) Since, **A**, **B**, **C** lies in the same plane so, $(\mathbf{A}\times\mathbf{B})\cdot\mathbf{C}$ is always zero as discussed in option (b).

$\therefore$ option (d) is false.

Q.10 It is found that $|\mathbf{A}+\mathbf{B}|=|\mathbf{A}|$. This necessarily implies

(a) $\mathbf{B}=0$

(b) **A**, **B** are anti-parallel

(c) **A**, **B** are perpendicular

(d) $\mathbf{A}\cdot\mathbf{B}\le 0$

Ans. ***(b)*** Given that, $|\mathbf{A}+\mathbf{B}|=|\mathbf{A}|$ or $|\mathbf{A}+\mathbf{B}|^2=|\mathbf{A}|^2$

$$\Rightarrow \quad |\mathbf{A}|^2+|\mathbf{B}|^2+2|\mathbf{A}||\mathbf{B}|\cos\theta=|\mathbf{A}|^2$$

where, θ is angle between **A** and **B**.

$$\Rightarrow \quad |\mathbf{B}|(|\mathbf{B}|+2|\mathbf{A}|\cos\theta)=0$$

$$\Rightarrow \quad |\mathbf{B}|=0$$

or

$$|\mathbf{B}|+2|\mathbf{A}|\cos\theta=0$$

$$\Rightarrow \quad \cos\theta=-\frac{|\mathbf{B}|}{2|\mathbf{A}|} \qquad \text{...(i)}$$

If **A** and **B** are anti-parallel, then $\theta=180°$

Hence, from Eq. (i),

$$-1=-\frac{|\mathbf{B}|}{2|\mathbf{A}|}\Rightarrow|\mathbf{B}|=2|\mathbf{A}|$$

Hence, correct answer will be **A** and **B** are anti-parallel provided $|\mathbf{B}|=2|\mathbf{A}|$.

Multiple Choice Questions (More Than One Options)

Q.11 Two particles are projected in air with speed v_0 at angles θ_1 and θ_2 (both acute) to the horizontal, respectively. If the height reached by the first particle is greater than that of the second, then tick the right choices.

(a) Angle of projection : $\theta_1 > \theta_2$
(b) Time of flight : $T_1 > T_2$
(c) Horizontal range : $R_1 > R_2$
(d) Total energy : $U_1 > U_2$

Thinking Process In this problem, we have to apply equation for maximum height reached, $H = \frac{u^2 \sin^2 \theta}{2g}$ where, θ is angle of projection and u is speed of projection of a projectile motion.

Ans. (a, b) According to formula, maximum height of a projections is

$$H = \frac{u^2 \sin^2 \theta}{2g}$$

(a) $H_1 > H_2$

$$\sin^2 \theta_1 > \sin^2 \theta_2$$

$$(\sin \theta_1 + \sin \theta_2)(\sin \theta_1 - \sin \theta_2) > 0$$

So, $$(\sin \theta_1 + \sin \theta_2) > 0$$

or $$(\sin \theta_1 - \sin \theta_2) > 0$$

So, $\theta_1 > \theta_2$ and θ lies between 0 and 90° i.e. acute.

(b) $\frac{T_1}{T_2} = \frac{\sin \theta_1}{\sin \theta_2}$

$$\frac{T_1}{T_2} = \frac{\sin \theta_1}{\sin \theta_2}$$

$$T_1 \sin \theta_2 = T_2 \sin \theta_1$$

Since, $$\sin \theta_1 > \sin \theta_2$$

Hence, $$T_1 > T_2$$

(c) θ_1 and θ_2 are acute angles. If $\theta_1 + \theta_2 = 90°$, then $R_1 = R_2$

So, option (c) is incorrect.

(d) As there is no external force on each particle, so energy is conserved in each case.

Initial speed of both the particles is same.

$\therefore$ Total energy, $U = \frac{1}{2} m v_0^2 = \text{constant}$

So, option (d) is incorrect.

Q.12 A particle slides down a frictionless parabolic ($y = x^2$) track ($A - B - C$) starting from rest at point A (figure). Point B is at the vertex of parabola and point C is at a height less than that of point A. After C, the particle moves freely in air as a projectile. If the particle reaches highest point at P, then

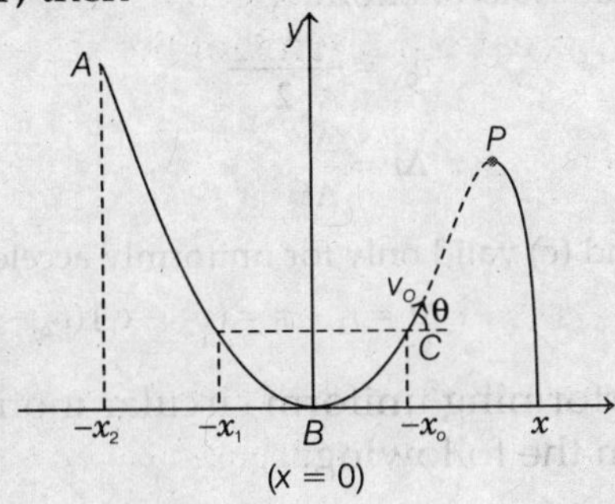

(a) KE at P = KE at B
(b) height at P = height at A
(c) total energy at P = total energy at A
(d) time of travel from A to B = time of travel from B to P

Thinking Process In this type of question, nature of track is very important for consider ration, as friction is not in this track, total energy of the particle will remain constant throughout the journey.

Ans. *(c)* (a) As the given track $y = x^2$ is a frictionless track, thus total energy (KE + PE) will be same throughout the journey.

Hence, total energy at A = total energy at P. At B, the particle is having only KE but at P some KE is converted to P.

Hence, $(\text{KE})_B > (\text{KE})_P$

(b) The motion of the particle is a constrained motion along ABC but after point C to point P it moves freely under gravity.

Hence, height at $P \neq$ height at A.

(c) There is no external force on the system hence, its total energy is conserved.

(d) Path length $AB >$ path length BP

Hence, time of travel from A to $B \neq$ time of travel from B to P.

Q.13 Following are four different relations about displacement, velocity and acceleration for the motion of a particle in general. Choose the incorrect one(s).

(a) $v_{av} = \frac{1}{2}[v(t_1) + v(t_2)]$
(b) $v_{av} = \frac{r(t_2) - r(t_1)}{t_2 - t_1}$
(c) $r = \frac{1}{2}[v(t_2) - v(t_1)](t_2 - t_1)$
(d) $a_{av} = \frac{v(t_2) - v(t_1)}{t_2 - t_1}$

Ans. *(a, c)* If an object undergoes a displacement Δr in time Δt, its average velocity is given by

$v = \frac{\Delta r}{\Delta t} = \frac{r_2 - r_1}{t_2 - t_1}$; where r_1 and r_2 are position vectors corresponding to time t_1 and t_2.

If the velocity of an object changes from v_1 to v_2 in time Δt. Average acceleration is given by

$$a_{av} = \frac{\Delta v}{\Delta t} = \frac{v_2 - v_1}{t_2 - t_1}$$

But when acceleration is non-uniform

$$v_{av} \neq \frac{v_1 + v_2}{2}$$

We can write $$\Delta v = \frac{\Delta r}{\Delta t}$$

Hence, option (a) and (c) valid only for uniformly accelerated motion.

$$\Delta r = r_2 - r_1 = (v_2 - v_1)(t_2 - t_1)$$

Q.14 For a particle performing uniform circular motion, choose the correct statement(s) from the following.

(a) Magnitude of particle velocity (speed) remains constant.
(b) Particle velocity remains directed perpendicular to radius vector.
(c) Direction of acceleration keeps changing as particle moves.
(d) Angular momentum is constant in magnitude but direction keeps changing.

Ans. ***(a, b, c)*** For a particle performing uniform circular motion

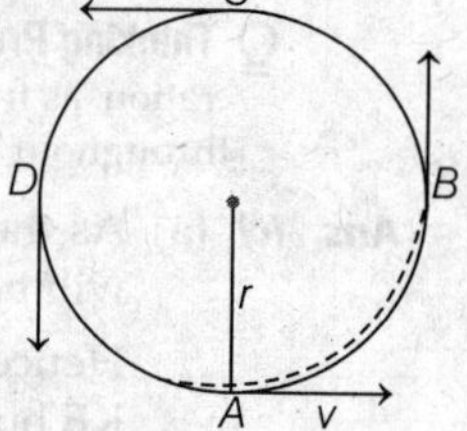

(a) speed will be constant throughout.
(b) velocity will be tangential in the direction of motion at a particular point. So it is always perpendicular to radius vector.
(c) acceleration, $a = \frac{v^2}{r}$ will always be towards centre of the circular path.
(d) angular momentum (mvr) is constant in magnitude and direction/out of the plane perpendicularly as well i.e. perpendicular to $\mathbf{r}$ as well as $\mathbf{v}$.

Note In uniform circular motion, magnitude of velocity and acceleration is constant but direction changes continuously.

Q.15 For two vectors **A** and **B**, $|\mathbf{A}+\mathbf{B}| = |\mathbf{A}-\mathbf{B}|$ is always true when

(a) $|\mathbf{A}| = |\mathbf{B}| \neq 0$
(b) $\mathbf{A} \perp \mathbf{B}$
(c) $|\mathbf{A}| = |\mathbf{B}| \neq 0$ and **A** and **B** are parallel or anti-parallel
(d) either $|\mathbf{A}|$ or $|\mathbf{B}|$ is zero

Ans. ***(b, d)*** Given, $|\mathbf{A}+\mathbf{B}| = |\mathbf{A}-\mathbf{B}|$

$$\Rightarrow \sqrt{|\mathbf{A}|^2 + |\mathbf{B}|^2 + 2|\mathbf{A}||\mathbf{B}|\cos\theta} = \sqrt{|\mathbf{A}|^2 + |\mathbf{B}|^2 - 2|\mathbf{A}||\mathbf{B}|\cos\theta}$$

$$\Rightarrow |\mathbf{A}|^2 + |\mathbf{B}|^2 + 2|\mathbf{A}||\mathbf{B}|\cos\theta = |\mathbf{A}|^2 + |\mathbf{B}|^2 - 2|\mathbf{A}||\mathbf{B}|\cos\theta$$

$$\Rightarrow 4|\mathbf{A}||\mathbf{B}|\cos\theta = 0$$

$$\Rightarrow |\mathbf{A}||\mathbf{B}|\cos\theta = 0$$

$$\Rightarrow |\mathbf{A}| = 0 \text{ or } |\mathbf{B}| = 0 \text{ or } \cos\theta = 0$$

$$\Rightarrow \theta = 90^\circ$$

When $\theta = 90°$, we can say that $\mathbf{A} \perp \mathbf{B}$

Now, if $|\mathbf{A}| = 0$, then $|\mathbf{A} + \mathbf{B}| = \mathbf{A} - \mathbf{B}|$

Similarly, if $|\mathbf{B}| = 0$, then $|\mathbf{A} + \mathbf{B}| = |\mathbf{A} - \mathbf{B}|$

Hence, (b) and (d) are correct.

Very Short Answer Type Questions

Q.16 A cyclist starts from centre O of a circular park of radius 1 km and moves along the path $OPRQO$ as shown in figure. If he maintains constant speed of 10 ms^{-1}, what is his acceleration at point R in magnitude and direction?

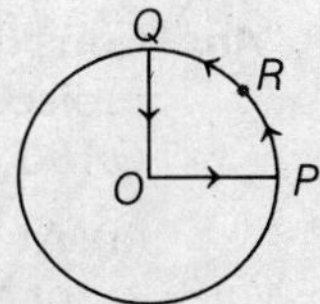

Ans. As shown in the adjacent figure, the cyclist covers the path $OPRQO$.

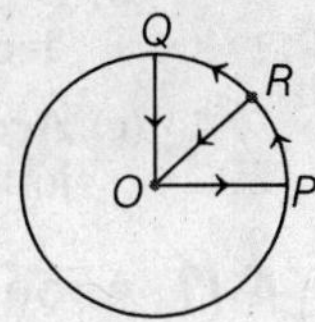

As an object is performing uniform circular motion, acceleration is called centripetal acceleration and is always directed towards the centre.

Hence, acceleration at R is $a = \dfrac{v^2}{r}$

$$\Rightarrow \qquad a = \frac{(10)^2}{1 \text{ km}} = \frac{100}{10^3} = 0.1 \text{ m/s}^2 \text{ along } RO.$$

Q.17 A particle is projected in air at some angle to the horizontal, moves along parabola as shown in figure, where x and y indicate horizontal and vertical directions, respectively. Shown in the diagram, direction of velocity and acceleration at points A, B and C.

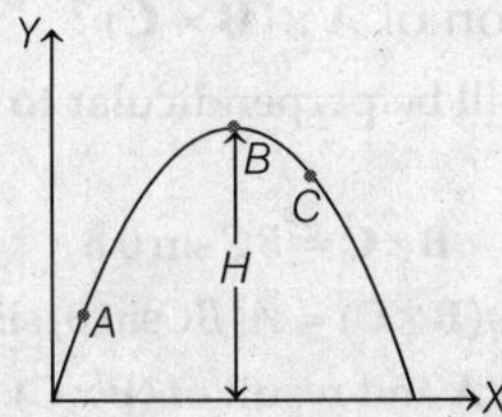

- **Concept Insight** In this problem we use the concept that, when a particle is under projectile motion, horizontal component of velocity will always be constant and acceleration is always vertically downward and is equal to g.

Ans. Consider the adjacent diagram in which a particle is projected at an angle θ.

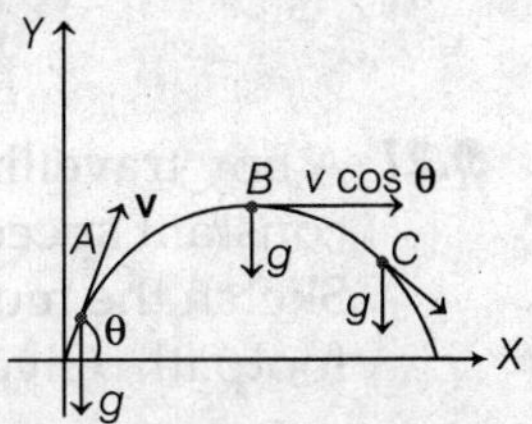

v_x = Horizontal component of velocity

$= v \cos \theta$ = constant.

v_y = Vertical component of velocity $= v \sin \theta$

Velocity will always be tangential to the curve in the direction of motion and acceleration is always vertically downward and is equal to g (acceleration due to gravity).

Q.18 A ball is thrown from a roof top at an angle of 45° above the horizontal. It hits the ground a few seconds later. At what point during its motion, does the ball have

(a) greatest speed (b) smallest speed

(c) greatest acceleration

Explain.

Ans. Consider the adjacent diagram in which a ball is projected from point O, and covering the path OABC.

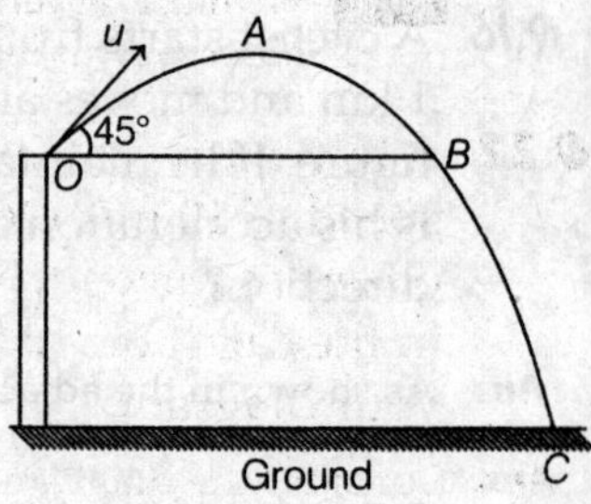

(a) At point C, because at this point, whole energy of ball (PE + KE) changes into KE only.

(b) During upward journey from O to A, speed decreases and will be minimum at point A.

(c) Acceleration is always constant throughout the journey and is vertically downward equal to g.

Q.19 A football is kicked into the air vertically upwards. What is its (a) acceleration and (b) velocity at the highest point?

Ans. (a) Consider the adjacent diagram in which a football is kicked into the air vertically upwards. Acceleration of the football will always be vertically downward and is equal to g.

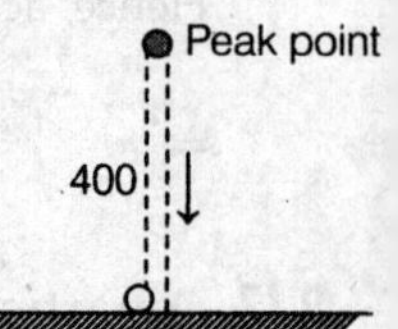

(b) When the football reaches the highest point, velocity will be zero as it is continuously retarded by acceleration due to gravity g.

Q.20 A, B and C are three non-collinear, non co-planar vectors. What can you say about direction of $\mathbf{A}\times(\mathbf{B}\times\mathbf{C})$?

Ans. The direction of $(\mathbf{B}\times\mathbf{C})$ will be perpendicular to the plane containing **B** and **C** by right hand rule.

$$\mathbf{B}\times\mathbf{C} = BC\sin\theta\,\hat{\mathbf{n}}$$

Now, $$\mathbf{A}\times(\mathbf{B}\times\mathbf{C}) = A(BC\sin\theta)\sin\alpha\,\hat{\mathbf{p}}$$

Where α is angle between **A** and result of $(\mathbf{B}\times\mathbf{C})$. $\hat{\mathbf{p}}$ has direction perpendicular to **A** as well as $\hat{\mathbf{n}}$. So, $\mathbf{A}\times(\mathbf{B}\times\mathbf{C})$ will be perpendicular to the plane containing vector **A** and vector $(\mathbf{B}\times\mathbf{C})$.

Short Answer Type Questions

Q.21 A boy travelling in an open car moving on a levelled road with constant speed tosses a ball vertically up in the air and catches it back. Sketch the motion of the ball as observed by a boy standing on the footpath. Give explanation to support your diagram.

Ans. The path of the ball observed by a boy standing on the footpath is parabolic. The horizontal speed of the ball is same as that of the car, therefore ball as well car travels equal horizontal distance.

Due to its vertical speed, the ball follows a parabolic path.

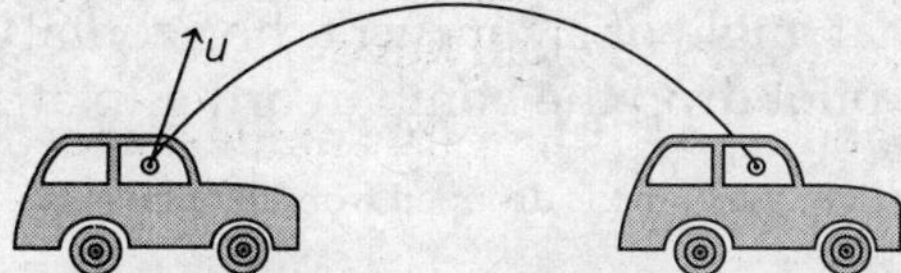

Note We must be very clear that we are working with respect to ground. When we observe with respect to the car, motion will be along vertical direction only.

Q.22 A boy throws a ball in air at 60° to the horizontal along a road with a speed of 10 m/s (36 km/h). Another boy sitting in a passing by car observes the ball. Sketch the motion of the ball as observed by the boy in the car, if car has a speed of (18 km/h). Give explanation to support your diagram.

Ans. Consider the diagram below

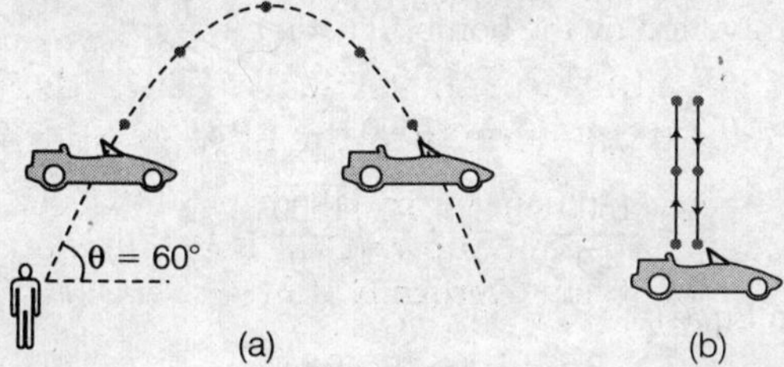

The boy is at rest and throws the ball at an angle of 60° with horizontal.

$\therefore$ Horizontal component of velocity $= u\cos\theta = (10\cos 60^\circ)$ m/s.

$$= 10 \times \frac{1}{2} = 5 \text{ m/s}$$

Speed of the car = 18 km/h = 5 m/s.

As horizontal speed of ball and car is same, hence relative velocity of car and ball in the horizontal direction will be zero.

Only vertical motion of the ball will be seen by the boy in the car as shown in Fig. (b).

Q.23 In dealing with motion of projectile in air, we ignore effect of air resistance on motion. This gives trajectory as a parabola as you have studied. What would the trajectory look like, if air resistance is included? Sketch such a trajectory and explain why you have drawn it that way.

Thinking Process When air resistance is included, the horizontal component of velocity will not be constant and obviously trajectory will change.

Ans. Due to air resistance, particle's energy as well as horizontal component of velocity keeps on decreasing making the fall steeper than rise as shown in the figure.

When we are neglecting air resistance, path was symmetric parabola (OAC). When air resistance is considered, path is asymmetric parabola (OAB).

Q.24 A fighter plane is flying horizontally at an altitude of 1.5 km with speed 720 km/h. At what angle of sight (w.r.t. horizontal) when the target is seen, should the pilot drop the bomb in order to attack the target?

Thinking Process When the bomb is dropped from the plane, the bomb will have same velocity as that of plane.

Ans. Consider the adjacent diagram. Let a fighter plane, when it be at position P, drops a bomb to hit a target T.

Plane P θ P' Target T

Let $\angle P'PT = \theta$

$$\text{Speed of the plane} = 720 \text{ km/h} = 720 \times \frac{5}{18} \text{ m/s}$$

$$= 200 \text{ m/s}$$

Altitude of the plane $(P'T) = 1.5 \text{ km} = 1500 \text{ m}$

If bomb hits the target after time t, then horizontal distance travelled by the bomb,

$$PP' = u \times t = 200t \quad \text{...(i)}$$

Vertical distance travelled by the bomb, $P't = u_y t + \frac{1}{2} g t^2$ [as $u_y = 0$]

$$\Rightarrow \quad P'T = \frac{1}{2} g t^2 \Rightarrow 1500 = \frac{1}{2} \times 9.8 t^2$$

$$\Rightarrow \quad t^2 = \frac{1500}{4.9} \Rightarrow t = \sqrt{\frac{1500}{4.9}} = 17.49 \text{ s}$$

Using value of t in Eq. (i),

$$PP' = 200 \times 17.49 \text{ m}$$

Now, $$\tan\theta = \frac{P'T}{P'P} = \frac{1500}{200 \times 17.49} = 0.42881$$

$$\Rightarrow \quad \theta = 23^\circ \, 21'$$

Note Angle is with respect to target. As seen by observer in the plane, motion of the bomb will be vertically downward below the plane.

Q.25 (a) Earth can be thought of as a sphere of radius 6400 km. Any object (or a person) is performing circular motion around the axis of the earth due to the earth rotation (period 1 day). What is acceleration of object on the surface of the earth (at equator) towards its centre? What is it at latitude θ? How does these accelerations compare with $g = 9.8 \text{ m/s}^2$?

(b) Earth also moves in circular orbit around the sun once every year with an orbital radius of 1.5×10^{11} m. What is the acceleration of the earth (or any object on the surface of the earth) towards the centre of the sun? How does this acceleration compare with $g = 9.8 \text{ m/s}^2$?

Ans. (a) Radius of the earth $(R) = 6400 \text{ km} = 6.4 \times 10^6 \text{ m}$

Time period $(T) = 1 \text{ day} = 24 \times 60 \times 60 \text{ s} = 86400 \text{ s}$

$$\text{Centripetal acceleration } (a_c) = \omega^2 R = R\left(\frac{2\pi}{T}\right)^2 = \frac{4\pi^2 R}{T} = \frac{4 \times (3.14)^2 \times 6.4 \times 10^6}{(24 \times 60 \times 60)^2}$$

$$= \frac{4 \times 484 \times 64 \times 10^6}{49 \times (24 \times 3600)^2} = 3.38 \times 10^{-2} \text{ m/s}^2$$

At equator, latitude $\theta = 0°$

$$\therefore \quad \frac{a_c}{g} = \frac{3.38 \times 10^{-2}}{9.8} = 3.4 \times 10^{-3}$$

which is smalles than 1.

(b) Orbital radius of the earth around the sun $(R) = 1.5 \times 10^{11}$ m

Time period = 1 yr = 365 day

$$= 365 \times 24 \times 60 \times 60 \text{ s} = 3.15 \times 10^7 \text{ s}$$

$$\text{Centripetal acceleration } (a_c) = R\omega^2 = \frac{4\pi^2 R}{T^2}$$

$$= \frac{4 \times (22/7)^2 \times 1.5 \times 10^{11}}{(3.15 \times 10^7)^2} = 5.97 \times 10^{-3} \text{ m/s}^2$$

$$\therefore \quad \frac{a_c}{g} = \frac{5.97 \times 10^{-3}}{9.8} = 6.09 \times 10^{-4}$$

Q.26 Given below in Column I are the relations between vectors **a**, **b** and **c** and in Column II are the orientations of **a**, **b** and **c** in the XY- plane. Match the relation in Column I to correct orientations in Column II.

Column I	Column II
(a) $\mathbf{a} + \mathbf{b} = \mathbf{c}$	(i) 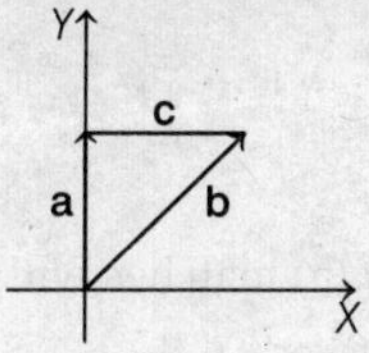
(b) $\mathbf{a} - \mathbf{c} = \mathbf{b}$	(ii) 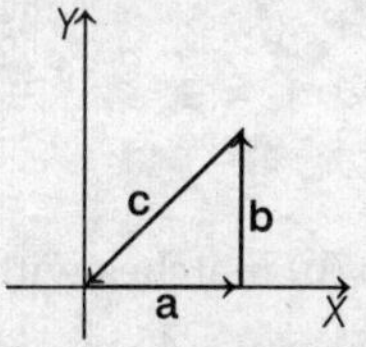
(c) $\mathbf{b} - \mathbf{a} = \mathbf{c}$	(iii) 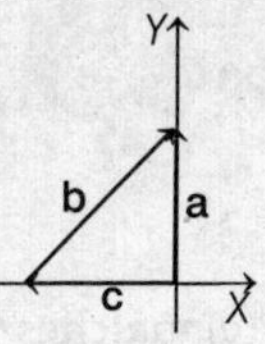
(d) $\mathbf{a} + \mathbf{b} + \mathbf{c} = 0$	(iv) 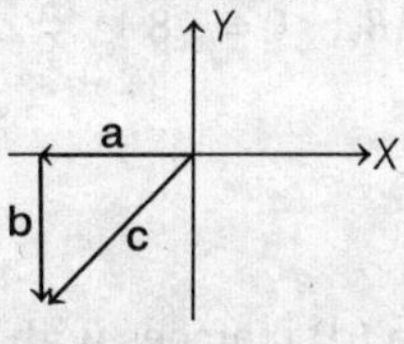

● **Concept Insight** In this problem, triangular law of vector addition concept will be applied. It states that when two vectors represented by two sides of a triangle in the same order, the third side of the triangle represents the resultant vector in magnitude and direction.

Ans. Consider the adjacent diagram in which vectors **A** and **B** are corrected by head and tail.

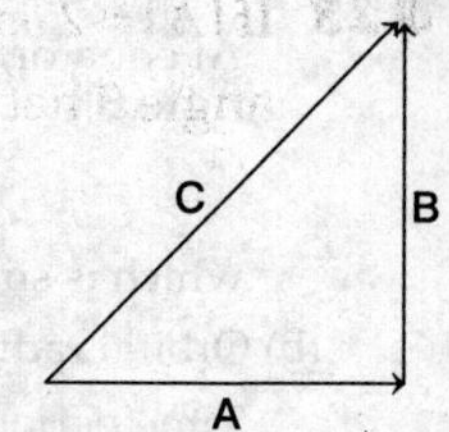

So, resultant vector $\mathbf{C} = \mathbf{A} + \mathbf{B}$

(a) From (iv) it is clear that $\mathbf{c} = \mathbf{a} + \mathbf{b}$

(b) From (iii) $\mathbf{c} + \mathbf{b} = \mathbf{a} \Rightarrow \mathbf{a} - \mathbf{c} = \mathbf{b}$

(c) From (i) $\mathbf{b} = \mathbf{a} + \mathbf{c} \Rightarrow \mathbf{b} - \mathbf{a} = \mathbf{c}$

(d) From (ii) $-\mathbf{c} = \mathbf{a} + \mathbf{b} \Rightarrow \mathbf{a} + \mathbf{b} + \mathbf{c} = 0$

Q.27 If $|\mathbf{A}| = 2$ and $|\mathbf{B}| = 4$, then match the relation in Column I with the angle θ between *A* and *B* in Column II.

Column I	Column II
(a) $\mathbf{A} \cdot \mathbf{B} = 0$	(i) $\theta = 0°$
(b) $\mathbf{A} \cdot \mathbf{B} = +8$	(ii) $\theta = 90°$
(c) $\mathbf{A} \cdot \mathbf{B} = 4$	(iii) $\theta = 180°$
(d) $\mathbf{A} \cdot \mathbf{B} = -8$	(iv) $\theta = 60°$

Ans. Given, $|\mathbf{A}| = 2$ and $|\mathbf{B}| = 4$

(a) $\mathbf{A} \cdot \mathbf{B} = AB\cos\theta = 0$

$$\Rightarrow \quad 2 \times 4 \cos\theta = 0$$
$$\Rightarrow \quad \cos\theta = 0 = \cos 90°$$
$$\Rightarrow \quad \theta = 90°$$

∴ Option (a) matches with option (ii).

(b) $\mathbf{A} \cdot \mathbf{B} = AB\cos\theta = 8$

$$\Rightarrow \quad 2 \times 4 \cos\theta = 8$$
$$\Rightarrow \quad \cos\theta = 1 = \cos 0°$$
$$\Rightarrow \quad \theta = 0°$$

∴ Option (b) matches with option (i).

(c) $\mathbf{A} \cdot \mathbf{B} = AB\cos\theta = 4$

$$\Rightarrow \quad 2 \times 4 \cos\theta = 4$$
$$\Rightarrow \quad \cos\theta = \frac{1}{2} = \cos 60°$$
$$\Rightarrow \quad \theta = 60°$$

∴ Option (c) matches with option (iv).

(d) $\mathbf{A} \cdot \mathbf{B} = AB\cos\theta = -8$

$$\Rightarrow \quad 2 \times 4 \cos\theta = -8$$
$$\Rightarrow \quad \cos\theta = -1 = \cos 180°$$
$$\Rightarrow \quad \theta = 180°$$

∴ Option (d) matches with option (iii).

Q.28 If $|\mathbf{A}| = 2$ and $|\mathbf{B}| = 4$, then match the relation in Column I with the angle θ between A and B in Column II.

Column I	Column II
(a) $\lvert\mathbf{A} \times \mathbf{B}\rvert = 0$	(i) $\theta = 30^\circ$
(b) $\lvert\mathbf{A} \times \mathbf{B}\rvert = 8$	(ii) $\theta = 45^\circ$
(c) $\lvert\mathbf{A} \times \mathbf{B}\rvert = 4$	(iii) $\theta = 90^\circ$
(d) $\lvert\mathbf{A} \times \mathbf{B}\rvert = 4\sqrt{2}$	(iv) $\theta = 0^\circ$

Ans. Given $|\mathbf{A}| = 2$ and $|\mathbf{B}| = 4$

(a) $|\mathbf{A} \times \mathbf{B}| = AB \sin\theta = 0$

$$\Rightarrow \quad 2 \times 4 \times \sin\theta = 0$$

$$\Rightarrow \quad \sin\theta = 0 = \sin 0^\circ$$

$$\Rightarrow \quad \theta = 0^\circ$$

$\therefore$ Option (a) matches with option (iv).

(b) $|\mathbf{A} \times \mathbf{B}| = AB \sin\theta = 8$

$$\Rightarrow \quad 2 \times 4 \sin\theta = 8$$

$$\Rightarrow \quad \sin\theta = 1 = \sin 90^\circ$$

$$\Rightarrow \quad \theta = 90^\circ$$

$\therefore$ Option (b) matches with option (iii).

(c) $|\mathbf{A} \times \mathbf{B}| = AB \sin\theta = 4$

$$\Rightarrow \quad 2 \times 4 \sin\theta = 4$$

$$\Rightarrow \quad \sin\theta = \frac{1}{2} = \sin 30^\circ$$

$$\Rightarrow \quad \theta = 30^\circ$$

$\therefore$ Option (c) matches with option (i).

(d) $|\mathbf{A} \times \mathbf{B}| = AB \sin\theta = 4\sqrt{2}$

$$\Rightarrow \quad 2 \times 4 \sin\theta = 4\sqrt{2}$$

$$\Rightarrow \quad \sin\theta = \frac{1}{\sqrt{2}} = \sin 45^\circ$$

$$\Rightarrow \quad \theta = 45^\circ$$

$\therefore$ Option (d) matches with option (ii).

Long Answer Type Questions

Q.29 A hill is 500 m high. Supplies are to be sent across the hill using a canon that can hurl packets at a speed of 125 m/s over the hill. The canon is located at a distance of 800 m from the foot of hill and can be moved on the ground at a speed of 2 m/s, so that its distance from the hill can be adjusted. What is the shortest time in which a packet can reach on the ground across the hill? (Take, $g = 10 \text{ m/s}^2$).

Ans. Given, speed of packets = 125 m/s

Height of the hill = 500 m.

To cross the hill, the vertical component of the velocity should be sufficient to cross such height.

$$u_y \geq \sqrt{2gh}$$
$$\geq \sqrt{2 \times 10 \times 500}$$
$$\geq 100 \text{ m/s}$$

But $$u^2 = u_x^2 + u_y^2$$

$\therefore$ Horizontal component of initial velocity,

$$u_x = \sqrt{u^2 - u_y^2} = \sqrt{(125)^2 - (100)^2} = 75 \text{ m/s}$$

Time taken to reach the top of the hill,

$$t = \sqrt{\frac{2h}{g}} = \sqrt{\frac{2 \times 500}{10}} = 10 \text{ s}$$

Time taken to reach the ground from the top of the hill, $t' = t = 10$ s. Horizontal distance travelled in 10 s,

$$x = u_x \times t = 75 \times 10 = 750 \text{ m}$$

$\therefore$ Distance through which canon has to be moved = 800 − 750 = 50 m

Speed with which canon can move = 2 m / s

$\therefore$ Time taken by canon $= \frac{50}{2} \Rightarrow t'' = 25$ s

$\therefore$ Total time taken by a packet to reach on the ground $= t'' + t + t' = 25 + 10 + 10 = 45$ s

Q.30 A gun can fire shells with maximum speed v_0 and the maximum horizontal range that can be achieved is $\mathbf{R} = \frac{v_0^2}{g}$. If a target farther away by distance Δx (beyond R) has to be hit with the same gun, show that it could be achieved by raising the gun to a height at least $h = \Delta x \left[1 + \frac{\Delta x}{R}\right]$.

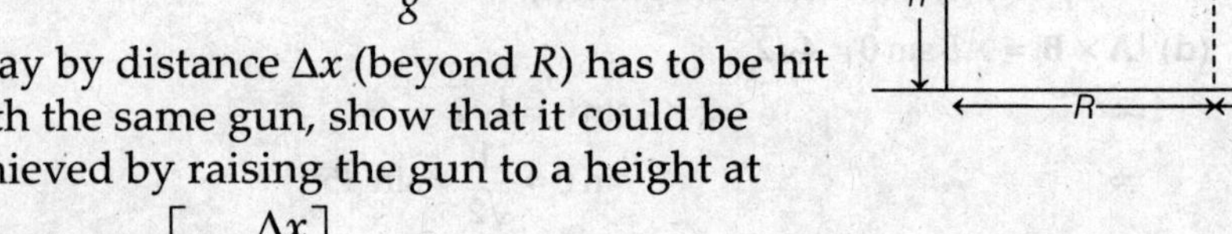

Thinking Process Horizontal range of a projectile is maximum when it is thrown at an angle 45° from the horizontal and $R_{max} = \frac{u^2}{g}$, where u is speed of projection of the projectile.

Ans. This problem can be approached in two different ways

(i) Refer to the diagram, target T is at horizontal distance $x = R + \Delta x$ and between point of projection $y = -h$.

(ii) From point P in the diagram, projection at speed v_0 at an angle θ above horizontal with height h and horizontal range $(R + \Delta x)$

Applying method (i)

Maximum horizontal range,

$$R = \frac{v_0^2}{g}, \text{ for } \theta = 45° \quad \text{...(i)}$$

Let the gun be raised through a height h from the ground, so that it can hit the target. Let vertically downward direction is taken as positive.

Horizontal component of initial velocity = $v_0 \cos\theta$

Vertical component of initial velocity = $-v_0 \sin\theta$

Taking motion in vertical direction,

$$h = (-v_0 \sin\theta)t + \frac{1}{2}gt^2 \quad \text{...(ii)}$$

Taking motion in horizontal direction,

$$(R+\Delta x) = v_0 \cos\theta \times t \Rightarrow t = \frac{(R+\Delta x)}{v_0 \cos\theta} \quad \text{...(iii)}$$

Substituting value of t in Eq. (ii), we get

$$h = (-v_0 \sin\theta) \times \left(\frac{R+\Delta x}{v_0 \cos\theta}\right) + \frac{1}{2}g\left(\frac{R+\Delta x}{v_0 \cos\theta}\right)^2$$

$$\Rightarrow \quad h = -(R+\Delta x)\tan\theta + \frac{1}{2}g\frac{(R+\Delta x)^2}{v_0^2 \cos^2\theta}$$

As angle of projection is $\theta = 45°$, therefore

$$h = -(R+\Delta x)\cdot \tan 45° + \frac{1}{2}g\frac{(R+\Delta x)^2}{v_0^2 \cos^2 45°}$$

$$\Rightarrow \quad h = -(R+\Delta x)\times 1 + \frac{1}{2}g\frac{(R+\Delta x)^2}{v_0^2 (1/2)} \quad \left[\because \tan 45° = 1 \text{ and } \cos 45° = \frac{1}{\sqrt{2}}\right]$$

or

$$h = -(R+\Delta x) + \frac{(R+\Delta x)^2}{R} \quad [\text{Using Eq. (i), } R = v_0^2/g]$$

$$= -(R+\Delta x) + \frac{1}{R}(R^2 + (\Delta x)^2 + 2R\Delta x)$$

$$= -R - \Delta x + \left(R + \frac{(\Delta x)^2}{R} + 2\Delta x\right) = \Delta x + \frac{(\Delta x)^2}{R}$$

$$\Rightarrow \quad h = \Delta x\left(1 + \frac{\Delta x}{R}\right)$$

Hence Proved.

Mistake Alert ! *We should not confuse with the positive direction of motion. Vertically upward direction or vertically downward direction is taken as positive according to convenience.*

Alternate Method

From figure, at point A, $u_y = u\sin\theta$ and $u_x = u\cos\theta$

$$\therefore \quad \Delta x = u\cos\theta \times t$$

Now,

$$h = u_y t + \frac{1}{2}gt^2$$

$$h = u\sin\theta\left(\frac{\Delta x}{u\cos\theta}\right) + \frac{g}{2}\left[\frac{\Delta x}{u\cos\theta}\right]^2 \quad [\because R_{max} = u^2/g \text{ and } \theta = 45°]$$

$$h = \Delta x \tan 45° + \frac{(\Delta x)^2}{2} \times \frac{2}{R}$$

$$h = \Delta x\left[1 + \frac{\Delta x}{R}\right]$$

Q.31 A particle is projected in air at an angle β to a surface which itself is inclined at an angle α to the horizontal (figure).

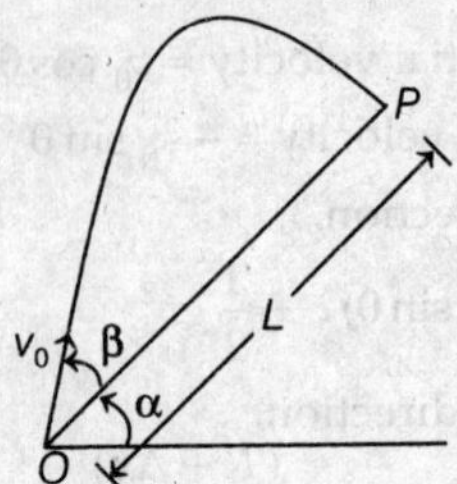

(a) Find an expression of range on the plane surface (distance on the plane from the point of projection at which particle will hit the surface).

(b) Time of flight.

(c) β at which range will be maximum.

Thinking Process To solve problems involving projectile motion on an inclined plane, we have to choose two mutually perpendicular axes, one along inclined plane and other perpendicular to the inclined plane.

Ans. Consider the adjacent diagram.

Mutually perpendicular X and Y-axes are shown in the diagram.

Particle is projected from the point O.

Let time taken in reaching from point O to point P is T.

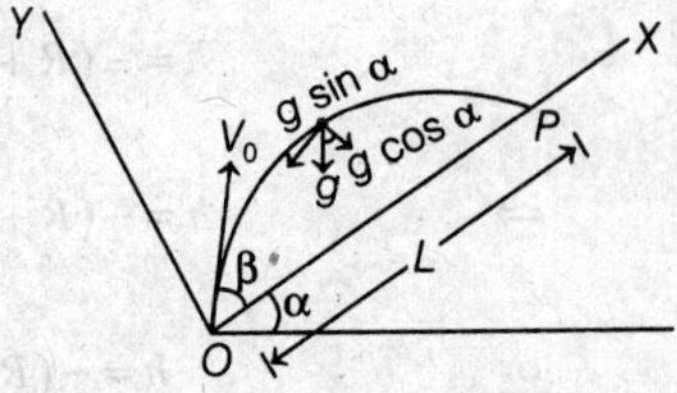

(b) Considering motion along vertical upward direction perpendicular to OX.

For the journey O to P,

$$y = 0,\ u_y = v_0 \sin \beta,\ a_y = -g \cos \alpha,\ t = T$$

Applying equation,

$$y = u_y t + \frac{1}{2} a_y t^2$$

$$\Rightarrow \quad 0 = v_0 \sin \beta T + \frac{1}{2}(-g\cos\alpha)\, T^2$$

$$\Rightarrow \quad T\left[v_0 \sin\beta - \frac{g \cos \alpha}{2} T\right] = 0$$

$$\Rightarrow \quad T = 0,\ T = \frac{2\, v_0 \sin\beta}{g \cos\alpha}$$

As $T = 0$, corresponding to point O

Hence, $$T = \text{Time of flight} = \frac{2\, v_0 \sin\beta}{g \cos\alpha}$$

(a) Considering motion along OX.

$$x = L,\ u_x = v_0 \cos \beta,\ a_x = -g \sin \alpha$$

$$t = T = \frac{2\, v_0 \sin\beta}{g \cos\alpha}$$

$$x = u_x t + \frac{1}{2} a_x t^2$$

$$\Rightarrow \quad L = v_0 \cos\beta\, T + \frac{1}{2}(-g \sin\alpha)\, T^2$$

$$\Rightarrow \quad L = v_0 \cos\beta T - \frac{1}{2} g \sin\alpha\, T^2$$

$$= T\,[v_0 \cos\beta - \frac{1}{2} g \sin\alpha\, T]$$

$$= T\left[v_0 \cos\beta - \frac{1}{2} g \sin\alpha \times \frac{2 v_0 \sin\beta}{g \cos\alpha}\right]$$

$$= \frac{2 v_0 \sin\beta}{g \cos\alpha}\left[v_0 \cos\beta - \frac{v_0 \sin\alpha \sin\beta}{\cos\alpha}\right]$$

$$= \frac{2 v_0^2 \sin\beta}{g \cos^2\alpha}[\cos\beta \cdot \cos\alpha - \sin\alpha \cdot \sin\beta]$$

$$\Rightarrow \quad L = \frac{2 v_0^2 \sin\beta}{g \cos^2\alpha} \cos(\alpha + \beta)$$

That is the required range.

(c) For range (L) to be maximum,

$\sin\beta \,.\, \cos(\alpha + \beta)$ should be maximum.

Let, $z = \sin\beta \cdot \cos(\alpha + \beta)$

$$= \sin\beta\,[\cos\alpha \cdot \cos\beta - \sin\alpha \cdot \sin\beta)$$

$$= \frac{1}{2}[\cos\alpha \cdot \sin 2\beta - 2\sin\alpha \cdot \sin^2\beta]$$

$$= \frac{1}{2}[\sin 2\beta \cdot \cos\alpha - \sin\alpha\,(1 - \cos 2\beta)]$$

$$\Rightarrow \quad z = \frac{1}{2}[\sin 2\beta \cdot \cos\alpha - \sin\alpha + \sin\alpha \cdot \cos 2\beta]$$

$$= \frac{1}{2}[\sin 2\beta \cdot \cos\alpha + \cos 2\beta \cdot \sin\alpha - \sin\alpha]$$

$$= \frac{1}{2}[\sin(2\beta + \alpha) - \sin\alpha]$$

For z to be maximum,

$$\sin(2\beta + \alpha) = 1 = \text{maximum}$$

$$\Rightarrow \quad 2\beta + \alpha = \frac{\pi}{2} \text{ or } \beta = \frac{\pi}{4} - \frac{\alpha}{2}$$

Q.32 A particle falling vertically from a height hits a plane surface inclined to horizontal at an angle θ with speed v_0 and rebounds elastically. Find the distance along the plane where it will hit second time.

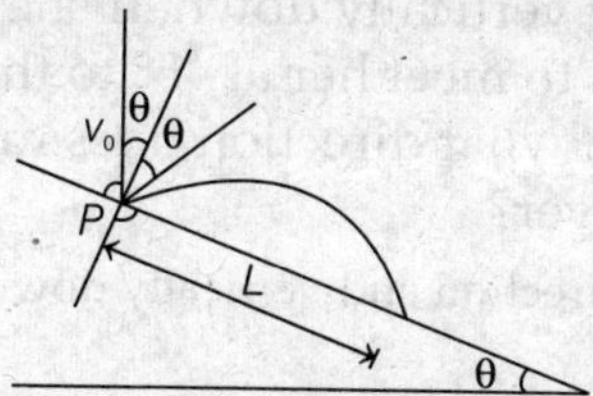

Thinking Process When particle rebounds elastically, speed remains same.

Ans. During elastic collision body rebounds with same speed but direction of velocity is interchanged.

Considering X and Y-axes as shown in the diagram.

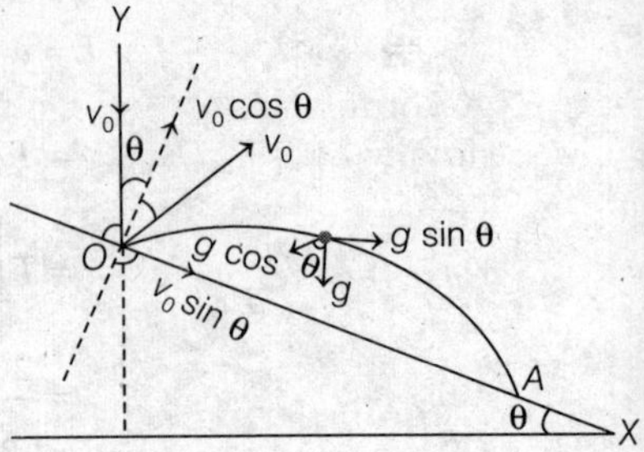

For the motion of the projectile from O to A.

$$y = 0,\ u_y = v_0 \cos\theta$$
$$a_y = -g\cos\theta,\ t = T$$

Applying equation of kinematics,

$$y = u_y t + \frac{1}{2} a_y t^2$$

$$\Rightarrow \quad 0 = v_0 \cos\theta\, T + \frac{1}{2}(-g\cos\theta)\, T^2$$

$$\Rightarrow \quad T\left[v_0 \cos\theta - \frac{g\cos\theta\, T}{2}\right] = 0$$

$$T = \frac{2\, v_0 \cos\theta}{g\cos\theta}$$

As $T = 0$, corresponds to point O

Hence, $$T = \frac{2v_0}{g}$$

Now considering motion along OX.

$$x = L,\ u_x = v_0 \sin\theta,\ a_x = g\sin\theta,\ t = T = \frac{2\, v_0}{g}$$

Applying equation of kinematics,

$$x = u_x t + \frac{1}{2} a_x t^2$$

$$\Rightarrow \quad L = (v_0 \sin\theta)(T) + \frac{1}{2} g\sin\theta\, T^2$$

$$= (v_0 \sin\theta)\left(\frac{2v_0}{g}\right) + \frac{1}{2} g\sin\theta \times \left(\frac{2\, v_0}{g}\right)^2$$

$$= \frac{2\, v_0^2}{g}\sin\theta + \frac{1}{2} g\sin\theta \times \frac{4v_0^2}{g^2} = \frac{2\, v_0^2}{g}[\sin\theta + \sin\theta]$$

$$\Rightarrow \quad L = \frac{4v_0^2}{g}\sin\theta$$

Q.33 A girl riding a bicycle with a speed of 5 m/s towards north direction, observes rain falling vertically down. If she increases her speed to 10 m/s, rain appears to meet her at 45° to the vertical. What is the speed of the rain? In what direction does rain fall as observed by a ground based observer?

Ans. Assume north to be $\hat{\mathbf{i}}$ direction and vertically downward to be $-\hat{\mathbf{j}}$. Let the rain velocity v_r be

$$\mathbf{v}_r = a\,\hat{\mathbf{i}} + b\,\hat{\mathbf{j}}$$

Case **I** Given velocity of girl $= \mathbf{v}_g = (5\ \text{m/s})\,\hat{\mathbf{i}}$

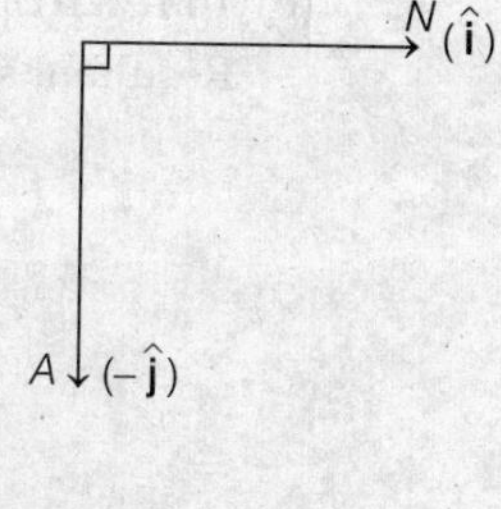

Let $\mathbf{v}_{rg}$ = velocity of rain w.r.t. girl

$$= \mathbf{v_r} - \mathbf{v_g} = (a\hat{\mathbf{i}} + b\hat{\mathbf{j}}) - 5\hat{\mathbf{i}}$$

$$= (a-5)\,\hat{\mathbf{i}} + b\hat{\mathbf{j}}$$

According to question, rain appears to fall vertically downward.

Hence, $$a - 5 = 0 \Rightarrow a = 5$$

***Case* II** Given velocity of the girl, $\mathbf{v_g} = (10\text{ m/s})\,\hat{\mathbf{i}}$

$$\therefore \quad \mathbf{v}_{rg} = \mathbf{v}_r - \mathbf{v}_g = (a\hat{\mathbf{i}} + b\hat{\mathbf{j}}) - 10\hat{\mathbf{i}} = (a-10)\,\hat{\mathbf{i}} + b\hat{\mathbf{j}}$$

According to question, rain appears to fall at 45° to the vertical, hence

$$\tan 45° = \frac{b}{a-10} = 1$$

$$\Rightarrow \quad b = a - 10 = 5 - 10 = -5$$

Hence, velocity of rain $\mathbf{v}_r = a\hat{\mathbf{i}} + b\hat{\mathbf{j}}$

$$\Rightarrow \quad \mathbf{v}_r = 5\hat{\mathbf{i}} - 5\hat{\mathbf{j}}$$

Speed of rain $= |\mathbf{v}_r| = \sqrt{(5)^2 + (-5)^2} = \sqrt{50} = 5\sqrt{2}\text{ m/s}$

Q.34 A river is flowing due east with a speed of 3 m/s. A swimmer can swim in still water at a speed of 4 m/s (figure).

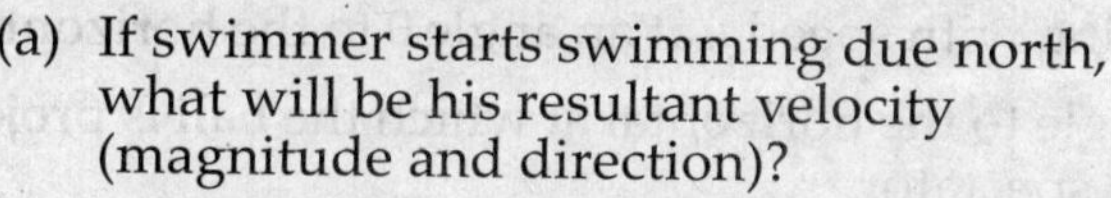

(a) If swimmer starts swimming due north, what will be his resultant velocity (magnitude and direction)?

(b) If he wants to start from point A on south bank and reach opposite point B on north bank,

(i) which direction should he swim?

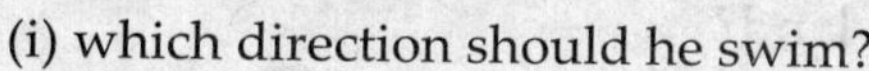

(ii) what will be his resultant speed?

(c) From two different cases as mentioned in (a) and (b) above, in which case will he reach opposite bank in shorter time?

Ans. Given, speed of the river $(v_r) = 3$ m/s (east)

Speed of swimmer $(v_s) = 4$ m/s (east)

(a) When swimmer starts swimming due north, then his resultant velocity,

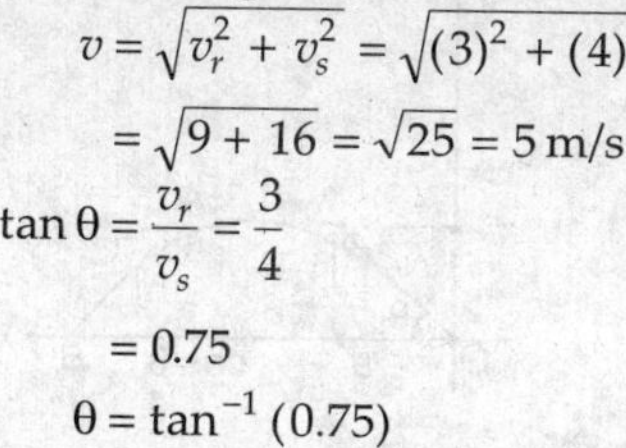

$$v = \sqrt{v_r^2 + v_s^2} = \sqrt{(3)^2 + (4)^2}$$

$$= \sqrt{9 + 16} = \sqrt{25} = 5\text{ m/s}$$

$$\tan\theta = \frac{v_r}{v_s} = \frac{3}{4}$$

$$= 0.75$$

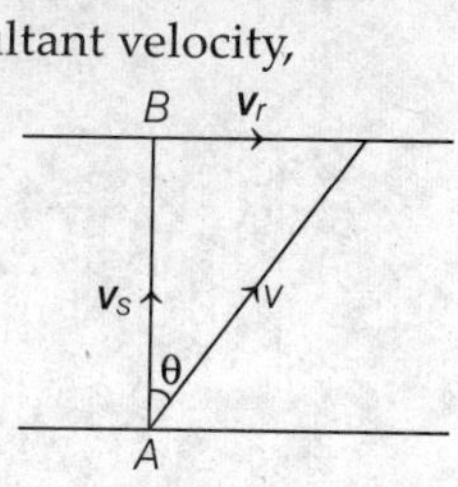

Hence, $$\theta = \tan^{-1}(0.75)$$

$$\theta = 36° \, 87'$$

(b) To reach opposite point B, the swimmer should swim at an angle θ of north.

Resultant speed of the swimmer,

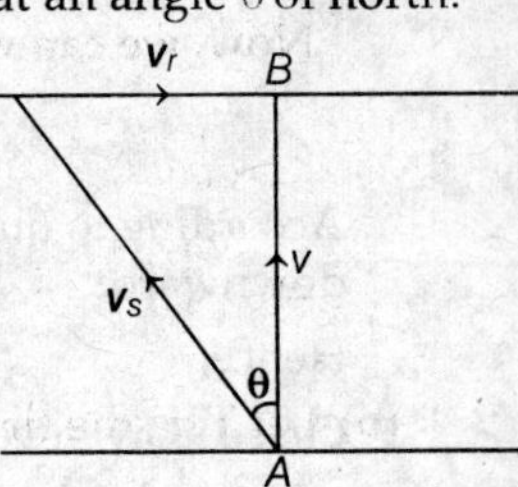

$$v = \sqrt{v_s^2 - v_r^2} = \sqrt{(4)^2 - (3)^2}$$

$$= \sqrt{16 - 9} = \sqrt{7} \text{ m/s}$$

$$\tan\theta = \frac{v_r}{v} = \frac{3}{\sqrt{7}}$$

$$\Rightarrow \quad \theta = \tan^{-1}\left(\frac{3}{\sqrt{7}}\right) \text{ of north}$$

(c) In case (a),

Time taken by the swimmer to cross the river, $t_1 = \frac{d}{v_s} = \frac{d}{4}$ s

In case (b),

Time taken by the swimmer to cross the river

$$t_1 = \frac{d}{v} = \frac{d}{\sqrt{7}}$$

As $\frac{d}{4} < \frac{d}{\sqrt{7}}$, therefore $t_1 < t_2$.

Hence, the swimmer will cross the river in shorter time in case (a).

Q.35 A cricket fielder can throw the cricket ball with a speed v_0. If he throws the ball while running with speed u at an angle θ to the horizontal, find

(a) the effective angle to the horizontal at which the ball is projected in air as seen by a spectator.

(b) what will be time of flight?

(c) what is the distance (horizontal range) from the point of projection at which the ball will land?

(d) θ at which he should throw the ball that would maximise the horizontal range as found in (iii).

(e) how does θ for maximum range change, if $u > v_0$, $u = v_0$, $u < v_0$?

(f) how does θ in (e) compare with that for $u = 0$ (*i.e.*, 45°)?

Ans. Consider the given diagram.

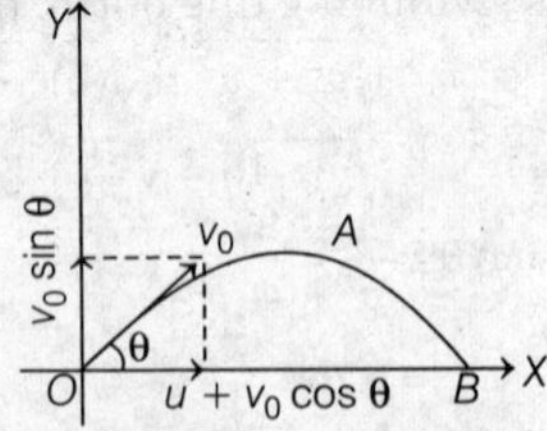

(a) Initial velocity in X-direction, $u_x = u + v_0 \cos\theta$

u_y = initial velocity in Y-direction

$= v_0 \sin\theta$

where, θ is angle of projection.

Now, we can write

$$\tan\theta = \frac{u_y}{u_x} = \frac{v_0 \sin\theta}{u + v_0 \cos\theta}$$

$$\Rightarrow \qquad \theta = \tan^{-1}\left(\frac{v_0 \sin\theta}{u + v_0 \cos\theta}\right)$$

(b) Let T be the time of flight.

As net displacement is zero over time period T.

$$y = 0,\ u_y = v_0 \sin\theta,\ a_y = -g,\ t = T$$

We know that, $y = u_y t + \frac{1}{2} a_y t^2$

$$\Rightarrow \qquad 0 = v_0 \sin\theta\, T + \frac{1}{2}(-g)\, T^2$$

$$\Rightarrow \qquad T\left[v_0 \sin\theta - \frac{g}{2} T\right] = 0 \ \Rightarrow\ T = 0, \frac{2v_0 \sin\theta}{g}$$

$T = 0$, corresponds to point O.

Hence, $T = \frac{2v_0 \sin\theta}{g}$

(c) Horizontal range, $R = (u + v_0 \cos\theta)\, T = (u + v_0 \cos\theta) \frac{2v_0 \sin\theta}{g}$

$$= \frac{v_0}{g}\,[2u \sin\theta + v_0 \sin 2\theta]$$

(d) For horizontal range to be maximum, $\frac{dR}{d\theta} = 0$

$$\frac{v_0}{g}[2u\cos\theta + v_0 \cos 2\theta \times 2] = 0$$

$$2u\cos\theta + 2v_0[2\cos^2\theta - 1] = 0$$

$$u\cos\theta + 2v_0 \cos^2\theta - v_0 = 0$$

$$2v_0 \cos^2\theta + u\cos\theta - v_0 = 0$$

$$\cos\theta = \frac{-u \pm \sqrt{u^2 + 8v_0}}{4v_0}$$

$$\theta = \cos^{-1}\left[\frac{-u \pm \sqrt{u^2 + 8v_0^2}}{4v_0}\right]$$

Since, the angle cannot be negative,

$$\therefore \qquad \theta_{max} = \cos^{-1}\left[\frac{-u + \sqrt{u^2 + 8v_0}}{4v_0}\right]$$

(e) If $u = v_0$,

$$\cos\theta = \frac{-v_0 \pm \sqrt{{v_0}^2 + 8{v_0}^2}}{4v_0} = \frac{-1+3}{4} = \frac{1}{2}$$

$$\Rightarrow \qquad \theta = 60^\circ$$

If $u < v_0$, then $8{v_0}^2 + u^2 \approx 8{v_0}^2$

$$\theta_{max} = \cos^{-1}\left[\frac{-u \pm 2\sqrt{2}v_0}{4v_0}\right] = \cos^{-1}\left[\frac{1}{\sqrt{2}} - \frac{u}{4v_0}\right]$$

If $u << v_0$, then $\theta_{max} = \cos^{-1}\left(\frac{1}{\sqrt{2}}\right) = \frac{\pi}{4}$

If $u > u_0$ and $u >> v_0$

$$\theta_{max} = \cos^{-1}\left[\frac{-u \pm u}{4v_0}\right] = 0 \Rightarrow \theta_{max} = \frac{\pi}{2}$$

(f) If $u = 0$, $\theta_{max} = \cos^{-1}\left[\frac{0 \pm \sqrt{8v_0^2}}{4v_0}\right] = \cos^{-1}\left(\frac{1}{\sqrt{2}}\right) = 45°$

Q.36 Motion in two dimensions in a plane can be studied by expressing position, velocity and acceleration as vectors in cartesian coordinates $\mathbf{A} = A_x\hat{\mathbf{i}} + A_y\hat{\mathbf{j}}$, where $\hat{\mathbf{i}}$ and $\hat{\mathbf{j}}$ are unit vectors along x and y-directions, respectively and A_x and A_y are corresponding components of $\mathbf{A}$. Motion can also be studied by expressing vectors in circular polar coordinates as $\mathbf{A} = A_r\hat{\mathbf{r}} + A_\theta\hat{\theta}$, where $\hat{\mathbf{r}} = \frac{\mathbf{r}}{r} = \cos\theta\,\hat{\mathbf{i}} + \sin\theta\,\hat{\mathbf{j}}$ and $\hat{\theta} = -\sin\theta\,\hat{\mathbf{i}} + \cos\theta\hat{\mathbf{j}}$ are unit vectors along direction in which r and θ are increasing.

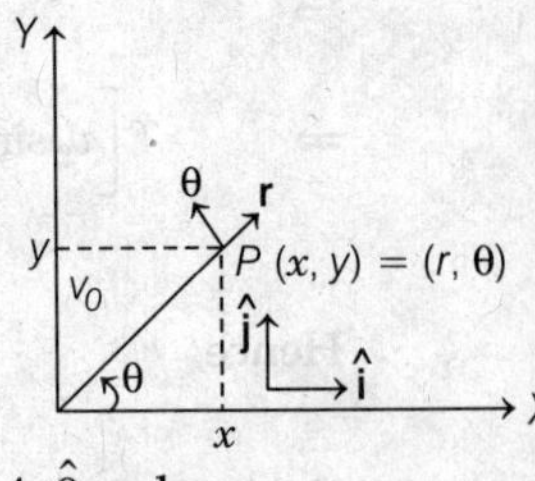

(a) Express $\hat{\mathbf{i}}$ and $\hat{\mathbf{j}}$ in terms of $\hat{\mathbf{r}}$ and $\hat{\theta}$.

(b) Show that both $\hat{\mathbf{r}}$ and $\hat{\theta}$ are unit vectors and are perpendicular to each other.

(c) Show that $\frac{d}{dt}(\hat{\mathbf{r}}) = \omega\hat{\theta}$, where $\omega = \frac{d\theta}{dt}$ and $\frac{d}{dt}(\hat{\theta}) = -\theta\hat{\mathbf{r}}$.

(d) For a particle moving along a spiral given by $r = a\theta\hat{\mathbf{r}}$, where $a = 1$ (unit), find dimensions of a.

(e) Find velocity and acceleration in polar vector representation for particle moving along spiral described in (d) above.

Ans. (a) Given, unit vector $\hat{\mathbf{r}} = \cos\theta\hat{\mathbf{i}} + \sin\theta\hat{\mathbf{j}}$ ...(i)

$$\hat{\theta} = -\sin\theta\hat{\mathbf{i}} + \cos\theta\hat{\mathbf{j}} \quad ...(ii)$$

Multiplying Eq. (i) by $\sin\theta$ and Eq. (ii) with $\cos\theta$ and adding

$$\hat{\mathbf{r}}\sin\theta + \hat{\theta}\cos\theta = \sin\theta\cdot\cos\theta\hat{\mathbf{i}} + \sin^2\theta\hat{\mathbf{j}} + \cos^2\theta\hat{\mathbf{j}} - \sin\theta\cdot\cos\theta\hat{\mathbf{i}}$$

$$= \hat{\mathbf{j}}(\cos^2\theta + \sin^2\theta) = \hat{\mathbf{j}}$$

$$\Rightarrow \quad \hat{\mathbf{r}}\sin\theta + \hat{\theta}\cos\theta = \hat{\mathbf{j}}$$

Similarly, multiplying Eq. (i) by $\cos\theta$ and Eq (ii) by $\sin\theta$, we get

$$(\hat{\mathbf{r}}\cos\theta - \hat{\theta}\sin\theta) = \hat{\mathbf{i}}$$

(b) $\hat{\mathbf{r}}\cdot\hat{\theta} = (\cos\theta\hat{\mathbf{i}} + \sin\theta\hat{\mathbf{j}})\cdot(-\sin\theta\hat{\mathbf{i}} + \cos\theta\hat{\mathbf{j}}) = -\cos\theta\,.\sin\theta + \sin\theta\,.\cos\theta = 0$

$$\Rightarrow \quad \theta = 90° \text{ (Angle between } \hat{\mathbf{r}} \text{ and } \hat{\theta}).$$

(c) Given, $\hat{\mathbf{r}} = \cos\theta\hat{\mathbf{i}} + \sin\theta\hat{\mathbf{j}}$

$$\frac{d\hat{\mathbf{r}}}{dt} = \frac{d}{dt}(\cos\theta\hat{\mathbf{i}} + \sin\theta\hat{\mathbf{j}}) = -\sin\theta\cdot\frac{d\theta}{dt}\hat{\mathbf{i}} + \cos\theta\cdot\frac{d\theta}{dt}\hat{\mathbf{j}}$$

$$= \omega[-\sin\theta\hat{\mathbf{i}} + \cos\theta\hat{\mathbf{j}}] \qquad \left[\because \omega = \frac{d\theta}{dt}\right]$$

$$= \omega\hat{\theta}$$

(d) Given, $\mathbf{r} = a\theta\hat{\mathbf{r}}$, here writing dimensions $[\mathbf{r}] = [a][\theta][\hat{\mathbf{r}}]$

Since, angle θ is dimensionless quantity, so dimension of 'a' is same as that of $[r]$ i.e. length [L]

(e) Given, $a = 1$ unit $\quad \mathbf{r} = \theta\hat{\mathbf{r}} = \theta[\cos\theta\hat{\mathbf{i}} + \sin\theta\hat{\mathbf{j}}]$

Velocity,
$$v = \frac{d\mathbf{r}}{dt} = \frac{d\theta}{dt}\hat{\mathbf{r}} + \theta\frac{d}{dt}\hat{\mathbf{r}} = \frac{d\theta}{dt}\hat{\mathbf{r}} + \theta\frac{d}{dt}[(\cos\theta\hat{\mathbf{i}} + \sin\theta\hat{\mathbf{j}})]$$

$$= \frac{d\theta}{dt}\hat{\mathbf{r}} + \theta\left[(-\sin\theta\hat{\mathbf{i}} + \cos\theta\hat{\mathbf{j}})\frac{d\theta}{dt}\right]$$

$$= \frac{d\theta}{dt}\hat{\mathbf{r}} + \theta\hat{\theta}\omega = \omega\hat{\mathbf{r}} + \omega\theta\hat{\theta}$$

Acceleration,
$$\mathbf{a} = \frac{d}{dt}[\omega\hat{\mathbf{r}} + \omega\theta\hat{\theta}] = \frac{d}{dt}\left[\frac{d\theta}{dt}\hat{\mathbf{r}} + \frac{d\theta}{dt}(\theta\hat{\theta})\right]$$

$$= \frac{d^2\theta}{dt^2}\hat{\mathbf{r}} + \frac{d\theta}{dt}\cdot\frac{d\hat{\mathbf{r}}}{dt} + \frac{d^2\theta}{dt^2}\theta\hat{\theta} + \frac{d\theta}{dt}\frac{d}{dt}(\theta\hat{\theta})$$

$$= \frac{d^2\theta}{dt^2}\hat{\mathbf{r}} + \omega^2[-\sin\theta\hat{\mathbf{i}} + \sin\theta\hat{\mathbf{j}}] + \frac{d^2\theta}{dt^2}\theta\hat{\theta} + \frac{\omega d}{dt}(\theta\hat{\theta})$$

$$[\because \hat{\mathbf{r}} = \cos\theta\hat{\mathbf{i}} + \sin\theta\hat{\mathbf{j}}]$$

$$= \frac{d^2\theta}{dt^2}\hat{\mathbf{r}} + \omega^2\hat{\theta} + \frac{d^2\theta}{dt^2}\times\theta\hat{\theta} + \omega^2\hat{\theta} + \omega^2(-\hat{\mathbf{r}})$$

$$= \left(\frac{d^2\theta}{dt^2} - \omega^2\right)\hat{\mathbf{r}} + \left(2\omega^2 + \frac{d^2\theta}{dt^2}\theta\right)\hat{\theta}$$

Q.37 A man wants to reach from A to the opposite corner of the square C. The sides of the square are 100 m. A central square of 50m × 50m is filled with sand. Outside this square, he can walk at a speed 1 m/s. In the central square, he can walk only at a speed of v m/s ($v < 1$). What is smallest value of v for which he can reach faster *via* a straight path through the sand than any path in the square outside the sand?

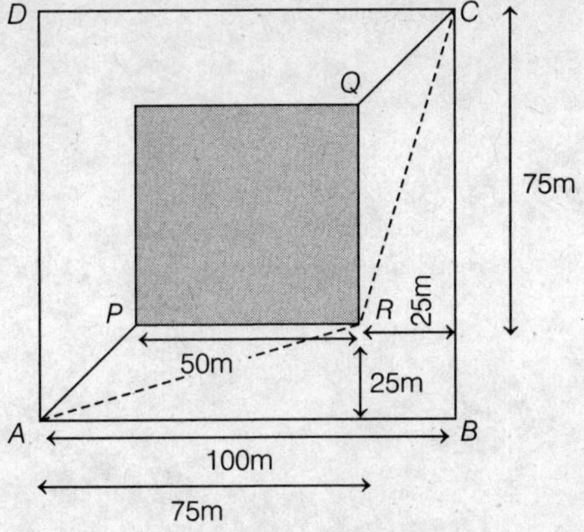

Ans. Consider given diagram.

Time taken to go from A to C *via* straight line path $APQC$ through the sand,

$$T_{\text{sand}} = \frac{AP + QC}{1} + \frac{PQ}{v} = \frac{25\sqrt{2} + 25\sqrt{2}}{1} + \frac{50\sqrt{2}}{v}$$

$$\left[\begin{array}{l} AC = 100\sqrt{2}\text{ m}, PQ = 50\sqrt{2}\text{ m}, \\ \therefore AP + QC = AC - PQ \end{array}\right]$$

$$= 50\sqrt{2} + \frac{50\sqrt{2}}{v} = 50\sqrt{2}\left(\frac{1}{v} + 1\right)$$

Clearly from figure, the shortest path outside the sand will be ARC.

Time taken to go from A to C *via* this path,

$$T_{\text{outside}} = \frac{AR + RC}{1}\text{ s}$$

Clearly, $$AR = \sqrt{75^2 + 25^2} = \sqrt{75 \times 75 + 25 \times 25}$$

$$= 5 \times 5\sqrt{9 + 1} = 25\sqrt{10}\text{ m}$$

$\therefore$ $$RC = AR = \sqrt{75^2 + 25^2} = 25\sqrt{10}\text{ m}$$

$\Rightarrow$ $$T_{\text{outside}} = 2AR = 2 \times 25\sqrt{10}\text{ s} = 50\sqrt{10}\text{ s}$$

For $$T_{\text{sand}} < T_{\text{outside}}$$

$\Rightarrow$ $$50\sqrt{2}\left(\frac{1}{v} + 1\right) < 2 \times 25\sqrt{10}$$

$\Rightarrow$ $$\frac{2\sqrt{2}}{2}\left(\frac{1}{v} + 1\right) < \sqrt{10}$$

$\Rightarrow$ $$\frac{1}{v} + 1 < \frac{2\sqrt{10}}{2\sqrt{2}}$$

$\Rightarrow$ $$\frac{1}{v} < \sqrt{5} - 1$$

$\Rightarrow$ $$v > \frac{1}{\sqrt{5} - 1} \approx 0.81\text{ m/s}$$

$\Rightarrow$ $$v > 0.81\text{ m/s}$$

Chapter

04

Laws of Motion

Multiple Choice Questions (MCQs)

Q.1 A ball is travelling with uniform translatory motion. This means that

(a) it is at rest

(b) the path can be a straight line or circular and the ball travels with uniform speed

(c) all parts of the ball have the same velocity (magnitude and direction) and the velocity is constant

(d) the centre of the ball moves with constant velocity and the ball spins about its centre uniformly

Ans. ***(c)*** In a uniform translatory motion, all parts of the ball have the same velocity in magnitude and direction and this velocity is constant.

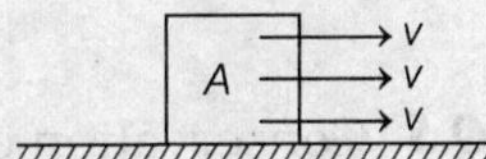

The situation is shown in adjacent diagram where a body *A* is in uniform translatory motion.

Q.2 A metre scale is moving with uniform velocity. This implies that

(a) the force acting on the scale is zero but a torque about the centre of mass can act on the scale

(b) the force acting on the scale is zero and the torque acting about centre of mass of the scale is also zero

(c) the total force acting on it need not to be zero but the torque on it is zero

(d) neither the force nor the torque need to be zero

Ans. ***(b)*** Using Newton's second law of motion, in terms of force and change in momentum,

$$F = \frac{dp}{dt}$$

Given that meter scale is moving with uniform velocity, hence $dp = 0$.

$$\text{Force, } F = 0$$

As all parts of the scale is moving with uniform velocity and total force is zero, hence torque will also be zero.

Q.3 A cricket ball of mass 150 g has an initial velocity $\mathbf{u} = (3\hat{\mathbf{i}} + 4\hat{\mathbf{j}})\ \text{ms}^{-1}$ and a final velocity $\mathbf{v} = -(3\hat{\mathbf{i}} + 4\hat{\mathbf{j}})\ \text{ms}^{-1}$, after being hit. The change in momentum (final momentum - initial momentum) is (in kgms^{-1})

(a) zero

(b) $-(0.45\hat{\mathbf{i}} + 0.6\hat{\mathbf{j}})$

(c) $-(0.9\hat{\mathbf{j}} + 1.2\hat{\mathbf{j}})$

(d) $-5(\hat{\mathbf{i}} + \hat{\mathbf{j}})\hat{\mathbf{i}}$

Ans. ***(c)*** Given, $\mathbf{u} = (3\hat{\mathbf{i}} + 4\hat{\mathbf{j}})$ m/s

and $\mathbf{v} = -(3\hat{\mathbf{i}} + 4\hat{\mathbf{j}})$ m/s

Mass of the ball = 150 g = 0.15 kg

$$\begin{aligned}\Delta\mathbf{p} &= \text{Change in momentum}\\ &= \text{Final momentum} - \text{Initial momentum}\\ &= m\mathbf{v} - m\mathbf{u}\\ &= m(\mathbf{v} - \mathbf{u}) = (0.15)\,[-(3\hat{\mathbf{i}} + 4\hat{\mathbf{j}}) - (3\hat{\mathbf{i}} + 4\hat{\mathbf{j}})]\\ &= (0.15)\,[-6\hat{\mathbf{i}} - 8\hat{\mathbf{j}}]\\ &= -[0.15 \times 6\hat{\mathbf{i}} + 0.15 \times 8\hat{\mathbf{j}}]\\ &= -[0.9\hat{\mathbf{i}} + 1.20\hat{\mathbf{j}}]\end{aligned}$$

Hence, $\Delta\mathbf{p} = -[0.9\hat{\mathbf{i}} + 1.2\hat{\mathbf{j}}]$ kgms^{-1}

Q.4 **In the previous problem (3), the magnitude of the momentum transferred during the hit is**

(a) zero (b) 0.75 kg ms^{-1} (c) 1.5 kg ms^{-1} (d) 14 kg ms^{-1}

Ans. ***(c)*** By previous solution, $\Delta\mathbf{p} = -(0.9\hat{\mathbf{i}} + 1.2\hat{\mathbf{j}})$

$$\text{Magnitude} = |\Delta\mathbf{p}| = \sqrt{(0.9)^2 + (1.2)^2}$$

$$= \sqrt{0.81 + 1.44} = 1.5 \text{ kg ms}^{-1}$$

Q.5 **Conservation of momentum in a collision between particles can be understood from**

(a) conservation of energy
(b) Newton's first law only
(c) Newton's second law only
(d) both Newton's second and third law

Thinking Process For conservation of momentum, we have to see whether net external force is acting on a system or not.

Ans. ***(d)*** We know that for a system, $F_{ext} = \frac{dp}{dt}$ [from Newton's second law]

If $F_{ext} = 0$, $dp = 0 \Rightarrow p = \text{constant}$

Hence, momentum of a system will remain conserved, if external force on the system is zero.

In case of collision between particles, equal and opposite forces will act on individual particles by Newton's third law.

Hence total force on the system will be zero.

Mistake Alert ! *We should not confuse with system and individual particles. As total force on the system of both particles is zero but force acts on individual particles.*

Q.6 **A hockey player is moving northward and suddenly turns westward with the same speed to avoid an opponent. The force that acts on the player is**

(a) frictional force along westward
(b) muscle force along southward
(c) frictional force along south-west
(d) muscle force along south-west

Ans. ***(c)*** Consider the below diagram.

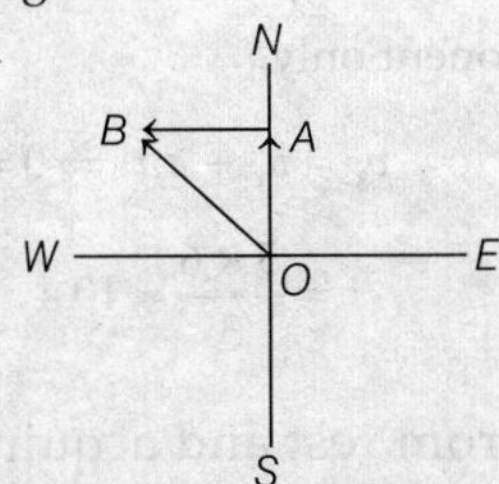

B $\mathbf{p}_2$ A $-\mathbf{p}_1$ R O

Let $\quad \mathbf{OA} = \mathbf{p}_1 =$ initial momentum of player northward

$\mathbf{AB} = \mathbf{p}_2 =$ final momentum of player towards west

Clearly, $\quad \mathbf{OB} = \mathbf{OA} + \mathbf{AB}$

Change in momentum $= \mathbf{p}_2 - \mathbf{p}_1$

$$= \mathbf{AB} - \mathbf{OA} = \mathbf{AB} + (-\mathbf{OA})$$

Clearly, resultant **AR** will be along south-west.

Q.7 A body of mass 2 kg travels according to the law $x(t) = pt + qt^2 + rt^3$ where, $q = 4\text{ms}^{-2}$, $p = 3\text{ms}^{-1}$ and $r = 5\text{ms}^{-3}$. The force acting on the body at $t = 2\text{s}$ is

(a) 136 N (b) 134 N (c) 158 N (d) 68 N

Thinking Process We have to apply differentiations to calculate acceleration and then Newton's second law will be applied.

Ans. ***(a)*** Given, mass = 2 kg

$$x(t) = pt + qt^2 + rt^3$$

$$v = \frac{dx}{dt} = p + 2qt + 3rt^2$$

$$a = \frac{dv}{dt} = 0 + 2q + 6rt$$

$$\text{at } t = 2\text{ s}; a = 2q + 6 \times 2 \times r$$

$$= 2q + 12r = 2 \times 4 + 12 \times 5$$

$$= 8 + 60 = 68 \text{ m/s}^2$$

$$\text{Force} = F = ma = 2 \times 68 = 136 \text{ N}$$

Q.8 A body with mass 5 kg is acted upon by a force $\mathbf{F} = (-3\hat{\mathbf{i}} + 4\hat{\mathbf{j}})$ N. If its initial velocity at $t = 0$ is $\mathbf{u} = (6\hat{\mathbf{i}} - 12\hat{\mathbf{j}})\text{ms}^{-1}$, the time at which it will just have a velocity along the Y–axis is

(a) never (b) 10 s (c) 2 s (d) 15 s

Ans. ***(b)*** Given, mass $= m = 5$ kg

Acting force $= \mathbf{F} = (-3\hat{\mathbf{i}} + 4\hat{\mathbf{j}})$ N

Given that initial velocity at $t = 0$ is $\mathbf{u} = (6\hat{\mathbf{i}} - 12\hat{\mathbf{j}})$ m / s

$$\text{Retardation, } \hat{\mathbf{a}} = \frac{\mathbf{F}}{m} = \left(-\frac{3\hat{\mathbf{i}}}{5} + \frac{4\hat{\mathbf{j}}}{5}\right) \text{m/s}^2$$

As final velocity is along Y-axis only, its x-component must be zero.

From $v = u + at$, for x-component only,

$$v_x = u_x + a_x t \Rightarrow 0 = 6\hat{\mathbf{i}} - \frac{3\hat{\mathbf{i}}}{5}t$$

$$\Rightarrow \quad t = \frac{5 \times 6}{3} = 10 \text{ s}$$

Q.9 A car of mass m starts from rest and acquires a velocity along east, $\mathbf{v} = v\hat{\mathbf{i}}$ $(v > 0)$ in two seconds. Assuming the car moves with uniform acceleration, the force exerted on the car is

(a) $\frac{mv}{2}$ eastward and is exerted by the car engine

(b) $\frac{mv}{2}$ eastward and is due to the friction on the tyres exerted by the road

(c) more than $\frac{mv}{2}$ eastward, exerted due to the engine and overcomes the friction of the road

(d) $\frac{mv}{2}$ exerted by the engine

Ans. ***(b)*** Given, mass of the car $= m$

As car starts from rest, $u = 0$

Velocity acquired along east $= v\hat{\mathbf{i}}$

Duration $= t = 2$s.

We know that, $\quad v = u + at \Rightarrow v\hat{\mathbf{i}} = 0 + a \times 2$

$$\Rightarrow \quad a = \frac{v}{2}\hat{\mathbf{i}}$$

Force, $\quad F = ma = \frac{mv}{2}\hat{\mathbf{i}}$

Hence, force acting on the car is $\frac{mv}{2}$ towards east. As external force on the system is only friction, hence the force $\frac{mv}{2}$ is by friction. Hence, force by engine is internal force.

Multiple Choice Questions (More Than One Options)

Q.10 The motion of a particle of mass m is given by $x = 0$ for $t < 0$ s, $x(t) = A \sin 4\pi t$ for $0 < t < (1/4)$s $(A > 0)$ and $x = 0$ for $t > (1/4)$ s. Which of the following statements are true?

(a) The force at $t = (1/8)$s on the particle is $-16\pi^2$A-m.

(b) The particle is acted upon by an impulse of magnitude $4\pi^2$A-m at $t = 0$ s and $t = (1/4)$ s.

(c) The particle is not acted upon by any force.

(d) The particle is not acted upon by a constant force.

(e) There is no impulse acting on the particle.

Thinking Process Here, position of the particle is given for different time intervals. Hence, we have to find velocity and acceleration corresponding to the intervals.

Ans. *(a, b, d)* Given,

$$x = 0; \text{ for } t < 0 \text{ s.}$$

$$x(t) = A\sin 4\pi t; \text{ for } 0 < t < \frac{1}{4} \text{ s}$$

$$x = 0; \text{ for } t > \frac{1}{4} \text{ s}$$

For $0 < t < \frac{1}{4}$ s;

$$v(t) = \frac{dx}{dt} = 4\pi\,(A\cos 4\pi t)$$

$$a(t) = \text{acceleration}$$

$$= \frac{dv(t)}{dt} = -16\,\pi^2 A\sin 4\pi t$$

$$\text{At } t = \frac{1}{8}\text{ s}, a(t) = -16\pi^2 A\sin\left(4\pi\times\frac{1}{8}\right) = -16\pi^2 A$$

$$F = ma\,(t) = -16\pi^2\ A\times m = -16\pi^2\,mA \qquad \text{[i.e. part } a\text{]}$$

$\Rightarrow$ Impulse = Change in linear momentum

$$\Rightarrow \quad F\times t = (-16\pi^2\ Am)\times\frac{1}{4}$$

$$= -4\pi^2\,Am \qquad \text{[i.e. part } b\text{]}$$

The impulse (change in linear momentum) at $t = 0$ is same as $t = \frac{1}{4}$ s. [i.e. part *d*]

Clearly, force depends upon *A* which is not constant. Hence, force is also not constant.

Mistake Alert ! *We have to keep in mind that the force is varying for different time intervals. Hence, we should apply differential formulae for each interval separately.*

Q.11 In figure, the coefficient of friction between the floor and the body *B* is 0.1. The coefficient of friction between the bodies *B* and *A* is 0.2. A force **F** is applied as shown on *B*. The mass of *A* is $m/2$ and of *B* is *m*. Which of the following statements are true?

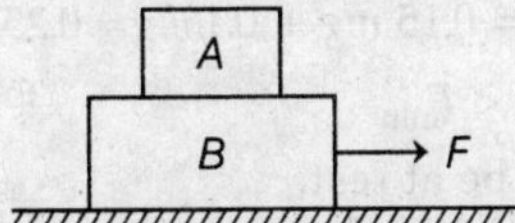

(a) The bodies will move together if **F** = 0.25 *mg*.
(b) The body *A* will slip with respect to *B* if **F** = 0.5 *mg*.
(c) The bodies will move together if **F** = 0.5 *mg*.
(d) The bodies will be at rest if **F** = 0.1 *mg*.
(e) The maximum value of **F** for which the two bodies will move together is 0.45 *mg*.

Thinking Process In this problem we have to find frictional forces on each surface and accordingly we will decide maximum force.

Ans. *(a, b, d, e)* Consider the adjacent diagram, frictional force on $B(f_1)$ and frictional force on $A\ (f_2)$ will be as shown.

Let *A* and *B* are moving together $a_{\text{common}} = \dfrac{F - f_1}{m_A + m_B} = \dfrac{F - f_1}{(m/2) + m} = \dfrac{2(F - f_1)}{3m}$

Pseudo force on $A = (m_A) \times a_{common}$

$$= m_A \times \frac{2(F - f_1)}{3m} = \frac{m}{2} \times \frac{2(F - f_1)}{3m} = \frac{(F - f_1)}{3}$$

The force (F) will be maximum when

Pseudo force on $A =$ Frictional force on A

$$\Rightarrow \quad \frac{F_{max} - f_1}{3} = \mu \, m_A g$$

$$= 0.2 \times \frac{m}{2} \times g = 0.1 mg$$

$$\Rightarrow \quad F_{max} = 0.3 \, mg + f_1$$

$$= 0.3 \, mg + \mu_B (m_A + m_B) g$$

$$= 0.3 \, mg + (0.1) \frac{3}{2} \, mg = 0.45 \, mg$$

$\Rightarrow$ Hence, maximum force upto which bodies will move together is $F_{max} = 0.45 \, mg$

(a) Hence, for $F = 0.25 \, mg < F_{max}$ bodies will move together.

(b) For $F = 0.5 \, mg > F_{max}$, body A will slip with respect to B.

(c) For $F = 0.5 \, mg > F_{max}$, bodies slip.

$$(f_1)_{max} = \mu \, m_B g = (0.1) \times \frac{3}{2} m \times g = 0.15 \, mg$$

$$(f_2)_{max} = \mu \, m_A g = (0.2) \left(\frac{m}{2}\right) (g) = 0.1 \, mg$$

Hence, minimum force required for movement of the system ($A + B$)

$$F_{min} = (f_1)_{max} + (f_2)_{max}$$

$$= 0.15 \, mg + 0.1 \, mg = 0.25 \, mg$$

(d) Given, force $F = 0.1 \, mg < F_{min}$.

Hence, the bodies will be at rest.

(e) Maximum force for combined movement $F_{max} = 0.45 \, mg$.

Q.12 Mass m_1 moves on a slope making an angle θ with the horizontal and is attached to mass m_2 by a string passing over a frictionless pulley as shown in figure. The coefficient of friction between m_1 and the sloping surface is μ. Which of the following statements are true?

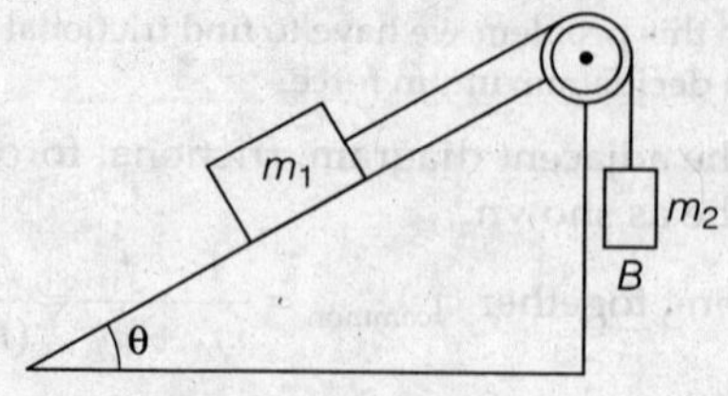

(a) If $m_2 > m_1 \sin\theta$, the body will move up the plane

(b) If $m_2 > m_1 (\sin\theta + \mu \cos\theta)$, the body will move up the plane

(c) If $m_2 < m_1 (\sin\theta + \mu \cos\theta)$, the body will move up the plane

(d) If $m_2 < m_1 (\sin\theta - \mu \cos\theta)$, the body will move down the plane

Thinking Process The friction force always have tendency to oppose the motion. Consider the adjacent diagram.

Ans. ***(b, d)*** Let m_1, moves up the plane. Different forces involved are shown in the diagram.

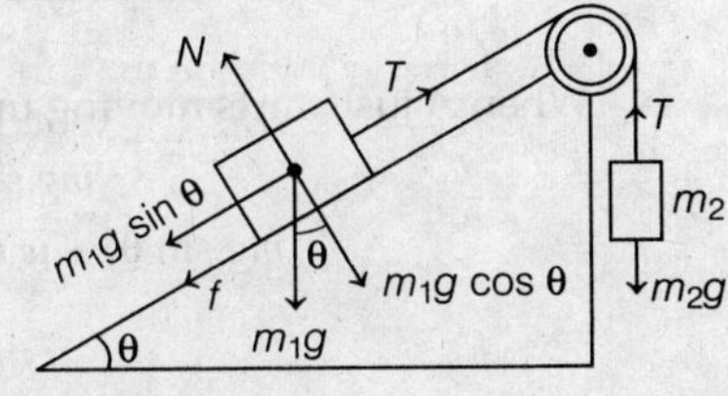

N = Normal reaction

f = Frictional force

T = Tension in the string

$f = \mu N = \mu m_1 g \cos\theta$

For the system $(m_1 + m_2)$ to move up

$$m_2 g - (m_1 g \sin\theta + f) > 0$$

$$\Rightarrow \quad m_2 g - (m_1 g \sin\theta + \mu m_1 g \cos\theta) > 0$$

$$\Rightarrow \quad m_2 > m_1 (\sin\theta + \mu \cos\theta)$$

Hence, option (b) is correct.

Let the body moves down the plane, in this case f acts up the plane.

Hence, $\quad m_1 g \sin\theta - f > m_2 g$

[Frictional force acts opposite to the motion of block]

$$\Rightarrow \quad m_1 g \sin\theta - \mu m_1 g \cos\theta > m_2 g$$

$$\Rightarrow \quad m_1 (\sin\theta - \mu \cos\theta) > m_2$$

$$\Rightarrow \quad m_2 < m_1 (\sin\theta - \mu \cos\theta)$$

Hence, option (d) is correct.

Q.13 In figure a body A of mass m slides on plane inclined at angle θ_1 to the horizontal and μ is the coefficent of friction between A and the plane. A is connected by a light string passing over a frictionless pulley to another body B, also of mass m, sliding on a frictionless plane inclined at an angle θ_2 to the horizontal. Which of the following statements are true?

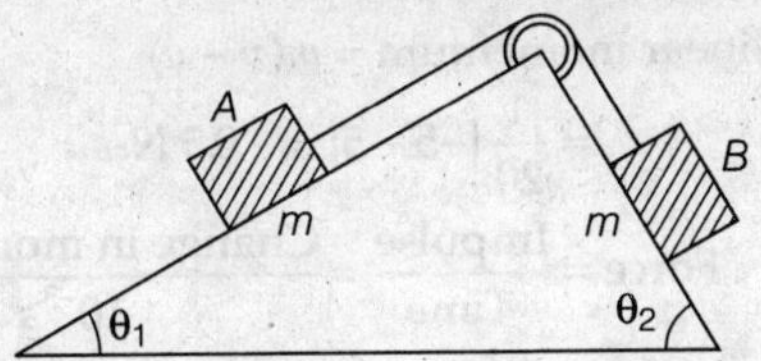

(a) A will never move up the plane.

(b) A will just start moving up the plane when $\mu = \dfrac{\sin\theta_2 - \sin\theta_1}{\cos\theta_1}$.

(c) For A to move up the plane, θ_2 must always be greater than θ_1.

(d) B will always slide down with constant speed.

Ans. ***(b, c)*** Let A moves up the plane frictional force on A will be downward as shown.

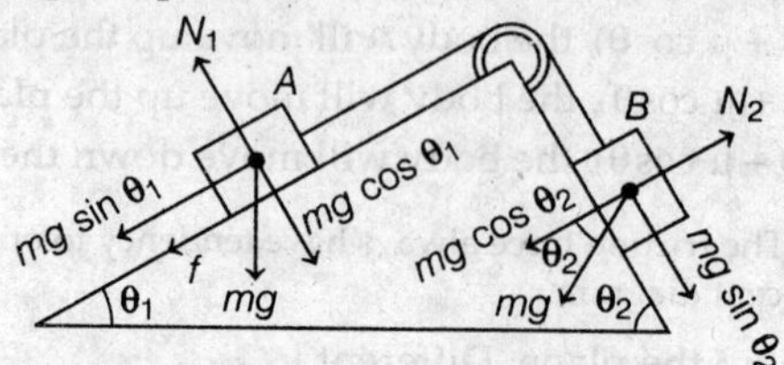

When A just starts moving up

$$mg\sin\theta_1 + f = mg\sin\theta_2$$

$$\Rightarrow \quad mg\sin\theta_1 + \mu\, mg\cos\theta_1 = mg\sin\theta_2$$

$$\Rightarrow \quad \mu = \frac{\sin\theta_2 - \sin\theta_1}{\cos\theta_1}$$

When A moves upwards

$$\mu > 0$$

So, $\sin\theta_2 > \sin\theta_1$ or $\theta_2 > \theta_1$

Hence, option (b) and (c) are correct.

Q.14 Two billiard balls A and B, each of mass 50g and moving in opposite directions with speed of 5 ms^{-1} each, collide and rebound with the same speed. If the collision lasts for 10^{-3} s, which of the following statements are true?

(a) The impulse imparted to each ball is 0.25 kg-ms^{-1} and the force on each ball is 250 N.

(b) The impulse imparted to each ball is 0.25 kg-ms^{-1} and the force exerted on each ball is 25×10^{-5} N.

(c) The impulse imparted to each ball is 0.5 N-s.

(d) The impulse and the force on each ball are equal in magnitude and opposite in directions.

Ans. ***(c, d)*** Given, $m_1 = m_2 = 50(g) = \frac{50}{1000}\text{ kg} = \frac{1}{20}\text{ kg}$

Initial velocity $(u) = u_1 = u_2 = 5\text{ m/s}$

Final velocity $(v) = v_1 = v_2 = -5\text{ m/s}$

Time duration of collision $= 10^{-3}$s .

Impulse = change in linear momentum $= m(v-u)$

$$= \frac{1}{20}[-5-5] = -0.5\text{ N-s.}$$

$$\text{Force} = \frac{\text{Impulse}}{\text{Time}} = \frac{\text{Change in momentum}}{10^{-3}\text{s}}$$

$$= \frac{0.5}{10^{-3}} = 500\text{ N}$$

Impulse and force are opposite in directions, because direction of change in momentum of B is opposite to that of A.

Q.15 A body of mass 10 kg is acted upon by two perpendicular forces, 6N and 8N. The resultant acceleration of the body is

(a) $1\ ms^{-2}$ at an angle of $\tan^{-1}\left(\frac{4}{3}\right)$ w.r.t. 6N force

(b) $0.2\ ms^{-2}$ at an angle of $\tan^{-1}\left(\frac{4}{3}\right)$ w.r.t. 6N force

(c) $1\ ms^{-2}$ at an angle of $\tan^{-1}\left(\frac{3}{4}\right)$ w.r.t. 8N force

(d) $0.2\ ms^{-2}$ at an angle of $\tan^{-1}\left(\frac{3}{4}\right)$ w.r.t. 8N force

- **Concept Insight** In this problem we use the concept of resultant of two vectors, which is perpendicular to the vector *A* and its magnitude is equal to half of the magnitude of vector *B*.

Ans. ***(a, c)*** Consider the adjacent diagram

Given, mass $= m = 10\,\text{kg}.$

$$F_1 = 6\text{N},\ F_2 = 8\text{N}$$

$$\text{Resultant force} = F = \sqrt{F_1^2 + F_2^2} = \sqrt{36 + 64}$$

$$= 10\ \text{N}$$

$$a = \frac{F}{m} = \frac{10}{10} = 1\ \text{m/s}^2;\ \text{along } R.$$

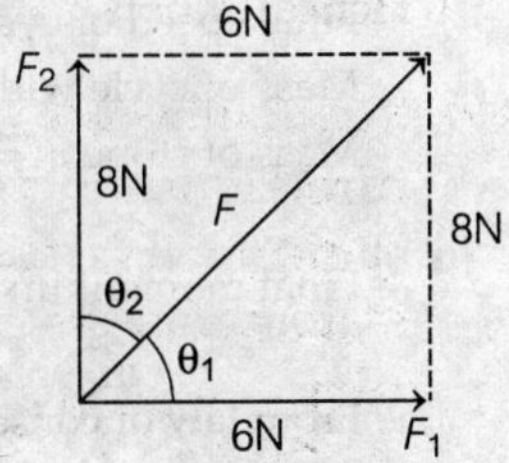

Let θ_1 be angle between R and F_1

$$\tan\theta_1 = \frac{8}{6} = \frac{4}{3}$$

$$\theta_1 = \tan^{-1}(4/3)\ \text{w.r.t. } F_1 = 6\,\text{N}$$

Let θ_2 be angle between F and F_2

$$\tan\theta_2 = \frac{6}{8} = \frac{3}{4}$$

$$\theta_2 = \tan^{-1}\left(\frac{3}{4}\right)\ \text{w.r.t. } F_2 = 8\ \text{N}$$

Very Short Answer Type Questions

Q.16 A girl riding a bicycle along a straight road with a speed of $5\ ms^{-1}$ throws a stone of mass 0.5 kg which has a speed of $15\ ms^{-1}$ with respect to the ground along her direction of motion. The mass of the girl and bicycle is 50 kg. Does the speed of the bicycle change after the stone is thrown? What is the change in speed, if so?

- **Concept Insight** In this problem we use the concept of conservation of linear momentum which is defined as the total momentum of a system of object remains constant unless an external force acts on it.

Ans. Given, total mass of girl, bicycle and stone $= m_1 = (50 + 0.5)\ \text{kg} = 50.5\,\text{kg}.$

Velocity of bicycle $u_1 = 5\ \text{m/s}$, Mass of stone $m_2 = 0.5\,\text{kg}$

Velocity of stone $u_2 = 15\ \text{m/s}$, Mass of girl and bicycle $m = 50$ kg

Yes, the speed of the bicycle changes after the stone is thrown.

Let after throwing the stone the speed of bicycle be v m/s.

According to law of conservation of linear momentum, (As no external force acts on system)

$$m_1 u_1 = m_2 u_2 + mv$$

$$50.5 \times 5 = 0.5 \times 15 + 50 \times v$$

$$252.5 - 7.5 = 50\, v$$

or $$v = \frac{245.0}{50}$$

$$v = 4.9 \text{ m/s}$$

Change in speed = 5 – 4.9 = 0.1 m/s.

Alternate Method

Given,

Initial speed of girl, cycle and stone,

$$u = 5\text{ms}^{-1}$$

Final speed of stone $v_1 = 15\,\text{ms}^{-1}$

Final speed of cycle with girl $v_2 = ?$

Mass of cycle with girl $M = 50$ kg

Mass of stone $m = 0.5$ kg

$$P_i = (50 + 0.5) \times 5 = 252 \cdot 5 \text{ kgms}^{-1}$$

Final momentum of the system

$$P_f = 50\,v_2 + 0.5 \times 15 = (50\,v_2 + 7.5) \text{ kgms}^{-1}$$

From law of conservation of momentum

$$P_f = P_i = 50v_2 + 7.5 - 252 \cdot 5 = 50v_2 = 245$$

$\Rightarrow$ $$v_2 = \frac{245}{50} = 4.9 \text{ ms}^{-1}$$

Change in speed = 5 – 4.9 = 0.1 ms^{-1}

Q.17 **A person of mass 50 kg stands on a weighing scale on a lift. If the lift is descending with a downward acceleration of 9 ms^{-2}, what would be the reading of the weighing scale? (g = 10 ms^{-2})**

Ans. When a lift descends with a downward acceleration a the apparent weight of a body of mass m is given by

$$w' = R = m(g - a)$$

Mass of the person $m = 50$ kg

Descending acceleration $a = 9 \text{ m/s}^2$

Acceleration due to gravity $g = 10 \text{ m/s}^2$

Apparent weight of the person,

$$R = m(g - a)$$

$$= 50\,(10 - 9) = 50 \text{ N}$$

$\therefore$ Reading of the weighing scale $= \frac{R}{g} = \frac{50}{10} = 5$ kg.

Q.18 The position-time graph of a body of mass 2 kg is as given in figure. What is the impulse on the body at $t = 0$ s and $t = 4$ s.

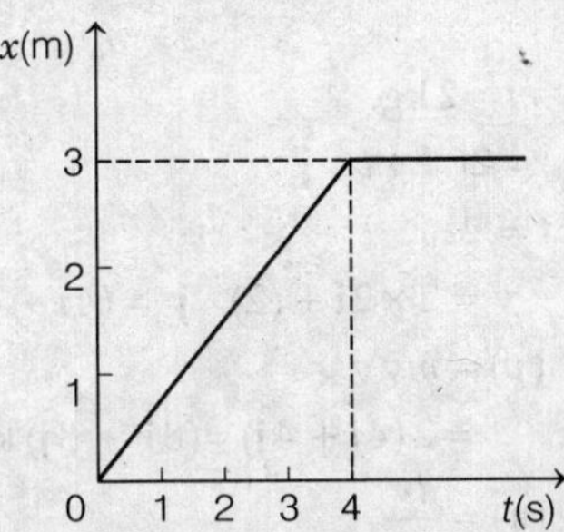

Ans. Given, mass of the body $(m) = 2$ kg

From the position-time graph, the body is at $x = 0$ when $t = 0$, *i.e.*, body is at rest $(u = 0)$.

From $t = 0$ s to $t = 4$ s, the position-time graph is a straight line, which shows that body moves with uniform velocity.

Beyond $t = 4s$, the graph is a straight line parallel to time axis, *i.e.*, body is at rest $(v = 0)$.

Velocity of the body between $t = 0$ to $t = 4$ sec is = slope of position-time graph

$$u' = \tan\theta = \frac{3}{4} \text{ m/s}$$

Impulse at $(t = 0)$ = change in momentum

$$= mu' - mu$$

$$= 2\left[\frac{3}{4} - 0\right]$$

$$= \frac{3}{2} = 1.5 \text{ kg m/s}$$

Impulse (at $t = 4$ s) = change in momentum

$$= mv - mu'$$

$$= m(v - u')$$

$$= 2\left(0 - \frac{3}{4}\right)$$

$$= -\frac{3}{2} \text{ kg-m/s} = -1.5 \text{ kg-m/s}$$

Q.19 A person driving a car suddenly applies the brakes on seeing a child on the road ahead. If he is not wearing seat belt, he falls forward and hits his head against the steering wheel. Why?

Ans. When a person driving a car suddenly applies the brakes, the lower part of the body slower down with the car while upper part of the body continues to move forward due to inertia of motion.

If driver is not wearing seat belt, then he falls forward and his head hit against the steering wheel.

Q.20 The velocity of a body of mass 2 kg as a function of t is given by $\mathbf{v}(t) = 2t\,\hat{\mathbf{i}} + t^2\,\hat{\mathbf{j}}$. Find the momentum and the force acting on it, at time $t = 2$s.

Ans. Given, mass of the body $m = 2$ kg.

Velocity of the body $\mathbf{v}(t) = 2t\,\hat{\mathbf{i}} + t^2\,\hat{\mathbf{j}}$

$\therefore$ Velocity of the body at $t = 2$s

$$\mathbf{v} = 2 \times 2\hat{\mathbf{i}} + (2)^2\,\hat{\mathbf{j}} = (4\hat{\mathbf{i}} + 4\hat{\mathbf{j}})$$

Momentum of the body $(p) = m\mathbf{v}$

$$= 2(4\hat{\mathbf{i}} + 4\hat{\mathbf{j}}) = (8\hat{\mathbf{i}} + 8\hat{\mathbf{j}})\text{ kg-m/s}$$

Acceleration of the body $(\mathbf{a}) = \dfrac{d\mathbf{v}}{dt}$

$$= \frac{d}{dt}(2t\,\hat{\mathbf{i}} + t^2\,\hat{\mathbf{j}})$$

$$= (2\hat{\mathbf{i}} + 2t\,\hat{\mathbf{j}})$$

At $t = 2$ s

$$\mathbf{a} = (2\hat{\mathbf{i}} + 2 \times 2\hat{\mathbf{j}}) = (2\hat{\mathbf{i}} + 4\hat{\mathbf{j}})$$

Force acting on the body $(\mathbf{F}) = m\mathbf{a}$

$$= 2(2\hat{\mathbf{i}} + 4\hat{\mathbf{j}})$$

$$= (4\hat{\mathbf{i}} + 8\hat{\mathbf{j}})\text{ N}$$

Q. 21 A block placed on a rough horizontal surface is pulled by a horizontal force F. Let f be the force applied by the rough surface on the block. Plot a graph of f *versus* F.

Ans. The approximate graph is shown in the diagram

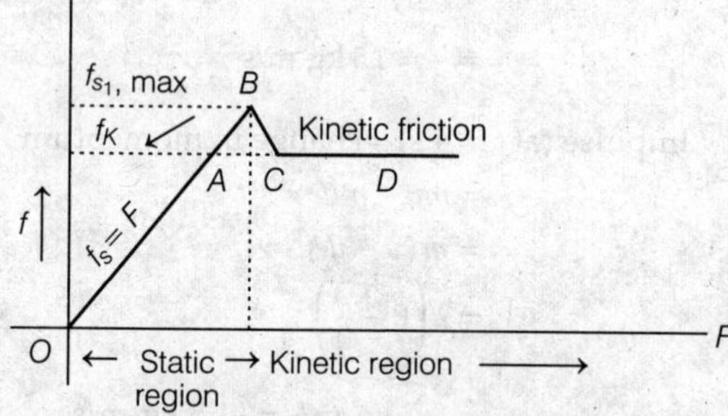

The frictional force f is shown on vertical axis and the applied force F is shown on the horizontal axis. The portion OA of graph represents static friction which is self adjusting. In this portion, $f = F$.

The point B corresponds to force of limiting friction which is the maximum value of static friction. $CD \parallel OF$ represents kinetic friction, when the body actually starts moving. The force of kinetic friction does not increase with applied force, and is slightly less than limiting friction.

Q.22 **Why are porcelain objects wrapped in paper or straw before packing for transportation?**

Ans. Porcelain objects are wrapped in paper or straw before packing to reduce the chances of damage during transportation. During transportation sudden jerks or even fall takes place, the force takes longer time to reach the porcelain objects through paper or straw for same change in momentum as $F = \frac{\Delta p}{\Delta t}$ and therefore, a lesser force acts on object.

Q.23 **Why does a child feel more pain when she falls down on a hard cement floor, than when she falls on the soft muddy ground in the garden?**

Ans. We know, $$F = \frac{\Delta p}{\Delta t}$$

When a child falls down on a hard cement floor, then time of impact is small as she comes to rest very soon. So, force on the child by the floor is more and the child feels more pain.

On the other hand, when child falls down on the soft muddy ground in the garden, then the time of impact is increased as the mud get depressed under her weight. So, force on the child by muddy ground is less and she feels lesser pain.

Q.24 **A woman throws an object of mass 500 g with a speed of 25 ms^{-1}.**

(a) What is the impulse imparted to the object?

(b) If the object hits a wall and rebounds with half the original speed, what is the change in momentum of the object?

Ans. Mass of the object (m) = 500 g = 0.5 kg

Speed of the object (v) = 25 m/s

(a) Impulse imparted to the object = change in momentum (initial velocity u is zero)

$$= mv - mu$$
$$= m(v - u)$$
$$= 0.5\,(25 - 0) = 12.5 \text{ N-s}$$

(b) Velocity of the object after rebounding

$$= -\frac{25}{2} \text{ m/s}$$
$$v' = -12.5 \text{ m/s}$$

$\therefore$ Change in momentum $= m(v' - v)$

$$= 0.5\,(-12.5 - 25) = -18.75 \text{ N-s}$$

Q.25 **Why are mountain roads generally made winding upwards rather than going straight up?**

Ans. While going up a mountain, the force of friction acting on a vehicle of mass m is $f = \mu, R = \mu\, mg\cos\theta$, where θ is the angle of slope of the road with the horizontal. To avoid skidding, force of friction (f) should be large and therefore, $\cos\theta$ should be large and hence, θ should be small.

That's why mountain roads are generally made winding upwards rather than going straight up to avoid skidding.

Short Answer Type Questions

Q.26 A mass of 2 kg is suspended with thread AB (figure). Thread CD of the same type is attached to the other end of 2 kg mass. Lower thread is pulled gradually, harder and harder in the downward direction, so as to apply force on AB. Which of the threads will break and why?

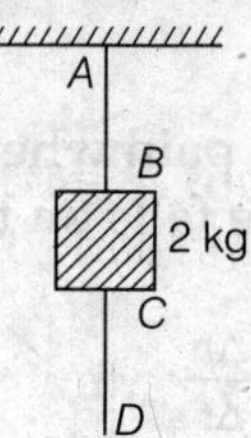

Ans. The thread AB will break earlier than the thread CD. This is because force acting on thread CD = applied force and force acting on thread AB = (applied force + weight of 2 kg mass).

Hence, force acting on thread AB is larger than the force acting on thread CD.

Q.27 In the above given problem if the lower thread is pulled with a jerk, what happens?

Ans. When the lower thread CD is pulled with a jerk, the thread CD itself breaks. Because pull on thread CD is not transmitted to the thread AB instantly due to inertia of rest.

Q.28 Two masses of 5 kg and 3 kg are suspended with help of massless inextensible strings as shown in figure. Calculate T_1 and T_2 when whole system is going upwards with acceleration = $2\,\text{m/s}^2$ (use $g = 9.8\,\text{ms}^{-2}$).

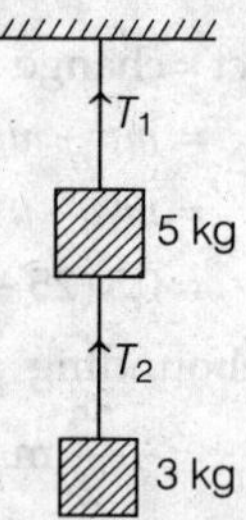

Thinking Process As the whole system is going upward with an acceleration we have to apply Newton's laws.

Ans. Given, $m_1 = 5$ kg, $m_2 = 3$ kg, $g = 9.8\,\text{m/s}^2$ and $a = 2\,\text{m/s}^2$

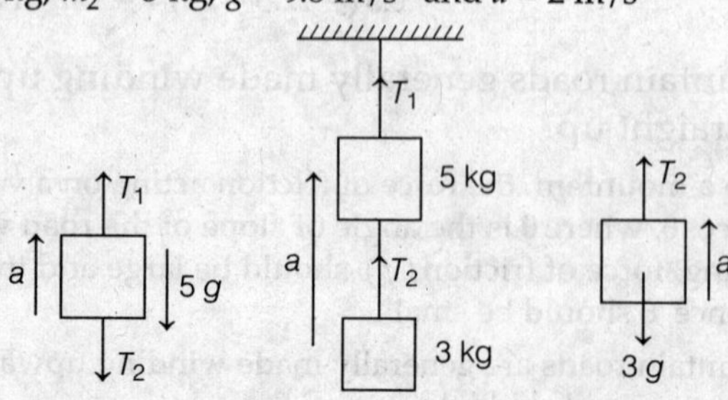

For the upper block $T_1 - T_2 - 5g = 5a$

$\Rightarrow$ $T_1 - T_2 = 5(g + a)$ ...(i)

For the lower block $T_2 - 3g = 3a$

$\Rightarrow$ $T_2 = 3(g + a) = 3(9.8 + 2) = 35.4\text{ N}$

From Eq. (i) $T_1 = T_2 + 5(g + a)$

$= 35.4 + 5(9.8 + 2) = 94.4\text{ N}$

Q.29 Block *A* of weight 100 N rests on a frictionless inclined plane of slope angle 30°. A flexible cord attached to *A* passes over a frictionless pulley and is connected to block *B* of weight *w*. Find the weight *w* for which the system is in equilibrium.

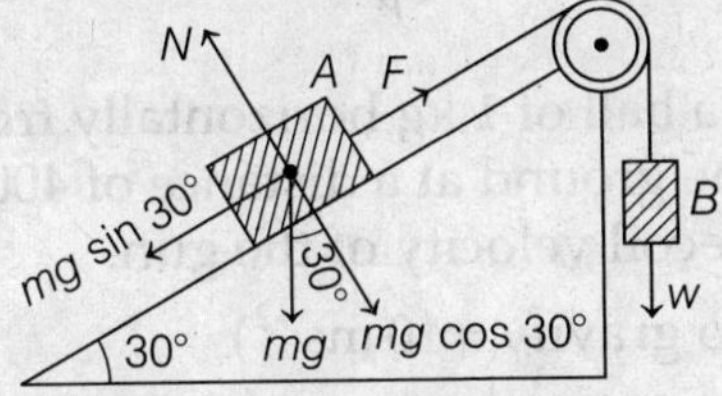

Ans. In equilibrium, the force $mg\sin\theta$ acting on block *A* parallel to the plane should be balanced by the tension in the string, *i.e.*,

$$mg\sin\theta = T = F \quad [\because T = F] \quad ...(i)$$

and for block *B*, $w = T = F$ ...(ii)

where, *w* is the weight of block *B*.

From Eqs. (i) and (ii), we get,

$\therefore$ $w = mg\sin\theta$

$= 100 \times \sin 30°$ $[\because mg = 100\text{ N}]$

$= 100 \times \frac{1}{2}\text{ N} = 50\text{ N}$

Mistake Alert ! *While finding normal reaction in such cases, we should be careful since it will be* $N = mg\cos\theta$, *where* θ *is angle of inclination.*

Q.30 A block of mass *M* is held against a rough vertical wall by pressing it with a finger. If the coefficient of friction between the block and the wall is μ and the acceleration due to gravity is *g*, calculate the minimum force required to be applied by the finger to hold the block against the wall.

Ans. Given, mass of the block = *M*

Coefficient of friction between the block and the wall = μ

Let a force *F* be applied on the block to hold the block against the wall. The normal reaction of mass be *N* acting opposite to *F*. Force of friction acting upward be *f*. In equilibrium, vertical and horizontal forces should be balanced separately.

$\therefore$ $f = Mg$ ...(i)

and $F = N$ ...(ii)

But force of friction $(f) = \mu N$

$= \mu F$ [using Eq. (ii)]

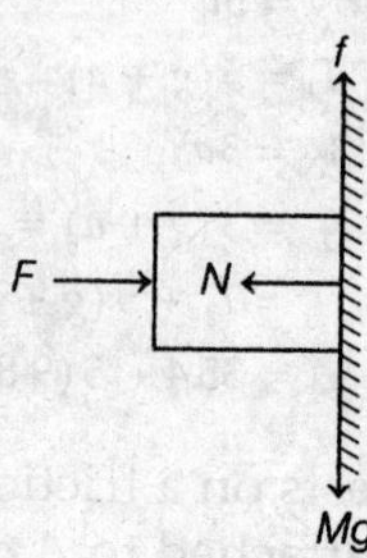

From Eqs. (i) and (iii), we get $\mu F = Mg$

or $$F = \frac{Mg}{\mu}$$

Q.31 **A 100 kg gun fires a ball of 1 kg horizontally from a cliff of height 500 m. It falls on the ground at a distance of 400 m from the bottom of the cliff. Find the recoil velocity of the gun.**

(acceleration due to gravity $= 10\ ms^{-2}$)

Ans. Given, mass of the gun $(m_1) = 100$ kg

Mass of the ball $(m_2) = 1$ kg

Height of the cliff $(h) = 500$ m

Horizontal distance travelled by the ball $(x) = 400$ m

$\therefore$ Now, $$h = u_y t + \frac{1}{2} g t^2$$

Since, $$u_y = 0 \Rightarrow h = \frac{1}{2} g t^2$$

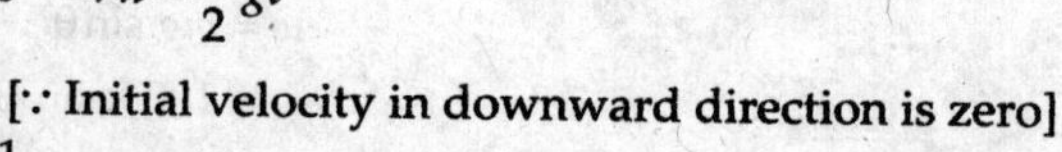
[∵ Initial velocity in downward direction is zero]

$$500 = \frac{1}{2} \times 10 t^2$$

$$t = \sqrt{100} = 10\ \text{s}$$

From $x = u_x t$, $$u_x = \frac{x}{t} = \frac{400}{10} = 40\ \text{m/s}$$

As ball was fired horizontally, so its velocity

$$u = 40\ \text{m/s}$$

If v is recoil velocity of gun, then according to principle of conservation of linear momentum,

$$m_1 v = m_2 u$$

$$v = \frac{m_2 u}{m_1} = \frac{1}{100} \times 40 = 0.4\ \text{m/s}$$

Q.32 Figure shows (x, t), (y, t) diagram of a particle moving in 2-dimensions.

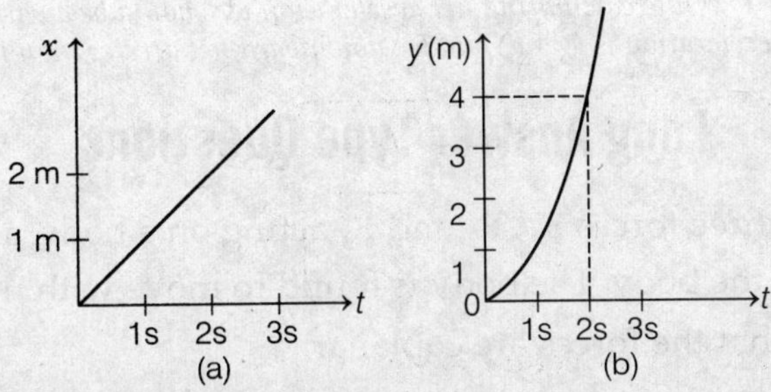

If the particle has a mass of 500 g, find the force (direction and magnitude) acting on the particle.

Thinking Process To solve this question, we have to find the relation for x and time (t), y and time (t) from the given diagram.

Ans. Clearly from diagram (a), the variation can be related as

$$v = \frac{dx}{dt} = 1\,\text{m/s}$$

$$a_x = 0 \quad \text{[As body has uniform velocity]}$$

Diagram (b) represents accelerated motion as slope of $x - t$ graph is increasing.

$$y = t^2$$

$$\Rightarrow \quad \frac{dy}{dt} = 2t \quad \text{or} \quad a_y = \frac{d^2y}{dt^2} = 2\,\text{m/s}^2$$

Hence, $F_y = ma_y = 500 \times 10^{-3} \times 2 = 1\text{N}$ $\quad [\because m = 500\,\text{g}]$

$$F_x = ma_x = 0$$

Hence, net force, $F = \sqrt{F_x^2 + F_y^2} = F_y = 1\text{N}$ $\quad$ [along y-axis]

Q.33 A person in an elevator accelerating upwards with an acceleration of 2 ms^{-2}, tosses a coin vertically upwards with a speed of 20 ms^{-1}. After how much time will the coin fall back into his hand? $(g = 10\text{ ms}^{-2})$

Ans. Here, initial speed of the coin $(u) = 20\,\text{m/s}$

Acceleration of the elevator $(a) = 2\,\text{m/s}^2$ $\quad$ [upwards]

Acceleration due to gravity $(g) = 10\,\text{m/s}^2$

$\therefore$ Effective acceleration $a' = -(g + a) = -(10 + 2) = -12\,\text{m/s}^2$

[here, acceleration is w.r.t. the lift]

If the time of ascent of the coin is t, then

$$v = u + at$$

$$0 = 20 + (-12) \times t$$

or $\quad t = \frac{20}{12} = \frac{5}{3}\,\text{s}$

Time of ascent = Time of desent

$\therefore$ Total time after which the coin fall back into hand $= \left(\frac{5}{3} + \frac{5}{3}\right) s = \frac{10}{3} s = 3.33 s$

Mistake Alert! *While calculating net acceleration we should be aware that if lift is going upward net acceleration is (g + a) and for downward net acceleration is (g − a).*

Long Answer Type Questions

Q.34 There are three forces $\mathbf{F_1}$, $\mathbf{F_2}$ and $\mathbf{F_3}$ acting on a body, all acting on a point P on the body. The body is found to move with uniform speed.

(a) Show that the forces are coplanar.

(b) Show that the torque acting on the body about any point due to these three forces is zero.

Thinking Process As the body is found to move with uniform velocity hence, we can say that total force acting will be zero.

Ans. As the body is moving with uniform speed (velocity) its acceleration $a = 0$.

$\therefore$ The sum of the forces is zero, $\mathbf{F_1 + F_2 + F_3 = 0}$

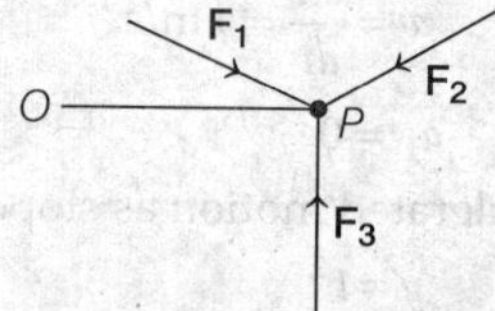

(a) Let $\mathbf{F_1}$, $\mathbf{F_2}$, $\mathbf{F_3}$ be the three forces passing through a point. Let $\mathbf{F_1}$ and $\mathbf{F_2}$ be in the plane A (one can always draw a plane having two intersecting lines such that the two lines lie on the plane). Then $\mathbf{F_1 + F_2}$ must be in the plane A.

Since, $\mathbf{F_3} = -(\mathbf{F_1 + F_2})$, $\mathbf{F_3}$ is also in the plane A.

(b) Consider the torque of the forces about P. Since, all the forces pass through P, the torque is zero. Now, consider torque about another point O. Then torque about O is

$$\text{Torque} = \mathbf{OP} \times (\mathbf{F_1 + F_2 + F_3})$$

Since, $$\mathbf{F_1 + F_2 + F_3} = 0,$$

$$\text{torque} = 0$$

Q.35 When a body slides down from rest along a smooth inclined plane making an angle of 45° with the horizontal, it takes time T. When the same body slides down from rest along a rough inclined plane making the same angle and through the same distance, it is seen to take time pT, where p is some number greater than 1. Calculate the coefficient of friction between the body and the rough plane.

Ans. Consider the diagram where a body slides down from along an inclined plane of inclination $\theta (= 45°)$.

On smooth inclined plane Acceleration of a body sliding down a smooth inclined plane

$$ma = mg \sin\theta$$

$$a = g \sin \theta$$

Here, $\theta = 45°$

$\therefore$ $a = g \sin 45° = \dfrac{g}{\sqrt{2}}$

N, mg sin θ, mg cos θ, mg, θ = 45°

Let the travelled distance be s.

Using equation of motion, $s = ut + \dfrac{1}{2} at^2$, we get

$$s = 0.t + \frac{1}{2} \frac{g}{\sqrt{2}} T^2$$

or $$s = \frac{gT^2}{2\sqrt{2}} \quad \text{...(i)}$$

On rough inclined plane

$$mg \sin\theta - F_f = ma$$

$$mg \sin\theta - \mu mg \cos\theta = ma$$

Acceleration of the body $a = g(\sin \theta - \mu \cos \theta)$

$$= g (\sin 45° - \mu \cos 45°)$$

$$= \frac{g(1-\mu)}{\sqrt{2}} \quad \left[\text{As, } \sin 45° = \cos 45° = \frac{1}{\sqrt{2}}\right]$$

Again using equation of motion, $s = ut + \dfrac{1}{2} at^2$, we get

$$s = 0(pT) + \frac{1}{2} \frac{g(1-\mu)}{\sqrt{2}} (pT)^2$$

or $$s = \frac{g(1-\mu)p^2T^2}{2\sqrt{2}} \quad \text{...(ii)}$$

From Eqs. (i) and (ii), we get

$$\frac{gT^2}{2\sqrt{2}} = \frac{g(1-\mu)p^2T^2}{2\sqrt{2}}$$

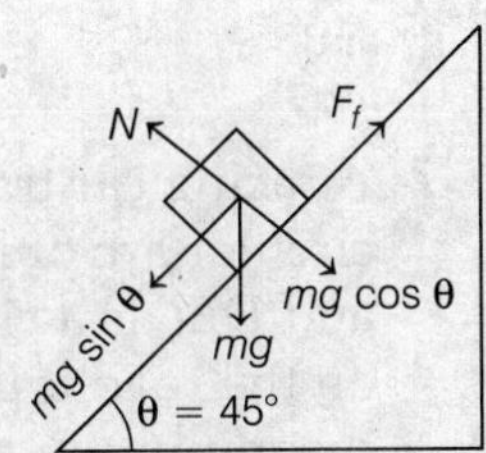

or $$(1-\mu)p^2 = 1$$

or $$1-\mu = \frac{1}{p^2}$$

or $$\mu = \left(1 - \frac{1}{p^2}\right)$$

Q.36 Figure shows (v_x, t) and (v_y, t) diagrams for a body of unit mass. Find the force as a function of time.

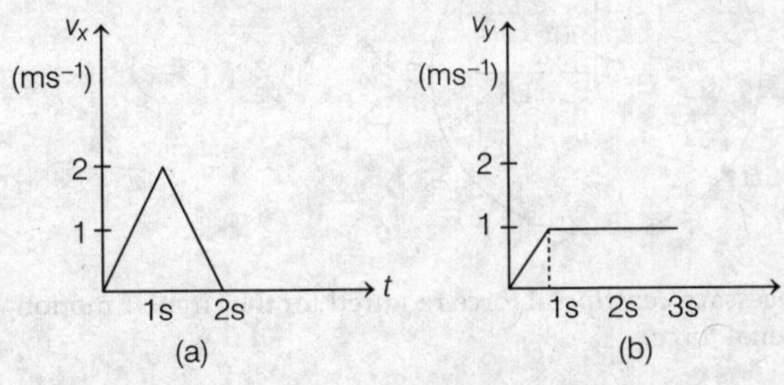

Ans. Consider figure (a)

$$v_x = 2t \text{ for } 0 < t < 1\text{s}$$
$$= 2(2-t) \text{ for } 1 < t < 2\text{s}$$
$$= 0 \text{ for } t > 2\text{s}.$$

From figure (b)

$$v_y = t \text{ for } 0 < t < 1\text{s}$$
$$= 1 \text{ for } t > 1\text{s}$$

$\therefore$

$$F_x = ma_x = m\frac{dv_x}{dt}$$
$$F_x = 1 \times 2 = 2, \quad \text{for } 0 < t < 1\text{s}$$
$$F_x = 1(-2) = 2 \quad \text{for } 1 < t < 2\text{s}$$

and

$$F_x = 0 = -2 \quad \text{for } t > 2\text{s}$$

(a) (b)

$$F_y = ma_y = m\frac{dv_y}{dt}$$
$$F_y = 1 \times 1 = 1 \quad \text{for } 0 < t < 1\text{s}$$

and

$$F_y = 0 \quad \text{for } t > 1\text{s}$$

Hence,

$$\mathbf{F} = F_x\hat{\mathbf{i}} + F_y\hat{\mathbf{j}}$$
$$\mathbf{F} = 2\hat{\mathbf{i}} + \hat{\mathbf{j}}, \quad \text{for } 0 < t < 1\text{s}$$
$$\mathbf{F} = -2\hat{\mathbf{i}}, \quad \text{for } 1 < t < 2\text{s}$$

and

$$\mathbf{F} = 0 \quad \text{for } t > 2\text{s}.$$

Q.37 A racing car travels on a track (without banking) *ABCDEFA*. *ABC* is a circular arc of radius 2 *R*. *CD* and *FA* are straight paths of length *R* and *DEF* is a circular arc of radius $R = 100$ m. The coefficient of friction on the road is $\mu = 0.1$. The maximum speed of the car is 50 ms^{-1}. Find the minimum time for completing one round.

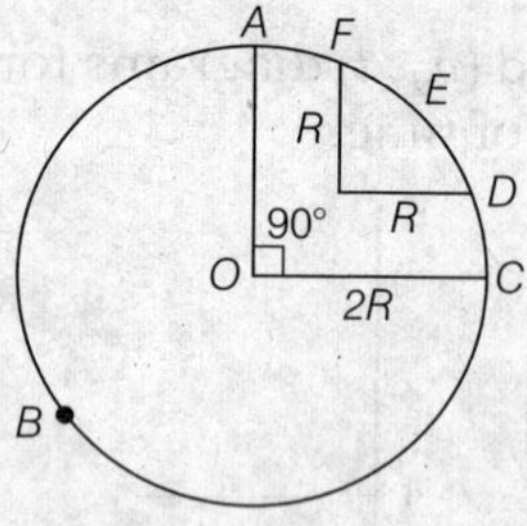

Thinking Process The necessary centripetal force required for the circular motion will be provided by the frictional force.

Ans. Balancing frictional force for centripetal force $\frac{mv^2}{r} = f = \mu N = \mu mg$

where, N is normal reaction.

$\therefore \quad v = \sqrt{\mu rg}$ [where, r is radius of the circular track]

For path ABC Path length $= \frac{3}{4}(2\pi\ 2R) = 3\pi\ R = 3\pi \times 100$

$$= 300\pi \text{ m}$$

$$v_1 = \sqrt{\mu 2Rg} = \sqrt{0.1 \times 2 \times 100 \times 10}$$

$$= 14.14 \text{ m/s}$$

$$\therefore \quad t_1 = \frac{300\pi}{14.14} = 66.6 \text{ s}$$

For path DEF Path length $= \frac{1}{4}(2\pi R) = \frac{\pi \times 100}{2} = 50\pi$

$$v_2 = \sqrt{\mu Rg} = \sqrt{0.1 \times 100 \times 10} = 10 \text{ m/s}$$

$$t_2 = \frac{50\pi}{10} = 5\pi \text{ s} = 15.7 \text{s}$$

For paths, CD and FA

Path length $= R + R = 2R = 200$ m

$$t_3 = \frac{200}{50} = 4.0 \text{ s.}$$

$\therefore$ Total time for completing one round

$$t = t_1 + t_2 + t_3 = 66.6 + 15.7 + 4.0 = 86.3 \text{ s}$$

Q.38 **The displacement vector of a particle of mass m is given by $\mathbf{r}(t) = \hat{\mathbf{i}} A \cos \omega t + \hat{\mathbf{j}} B \sin \omega t$.**

(a) Show that the trajectory is an ellipse.

(b) Show that $\mathbf{F} = -m\omega^2 \mathbf{r}$.

Thinking Process To find trajectory, we will relate x and y in terms of constants A and B.

Ans. (a) Displacement vector of the particle of mass m is given by

$$\mathbf{r}(t) = \hat{\mathbf{i}} A \cos \omega t + \hat{\mathbf{j}} B \sin \omega t$$

$\therefore$ Displacement along x-axis is,

$$x = A \cos \omega t$$

or $$\frac{x}{A} = \cos \omega t \quad \text{...(i)}$$

Displacement along y-axis is,

$$y = B \sin \omega t$$

or $$\frac{y}{B} = \sin \omega t \quad \text{...(ii)}$$

Squaring and then adding Eqs. (i) and (ii), we get

$$\frac{x^2}{A^2} + \frac{y^2}{B^2} = \cos^2 \omega t + \sin^2 \omega t = 1$$

This is an equation of ellipse.

Therefore, trajectory of the particle is an ellipse.

(b) Velocity of the particle

$$\mathbf{v} = \frac{d\mathbf{r}}{dt} = \hat{\mathbf{i}}\frac{d}{dt}(A\cos\omega t) + \hat{\mathbf{j}}\frac{d}{dt}(B\sin\omega t)$$

$$= \hat{\mathbf{i}}[A(-\sin\omega t).\omega] + \hat{\mathbf{j}}[B(\cos\omega t).\omega]$$

$$= -\hat{\mathbf{i}}A\omega\sin\omega t + \hat{\mathbf{j}}\ B\omega\cos\omega t$$

Acceleration of the particle $(\mathbf{a}) = \dfrac{d\mathbf{v}}{dt}$

or
$$\mathbf{a} = -\hat{\mathbf{i}}A\omega\frac{d}{dt}(\sin\omega t) + \hat{\mathbf{j}}B\omega\frac{d}{dt}(\cos\omega t)$$

$$= -\hat{\mathbf{i}}A\omega[\cos\omega t]\cdot\omega + \hat{\mathbf{j}}B\omega[-\sin\omega t].\omega$$

$$= -\hat{\mathbf{i}}A\omega^2\cos\omega t - \hat{\mathbf{j}}B\omega^2\sin\omega t$$

$$= -\omega^2[\hat{\mathbf{i}}A\cos\omega t + \hat{\mathbf{j}}B\sin\omega t]$$

$$= -\omega^2\mathbf{r}$$

$\therefore$ Force acting on the particle,

$$\mathbf{F} = m\mathbf{a} = -m\omega^2\mathbf{r},$$ **Hence Proved.**

Q.39 A cricket bowler releases the ball in two different ways

(a) giving it only horizontal velocity, and

(b) giving it horizontal velocity and a small downward velocity.

The speed v_s at the time of release is the same. Both are released at a height H from the ground. Which one will have greater speed when the ball hits the ground ? Neglect air resistance.

Thinking Process The horizontal component of velocity will remain unaffected by gravity.

Ans. (a) **When ball is given only horizontal velocity** Horizontal velocity at the time of release $(u_x) = v_s$

During projectile motion, horizontal velocity remains unchanged,

Therefore, $v_x = u_x = v_s$

In vertical direction, $v_y^2 = u_y^2 + 2gH$

$$v_y = \sqrt{2gH} \qquad (\because u_y = 0)$$

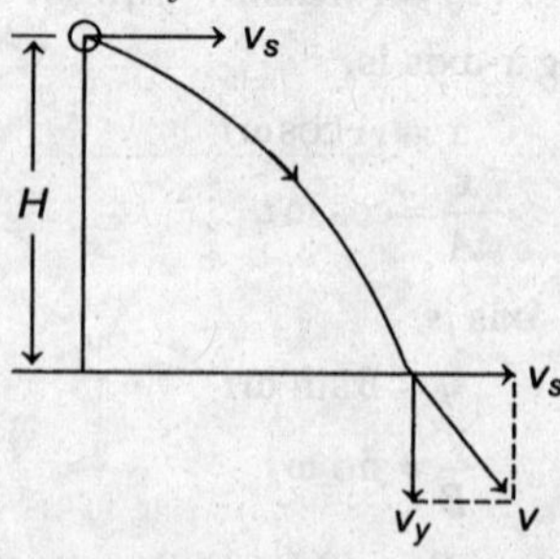

$\therefore$ Resultant speed of the ball at bottom,

$$v = \sqrt{v_x^2 + v_y^2}$$

$$= \sqrt{v_s^2 + 2gH} \qquad \text{...(i)}$$

(b) **When ball is given horizontal velocity and a small downward velocity**

Let the ball be given a small downward velocity u.

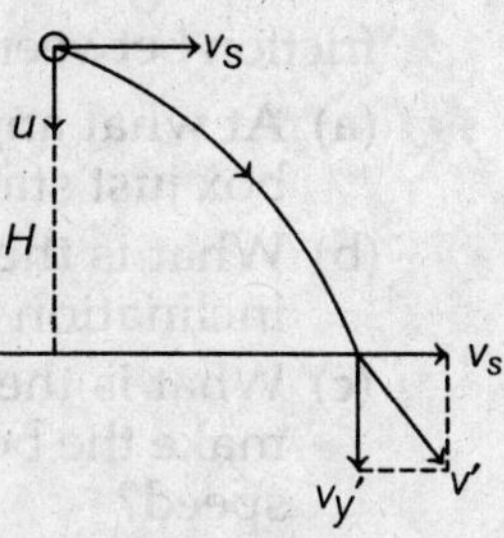

In horizontal direction $v'_x = u_x = v_s$

In vertical direction $v'^2_y = u^2 + 2gH$

or $v'_y = \sqrt{u^2 + 2gH}$

$\therefore$ Resultant speed of the ball at the bottom

$$v' = \sqrt{v'^2_x + v'^2_y} = \sqrt{v_s^2 + u^2 + 2gH} \quad \text{...(ii)}$$

From Eqs. (i) and (ii), we get $v' > v$

Q.40 There are four forces acting at a point P produced by strings as shown in figure, which is at rest. Find the forces $\mathbf{F}_1$ and $\mathbf{F}_2$.

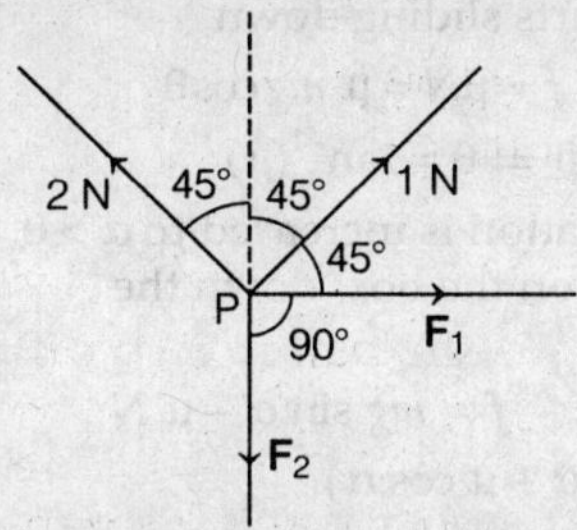

Thinking Process To balance the forces, we have to resolve them along two mutually perpendicular directions.

Ans. Consider the adjacent diagram, in which the net force acting at point P is zero. Since the system is in equilibrium.

So, the x and y-components of forces must be zero.

$$\therefore \quad F_x = \mathbf{F}_1 + \cos 45° - 2\sin 45° = 0$$

$$F_y = \mathbf{F}_2 - 2\cos 45° - \cos 45° = 0$$

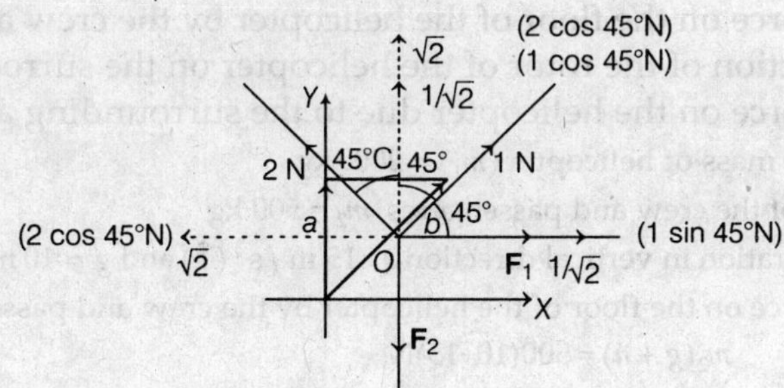

$$\therefore \quad F_1 + \frac{1}{\sqrt{2}} = \sqrt{2}$$

$$F_1 = \sqrt{2} - \frac{1}{\sqrt{2}} = \frac{2-1}{\sqrt{2}} = \frac{1}{\sqrt{2}} = 0.707 \text{ N}$$

and $$F_2 = \sqrt{2} + \frac{1}{\sqrt{2}} = \frac{2+1}{\sqrt{2}} \text{ N} = \frac{3}{\sqrt{2}} \text{ N} = 2.121 \text{ N}$$

Q.41 A rectangular box lies on a rough inclined surface. The coefficient of friction between the surface and the box is μ. Let the mass of the box be m.

(a) At what angle of inclination θ of the plane to the horizontal will the box just start to slide down the plane?

(b) What is the force acting on the box down the plane, if the angle of inclination of the plane is increased to $\alpha > \theta$?

(c) What is the force needed to be applied upwards along the plane to make the box either remain stationary or just move up with uniform speed?

(d) What is the force needed to be applied upwards along the plane to make the box move up the plane with acceleration a?

Ans. (a) Consider the adjacent diagram, force of friction on the box will act up the plane. For the box to just starts sliding down

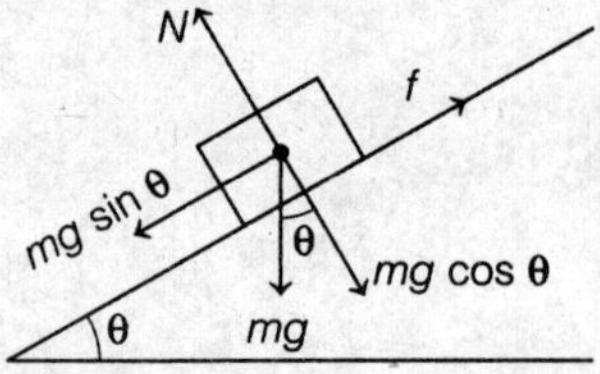

$$mg\sin\theta = f = \mu N = \mu\, mg\cos\theta$$

or $$\tan\theta = \mu \Rightarrow \theta = \tan^{-1}(\mu)$$

(b) When angle of inclination is increased to $\alpha > \theta$, then net force acting on the box, down the plane is

$$F_1 = mg\sin\alpha - f = mg\sin\alpha - \mu N$$
$$= mg(\sin\alpha - \mu\cos\alpha).$$

(c) To keep the box either stationary or just move it up with uniform speed, upward force needed, $F_2 = mg\sin\alpha + f = mg(\sin\alpha + \mu\cos\alpha)$ (In this case, friction would act down the plane).

(d) If the box is to be moved with an upward acceleration a, then upward force needed, $F_3 = mg(\sin\alpha + \mu\cos\alpha) + ma$.

Q.42 A helicopter of mass 2000 kg rises with a vertical acceleration of 15 ms^{-2}. The total mass of the crew and passengers is 500 kg. Give the magnitude and direction of the (g=10 ms^{-2})

(a) force on the floor of the helicopter by the crew and passengers.

(b) action of the rotor of the helicopter on the surrounding air.

(c) force on the helicopter due to the surrounding air.

Ans. Given, mass of helicopter $(m_1) = 2000$ kg

Mass of the crew and passengeres $m_2 = 500$ kg

Acceleration in vertical direction $a = 15\ m/s^2\ (\uparrow)$ and $g = 10\ m/s^2\ (\downarrow)$

(a) Force on the floor of the helicopter by the crew and passengers

$$m_2(g+a) = 500(10+15)\text{N}$$
$$= 500 \times 25\ \text{N} = 12500\ \text{N}$$

(b) Action of the rotor of the helicopter on the surrounding air $= (m_1 + m_2)(g+a)$

$$= (2000 + 500) \times (10 + 15) = 2500 \times 25 = 62500\ \text{N (downward)}$$

(c) Force on the helicopter due to the surrounding air

= reaction of force applied by helicopter.

= 62500 N (upward)

Mistake Alert! *We should be very clear when we are balancing action and reaction forces. We must know that which part is action and which part is reaction due to the action.*

Chapter

05

Work, Energy and Power

Multiple Choice Questions (MCQs)

Q.1 An electron and a proton are moving under the influence of mutual forces. In calculating the change in the kinetic energy of the system during motion, one ignores the magnetic force of one on another. This is, because,

(a) the two magnetic forces are equal and opposite, so they produce no net effect.
(b) the magnetic forces do not work on each particle.
(c) the magnetic forces do equal and opposite (but non-zero) work on each particle.
(d) the magnetic forces are necessarily negligible.

Thinking Process In this problem as the electron and proton are moving under the influence of mutual forces, they will perform circular motion about their centre (i.e. about middle point of the line joining them).

Ans. *(b)* When electron and proton are moving under influence of their mutual forces, the magnetic forces will be perpendicular to their motion hence, no work is done by these forces.

[Work done per second $= \frac{\mathbf{F} \cdot \mathbf{S}}{t} = \mathbf{F} \cdot \mathbf{V} = FV \cos 90° = 0$]

Q.2 A proton is kept at rest. A positively charged particle is released from rest at a distance d in its field. Consider two experiments; one in which the charged particle is also a proton and in another, a positron. In the same time t, the work done on the two moving charged particles is

(a) same as the same force law is involved in the two experiments.
(b) less for the case of a positron, as the positron moves away more rapidly and the force on it weakens.
(c) more for the case of a positron, as the positron moves away a larger distance.
(d) same as the work done by charged particle on the stationary proton.

Ans. *(c)* Force between two protons is same as that of between proton and a positron.

As positron is much lighter than proton, it moves away through much larger distance compared to proton.

We know that work done = force × distance. As forces are same in case of proton and positron but distance moved by positron is larger, hence, work done will be more.

Q. 3 A man squatting on the ground gets straight up and stand. The force of reaction of ground on the man during the process is

(a) constant and equal to mg in magnitude
(b) constant and greater than mg in magnitude
(c) variable but always greater than mg
(d) at first greater than mg and later becomes equal to mg

Ans. *(d)* When the man is squatting on the ground, he is tilted somewhat, hence he also has to balance frictional force besides his weight in this case.

$$R = \text{reactional force} = \text{friction} + mg$$

$$\Rightarrow \quad R > mg$$

When the man gets straight up in that case friction ≈ 0

$$\Rightarrow \quad \text{Reactional force} \approx mg$$

Q.4 A bicyclist comes to a skidding stop in 10 m. During this process, the force on the bicycle due to the road is 200N and is directly opposed to the motion. The work done by the cycle on the road is

(a) + 2000 J (b) – 200 J (c) zero (d) – 20, 000 J

Thinking Process In this problem, energy will be lost due to dissipation by friction.

Ans. *(c)* Here, work is done by the frictional force on the cycle and is equal to $-200 \times 10 = -2000$ J.

As the road is not moving, hence, work done by the cycle on the road = zero.

Mistake Alert ! *We should be aware that here the energy of bicyclist is lost during the motion, but it is lost due to friction in the form of heat.*

Q.5 A body is falling freely under the action of gravity alone in vaccum. Which of the following quantities remain constant during the fall?

(a) Kinetic energy (b) Potential energy
(c) Total mechanical energy (d) Total linear momentum

Ans. *(c)* As the body is falling freely under gravity, the potential energy decreases and kinetic energy increases but total mechanical energy (PE + KE) of the body will be constant as external force on the system is zero.

Q.6 During inelastic collision between two bodies, which of the following quantities always remain conserved?

(a) Total kinetic energy (b) Total mechanical energy
(c) Total linear momentum (d) Speed of each body

Thinking Process In an inelastic collision between two bodies due to some deformation, energy may be lost in the form of heat and sound etc.

Ans. *(c)* When we are considering the two bodies as system and total external force on the system is zero.

Then, total linear momentum of the system remain conserved.

Q.7 Two inclined frictionless tracks, one gradual and the other steep meet at A from where two stones are allowed to slide down from rest, one on each track as shown in figure.

Which of the following statement is correct?

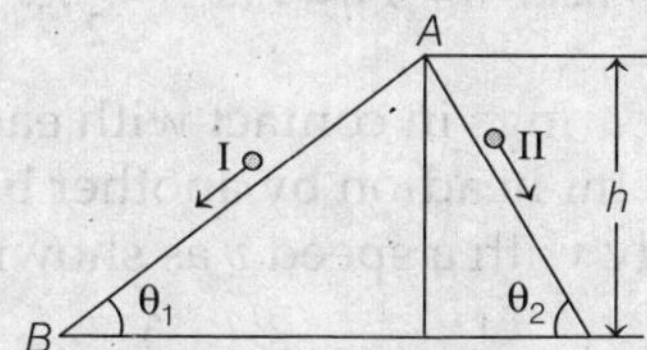

(a) Both the stones reach the bottom at the same time but not with the same speed.
(b) Both the stones reach the bottom with the same speed and stone I reaches the bottom earlier than stone II.
(c) Both the stones reach the bottom with the same speed and stone II reaches the bottom earlier than stone I.
(d) Both the stones reach the bottom at different times and with different speeds.

Ans. *(c)* As the given tracks are frictionless, hence, mechanical energy will be conserved. As both the tracks having common height, h.

From conservation of mechanical energy,

$$\frac{1}{2}mv^2 = mgh \qquad \text{(for both tracks I and II)}$$

$$v = \sqrt{2gh}$$

Hence, speed is same for both stones. For stone I, a_1 = acceleration along inclined plane $= g \sin \theta_1$

Similarly, for stone II $a_2 = g \sin \theta_2$ as $\theta_2 > \theta_1$ hence, $a_2 > a_1$.

And length for track II is also less hence, stone II reaches earlier than stone I.

Q.8 The potential energy function for a particle executing linear SHM is given by $V(x) = \frac{1}{2}kx^2$ where k is the force constant of the oscillator (Fig). For $k = 0.5$ N/m, the graph of $V(x)$ *versus* x is shown in the figure. A particle of total energy E turns back when it reaches $x = \pm x_m$. If V and K indicate the PE and KE, respectively of the particle at $x = +x_m$, then which of the following is correct?

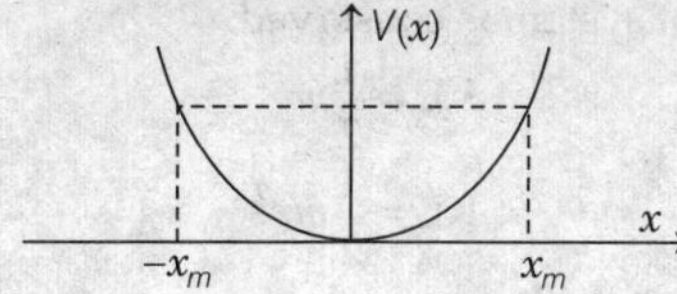

(a) $V = O$, $K = E$
(b) $V = E$, $K = O$
(c) $V < E$, $K = O$
(d) $V = O$, $K < E$

Ans. *(b)* Total energy is $E = \text{PE} + \text{KE} = \frac{1}{2} Kx^2 + \frac{1}{2} mv^2$ ...(i)

When particle is at $x = x_m$ i.e. at extreme position, its speed becomes zero and it returns back. Hence, at $x = x_m$; $v = 0$; KE $= 0$

From Eq. (i) $E = \text{PE} + 0 = \text{PE} = V(x_m) = \frac{1}{2} kx_m^2$

Q.9 Two identical ball bearings in contact with each other and resting on a frictionless table are hit head-on by another ball bearing of the same mass moving initially with a speed v as shown in figure.

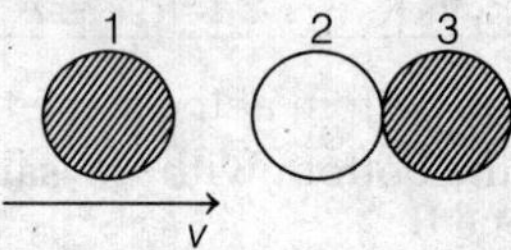

If the collision is elastic, which of the following (figure) is a possible result after collision?

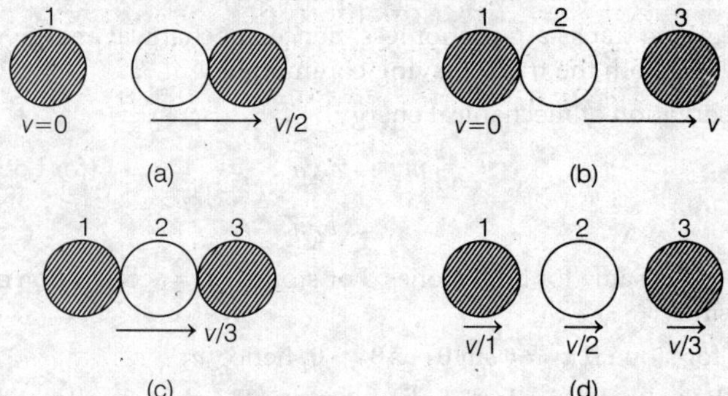

Ans. *(b)* When two bodies of equal masses collides elastically, their velocities are interchanged.

When ball 1 collides with ball-2, then velocity of ball-1, v_1 becomes zero and velocity of ball-2, v_2 becomes v, i.e. similarly.

$$v_1 = 0 \Rightarrow v_2 = v$$

when ball 2 collides will ball 3 $\quad v_2 = 0, v_3 = v$

Alternate Method

In elastic collision KE of system is conserved

So, Initial $\quad \text{KE} = \frac{1}{2} mv^2$

Only in fig (b) Final $\quad \text{KE} = \frac{1}{2} mv^2$

So, option (b) is correct.

Q.10 A body of mass 0.5 kg travels in a straight line with velocity $v = a\,x^{3/2}$ where $a = 5\ \text{m}^{-1/2}\text{s}^{-1}$. The work done by the net force during its displacement from $x = 0$ to $x = 2$ m is

(a) 1.5 J (b) 50 J (c) 10 J (d) 100 J

Ans. Given, $v = ax^{3/2}$

$m = 0.5\,\text{kg},\ a = 5\,\text{m}^{-1/2}\text{s}^{-1}$, work done $(W) = ?$

We know that

Acceleration $$a_0 = \frac{dv}{dt} = v\frac{dv}{dx} = ax^{3/2}\,\frac{d}{dx}(ax^{3/2})$$

$$= ax^{3/2} \times a \times \frac{3}{2} \times x^{1/2} = \frac{3}{2}\,a^2x^2$$

Now, $$\text{Force} = ma_0 = m\,\frac{3}{2}\,a^2x^2$$

$$\text{Work done} = \int_{x=0}^{x=2} F\,dx = \int_0^2 \frac{3}{2}\,ma^2x^2\,dx$$

$$= \frac{3}{2}\,ma^2 \times (x^3/3)_0^2 = \frac{3}{2}\,ma^2\left[\frac{(2)^3}{3} - 0\right]$$

$$= \frac{1}{2}\,ma^2 \times 8 = \frac{1}{2} \times (0.5) \times (25) \times 8 = 50\,\text{J}$$

Q.11 **A body is moving unidirectionally under the influence of a source of constant power supplying energy. Which of the diagrams shown in figure correctly shown the displacement-time curve for its motion?**

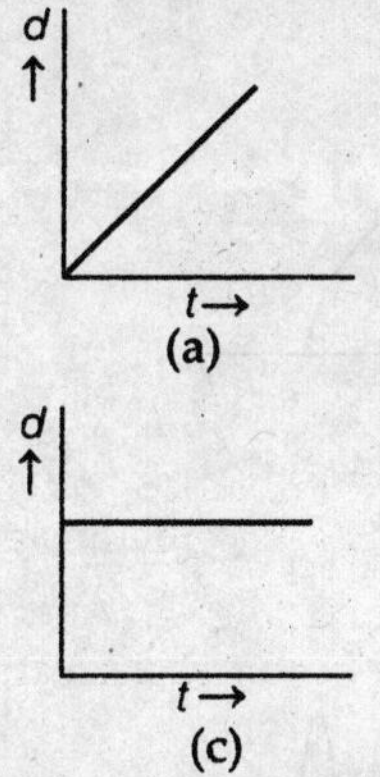

(a)

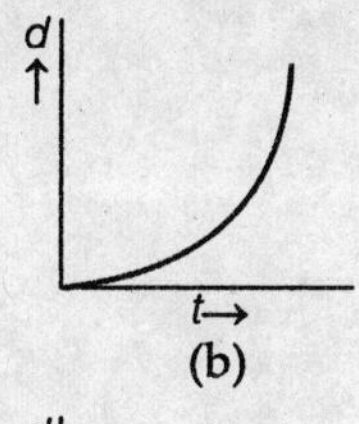

(b)

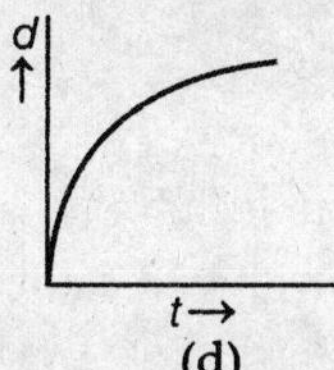

(c)

(d)

Ans. ***(b)*** Given, power = constant

We know that power (P)

$$P = \frac{dW}{dt} = \frac{\mathbf{F}\cdot\mathbf{ds}}{dt} = \frac{F\,ds}{dt} \qquad [\because \text{body is moving unidirectionally}]$$

Hence, $$F.ds = Fds\cos 0°$$

$$P = \frac{Fds}{dt} = \text{constant} \qquad [\because P = \text{constant by question}]$$

Now, writing dimensions

$$[\text{F}]\,[\text{v}] = \text{constant}$$

$\Rightarrow$ $$[\text{MLT}^{-2}]\,[\text{LT}^{-1}] = \text{constant}$$

$\Rightarrow$ $$\text{L}^2\,\text{T}^{-3} = \text{constant} \qquad [\because \text{mass is constant}]$$

$\Rightarrow$ $$L \propto T^{3/2}$$

$\Rightarrow$ $$\text{Displacement}\,(d) \propto t^{3/2}$$

Q.12 Which of the diagrams shown in figure most closely shows the variation in kinetic energy of the earth as it moves once around the sun in its elliptical orbit?

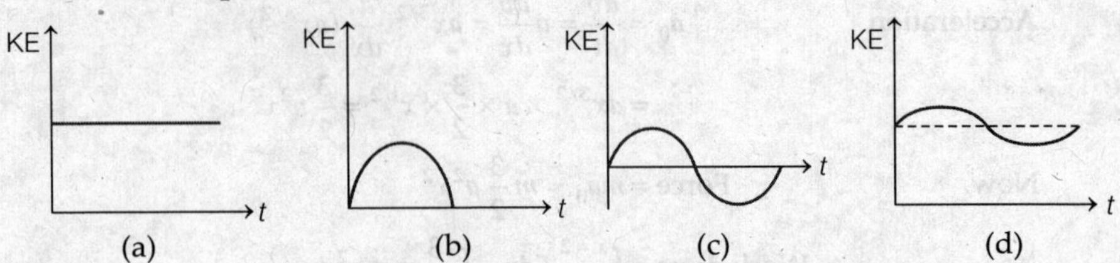

Thinking Process KE may be zero or positive but it can not be negative while PE may be zero, positive or negative.

Ans. ***(d)*** When the earth is closest to the sun, speed of the earth is maximum, hence, KE is maximum. When the earth is farthest from the sun speed is minimum hence, KE is minimum but never zero and negative.

This variation is correctly represented by option(d).

Q.13 Which of the diagrams shown in figure represents variation of total mechanical energy of a pendulum oscillating in air as function of time?

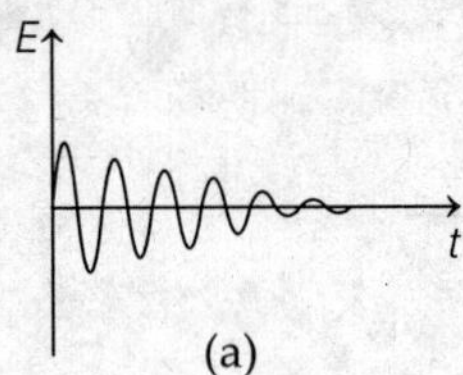

(a)

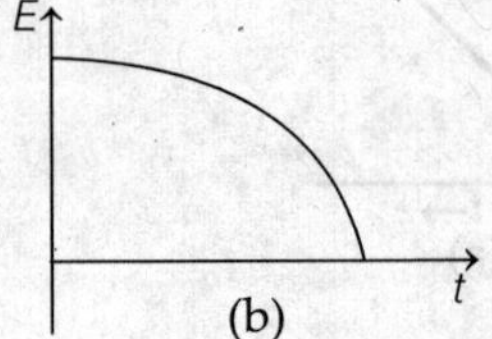

(b)

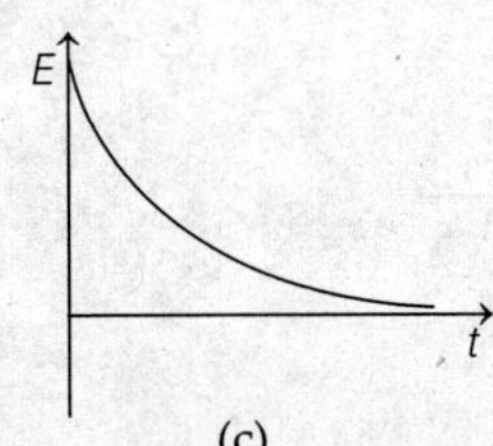

(c)

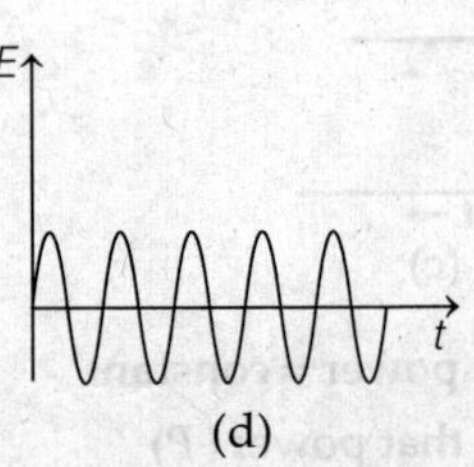

(d)

Ans. ***(c)*** When a pendulum oscillates in air, it will lose energy continuously in overcoming resistance due to air. Therefore, total mechanical energy of the pendulum decreases continuously with time.

The variation is correctly represented by curve (c).

Q.14 A mass of 5 kg is moving along a circular path of radius 1 m. If the mass moves with 300 rev/min, its kinetic energy would be

(a) $250\pi^2$ (b) $100\pi^2$
(c) $5\pi^2$ (d) 0

Ans. ***(a)*** Given, mass $= m = 5\,\text{kg}$

$$\text{Radius} = 1\text{ m} = R$$

Revolution per minute $\omega = 2\pi n$

$$= (300 \times 2\pi)\text{ rad/min}$$

$$= \frac{300 \times 2\pi}{60} = 10\pi\text{ rad/sec}$$

$\Rightarrow$ linear speed $= v = \omega R$

$$= \left(\frac{300 \times 2\pi}{60}\right)(1)$$

$$= 10\pi\text{ m/s}$$

$$\text{KE} = \frac{1}{2}mv^2$$

$$= \frac{1}{2} \times 5 \times (10\pi)^2$$

$$= 100\pi^2 \times 5 \times \frac{1}{2} = 250\,\pi^2\text{ J}$$

Q.15 A raindrop falling from a height h above ground, attains a near terminal velocity when it has fallen through a height $(3/4)h$. Which of the diagrams shown in figure correctly shows the change in kinetic and potential energy of the drop during its fall up to the ground?

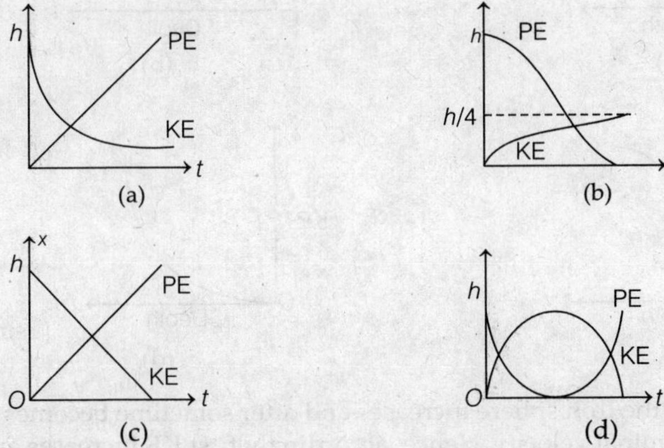

Ans. ***(b)*** When drop falls first velocity increases, hence, first KE also increases. After sometime speed (velocity) is constant this is called terminal velocity, hence, KE also become constant. PE decreases continuously as the drop is falling continuously. The variation in PE and KE is best represented by (b).

Q.16 In a shotput event an athlete throws the shotput of mass 10 kg with an initial speed of 1 m s^{-1} at 45° from a height 1.5 m above ground. Assuming air resistance to be negligible and acceleration due to gravity to be 10 m s^{-2}, the kinetic energy of the shotput when it just reaches the ground will be

(a) 2.5 J (b) 5.0 J (c) 52.5 J (d) 155.0 J

Ans. ***(d)*** Given, $h = 1.5$ m, $v = 1$ m/s, $m = 10$ kg, $g = 10$ ms^{-2}

From law of conservation of mechanical energy. [As air resistance is negligible]

$$(PE)_i + (KE)_i = (PE)_f + (KE)_f$$

$$\Rightarrow \quad mgh + \frac{1}{2}mv^2 = 0 + (KE)_f$$

$$\Rightarrow \quad (KE)_f = mgh + \frac{1}{2}mv^2$$

$$\Rightarrow \quad (KE)_f = 10 \times 10 \times 1.5 + \frac{1}{2} \times 10 \times (1)^2$$

$$= 150 + 5 = 155 \text{ J}$$

Mistake Alert ! *We should be careful about the reference taken for PE, it may or may not be the ground.*

Q.17 Which of the diagrams in figure correctly shows the change in kinetic energy of an iron sphere falling freely in a lake having sufficient depth to impart it a terminal velocity?

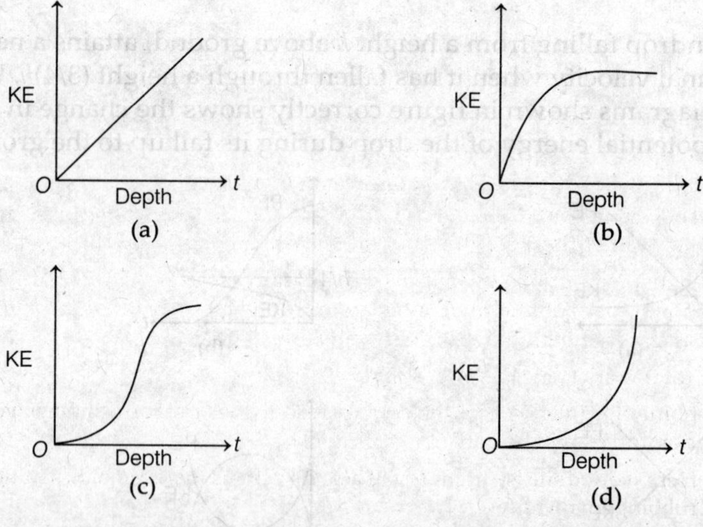

Ans. ***(b)*** First velocity of the iron sphere increases and after sometime becomes constant, called terminal velocity. Hence, accordingly first KE increases and then becomes constant which is best represented by (b).

Q.18 A cricket ball of mass 150 g moving with a speed of 126 km/h hits at the middle of the bat, held firmly at its position by the batsman. The ball moves straight back to the bowler after hitting the bat. Assuming that collision between ball and bat is completely elastic and the two remain in contact for 0.001s, the force that the batsman had to apply to hold the bat firmly at its place would be

(a) 10.5 N
(b) 21 N
(c) 1.05×10^4 N
(d) 2.1×10^4 N

Ans. ***(c)*** Given, $m = 150\text{ g} = \frac{150}{1000}\text{ kg} = \frac{3}{20}\text{ kg}$

$$\Delta t = \text{time of contact} = 0.001\text{ s}$$

$$u = 126\text{ km/h} = \frac{126 \times 1000}{60 \times 60}\text{ m/s} = 35\text{ m/s}$$

$$v = -126\text{ km/h} = -35\text{ m/s}$$

Change in momentum of the ball

$$\Delta p = m(v-u) = \frac{3}{20}(-35-35)\text{ kg-m/s}$$

$$= \frac{3}{20}(-70) = -\frac{21}{2}$$

We know that force $F = \frac{\Delta p}{\Delta t} = \frac{-21/2}{0.001}\text{ N} = -1.05 \times 10^4\text{ N}$

Here, – *ve* sign shown that force will be opposite to the direction of movement of the ball before hitting.

Multiple Choice Questions (More Than One Options)

Q.19 A man of mass m, standing at the bottom of the staircase, of height L climbs it and stands at its top.

(a) Work done by all forces on man is equal to the rise in potential energy mgL.

(b) Work done by all forces on man is zero.

(c) Work done by the gravitational force on man is mgL.

(d) The reaction force from a step does not do work because the point of application of the force does not move while the force exists.

Ans. ***(b, d)*** When a man of mass m climbs up the staircase of height L, work done by the gravitational force on the man is-mgL work done by internal muscular forces will be mgL as the change in kinetic energy is almost zero.

Hence, total work done $= -mgL + mgL = 0$

As the point of application of the contact forces does not move hence work done by reaction forces will be zero.

Note Here work done by friction will also be zero as there is no dissipation or rubbing involved.

Q.20 A bullet of mass m fired at 30° to the horizontal leaves the barrel of the gun with a velocity v. The bullet hits a soft target at a height h above the ground while it is moving downward and emerge out with half the kinetic energy it had before hitting the target.

Which of the following statements are correct in respect of bullet after it emerges out of the target?

(a) The velocity of the bullet will be reduced to half its initial value.

(b) The velocity of the bullet will be more than half of its earlier velocity.

(c) The bullet will continue to move along the same parabolic path.

(d) The bullet will move in a different parabolic path.

(e) The bullet will fall vertically downward after hitting the target

(f) The internal energy of the particles of the target will increase

Ans. *(b, d, f)* Consider the adjacent diagram for the given situation in the question.

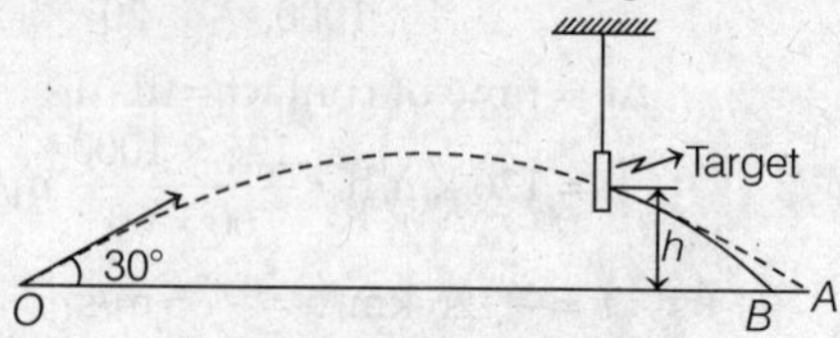

(b) Conserving energy between "O" and "A"

$$U_i + K_i = U_f + K_f$$

$$\Rightarrow \quad 0 + \frac{1}{2} mv^2 = mgh + \frac{1}{2} mv'^2$$

$$\Rightarrow \quad \frac{(v')^2}{2} = \frac{v^2}{2} - gh$$

$$\Rightarrow \quad (v')^2 = v^2 - 2\,gh \Rightarrow v' = \sqrt{v^2 - 2\,gh} \quad \text{...(i)}$$

where v' is speed of the bullet just before hitting the target. Let speed after emerging from the target is v'' then,

By question, $= \frac{1}{2}(mv'')^2 = \frac{1}{2}\left[\frac{1}{2} m(v')^2\right]$

$$\frac{1}{2} m(v'')^2 = \frac{1}{4} m(v')^2 = \frac{1}{4} m[v^2 - 2\,gh]$$

$$\Rightarrow \quad (v'')^2 = \frac{v^2 - 2\,gh}{2} = \frac{v'^2}{2}$$

$$\Rightarrow \quad v'' = \frac{v'}{\sqrt{2}} \quad \text{...(ii)}$$

$$\Rightarrow \text{or} \quad v' > \frac{v}{2}$$

Hence, after emerging from the target velocity of the bullet (v'') is more than half of its earlier velocity v' (velocity before emerging into the target).

(d) As the velocity of the bullet changes to v' which is less than v'' hence, path, followed will change and the bullet reaches at point B instead of A', as shown in the figure.

(f) As the bullet is passing through the target the loss in energy of the bullet is transferred to particles of the target. Therefore, their internal energy increases.

Q.21 Two blocks M_1 and M_2 having equal mass are free to move on a horizontal frictionless surface. M_2 is attached to a massless spring as shown in figure. Initially M_2 is at rest and M_1 is moving toward M_2 with speed v and collides head-on with M_2.

(a) While spring is fully compressed all the KE of M_1 is stored as PE of spring.
(b) While spring is fully compressed the system momentum is not conserved, though final momentum is equal to initial momentum.
(c) If spring is massless, the final state of the M_1 is state of rest.
(d) If the surface on which blocks are moving has friction, then collision cannot be elastic.

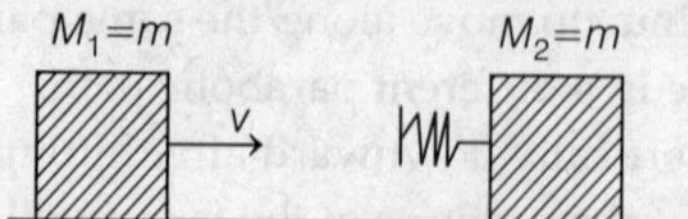

Ans. *(c, d)* Consider the adjacent diagram when M_1 comes in contact with the spring, M_1 is retarded by the spring force and M_2 is accelerated by the spring force.

(a) The spring will continue to compress until the two blocks acquire common velocity and hence, some KE of M_1 will be stored in the spring as PE and the rest will be imparted to M_2 in the form of KE.

(b) As surfaces are frictionalless momentum of the system will be conserved.

(c) If spring is massless whole energy of M_1 will be imparted to M_2 and M_1 will eventually come to rest.

(d) Collision is inelastic, as there will be loss in kinetic energy due to friction.

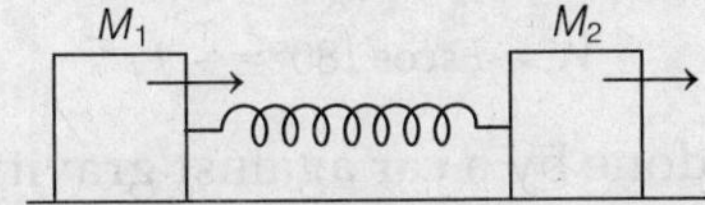

Very Short Answer Type Questions

Q.22 A rough inclined plane is placed on a cart moving with a constant velocity u on horizontal ground. A block of mass M rests on the incline. Is any work done by force of friction between the block and incline? Is there then a dissipation of energy?

Ans. Consider the adjacent diagram. As the block M is at rest.

Hence, f = frictional force = $Mg \sin \theta$

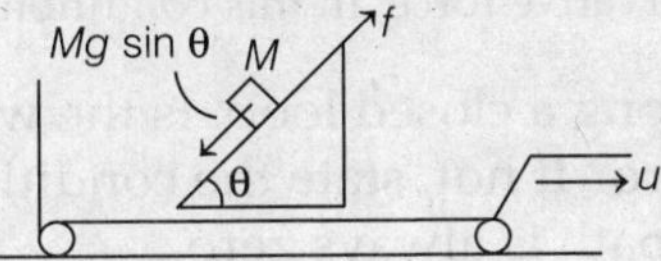

The force of friction acting between the block and incline opposes the tendency of sliding of the block. Since, block is not in motion, therefore, no work is done by the force of friction. Hence, no dissipation of energy takes place.

Q.23 Why is electrical power required at all when the elevator is descending? Why should there be a limit on the number of passengers in this case?

Ans. When the elevator is descending, then electric power is required to prevent it from falling freely under gravity and to control its speed.

Also, as the weight inside the elevator increases, its speed of descending increases, therefore, there should be a limit on the number of passengers in the elevator to prevent the elevator from descending with large velocity.

Q.24 A body is being raised to a height h from the surface of earth. What is the sign of work done by

(a) applied force and

(b) gravitational force?

Ans. (a) Force is applied on the body to lift it in upward direction and displacement of the body is also in upward direction, therefore, angle between the applied force and displacement is $\theta = 0°$

$\therefore$ Work done by the applied force

$$W = Fs\cos\theta = Fs\cos 0° = Fs \quad [\because \cos 0° = 1]$$

i.e. W = Positive

(b) The gravitational force acts in downward direction and displacement in upward direction, therefore, angle between them is $\theta = 180°$.

$\therefore$ Work done by the gravitational force

$$W = Fs\cos 180° = -Fs \quad [\because \cos 180° = -1]$$

Q.25 **Calculate the work done by a car against gravity in moving along a straight horizontal road. The mass of the car is 400 kg and the distance moved is 2 m.**

Ans. Force of gravity acts on the car vertically downward while car is moving along horizontal road, i.e. angle between force and direction of motion is 90°.

Work done by the car against gravity

$$W = Fs\cos 90° = 0 \quad [\because \cos 90° = 0]$$

Q.26 **A body falls towards earth in air. Will its total mechanical energy be conserved during the fall? Justify.**

Ans. No, total mechanical energy of the body falling freely under gravity is not conserved, because a small part of its energy is utilised against resistive force of air, which is non-conservative force. In this condition, gain in KE < loss in PE.

Q.27 **A body is moved along a closed loop. Is the work done in moving the body necessarily zero? If not, state the condition under which work done over a closed path is always zero.**

Ans. No, work done in moving along a closed loop is not necessarily zero. It is zero only when all the forces are conservative forces. If force is non-conservative like frictional force, then work done in moving body over closed loop is not zero.

Q.28 **In an elastic collision of two billiard balls, which of the following quantities remain conserved during the short time of collision of the balls (*i.e.*, when they are in contact)?**

(a) Kinetic energy.

(b) Total linear momentum.

Give reason for your answer in each case.

Ans. Total linear momentum of the system of two balls is always conserved. While balls are in contact, there may be deformation which means elastic PE which came from part of KE Therefore, KE may not be conserved.

Q.29 Calculate the power of a crane in watts, which lifts a mass of 100 kg to a height of 10 m in 20s.

Ans. Given, mass $= m = 100$ kg

height $= h = 10$ m, time duration $t = 20$s

$$\text{power} = \text{Rate of work done}$$
$$= \frac{\text{change of PE}}{\text{time}} = \frac{mgh}{t}$$
$$= \frac{100 \times 9.8 \times 10}{20} = 5 \times 98 = 490 \text{ W}$$

Q.30 The average work done by a human heart while it beats once is 0.5 J. Calculate the power used by heart if it beats 72 times in a minute.

Ans. Given, average work done by a human heart per beat = 0.5 J

Total work done during 72 beats = $72 \times 0.5 \text{ J} = 36 \text{ J}$

$$\text{Power} = \frac{\text{Work done}}{\text{Time}} = \frac{36 \text{ J}}{60 \text{ s}} = 0.6 \text{ W}$$

Mistake Alert! *Carefully calculate total work done and ensure the time is in second for power calculation.*

Q.31 Give example of a situation in which an applied force does not result in a change in kinetic energy.

Ans. When a charged particle moves in a uniform normal magnetic field, the path of the particle is circular, as given field is uniform hence, radius of the circular path is also constant.

As the force is acting towards center of circular path and movement is tangential so work done by the force is zero. As speed is also constant. We can say that $\Delta K = 0$.

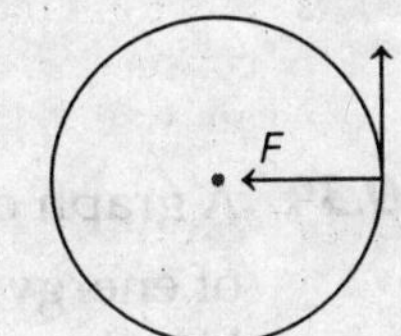

Q.32 Two bodies of unequal mass are moving in the same direction with equal kinetic energy. The two bodies are brought to rest by applying retarding force of same magnitude. How would the distance moved by them before coming to rest compare?

Ans. According to work-energy theorem,

Change in KE = Work done by the retarding force

KE of the body = Retarding force × Displacement

As KE of the bodies and retarding forces applied on them are same, therefore, both bodies will travel equal distances before coming to rest.

Q.33 A bob of mass m suspended by a light string of length L is whirled into a vertical circle as shown in figure. What will be the trajectory of the particle, if the string is cut at

(a) point B? (b) point C?

(c) point X?

Thinking Process In a uniform circular motion, velocity is always tangential in the direction of motion at any point.

Ans. When bob is whirled into a vertical circle, the required centripetal force is obtained from the tension in the string. When string is cut, tension in string becomes zero and centripetal force is not provided, hence, bob start to move in a straight line path along the direction of its velocity.

(a) At point B, the velocity of B is vertically downward, therefore, when string is cut at B, bob moves vertically downward.

(b) At point C, the velocity is along the horizontal towards right, therefore, when string is cut at C, bob moves horizontally towards right and follows a parabolic path, under the influence of gravity and horizontal speed.

(c) At point X, the velocity of the bob is along the tangent drawn at point X, therefore when string is cut at point C, bob moves along the tangent at that point X.

Also, the bob moves under gravity simultaneously with horizontal uniform speed. So, it traversed on a parabolic path with vertex at higher than C.

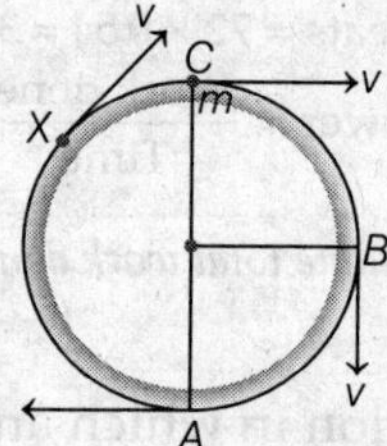

Short Answer Type Questions

Q.34 A graph of potential energy $V(x)$ *versus* x is shown in figure. A particle of energy E_0 is executing motion in it. Draw graph of velocity and kinetic energy *versus* x for one complete cycle AFA.

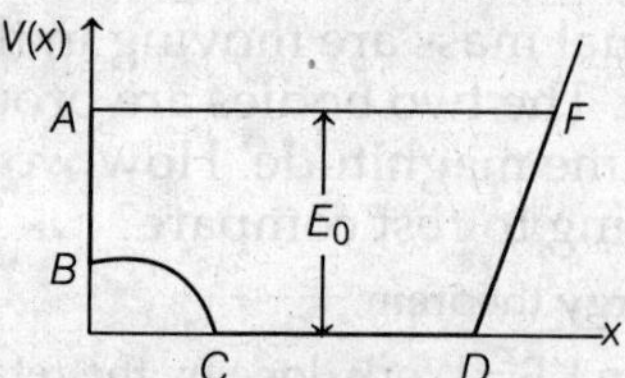

Thinking Process We will assume total mechanical energy of the system to be constant.

Ans. KE *versus* x graph

We know that Total ME = KE + PE

$\Rightarrow \quad E_0 = \text{KE} + V(x)$

$\Rightarrow \quad \text{KE} = E_0 - V(x)$

at $A, x = 0, V(x) = E_0$

$\Rightarrow \quad \text{KE} = E_0 - E_0 = 0$

at $B, V(x) < E_0$

$\Rightarrow \quad \text{KE} > 0$ [positive]

at C and D, $V(x) = 0$. So, KE is maximum

$\Rightarrow$ at $F, V(x) = E_o$

Hence, KE = 0

The variation is shown in adjacent diagram.

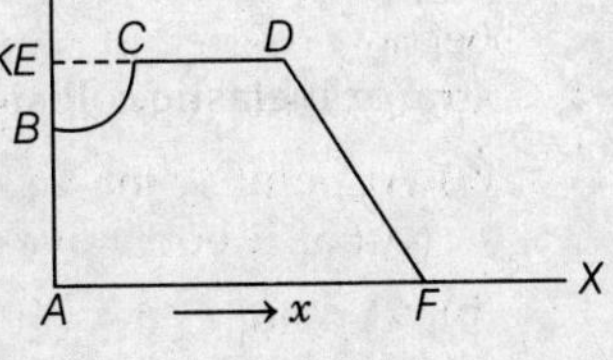

Velocity *versus* x graph

As $$KE = \frac{1}{2} mv^2$$

$\therefore$ At A and F, where KE = 0, $v = 0$.

At C and D, KE is maximum. Therefore, v is $\pm$ max.

At B, KE is positive but not maximum.

Therefore, v is $\pm$ some value (< max)

The variation is shown in the diagram.

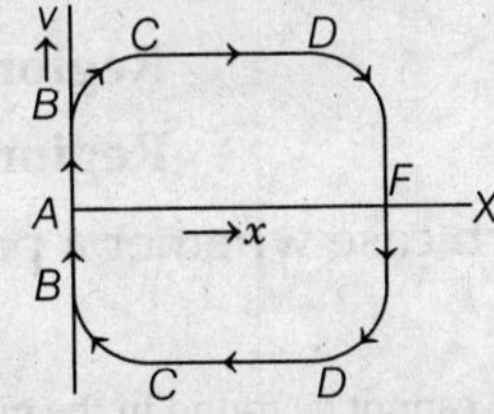

Q.35 A ball of mass m, moving with a speed $2v_0$, collides inelastically ($e > 0$) with an identical ball at rest. Show that

(a) for head-on collision, both the balls move forward.

(b) for a general collision, the angle between the two velocities of scattered balls is less than 90°.

Ans. (a) Let v_1 and v_2 are velocities of the two balls after collision.

Now, by the principle of conservation of linear momentum,

$$2mv_0 = mv_1 + mv_2$$

or $$2v_0 = v_1 + v_2$$

and $$e = \frac{v_2 - v_1}{2v_0}$$

$\Rightarrow$ $$v_2 = v_1 + 2v_0 e \text{ or } 2v_1 = 2v_0 - 2ev_0$$

$\therefore$ $$2v_0 = v_1 + v_1 + 2v_0\, e$$

$\therefore$ $$v_1 = v_0\,(1 - e)$$

Since, $e < 1 \Rightarrow v_1$ has the same sign as v_0, therefore, the ball moves in same direction after collision.

(b) Consider the diagram below for a general collision.

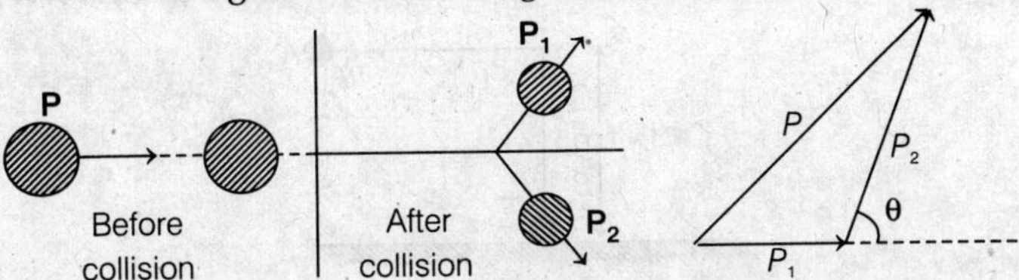

By principle of conservation of linear momentum,

$$\mathbf{P} = \mathbf{P}_1 + \mathbf{P}_2 \text{ or } 2\mathbf{v}_0 = \mathbf{v}_1 + \mathbf{v}_2$$

For inelastic collision some KE is lost, hence

$$\frac{p^2}{2m} > \frac{p_1^2}{2m} + \frac{p_2^2}{2m}$$

$$\therefore \qquad p^2 > p_1^2 + p_2^2$$

Thus, **p**, $\mathbf{p}_1$ and $\mathbf{p}_2$ are related as shown in the figure.

θ is acute (less than 90°) ($p^2 = p_1^2 + p_2^2$ would given $\theta = 90°$)

Q.36 Consider a one-dimensional motion of a particle with total energy E. There are four regions A, B, C and D in which the relation between potential energy V, kinetic energy (K) and total energy E is as given below

Region A : $V > E$ **Region B** : $V < E$

Region C : $K > E$ **Region D** : $V > K$

State with reason in each case whether a particle can be found in the given region or not.

Thinking Process A particle cannot be found in the given region when KE < 0.

Ans. We know that

$$\text{Total energy } E = \text{PE} + \text{KE}$$

$$\Rightarrow \qquad E = V + K \qquad \text{...(i)}$$

For region A Given, $V > E$, From Eq. (i)

$$K = E - V$$

as $$V > E \Rightarrow E - V < 0$$

Hence, $K < 0$, this is not possible.

For region B Given, $V < E \Rightarrow E - V > 0$

This is possible because total energy can be greater than PE (V).

For region C Given, $K < E \Rightarrow K - E > 0$

from Eq. (i) PE $= V = E - K < 0$

Which is possible, because PE can be negative.

For region D Given, $V > K$

This is possible because for a system PE (V) may be greater than KE (K).

Q.37 The bob A of a pendulum released from horizontal to the vertical hits another bob B of the same mass at rest on a table as shown in figure.

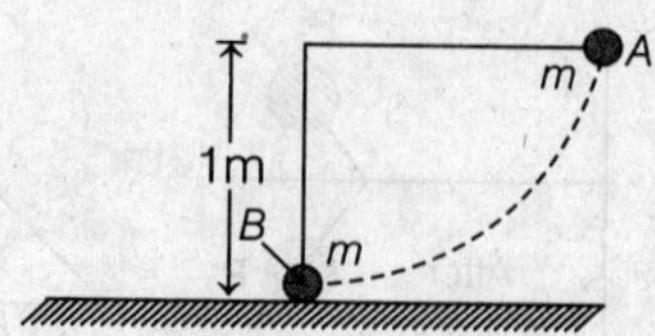

If the length of the pendulum is 1m, calculate

(a) the height to which bob A will rise after collision.

(b) the speed with which bob B starts moving.

Neglect the size of the bobs and assume the collision to be elastic.

Thinking Process When two bodies of equal masses collides elastically momentum is interchanged. At the bottom point bob A is having almost horizontal velocity.

Ans. When ball A reaches bottom point its velocity is horizontal, hence, we can apply conservation of linear momentum in the horizontal direction.

(a) Two balls have same mass and the collision between them is elastic, therefore, ball A transfers its entire linear momentum to ball B. Hence, ball A will come to at rest after collision and does not rise at all.

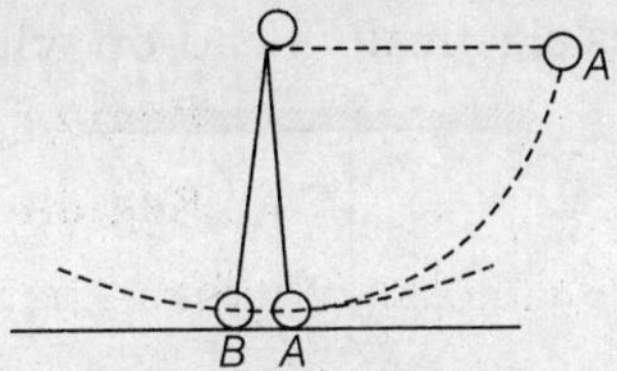

(b) Speed with which bob B starts moving

$$= \text{Speed with which bob } A \text{ hits bob } B$$
$$= \sqrt{2gh}$$
$$= \sqrt{2 \times 9.8 \times 1}$$
$$= \sqrt{19.6}$$
$$= 4.42 \text{ m/s}$$

Note When the bob A is at the bottommost point, its velocity is horizontal and tension is the external force on the bob but still momentum can be considered to be conserved in horizontal direction, because the tension has no effect in horizontal direction at the bottommost point.

Q.38 A raindrop of mass 1.00 g falling from a height of 1 km hits the ground with a speed of 50 m s^{-1}. Calculate

(a) the loss of PE of the drop.

(b) the gain in KE of the drop.

(c) is the gain in KE equal to loss of PE? If not why?

(Take, $g = 10$ ms^{-2}.)

Ans. Given, mass of the rain drop $(m) = 1.00$ g

$$= 1 \times 10^{-3} \text{ kg}$$

Height of falling $(h) = 1 \text{ km} = 10^3$ m

$$g = 10 \text{ m/s}^2$$

Speed of the rain drop $(v) = 50$ m/s (when it hits the ground)

(a) Loss of PE of the drop $= mgh$

$$= 1 \times 10^{-3} \times 10 \times 10^3 = 10 \text{ J}$$

(b) Gain in KE of the drop $= \frac{1}{2} mv^2$

$$= \frac{1}{2} \times 1 \times 10^{-3} \times (50)^2$$

$$= \frac{1}{2} \times 10^{-3} \times 2500$$

$$= 1.250 \text{ J}$$

(c) No, gain in KE is not equal to the loss in its PE, because a part of PE is utilised in doing work against the viscous drag of air.

Q.39 Two pendulums with identical bobs and lengths are suspended from a common support such that in rest position the two bobs are in contact (figure). One of the bobs is released after being displaced by 10°, so that it collides elastically head-on with the other bob.

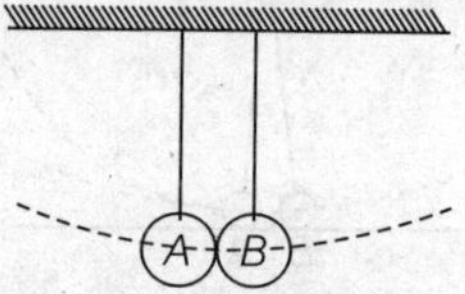

(a) Describe the motion of two bobs.

(b) Draw a graph showing variation in energy of either pendulum with time, for $0 \leq t \leq 2T$, where T is the period of each pendulum.

- **Concept Insight** In this problem, we use the concept of principle of energy conversion, which states that the energy can neither nor can be destroyed.

Ans. (a) Consider the adjacent diagram in which the bob B is displaced through an angle θ and released.

At $t = 0$, bob B is displaced by $\theta = 10°$ to the right. It is given potential energy $E_1 = E$. Energy of A, $E_2 = 0$.

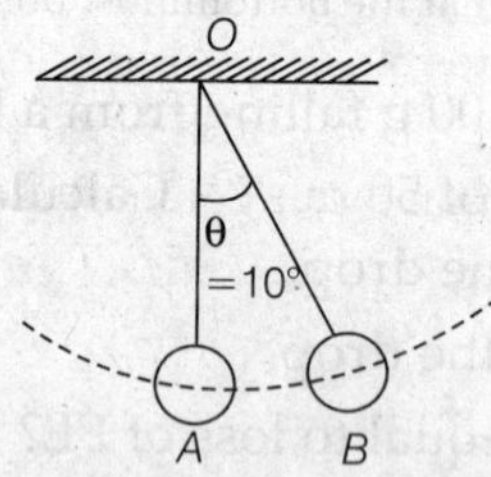

When B is released, it strikes A at $t = T/4$. In the head-on elastic collision between B and A comes to rest and A gets velocity of B. Therefore, $E_1 = 0$ and $E_2 = E$. At $t = 2\,T/4$, B reaches its extreme right position when KE of A is converted into PE $= E_2 = E$. Energy of B, $E_1 = 0$.

At $t = 3\,T/4$, A reaches its mean position, when its PE is converted into KE $= E_2 = E$. It collides elastically with B and transfers whole of its energy to B. Thus, $E_2 = 0$ and $E_1 = E$. The entire process is repeated.

(b) The values of energies of B and A at different time intervals are tabulated here. The plot of energy with time $0 \leq t \leq 2\,T$ is shown separately for B and A in the figure below.

Time (t)	Energy of A (E_1)	Energy of B (E_2)
0	E	0
$T/4$	0	E
$2T/4$	0	E
$3T/4$	E	0
$4T/4$	E	0
$5T/4$	0	E
$6T/4$	0	E
$7T/4$	E	0
$8T/4$	E	0

Q.40 **Suppose the average mass of raindrops is 3.0×10^{-5} kg and their average terminal velocity 9 m s^{-1}. Calculate the energy transferred by rain to each square metre of the surface at a place which receives 100cm of rain in a year.**

Ans. Given, average mass of rain drop

$$(m) = 3.0 \times 10^{-5} \text{ kg}$$

Average terminal velocity $(v) = 9$ m/s.

$$\text{Height } (h) = 100 \text{ cm} = 1 \text{ m}$$

$$\text{Density of water } (\rho) = 10^3 \text{ kg/m}^3$$

$$\text{Area of the surface } (A) = 1 \text{ m}^2$$

Volume of the water due to rain (V) = Area $\times$ height

$$= A \times h = 1 \times 1 = 1 \text{ m}^3$$

Mass of the water due to rain (M) = Volume $\times$ density

$$= V \times \rho = 1 \times 10^3 = 10^3 \text{ kg}$$

$$\therefore \text{ Energy transferred to the surface} = \frac{1}{2} mv^2 = \frac{1}{2} \times 10^3 \times (9)^2$$

$$= 40.5 \times 10^3 = 4.05 \times 10^4 \text{ J}$$

Q.41 **An engine is attached to a wagon through a shock absorber of length 1.5 m. The system with a total mass of 50,000 kg is moving with a speed of 36 kmh^{-1} when the brakes are applied to bring it to rest. In the process of the system being brought to rest, the spring of the shock absorber gets compressed by 1.0 m. If 90% of energy of the wagon is lost due to friction, calculate the spring constant.**

Ans. Given, mass of the system $(m) = 50{,}000$ kg

$$\text{Speed of the system } (v) = 36 \text{ km/h} = \frac{36 \times 1000}{60 \times 60} = 10 \text{ m/s}$$

Compression of the spring $(x) = 1.0$ m

$$\text{KE of the system} = \frac{1}{2}mv^2 = \frac{1}{2} \times 50000 \times (10)^2$$

$$= 25000 \times 100 \text{ J} = 2.5 \times 10^6 \text{ J}$$

Since, 90% of KE of the system is lost due to friction, therefore, energy transferred to shock absorber, is given by

$$\Delta E = \frac{1}{2}kx^2 = 10\% \text{ of total KE of the system}$$

$$\frac{1}{2}k \times (1)^2 = \frac{10}{100} \times 2.5 \times 10^6$$

$$k = 5 \times 10^5 \text{ N/m}$$

Q.42 An adult weighting 600 N raises the centre of gravity of his body by 0.25m while taking each step of 1 m length in jogging. If he jogs for 6 km, calculate the energy utilised by him in jogging assuming that there is no energy loss due to friction of ground and air. Assuming that the body of the adult is capable of converting 10% of energy intake in the form of food, calculate the energy equivalents of food that would be required to compensate energy utilised for jogging.

Thinking Process Here, shift in centre of gravity of his body is equal to the height of each step.

Ans. Given, weight of the adult $(w) = mg = 600$ N

Height of each step $= h = 0.25$ m

Length of each step $= 1$ m

Total distance travelled $= 6$ km $= 6000$ m

$$\therefore \quad \text{Total number of steps} = \frac{6000}{1} = 6000$$

$$\text{Total energy utilised in jogging} = n \times mgh$$

$$= 6000 \times 600 \times 0.25 = 9 \times 10^5 \text{ J}$$

Since, 10% of intake energy is utilised in jogging.

$$\therefore \text{ Total intake energy} = \frac{1}{0.1} \times 9 \times 10^5 \text{ J} = 9 \times 10^6 \text{ J.}$$

Q.43 On complete combustion a litre of petrol gives off heat equivalent to 3×10^7 J. In a test drive, a car weighing 1200 kg including the mass of driver, runs 15 km per litre while moving with a uniform speed on a straight track. Assuming that friction offered by the road surface and air to be uniform, calculate the force of friction acting on the car during the test drive, if the efficiency of the car engine were 0.5.

Ans. Energy is given by the petrol in the form of heat of combustion.

Thus, by question,

Energy given by 1 litre of petrol $= 3 \times 10^7$ J

Efficiency of the car engine $= 0.5$

$\therefore$ Energy used by the car $= 0.5 \times 3 \times 10^7$ J

$$E = 1.5 \times 10^7 \text{ J}$$

Total distance travelled (s) = 15 km = 15×10^3 m

If f is the force of friction then,

$$E = f \times s$$

[$\because$ Energy is utilised in working against friction]

$$1.5 \times 10^7 = f \times 15 \times 10^3$$

$$\Rightarrow \quad f = \frac{1.5 \times 10^7}{15 \times 10^3} = 10^3 \text{ N}$$

$$f = 1000 \text{ N}$$

Long Answer Type Questions

Q.44 A block of mass 1 kg is pushed up a surface inclined to horizontal at an angle of 30° by a force of 10 N parallel to the inclined surface (figure). The coefficient of friction between block and the incline is 0.1. If the block is pushed up by 10 m along the incline, calculate

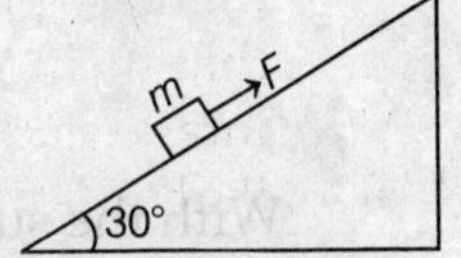

(a) work done against gravity (b) work done against force of friction

(c) increases in potential energy (d) increase in kinetic energy

(e) work done by applied force

Ans. Consider the adjacent diagram the block is pushed up by applying a force F.

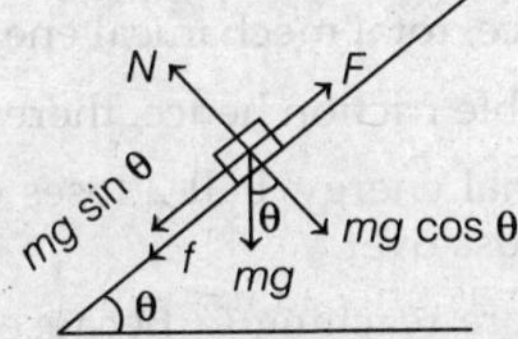

Normal reaction (N) and frictional force (f) is shown.

Given, mass = m = 1 kg, $\theta = 30°$, $F = 10$ N, $\mu = 0.1$ and s = distance moved by the block along the inclined plane = 10 m.

(a) Work done against gravity = Increase in PE of the block

$= mg \times$ Vertical distance travelled

$= mg \times s\,(\sin\theta) = (mgs)\sin\theta$

$= 1 \times 10 \times 10 \times \sin 30° = 50$ J [$\because g = 10 \text{ m/s}^2$]

(b) Work done against friction

$$W_f = f \times s = \mu N \times s = \mu\, mg \cos\theta \times s$$

$$= 0.1 \times 1 \times 10 \times \cos 30° \times 10 = 10 \times 0.866 = 8.66 \text{ J}$$

(c) Increase in PE = $mgh = mg\,(s \sin\theta) = 1 \times 10 \times 10 \times \sin 30°$

$$= 100 \times \frac{1}{2} = 50 \text{ J}$$

(d) By work-energy theorem, we know that work done by all the forces = change in KE

$$(W) = \Delta K$$

$$\Delta K = W_g + W_f + W$$

$$\Rightarrow \quad = -mgh - fs + FS$$

$$= -50 - 8.66 + 10 \times 10$$

$$= 50 - 8.66 = 41.34 \text{ J}$$

(e) Work done by applied force, $W = FS = (10)(10) = 100$ J

Q.45 A curved surface is shown in figure. The portion BCD is free of friction. There are three spherical balls of identical radii and masses. Balls are released from rest one by one from A which is at a slightly greater height than C.

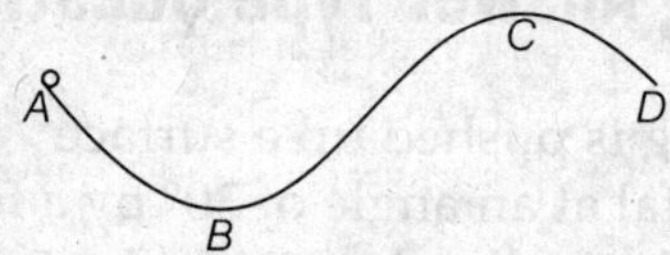

With the surface AB, ball 1 has large enough friction to cause rolling down without slipping; ball 2 has a small friction and ball 3 has a negligible friction.

(a) For which balls is total mechanical energy conserved?

(b) Which ball (s) can reach D?

(c) For balls which do not reach D, which of the balls can reach back A?

Ans. (a) As ball 1 is rolling down without slipping there is no dissipation of energy because of friction hence, total mechanical energy is conserved.

Ball 3 is having negligible friction hence, there is no loss of energy.

(b) Ball 1 acquires rotational energy, ball 2 loses energy by friction. They cannot cross at C. Ball 3 can cross over.

(c) Ball 1, 2 turn back before reaching C. Because of loss of energy, ball 2 cannot reach back to A. Ball 1 has a rotational motion in "wrong" (i.e. in opposite direction) sense when it reaches B. It cannot roll back to A, because of kinetic friction.

Q.46 A rocket accelerates straight up by ejecting gas downwards. In a small time interval Δt, it ejects a gas of mass Δm at a relative speed u. Calculate KE of the entire system at $t + \Delta t$ and t and show that the device that ejects gas does work $= (1/2)\,\Delta m u^2$ in this time interval (neglect gravity).

Thinking Process As the gas is ejected, the rocket gets propelled in forward direction due to upward thrust.

Ans. Let M be the mass of rocket at any time t and v_1 the velocity of rocket at the same time t.

Let Δm = mass of gas ejected in time interval Δt.

Relative speed of gas ejected = u.

Consider at time $t+\Delta t$

$$\text{KE at time } (t+\Delta t) = \text{KE of rocket} + \text{KE of gas}$$

$$= \frac{1}{2}(M-\Delta m)(v+\Delta v)^2 + \frac{1}{2}\Delta m(v-u)^2$$

$$= \frac{1}{2}[(M-\Delta m)(v^2+\Delta v^2+2v\Delta v] + \frac{1}{2}\Delta m(v^2+u^2-2uv)$$

$$= \frac{1}{2}[Mv^2 + M\Delta v^2 + 2Mv\Delta v - \Delta m(v^2) - \Delta m\Delta v^2 - 2v\Delta m\Delta v + \Delta mv^2 + \Delta mu^2 - 2uv\Delta m]$$

Neglecting terms containing Δv^2 and $\Delta m\Delta v$, we have.

$$= \frac{1}{2}Mv^2 + Mv\Delta v - \Delta mvu + \frac{1}{2}\Delta mu^2$$

$$(\text{KE})_t = \text{KE of the rocket at time } t = \frac{1}{2}Mv^2$$

$$\Delta K = (\text{KE})_{t+\Delta t} - (\text{KE})_t$$

$$= (M\Delta v - \Delta mu)\,v + \frac{1}{2}\Delta mu^2$$

Since, action-reaction forces are equal.

Hence, $$M\frac{dv}{dt} = \frac{dm}{dt}|u|$$

$\Rightarrow$ $$M\Delta v = \Delta mu$$

$$\Delta K = \frac{1}{2}\Delta mu^2$$

Now, by work-energy theorem,

$$\Delta K = \Delta W$$

$\Rightarrow$ $$\Delta W = \frac{1}{2}\Delta mu^2$$

Q.47 Two identical steel cubes (masses 50g, side 1 cm) collide head-on face to face with a speed of 10 cm/s each. Find the maximum compression of each. Young's modulus for steel = $Y = 2\times 10^{11}$ N/m^2.

Ans. Let $$m = 50g = 50\times 10^{-3}\text{ kg}$$

$$\text{Side} = L = 1\text{ cm} = 0.01\text{ m}$$

$$\text{Speed} = v = 10\text{ cm/s} = 0.1\text{ m/s}$$

$$\text{Young's modulus} = Y = 2\times 10^{11}\text{ N/m}^2$$

$$\text{Maximum compression } \Delta L = ?$$

In this case, all KE will be converted to PE

By Hooke's law, $$\frac{F}{A} = Y\frac{\Delta L}{L} \quad \ldots\text{(i)}$$

where A is the surface area and L is length of the side of the cube. If k is spring or compression constant, then

$$\text{force } F = k\,\Delta L \quad \ldots\text{(ii)}$$

$\therefore$ From equation (i)

$$k = Y\frac{A}{L} = YL = 2\times10^{11}\times10^{-2} = 2\times10^{9}\ \text{N/m}$$

$$\text{Initial KE} = 2\times\frac{1}{2}mv^2 = 5\times10^{-4}\ \text{J}$$

$$\text{Final KE} = 2\times\frac{1}{2}k(\Delta L)^2$$

$$\therefore \qquad \Delta L = \sqrt{\frac{\text{KE}}{k}} = \sqrt{\frac{\text{KE}}{YL}} = \sqrt{\frac{5\times10^{-4}}{2\times10^{11}\times0.01}}$$

$$\Delta L = \sqrt{\frac{50}{2}\times10^{-14}} = 5\times10^{-7}\ \text{m}$$

Q.48 A balloon filled with helium rises against gravity increasing its potential energy. The speed of the balloon also increases as it rises. How do you reconcile this with the law of conservation of mechanical energy? You can neglect viscous drag of air and assume that density of air is constant.

Thinking Process In this problem, as viscous drag of air is neglected, hence there is no dissipation of energy.

Ans. Let m = Mass of balloon, V = Volume of balloon

ρ_{He} = Density of helium, ρ_{air} = Density of air

Volume V of balloon displaces volume V of air.

So, $$V(\rho_{air} - \rho_{He})g = ma = m\frac{dv}{dt} = \text{up thrust on balloon} \qquad \text{...(i)}$$

Integrating with respect to t,

$$V(\rho_{air} - \rho_{He})gt = mv \qquad \text{...(ii)}$$

$$\Rightarrow \quad \text{KE} = \frac{1}{2}mv^2 = \frac{1}{2m}V^2(\rho_{air} - \rho_{He})^2 g^2 t^2 \qquad \left[\text{KE} = \frac{p^2}{2m} = \frac{m^2v^2}{2m}\right]$$

If the balloon rises to a height h, from $s = ut + \frac{1}{2}at^2$,

$$\text{We get } h = \frac{1}{2}at^2 = \frac{1}{2}\frac{V(\rho_{air} - \rho_{He})}{m}gt^2 \qquad \text{...(iii)}$$

From Eqs. (iii) and (ii),

$$\frac{1}{2}mv^2 = [V(\rho_a - \rho_{He})g]\left[\frac{1}{2m}V(\rho_{air} - \rho_{He})gt^2\right]$$

$$= V(\rho_a - \rho_{He})gh$$

Rearranging the terms,

$$\Rightarrow \quad \frac{1}{2}mv^2 + V\rho_{He}gh = V\rho_{air}hg$$

$$\Rightarrow \quad \text{KE}_{balloon} + \text{PE}_{balloon} = \text{Change in PE of air.}$$

So, as the balloon goes up, an equal volume of air comes down, increase in PE and KE of the balloon is at the cost of PE of air [which comes down].

Chapter

06

System of Particles and Rotational Motion

Multiple Choice Questions (MCQs)

Q.1 For which of the following does the centre of mass lie outside the body?

(a) A pencil
(b) A shotput
(c) A dice
(d) A bangle

Ans. *(d)* A bangle is in the form of a ring as shown in figure. The centre of mass lies at the centre, which is outside the body (boundary).

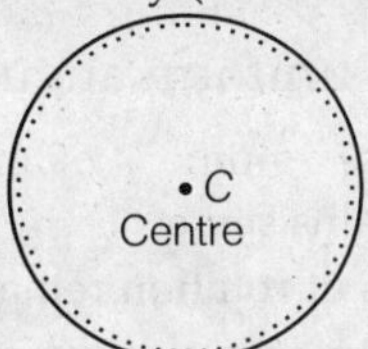

Q.2 Which of the following points is the likely position of the centre of mass of the system shown in figure?

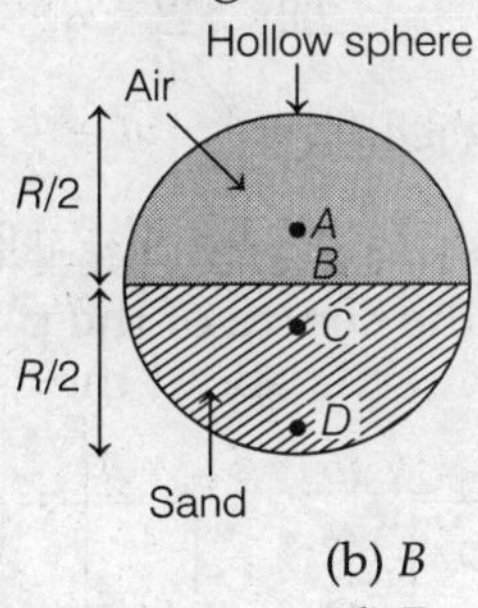

(a) A
(b) B
(c) C
(d) D

Thinking Process In a system of particles, the centre of mass of a body lies closer to heavier mass or masses.

Ans. *(c)* Centre of mass of a system lies towards the part of the system, having bigger mass. In the above diagram, lower part is heavier, hence CM of the system lies below the horizontal diameter.

Q.3 A particle of mass m is moving in yz-plane with a uniform velocity v with its trajectory running parallel to +ve y-axis and intersecting z-axis at $z = a$ in figure. The change in its angular momentum about the origin as it bounces elastically from a wall at y = constant is

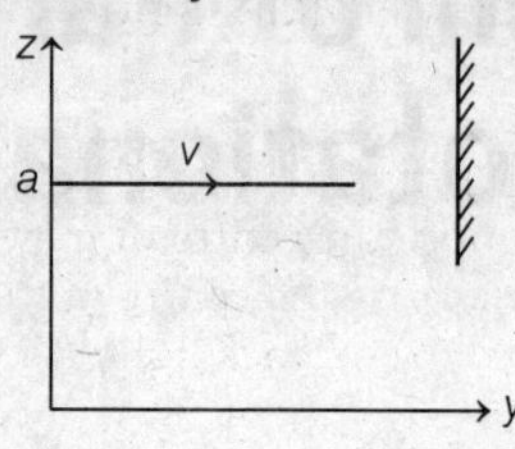

(a) $mva\ \hat{\mathbf{e}}_x$ (b) $2\ mva\ \hat{\mathbf{e}}_x$ (c) $ymv\ \hat{\mathbf{e}}_x$ (d) $2\ ymv\ \hat{\mathbf{e}}_x$

Thinking Process In elastic collision, KE of the system remains conserved. Therefore, the ball will bounce back with the same speed v but in opposite direction i.e. along $-ve$ y-axis.

Ans. ***(b)*** The initial velocity is $\mathbf{v}_i = v\hat{\mathbf{e}}_y$ and after reflection from the wall, the final velocity is $\mathbf{v}_f = -\ v\hat{\mathbf{e}}_y$. The trajectory is described as position vector $\mathbf{r} = y\hat{\mathbf{e}}_y + a\hat{\mathbf{e}}_z$. Hence, the change in angular momentum is $\Delta\mathbf{L} = \mathbf{r} \times m\Delta\mathbf{v}$

$$\Delta\mathbf{L} = (y\hat{\mathbf{e}}_y + a\hat{\mathbf{e}}_z) \times (-mv\hat{\mathbf{e}}_y - mv\hat{\mathbf{e}}_y) = 2mva\,\hat{\mathbf{e}}_x \qquad [\because \hat{\mathbf{e}}_z \times \hat{\mathbf{e}}_y = -\,\hat{\mathbf{e}}_x]$$

Q.4 When a disc rotates with uniform angular velocity, which of the following is not true?

(a) The sense of rotation remains same

(b) The orientation of the axis of rotation remains same

(c) The speed of rotation is non-zero and remains same

(d) The angular acceleration is non-zero and remains same

Ans. ***(d)*** When disc is rotating with uniform angular velocity, so angular acceleration is

$$\Rightarrow \qquad \alpha = \frac{d\omega}{dt} = \frac{0}{dt} = 0$$

Hence, angular acceleration is zero.

Q.5 A uniform square plate has a small piece Q of an irregular shape removed and glued to the centre of the plate leaving a hole behind in figure. The moment of inertia about the z-axis is then

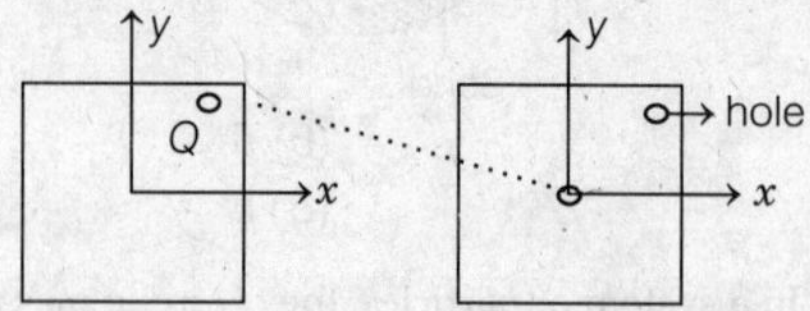

(a) increased (b) decreased

(c) the same (d) changed in unpredicted manner

Thinking Process For two bodies having same mass, the body having mass distributed at greater distance from an axis, will have more moment of inertia.

Ans. *(b)* Initially, when the square plate had a uniform mass distribution, the centre of mass was at the geometric centre that is at the origin of the *XY*-coordinate shown in the figure.

Q.6 In problem 5, the CM of the plate is now in the following quadrant of *x-y* plane.

(a) I (b) II (c) III (d) IV

Ans. *(c)* Now, after the modification, the centre of mass shifts towards the third quadrant of the *XY*-plane because the centre of the plate becomes heavier and the portion containing the piece *Q* becomes lighter.

Q.7 The density of a non-uniform rod of length 1m is given by $\rho(x) = a(1 + bx^2)$ where, *a* and *b* are constants and $0 \le x \le 1$. The centre of mass of the rod will be at

(a) $\frac{3(2+b)}{4(3+b)}$ (b) $\frac{4(2+b)}{3(3+b)}$ (c) $\frac{3(3+b)}{4(2+b)}$ (d) $\frac{4(3+b)}{3(2+b)}$

Ans. *(a)* Let us consider that the rod lies along the *X*-axis with one of its side lying at the origin.

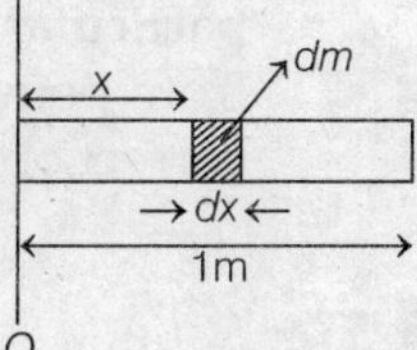

The density of the rod is $\rho(x) = a(1 + bx^2)$

Let us consider an element mass *dm* at a distance *x* from the origin.

The total mass, $M = \int_0^1 \rho(x)\, dx$

$$\Rightarrow \quad M = \int_0^1 a(1 + bx^2)dx = \left[ax + \frac{abx^3}{3}\right]_0^1$$

$$\Rightarrow \quad M = a + \frac{ab}{3} = a\left(\frac{3+b}{3}\right)$$

The centre of mass of the rod X_{cm} can be found as

$$X_{cm} = \frac{1}{M}\int_0^1 x\rho(x)\, dx = \frac{1}{M}\int_0^1 ax(1 + bx^2)dx$$

$$= \frac{1}{M}\left[\frac{ax^2}{2} + \frac{abx^4}{4}\right]_0^1 = \frac{1}{a\left(\frac{3+b}{3}\right)} \times a\left(\frac{1}{2} + \frac{b}{4}\right) = \frac{3(2+b)}{4(3+b)}$$

Q.8 A merry-go-round, made of a ring-like platform of radius *R* and mass *M*, is revolving with angular speed ω. A person of mass *M* is standing on it. At one instant, the person jumps off the round, radially away from the centre of the round (as seen from the round). The speed of the round of afterwards is

(a) 2 ω (b) ω (c) $\frac{\omega}{2}$ (d) 0

Ans. *(b)* As no external torque acts on the system, angular momentum should be conserved. Hence ω remains constant.

Multiple Choice Questions (More Than One Options)

Q.9 Choose the correct alternatives.

(a) For a general rotational motion, angular momentum **L** and angular velocity ω need not be parallel.

(b) For a rotational motion about a fixed axis, angular momentum **L** and angular velocity ω are always parallel.

(c) For a general translational motion, momentum **p** and velocity **v** are always parallel.

(d) For a general translational motion, acceleration **a** and velocity **v** are always parallel.

Ans. *(a, c)* For a general rotational motion ,where axis of rotation is not symmetric. Angular momentum **L** and angular velocity ω need not be parallel. For a general translational motion momentum $\mathbf{p} = m\mathbf{v}$, hence, **p** and **v** are always parallel.

Q.10 Figure shows two identical particles 1 and 2, each of mass m, moving in opposite directions with same speed **v** along parallel lines. At a particular instant $\mathbf{r}_1$ and $\mathbf{r}_2$ are their respective position vectors drawn from point A which is in the plane of the parallel lines. Choose the correct options.

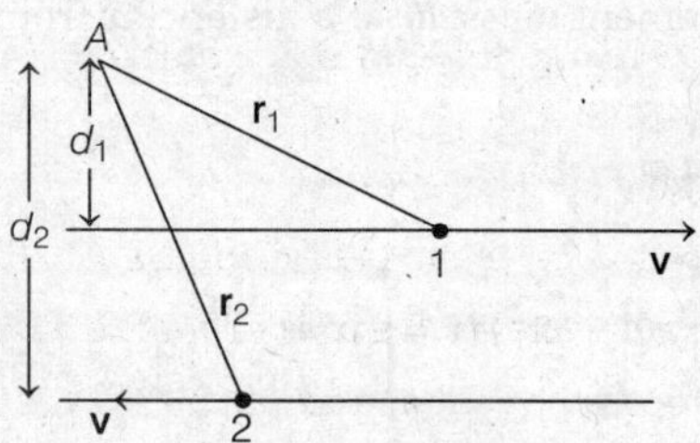

(a) Angular momentum L_1 of particle 1 about A is $L_1 = mv(d_1)\odot$

(b) Angular momentum L_2 of particle 2 about A is $L_2 = mv\,\mathbf{r}_2\odot$

(c) Total angular momentum of the system about A is $L = mv(\mathbf{r}_1 + \mathbf{r}_2)\odot$

(d) Total angular momentum of the system about A is $L = mv(d_2 - d_1)\otimes$

$\odot$ represents a unit vector coming out of the page.

$\otimes$ represents a unit vector going into the page.

Ans. *(a, d)*

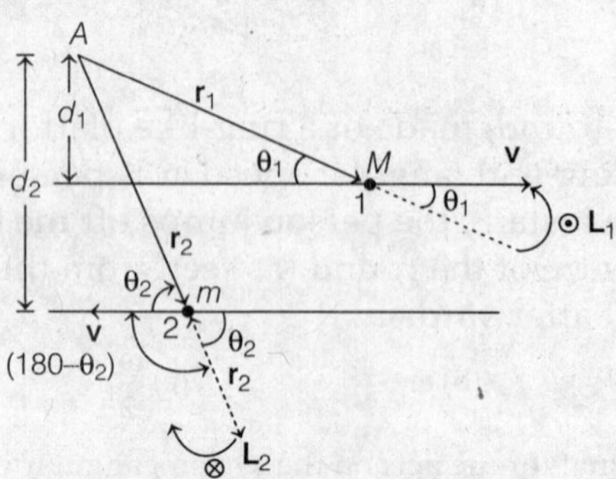

$$L_1 = \mathbf{r}_1 \times \mathbf{p}_1 = m(\mathbf{r}_1 \times \mathbf{v})$$

$$L_1 = mr_1 v \sin\theta$$

$$L_1 = mvd_1 \qquad [\because d_1 = r_1 \sin\theta]$$

$$L_2 = \mathbf{r}_2 \times \mathbf{p}_2 = m(\mathbf{r}_2 \times \mathbf{v}) = mr_2 v \sin\theta_2$$

$$= md_2 v \qquad [\because r_2 \sin\theta_2 = d_2]$$

$\therefore$ Net angular momentum $\mathbf{L} = \mathbf{L}_1 + \mathbf{L}_2$

$\Rightarrow \qquad \mathbf{L} = mvd_1 \odot + mvd_2 \otimes$

$\Rightarrow \qquad \mathbf{L} = mv(d_2 - d_1) \otimes \qquad [\because d_2 > d_1]$

Hence (a) and (d) are correct options.

Note In the expression of angular momentum $L = \mathbf{r} \times \mathbf{p}$ the direction of **L** is taken by right hand rule.

Q.11 The net external torque on a system of particles about an axis is zero. Which of the following are compatible with it?

(a) The forces may be acting radially from a point on the axis.
(b) The forces may be acting on the axis of rotation.
(c) The forces may be acting parallel to the axis of rotation.
(d) The torque caused by some forces may be equal and opposite to that caused by other forces.

Ans. *(a, b, c, d)* We know that torque on a system of particles $\tau = \mathbf{r} \times \mathbf{F} = \mathbf{r}\,\mathbf{F}\sin\theta\,\hat{\mathbf{n}}$ ...(i)

where, θ is angle between **r** and **F**, and $\hat{\mathbf{n}}$ is a unit vector perpendicular to both **r** and **F**.

(a) When forces act radially, $\theta = 0°$ hence $|\tau| = 0$. [from Eq. (i)]

(b) When forces are acting on the axis of rotation, $\mathbf{r} = 0, |\tau| = 0$. [from Eq. (i)]

(c) When forces acting parallel to the axis of rotation $\theta = 0°, |\tau| = 0$. [from Eq. (i)]

(d) When torque by forces are equal and opposite, $\tau_{net} = \tau_1 - \tau_2 = 0$.

Q.12 Figure shows a lamina in *xy*-plane. Two axes *z* and *z'* pass perpendicular to its plane. A force **F** acts in the plane of lamina at point *P* as shown. Which of the following are true? (The point *P* is closer to *z'*-axis than the *z*-axis.)

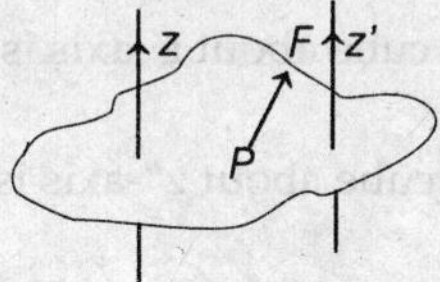

(a) Torque τ caused by **F** about *z*-axis is along $-\hat{\mathbf{k}}$.

(b) Torque τ' caused by **F** about *z'*-axis is along $-\hat{\mathbf{k}}$.

(c) Torque τ caused by **F** about *z*-axis is greater in magnitude than that about *z*-axis

(d) Total torque is given be $\tau = \tau + \tau'$.

Thinking Process Torque of a force **F** about an axis is $\mathbf{r} \times \mathbf{F}$ which is perpendicular to the plane containing **r** and **F**.

Ans. ***(b, c)***

(a) Consider the adjacent diagram, where $r > r'$

Torque τ about z-axis $\tau = \mathbf{r} \times \mathbf{F}$ which is along $\hat{\mathbf{k}}$

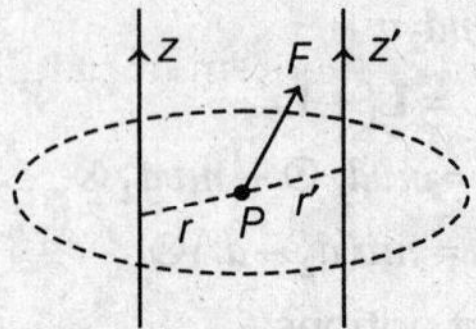

(b) $\tau' = \mathbf{r}' \times \mathbf{F}$ which is along $-\hat{\mathbf{k}}$

(c) $|\tau|_z = Fr_\perp$ = magnitude of torque about z-axis where $r_\perp$ is perpendicular distance between F and z-axis.

Similarly, $|\tau|_{z'} = F r_\perp'$

Clearly $r_\perp > r_\perp' \Rightarrow |\tau|_z > |\tau|_{z'}$

(d) We are always calculating resultant torque about a common axis.

Hence, total torque $\tau \neq \tau + \tau'$, because τ and τ' are not about common axis.

Q.13 With reference to figure of a cube of edge a and mass m, state whether the following are true or false. (O is the centre of the cube.)

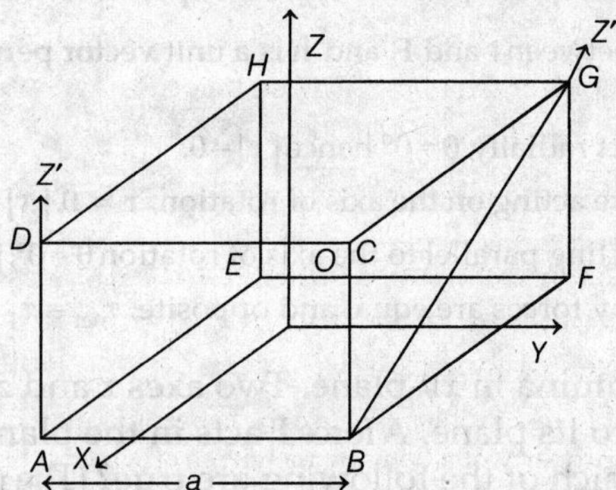

(a) The moment of inertia of cube about z-axis is $I_z = I_x + I_y$.

(b) The moment of inertia of cube about z′-axis is $I_{z'} = I_z + \frac{ma^2}{2}$.

(c) The moment of inertia of cube about z″-axis is $I_{z''} = I_z + \frac{ma^2}{2}$.

(d) $I_x = I_y$

Thinking Process Moment of inertia about two symmetrical axes are same. To calculate net moment of inertia we can apply the concept of symmetry.

Ans. ***(b, d)***

(a) Theorem of perpendicular axes is applicable only for laminar (plane) objects. Thus, option (a) is false.

(b) As z′ || z and distance between them $= a\frac{\sqrt{2}}{2} = \frac{a}{\sqrt{2}}$

Now, by theorem of parallel axes

$$I_{z'} = I_z + m\left(\frac{a}{\sqrt{2}}\right)^2 = I_z + \frac{ma^2}{2}$$

Hence, option (b) is true.

(c) z'' is not parallel to z hence, theorem of parallel axis cannot be applied.

Thus, option (c) is false.

(d) As x and y-axes are symmetrical.

Hence, $I_x = I_y$

Thus, option (d) is true.

Very Short Answer Type Questions

Q.14 The centre of gravity of a body on the earth coincides with its centre of mass for a small object whereas for an extended object it may not. What is the qualitative meaning of small and extended in this regard? For which of the following two coincides? A building, a pond, a lake, a mountain?

Thinking Process Centre of gravity is centre of a given structure but centre of mass is a point where whole mass of the body can be assumed to be concentrated.

Ans. When the vertical height of the object is very small as compared to the earth's radius, we call the object small, otherwise it is extended.

(i) Building and pond are small objects.

(ii) A deep lake and a mountain are examples of extended objects.

Q.15 Why does a solid sphere have smaller moment of inertia than a hollow cylinder of same mass and radius, about an axis passing through their axes of symmetry?

- **Concept Insight** In this problem we use the concept of moment of inertia which is defined as the property of a body by the virtue of which it opposes the torque tending to change its state of rest or of uniform rotation about an axis is called moment of interia.

Ans. The moment of inertia of a body is given by $I = \Sigma m_i r_i^2$ [sum of moment of inertia of each constituent particles]

All the mass in a cylinder lies at distance R from the axis of symmetry but most of the mass of a solid sphere lies at a smaller distance than R. Hence $I_{\text{sphere}} < I_{\text{hollow cylinder.}}$

Q.16 The variation of angular position θ, of a point on a rotating rigid body, with time t is shown in figure. Is the body rotating clockwise or anti-clockwise?

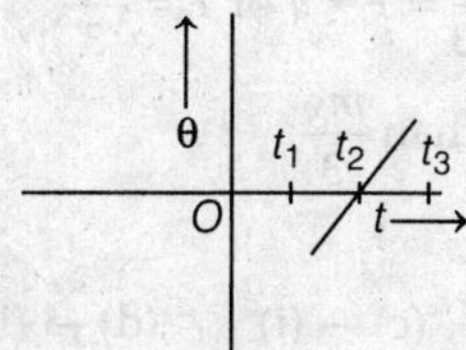

Ans. As the slope of θ-t graph i.e. $\frac{d\theta}{dt}$ is positive and positive slope indicates anti-clockwise rotation which is traditionally taken as positive.

Q.17 A uniform cube of mass m and side a is placed on a frictionless horizontal surface. A vertical force F is applied to the edge as shown in figure. Match the following (most appropriate choice)

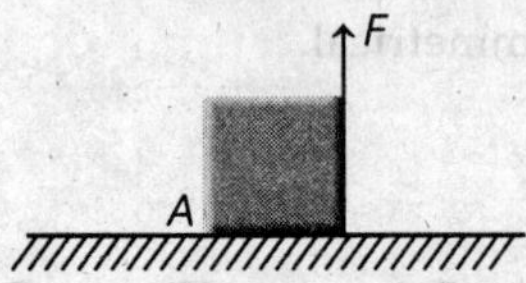

(a)	$mg/4 < F < mg/2$	(i)	Cube will move up.
(b)	$F > mg/2$	(ii)	Cube will not exhibit motion.
(c)	$F > mg$	(iii)	Cube will begin to rotate and slip at A.
(d)	$F = mg/4$	(iv)	Normal reaction effectively at $a/3$ from A, no motion.

Ans. Consider the below diagram

Moment of the force F about point A, $\tau_1 = F \times a$ (anti-clockwise)

Moment of weight mg of the cube about point A,

$$\tau_2 = mg \times \frac{a}{2} \text{ (clockwise)}$$

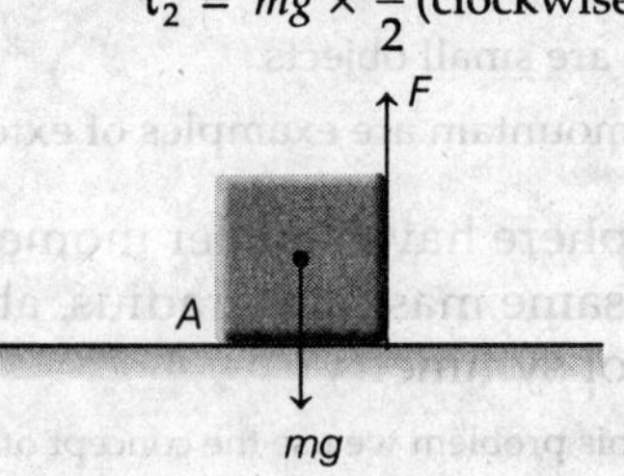

Cube will not exhibit motion, if $\tau_1 = \tau_2$

[$\because$ In this case, both the torque will cancel the effect of each other]

$$\therefore \quad F \times a = mg \times \frac{a}{2} \Rightarrow F = \frac{mg}{2}$$

Cube will rotate only when, $\tau_1 > \tau_2$

$$\Rightarrow \quad F \times a > mg \times \frac{a}{2} \Rightarrow F > \frac{mg}{2}$$

Let normal reaction is acting at $\frac{a}{3}$ from point A, then

$$mg \times \frac{a}{3} = F \times a \text{ or } F = \frac{mg}{3}$$ [For no motion]

When $F = \frac{mg}{4}$ which is less than $\frac{mg}{3}$, $\left[F < \frac{mg}{3}\right]$

there will be no motion.

$\therefore$ (a) $\rightarrow$ (ii) (b) $\rightarrow$ (iii) (c) $\rightarrow$ (i) (d) $\rightarrow$ (iv)

Q.18 A uniform sphere of mass m and radius R is placed on a rough horizontal surface (figure). The sphere is struck horizontally at a height h from the floor. Match the following

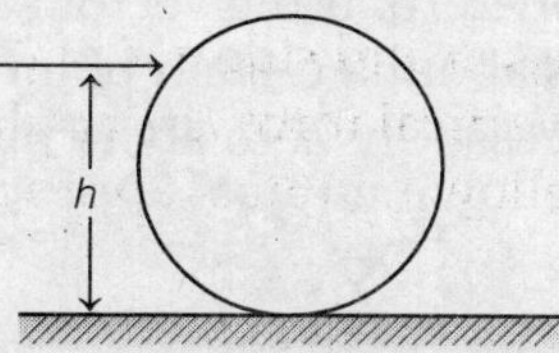

(a) $h = R/2$	(i)	Sphere rolls without slipping with a constant velocity and no loss of energy.
(b) $h = R$	(ii)	Sphere spins clockwise, loses energy by friction.
(c) $h = 3R/2$	(iii)	Sphere spins anti-clockwise, loses energy by friction.
(d) $h = 7R/5$	(iv)	Sphere has only a translational motion, looses energy by friction.

Ans. Consider the diagram where a sphere of m and radius R, struck horizontally at height h above the floor

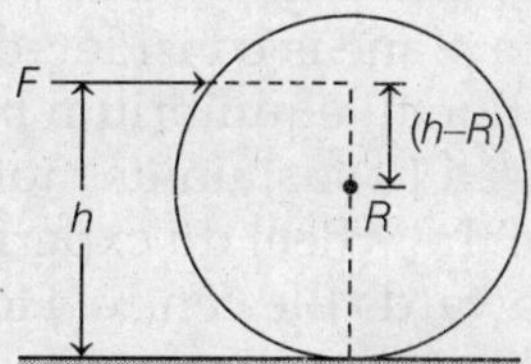

The sphere will roll without slipping when $\omega = \frac{v}{r}$, where, v is linear velocity and ω is angular velocity of the sphere.

Now, angular momentum of sphere, about centre of mass

[We are applying conservation of angular momentum just before and after struck]

$$mv(h - R) = I\omega = \left(\frac{2}{5}mR^2\right)\left(\frac{v}{R}\right)$$

$$\Rightarrow \quad mv(h - R) = \frac{2}{5}mvR$$

$$h - R = \frac{2}{5}R \quad \Rightarrow \quad h = \frac{7}{5}R$$

Therefore, the sphere will roll without slipping with a constant velocity and hence, no loss of energy, so (d) → (i)

Torque due to applied force, F about centre of mass

$$\tau = F(h - R) \qquad \text{(clockwise)}$$

For $\tau = 0$, $h = R$, sphere will have only translational motion. It would lose energy by friction.

Hence, (b) → (iv)

The sphere will spin clockwise when $\tau > 0 \Rightarrow h > R$

Therefore, (c) → (ii)

The sphere will spin anti-clockwise when $\tau < 0 \Rightarrow h < R$, (a) → (iii)

Short Answer Type Questions

Q.19 The vector sum of a system of non-collinear forces acting on a rigid body is given to be non-zero. If the vector sum of all the torques due to the system of forces about a certain point is found to be zero, does this mean that it is necessarily zero about any arbitrary point?

Ans. *No*, not necessarily.

Given, $\sum_i F_i \neq 0$

The sum of torques about a certain point O, $\sum_i \mathbf{r}_i \times \mathbf{F}_i = 0$

The sum of torques about any other point O

$$\sum_i (\mathbf{r}_i - \mathbf{a}) \times \mathbf{F}_i = \sum_i \mathbf{r}_i \times \mathbf{F}_i - \mathbf{a} \times \sum_i \mathbf{F}_i$$

Here, the second term need not vanish.

Therefore, sum of all the torques about any arbitrary point need not be zero necessarily.

Q.20 A wheel in uniform motion about an axis passing through its centre and perpendicular to its plane is considered to be in mechanical (translational plus rotational) equilibrium because no net external force or torque is required to sustain its motion. However, the particles that constitute the wheel do experience a centripetal acceleration directed towards the centre. How do you reconcile this fact with the wheel being in equilibrium?

How would you set a half wheel into uniform motion about an axis passing through the centre of mass of the wheel and perpendicular to its plane? Will you require external forces to sustain the motion?

Ans. Wheel is a rigid body. The particles that constitute the wheel do experience a centripetal acceleration directed towards the centre. This acceleration arises due to internal elastic forces, which cancel out in pairs.

In a half wheel, the distribution of mass about its centre of mass (through which axis of rotation passes) is not symmetrical. Therefore, the direction of angular momentum of the wheel does not coincide with the direction of its angular velocity. Hence, an external torque is required to maintain the motion of the half wheel.

Q.21 A door is hinged at one end and is free to rotate about a vertical axis (figure). Does its weight cause any torque about this axis? Give reason for your answer.

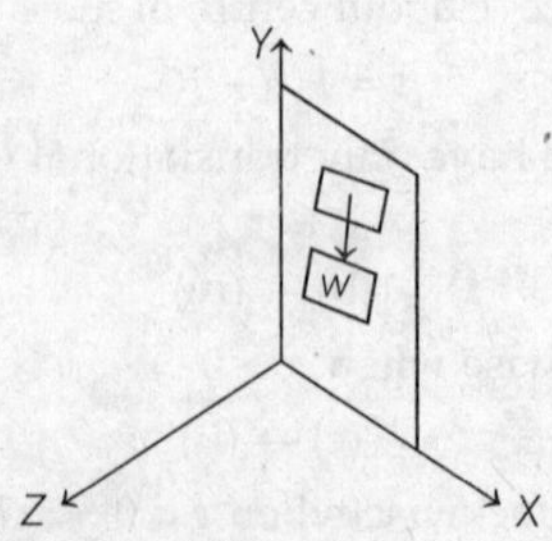

Ans. Consider the diagram, where weight of the door acts along negative y-axis.

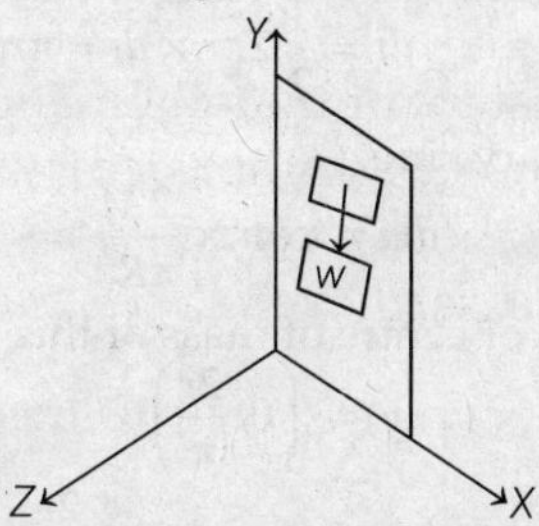

A force can produce torque only along a direction normal to itself as $\tau = \mathbf{r} \times \mathbf{F}$. So, when the door is in the xy-plane, the torque produced by gravity can only be along $\pm z$ direction, but never about an axis passing through y-direction.

Hence, the weight will not produce any torque about y-axis.

Q.22 $(n-1)$ equal point masses each of mass m are placed at the vertices of a regular n-polygon. The vacant vertex has a position vector $\mathbf{a}$ with respect to the centre of the polygon. Find the position vector of centre of mass.

Thinking Process The centre of mass of a regular n-polygon lies at its geometrical centre.

Ans. Let $\mathbf{b}$ be the position vector of the centre of mass of a regular n-polygon. $(n-1)$ equal point masses are placed at $(n-1)$ vertices of the regular n-polygon, therefore, for its centre of mass

$$\mathbf{r}_{CM} = \frac{(n-1)\,m\mathbf{b} + m\mathbf{a}}{(n-1)\,m + m} = 0 \qquad [\because \text{Centre of mass lies at centre}]$$

$$\Rightarrow \qquad (n-1)\,m\mathbf{b} + m\mathbf{a} = 0$$

$$\Rightarrow \qquad \mathbf{b} = -\frac{\mathbf{a}}{(n-1)}$$

Long Answer Type Questions

Q.23 Find the centre of mass of a uniform (a) half-disc, (b) quarter-disc.

Ans. Let M and R be the mass and radius of the half-disc, mass per unit area of the half-disc

$$m = \frac{M}{\frac{1}{2}\pi R^2} = \frac{2M}{\pi R^2}$$

(a) The half-disc can be supposed to be consists of a large number of semicircular rings of mass dm and thickness dr and radii ranging from $r = 0$ to $r = R$.

Surface area of semicircular ring of radius r and of thickness

$$dr = \frac{1}{2} 2\pi r \times dr = \pi r dr$$

$\therefore$ Mass of this elementary ring,

$$dm = \pi r dr \times \frac{2M}{\pi R^2} \Rightarrow dm = \frac{2M}{R^2} r dr$$

If (x, y) are coordinates of centre of mass of this element,

then, $$(x, y) = \left(0, \frac{2r}{\pi}\right)$$

Therefore, $$x = 0 \text{ and } y = \frac{2r}{\pi}$$

Let x_{CM} and y_{CM} be the coordinates of the centre of mass of the semicircular disc.

Then $$x_{CM} = \frac{1}{M}\int_0^R x\, dm = \frac{1}{M}\int_0^R 0\, dm = 0$$

$$y_{CM} = \frac{1}{M}\int_0^R y dm = \frac{1}{M}\int_0^R \frac{2r}{\pi} \times \left(\frac{2M}{R^2} r dr\right)$$

$$= \frac{4}{\pi R^2}\int_0^R r^2 dr = \frac{4}{\pi R^2}\left[\frac{r^3}{3}\right]_0^R = \frac{4}{\pi R^2} \times \left(\frac{R^3}{3} - 0\right) = \frac{4R}{3\pi}$$

$\therefore$ Centre of mass of the semicircular disc $= \left(0, \frac{4R}{3\pi}\right)$

(b) Centre of mass of a uniform quarter disc.

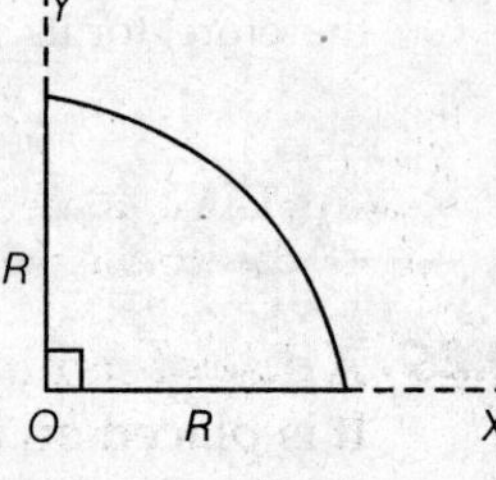

Mass per unit area of the quarter disc $= \dfrac{M}{\frac{\pi R^2}{4}} = \dfrac{4M}{\pi R^2}$

Using symmetry

For a half-disc along y-axis centre of mass will be at $x = \dfrac{4R}{3\pi}$

For a half-disc along x-axis centre of mass will be at $x = \dfrac{4R}{3\pi}$

Hence, for the quarter disc centre of mass $= \left(\dfrac{4R}{3\pi}, \dfrac{4R}{3\pi}\right)$

Q.24 Two discs of moments of inertia I_1 and I_2 about their respective axes (normal to the disc and passing through the centre), and rotating with angular speed ω_1 and ω_2 are brought into contact face to face with their axes of rotation coincident.

(a) Does the law of conservation of angular momentum apply to the situation? Why?

(b) Find the angular speed of the two discs system.

(c) Calculate the loss in kinetic energy of the system in the process.

(d) Account for this loss.

Thinking Process Due to friction between the two discs, the system will acquire common angular speed after sometime.

Ans. Consider the diagram below

Let the common angular velocity of the system is ω.

(a) *Yes*, the law of conservation of angular momentum can be applied. Because, there is no net external torque on the system of the two discs.

External forces, gravitation and normal reaction, act through the axis of rotation, hence, produce no torque, as perpendicular distance from axis of rotation is zero.

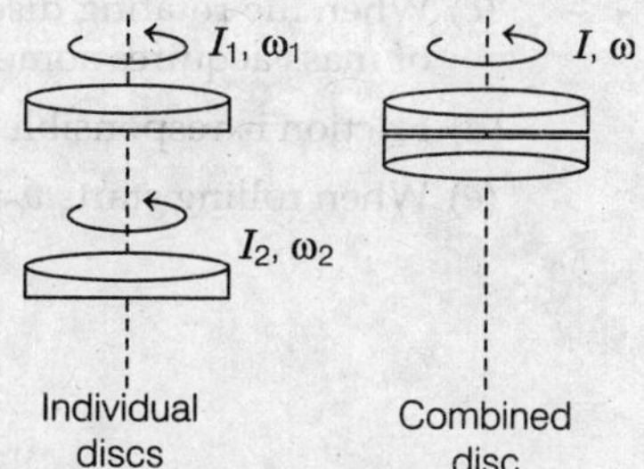

(b) By conservation of angular momentum

$$L_f = L_i$$

$$\Rightarrow \quad I\omega = I_1\omega_1 + I_2\omega_2$$

$$\Rightarrow \quad \omega = \frac{I_1\omega_1 + I_2\omega_2}{I} = \frac{I_1\omega_1 + I_2\omega_2}{I_1 + I_2}$$

[∵ $I = I_1 + I_2$ as their axis of rotation concide]

(c) $K_f = \frac{1}{2}(I_1 + I_2)\frac{(I_1\omega_1 + I_2\omega_2)^2}{(I_1 + I_2)^2} = \frac{1}{2}\frac{(I_1\omega_1 + I_2\omega_2)^2}{(I_1 + I_2)}$

$$K_i = \frac{1}{2}(I_1\omega_1^2 + I_2\omega_2^2)$$

$$\Delta K = K_f - K_i = -\frac{I_1 I_2}{2(I_1 + I_2)}(\omega_1 - \omega_2)^2 < 0$$

(d) Hence, there is loss in KE of the system. The loss in kinetic energy is mainly due to the work against the friction between the two discs.

Q.25 A disc of radius R is rotating with an angular ω_0 about a horizontal axis. It is placed on a horizontal table. The coefficient of kinetic friction is μ_K.

(a) What was the velocity of its centre of mass before being brought in contact with the table?

(b) What happens to the linear velocity of a point on its rim when placed in contact with the table?

(c) What happens to the linear speed of the centre of mass when disc is placed in contact with the table?

(d) Which force is responsible for the effects in (b) and (c)?

(e) What condition should be satisfied for rolling to begin?

(f) Calculate the time taken for the rolling to begin.

Ans. (a) Before being brought in contact with the table the disc was in pure rotational motion about its horizontal axis, hence, $v_{CM} = 0$.

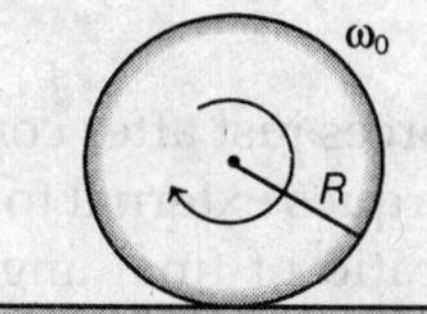

(b) When the disc is placed in contact with the table due to friction between table and disc velocity of a point on the rim decreases.

(c) When the rotating disc is placed in contact with the table due to friction centre of mass acquires some linear velocity.

(d) Friction is responsible for the effects in (b) and (c).

(e) When rolling starts $v_{CM} = \omega R$.

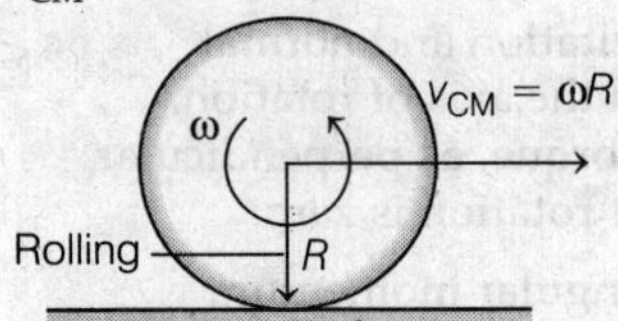

where ω is angular speed of the disc when rolling just starts.

(f) Acceleration produced in centre of mass due to friction

$$a_{CM} = \frac{F}{m} = \frac{\mu_k mg}{m} = \mu_k g. \qquad \ldots(i)$$

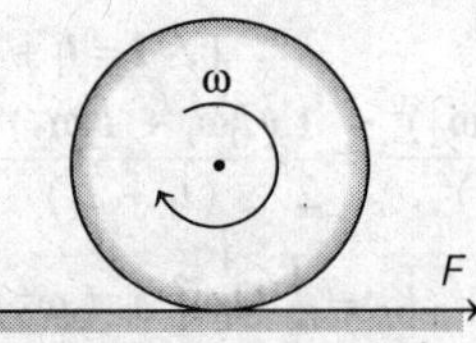

Angular retardation produced by the torque due to friction.

$$\alpha = \frac{\tau}{I} = \frac{\mu_k mgR}{I} \qquad \ldots(ii)\ [\because \tau = (\mu_k N)R = \mu_k mgR]$$

$\therefore$ $$v_{CM} = u_{CM} + a_{CM}t$$

$\Rightarrow$ $$v_{CM} = \mu_k gt \qquad \ldots(iii)\ [\because u_{CM} = 0]$$

and $$\omega = \omega_0 + \alpha t$$

$\Rightarrow$ $$\omega = \omega_0 - \frac{\mu_k mgR}{I}t \qquad \ldots(iv)\ [\text{using Eq. (ii)}]$$

For rolling without slipping, $\frac{v_{CM}}{R} = \omega$

$\Rightarrow$ $$\frac{v_{CM}}{R} = \omega_0 - \frac{\mu_k mgR}{I}t \qquad [\text{using Eq. (iii)}]$$

$$\frac{\mu_k gt}{R} = \omega_0 - \frac{\mu_k mgR}{I}t \Rightarrow t = \frac{R\omega_0}{\mu_k g\left(1 + \frac{mR^2}{I}\right)}$$

Note In this problem, frictional force helps in setting pure rolling motion.

Q.26 Two cylindrical hollow drums of radii R and $2R$, and of a common height h, are rotating with angular velocities ω (anti-clockwise) and ω (clockwise), respectively. Their axes, fixed are parallel and in a horizontal plane separated by $(3R + \delta)$. They are now brought in contact$(\delta \to 0)$

(a) Show the frictional forces just after contact.

(b) Identify forces and torques external to the system just after contact.

(c) What would be the ratio of final angular velocities when friction ceases?

Ans. (a) Consider the situation shown below, we have shown the frictional forces.

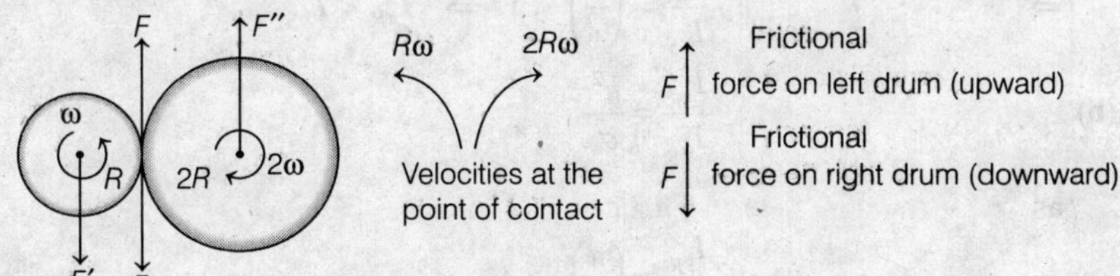

(b) $F' = F = F''$ where F' and F'' are external forces through support.

$\Rightarrow$ $F_{net} = 0$ [one each cylinder]

External torque $= F \times 3R$, (anti-clockwise)

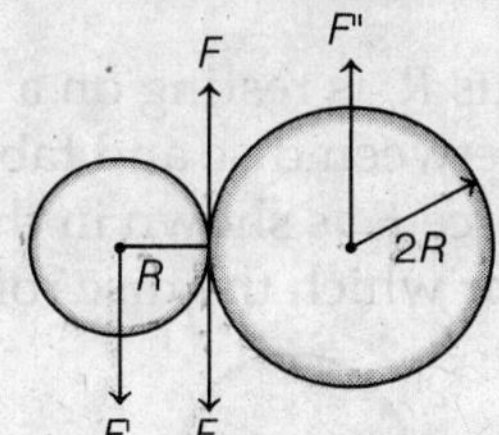

(c) Let ω_1 and ω_2 be final angular velocities of smaller and bigger drum respectively (anti-clockwise and clockwise respectively)

Finally, there will be no friction.

Hence, $R\omega_1 = 2R\omega_2 \Rightarrow \frac{\omega_1}{\omega_2} = 2$

Mistake Alert ! *We should be very careful while indicating direction of frictional forces.*

Q.27 A uniform square plate S (side c) and a uniform rectangular plate R (sides b, a) have identical areas and masses.

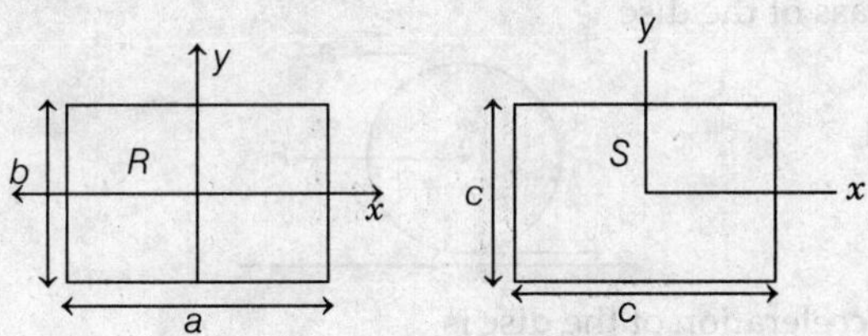

Show that

(a) $I_{xR} / I_{xS} < 1$ (b) $I_{yR} / I_{yS} > 1$ (c) $I_{zR} / I_{zS} > 1$

Ans. By given question

Area of square = Area of rectangular plate

$\Rightarrow$ $c^2 = a \times b \Rightarrow c^2 = ab$

Now by definition

(a) $$\frac{I_{xR}}{I_{xS}} = \frac{b^2}{c^2}$$ $[\because I \propto (\text{area})^2]$

From the diagram $b < c$

$$\Rightarrow \quad \frac{I_{xR}}{I_{xS}} = \left(\frac{b}{c}\right)^2 < 1 \Rightarrow I_{xR} < I_{xS}$$

(b) $$\frac{I_{yR}}{I_{yS}} = \frac{a^2}{c^2}$$

as $$a > c$$

$$\frac{I_{yR}}{I_{yS}} = \left(\frac{a}{c}\right)^2 > 1$$

(c) $I_{zR} - I_{zS} \propto (a^2 + b^2 - 2c^2) = a^2 + b^2 - 2ab = (a-b)^2$ $[\because c^2 = ab]$

$$\Rightarrow \quad (I_{zR} - I_{zS}) > 0 \Rightarrow \frac{I_{zR}}{I_{zS}} > 1$$

Q.28 A uniform disc of radius R, is resting on a table on its rim. The coefficient of friction between disc and table is μ (figure). Now, the disc is pulled with a force F as shown in the figure. What is the maximum value of F for which the disc rolls without slipping?

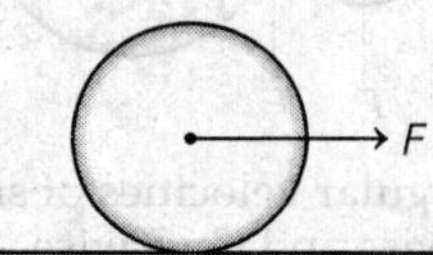

Thinking Process Frictional force on the disc will be in opposite direction of F and supports the rotation of the disc in clockwise direction.

Ans. Consider the diagram below

Frictional force (f) is acting in the opposite direction of F.

Let the acceleration of centre of mass of disc be a then

$$F - f = Ma \quad \text{...(i)}$$

where M is mass of the disc

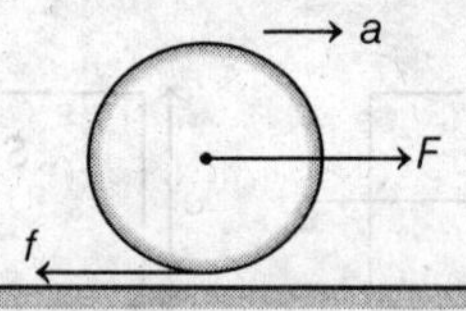

The angular acceleration of the disc is

$$\alpha = a/R \quad \text{[for pure rolling]}$$

from $$\tau = I\alpha$$

$$\Rightarrow \quad fR = \left(\frac{1}{2}MR^2\right)\alpha \Rightarrow fR = \left(\frac{1}{2}MR^2\right)\left(\frac{a}{R}\right)$$

$$\Rightarrow \quad Ma = 2f \quad \text{...(ii)}$$

From Eqs. (i) and (ii), we get

$$f = F/3 \quad [\because N = Mg]$$

$$\Rightarrow \quad f \le \mu N = \mu Mg$$

$$\frac{F}{3} \le \mu Mg \Rightarrow F \le 3\mu Mg$$

$$\Rightarrow \quad F_{max} = 3\mu Mg$$

Chapter 07 Gravitation

Multiple Choice Questions (MCQs)

Q.1 The earth is an approximate sphere. If the interior contained matter which is not of the same density everywhere, then on the surface of the earth, the acceleration due to gravity

(a) will be directed towards the centre but not the same everywhere.
(b) will have the same value everywhere but not directed towards the centre.
(c) will be same everywhere in magnitude directed towards the centre.
(d) cannot be zero at any point.

Ans. *(d)* If we assume the earth as a sphere of uniform density, then it can be treated as point mass placed at its centre. In this case acceleration due to gravity $g = 0$, at the centre.

But if the earth is considered as a sphere of non-uniform density, in that case value of g will be different at different points and cannot be zero at any point.

Q.2 As observed from the earth, the sun appears to move in an approximate circular orbit. For the motion of another planet like mercury as observed from the earth, this would

(a) be similarly true.
(b) not be true because the force between the earth and mercury is not inverse square law.
(c) not be true because the major gravitational force on mercury is due to the sun.
(d) not be true because mercury is influenced by forces other than gravitational forces.

Ans. *(c)* As observed from the earth, the sun appears to move in an approximate circular orbit. The gravitational force of attraction between the earth and the sun always follows inverse square law.

Due to relative motion between the earth and mercury, the orbit of mercury, as observed from the earth will not be approximately circular, since the major gravitational force on mercury is due to the sun, as compare to gravitational force between earth and mercury.

Q.3 Different points in the earth are at slightly different distances from the sun and hence experience different forces due to gravitation. For a rigid body, we know that if various forces act at various points in it, the resultant motion is as if a net force acts on the CM (centre of mass) causing translation and a net torque at the CM causing rotation around an axis through the CM.

For the earth-sun system (approximating the earth as a uniform density sphere).

(a) the torque is zero.

(b) the torque causes the earth to spin.

(c) the rigid body result is not applicable since the earth is not even approximately a rigid body.

(d) the torque causes the earth to move around the sun.

Ans. *(a)* As the earth is revolving around the sun in a circular motion due to gravitational attraction. The force of attraction will be of radial nature i.e. angle between position vector **r** and force **F** is zero. So, torque $= |\tau| = |\mathbf{r} \times \mathbf{F}| = rF\sin 0° = 0$

Q.4 Satellites orbitting the earth have finite life and sometimes debris of satellites fall to the earth. This is because

(a) the solar cells and batteries in satellites run out.

(b) the laws of gravitation predict a trajectory spiralling inwards.

(c) of viscous forces causing the speed of satellite and hence height to gradually decrease.

(d) of collisions with other satellites.

Ans. *(c)* As the total energy of the earth satellite bounded system is negative $\left(\dfrac{-GM_eM}{2a}\right)$.

Where, a is radius of the satellite and M_e is mass of the earth and M is mass of satellite.

Due to the viscous force acting on satellite, energy decreases continuously and radius of the orbit or height decreases gradually.

Q.5 Both the earth and the moon are subject to the gravitational force of the sun. As observed from the sun, the orbit of the moon

(a) will be elliptical.

(b) will not be strictly elliptical because the total gravitational force on it is not central.

(c) is not elliptical but will necessarily be a closed curve.

(d) deviates considerably from being elliptical due to influence of planets other than the earth.

Ans. *(b)* As observed from the sun, two types of forces are acting on the moon one is due to gravitational attraction between the sun and the moon and the other is due to gravitational attraction between the earth and the moon. Hence, total force on the moon is not central.

Q.6 In our solar system, the inter-planetary region has chunks of matter (much smaller in size compared to planets) called asteroids. They

(a) will not move around the sun, since they have very small masses compared to the sun.

(b) will move in an irregular way because of their small masses and will drift away into outer space.

(c) will move around the sun in closed orbits but not obey Kepler's laws.

(d) will move in orbits like planets and obey Kepler's laws .

Ans. *(d)* Asteroids are also being acted upon by central gravitational forces, hence they are moving in circular orbits like planets and obey Kepler's laws.

Q.7 Choose the wrong option.

(a) Inertial mass is a measure of difficulty of accelerating a body by an external force whereas the gravitational mass is relevant in determining the gravitational force on it by an external mass.

(b) That the gravitational mass and inertial mass are equal is an experimental result.

(c) That the acceleration due to gravity on the earth is the same for all bodies is due to the equality of gravitational mass and inertial mass.

(d) Gravitational mass of a particle like proton can depend on the presence of neighbouring heavy objects but the inertial mass cannot.

Ans. ***(d)*** Gravitational mass of proton is equivalent to its inertial mass and is independent of presence neighbouring heavy objects.

Q.8 Particles of masses $2M$, m and M are respectively at points A, B and C with $AB = \frac{1}{2}(BC)$. m is much-much smaller than M and at time $t = 0$, they are all at rest as given in figure.
At subsequent times before any collision takes place.

A B C
2M m M

(a) m will remain at rest
(b) m will move towards M
(c) m will move towards $2M$
(d) m will have oscillatory motion

Thinking Process The particle B will move towards the greater force, between forces by A and B.

Ans. ***(c)*** Force on B due to $A = F_{BA} = \dfrac{G(2Mm)}{(AB)^2}$ towards BA

Force on B due to $C = F_{BC} = \dfrac{GMm}{(BC)^2}$ towards BC

As, $(BC) = 2AB$

$\Rightarrow$ $F_{BC} = \dfrac{GMm}{(2AB)^2} = \dfrac{GMm}{4(AB)^2}$ towards BC

Net force on m is

$$F_{net} = F_{BA} - F_{BC}$$

$$= \frac{GMm}{(AB)^2}\left[2 - \frac{1}{4}\right] = \frac{7GMm}{4AB^2}$$

So 'm' will move towards $2M$ i.e towards A.

Multiple Choice Questions (More Than One Options)

Q.9 Which of the following options are correct?

(a) Acceleration due to gravity decreases with increasing altitude
(b) Acceleration due to gravity increases with increasing depth (assume the earth to be a sphere of uniform density)
(c) Acceleration due to gravity increases with increasing latitude
(d) Acceleration due to gravity is independent of the mass of the earth

- **Concept Insight** Acceleration due to gravity is maximum on the surface of the earth, it decreases in both cases while going upward or at a depth.

Ans. ***(a, c, d)*** Acceleration due to gravity at altitude h, $g_h = \dfrac{g}{(1+h/R)^2} \approx g\left(1-\dfrac{2h}{R}\right)$

As h increases g decreases

At depth d, $$g_d = g\left(1-\frac{d}{R}\right)$$

As d increases g decreases.

At latitude ϕ, $$g_\phi = g - \omega^2 R\cos^2\phi$$

As ϕ increases g_ϕ increases.

Also, we can conclude from the formulae, that it is independent of mass of earth only if earth is considered to be of uniform density and perfectly spherical.

Q.10 If the law of gravitation, instead of being inverse square law, becomes an inverse cube law

(a) planets will not have elliptic orbits
(b) circular orbits of planets is not possible
(c) projectile motion of a stone thrown by hand on the surface of the earth will be approximately parabolic
(d) there will be no gravitational force inside a spherical shell of uniform density

Ans. ***(a, b, c)*** If the law of gravitation becomes an inverse cube law, then we can write, for a planet of mass m revolving around the sun of mass M,

$$F = \frac{GMm}{a^3} = \frac{mv^2}{a}$$ [where a is radius of orbiting planet]

$\Rightarrow$ $$v = \text{orbital speed} = \frac{\sqrt{GM}}{a} \Rightarrow v \propto \frac{1}{a}$$

Time period of revolution of a planet $T = \dfrac{2\pi a}{v} = \dfrac{2\pi a}{\dfrac{\sqrt{GM}}{a}} = \dfrac{2\pi a^2}{\sqrt{GM}}$

$\Rightarrow$ $$T^2 \propto a^4$$

Hence, orbit will not be elliptical. [for elliptical orbit $T^2 \propto a^3$]

Similarly due to new gravitational law circular orbits of planets is not possible.

As force $$F = \left(\frac{GM}{a^3}\right)m = g'm$$

where, $$g' = \frac{GM}{a^3}$$

As g', acceleration due to gravity is constant, hence path followed by a projectile will be approximately parabolic. [as $T \propto a^2$]

Q.11 If the mass of the sun were ten times smaller and gravitational constant G were ten times larger in magnitude. Then,

(a) walking on ground would become more difficult.

(b) the acceleration due to gravity on the earth will not change.

(c) raindrops will fall much faster.

(d) airplanes will have to travel much faster.

Ans. *(a, c, d)*

Given, $G' = 10\,G$

Consider the adjacent diagram.

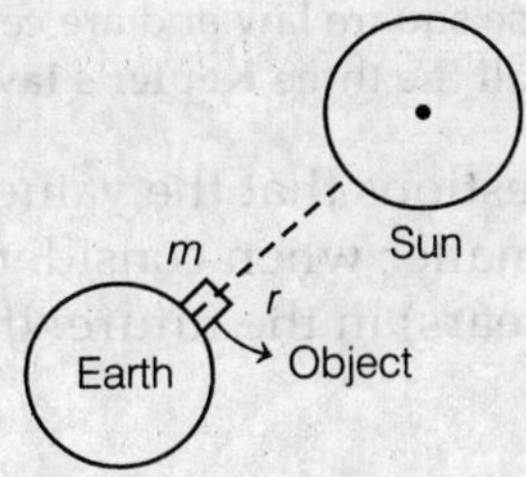

Force on the object due to the earth $= \dfrac{G' M_e m}{R^2} = \dfrac{10 G M_e m}{R^2}$ $[\because G' = 10\,G \text{ given}]$

$$= 10\left(\frac{GM_e m}{R^2}\right)$$

$$= (10g)\, m = 10\, mg \qquad \left[\because g = \frac{GM_e}{R^2}\right] \quad ...(i)$$

Force on the object due to the sun $F = \dfrac{G' M_s' m}{r^2}$

$$= 10\,\frac{G(M_s)m}{10r^2} = \frac{GM_s m}{r^2} \qquad \left[\because M_s' = \frac{M_s}{10} \text{ (given)}\right]$$

As $r >> R$ (radius of the earth) $\Rightarrow F$ will be very small.

So, the effect of the sun will be small.

Now, as $g' = 10\,g$

Hence, weight of person $= mg' = 10\,mg$ [from Eq. (i)]

i.e. gravity pull on the person will increase. Due to it, walking on ground would become more difficult.

Critical velocity, v_c is proportional to g i.e.

$$v_c \propto g$$

As, $g' > g$

$\Rightarrow$ $v_c' > v_c$

Hence, rain drops will fall much faster.

To overcome the increased gravitational force of the earth, the aeroplanes will have to travel much faster.

Q.12 If the sun and the planets carried huge amounts of opposite charges,

(a) all three of Kepler's laws would still be valid.
(b) only the third law will be valid.
(c) the second law will not change.
(d) the first law will still be valid.

Thinking Process Electrostatic force of attraction acts between two opposite charges.

Ans. *(a, c, d)* Due to huge amounts of opposite charges on the sun and the earth electrostatic force of attraction will be large. Gravitational force is also attractive in nature have both forces will be added.

Both the forces obey inverse square law and are central forces. As both the forces are of same nature, hence all the three **Kepler's laws** will be valid.

Q.13 There have been suggestions that the value of the gravitational constant G becomes smaller when considered over very large time period (in billions of years) in the future. If that happens, for our earth,

(a) nothing will change.
(b) we will become hotter after billions of years.
(c) we will be going around but not strictly in closed orbits.
(d) after sufficiently long time we will leave the solar system .

Ans. *(c, d)*

We know that gravitational force between the earth and the sun, provides centripetal force due to which earth revolves around sun in elliptical orbits.

Now, $F_G = \frac{GMm}{r^2}$, where M is mass of the sun and m is mass of the earth.

When G decreases with time, the gravitational force F_G will become weaker with time. As F_G is changing with time. Due to it, the earth will be going around the sun not strictly in closed orbit and radius also increases, since the attraction force is getting weaker.

Hence, after long time the earth will leave the solar system.

Q.14 Supposing Newton's law of gravitation for gravitation forces $\mathbf{F}_1$ and $\mathbf{F}_2$ between two masses m_1 and m_2 at positions $\mathbf{r}_1$ and $\mathbf{r}_2$ read

$$\mathbf{F}_1 = -\mathbf{F}_2 = -\frac{\mathbf{r}_{12}}{r_{12}^3} \text{GM}^2{}_0 \left(\frac{m_1 m_2}{M_0^2}\right)^n$$

where M_0 is a constant of dimension of mass, $\mathbf{r}_{12} = \mathbf{r}_1 - \mathbf{r}_2$ and n is a number. In such a case,

(a) the acceleration due to gravity on the earth will be different for different objects.
(b) None of the three laws of Kepler will be valid.
(c) Only the third law will become invalid.
(d) for n negative, an object lighter than water will sink in water.

Ans. ***(a,c, d)*** Given,
$$\mathbf{F}_1 = -\mathbf{F}_2 = \frac{-\mathbf{r}_{12}}{\mathbf{r}_{12}^3} GM_0^2 \left(\frac{m_1 m_2}{M_0^2}\right)^n$$
$$\mathbf{r}_{12} = \mathbf{r}_1 - \mathbf{r}_2$$

Acceleration due to gravity, $g = \dfrac{|F|}{\text{mass}}$
$$= \frac{GM_0^2 (m_1 m_2)^n}{r_{12}^2 (M_0)^{2n}} \times \frac{1}{(\text{mass})}$$

Since, g depends upon position vector, hence it will be different for different objects. As g is not constant, hence constant of proportionality will not be constant in Kepler's third law. Hence, Kepler's third law will not be valid.

As the force is of central nature. $\left[\because \text{force} \propto \dfrac{1}{r^2}\right]$

Hence, first two Kepler's laws will be valid.

For negative n,
$$g = \frac{GM_0^2 (m_1 m_2)^{-n}}{r_{12}^2 (M_0)^{-2n}} \times \frac{1}{(\text{mass})}$$
$$= \frac{GM_0^{2(1+n)}}{r_{12}^2} \frac{(m_1 m_2)^{-n}}{(\text{mass})}$$
$$g = \frac{GM_0^2}{r_{12}^2} \left(\frac{M_0^2}{m_1 m_2}\right)^n \times \frac{1}{\text{mass}}$$

As $M_0 > m_1$ or m_2

$g > 0$, hence in this case situation will reverse i.e. object lighter than water will sink in water.

Alternate Method

Given,
$$\mathbf{F}_1 = \mathbf{F}_2 = -\frac{r_{12}}{r^3{}_{12}} GM_0^2 \left(\frac{m_1 m_2}{M_0^2}\right)^n$$

or
$$F = \frac{GM_0^{2(1-n)}}{r_{12}^2} (m_1 m_2)^n$$

Take, $m_1 = m$ [mass of the object]

$m_2 = M$ [mass of the earth]

$r_{12} = R$ [radius of earth]

$\therefore$
$$F = \left(\frac{GM_0^{2(1-n)} M^n}{R^2}\right) m^n = km^n$$

Where, K is constant.

Also, $F = mg = km^n \Rightarrow g = km^{(n-1)}$

Hence, g depends on the mass of object. In this way, Keplar's third law will not be valid.

When, n is negative, then
$$F = \frac{K}{m^n}$$

It shows that lighter object experiences greater force and vice versa. Hence, an object lighter than water will sink in water.

***Q.15** Which of the following are true?

(a) A polar satellite goes around the earth's pole in north-south direction.
(b) A geostationary satellite goes around the earth in east-west direction.
(c) A geostationary satellite goes around the earth in west-east direction.
(d) A polar satellite goes around the earth in east-west direction .

Ans. ***(a, c)*** A geostationary satellite is having same sense of rotation as that of earth *i.e.*, west-east direction.

A polar satellite goes around the earth's pole in north-south direction.

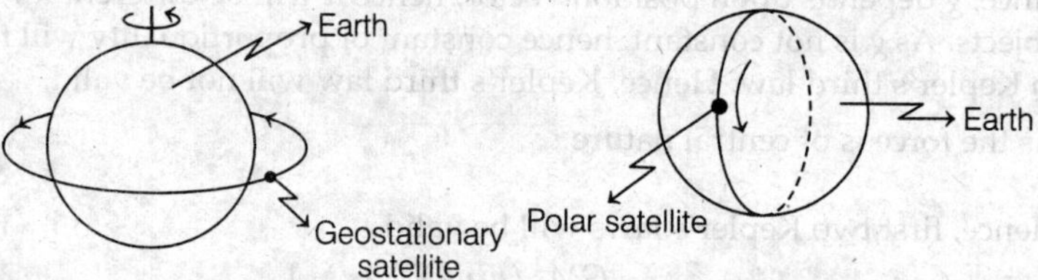

Q.16 The centre of mass of an extended body on the surface of the earth and its centre of gravity

(a) are always at the same point for any size of the body
(b) are always at the same point only for spherical bodies
(c) can never be at the same point
(d) is close to each other for objects, say of sizes less than 100 m
(e) both can change if the object is taken deep inside the earth

Ans. ***(d)*** For small objects, say of sizes less than 100 m centre of mass is very close with the centre of gravity of the body. But when the size of object increases, its weight changes as a result its CM and CG become far from each other.

Alternate Method

For smaller bodies, the COM and COG usually coincide. For extended objects like mountains and lake, they are far away. COG is the point in a body where net torque due to gravity is 0. The COM is where the whole mass of a body is supposed to be concentrated.

Very Short Answer Type Questions

Q.17 Molecules in air in the atmosphere are attracted by gravitational force of the earth. Explain why all of them do not fall into the earth just like an apple falling from a tree.

Ans. Air molecules in the atmosphere are attracted vertically downward by gravitational force of the earth just like an apple falling from a tree. But air molecules move randomly due to their thermal velocity and hence the resultant motion of air molecules is not exactly in the vertical downward direction.

But in case of apple, only vertical motion dominates because of being heavier than air molecules. But due to gravity, the density of atmosphere increases near to the earth's surface.

Note (*) *Topics related to these question have been removed from latest NCERT.*

***Q.18** Give one example each of central force and non-central force.

Ans. Example of central force Gravitational force, electrostatic force etc.

Example of non-central force Nuclear force, magnetic force acting between two current carrying loops etc.

***Q.19** Draw areal velocity *versus* time graph for mars.

Ans. Areal velocity of a planet revolving around the sun is constant with time. Therefore, graph between areal velocity and time is a straight line (*AB*) parallel to time axis.(Kepler's second law).

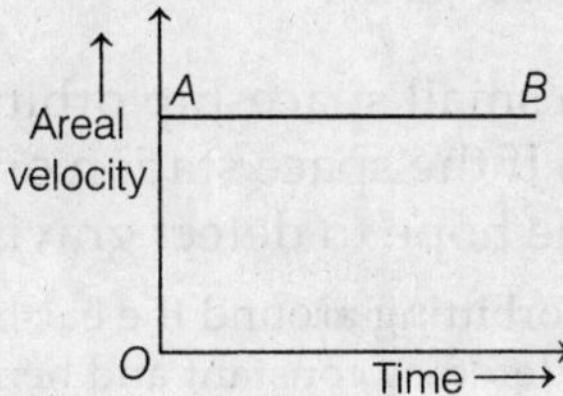

***Q.20** What is the direction of areal velocity of the earth around the sun?

Ans. Areal velocity of the earth around the sun is given by

$$\frac{d\mathbf{A}}{dt} = \frac{\mathbf{L}}{2m}$$

where, **L** is the angular momentum and m is the mass of the earth.

But angular momentum $\mathbf{L} = \mathbf{r} \times \mathbf{p} = \mathbf{r} \times m\mathbf{v}$

$\therefore$ Areal velocity $\left(\frac{dA}{dt}\right) = \frac{1}{2m}(\mathbf{r} \times m\mathbf{v}) = \frac{1}{2}(\mathbf{r} \times \mathbf{v})$

Therefore, the direction of areal velocity $\left(\frac{d\mathbf{A}}{dt}\right)$ is in the direction of $(\mathbf{r} \times \mathbf{v})$, i.e. perpendicular to the plane containing **r** and **v** and directed as given by right hand rule.

Q.21 How is the gravitational force between two point masses affected when they are dipped in water keeping the separation between them the same?

Ans. Gravitational force acting between two point masses m_1 and m_2, $F = \frac{Gm_1m_2}{r^2}$, is independent of the nature of medium between them. Therefore, gravitational force acting between two point masses will remain unaffected when they are dipped in water.

Q.22 Is it possible for a body to have inertia but no weight?

Ans. *Yes,* a body can have inertia (i.e. mass) but no weight. Everybody always have inertia (i.e. mass) but its weight (mg) can be zero, if $g = 0$ for e.g. when it is taken at the centre of, the earth or during free fall under gravity.

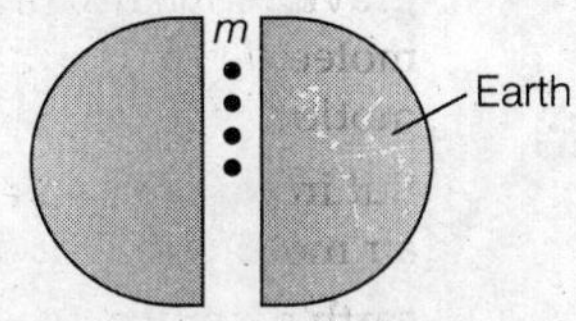

Note (*) *Topics related to these question have been removed from latest NCERT.*

e.g. In the tunnel through the centre of the earth, the object moves only due to inertia at the centre while its weight becomes zero.

Q.23 We can shield a charge from electric fields by putting it inside a hollow conductor. Can we shield a body from the gravitational influence of nearby matter by putting it inside a hollow sphere or by some other means?

Ans. A body cannot be shielded from the gravitational influence of nearby matter, because gravitational force between two point mass bodies is independent of the intervening medium between them.

Q.24 An astronaut inside a small spaceship orbitting around the earth cannot detect gravity. If the space station orbitting around the earth has a large size, can he hope to detect gravity?

Ans. Inside a small spaceship orbitting around the earth, the value of acceleration due to gravity g, can be considered as constant and hence astronaut feels weightlessness.

If the space station orbitting around the earth has a large size, such that variation in g matters. In that case astronaut inside the spaceship will experience gravitational force and hence can detect gravity. *e.g.*, On the moon, due to larger size gravity can be detected.

Q.25 The gravitational force between a hollow spherical shell (of radius R and uniform density) and a point mass is F. Show the nature of F *versus* r graph where r is the distance of the point from the centre of the hollow spherical shell of uniform density.

Ans. Consider the diagram, density of the shell is constant.

Let it is ρ.

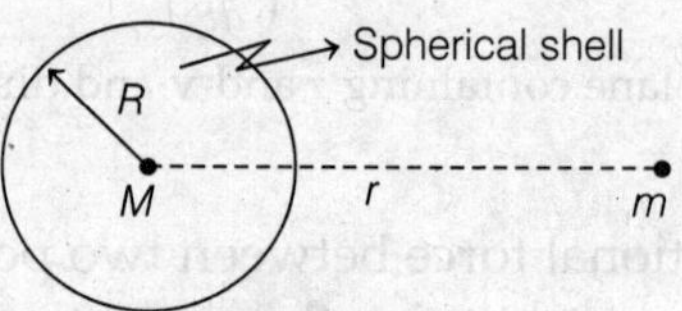

Mass of the shell = (density) × (volume)

$$= (\rho) \times \frac{4}{3}\pi R^3 = M$$

As the density of the shell is uniform, it can be treated as a point mass placed at its centre.

Therefore, F = gravitational force between M and $m = \dfrac{GMm}{r^2}$

$$F = 0 \text{ for } r < R \quad \text{[i.e. force inside the shell is zero]}$$

$$= \frac{GMm}{r^2} \text{ for } r \geq R$$

The variation of F *versus* r is shown in the diagram.

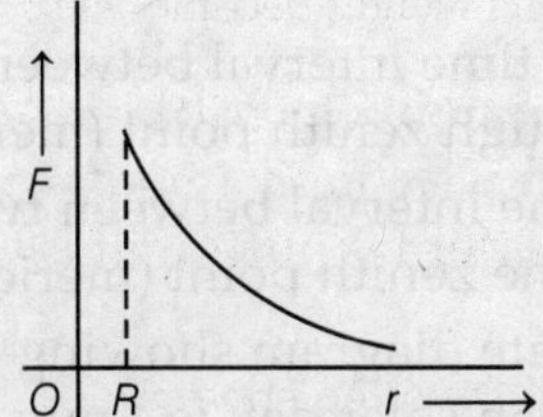

Note When r tends to infinity, force tends to zero, also force is maximum on the surface of the hollow spherical shell.

Q.26 Out of aphelion and perihelion, where is the speed of the earth more and why?

Ans. Aphelion is the location of the earth where it is at the greatest distance from the sun and perihelion is the location of the earth where it is at the nearest distance from the sun.

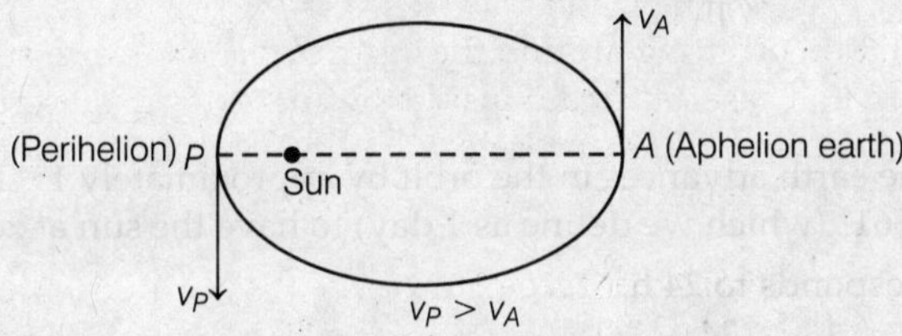

The areal velocity $\left|\frac{1}{2}\mathbf{r}\times\mathbf{v}\right|$ of the earth around the sun is constant (Kepler's IInd law).

Therefore, the speed of the earth is more at the perihelion than at the aphelion.

***Q.27** What is the angle between the equatorial plane and the orbital plane of

(a) polar satellite?

(b) geostationary satellite?

Ans. Consider the diagram where plane of geostationary and polar satellite are shown.

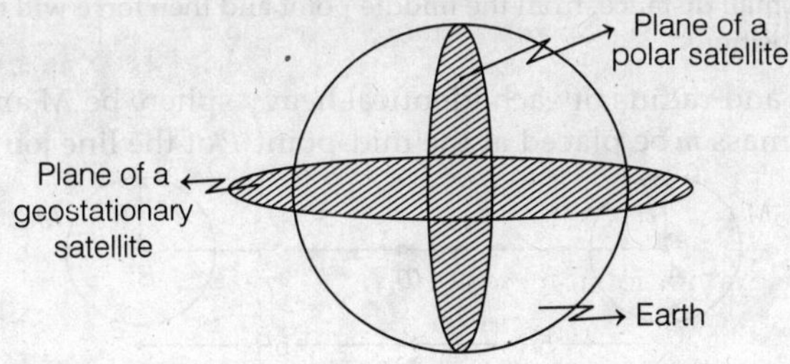

(a) Angle between the equatorial plane and orbital plane of a polar satellite is 90°.

(b) Angle between equatorial plane and orbital plane of a geostationary satellite is 0°.

Note (*) *Topics related to these question have been removed from latest NCERT.*

Short Answer Type Questions

Q.28 Mean solar day is the time interval between two successive noon when sun passes through zenith point (meridian).

Sidereal day is the time interval between two successive transit of a distant star through the zenith point (meridian).

By drawing appropriate diagram showing the earth's spin and orbital motion, show that mean solar day is 4 min longer than the sidereal day. In other words, distant stars would rise 4 min early every successive day.

Ans. Consider the diagram below, the earth moves from the point P to Q in one solar day.

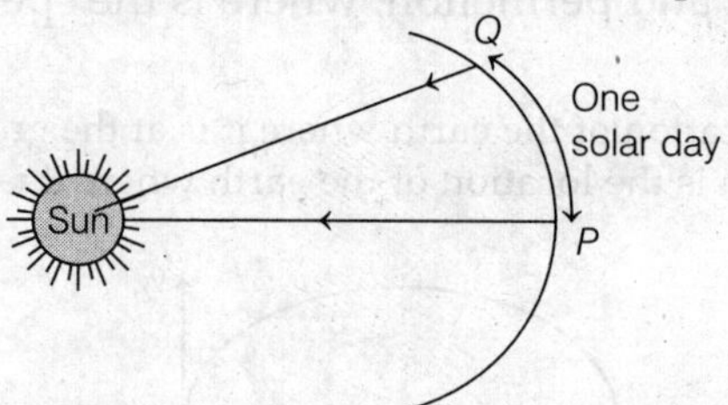

Every day the earth advances in the orbit by approximately 1°. Then, it will have to rotate by 361° (which we define as 1 day) to have the sun at zenith point again.

$\because$ 361° corresponds to 24 h.

$\therefore$ 1° corresponds to $\frac{24}{361} \times 1 = 0.066 \text{ h} = 3.99 \text{ min} \approx 4 \text{ min}$

Hence, distant stars would rise 4 min early every successive day.

Q.29 Two identical heavy spheres are separated by a distance 10 times their radius. Will an object placed at the mid-point of the line joining their centres be in stable equilibrium or unstable equilibrium? Give reason for your answer.

Thinking Process To determine the nature of equilibrium, we have to displace the object through a small distance, from the middle point and then force will be calculated in displaced position.

Ans. Let the mass and radius of each identical heavy sphere be M and R respectively. An object of mass m be placed at the mid-point P of the line joining their centres.

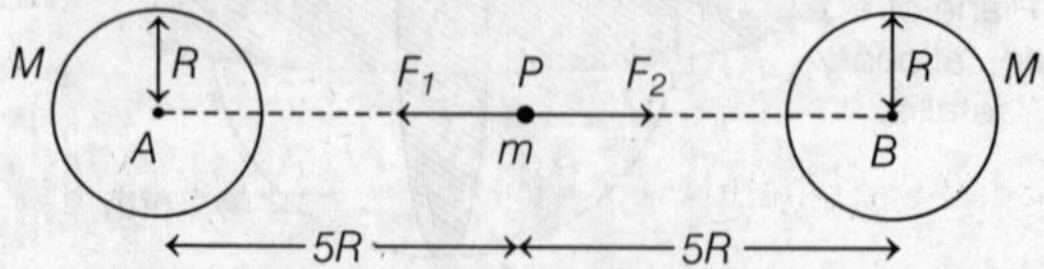

Force acting on the object placed at the mid-point,

$$F_1 = F_2 = \frac{GMm}{(5R)^2}$$

The direction of forces are opposite, therefore net force acting on the object is zero. To check the stability of the equilibrium, we displace the object through a small distance x towards sphere A.

Now, force acting towards sphere A, $F_1' = \dfrac{GMm}{(5R-x)^2}$

Force acting towards sphere B, $F_2' = \dfrac{GMm}{(5R+x)^2}$

As $F_1' > F_2'$, therefore a resultant force $(F_1' - F_2')$ acts on the object towards sphere A, therefore object start to move towards sphere A and hence equilibrium is unstable.

Q.30 Show the nature of the following graph for a satellite orbitting the earth.

(a) KE *versus* orbital radius R

(b) PE *versus* orbital radius R

(c) TE *versus* orbital radius R

Ans. Consider the diagram, where a satellite of mass m, moving around the earth in a circular orbit of radius R.

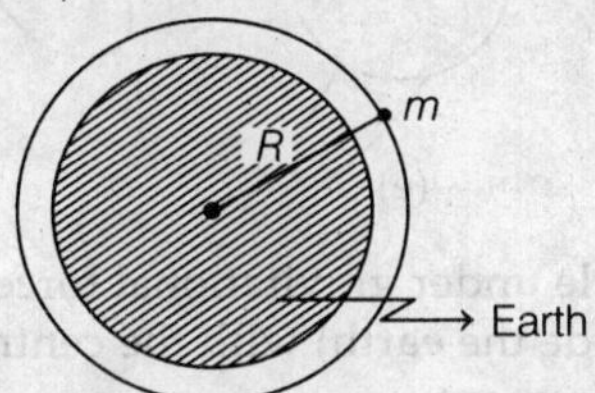

Orbital speed of the satellite orbitting the earth is given by $v_o = \sqrt{\dfrac{GM}{R}}$

where, M and R are the mass and radius of the earth.

(a) $\therefore$ KE of a satellite of mass m, $E_K = \dfrac{1}{2}mv_o^2 = \dfrac{1}{2}m \times \dfrac{GM}{R}$

$\therefore$ $E_K \propto \dfrac{1}{R}$

It means the KE decreases exponentially with radius.

The graph for KE *versus* orbital radius R is shown in figure.

E_K (vertical axis), R (horizontal axis)

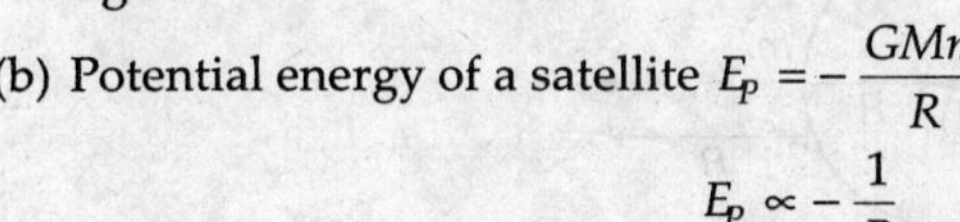

(b) Potential energy of a satellite $E_P = -\dfrac{GMm}{R}$

$E_P \propto -\dfrac{1}{R}$

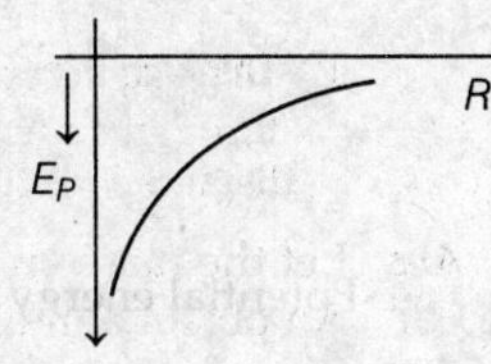

The graph for PE *versus* orbital radius R is shown in figure.

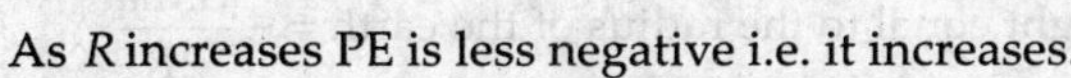

As R increases PE is less negative i.e. it increases.

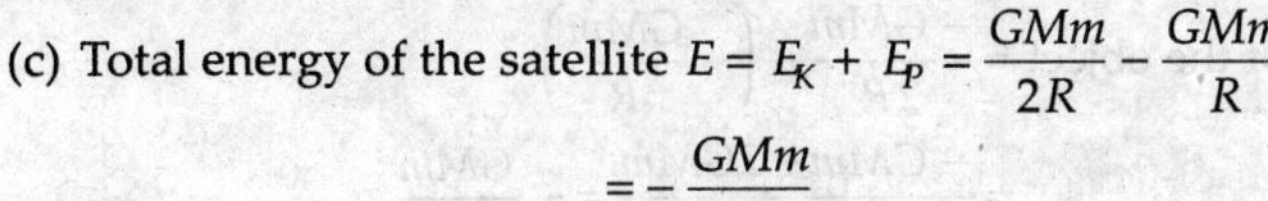

(c) Total energy of the satellite $E = E_K + E_P = \dfrac{GMm}{2R} - \dfrac{GMm}{R}$

$= -\dfrac{GMm}{2R}$

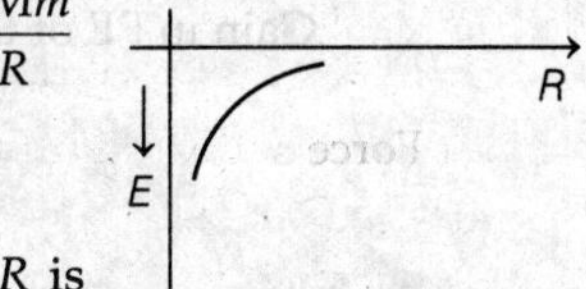

The graph for total energy *versus* orbital radius R is shown in the figure.

Mistake Alert ! *We should keep in mind that Potential Energy (PE) and Total Energy (TE) of the satellite-earth system is always negative.*

Q.31 Shown are several curves [fig. (a), (b), (c), (d), (e), (f)]. Explain with reason, which ones amongst them can be possible trajectories traced by a projectile (neglect air friction).

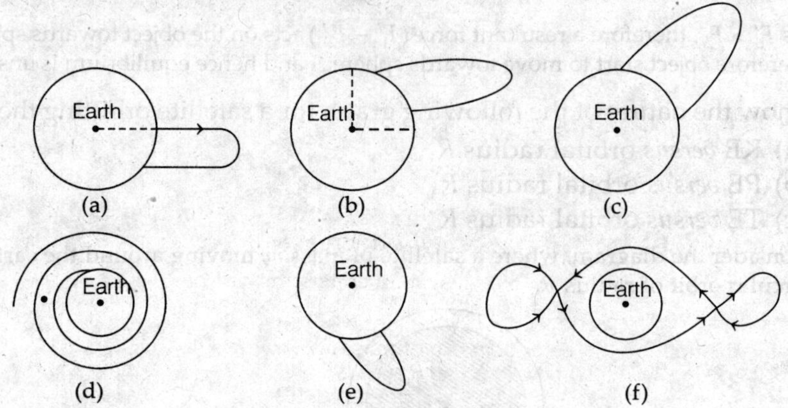

Ans. The trajectory of a particle under gravitational force of the earth will be a conic section (for motion outside the earth) with the centre of the earth as a focus. Only (c) meets this requirement.

Note The trajectory of the particle depends upon the velocity of projection. Depending upon the magnitude and direction of velocity it may be parabolic or elliptical.

Q.32 An object of mass m is raised from the surface of the earth to a height equal to the radius of the earth, that is, taken from a distance R to $2R$ from the centre of the earth. What is the gain in its potential energy?

Ans. Consider the diagram where an object of mass m is raised from the surface of the earth to a distance (height) equal to the radius of the earth (R).

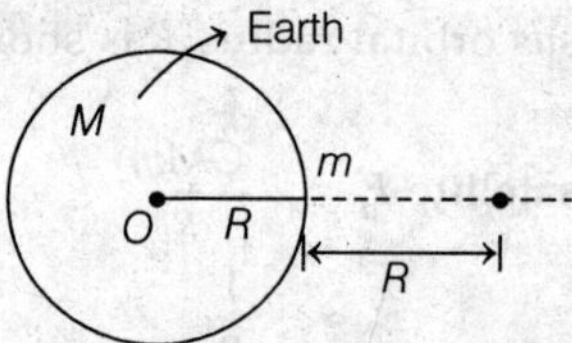

Potential energy of the object at the surface of the earth $= -\frac{GMm}{R}$

PE of the object at a height equal to the radius of the earth $= -\frac{GMm}{2R}$

$\therefore$ Gain in PE of the object $= \frac{-GMm}{2R} - \left(-\frac{GMm}{R}\right)$

$$= \frac{-GMm + 2GMm}{2R} = +\frac{GMm}{2R}$$

$$= \frac{gR^2 \times m}{2R} = \frac{1}{2}mgR \qquad [\because GM = gR^2]$$

Q.33 A mass m is placed at P a distance h along the normal through the centre O of a thin circular ring of mass M and radius r (figure).

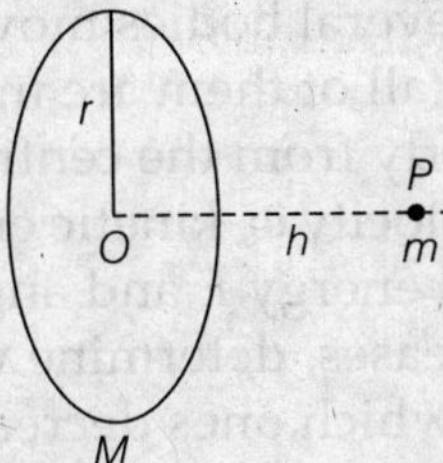

If the mass is moved further away such that OP becomes $2h$, by what factor the force of gravitation will decrease, if $h = r$?

Ans. Consider the diagram, in which a system consisting of a ring and a point mass is shown.

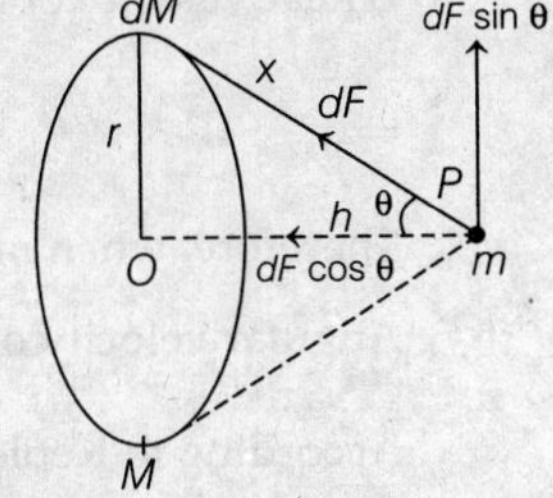

Now, consider small element of ring of mass dM, then

$$dF = \frac{Gm(dM)}{x^2} = \frac{Gm(dM)}{(r^2 + h^2)}$$

Similarly, consider identical small element of ring of mass dM on opposite side, then by symmetry net force on mass m is

$$F = \int dF \cos\theta = \int \frac{Gm(dM)}{(r^2 + h^2)} \cdot \frac{h}{(r^2 + h^2)^{\frac{1}{2}}}$$

Gravitational force acting on an object of mass m, placed at point P at a distance h along the normal through the centre of a circular ring of mass M and radius r is given by

$$F = \frac{GMmh}{(r^2 + h^2)^{3/2}} \qquad \text{(along } PO) \text{ ...(i)}$$

Similarly when mass is displaced upto distance $2h$, then

$$F' = \frac{GMm \times 2h}{[r^2 + (2h)^2]^{3/2}} \qquad [\because h = 2r]$$

$$= \frac{2GMmh}{(r^2 + 4h^2)^{3/2}} \qquad \text{...(ii)}$$

When $h = r$, then from Eq.(i)

$$F = \frac{GMm \times r}{(r^2 + r^2)^{3/2}}$$

$$\Rightarrow \quad F = \frac{GMm}{2r\sqrt{2r^2}}$$

and $$F' = \frac{2GMmr}{(r^2 + 4r^2)^{3/2}} = \frac{2GMm}{5r\sqrt{5r^2}} \qquad \text{[From Eq. (ii) substituting } h = r]$$

$$\therefore \quad \frac{F'}{F} = \frac{4\sqrt{2}}{5\sqrt{5}}$$

$$\Rightarrow \quad F' = \frac{4\sqrt{2}}{5\sqrt{5}} F$$

Long Answer Type Questions

Q.34 A star like the sun has several bodies moving around it at different distances. Consider that all of them are moving in circular orbits. Let r be the distance of the body from the centre of the star and let its linear velocity be v, angular velocity ω, kinetic energy K, gravitational potential energy U, total energy E and angular momentum l. As the radius r of the orbit increases, determine which of the above quantities increase and which ones decrease.

Ans. The situation is shown in the diagram, where a body of mass m is revolving around a star of mass M.

Linear velocity of the body $v = \sqrt{\dfrac{GM}{r}}$

$$\Rightarrow \qquad v \propto \frac{1}{\sqrt{r}}$$

Therefore, when r increases, v decreases.

Angular velocity of the body $\omega = \dfrac{2\pi}{T}$

According to Kepler's law of period,

$$T^2 \propto r^3 \Rightarrow T = kr^{3/2}$$

where k is a constant

$$\therefore \qquad \omega = \frac{2\pi}{kr^{3/2}} \Rightarrow \omega \propto \frac{1}{r^{3/2}} \qquad \left[\because \omega = \frac{2\pi}{T}\right]$$

Therefore, when r increases, ω decreases.

Kinetic energy of the body $K = \dfrac{1}{2}mv^2 = \dfrac{1}{2}m \times \dfrac{GM}{r} = \dfrac{GMm}{2r}$

$$\therefore \qquad K \propto \frac{1}{r}$$

Therefore, when r increases, KE decreases.

Gravitational potential energy of the body,

$$U = -\frac{GMm}{r} \Rightarrow U \propto -\frac{1}{r}$$

Therefore, when r increases, PE becomes less negative *i.e.*, increases.

Total energy of the body $\quad E = \text{KE} + \text{PE} = \dfrac{GMm}{2r} + \left(-\dfrac{GMm}{r}\right) = -\dfrac{GMm}{2r}$

Therefore, when r increases, total energy becomes less negative, *i.e.*, increases.

Angular momentum of the body $L = mvr = mr\sqrt{\dfrac{GM}{r}} = m\sqrt{GMr}$

$$\therefore \qquad L \propto \sqrt{r}$$

Therefore, when r increases, angular momentum L increases.

Note In this case, we have not considered the sun-object system as isolated and the force on the system is not zero. So, angular momentum is not conserved.

Q.35 Six point masses of mass m each are at the vertices of a regular hexagon of side l. Calculate the force on any of the masses.

- **Concept Insight** In this problem, we will apply concept of principle of super position i.e. the total gravitational force acting on an object is the vector sum of the force exerted by individual masses on that object.

Ans. Consider the diagram below, in which six point masses are placed at six vertices A, B, C, D, E and F.

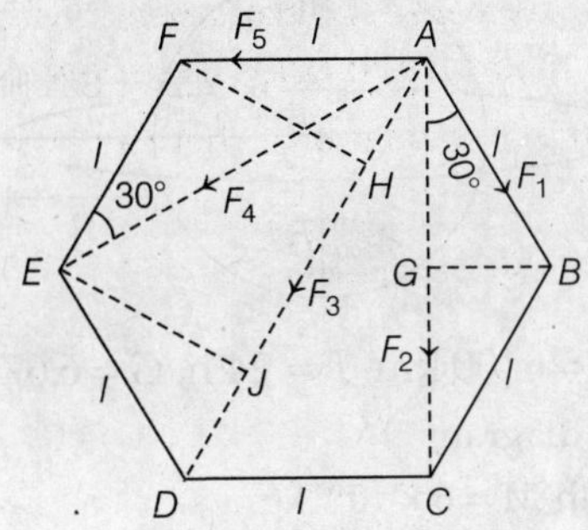

$$AC = AG + GC = 2AG$$
$$= 2l\cos 30° = 2l\sqrt{3}/2 = \sqrt{3}l = AE$$
$$AD = AH + HJ + JD$$
$$= l\sin 30° + l + l\sin 30° = 2l$$

Force on mass m at A due to mass m at B is, $F_1 = \frac{Gmm}{l^2}$ along AB.

Force on mass m at A due to mass m at C is, $F_2 = \frac{Gm \times m}{(\sqrt{3}l)^2} = \frac{Gm^2}{3l^2}$ along AC.

$[\because AC = \sqrt{3}l]$

Force on mass m at A due to mass m at D is, $F_3 = \frac{Gm \times m}{(2l)^2} = \frac{Gm^2}{4l^2}$ along AD.

$[\because AD = 2l]$

Force on mass m at A due to mass m at E is, $F_4 = \frac{Gm \times m}{(\sqrt{3}l)^2} = \frac{Gm^2}{3l^2}$ along AE.

Force on mass m at A due to mass m at F is, $F_5 = \frac{Gm \times m}{l^2} = \frac{Gm^2}{l^2}$ along AF.

Resultant force due to F_1 and F_5 is, $F' = \sqrt{F_1^2 + F_5^2 + 2F_1F_5\cos 120°} = \frac{Gm^2}{l^2}$ along AD.

$[\because$ Angle between F_1 and $F_5 = 120°]$

Resultant force due to F_2 and F_4 is, $F'' = \sqrt{F_2^2 + F_4^2 + 2F_2F_4\cos 60°}$

$$= \frac{\sqrt{3}\,Gm^2}{3l^2} = \frac{Gm^2}{\sqrt{3}l^2} \text{ along } AD.$$

So, net force along $AD = F' + F'' + F_3 = \frac{Gm^2}{l^2} + \frac{Gm^2}{\sqrt{3}l^2} + \frac{Gm^2}{4l^2} = \frac{Gm^2}{l^2}\left(1 + \frac{1}{\sqrt{3}} + \frac{1}{4}\right).$

$$= \frac{Gm}{l^2}\left[\frac{5}{4} + \frac{1}{\sqrt{3}}\right]$$

Q.36 A satellite is to be placed in equatorial geostationary orbit around the earth for communication.

(a) Calculate height of such a satellite.

(b) Find out the minimum number of satellites that are needed to cover entire earth, so that atleast one satellite is visible from any point on the equator.

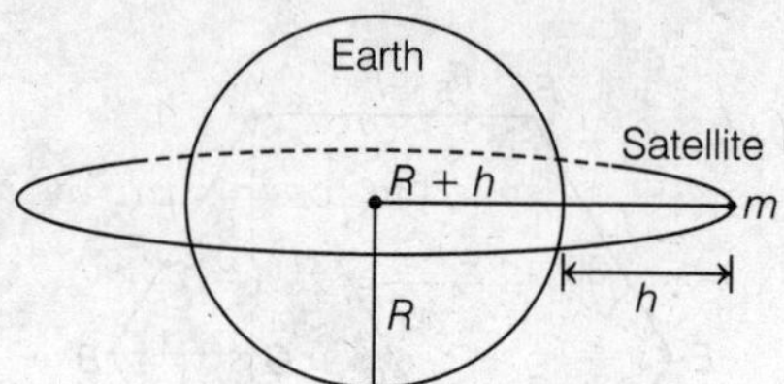

$[M = 6 \times 10^{24}$ kg, $R = 6400$ km, $T = 24$ h, $G = 6.67 \times 10^{-11}$ SI unit]

Ans. Consider the adjacent diagram

Given, mass of the earth $M = 6 \times 10^{24}$ kg

Radius of the earth, $R = 6400 \text{ km} = 6.4 \times 10^6$ m

Time period $T = 24 \text{ h} = 24 \times 60 \times 60 = 86400$ s

$G = 6.67 \times 10^{-11} \text{ N-m}^2/\text{kg}^2$

(a) Time period $T = 2\pi\sqrt{\dfrac{(R+h)^3}{GM}}$ $\left[\because v_o = \sqrt{\dfrac{GM}{R+h}} \text{ and } T = \dfrac{2\pi(R+h)}{v_o}\right]$

$$\Rightarrow \quad T^2 = 4\pi^2 \frac{(R+h)^3}{GM}$$

$$\Rightarrow \quad (R+h)^3 = \frac{T^2 GM}{4\pi^2}$$

$$\Rightarrow \quad R + h = \left(\frac{T^2 GM}{4\pi^2}\right)^{1/3} \Rightarrow h = \left(\frac{T^2 GM}{4\pi^2}\right)^{1/3} - R$$

$$\Rightarrow \quad h = \left[\frac{(24 \times 60 \times 60)^2 \times 6.67 \times 10^{-11} \times 6 \times 10^{24}}{4 \times (3.14)^2}\right]^{1/3} - 6.4 \times 10^6$$

$$= 4.23 \times 10^7 - 6.4 \times 10^6$$

$$= (42.3 - 6.4) \times 10^6 = 35.9 \times 10^6 \text{ m} = 3.59 \times 10^7 \text{ m}$$

(b) If satellite is at height h from the earth's surface, then according to the diagram.

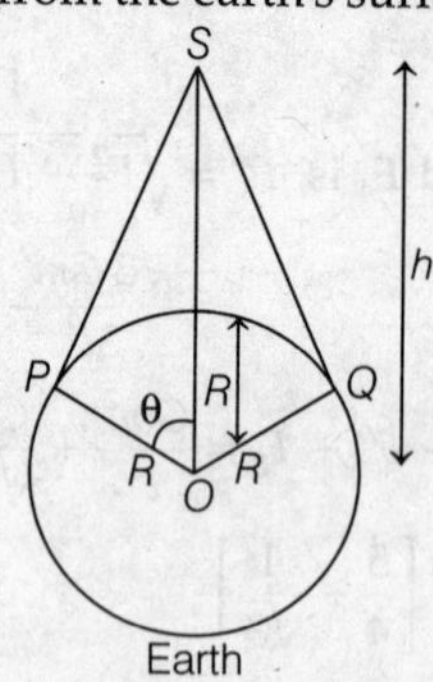

$$\cos\theta = \frac{R}{R+h} = \frac{1}{\left(1+\frac{h}{R}\right)} = \frac{1}{\left(1+\frac{3.59\times10^7}{6.4\times10^6}\right)}$$

$$= \frac{1}{1+5.61} = \frac{1}{6.61} = 0.1513$$

$$\theta = \cos^{-1}(0.1513)$$

$$\theta = 81°18'$$

$\therefore$ $$2\theta = 2\times(81°18') = 162°36'$$

If n is the number of satellites needed to cover entire the earth, then

$$n = \frac{360°}{2\theta} = \frac{360°}{162°36'} = 2.31 \simeq 3$$

$\therefore$ Minimum 3 satellites are required to cover entire the earth.

Q.37 Earth's orbit is an ellipse with eccentricity 0.0167. Thus, the earth's distance from the sun and speed as it moves around the sun varies from day-to-day. This means that the length of the solar day is not constant through the year. Assume that the earth's spin axis is normal to its orbital plane and find out the length of the shortest and the longest day. A day should be taken from noon to noon. Does this explain variation of length of the day during the year?

Thinking Process As the earth orbits the sun, the angular momentum is conserved and areal velocity is constant.

Ans. Consider the diagram. Let m be the mass of the earth, v_p and v_a be the velocity of the earth at perigee and apogee respectively. Similarly, ω_p and ω_a are corresponding angular velocities.

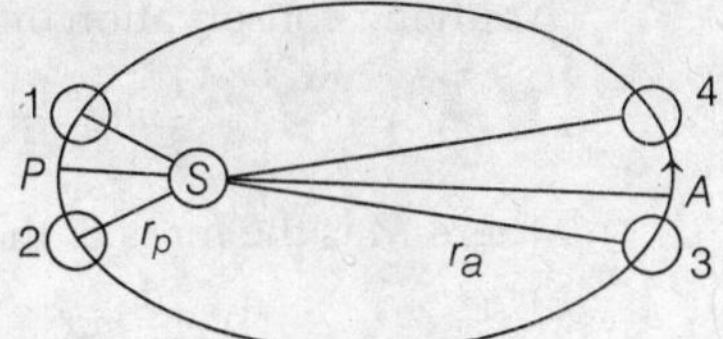

Angular momentum and areal velocity are constant as the earth orbits the sun.

$$Mv_pr_p = Mv_ar_a \Rightarrow r_p^2\,\omega_p = r_a^2\,\omega_a$$

$$\frac{\omega_p}{\omega_a} = \frac{r_a^2}{r_p^2} \quad \text{...(i)}$$

If a is the semi-major axis of the earth's orbit, then $r_p = a(1-e)$ and $r_a = a(1+e)$ ...(ii)

$\therefore$ $$\frac{\omega_p}{\omega_a} = \left(\frac{1+e}{1-e}\right)^2, \; e = 0.0167 \quad \text{[from Eqs. (i) and (ii)]}$$

$\therefore$ $$\frac{\omega_p}{\omega_a} = 1.0691$$

Let ω be angular speed which is geometric mean of ω_p and ω_a and corresponds to mean solar day,

$\therefore$ $$\left(\frac{\omega_p}{\omega}\right)\left(\frac{\omega}{\omega_a}\right) = 1.0691$$

$\therefore$ $$\frac{\omega_p}{\omega} = \frac{\omega}{\omega_a} = 1.034$$

If ω corresponds to 1° per day (mean angular speed), then $\omega_p = 1.034°$ per day and $\omega_a = 0.967°$ per day. Since, $361° = 24$, mean solar day, we get 361.034° which corresponds to 24 h, 8.14″ (8.1″ longer) and 360.967° corresponds to 23 h 59 min 52″ (7.9″ smaller).

This does not explain the actual variation of the length of the day during the year.

Q.38 A satellite is in an elliptic orbit around the earth with aphelion of $6R$ and perihelion of $2R$, where $R = 6400$ km is the radius of the earth. Find eccentricity of the orbit. Find the velocity of the satellite at apogee and perigee. What should be done if this satellite has to be transferred to a circular orbit of radius $6R$? [$G = 6.67 \times 10^{-11}$ SI unit and $M = 6 \times 10^{24}$ kg]

Ans. Given,
$$r_p = \text{radius of perihelion} = 2R$$
$$r_a = \text{radius of apnelion} = 6R$$

Hence, we can write
$$r_a = a(1+e) = 6R \quad \text{...(i)}$$
$$r_p = a(1-e) = 2R \quad \text{...(ii)}$$

Solving Eqs. (i) and (ii), we get eccentricity, $e = \dfrac{1}{2}$

By conservation of angular momentum, angular momentum at perigee = angular momentum at apogee
$$\therefore \quad mv_p r_p = mv_a r_a$$
$$\therefore \quad \frac{v_a}{v_p} = \frac{1}{3}$$

where m is mass of the satellite.

Applying conservation of energy, energy at perigee = energy at apogee
$$\frac{1}{2}mv_p^2 - \frac{GMm}{r_p} = \frac{1}{2}mv_a^2 - \frac{GMm}{r_a}$$

where M is the mass of the earth.
$$\therefore \quad \frac{1}{2}mv_p^2 - \frac{1}{2}mv_a^2 = \frac{GMm}{r_p} - \frac{GMm}{r_a}$$
$$v_p^2 - v_a^2 = 2GM\left[-\frac{1}{r_a} + \frac{1}{r_p}\right]$$
$$v_p^2 \times \left(1 - \frac{1}{9}\right) = 2GM\left[-\frac{1}{6R} + \frac{1}{2R}\right]$$
$$v_p^2 = \frac{9}{8} \times 2GM\left[\frac{1}{3R}\right] = \frac{3}{4}\frac{GM}{R}$$
$$v_p = \sqrt{\frac{3GM}{4R}} = 6.85 \text{ km/s}$$
$$v_p = 6.85 \text{ km/s}, \; v_a = 2.28 \text{ km/s}$$

For circular orbit of radius r,
$$v_c = \text{orbital velocity} = \sqrt{\frac{GM}{r}}$$

For
$$r = 6R, \; v_c = \sqrt{\frac{GM}{6R}} = 3.23 \text{ km/s.}$$

Hence, to transfer to a circular orbit at apogee, we have to boost the velocity by $\Delta = (3.23 - 2.28) = 0.95$ km/s. This can be done by suitably firing rockets from the satellite.

Chapter 08

Mechanical Properties of Solids

Multiple Choice Questions (MCQs)

Q.1 Modulus of rigidity of ideal liquids is

(a) infinity
(b) zero
(c) unity
(d) some finite small non-zero constant value

Ans. *(b)* No frictional (viscous) force exists in case of ideal fluid, hence, tangential forces are zero so there is no stress developed.

Q.2 The maximum load a wire can withstand without breaking, when its length is reduced to half of its original length, will

(a) be double (b) be half (c) be four times (d) remain same

Ans. *(d)* We know that, $\text{Breaking stress} = \dfrac{\text{Breaking force}}{\text{Area of cross - section}}$ ... (i)

When length of the wire changes, area of cross-section remains same.

Hence, breaking force will be same when length changes as breaking stress for given material is constant quantity.

Q.3 The temperature of a wire is doubled. The Young's modulus of elasticity

(a) will also double (b) will become four times
(c) will remain same (d) will decrease

Ans. *(d)* We know that with increase in temperature length of a wire changes as

$$L_t = L_o (1 + \alpha \Delta T)$$

where ΔT is change in the temperature, L_0 is original length, α is coefficient of linear expansion and L_t is Length at temperature T.

Now we can write $\Delta L = L_t - L_o = L_o \alpha \Delta T$

where α is coefficient of linear expansion.

$$\text{Young's modulus } (Y) = \frac{\text{Stress}}{\text{Strain}} = \frac{F L_o}{A \times \Delta L} = \frac{FL_o}{AL_o \alpha \Delta T} \propto \frac{1}{\Delta T}$$

As, $Y \propto \dfrac{1}{\Delta T}$

When temperature ΔT increases hence, Y decreases.

Q.4 A spring is stretched by applying a load to its free end. The strain produced in the spring is

(a) volumetric (b) shear
(c) longitudinal and shear (d) longitudinal

Ans. *(c)* Consider the diagram where a spring is stretched by applying a load to its free end. Clearly the length and shape of the spring changes.

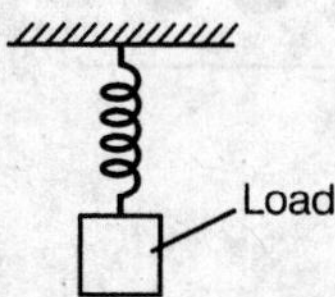

The change in length corresponds to longitudinal strain and change in shape corresponds to shearing strain.

Q.5 A rigid bar of mass M is supported symmetrically by three wires each of length l. Those at each end are of copper and the middle one is of iron. The ratio of their diameters, if each is to have the same tension, is equal to

(a) Y_{copper} / Y_{iron} (b) $\sqrt{\dfrac{Y_{iron}}{Y_{copper}}}$ (c) $\dfrac{Y^2_{iron}}{Y^2_{copper}}$ (d) $\dfrac{Y_{iron}}{Y_{copper}}$

Ans. *(b)* Let T be the tension in each wire is D, then

$$Y = \frac{\text{Stress}}{\text{Strain}} = \frac{F/A}{\Delta L/L} = F/A \times \frac{L}{\Delta L}$$

$$Y = \frac{F}{\pi (D/2)^2} \times \frac{L}{\Delta L} = \frac{4\,FL}{\pi\, D^2 \Delta L}$$

$$\Rightarrow \quad D^2 = \frac{4\,FL}{\pi\, \Delta L Y} \quad \Rightarrow \quad D = \sqrt{\frac{4\,FL}{\pi \Delta L Y}}$$

As F and $\dfrac{L}{\Delta L}$ are constants. [Given]

Hence, $D \propto \sqrt{\dfrac{1}{Y}}$ or $D = \dfrac{K}{\sqrt{Y}}$

$\therefore$ K is the proportionality constant.

Now, we can find ratio as $\dfrac{D_{copper}}{D_{iron}} = \sqrt{\dfrac{Y_{iron}}{Y_{copper}}}$

Q.6 A mild steel wire of length $2L$ and cross-sectional area A is stretched, well within elastic limit, horizontally between two pillars (figure). A mass m is suspended from the mid-point of the wire. Strain in the wire is

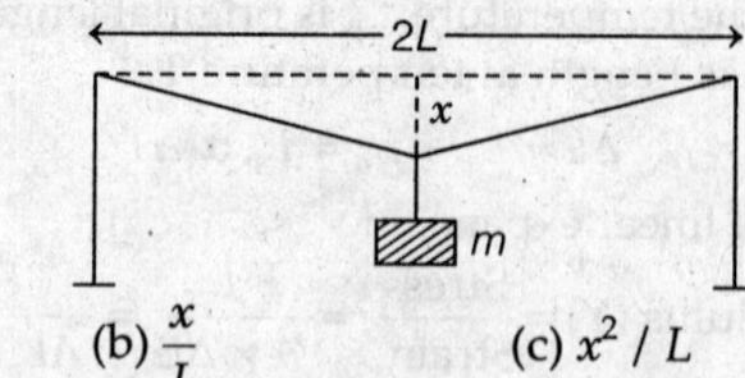

(a) $\dfrac{x^2}{2L^2}$ (b) $\dfrac{x}{L}$ (c) x^2 / L (d) $x^2 / 2L$

Thinking Process We will assume the vertical displacement x to be very small compared to L. Change in the length will be calculated by difference of final total length and initial length $2L$.

Ans. (a) Consider the diagram below

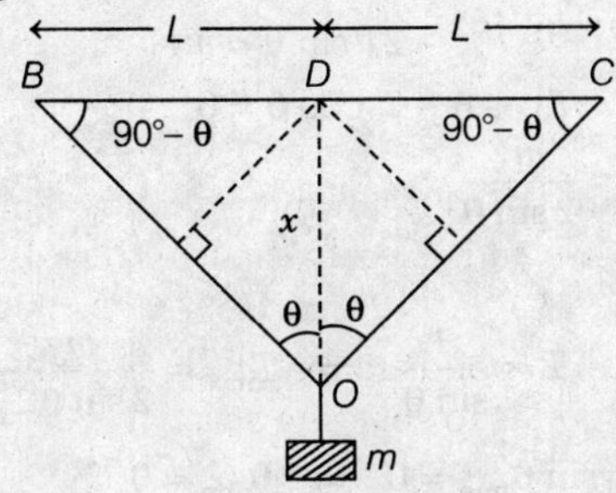

Hence, change in length

$$\Delta L = BO + OC - (BD + DC)$$
$$= 2BO - 2BD \qquad [\because BO = OC, BD = DC]$$
$$= 2[BO - BD]$$
$$= 2[(x^2 + L^2)^{1/2} - L] = 2\left[L\left(\frac{x^2}{L^2} + 1\right)^{1/2} - L\right]$$
$$= 2L\left[\left(1 + \frac{x^2}{L^2}\right)^{1/2} - 1\right] \approx 2L\left[1 + \frac{1}{2}\frac{x^2}{L^2} - 1\right] = \frac{x^2}{L}$$

[$\because x << L$, so higher terms are neglected]

$$\therefore \qquad \text{Strain} = \frac{\Delta L}{2L} = \frac{x^2/L}{2L} = \frac{x^2}{2L^2}$$

Q.7 A rectangular frame is to be suspended symmetrically by two strings of equal length on two supports (figure). It can be done in one of the following three ways;

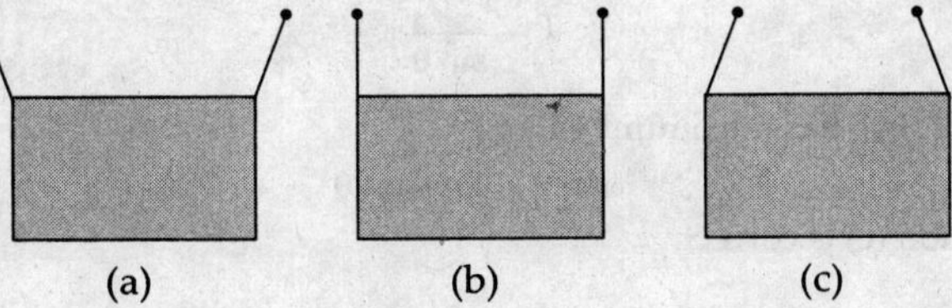

The tension in the strings will be

(a) the same in all cases
(b) least in (a)
(c) least in (b)
(d) least in (c)

Ans. (c) Consider the FBD diagram of the rectangular frame

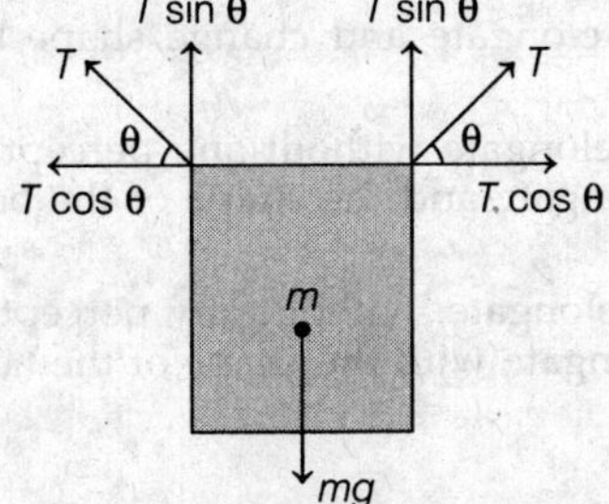

Balancing vertical forces $2T \sin \theta - mg = 0$ [T is tension in the string]

$\Rightarrow$ $$2T \sin \theta = mg \quad ...(i)$$

Total horizontal force $= T \cos \theta - T \cos \theta = 0$

Now from Eq. (i), $T = \dfrac{mg}{2 \sin \theta}$

As mg is constant

$\Rightarrow$ $$T \propto \frac{1}{\sin \theta} \Rightarrow T_{max} = \frac{mg}{2 \sin \theta_{min}}$$

$$\sin \theta_{min} = 0 \Rightarrow \theta_{min} = 0$$

No option matches with $\theta = 0°$

$$T_{min} = \frac{mg}{2 \sin \theta_{max}} \quad (\text{since, } \sin \theta_{max} = 1)$$

$$\sin \theta_{max} = 1 \Rightarrow \theta = 90°$$

Matches with option (c)

Hence, tension is least for the case (b).

Mistake Alert ! *We should be careful when measuring the angle, it must be in the direction as given in the diagram.*

Alternate Method

Let M be the mass of rectangular frame and θ be the angle which the tension T in the string makes with the horizontal as shown in the figure.

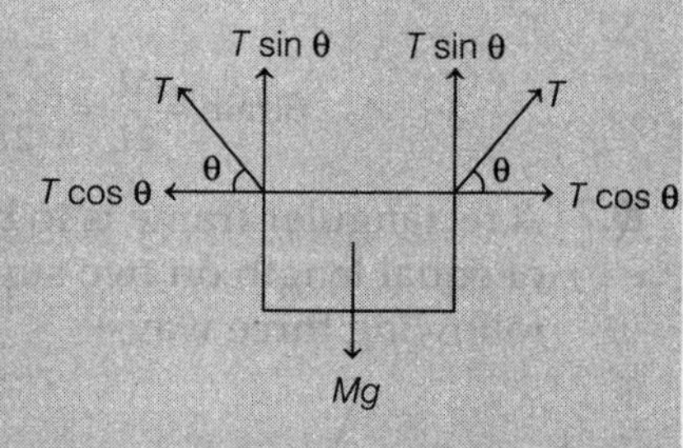

$\therefore$ $$2T \sin\theta = Mg$$

or $$T = \frac{Mg}{2\sin\theta}$$

or $$T \propto \frac{1}{\sin \theta}$$

T is least if $\sin \theta$ has maximum value i.e.

$$\sin \theta = 1 = \sin 90°$$

Thus, option (c) is correct.

Q.8 Consider two cylindrical rods of identical dimensions, one of rubber and the other of steel. Both the rods are fixed rigidly at one end to the roof. A mass M is attached to each of the free ends at the centre of the rods.

(a) Both the rods will elongate but there shall be no perceptible change in shape.

(b) The steel rod will elongate and change shape but the rubber rod will only elongate.

(c) The steel rod will elongate without any perceptible change in shape, but the rubber rod will elongate and the shape of the bottom edge will change to an ellipse.

(d) The steel rod will elongate, without any perceptible change in shape, but the rubber rod will elongate with the shape of the bottom edge tapered to a tip at the centre.

Ans. ***(d)*** Consider the diagram.

A mass M is attached at the centre. As the mass is attached to both the rods, both rod will be elongated due to action and reaction force but due to different elastic properties of material rubber changes shape also.

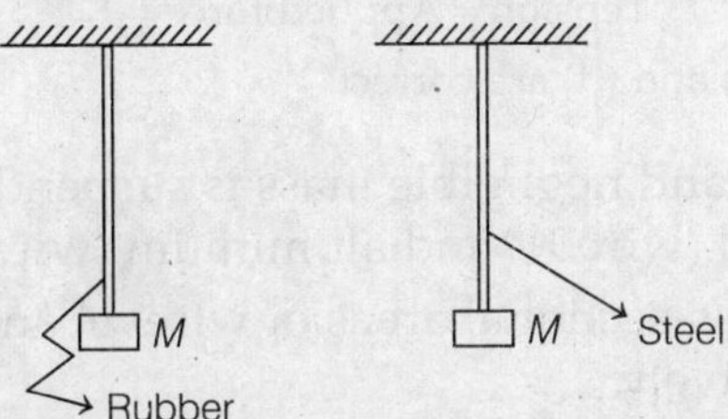

Multiple Choice Questions (More Than One Options)

Q.9 The stress-strain graphs for two materials are shown in figure. (assume same scale)

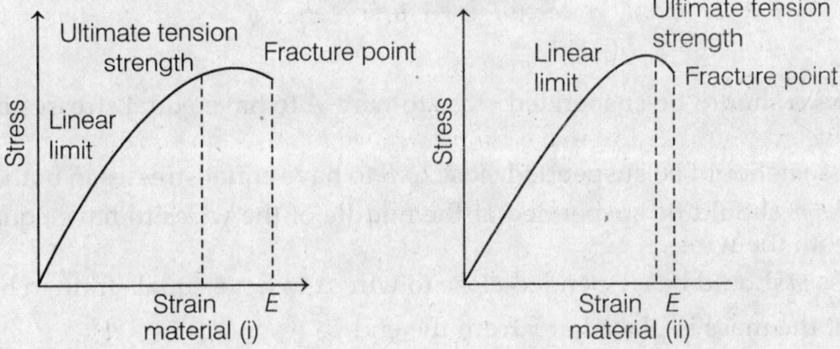

(a) Material (ii) is more elastic than material (i) and hence material (ii) is more brittle.

(b) Material (i) and (ii) have the same elasticity and the same brittleness.

(c) Material (ii) is elastic over a larger region of strain as compared to (i).

(d) Material (ii) is more brittle than material (i).

Thinking Process We have to compare ultimate tensile strength for each material. Material having more ultimate tensile strength will be elastic over larger region.

Ans. ***(c, d)*** It is clear from the two graphs, the ultimate tensile strength for material (ii) is greater (slope of stress versus strain graph is more) hence material (ii) is elastic over larger region as compared to material (i).

For material (ii) fracture point is nearer, hence it is more brittle.

Q.10 A wire is suspended from the ceiling and stretched under the action of a weight F suspended from its other end. The force exerted by the ceiling on it is equal and opposite to the weight.

(a) Tensile stress at any cross-section A of the wire is F/A.

(b) Tensile stress at any cross-section is zero.

(c) Tensile stress at any cross-section A of the wire is $2F/A$.

(d) Tension at any cross-section A of the wire is F.

Ans. ***(a, d)*** As shown in the diagram

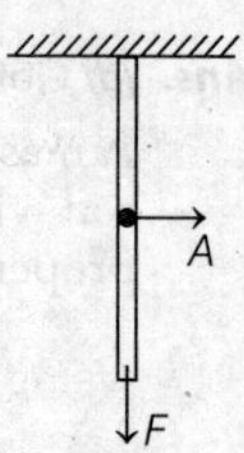

Clearly, forces at each cross-section is F.

Now applying formula, $\text{Stress} = \dfrac{\text{Tension}}{\text{Area}} = \dfrac{F}{A}$

We know that, Tension = Applied force = F

Therefore, option (a) and (d) are correct.

Q.11 A rod of length l and negligible mass is suspended at its two ends by two wires of steel (wire A) and aluminium (wire B) of equal lengths (figure). The cross-sectional areas of wires A and B are 1.0 mm^2 and 2.0 mm^2, respectively.

$(Y_{Al} = 70 \times 10^9 \text{Nm}^{-2}$ and $Y_{steel} = 200 \times 10^9 \text{Nm}^{-2})$

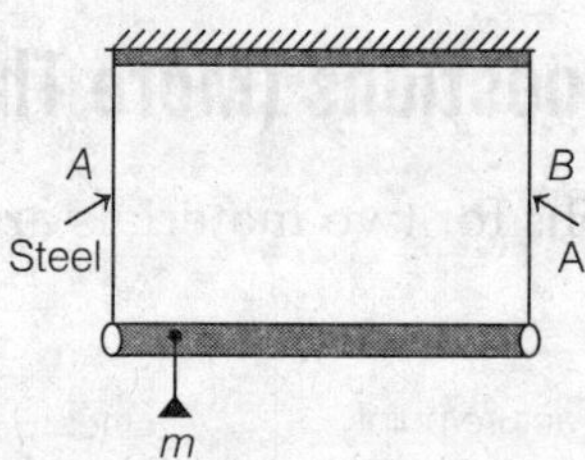

(a) Mass m should be suspended close to wire A to have equal stresses in both the wires.

(b) Mass m should be suspended close to B to have equal stresses in both the wires.

(c) Mass m should be suspended at the middle of the wires to have equal stresses in both the wires.

(d) Mass m should be suspended close to wire A to have equal strain in both wires.

Ans. ***(b, d)*** Let the mass is placed at x from the end B.

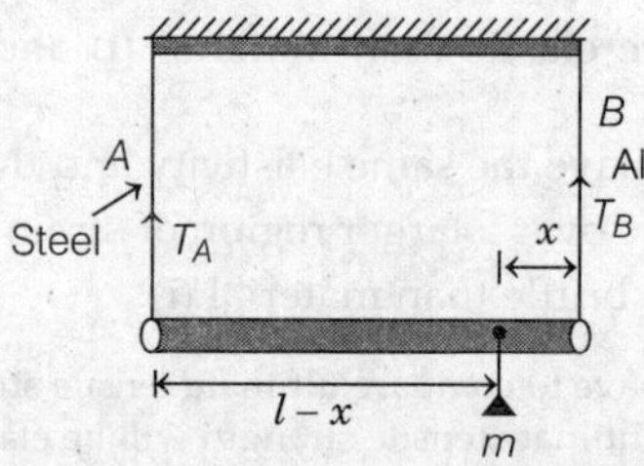

Let T_A and T_B be the tensions in wire A and wire B respectively.

For the rotational equilibrium of the system,

$$\Sigma \tau = 0 \qquad \text{[Total torque = 0]}$$

$$\Rightarrow \quad T_B x - T_A (l - x) = 0$$

$$\Rightarrow \quad \frac{T_B}{T_A} = \frac{l - x}{x} \qquad \text{...(i)}$$

$$\text{Stress in wire } A = S_A = \frac{T_A}{a_A}$$

$$\text{Stress in wire } B = S_B = \frac{T_B}{a_B}$$

where a_A and a_B are cross-sectional areas of wire A and B respectively.

By question $a_B = 2\,a_A$

Now, **for equal stress** $S_A = S_B$

$$\Rightarrow \frac{T_A}{a_A} = \frac{T_B}{a_B} \Rightarrow \frac{T_B}{T_A} = \frac{a_B}{a_A} = 2 \quad \text{...(ii)}$$

Using equation (ii), equation (i) becomes

$$\Rightarrow \frac{l-x}{x} = 2 \Rightarrow \frac{l}{x} - 1 = 2$$

$$\Rightarrow x = \frac{l}{3} \Rightarrow l - x = l - l/3 = \frac{2\,l}{3}$$

Hence, mass m should be placed closer to B.

For equal strain, $(\text{strain})_A = (\text{strain})_B$

$$\Rightarrow \frac{(Y_A)}{S_A} = \frac{Y_B}{S_B} \quad \text{[where } Y_A \text{ and } Y_B \text{ are Young modulii]}$$

$$\Rightarrow \frac{Y_{\text{steel}}}{T_A/a_A} = \frac{Y_{\text{Al}}}{T_B/a_B}$$

$$\Rightarrow \frac{Y_{\text{steel}}}{Y_{\text{Al}}} = \frac{T_A}{T_B} \times \frac{a_B}{a_A} = \left(\frac{x}{l-x}\right)\left(\frac{2a_A}{a_A}\right)$$

$$\Rightarrow \frac{200 \times 10^9}{70 \times 10^9} = \frac{2x}{l-x} \Rightarrow \frac{20}{7} = \frac{2x}{l-x}$$

$$\Rightarrow \frac{10}{7} = \frac{x}{l-x} \Rightarrow 10l - 10x = 7x$$

$$\Rightarrow 17x = 10l \Rightarrow x = \frac{10\,l}{17}$$

$$l - x = l - \frac{10l}{17} = \frac{7l}{17}$$

Hence, mass m should be placed closer to wire A.

Q.12 For an ideal liquid,

(a) the bulk modulus is infinite (b) the bulk modulus is zero

(c) the shear modulus is infinite (d) the shear modulus is zero

Ans. ***(a, d)*** The property of an ideal liquid is that it is not compressible.

Hence, change in volume, $\Delta V = 0$

$$\text{Bulk modulus } B = \frac{\text{Stress}}{\text{Volume strain}} = \frac{F/A}{\Delta V/V} = \frac{F}{A} \times \frac{V}{\Delta V} = \infty$$

$$\text{Compressibility, } K = \frac{1}{B} = \frac{1}{\infty} = 0$$

As there is no tangential (viscous) force exists in case of an ideal fluid, hence, shear modulus = 0.

Q.13 A copper and a steel wire of the same diameter are connected end to end. A deforming force F is applied to this composite wire which causes a total elongation of 1 cm. The two wires will have

(a) the same stress (b) different stress

(c) the same strain (d) different strain

Ans. *(a, d)* Consider the diagram where a deforming force F is applied to the combination.

$$\text{For steel wire, } Y_{\text{steel}} = \frac{\text{Stress}}{\text{Strain}} = \frac{F/A}{\text{Strain}}$$

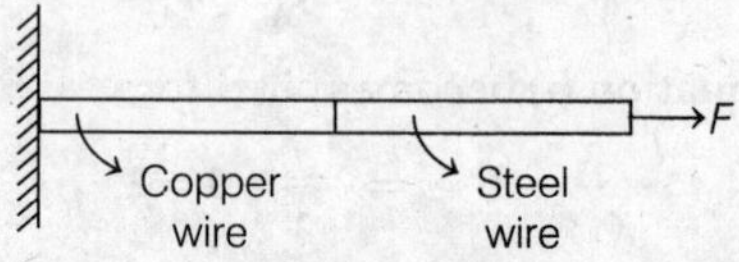

where F is tension in each wire and A is cross-section area of each wires.

As F and A are same for both the wire, hence, stress will be same for both the wire. i.e. option (a)

Now, $$(\text{Strain})_{\text{steel}} = \frac{\text{Stress}}{Y_{\text{steel}}}, (\text{Strain})_{\text{copper}} = \frac{\text{Stress}}{Y_{\text{copper}}}$$

As, $$Y_{\text{steel}} \neq Y_{\text{copper}}$$

Hence, the two wires will have differents strain.

Alternate Method

We know, $$\text{Stress} = \frac{F}{A}, \text{Strain} = \frac{\text{Stress}}{Y}$$

Both wires have same diameter i.e. they have same cross sectional area.

It deforming force, F is same on the wire, the equal stress will be developed.

For some stress, strain $\propto \frac{1}{Y}$. So, two wire will have different strain due to different value of Y.

Very Short Answer Type Questions

Q.14 The Young's modulus for steel is much more than that for rubber. For the same longitudinal strain, which one will have greater tensile stress?

Ans. $$\text{Young's modulus } (Y) = \frac{\text{Stress}}{\text{Longitudinal strain}}$$

For same longitudinal strain, $Y \propto$ stress

$$\therefore \quad \frac{Y_{\text{steel}}}{Y_{\text{rubber}}} = \frac{(\text{stress})_{\text{steel}}}{(\text{stress})_{\text{rubber}}} \quad \text{...(i)}$$

But $$Y_{\text{steel}} > Y_{\text{rubber}}$$

$$\therefore \quad (\text{stress})_{\text{steel}} > (\text{stress})_{\text{rubber}}$$

Hence, for same longitudinal strain, steel will have greater tensile stress than that of rubber.

Q.15 Is stress a vector quantity?

Ans. $$\text{Stress} = \frac{\text{Magnitude of internal reaction force}}{\text{Area of cross - section}}$$

Therefore, stress is a scalar quantity not a vector quantity.

Q.16 Identical springs of steel and copper are equally stretched. On which, more work will have to be done?

Ans. Work done in stretching a wire is given by $W = \frac{1}{2} F \times \Delta l$

[where F is applicd force and Δl is extension in the wire]

As $$Y = \frac{FL}{A\Delta l} \Rightarrow F = \frac{YA\Delta l}{L}$$

$\therefore$ $$W = \frac{1}{2}\frac{YA\Delta l^2}{L}$$

For identical springs which are equally streched

$\therefore$ $$W \propto Y$$

Hence, more work will be done in steel wire $(Y_S > Y_{cu})$

Alternate Method

In stretching a wire, work is done against internal restoring forces. This work is stored in the wire as elastic potential energy or strain energy.

$$\text{Work done} = \frac{1}{2} \times \text{stress} \times \text{strain}$$
$$= \frac{1}{2} \times Y \times (\text{strain})^2$$

Since, elasticity of steel is more than copper, hence more work has to be done in order to stretch the steel.

Q.17 What is the Young's modulus for a perfect rigid body?

Ans. Young's modulus $(Y) = \frac{F}{A} \times \frac{l}{\Delta l}$

For a perfectly rigid body, change in length $\Delta l = 0$

$\therefore$ $$Y = \frac{F}{A} \times \frac{l}{0} = \infty$$

Therefore, Young's modulus for a perfectly rigid body is infinite(∞).

Q.18 What is the Bulk modulus for a perfect rigid body?

Ans. Bulk modulus $(K) = \frac{p}{\Delta V / V} = \frac{pV}{\Delta V}$

For perfectly rigid body, change in volume $\Delta V = 0$

$\therefore$ $$K = \frac{pV}{0} = \infty$$

Therefore, bulk modulus for a perfectly rigid body is infinity (∞).

Q.19 A wire of length L and radius r is clamped rigidly at one end. When the other end of the wire is pulled by a force f, its length increases by l. Another wire of the same material of length $2L$ and radius $2r$, is pulled by a force $2f$. Find the increase in length of this wire.

- **Concept Insight** In this problem, we apply the concept of Hooke's law which states that within elastic limit, the stress developed is directly proportional to the strain produced in a body.

  i.e. $$\text{stress} = Y \times \text{strain}$$

Ans. The situation is shown in the diagram.

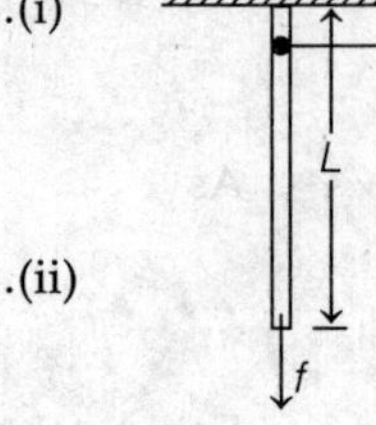

Now, Young's modulus $(Y) = \dfrac{f}{A} \times \dfrac{L}{l}$

For first wire, $Y = \dfrac{f}{\pi r^2} \times \dfrac{L}{l}$ ...(i)

For second wire, $Y = \dfrac{2f}{\pi(2r)^2} \times \dfrac{2L}{l'}$

$= \dfrac{f}{\pi r^2} \times \dfrac{L}{l'}$ ...(ii)

From Eqs. (i) and (ii), $\dfrac{f}{\pi r^2} \times \dfrac{L}{l} = \dfrac{f}{\pi r^2} \times \dfrac{L}{l'}$

$\therefore \quad l = l'$

[$\because$ Both wires are of same material, hence, Young's modulus will be same.]

Q. 20 A steel rod ($Y = 2.0 \times 10^{11}$ N/m^2 and $\alpha = 10^{-5}$ °C^{-1}) of length 1 m and area of cross-section 1 cm^2 is heated from 0°C to 200° C, without being allowed to extend or bend. What is the tension produced in the rod?

Thinking Process Due to increase in temperature of the rod, length, increases. The equation of thermal expansion for linear expansion will be applied.

Ans. Given, Young's modulus of steel $Y = 2.0 \times 10^{11}$ N/m^2

Coefficient of thermal expansion $\alpha = 10^{-5}$ °C^{-1}

Length $l = 1$ m

Area of cross-section $A = 1\,\text{cm}^2 = 1 \times 10^{-4}\,\text{m}^2$

Increase in temperature $\Delta t = 200°\text{C} - 0°\text{C} = 200°\text{C}$

Tension produced in steel rod $(F) = YA\alpha\Delta t$

$= 2.0 \times 10^{11} \times 1 \times 10^{-4} \times 10^{-5} \times 200 \quad \left[Y = \dfrac{FL}{A\Delta l} = \dfrac{FL}{AL\alpha\,\Delta t}\right]$

$= 4 \times 10^4$ N

Q.21 To what depth must a rubber ball be taken in deep sea so that its volume is decreased by 0.1%. (The bulk modulus of rubber is 9.8×10^8 N/m^2; and the density of sea water is 10^3 kg/m^3)

Ans. Given, Bulk modulus of rubber $(K) = 9.8 \times 10^8$ N / m^2

Density of sea water $(\rho) = 10^3$ kg/m^3

Percentage decrease in volume, $\left(\dfrac{\Delta V}{V} \times 100\right) = 0.1 \Rightarrow \dfrac{\Delta V}{V} = \dfrac{0.1}{100}$

$\Rightarrow \quad \dfrac{\Delta V}{V} = \dfrac{1}{1000}$

Let the rubber ball be taken upto depth h.

$\therefore$ Change in pressure $(p) = h\rho g$

$\therefore$ Bulk modulus $(K) = \left|\dfrac{p}{\Delta V / V}\right| = \dfrac{h\rho g}{(\Delta V / V)}$

$\Rightarrow \quad h = \dfrac{K \times (\Delta V / V)}{\rho g} = \dfrac{9.8 \times 10^8 \times \dfrac{1}{1000}}{10^3 \times 9.8} = 100\,\text{m}$

Q.22 A truck is pulling a car out of a ditch by means of a steel cable that is 9.1 m long and has a radius of 5 mm. When the car just begins to move, the tension in the cable is 800 N. How much has the cable stretched? (Young's modulus for steel is 2×10^{11} N/m^2)

Ans. Length of steel cable $l = 9.1\,\text{m}$

$$\text{Radius } r = 5\,\text{mm} = 5\times10^{-3}\text{ m}$$

$$\text{Tension in the cable } F = 800\,\text{N}$$

$$\text{Young's modulus for steel } Y = 2\times10^{11}\,\text{N/m}^2$$

$$\text{Change in length } \Delta l = ?$$

$$\text{Young's modulus } (Y) = \frac{F}{A}\times\frac{l}{\Delta l}$$

$$\Rightarrow \quad \Delta l = \frac{F}{\pi r^2}\times\frac{l}{Y}$$

$$= \frac{800}{3.14\times(5\times10^{-3})^2}\times\frac{9.1}{2\times10^{11}}$$

$$= 4.64\times10^{-4}\text{ m}$$

Q.23 Two identical solid balls, one of ivory and the other of wet-clay, are dropped from the same height on the floor. Which one will rise to a greater height after striking the floor and why?

Ans. Since, ivory ball is more elastic than wet-clay ball, therefore, ivory ball tries to regain its original shape quickly. Hence, more energy and momentum is transferred to the ivory ball in comparison to the wet clay ball and therefore, ivory ball will rise higher after striking the floor.

Long Answer Type Questions

Q.24 Consider a long steel bar under a tensile stress due to forces F acting at the edges along the length of the bar (figure). Consider a plane making an angle θ with the length. What are the tensile and shearing stresses on this plane?

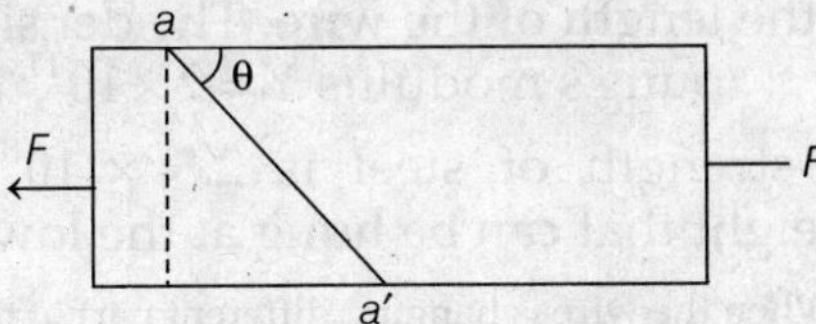

(a) For what angle is the tensile stress a maximum?
(b) For what angle is the shearing stress a maximum?

Thinking Process To solve this question, we have to resolve the force along and perpendicular to the inclined plane. Now, we can easily calculate the tensile and shearing stress.

Ans. Consider the adjacent diagram.

Let the cross-sectional area of the bar be A. Consider the equilibrium of the plane aa'.

A force F must be acting on this plane making an angle $\frac{\pi}{2}-\theta$ with the normal ON.

Resolving F into components, along the plane (i.e. parallel, P) and normal (N) to the plane.

$$F_P = F\cos\theta$$
$$F_N = F\sin\theta$$

Let the area of the face aa' be A', then

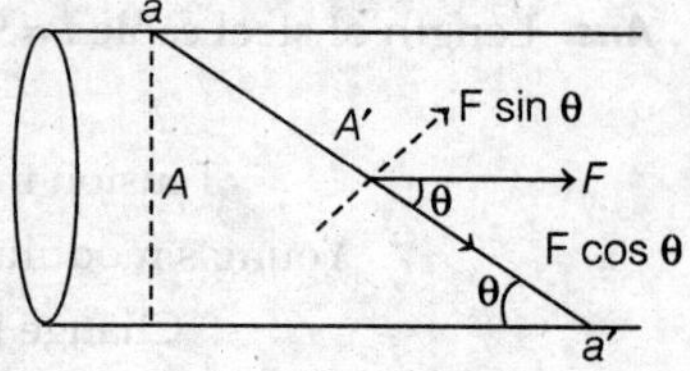

$$\frac{A}{A'} = \sin\theta$$

$$\therefore \quad A' = \frac{A}{\sin\theta}$$

$$\text{The tensile stress} = \frac{\text{Normal force}}{\text{Area}} = \frac{F\sin\theta}{A'}$$

$$= \frac{F\sin\theta}{A/\sin\theta} = \frac{F}{A}\sin^2\theta$$

$$\text{Shearing stress} = \frac{\text{Parallel force}}{\text{Area}} = \frac{F\cos\theta}{A/\sin\theta} = \frac{F}{A}\sin\theta.\cos\theta$$

$$= \frac{F}{2A}(2\sin\theta.\cos\theta) = \frac{F}{2A}\sin 2\theta$$

(a) For tensile stress to be maximum, $\sin^2\theta = 1$

$$\Rightarrow \quad \sin\theta = 1 \Rightarrow \theta = \frac{\pi}{2}$$

(b) For shearing stress to be maximum,

$$\sin 2\theta = 1$$

$$\Rightarrow \quad 2\theta = \frac{\pi}{2} \Rightarrow \theta = \frac{\pi}{4}$$

Note We must not apply the formula for stress directly, forces must be resolved.

Q.25 (a) A steel wire of mass μ per unit length with a circular cross-section has a radius of 0.1 cm. The wire is of length 10 m when measured lying horizontal, and hangs from a hook on the wall. A mass of 25 kg is hung from the free end of the wire. Assuming, the wire to be uniform and lateral strains << longitudinal strains, find the extension in the length of the wire. The density of steel is 7860 kg m^{-3}. (Young's modulus $Y = 2 \times 10^{11}$ Nm^{-2}.)

(b) If the yield strength of steel is 2.5×10^8 Nm^{-2}, what is the maximum weight that can be hung at the lower end of the wire?

Thinking Process When the wire is hanging different part of the wire will be acted upon by different forces. To find the tension due to whole wire, consider a small element and find the tension there and then integrate for the whole wire.

Ans. Consider the diagram when a small element of length dx is considered at x from the load ($x = 0$).

(a) Let $T(x)$ and $T(x + dx)$ are tensions on the two cross-sections a distance dx apart, then $T[x + dx] - T(x) = dmg = \mu g\, dx$ (where μ is the mass/length).

$$[\because dm = \mu dx]$$

$$dT = \mu g dx \qquad [\because dT = T(x + dx) - T(x)]$$

$$\Rightarrow \quad T(x) = \mu g x + C \qquad \text{[on integrating]}$$

At $x = 0$, $T(0) = Mg \Rightarrow C = Mg$

$\therefore$ $T(x) = \mu gx + Mg$

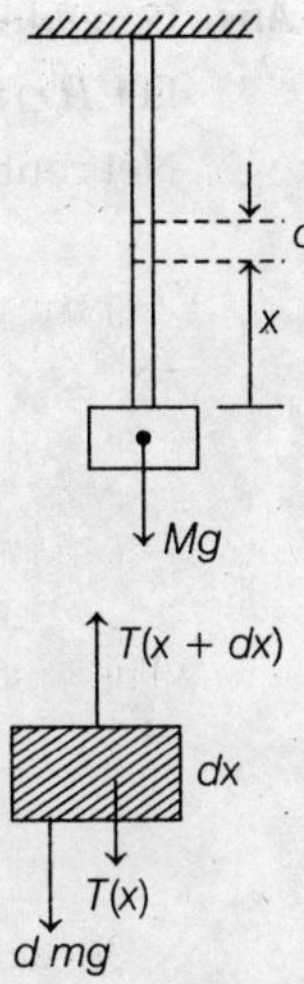

Let the length dx at x increase by dr, then

$$\text{Young's modulus } Y = \frac{\text{Stress}}{\text{Strain}}$$

$$\frac{T(x)/A}{dr/dx} = Y$$

$$\Rightarrow \quad \frac{dr}{dx} = \frac{1}{YA}T(x)$$

$$\Rightarrow \quad r = \frac{1}{YA}\int_0^L (\mu gx + Mg)\,dx$$

$$= \frac{1}{YA}\left[\frac{\mu gx^2}{2} + Mgx\right]_0^L$$

$$= \frac{1}{YA}\left[\frac{\mu gL^2}{2} + MgL\right]$$

$$= \frac{1}{YA}\left[\frac{mgL}{2} + MgL\right] \quad [m \text{ is the mass of the wire}]$$

dx, x, Mg, T(x + dx), dx, T(x), d mg

$$A = \pi \times (10^{-3})^2 \text{ m}^2$$

$$Y = 2 \times 10^{11} \text{ Nm}^{-2}$$

$$m = \pi \times (10^{-3})^2 \times 10 \times 7860 \text{ kg}$$

$$\therefore \quad r = \frac{1}{2 \times 10^{11} \times \pi \times 10^{-6}}\left[\frac{\pi \times 786 \times 10^{-4} \times 10 \times 10}{2} + 25 \times 10 \times 10\right]$$

$$= [196.5 \times 10^{-6} + 3.98 \times 10^{-3}] \approx 4 \times 10^{-3} \text{m}$$

(b) Clearly tension will be maximum at $x = L$

$$\therefore \quad T = \mu gL + Mg = (m + M)g \quad [\because m = \mu L]$$

The yield force = (Yield strength Y) area $= 250 \times 10^6 \times \pi \times (10^{-3})^2 = 250 \times \pi$ N

At yield point $\quad T =$ Yield force

$$\Rightarrow \quad (m + M)g = 250 \times \pi$$

$$m = \pi \times (10^{-3})^2 \times 10 \times 7860 << M$$

$$\therefore \quad Mg \approx 250 \times \pi$$

Hence, $$M = \frac{250 \times \pi}{10} = 25 \times \pi \approx 78.5 \text{ kg.}$$

Q.26 A steel rod of length $2l$, cross-sectional area A and mass M is set rotating in a horizontal plane about an axis passing through the centre. If Y is the Young's modulus for steel, find the extension in the length of the rod. (assume the rod is uniform)

Thinking Process To solve this question, we have to consider a small element, find tension in the rod at this element and then calculate for the whole rod.

Ans. Consider an element of width dr at r as shown in the diagram.

Let $T(r)$ and $T(r + dr)$ be the tensions at r and $r + dr$ respectively.

Net centrifugal force on the element $= \omega^2 r\,dm$

[where ω is angular velocity of the rod]

$$= \omega^2 r \mu dr \qquad [\because \mu = \text{mass/length}]$$

$$\Rightarrow \quad T(r) - T(r + dr) = \mu\, \omega^2 r dr \;\Rightarrow\; -dT = \mu\omega^2 r dr$$

[$\because$ Tension and centrifugal forces are opposite]

$$\therefore \quad -\int_{T=0}^{T} dT = \int_{r=l}^{r=r} \mu\omega^2 r dr \qquad [\because T = 0 \text{ at } r = l]$$

$$\Rightarrow \quad T(r) = \frac{\mu\omega^2}{2}(l^2 - r^2)$$

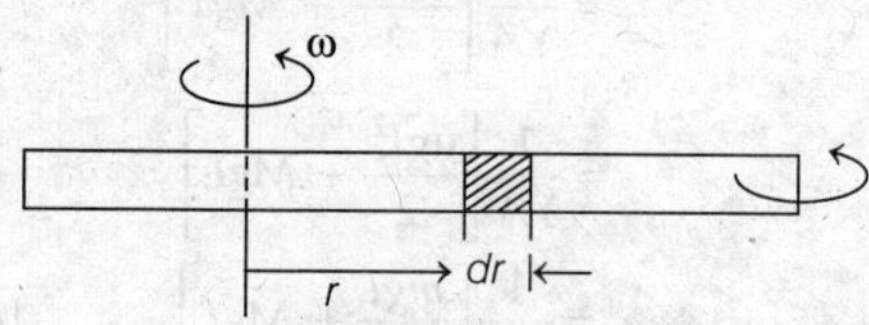

Let the increase in length of the element dr be Δr

So, Young's modulus $Y = \dfrac{\text{Stress}}{\text{Strain}} = \dfrac{T(r)/A}{\dfrac{\Delta r}{dr}}$

ω²r dm ω² (r + dr)

$$\therefore \quad \frac{\Delta r}{dr} = \frac{T(r)}{YA} = \frac{\mu\omega^2}{2YA}(l^2 - r^2)$$

$$\therefore \quad \Delta r = \frac{1}{YA}\frac{\mu\omega^2}{2}(l^2 - r^2)\,dr$$

$$\therefore \quad \Delta = \text{change in length in right part} = \frac{1}{YA}\frac{\mu\omega^2}{2}\int_0^l (l^2 - r^2)\,dr$$

$$= \left(\frac{1}{YA}\right)\frac{\mu\omega^2}{2}\left[l^3 - \frac{l^3}{3}\right] = \frac{1}{3YA}\mu\omega^2 l^2$$

$$\therefore \quad \text{Total change in length} = 2\Delta = \frac{2}{3YA}\mu\omega^2 l^2$$

Q.27 In nature, the failure of structural members usually result from large torque because of twisting or bending rather than due to tensile or compressive strains. This process of structural breakdown is called buckling and in cases of tall cylindrical structures like trees, the torque is caused by its own weight bending the structure. Thus, the vertical through the centre of gravity does not fall within the base. The elastic torque caused because of this bending about the central axis of the tree is given by $\dfrac{Y\pi r^4}{4R}$. Y is the Young's modulus, r is the radius of the trunk and R is the radius of curvature of the bent surface along the height of the tree containing the centre of gravity (the neutral surface). Estimate the critical height of a tree for a given radius of the trunk.

Thinking Process In this question, the elastic torque is given we have to find the torque caused by the weight due to bending and equate with the given value.

Ans. Consider the diagram according to the question, the bending torque on the trunk of radius r of the tree $= \dfrac{Y\pi r^4}{4R}$

where R is the radius of curvature of the bent surface.

When the tree is about to buckle $Wd = \dfrac{Y\pi r^4}{4R}$

If $R \gg h$, then the centre of gravity is at a height $l \approx \dfrac{1}{2}h$ from the ground.

From ΔABC $\quad R^2 \simeq (R-d)^2 + \left(\dfrac{1}{2}h\right)^2$

if $d \ll R$, $\quad R^2 \simeq R^2 - 2Rd + \dfrac{1}{4}h^2$

$$\therefore \quad d = \frac{h^2}{8R}$$

If ω_0 is the weight/volume

$$\frac{Y\pi r^4}{4R} = \omega_0 (\pi r^2 h)\frac{h^2}{8R} \qquad [\because \text{Torque is caused by the weight}]$$

$$\Rightarrow \qquad h \simeq \left(\frac{2Y}{\omega_0}\right)^{1/3} r^{2/3}$$

Hence, critical height $= h = \left(\dfrac{2Y}{\omega_0}\right)^{1/3} r^{2/3}$.

Q.28 A stone of mass m is tied to an elastic string of negligble mass and spring constant k. The unstretched length of the string is L and has negligible mass. The other end of the string is fixed to a nail at a point P. Initially the stone is at the same level as the point P. The stone is dropped vertically from point P.

(a) Find the distance y from the top when the mass comes to rest for an instant, for the first time.

(b) What is the maximum velocity attained by the stone in this drop?

(c) What shall be the nature of the motion after the stone has reached its lowest point?

- **Concept Insight** In this problem ,the given string is elastic and there is no dissipation of energy so, we can use the concept of conservation of mechanical energy, which states that the total amount of mechanical energy in a closed system in the absence of dissipative force remains constant.

Ans. Consider the diagram the stone is dropped from point p.

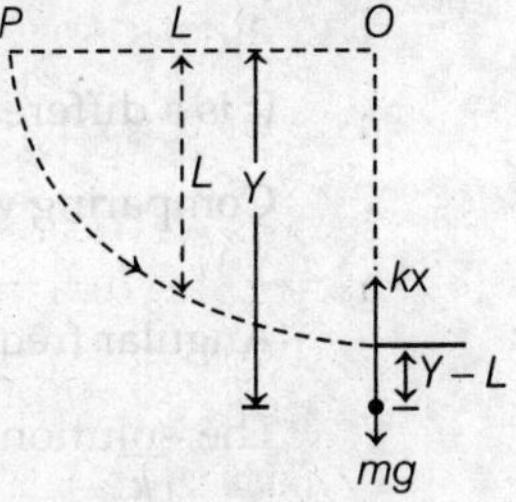

(a) Till the stone drops through a length L it will be in free fall. After that the elasticity of the string will force it to a SHM. Let the stone come to rest instantaneously at y.

The loss in PE of the stone is the PE stored in the stretched string.

$$mgy = \frac{1}{2}k(y-L)^2$$

where Y is total length of string after extension.

$$\Rightarrow \qquad mgy = \frac{1}{2}ky^2 - kyL + \frac{1}{2}kL^2$$

$$\Rightarrow \qquad \frac{1}{2}ky^2 - (kL + mg)y + \frac{1}{2}kL^2 = 0$$

$$y = \frac{(kL + mg) \pm \sqrt{(kL + mg)^2 - k^2L^2}}{k}$$

$$= \frac{(kL + mg) \pm \sqrt{2mgkL + m^2g^2}}{k}$$

Retain the positive sign.

$$\therefore \qquad y = \frac{(kL + mg) + \sqrt{2mgkL + m^2g^2}}{k}$$

(b) In SHM, the maximum velocity is attained when the body passes, through the "equilibrium, position" i.e. when the instantaneous acceleration is zero. In this situation $mg - kx = 0$, where x is the extension from L.

$$\Rightarrow \qquad mg = kx$$

Let the velocity be v. Then,

$$\frac{1}{2}mv^2 + \frac{1}{2}kx^2 = mg(L + x) \qquad \text{[from conservation of energy]}$$

$$\frac{1}{2}mv^2 = mg(L + x) - \frac{1}{2}kx^2$$

Now, $\qquad mg = kx \Rightarrow x = \frac{mg}{k}$

$$\therefore \qquad \frac{1}{2}mv^2 = mg\left(L + \frac{mg}{k}\right) - \frac{1}{2}k\frac{m^2g^2}{k^2} = mgL + \frac{m^2g^2}{k} - \frac{1}{2}\frac{m^2g^2}{k}$$

$$\frac{1}{2}mv^2 = mgL + \frac{1}{2}\frac{m^2g^2}{k}$$

$$\therefore \qquad v^2 = 2gL + mg^2/k$$

$$v = (2gL + mg^2/k)^{1/2}$$

(c) When stone is at the lowest position i.e. at instantaneous distance Y from P, then equation of motion of the stone is

$$\frac{md^2y}{dt^2} = mg - k(y - L) \Rightarrow \frac{d^2y}{dt^2} + \frac{k}{m}(y - L) - g = 0$$

Make a transformation of variables, $z = \frac{k}{m}(y - L) - g$

$$\therefore \qquad \frac{d^2z}{dt^2} + \frac{k}{m}z = 0$$

It is a differential equation of second order which represents SHM.

Comparing with equation $\frac{d^2z}{dt^2} + \omega^2 z = 0$

Angular frequency of harmonic motion $\omega = \sqrt{\frac{k}{m}}$

The solution of above equation will be of the type $z = A\cos(\omega t + \phi)$; where $\omega = \sqrt{\frac{k}{m}}$

$$y = \left(L + \frac{mg}{k}\right) + A' \cos(\omega t + \phi)$$

Thus, the stone will perform SHM with angular frequency $\omega = \sqrt{k/m}$ about a point $y_0 = L + \frac{mg}{k}$.

Mistake Alert ! *Ensure that students correctly account for both KE and PE at different points in the motion. For instance, the spring potential energy is $\frac{1}{2}Kx^2$ and gravitational potential energy is mgh. They must clearly identity the reference points.*

Q.29 An equilateral triangle ABC is formed by two Cu rods AB and BC and one Al rod. It is heated in such a way that temperature of each rod increases by ΔT. Find change in the angle ABC. [Coeffecient of linear expansion for Cu is α_1, coefficient of linear expansion for Al is α_2]

Thinking Process Due to increase in temperature length of each side will change, hence, the angle corresponding to any vertex also changes.

Ans. Consider the diagram shown

Let $l_1 = AB, l_2 = AC, l_3 = BC$

$\therefore \quad \cos\theta = \frac{l_3^2 + l_1^2 - l_2^2}{2l_3 l_1}$ [assume $\angle ABC = \theta$]

$\Rightarrow \quad 2l_3 l_1 \cos\theta = l_3^2 + l_1^2 - l_2^2$

Differentiating $2(l_3\, dl_1 + l_1 dl_3)\cos\theta - 2l_1 l_3 \sin\theta d\theta$

$$= 2l_3\, dl_3 + 2l_1\, dl_1 - 2l_2\, dl_2$$

Now, $dl_1 = l_1\alpha_1\,\Delta t$ [where, Δt = change in temperature]

$dl_2 = l_2\alpha_1\,\Delta t$

$\Rightarrow \quad dl_3 = l_3\alpha_2\Delta t$

and $l_1 = l_2 = l_3 = l$

$$(l^2\alpha_1\Delta t + l^2\alpha_1\Delta t)\cos\theta + l^2\sin\theta d\theta = l^2\alpha_1\Delta t + l^2\alpha_1\Delta t - l^2\alpha_2\Delta t$$

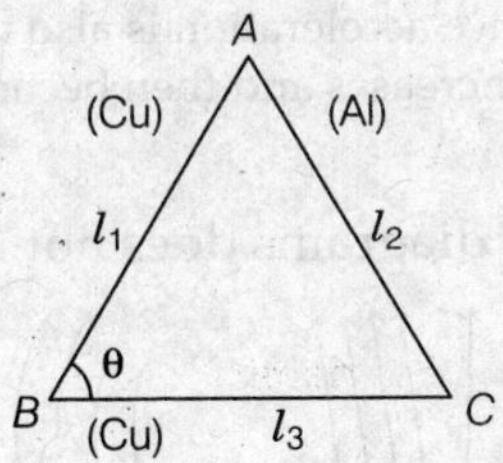

$$\sin\theta d\theta = 2\alpha_1\Delta t(1 - \cos\theta) - \alpha_2\Delta t$$

Putting $\theta = 60°$ [for equilateral triangle]

$$d\theta \times \sin 60° = 2\alpha_1\Delta t(1 - \cos 60°) - \alpha_2\Delta t$$

$$= 2\alpha_1\Delta t \times \frac{1}{2} - \alpha_2\Delta t = (\alpha_1 - \alpha_2)\Delta t$$

$\Rightarrow \quad d\theta$ = change in the angle $\angle ABC$

$$= \frac{(\alpha_1 - \alpha_2)\Delta T}{\sin 60°} = \frac{2(\alpha_1 - \alpha_2)\Delta T}{\sqrt{3}}$$ [$\because \Delta t = \Delta T$ given]

Chapter

09 Mechanical Properties of Fluids

Multiple Choice Questions (MCQs)

Q.1 A tall cylinder is filled with viscous oil. A round pebble is dropped from the top with zero initial velocity. From the plot shown in figure, indicate the one that represents the velocity (v) of the pebble as a function of time (t).

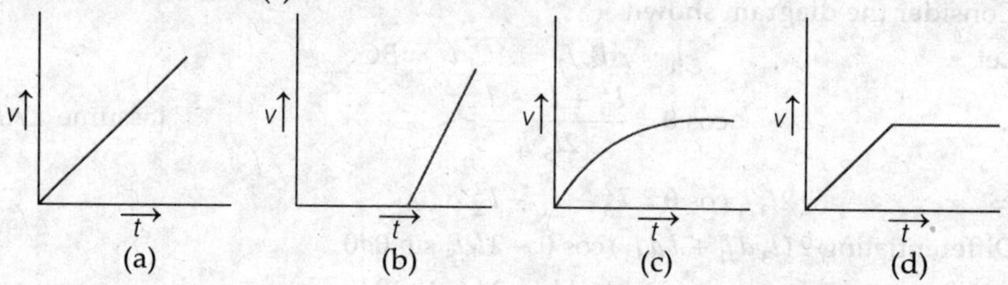

Thinking Process When the pebble is dropped from the top, a variable force called viscous force will act which increases with increase in speed. And at equilibrium this velocity becomes constant.

Ans. *(c)* When the pebble is falling through the viscous oil the viscous force is

$$F = 6\pi\eta r v$$

where r is radius of the pebble, v is instantaneous speed, η is coefficient of viscosity. As the force is variable, hence acceleration is also variable so v-t graph will not be straight line.First velocity increases and then becomes constant known as terminal velocity.

Q. 2 Which of the following diagrams does not represent a streamline flow?

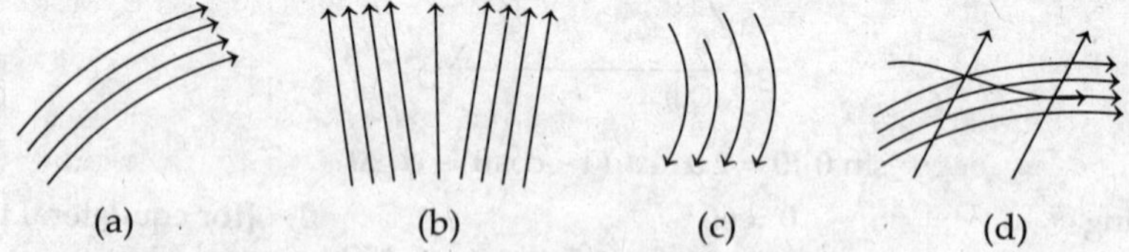

Concept Insight In this problem we use the concept of Streamline. Flow which is defined as a type of flow of fluid which travels in regular paths. In streamline flow, the velocity, pressure and other such properties remain constant in fluid at each point.

Ans. *(d)* In a streamline flow at any given point, the velocity of each passing fluid particles remains constant. If we consider a cross-sectional area, then a point on the area cannot have different velocities at the same time, hence two streamlines of flow cannot cross each other.

Q.3 A long a streamline,

(a) the velocity of a fluid particle remains constant

(b) the velocity of all fluid particles crossing a given position is constant

(c) the velocity of all fluid particles at a given instant is constant

(d) the speed of a fluid particle remains constant

Ans. ***(b)*** As we know for a streamline flow of a liquid velocity of each particle at a particular cross-section is constant, because $Av =$ constant (law of continuity) between two cross-section of a tube of flow.

Q.4 An ideal fluid flows through a pipe of circular cross-section made of two sections with diameters 2.5 cm and 3.75 cm. The ratio of the velocities in the two pipes is

(a) 9 : 4 (b) 3 : 2 (c) $\sqrt{3}:\sqrt{2}$ (d) $\sqrt{2}:\sqrt{3}$

Ans. ***(a)*** Consider the diagram, where an ideal fluid is flowing through a pipe.

As given

$d_1 =$ Diameter at 1st point is 2.5.

$d_2 =$ Diameter at 2nd point is 3.75.

Applying equation of continuity for cross-sections A_1 and A_2.

$$\Rightarrow \quad A_1v_1 = A_2v_2$$

$$\Rightarrow \quad \frac{v_1}{v_2} = \frac{A_2}{A_1} = \frac{\pi(r_2^2)}{\pi(r_1^2)} = \left(\frac{r_2}{r_1}\right)^2 = \left(\frac{\frac{3.75}{2}}{\frac{2.5}{2}}\right)^2 = \left(\frac{3.75}{2.5}\right)^2 = \frac{9}{4} \quad \left[\because r_2 = \frac{d_2}{2},\ r_1 = \frac{d_1}{2}\right]$$

Q.5 The angle of contact at the interface of water-glass is 0°, ethyl alcohol-glass is 0°, mercury-glass is 140° and methyliodide-glass is 30°. A glass capillary is put in a trough containing one of these four liquids. It is observed that the meniscus is convex. The liquid in the trough is

(a) water (b) ethylalcohol (c) mercury (d) methyliodide

Ans. ***(c)*** According to the question, the observed meniscus is of convex figure shape. Which is only possible when angle of contact is obtuse. Hence, the combination will be of mercury-glass (140°)

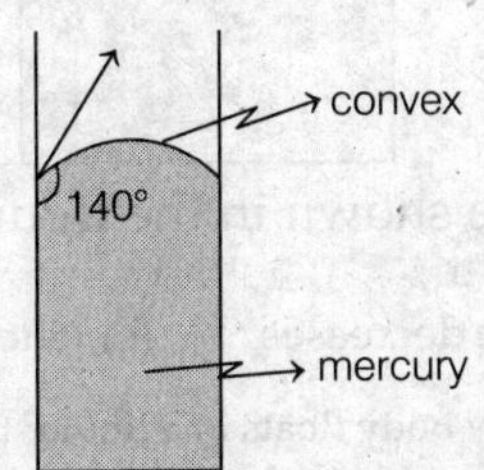

Multiple Choice Questioins (More Than One Options)

Q.6 For a surface molecule,

(a) the net force on it is zero
(b) there is a net downward force
(c) the potential energy is less than that of a molecule inside
(d) the potential energy is more than that of a molecule inside

Ans. ***(b, d)*** Consider the diagram where two molecules of a liquid are shown. One is well inside the liquid i.e. below surface film and other is on the surface. The molecule (A) which is well inside experiences equal forces from all directions, hence net force on it will be zero.

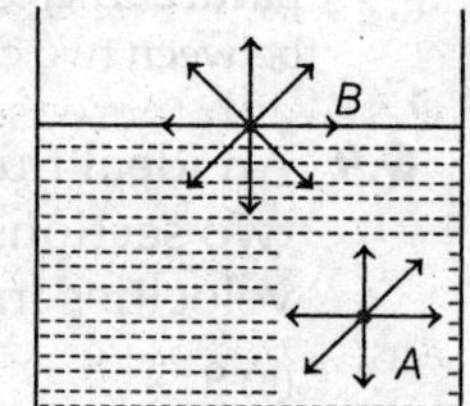

And molecules on the liquid surface or in surface film have some extra energy as it surrounded surraind by only lower half side of liquid molecules.

Alternate Method

For molecule A insides the liquid, the liquid molecules will exert force on molecule A from all sides. Hence the net force on molecule A will be zero. But for the molecule at the surface, the net force will be downwards because for surface molecules the conhesive force between liquid and liquid molecules is more than the adhesive force between air and liquid molecules.

Also; the potential energy of the molecules on the surface is larger than the potential energy of the molecules inside the liquid.

Hence, the correct option are (b) and (d).

Q.7 Pressure is a scalar quantity, because

(a) it is the ratio of force to area and both force and area are vectors
(b) it is the ratio of the magnitude of the force to area
(c) it is the ratio of the component of the force normal to the area
(d) it does not depend on the size of the area chosen

Ans. ***(c, d)*** Pressure is defined as the ratio of magnitude of component of the force normal to the area under consideration.

As magnitude of component is considered, hence, it will not have any direction. So, pressure is a scalar quantity.

Q.8 A wooden block with a coin placed on its top, floats in water as shown in figure.

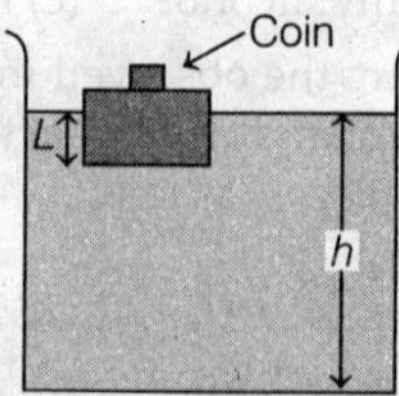

The distance l and h are shown in the figure. After sometime, the coin falls into the water. Then,

(a) l decreases (b) h decreases (c) l increases (d) h increases

Thinking Process When any body floats in a liquid, the upthrust force acting on the body due to the displaced liquid is balanced by its weight.

Ans. *(a,b)* When the coin falls into the water, weight of the (block + coin) system decreases, which was balanced by the upthrust force earlier. As weight of the system decreases, hence upthrust force will also decrease which is only possible when l decreases.

As l decreases volume of water displaced by the block decreases, hence h decreases.

Note As the coin falls into water, it displaces some volume of water which is very less hence, we neglect volume of the coin.

Q.9 With increase in temperature, the viscosity of

(a) gases decreases (b) liquids increases

(c) gases increases (d) liquids decreases

Ans. *(c, d)* For liquids coefficient of viscosity, $\eta \propto \frac{1}{\sqrt{T}}$

i.e. with increase in temperature η decreases.

For gases coefficient of viscosity, $\eta \propto \sqrt{T}$

i.e. with increase in temperature η increases.

Q.10 Streamline flow is more likely for liquids with

(a) high density (b) high viscosity

(c) low density (d) low viscosity

Ans. *(b, c)* Streamline flow is more likely for liquids having low density. We know that greater the coefficient of viscosity of a liquid more will be velocity gradient hence, each line of flow can be easily differentiated. Also higher the coefficient of viscosity lower will be Reynolds number, hence flow more like to be streamline.

$$\text{Critical Velocity } (V_c) \propto \frac{\eta}{\rho}$$

Very Short Answer Type Questions

Q.11 Is viscosity a vector?

Ans. Viscosity is a property of liquid having no direction, hence it is a scalar quantity.

Q.12 Is surface tension a vector?

Ans. No, surface tension is a scalar quantity.

As surface tension $= \frac{\text{Work done}}{\text{Surface area}}$, where work done and surface area both are scalar quantities.

Q.13 Iceberg floats in water with part of it submerged. What is the fraction of the volume of iceberg submerged, if the density of ice is $\rho_i = 0.917 \text{ g cm}^{-3}$?

Ans. Given, density of ice $(\rho_{ice}) = 0.917 \text{g /cm}^3$

Density of water $(\rho_w) = 1 \text{g/cm}^3$

Let V be the total volume of the iceberg and V' of its volume be submerged in water.

In floating condition.

Weight of the iceberg = Weight of the water displaced by the submerged part by ice

$$V\rho_{ice}\, g = V'\rho_w g$$

or $\dfrac{V'}{V} = \dfrac{\rho_{ice}}{\rho_w} = \dfrac{0.917}{1} = 0.917$ [$\because$ Weight $= mg = v\rho g$]

Q.14 **A vessel filled with water is kept on a weighing pan and the scale adjusted to zero. A block of mass M and density ρ is suspended by a massless spring of spring constant k. This block is submerged inside into the water in the vessel. What is the reading of the scale?**

Ans. Consider the diagram,

The scale is adjusted to zero, therefore, when the block suspended to a spring is immersed in water, then the reading of the scale will be equal to the thrust on the block due to water.

Thrust = weight of water displaced

$= V\rho_w g$ (where V is volume of the block and ρ_w is density of water)

$= \dfrac{m}{\rho}\rho_w g = \left(\dfrac{\rho_w}{\rho}\right) mg$ [$\because$ Density of the block $\rho = \dfrac{\text{mass}}{\text{volume}} = \dfrac{m}{V}$]

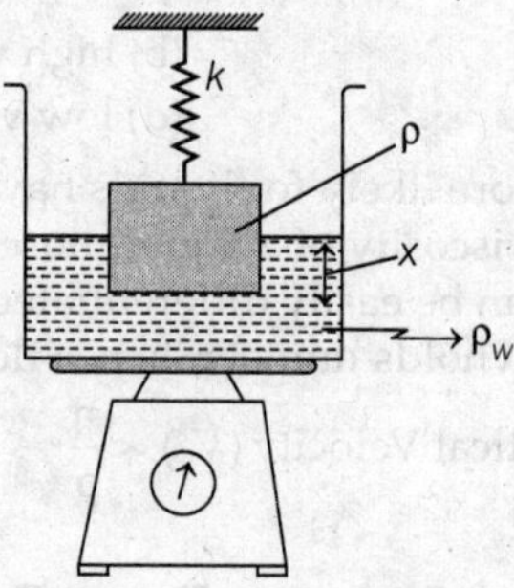

Q.15 **A cubical block of density ρ is floating on the surface of water. Out of its height L, fraction x is submerged in water. The vessel is in an elevator accelerating upward with acceleration a. What is the fraction immersed?**

Thinking Process As the elevator is accelerating upward the net acceleration of the block with respect to the elevator can be calculate by the concept of pseudo force.

Ans. Consider the diagram.

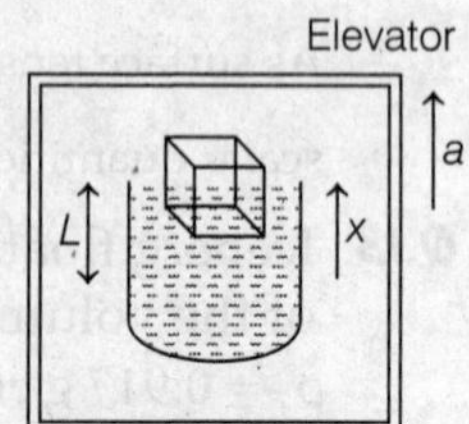

Let the density of water be ρ_w and a cubical block of ice of side L be floating in water with x of its height (L) submerged in water.

$$\text{Volume of the block } (V) = L^3$$

$$\text{Mass of the block } (m) = V\rho = L^3\rho$$

$$\text{Weight of the block} = mg = L^3\rho g$$

1st case

Volume of the water displaced by the submerged part of the block $= x\,L^2$

$\therefore$ Weight of the water displaced by the block

In floating condition, $x\,L^2\rho_w\, g$ [weight $= V_d \times$ density $\times g$]

Weight of the block = Weight of the water displaced by the block

$$L^3\rho g = x L^2\rho_w g \text{ or } \frac{x}{L} = \frac{\rho}{\rho_w} = x$$

2nd case

When elevator is accelerating upward with an acceleration a, then effective acceleration

$$= (g + a) \qquad [\because \text{ Pseudo force is downward}]$$

Then, weight of the block $= m(g + a)$

$$= L^3\rho (g + a)$$

Let x_1 fraction be submerged in water when elevator is accelerating upwards.

Now, in the floating condition, weight of the block = weight of the displaced water

$$L^3\rho(g + a) = (x_1 L^2)\rho_w(g + a) \text{ or } \frac{x_1}{L} = \frac{\rho}{\rho_w} = x$$

From 1st and 2nd case,

We see that,the fraction of the block submerged in water is independent of the acceleration of the elevator.

Mistake Alert ! *We should not confuse with the concept of pseudo force, i.e. pseudo force is downward, hence fraction will change due to increased force.*

Short Answer Type Questions

Q.16 **The sap in trees, which consists mainly of water in summer, rises in a system of capillaries of radius $r = 2.5 \times 10^{-5}$ m. The surface tension of sap is $T = 7.28 \times 10^{-2}$ Nm^{-1} and the angle of contact is 0°. Does surface tension alone account for the supply of water to the top of all trees?**

Ans. Given, radius $(r) = 2.5 \times 10^{-5}$ m

Surface tension $(S) = 7.28 \times 10^{-2}$ N/m

Angle of contact $(\theta) = 0°$

The maximum height to which sap can rise in trees through capillarity action is given by

$$h = \frac{2S\cos\theta}{r\rho g} \text{ where } S = \text{Surface tension}, \ \rho = \text{Density}, \ r = \text{Radius}$$

$$= \frac{2 \times 7.28 \times 10^{-2} \times \cos 0°}{2.5 \times 10^{-5} \times 1 \times 10^{-3} \times 9.8} = 0.6 \text{ m}$$

This is the maximum height upto which the sap can rise due to surface tension. Since, many trees have heights much more than this, capillary action alone cannot account for the rise of water in all trees.

Q.17 **The free surface of oil in a tanker, at rest, is horizontal. If the tanker starts accelerating the free surface will be titled by an angle θ. If the acceleration is a ms^{-2}, what will be the slope of the free surface?**

Thinking Process As the tanker starts accelerating, free surface of the tanker will not be horizontal because pseudo force acts.

Ans. Consider the diagram where a tanker is accelerating along X-axis, then water will bulge at the back of the tanker as shown in figure

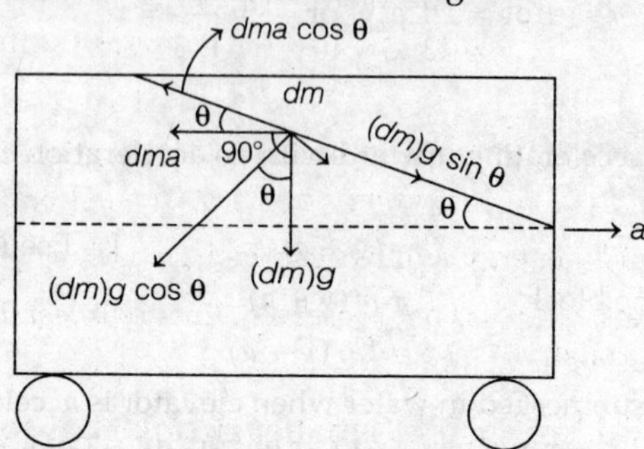

Consider an elementary particle of the fluid of mass dm.

The acting forces on the particle with respect to the tanker are shown above.

Now, balancing forces (as the particle is in equilibrium) along the inclined direction component of weight = component of pseudo force $dmg\sin\theta = dma\cos\theta$ (we have assumed that the surface is inclined at an angle θ) where, dma is pseudo force

$\Rightarrow$ $$g\sin\theta = a\cos\theta$$

$\Rightarrow$ $$a = g\tan\theta$$

$\Rightarrow$ $$\tan\theta = \frac{a}{g} = \text{slope}$$

Q.18 Two mercury droplets of radii 0.1 cm and 0.2 cm collapse into one single drop. What amount of energy is released? The surface tension of mercury $T = 435.5 \times 10^{-3}\ \text{Nm}^{-1}$.

Thinking Process In this process, conservation of mass will be applied. Before and after collapse, mass and hence, volume of the system remains conserved.

Ans. Consider the diagram.

Radii of mercury droplets, $r_1 = 0.1\ \text{cm} = 1 \times 10^{-3}\ \text{m}$

$r_2 = 0.2\ \text{cm} = 2 \times 10^{-3}\ \text{m}$

Surface tension $(T) = 435.5 \times 10^{-3}\ \text{N/m}$

Let the radius of the big drop formed by collapsing be R.

$\therefore$ Volume of big drop = Volume of small droplets

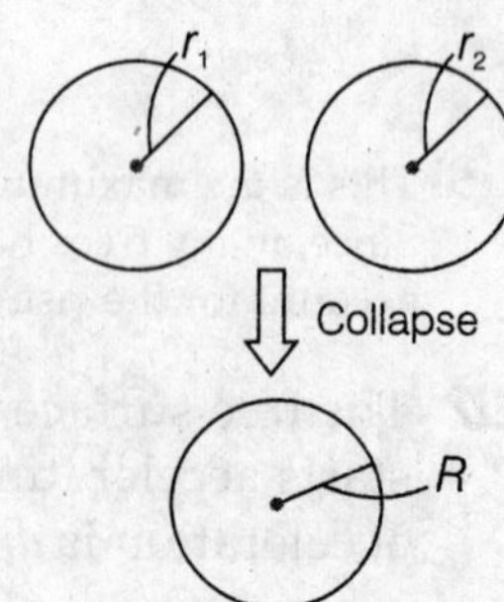

$$\frac{4}{3}\pi R^3 = \frac{4}{3}\pi r_1^3 + \frac{4}{3}\pi r_2^3$$

or $$R^3 = r_1^3 + r_2^3$$

$$= (0.1)^3 + (0.2)^3$$

$$= 0.001 + 0.008$$

$$= 0.009$$

or $$R = 0.21\ \text{cm} = 2.1 \times 10^{-3}\ \text{m}$$

$\therefore$ Change in surface area $\Delta A = 4\pi R^2 - (4\pi r_1^2 + 4\pi r_2^2)$

$$= 4\pi[R^2 - (r_1^2 + r_2^2)]$$

$\therefore$ Energy released $= T \cdot \Delta A$ [where T is surface tension of mercury]

$$= T \times 4\pi[R^2 - (r_1^2 + r_2^2)]$$

$$= 435.5 \times 10^{-3} \times 4 \times 3.14[(2.1 \times 10^{-3})^2 - (1 \times 10^{-6} + 4 \times 10^{-6})]$$

$$= 435.5 \times 4 \times 3.14[4.41 - 5] \times 10^{-6} \times 10^{-3}$$

$$= -32.23 \times 10^{-7}$$ (Negative sign shows absorption)

Therefore, 3.22×10^{-6} J energy will be absorbed.

Note In this process, energy is not conserved. Energy is last due to the collapsing, in the form of radiations.

Q.19 **If a drop of liquid breaks into smaller droplets, it results in lowering of temperature of the droplets. Let a drop of radius R, break into N small droplets each of radius r. Estimate the drop in temperature.**

Ans. When a big drop of radius R, breaks into N droplets each of radius r, the volume remains constant.

$\therefore$ Volume of big drop $= N \times$ Volume of each small drop

$$\frac{4}{3}\pi R^3 = N \times \frac{4}{3}\pi r^3$$

or $$R^3 = Nr^3$$

or $$N = \frac{R^3}{r^3}$$

Now, change in surface area $= 4\pi R^2 - N4\pi r^2$

$$= 4\pi(R^2 - Nr^2)$$

Energy released $= T \times \Delta A = T \times 4\pi(R^2 - Nr^2)$ [T = Surface tension]

Due to releasing of this energy, the temperature is lowered.

If ρ is the density and s is specific heat of liquid and its temperature is lowered by $\Delta\theta$, then energy released $= ms\Delta\theta$ [s = specific heat, $\Delta\theta$ = change in temperature]

$$T \times 4\pi(R^2 - Nr^2) = \left(\frac{4}{3}\pi R^3 \rho\, s\Delta\theta\right) \quad \left[\therefore m = V\rho = \frac{4}{3}\pi R^3 \rho\right]$$

$$\Rightarrow \quad \Delta\theta = \frac{T \times 4\pi(R^2 - Nr^2)}{\frac{4}{3}\pi R^3 \rho \times s} = \frac{3T}{\rho s}\left[\frac{R^2}{R^3} - \frac{Nr^2}{R^3}\right]$$

$$= \frac{3T}{\rho s}\left[\frac{1}{R} - \frac{(R^3/r^3) \times r^2}{R^3}\right] = \frac{3T}{\rho s}\left[\frac{1}{R} - \frac{1}{r}\right]$$

As $R > r$, so ΔQ is negative. Hence temperature of droplet falls.

Q.20 **The surface tension and vapour pressure of water at 20°C is 7.28×10^{-2} Nm^{-1} and 2.33×10^3 Pa, respectively. What is the radius of the smallest spherical water droplet which can form without evaporating at 20°C?**

Ans. Given, surface tension of water $(S) = 7.28 \times 10^{-2}$ N/m

Vapour pressure $(p) = 2.33 \times 10^3$ Pa

The drop will evaporate, if the water pressure is greater than the vapour pressure.

Let a water droplet of radius R formed without evaporating.

Vapour pressure = Excess pressure in drop.

$$\therefore \quad p = \frac{2S}{R} \text{ or } R = \frac{2S}{p} = \frac{2 \times 7.28 \times 10^{-2}}{2.33 \times 10^{3}} = 6.25 \times 10^{-5} \text{ m}$$

Long Answer Type Questions

Q.21 (a) Pressure decreases as one ascends the atmosphere. If the density of air is ρ, what is the change in pressure dp over a differential height dh?

(b) Considering the pressure p to be proportional to the density, find the pressure p at a height h if the pressure on the surface of the earth is p_0.

(c) If $p_0 = 1.03 \times 10^5 \text{ Nm}^{-2}$, $\rho_0 = 1.29 \text{ kg m}^{-3}$ and $g = 9.8 \text{ ms}^{-2}$, at what height will be pressure drop to (1/10) the value at the surface of the earth?

(d) This model of the atmosphere works for relatively small distances. Identify the underlying assumption that limits the model.

Thinking Process As we are going up in the atmosphere, thickness of the gases above us decreases hence, pressure also decreases.

Ans. (a) Consider a horizontal parcel of air with cross-section A and height dh.

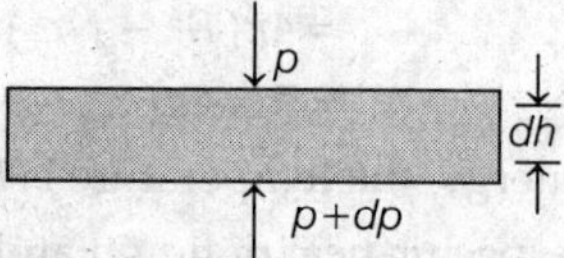

Let the pressure on the top surface and bottom surface be p and $p + dp$. If the parcel is in equilibrium, then the net upward force must be balanced by the weight.

i.e. $$(p + dp)A - pA = -\rho gAdh \quad [\because \text{Weight} = \text{Density} \times \text{Volume} \times g]$$

$$= -\rho \times Adh \times g$$

$$\Rightarrow \quad dp = -\rho gdh. \quad [\rho = \text{density of air}]$$

Negative sign shows that pressure decreases with height.

(b) Let ρ_o be the density of air on the surface of the earth.

As per question, pressure $\propto$ density

$$\Rightarrow \quad \frac{p}{p_o} = \frac{\rho}{\rho_o} \Rightarrow \rho = \frac{\rho_o}{p_o} p$$

$$\therefore \quad dp = -\frac{\rho_o g}{p_o} pdh \quad [\because dp = -\rho gdh]$$

$$\Rightarrow \quad \frac{dp}{p} = -\frac{\rho_o g}{p_o} dh$$

$$\Rightarrow \quad \int_{p_o}^{p} \frac{dp}{p} = -\frac{\rho_o g}{p_o} \int_0^h dh \qquad \begin{bmatrix} \because \text{at } h = 0, p = p_o \\ \text{and at } h = h, p = p \end{bmatrix}$$

$$\Rightarrow \quad \ln \frac{p}{p_o} = -\frac{\rho_o g}{p_o} h \qquad \ldots(i)$$

By removing log,

$$p = p_o \exp\left(\frac{-\rho_0 gh}{p_o}\right)$$

(c)

$$\rho_0 = 1.29 \text{ kgm}^{-3}$$

$$g = 9.8 \text{ ms}^{-1}$$

$$p = \frac{p_0}{10} \qquad \text{[given]}$$

$$h = ?$$

Using these values in Eq. (i)

$$\ln \frac{1}{10} = -\frac{1.29 \times 9.8}{1.013 \times 10^5} \times h$$

$$\Rightarrow \quad -2.30 = -\frac{12.642}{1.013 \times 10^5} h$$

$$-2.30 = -\frac{12.642}{1.013 \times 10^5} h$$

$$h = \frac{2.3 \times 1.013 \times 10^5}{12.642} = 0.1843 \times 10^5$$

$$h = 18.43 \text{ km}$$

(d) We know that $p \propto \rho$ [when T = constant i.e. isothermal pressure]

Temperature (T) remains constant only near the surface of the earth, not at greater heights.

Q.22 Surface tension is exhibited by liquids due to force of attraction between molecules of the liquid. The surface tension decreases with increase in temperature and vanishes at boiling point. Given that the latent heat of vaporisation for water $L_v = 540$ k cal kg^{-1}, the mechanical equivalent of heat $J = 4.2$ J cal^{-1}, density of water $\rho_w = 10^3$ kg/m^3, Avagadro's number $N_A = 6.0 \times 10^{26}$ k mole^{-1} and the molecular weight of water $M_A = 18$ kg for 1 k mole.

(a) Estimate the energy required for one molecule of water to evaporate.

(b) Show that the inter-molecular distance for water is $d = \left[\frac{M_A}{N_A} \times \frac{1}{\rho_w}\right]^{1/3}$ and find its value.

(c) 1 g of water in the vapour state at 1 atm occupies 1601 cm^3. Estimate the inter-molecular distance at boiling point, in the vapour state.

(d) During vaporisation a molecule overcomes a force F, assumed constant, to go from an inter-molecular distance d to d'. Estimate the value of F.

(e) Calculate F / d, which is a measure of the surface tension.

Ans. (a) Given , $L_v = 540\,\text{kcal kg}^{-1}$

$$= 540 \times 10^3 \text{ cal kg}^{-1} = 540 \times 10^3 \times 4.2\,\text{J kg}^{-1}$$

$\because$ Energy required to evaporate 1 kg of water = L_v kcal

$\therefore$ M_A kg of water requires $M_A L_v$ kcal [$\because Q = mL$]

Since, there are N_A molecules in M_A kg of water the energy required for 1 molecule to evaporate is

$$U = \frac{M_A L_v}{N_A}\,\text{J} \quad [\text{where } N_A = 6 \times 10^{26} = \text{Avogadro number}]$$

$$= \frac{18 \times 540 \times 4.2 \times 10^3}{6 \times 10^{26}}\,\text{J}$$

$$= 90 \times 18 \times 4.2 \times 10^{-23} = 6.8 \times 10^{-20}\,\text{J}$$

(b) Let the water molecules to be points and are separated at distance d from each other.

Volume of N_A molecule of water $= \dfrac{M_A}{\rho_w}$ $\left[\because V = \dfrac{M}{\rho}\right]$

Thus, the volume around one molecule is

$$= \frac{M_A}{N_A \rho_w}\left(\frac{\text{volume of 1 kmol}}{\text{number of molecules / kmol}}\right)$$

The volume around one molecule is

$$d^3 = (M_A / N_A \rho_w)$$

$$\therefore \quad d = \left(\frac{M_A}{N_A \rho_w}\right)^{1/3} = \left(\frac{18}{6 \times 10^{26} \times 10^3}\right)^{1/3}$$

$$d = (30 \times 10^{-30})^{1/3}\,\text{m} \approx 3.1 \times 10^{-10}\,\text{m}$$

(c) $\because$ 1 kg of vapour occupies volume = $1601 \times 10^{-3}\,\text{m}^3$

$\therefore$ 18 kg of vapour occupies $18 \times 1601 \times 10^{-3}\,\text{m}^3$

6×10^{26} molecules occupies $18 \times 1601 \times 10^{-3}\,\text{m}^3$

$\therefore$ 1 molecule occupies $\dfrac{18 \times 1601 \times 10^{-3}}{6 \times 10^{26}}\,\text{m}^3$

If d is the inter- molecular distance, then

$$d_1^3 = (3 \times 1601 \times 10^{-29})\,\text{m}^3$$

$$\therefore \quad d_1 = (30 \times 1601)^{1/3} \times 10^{-10} = 36.3 \times 10^{-10}\,\text{m}$$

(d) Work done to change the distance from d to d' is = $F(d' - d)$

This work done is equal to energy required to evaporate 1 molecule.

$$\therefore \quad F(d' - d) = 6.8 \times 10^{-20}$$

or
$$F = \frac{6.8 \times 10^{-20}}{d' - d} = \frac{6.8 \times 10^{-20}}{(36.3 \times 10^{-10} - 3.1 \times 10^{-10})}$$

$$= 2.05 \times 10^{-11}\,\text{N}$$

(e) Surface tension $= \dfrac{F}{d} = \dfrac{2.05 \times 10^{-11}}{3.1 \times 10^{-10}} = 6.6 \times 10^{-2}$ N/m.

Q.23 A hot air balloon is a sphere of radius 8 m. The air inside is at a temperature of 60°C. How large a mass can the balloon lift when the outside temperature is 20°C? (Assume air in an ideal gas, $R = 8.314$ J mole^{-1}K^{-1}, 1 atm $= 1.013 \times 10^5$ Pa, the membrane tension is 5 Nm^{-1}).

- **Concept Insight** In this problem we also use the concept of buoyancy principle i.e. buoyancy principle also known as Archimede's principle which states that any object submerged in a fluid (liquid or gas) experiences an upward force equal to the weight of the fluid displaced by the object.

Ans. Let the pressure inside the balloon be p_i and the outside pressure be p_o, then excess pressure is $p_i - p_o = \frac{2S}{r}$.

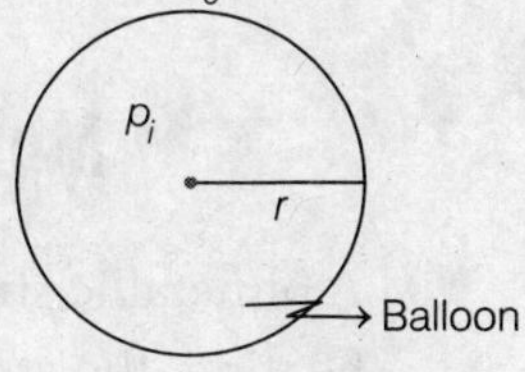

where, S = Surface tension, r = radius of balloon

Considering the air to be an ideal gas $p_i V = n_i RT_i$ where, V is the volume of the air inside the balloon, n_i is the number of moles inside and T_i is the temperature inside, and $p_o V = n_o RT_o$ where V is the volume of the air displaced and n_o is the number of moles displaced and T_o is the temperature outside.

So. $$n_i = \frac{p_i V}{RT_i} = \frac{M_i}{M_A} \quad \text{[As } PV = nRT\text{]}$$

where, M_i is the mass of air inside and M_A is the molar mass of air

and $$n_o = \frac{p_o V}{RT_o} = \frac{M_o}{M_A}$$

where, M_o is the mass of air outside that has been displaced. If w is the load it can raise, then

$$w + M_i g = M_o g \Rightarrow w = M_o g - M_i g$$

As in atmosphere 21% O_2 and 79% N_2-is present

$\therefore$ Molar mass of air $$M_A = 0.21 \times 32 + 0.79 \times 28 = 28.84 \text{ g}$$
$$= 28.84 \times 10^{-3} \text{ kg}$$

$\therefore$ Weight raised by the balloon

$$w = (M_o - M_i)\,g = \left(\frac{p_0 V M_A}{RT_0} - \frac{p_i V M_A}{RT_i}\right) g$$

$$\Rightarrow \quad w = \frac{M_A V}{R}\left(\frac{p_o}{T_o} - \frac{p_i}{T_i}\right) g$$

$$= \frac{0.02884 \times \frac{4}{3}\pi \times 8^3 \times 9.8}{8.314}\left(\frac{1.013 \times 10^5}{293} - \frac{1.013 \times 10^5}{333}\right) \begin{bmatrix} T_0 = 273 + 20 = 293 \text{ K} \\ T_i = 273 + 60 = 333 \text{ K} \end{bmatrix}$$

$$= \frac{0.02884 \times \frac{4}{3}\pi \times 8^3}{8.314} \times 1.013 \times 10^5 \left(\frac{1}{293} - \frac{1}{333}\right) \times 9.8 = 3044.2 \text{ N}$$

$\therefore$ Mass lifted by the balloon $= \frac{w}{g} = \frac{3044.2}{10} \approx 304.42$ kg.

$$\approx 305 \text{ kg}.$$

Mistake Alert! *A mistake might occur in calculating the average molar mass of air which is a mixture of Oxygen (O_2) and Nitrogen (N_2). Make sure that the ratio of 21% O_2 and 79% N_2 is applied properly.*

Chapter 10

Thermal Properties of Matter

Multiple Choice Questions (MCQs)

Q.1 A bimetallic strip is made of aluminium and steel ($\alpha_{Al} > \alpha_{steel}$). On heating, the strip will

(a) remain straight

(b) get twisted

(c) will bend with aluminium on concave side

(d) will bend with steel on concave side

Thinking Process The metallic strip with higher coefficient of linear expansion (α_{Al}) will expand more.

Ans. *(d)* As $\alpha_{Al} > \alpha_{steel}$, aluminium will expand more. So, it should have larger radius of curvature. Hence, aluminium will be on convex side.

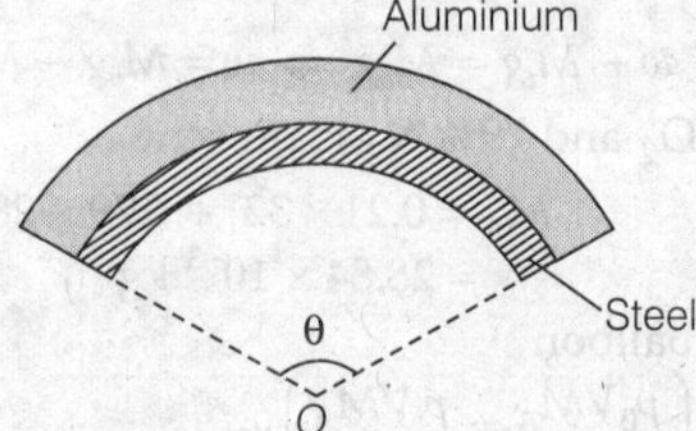

Q.2 A uniform metallic rod rotates about its perpendicular bisector with constant angular speed. If it is heated uniformly to raise its temperature slightly

(a) its speed of rotation increases

(b) its speed of rotation decreases

(c) its speed of rotation remains same

(d) its speed increases because its moment of inertia increases

Ans. *(b)* As the rod is heated, it expands. No external torque is acting on the system so angular momentum should be conserved.

$$L = \text{Angular momentum} = I\omega = \text{constant}$$

$\Rightarrow$ $$I_1\omega_1 = I_2\omega_2$$

Due to expansion of the rod $I_2 > I_1$

$\Rightarrow$ $$\omega_2 < \omega_1$$

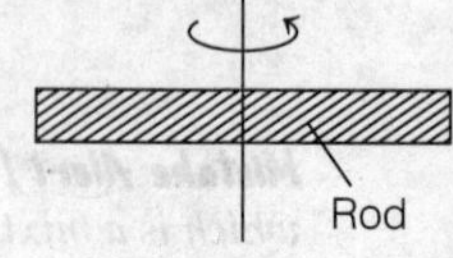

So, angular velocity (speed of rotation) decreases.

Q.3 The graph between two temperature scales A and B is shown in figure. Between upper fixed point and lower fixed point there are 150 equal division on scale A and 100 on scale B. The relationship for conversion between the two scales is given by

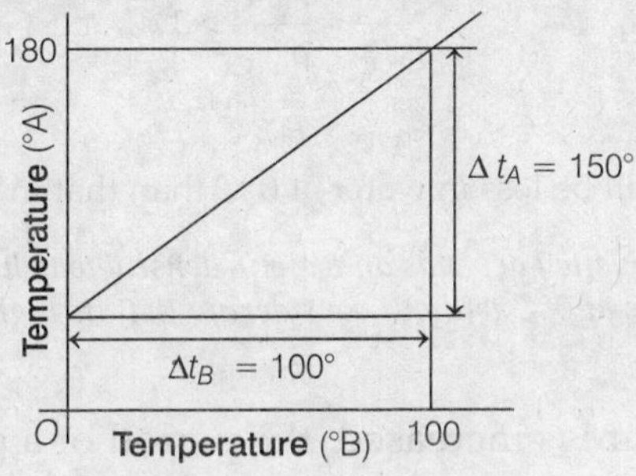

(a) $\frac{t_A - 180}{100} = \frac{t_B}{150}$ (b) $\frac{t_A - 30}{150} = \frac{t_B}{100}$ (c) $\frac{t_B - 180}{150} = \frac{t_A}{100}$ (d) $\frac{t_B - 40}{100} = \frac{t_A}{180}$

Ans. ***(b)*** It is clear from the graph that lowest point for scale A is 30° and lowest point for scale B is 0°. Highest point for the scale A is 180° and for scale B is 100°. Hence, correct relation is

$$\frac{t_A - (\text{LFP})_A}{(\text{UFP})_A - (\text{LFP})_A} = \frac{t_B - (\text{LFP})_B}{(\text{UFP})_B - (\text{LFP})_B}$$

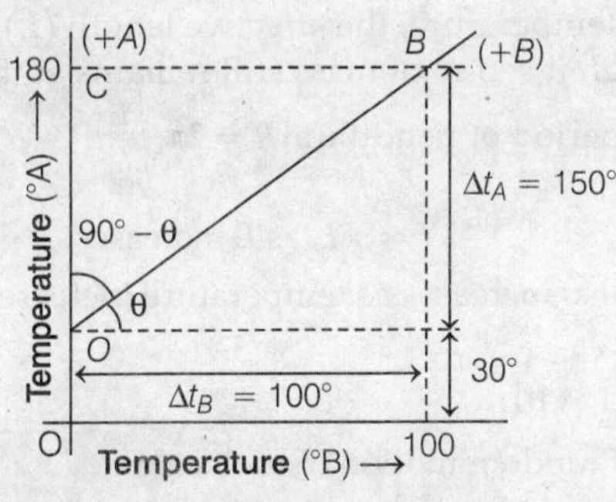

$$\Rightarrow \quad \frac{t_A - 30}{180 - 30} = \frac{t_B - 0}{100 - 0} \Rightarrow \frac{t_A - 30}{150} = \frac{t_B}{100}$$

where, LFP → Lower fixed point

UFP → Upper fixed point

Q.4 An aluminium sphere is dipped into water. Which of the following is true?

(a) Buoyancy will be less in water at 0°C than that in water at 4°C.
(b) Buoyancy will be more in water at 0°C than that in water at 4°C.
(c) Buoyancy in water at 0°C will be same as that in water at 4°C.
(d) Buoyancy may be more or less in water at 4°C depending on the radius of the sphere.

- **Concept Insight** In this problem we use the concept of Anomalous expansion of water i.e. the unusual property of water that cause it to expand instead of contract when then temperature decreases from 4°C to 0°C.

Ans. ***(a)*** Let volume of the sphere is V and ρ is its density, then we can write buoyant force

$$F = V\rho g \qquad [g = \text{acceleration due to gravity}]$$

$$\Rightarrow \quad F \propto \rho \qquad [\because V \text{ and } g \text{ are almost constant}]$$

$$\Rightarrow \quad \frac{F_{4^\circ C}}{F_{0^\circ C}} = \frac{\rho_{4^\circ C}}{\rho_{0^\circ C}} > 1 \qquad [\because \rho_{4^\circ C} > \rho_{0^\circ C}]$$

$$\Rightarrow \quad F_{4^\circ C} > F_{0^\circ C}$$

Hence, buoyancy will be less in water at 0°C than that in water at 4°C.

Mistakes Alert ! *Buoyancy depends on water's density which is highest at 4°C. Assuming it increases at 0°C without considering that its highest at 4°C will lead to errors.*

Q.5 As the temperature is increased, the period of a pendulum

(a) increases as its effective length increases even though its centre of mass still remains at the centre of the bob

(b) decreases as its effective length increases even though its centre of mass still remains at the centre of the bob

(c) increases as its effective length increases due to shifting to centre of mass below the centre of the bob

(d) decreases as its effective length remains same but the centre of mass shifts above the centre of the bob

Ans. ***(a)*** With increase in temperature, the effective length (L) of the pendulum increases even though it centre of mass still remains at the centre of the bob.

We know that time period of pendulum $T = 2\pi\sqrt{\frac{L}{g}}$

$$\Rightarrow \quad T \propto \sqrt{L}, \text{ as } L \text{ increases.}$$

So, time period (T) also increases as temperature increases.

L

Pendulum

Q.6 Heat is associated with

(a) kinetic energy of random motion of molecules

(b) kinetic energy of orderly motion of molecules

(c) total kinetic energy of random and orderly motion of molecules

(d) kinetic energy of random motion in some cases and kinetic energy of orderly motion in other

Ans. ***(a)*** We know that as temperature increases vibration of molecules about their mean position increases hence, kinetic energy associated with random motion of molecules increases.

Q.7 The radius of a metal sphere at room temperature T is R and the coefficient of linear expansion of the metal is α. The sphere heated a little by a temperature ΔT so that its new temperature is $T + \Delta T$. The increase in the volume of the sphere is approximately.

(a) $2\pi R\alpha\Delta T$ (b) $\pi R^2\alpha\Delta T$

(c) $4\pi R^3\alpha\Delta T / 3$ (d) $4\pi R^3\alpha\Delta T$

Ans. ***(d)*** Let the radius of the sphere is R. As the temperature increases radius of the sphere increases as shown.

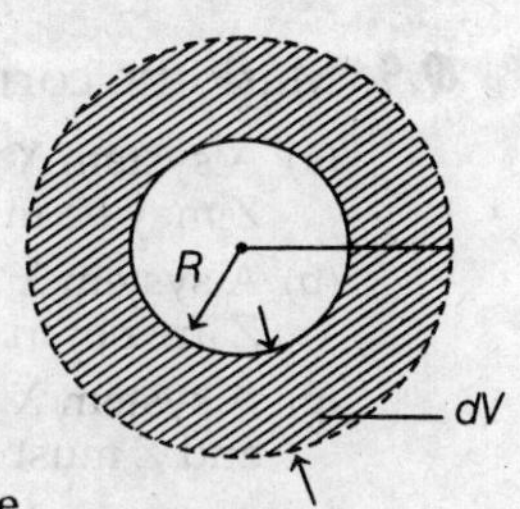

$$\text{Original volume } V_o = \frac{4}{3}\pi R^3$$

Coefficient of linear expansion $= \alpha$

$\therefore$ Coefficient of volume expansion $\gamma = 3\alpha$

$$dV = \gamma V dT$$

$$\Rightarrow \quad dV = 3V\alpha dT \simeq 4\pi R^3 \alpha \Delta T$$

$=$ Increase in the volume

Q.8 A sphere, a cube and a thin circular plate, all of same material and same mass are initially heated to same high temperature.

(a) Plate will cool fastest and cube the slowest
(b) Sphere will cool fastest and cube the slowest
(c) Plate will cool fastest and sphere the slowest
(d) Cube will cool fastest and plate the slowest

Thinking Process In this problem the cooling will be in the form of radiations as described by Stefan's law. Since, emissive power directly proportional to surface area. Here, for given volume, sphere have least surface area and circular plate of greatest surface area.

Ans. ***(c)*** Consider the diagram where all the three objects are heated to same temperature T. We know that density, $\rho = \frac{\text{mass}}{\text{volume}}$ as ρ is same for all the three objects hence, volume will also be same.

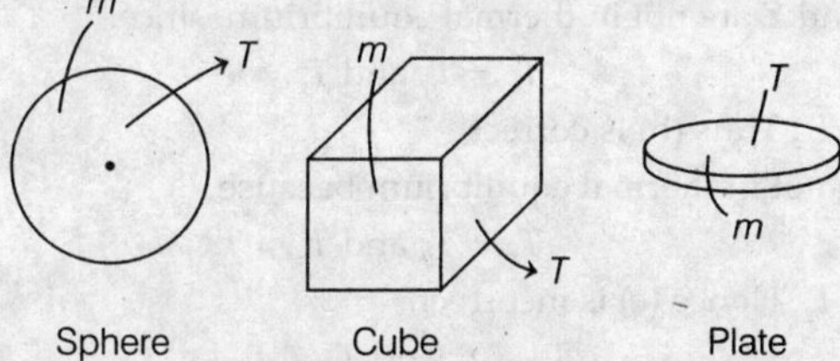

As thickness of the plate is least hence, surface area of the plate is maximum.

We know that, according to Stefan's law of heat loss $H \propto AT^4$

where, A is surface area of for object and T is temperature.

Hence, $\quad H_{\text{sphere}} : H_{\text{cube}} : H_{\text{plate}} = A_{\text{sphere}} : A_{\text{cube}} : A_{\text{plate}}$

As A_{plate} is maximum.

Hence, the plate will cool fastest.

As, the sphere is having minimum surface area hence, the sphere cools slowest.

Alternate Method

The circular plate has maximum surface area and such it cools the fastest. For a given volume, a sphere has the least surface area and accordingly cools the lowest.

Multiple Choice Questions (More Than One Options)

Q.9 Mark the correct options

(a) A system X is in thermal equilibrium with Y but not with Z. The systems Y and Z may be in thermal equilibrium with each other.

(b) A system X is in thermal equilibrium with Y but not with Z. The systems Y and Z are not in thermal equilibrium with each other.

(c) A system X is neither in thermal equilibrium with Y nor with Z. The systems Y and Z must be in thermal equilibrium with each other.

(d) A system X is neither in thermal equilibrium with Y nor with Z. The systems Y and Z may be in thermal equilibrium with each other.

Ans. ***(b, d)*** According to question

$$T_x = T_y \quad [\because x \text{ and } y \text{ are in thermal equilibrium}]$$

$$T_x \neq T_z \quad [\because x \text{ is not in thermal equilibrium with } z]$$

Clearly, $T_y \neq T_z$

Hence, y and z are not in thermal equilibrium.

(d) Given, $T_x \neq T_y$

and $T_x \neq T_z$

We cannot say about equilibrium of Y and Z, they may or may not be in equilibrium.

Alternate Method

(a) Here, Y and Z are not in thermal equilibrium. Since,

$$T_x = T_y \text{ and } T_x \text{ is not equal to } T_z$$

Thus, $T_x = T_y \neq T_z$. Hence, (a) is incorrect.

(b) System Y and Z are not in thermal equilibrium, since.

$$T_x = T_y \text{ and } T_x \neq T_z$$

Thus, $T_y \neq T_z$. Thus (b) is correct.

(c) Y and Z are not in thermal equilibrium because,

$$T_x \neq T_y \text{ and } T_x \neq T_z$$

Thus, $T_y \neq T_z$. Hence (c) is incorrect.

(d) Here, $T_x \neq T_y$ and $T_x \neq T_z$

Here, T_z may be equal to T_y

Hence (d) is correct.

Q.10 Gulab Jamuns (assumed to be spherical) are to be heated in an oven. They are available in two sizes, one twice bigger (in radius) than the other. Pizzas (assumed to be discs) are also to be heated in oven. They are also in two sizes, one twice bigger (in radius) than the other. All four are put together to be heated to oven temperature. Choose the correct option from the following.

(a) Both size gulab jamuns will get heated in the same time.

(b) Smaller gulab jamuns are heated before bigger ones.

(c) Smaller pizzas are heated before bigger ones.

(d) Bigger pizzas are heated before smaller ones.

Ans. ***(b, c)*** Smaller gulab jamuns are having least surface area hence, they will be heated first.

As in case of smaller gulab jamun heat radiates will be less.

Similarly, smaller pizzas are heated before bigger ones because they are of small surface areas.

$\therefore$ Rate of heat transfer, $\frac{dH}{dt} = KA\frac{dT}{dx}$

or, $\frac{dh}{dt} \propto A$ [Area of hot surface]

Q.11 Refer to the plot of temperature *versus* time (figure) showing the changes in the state if ice on heating (not to scale). Which of the following is correct?

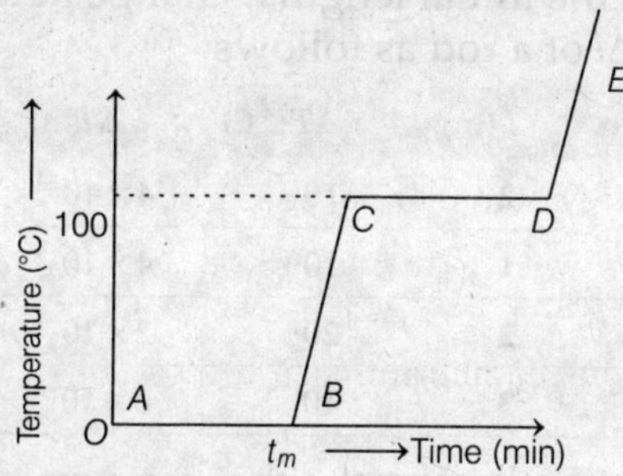

(a) The region AB represent ice and water in thermal equilibrium.

(b) At B water starts boiling.

(c) At C all the water gets converted into steam.

(d) C to D represents water and steam in equilibrium at boiling point.

Thinking Process During phase change process, temperature of the system remains constant.

Ans. ***(a, d)*** During the process AB temperature of the system is 0°C. Hence, it represents phase change that is transformation of ice into water while temperature remains 0°C.

BC represents rise in temperature of water from 0°C to 100°C (at C).

Now, water starts converting into steam which is represent by CD, and temperature remains same to 100°C.

Q.12 A glass full of hot milk is poured on the table. It begins to cool gradually. Which of the following is correct?

(a) The rate of cooling is constant till milk attains the temperature of the surrounding.

(b) The temperature of milk falls off exponentially with time.

(c) While cooling, there is a flow of heat from milk to the surrounding as well as from surrounding to the milk but the net flow of heat is from milk to the surrounding and that is why it cools.

(d) All three phenomenon, conduction, convection and radiation are responsible for the loss of heat from milk to the surroundings.

Ans. ***(b, c, d)*** When hot milk spread on the table heat is transferred to the surroundings by conduction, convection and radiation.

According to Newton's law of cooling temperature of the milk falls off exponentially. Heat also will be transferred from surroundings to the milk but will be lesser than that of transferred from milk to the surroundings.

Very Short Answer Type Questions

Q.13 Is the bulb of a thermometer made of diathermic or adiabatic wall?

Ans. As diathermic walls allow exchange of heat energy between two systems and adiabatic walls do not hence, diathermic walls are used to make the bulb of a thermometer.

Q.14 A student records the initial length l, change in temperature ΔT and change in length Δl of a rod as follows

S. No.	l (m)	ΔT (°C)	Δl (m)
1.	2	10	4×10^{-4}
2.	1	10	4×10^{-4}
3.	2	20	2×10^{-4}
4.	3	10	6×10^{-4}

If the first observation is correct, what can you say about observation 2, 3 and 4.

Ans. From the 1st observation $\alpha = \dfrac{\Delta l}{l\Delta T} \Rightarrow \alpha = \dfrac{4\times10^{-4}}{2\times10} = 2\times10^{-5}\,°\text{C}^{-1}$

For 2nd observation $\quad \Delta l = \alpha l \Delta T$

$= 2\times10^{-5}\times1\times10 = 2\times10^{-4}\text{ m} \neq 4\times10^{-4}\text{ m}$ (Wrong)

For 3rd observation $\quad \Delta l = \alpha l \Delta T$

$= 2\times10^{-5}\times2\times20 = 8\times10^{-4}\text{ m} \neq 2\times10^{-4}\text{ m}$ (Wrong)

For 4th observation $\quad \Delta l = \alpha l \Delta T$

$= 2\times10^{-5}\times3\times10 = 6\times10^{-4}\text{ m} = 6\times10^{-4}\text{ m}$

[i.e. observed value (Correct)]

Q.15 Why does a metal bar appear hotter than a wooden bar at the same temperature? Equivalently it also appears cooler than wooden bar if they are both colder than room temperature.

Thinking Process According to Kirchhoff's law, good radiator are good absorbers, of heat.

Ans. Due to difference in conductivity, metals having high conductivity compared to wood. On touch with a finger, heat from the surrounding flows faster to the finger from metals and so one feels the heat.

Similarly, when one touches a cold metal the heat from the finger flows away to the surroundings faster.

Q.16 Calculate the temperature which has same numeral value on Celsius and Fahrenheit scale.

Ans. Let Q be the value of temperature having same value an Celsius and Fahrenheit scale.

Now, we can write

$$\frac{°F - 32}{180} = \frac{°C}{100}$$

$\Rightarrow$ Let $F = C = Q$

$$\Rightarrow \frac{Q - 32}{180} = \frac{Q}{100} \Rightarrow Q = -40°\text{C or } -40°\text{F}$$

Q.17 These days people use steel utensiles with copper bottom. This is supposed to be good for uniform heating of food. Explain this effect using the fact that copper is the better conductor.

Ans. As copper is a better conductor of heat as compared to steel. Therefore steel utensils with copper bottom absorbs heat more quickly than steel and give it to the food in utensil. As a result of it, the food in utensil is heated uniformly and quickly.

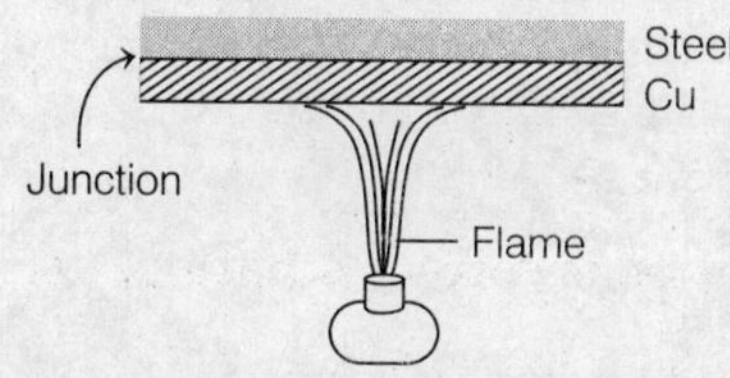

Short Answer Type Questions

Q.18 Find out the increase in moment of inertia I of a uniform rod (coefficient of linear expansion α) about its perpendicular bisector when its temperature is slightly increased by ΔT.

Thinking Process As temperature increases length of the rod also increases hence, moment of inertia of the rod also increases.

Ans. Let the mass and length of a uniform rod be M and l respectively.

Moment of inertia of the rod about its perpendicular bisector, $(I) = \frac{Ml^2}{12}$

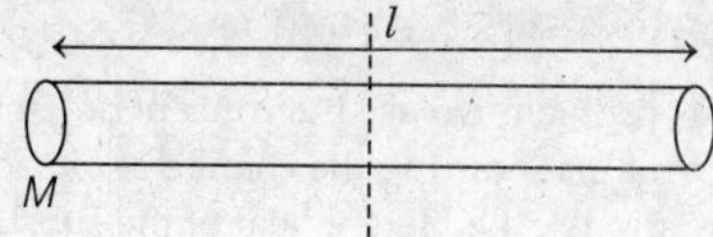

Increase in length of the rod when temperature is increased by ΔT, is given by

$$\Delta l = l \cdot \alpha \Delta T \quad \text{...(i)}$$

$\therefore$ New moment of inertia of the rod $(I') = \frac{M}{12}(l + \Delta l)^2 = \frac{M}{12}(l^2 + \Delta l^2 + 2l\Delta l)$

As change in length Δl is very small, therefore, neglecting $(\Delta l)^2$, we get

$$I' = \frac{M}{12}(l^2 + 2l\Delta l)$$

$$= \frac{Ml^2}{12} + \frac{Ml\Delta l}{6} = I + \frac{Ml\Delta l}{6}$$

$\therefore$ Increase in moment of inertia

$$\Delta I = I' - I = \frac{Ml\Delta l}{6} = 2\times\left(\frac{Ml^2}{12}\right)\frac{\Delta l}{l}$$

$$\Delta I = 2\cdot I\alpha\,\Delta T \qquad \text{[Using Eq. (i)]}$$

Q.19 During summers in India, one of the common practice to keep cool is to make ice balls of crushed ice, dip it in flavoured sugar syrup and sip it. For this a stick is inserted into crushed ice and is squeezed in the palm to make it into the ball. Equivalently in winter in those areas where it snows, people make snow balls and throw around. Explain the formation of ball out of crushed ice or snow in the light of p-T diagram of water.

Ans. From p-T diagram of water and double headed arrow. Increasing pressure at 0°C and 1 atm takes ice into liquid state and decreasing pressure in liquid state at 0°C and 1 atm takes water to ice state.

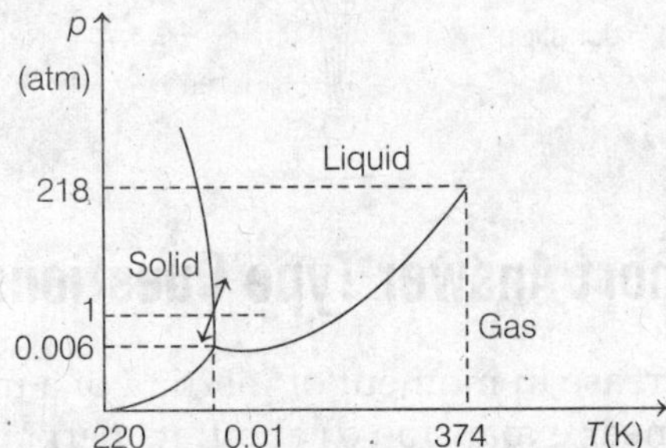

When crushed ice is squeezed, some of it melts, filling up gap between ice flakes upon releasing pressure. This water freezes, binding all ice flakes and making the ball more stable.

Q.20 100 g of water is supercooled to −10° C. At this point, due to some disturbance mechanised or otherwise some of it suddenly freezes to ice. What will be the temperature of the resultant mixture and how much mass would freeze? $[S_w = 1\ \text{cal/g/°C}$ and $L^w_{\text{Fusion}} = 80\ \text{cal/g}]$

- **Concept Insight** In this problem we use the concept of latent heat i.e. The amount of heat transferred per unit mass during the change of phase of a substance without any change in its temperature is called latent heat of the substance for particular change. i.e. Latent heat, $L = Q/m$

Ans. Given, mass of water $(m) = 100$ g

Change in temperature $\Delta T = 0 - (-10) = 10°\text{C}$

Specific heat of water $(S_w) = 1$ cal / g/°C

Latent heat of fusion of water $L^w_{\text{fusion}} = 80$ cal / g

Heat required to bring water in super cooling from –10°C to 0°C,

$$Q = ms_w \Delta T = 100 \times 1 \times 10 = 1000 \text{ cal}$$

Let m gram of ice be melted.

$\therefore$ $$Q = mL$$

or $$m = \frac{Q}{L} = \frac{1000}{80} = 12.5 \text{ g}$$

As small mass of ice is melted, therefore the temperature of the mixture will remain 0°C.

Mistake Alert! *To find the temperature of the mixture we must go through the two steps ($Q = ms\,\Delta T$) and ($Q = mL$), we should not directly apply first one without considering the phase change.*

Q.21 One day in the morning, Ramesh filled up 1/3 bucket of hot water from geyser, to take bath. Remaining 2/3 was to be filled by cold water (at room temperature) to bring mixture to a comfortable temperature. Suddenly Ramesh had to attend to something which would take some times, say 5-10 min before he could take bath. Now, he had two options (i) fill the remaining bucket completely by cold water and then attend to the work, (ii) first attend to the work and fill the remaining bucket just before taking bath. Which option do you think would have kept water warmer? Explain

- **Concept Insight** We should apply logic in this problem in the concept of Newton's law of cooling that rate of fall of temperature of a body with respect to the difference of temperature of body and surroundings. i.e. $\frac{d(T)}{dt} \propto (T - T_0)$

Ans. The first option would have kept water warmer because according to Newton's law of cooling, the rate of loss of heat is directly proportional to the difference of temperature of the body and the surrounding and in the first case the temperature difference is less, so, rate of loss of heat will be less.

Long Answers Type Questions

Q.22 We would like to prepare a scale whose length does not change with temperature. It is proposed to prepare a unit scale of this type whose length remains, say 10 cm. We can use a bimetallic strip made of brass and iron each of different length whose length (both components) would change in such a way that difference between their length B remain constant. If $\alpha_{\text{iron}} = 1.2 \times 10^{-5}$ / K and $\alpha_{\text{brass}} = 1.8 \times 10^{-5}$ / K, what should we take as length of each strip?

Ans. According to question $l_{\text{iron}} - l_{\text{brass}} = 10$ cm = constant at all temperatures ...(i)

Let l_0 be length at temperature 0°C and l be the length after change in temperature of Δt.

Now, we can write $$l_{\text{iron}} - l_{\text{brass}} = 10 \text{ cm at all temperatures}$$

$$l_{\text{iron}}(1 + \alpha_{\text{iron}}\Delta t) - l_{\text{brass}}(1 + \alpha_{\text{brass}}\Delta t) = 10 \text{ cm} \qquad [\text{As } l_{\text{iron}} - l_{\text{brass}} = 10 \text{ cm}]$$

$$l_{\text{iron}}\,\alpha_{\text{iron}} = l_{\text{brass}}\,\alpha_{\text{brass}}$$

$$\therefore \qquad \frac{l_{\text{iron}}}{l_{\text{brass}}} = \frac{1.8}{1.2} = \frac{3}{2}$$

In Eq. (i) $\quad \frac{3}{2} l_{\text{brass}} - l_{\text{brass}} = 10 \text{ cm}$

$$\therefore \qquad \frac{1}{2} l_{\text{brass}} = 10 \text{ cm}$$

$$\Rightarrow \qquad l_{\text{brass}} = 20 \text{ cm and } l_{\text{iron}} = 30 \text{ cm}$$

Q.23 We would like to make a vessel whose volume does not change with temperature (take a hint from the problem above). We can use brass and iron ($\beta_{\text{vbrass}} = 6 \times 10^{-5} / \text{K}$ and $\beta_{\text{viron}} = 3.55 \times 10^{-5} /\text{K}$) to create a volume of 100 cc. How do you think you can achieve this?

Ans. In the previous problem the difference in the length was constant.

In this problem the difference in volume is constant.

The situation is shown in the diagram.

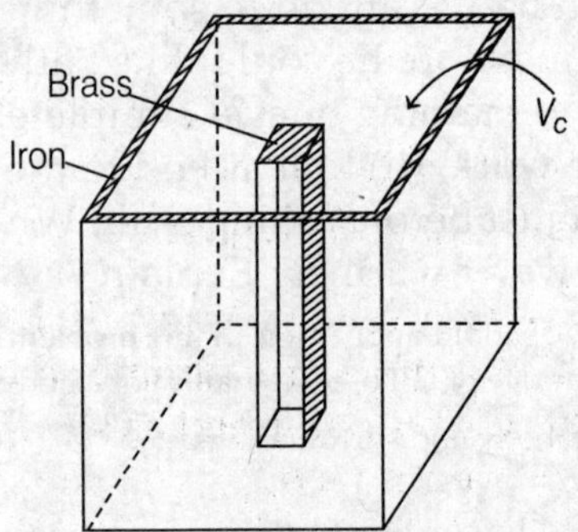

Let V_{io}, V_{bo} be the volume of iron and brass vessel at 0°C

V_i, V_b be the volume of iron and brass vessel at $\Delta\theta$ °C,

γ_i, γ_b be the coefficicnt, of volume expansion of iron and brass.

As per question, $\quad V_{io} - V_{bo} = 100 \text{ cc} = V_i - V_b \quad$ ...(i)

Now, $\quad V_i = V_{io}(1 + \gamma_i \Delta\theta)$

$$V_b = V_{bo}(1 + \gamma_b \Delta\theta)$$

$$V_i - V_b = (V_{io} - V_{bo}) + \Delta\theta (V_{io}\gamma_i - V_{bo}\gamma_b)$$

Since, $V_i - V_b = \text{constant}$.

So, $\quad V_{io}\gamma_i = V_{bo}\gamma_b$

$$\Rightarrow \qquad \frac{V_{io}}{V_{bo}} = \frac{\gamma_b}{\gamma_i} = \frac{\frac{3}{2}\beta_b}{\frac{3}{2}\beta_i} = \frac{\beta_b}{\beta_i} = \frac{6 \times 10^{-5}}{3.55 \times 10^{-5}} = \frac{6}{3.55} \qquad \left[\because \alpha = \frac{\beta}{2} = \frac{\gamma}{3}\right.$$

$$\frac{V_{io}}{V_{bo}} = \frac{6}{3.55} \qquad \text{...(ii)}$$

Solving Eqs. (i) and (ii), we get

$$V_{io} = 244.9 \text{ cc}$$

$$V_{bo} = 144.9 \text{ cc}$$

Q.24 Calculate the stress developed inside a tooth cavity filled with copper when hot tea at temperature of 57°C is drunk. You can take body (tooth) temperature to be 37°C and $\alpha = 1.7 \times 10^{-5}/°C$ bulk modulus for copper $= 140 \times 10^9$ N/m^2.

Ans. Given, change in temperature $(\Delta t) = 57 - 37 = 20°C$

Coefficient of linear expansion $(\alpha) = 1.7 \times 10^{-5}/°C$

Bulk modulus for copper $(B) = 140 \times 10^9$ N/m^2

Coefficient of cubical expansion $(\gamma) = 3\alpha = 5.1 \times 10^{-5}/°C$

Let initial volume of the cavity be V and its volume increases by ΔV due to increase in temperature.

$$\therefore \quad \Delta V = \gamma V \Delta t$$

$$\Rightarrow \quad \frac{\Delta V}{V} = \gamma \Delta t \quad \text{...(i)}$$

Thermal stress produced = $B \times$ Volumetric strain

$$= B \times \frac{\Delta V}{V} = B \times \gamma \Delta t$$

$$= 140 \times 10^9 \times (5.1 \times 10^{-5} \times 20)$$

$$= 1.428 \times 10^8 \text{ N/m}^2$$

This is about 10^3 times of atmospheric pressure.

Q.25 A rail track made of steel having length 10 m is clamped on a railway line at its two ends (figure). On a summer day due to rise in temperature by 20° C. It is deformed as shown in figure. Find x (displacement of the centre) if $\alpha_{steel} = 1.2 \times 10^{-5}/°C$.

Ans. Consider the diagram.

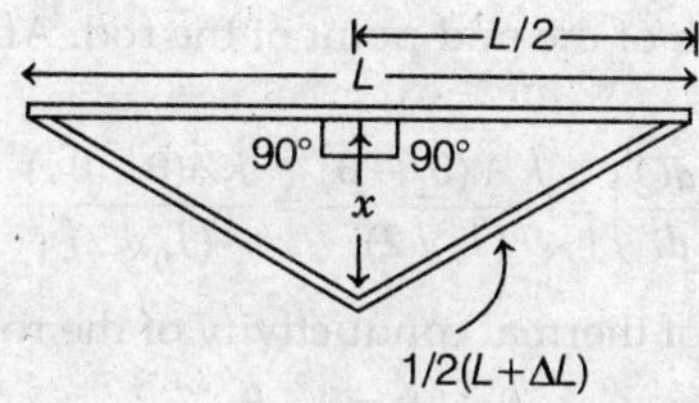

Applying Pythagorus theorem in right angled triangle in figure.

$$\left(\frac{L + \Delta L}{2}\right)^2 = \left(\frac{L}{2}\right)^2 + x^2$$

$$\Rightarrow \quad x = \sqrt{\left(\frac{L + \Delta L}{2}\right)^2 - \left(\frac{L}{2}\right)^2}$$

$$= \frac{1}{2}\sqrt{(L + \Delta L)^2 - L^2}$$

$$= \frac{1}{2}\sqrt{(L^2 + \Delta L^2 + 2L\Delta L) - L^2}$$

$$= \frac{1}{2}\sqrt{(\Delta L^2 + 2L\Delta L)}$$

As increase in length ΔL is very small, therefore, neglecting $(\Delta L)^2$, we get

$$x = \frac{1}{2} \times \sqrt{2L\Delta L} \quad \text{...(i)}$$

But $$\Delta L = L\alpha\Delta t \quad \text{...(ii)}$$

Substituting value of ΔL in Eq. (i) from Eq. (ii)

$$x = \frac{1}{2}\sqrt{2L \times L\alpha\,\Delta t}$$

$$= \frac{1}{2} L\sqrt{2\alpha\,\Delta t}$$

$$= \frac{10}{2} \times \sqrt{2 \times 1.2 \times 10^{-5} \times 20}$$

$$= 5 \times \sqrt{4 \times 1.2 \times 10^{-4}}$$

$$= 5 \times 2 \times 1.1 \times 10^{-2}$$

$$= 0.11\,\text{m} = 11\,\text{cm}$$

Note Here we have assumed ΔL to be very small so that it can be neglected compared to L.

Q.26 A thin rod having length L_0 at 0°C and coefficient of linear expansion α has its two ends maintained at temperatures θ_1 and θ_2, respectively. Find its new length.

Thinking Process When temperature of a rod varies linearly, temperature of the middle point of the rod can be taken as mean of temperatures at the two ends.

Ans. Consider the diagram

θ_1 θ_2

Let θ be the temperature of the mid-point of the rod. At steady state,

Rate of flow of heat,

$$\left(\frac{dQ}{dt}\right) = \frac{KA\,(\theta_1 - \theta)}{(L_0/2)} = \frac{KA(\theta - \theta_2)}{(L_0/2)}$$

where, K is coefficient of thermal conductivity of the rod.

$$\Rightarrow \quad \theta_1 - \theta = \theta - \theta_2$$

$$\Rightarrow \quad \theta = \frac{\theta_1 + \theta_2}{2}$$

Now, using relation, $$L = L_0\,(1 + \alpha\,\theta)$$

or $$L = L_0\left[1 + \alpha\left(\frac{\theta_1 + \theta_2}{2}\right)\right]$$

Q.27 According to Stefan's law of radiation, a black body radiates energy σT^4 from its unit surface area every second where T is the surface temperature of the black body and $\sigma = 5.67 \times 10^{-8}$ W/ m^{2}K^4 is known as Stefan's constant. A nuclear weapon may be thought of as a ball of radius 0.5 m. When detonated, it reaches temperature of 10^6K and can be treated as a black body.

(a) Estimate the power it radiates.

(b) If surrounding has water at 30° C, how much water can 10% of the energy produced evaporate in 1 s?
[$S_w = 4186.0$J / kg K and $L_v = 22.6 \times 10^5$ J / kg]

(c) If all this energy U is in the form of radiation, corresponding momentum is $p = U / c$. How much momentum per unit time does it impart on unit area at a distance of 1 km?

Ans. Given, $\sigma = 5.67 \times 10^{-8}$ W/m^2 K^{-4}

Radius, = $R = 0.5$ m, $T = 10^6$ K

(a) Power radiated by Stefan's law

$$P = \sigma A T^4 = \sigma(4\pi R^2)T^4$$
$$= 5.67 \times 10^{-4} \times 4 \times (3.14) \times (0.5)^2 \times (10^6)^4$$
$$= 1.78 \times 10^{17} \text{ J/s} = 1.8 \times 10^{17} \text{ J/s}$$

(b) Energy available per second, $U = 1.8 \times 10^{17}$ J / s = 18×10^{16} J / s

Actual energy required to evaporate water = 10% of 1.8×10^{17} J/s

$$= 1.8 \times 10^{16} \text{ J/s}$$

Energy used per second to raise the temperature of m kg of water from 30°C to 100°C and then into vapour at 100°C

$$= ms_w \, \Delta\theta + m \, L_v = m \times 4186 \times (100 - 30) + m \times 22.6 \times 10^5$$
$$= 2.93 \times 10^5 \, m + 22.6 \times 10^5 \, m = 25.53 \times 10^5 \, m \text{ J/s}$$

As per question, $25.53 \times 10^5 \, m = 1.8 \times 10^{16}$

or
$$m = \frac{1.8 \times 10^{16}}{25.33 \times 10^5} = 7.0 \times 10^9 \text{ kg}$$

(c) Moment per unit times

$$P = \frac{U}{c}$$

The radiation spread in an area of $4\pi r^2$

Here, $r = 1$ km $= 10^3$ m

Momentum imparted per unit time on a unit area at a distance r,

$$\frac{(u/c)}{4\pi r^2} = \frac{U}{4\pi c r^2} = \frac{1.8 \times 10^{17}}{4 \times 3.14 \times 3 \times 10^8 \times 10^6} = 47.7 \text{ Nm}^{-2}$$

Chapter 11

Thermodynamics

Multiple Choice Questions (MCQs)

Q.1 An ideal gas undergoes four different processes from the same initial state (figure). Four processes are adiabatic, isothermal, isobaric and isochoric. Out of 1, 2, 3 and 4 which one is adiabatic?

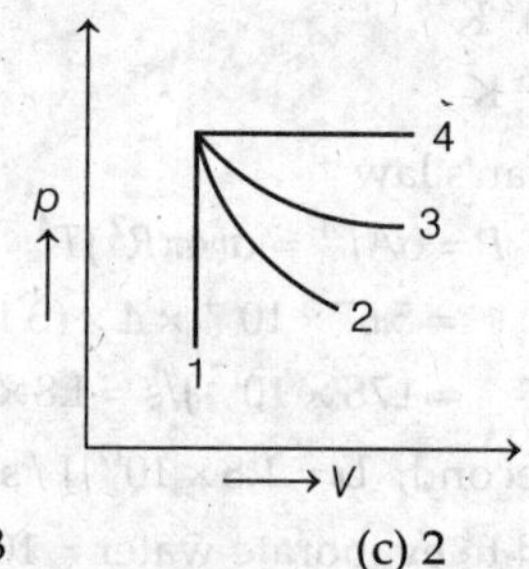

(a) 4 (b) 3 (c) 2 (d) 1

Thinking Process The slope of the curve for the adiabatic process will be more that is the curve will be steeper. Slope of p-V curve in adiabatic process $= -\gamma (p/V)$ where as slope of isothermal process $= -p/V$

Ans. ***(c)*** For the curve 4 pressure is constant, so this is an isobaric process.

For the curve 1, volume is constant, so it is isochoric process. Between curves 3 and 2, curve 2 is steeper, so it is adiabatic and 3 is isothermal.

Mistake Alert ! *We should be careful while deciding between isothermal and adiabatic curves because these curves look similar.*

Q.2 If an average person jogs, he produces 14.5×10^3 cal/min. This is removed by the evaporation of sweat. The amount of sweat evaporated per minute (assuming 1 kg requires 580×10^3 cal for evaporation) is

(a) 0.025 kg (b) 2.25 kg (c) 0.05 kg (d) 0.20 kg

Ans. ***(a)*** Amount of sweat evaporated/minute

$$= \frac{\text{Sweat produced / minute}}{\text{Number of calories required for evaporation / kg}}$$

$$= \frac{\text{Amount of heat produced per minute in jogging}}{\text{Latent heat (in cal / kg)}}$$

$$= \frac{14.5 \times 10^3}{580 \times 10^3} = \frac{145}{5800} = 0.025 \text{ kg}$$

Q.3 Consider p-V diagram for an ideal gas shown in figure.

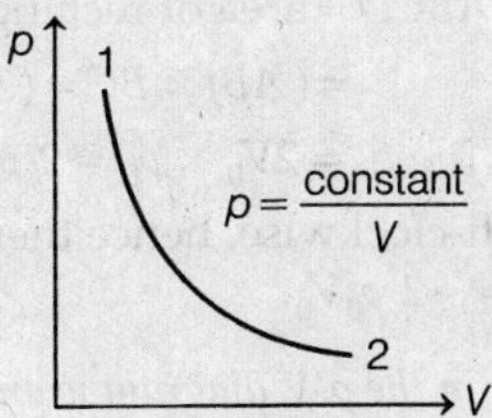

Out of the following diagrams, which figure represents the T-p diagram?

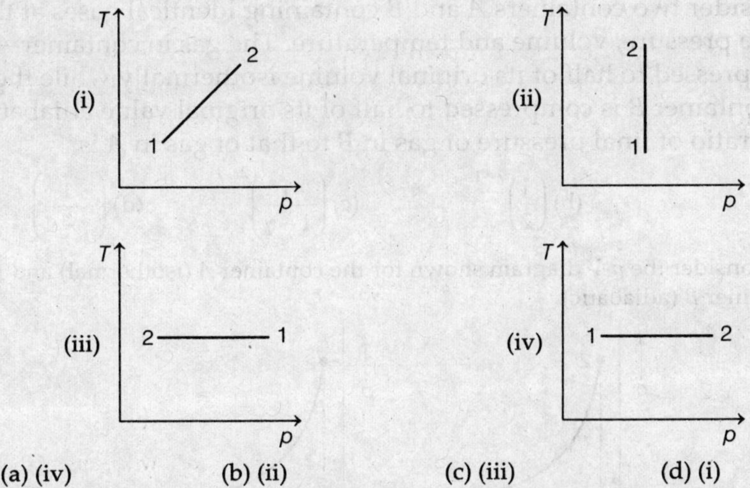

(a) (iv) (b) (ii) (c) (iii) (d) (i)

Ans. *(c)* According to the question given that $pV =$ constant

Hence, we can say that the gas is going through an isothermal process.

$[PV = nRT$ and here $PV =$ constant$]$

Clearly, from the graph that between process 1 and 2 temperature is constant and the gas expands and pressure decreases i.e. $p_2 < p_1$ which corresponds to diagram (iii).

Q.4 An ideal gas undergoes cyclic process $ABCDA$ as shown in given p-V diagram. The amount of work done by the gas is

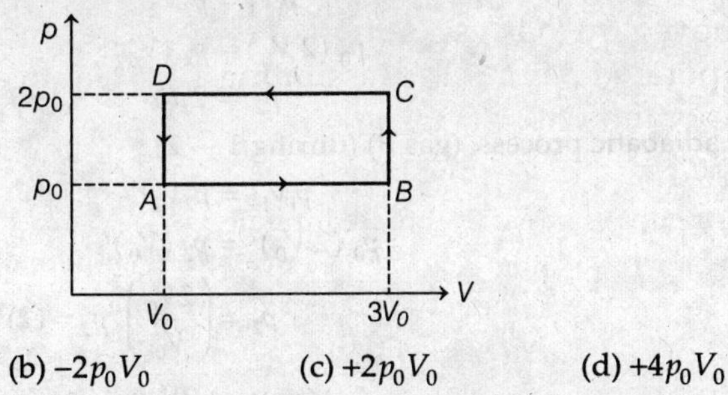

(a) $6p_0V_0$ (b) $-2p_0V_0$ (c) $+2p_0V_0$ (d) $+4p_0V_0$

Thinking Process Work done in a process by which a gas is going through can be calculated by area of the p-V diagram.

Ans. ***(b)*** Consider the *p-V* diagram given in the question.

Work done in the process $ABCD$ = area of rectangle $ABCDA$

$$= (AB) \times BC = (3V_0 - V_0) \times (2p_0 - p_0)$$

$$= 2V_0 \times p_0 = 2\, p_0\, V_0$$

As the process is going anti-clockwise, hence there is a net compression in the gas. So, work done by the gas $= -2\, p_0 V_0$.

Mistake Alert ! *The process in the p-V diagram is anticlockwise meaning the gas is being compressed. It someone incorrectly assumes it is clockwise, they may calculate the work as positive instead of negative.*

Q.5 Consider two containers A and B containing identical gases at the same pressure, volume and temperature. The gas in container A is compressed to half of its original volume isothermally while the gas in container B is compressed to half of its original value adiabatically. The ratio of final pressure of gas in B to that of gas in A is

(a) $2^{\gamma-1}$ (b) $\left(\frac{1}{2}\right)^{\gamma-1}$ (c) $\left(\frac{1}{1-\gamma}\right)^2$ (d) $\left(\frac{1}{\gamma-1}\right)^2$

Ans. ***(a)*** Consider the *p-V* diagram shown for the container A (isothermal) and for container B (adiabatic).

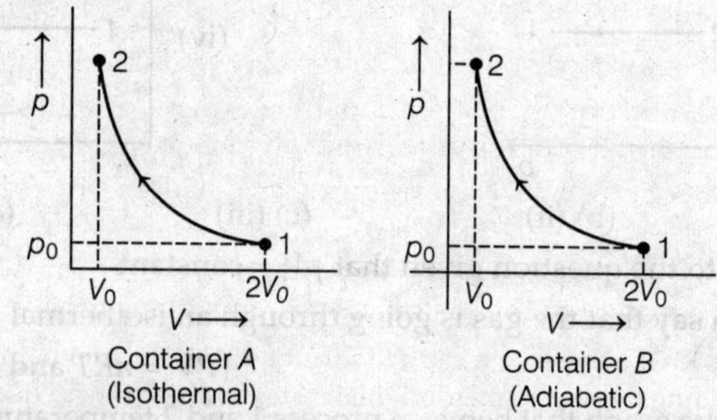

Container *A* (Isothermal) Container *B* (Adiabatic)

Both the process involving compression of the gas.

For isothermal process (gas A) (during $1 \to 2$)

$$p_1 V_1 = p_2 V_2$$

$$\Rightarrow \quad p_0 (2V_0) = p_2 (V_0)$$

$$\Rightarrow \quad p_2 = 2p_0$$

For adiabatic process, (gas B) (during $1 \to 2$)

$$p_1 V_1^{\gamma} = p_2 V_2^{\gamma}$$

$$\Rightarrow \quad p_0 (2V_0)^{\gamma} = p_2 (V_0)^{\gamma}$$

$$\Rightarrow \quad p_2 = \left(\frac{2V_0}{V_0}\right)^{\gamma} p_0 = (2)^{\gamma} p_0$$

Hence, $$\frac{(p_2)_B}{(p_2)_A} = \frac{(2)^{\gamma} p_0}{2p_0} = 2^{\gamma-1}$$

where, γ is ratio of specific heat capacities for the gas.

Q.6 Three copper blocks of masses M_1, M_2 and M_3 kg respectively are brought into thermal contact till they reach equilibrium. Before contact, they were at T_1, T_2, T_3 $(T_1 > T_2 > T_3)$. Assuming there is no heat loss to the surroundings, the equilibrium temperature T is (s is specific heat of copper)

(a) $T = \dfrac{T_1 + T_2 + T_3}{3}$ (b) $T = \dfrac{M_1T_1 + M_2T_2 + M_3T_3}{M_1 + M_2 + M_3}$

(c) $T = \dfrac{M_1T_1 + M_2T_2 + M_3T_3}{3(M_1 + M_2 + M_3)}$ (d) $T = \dfrac{M_1T_1s + M_2T_2s + M_3T_3s}{M_1 + M_2 + M_3}$

Ans. ***(b)*** If the equilibrium temperature $T < T_1$ and T_2 but greater than T_3, then heat loss by M_1 and M_2 = heat gained by M_3

$$M_1S(T_1 - T) + M_2S(T_2 - T) = M_3S(T - T_3)$$

$$M_1T_1 + M_2T_2 + M_3T_3 = (M_1 + M_2 + M_3)\,T$$

$$\Rightarrow \qquad T = \frac{M_1T_1 + M_2T_2 + M_3T_3}{M_1 + M_2 + M_3}$$

Multiple Choice Questions (More Than One Options)

Q.7 Which of the processes described below are irreversible?

(a) The increase in temperature of an iron rod by hammering it.

(b) A gas in a small container at a temperature T_1 is brought in contact with a big reservoir at a higher temperature T_2 which increases the temperature of the gas.

(c) A quasi-static isothermal expansion of an ideal gas in cylinder fitted with a frictionless piston.

(d) An ideal gas is enclosed in a piston cylinder arrangement with adiabatic walls. A weight w is added to the piston, resulting in compression of gas.

- **Concept Insight** If any process can be returned back such that both, the system and the surroundings return to their original states, with no other change anywhere else in the universe, then this process is called reversible process.

Ans. ***(a, b, d)***

(a) When the rod is hammered, the external work is done on the rod which increases its temperature. The process cannot be retraced itself.

(b) In this process energy in the form of heat is transferred to the gas in the small container by big reservoir at temperature T_2. This process is irreversible because heat cannot flow from smaller container (at lower temperature) to the larger container (at higher container).

(d) As the weight is added to the cylinder arrangement in the form of external pressure hence, it cannot be reversed back itself.

Q.8 An ideal gas undergoes isothermal process from some initial state i to final state f. Choose the correct alternatives.

(a) $dU = 0$ (b) $dQ = 0$ (c) $dQ = dU$ (d) $dQ = dW$

Ans. ***(a, d)*** For an isothermal process change in temperature of the system $dT = 0 \Rightarrow T = \text{constant}$.

Therefore in isothermal process an ideal gas dU = change in internal energy

$$= nC_V\, dT = 0$$

[where, n is number of moles and C_V is specific heat capacity at constant volume]

From first law of thermodynamics,

$$dQ = dU + dW = 0 + dW \Rightarrow dQ = dW$$

Q.9 Figure shows the p-V diagram of an ideal gas undergoing a change of state from A to B. Four different parts I, II, III and IV as shown in the figure may lead to the same change of state.

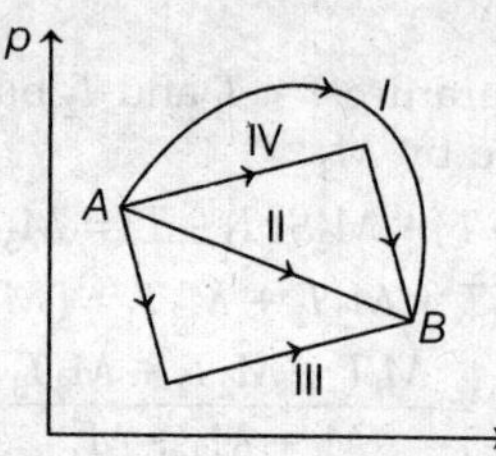

(a) Change in internal energy is same in IV and III cases, but not in I and II.
(b) Change in internal energy is same in all the four cases.
(c) Work done is maximum in case I.
(d) Work done is minimum in case II.

- **Concept Insight** Internal energy is a state function and work done by the gas is a path dependent function.The work done in a thermodynamical process is equal to the area bounded between p-V curve.

Ans. ***(b, c)*** Change in internal energy depends only upon the initial and final positions and not on the path followed.

Hence, change in internal energy is the same for all the cases. The work done is dependent upon the path followed.

Work done for A to B, $dW_{A \rightarrow B}$ = Area under the p-V curve which is maximum for the path I.

Q.10 Consider a cycle followed by an engine (figure.)

1 to 2 is isothermal

2 to 3 is adiabatic

3 to 1 is adiabatic

Such a process does not exist, because

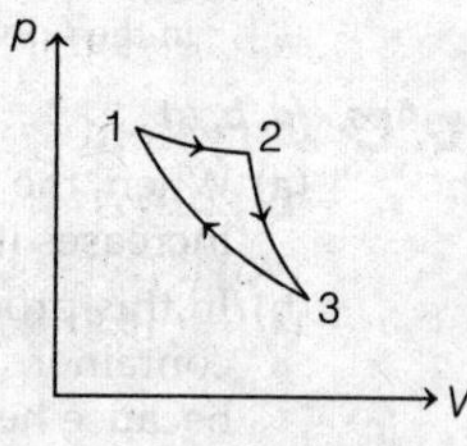

(a) heat is completely converted to mechanical energy in such a process, which is not possible.
(b) mechanical energy is completely converted to heat in this process, which is not possible.
(c) curves representing two adiabatic processes don't intersect.
(d) curves representing an adiabatic process and an isothermal process don't intersect.

Ans. ***(a)*** The given process is a cyclic process i.e., it returns to the original state 1.

Hence, change in internal energy $dU = 0$

$$\Rightarrow \quad dQ = dU + dW = 0 + dW = dW$$

Hence, total heat supplied is converted to work done by the gas (mechanical energy) which is not possible by second law of thermodynamics.

Q.11 Consider a heat engine as shown in figure. Q_1 and Q_2 are heat added both to T_1 and heat taken from T_2 in one cycle of engine. W is the mechanical work done on the engine.

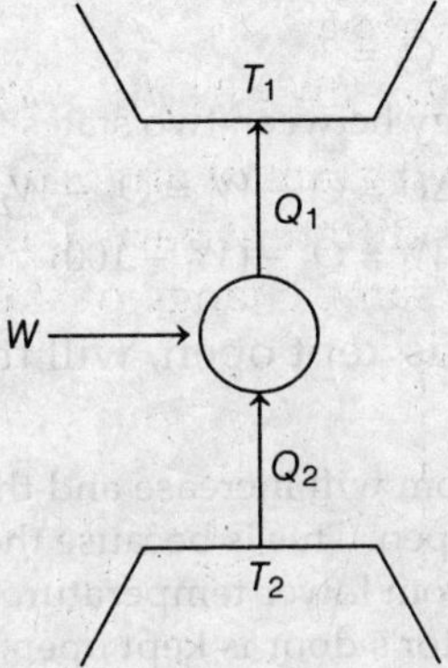

If $W > 0$, then possibilities are

(a) $Q_1 > Q_2 > 0$ (b) $Q_2 > Q_1 > 0$ (c) $Q_2 < Q_1 < 0$ (d) $Q_1 < 0, Q_2 > 0$

Ans. *(a, c)* Consider the figure we can write

$$Q_1 = W + Q_2$$

$\Rightarrow$ $W = Q_1 - Q_2 > 0$ [By question]

$\Rightarrow$ $Q_1 > Q_2 > 0$ [If both Q_1 and Q_2 are positive]

We can also, write $Q_2 < Q_1 < 0$ [If both Q_1 and Q_2 are negative].

Very Short Answer Type Questions

Q. 12 Can a system be heated and its temperature remains constant?

Ans. *Yes,* this is possible when the entire heat supplied to the system is utilised in expansion. i.e. its working against the surroundings and temperature of system remains same.

Q. 13 A system goes from P to Q by two different paths in the p-V diagram as shown in figure. Heat given to the system in path 1 is 1000 J. The work done by the system along path 1 is more than path 2 by 100 J. What is the heat exchanged by the system in path 2?

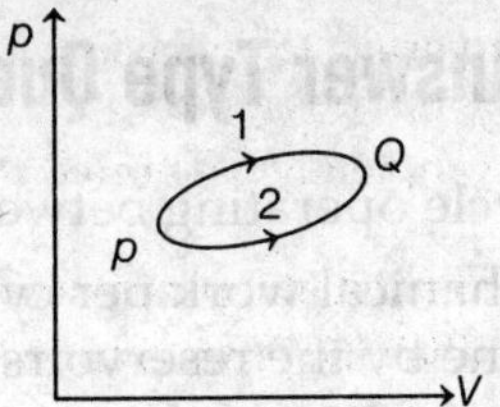

Thinking Process We have to apply first law of thermodynamics for each path.

Ans. **For path 1,** Heat given $Q_1 = +1000\,\text{J}$

Work done $= W_1$ (let)

For path 2, Work done $(W_2) = (W_1 - 100)\,\text{J}$

Heat given $Q_2 = ?$

As change in internal energy between two states for different path is same.

$$\therefore \quad \Delta U = Q_1 - W_1 = Q_2 - W_2$$

$$1000 - W_1 = Q_2 - (W_1 - 100) \Rightarrow Q_2 = 1000 - 100 = 900\,\text{J}$$

Q.14 If a refrigerator's door is kept open, will the room become cool or hot? Explain.

Ans. The temperature of the room will increase and the room will become hot if a refrigerator's door is left open. This is because the refrigerator, being a heat engine, extracts the heat from lower temperature and transfers to higher temperature. If a refrigerator's door is kept open, the refrigerator will transfer more heat inside the room than earlier.

Q.15 Is it possible to increase the temperature of a gas without adding heat to it? Explain.

Ans. *Yes,* during adiabatic compression the temperature of a gas increases while no heat is given to it.

In adiabatic compression, $dQ = 0$

$\therefore$ From first law of thermodynamics, $dU = dQ - dW$

$$dU = -dW$$

In compression work, is done on the gas i.e. work done is negative.

Therefore, $dU =$ Positive

Hence, internal energy of the gas increases due to which its temperature increases.

Q.16 Air pressure in a car tyre increases during driving. Explain.

Ans. During driving, temperature of the gas increases while its volume remains constant.

So, according to Charle's law, at constant volume (V),

Pressure (p) $\propto$ Temperature (T)

Therefore, pressure of gas increases.

Short Answer Type Questions

Q.17 Consider a Carnot's cycle operating between $T_1 = 500\,\text{K}$ and $T_2 = 300\,\text{K}$ producing 1 kJ of mechanical work per cycle. Find the heat transferred to the engine by the reservoirs.

Thinking Process The efficiency of a Carnot's engine is $\eta = 1 - \frac{T_2}{T_1}$,

where, T_2 is temperature of the sink and T_1 is temperature of the source.

Ans. Given, temperature of the source $T_1 = 500\,\text{K}$

Temperature of the sink $T_2 = 300\,\text{K}$

$$\text{Work done per cycle } W = 1\text{kJ} = 1000 \text{ J}$$

Heat transferred to the engine per cycle $Q_1 = ?$

Efficiency of a Carnot engine $(\eta) = 1 - \frac{T_2}{T_1} = 1 - \frac{300}{500} = \frac{200}{500} = \frac{2}{5}$

and $\eta = \frac{W}{Q_1}$

$\Rightarrow \quad Q_1 = \frac{W}{\eta} = \frac{1000}{(2/5)} = 2500 \text{ J}$

Heat transfer to the engine by the reservoir is $= Q_1 - W = 1500 \text{ J}$.

Q.18 Consider a cycle tyre being filled with air by a pump. Let V be the volume of the tyre (fixed) and at each stroke of the pump $\Delta V (<< V)$ of air is transferred to the tube adiabatically. What is the work done when the pressure in the tube is increased from p_1 to p_2?

Thinking Process There is no exchange of heat in the process, hence this can be considered as an adiabatic process.

Ans. Let, volume is increased by ΔV and pressure is increased by Δp by an stroke.

For just before and after an stroke, we can write

$$p_1 V_1^\gamma = p_2 V_2^\gamma$$

$\Rightarrow \quad p(V + \Delta V)^\gamma = (p + \Delta p) V^\gamma \quad$ [$\because$ volume is fixed]

$\Rightarrow \quad pV^\gamma \left(1 + \frac{\Delta V}{V}\right)^\gamma = p\left(1 + \frac{\Delta p}{p}\right) V^\gamma$

$\Rightarrow \quad pV^\gamma \left(1 + \gamma \frac{\Delta V}{V}\right) \approx pV^\gamma \left(1 + \frac{\Delta p}{p}\right) \quad$ [$\because \Delta V << V$]

$\Rightarrow \quad \gamma \frac{\Delta V}{V} = \frac{\Delta p}{p} \Rightarrow \Delta V = \frac{1}{\gamma} \frac{V}{p} \Delta p$

$\Rightarrow \quad dV = \frac{1}{\gamma} \frac{V}{p} dp$

Hence, work done is increasing the pressure from p_1 to p_2

$$W = \int_{p_1}^{p_2} p dV = \int_{p_1}^{p_2} p \times \frac{1}{\gamma} \frac{V}{p} dp = \frac{V}{\gamma} \int_{p_1}^{p_2} dp = \frac{V}{\gamma}(p_2 - p_1)$$

$\Rightarrow \quad W = \frac{(p_2 - p_1)}{\gamma} V$

Q.19 In a refrigerator one removes heat from a lower temperature and deposits to the surroundings at a higher temperature. In this process, mechanical work has to be done, which is provided by an electric motor. If the motor is of 1kW power and heat transferred from $-3°$C to $27°$C, find the heat taken out of the refrigerator per second assuming its efficiency is 50% of a perfect engine.

- **Concept Insight** The Carnot engine is the most efficient heat engine operating between two given temperature. This is why it is known as perfect engine. The efficiency of Carnot engine is $\eta = 1 - \frac{T_2}{T_1}$.

Ans. Given, temperature of the source is 27°C

$\Rightarrow \quad T_1 = (27 + 273)\text{K} = 300\text{K}$

Temperature of sink $\quad T_2 = (-3 + 273)\text{K} = 270\text{K}$

Efficiency of a perfect heat engine is given by

$$\eta = 1 - \frac{T_2}{T_1} = 1 - \frac{270}{300} = \frac{1}{10}$$

Efficiency of refrigerator is 50% of a perfect engine

$$\therefore \quad \eta' = 0.5 \times \eta = \frac{1}{2}\eta = \frac{1}{20}$$

$\therefore$ Coefficient of performance of the refrigerator

$$\beta = \frac{Q_2}{W} = \frac{1-\eta'}{\eta'}$$

$$\frac{Q_2}{W} = \frac{1-(1/20)}{(1/20)} = \frac{19/20}{1/20} = 19$$

$$\Rightarrow \quad Q_2 = \beta W = 19W \qquad \left[\because \beta = \frac{Q_2}{W}\right]$$

$$= 19 \times (1\text{kW})$$

$$= 19\,\text{kW} = 19\,\text{kJ/s}.$$

Therefore, heat is taken out of the refrigerator at a rate of 19 kJ per second.

Q.20 **If the coefficient of performance of a refrigerator is 5 and operates at the room temperature (27° C), find the temperature inside the refrigerator.**

Thinking Process Coefficient of performance (β) of a refrigerator is ratio of quantity of heat removed per cycle (Q_2) to the amount of work done on the refrigerator.

Ans. Given, coefficient of performance (β) = 5

$$T_1 = (27 + 273)\ K = 300\ \text{K},\ T_2 = ?$$

Coefficient of performance (β) $= \dfrac{T_2}{T_1 - T_2}$

$$5 = \frac{T_2}{300 - T_2} \Rightarrow 1500 - 5T_2 = T_2$$

$$\Rightarrow \quad 6T_2 = 1500 \Rightarrow T_2 = 250\ \text{K}$$

$$\Rightarrow \quad T_2 = (250 - 273)°\text{C} = -23°\text{C}$$

Q.21 **The initial state of a certain gas is (p_i, V_i, T_i). It undergoes expansion till its volume becomes V_f. Consider the following two cases**

(a) the expansion takes place at constant temperature.

(b) the expansion takes place at constant pressure.

Plot the *p-V* diagram for each case. In which of the two cases, is the work done by the gas more?

Ans. Consider the diagram p-V, where variation is shown for each process.

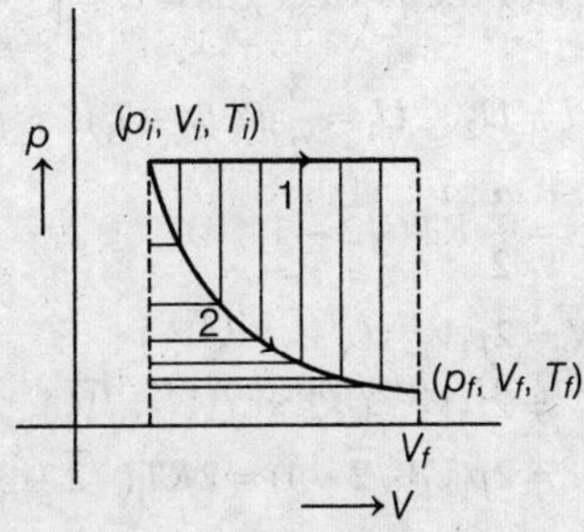

Process 1 is isobaric and process 2 is isothermal.

Since, work done = area under the p-V curve. Here, area under the p-V curve 1 is more . So, work done is more when the gas expands in isobaric process.

Long Answer Type Questions

Q.22 Consider a p-V diagram in which the path followed by one mole of perfect gas in a cylindrical container is shown in figure.

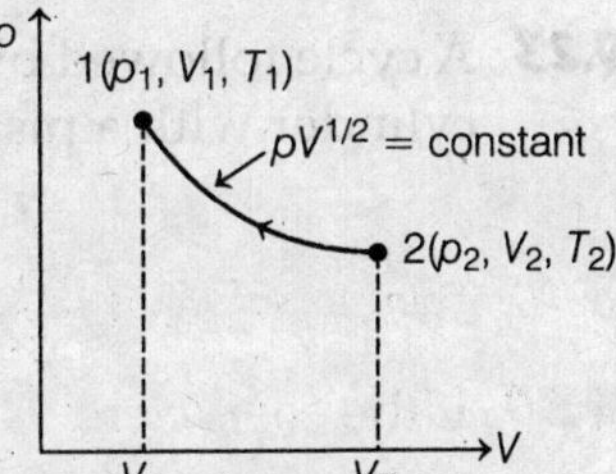

(a) Find the work done when the gas is taken from state 1 to state 2.

(b) What is the ratio of temperature T_1/T_2, if $V_2 = 2V_1$?

(c) Given the internal energy for one mole of gas at temperature T is $(3/2)RT$, find the heat supplied to the gas when it is taken from state 1 to 2, with $V_2 = 2V_1$.

Ans. Let $pV^{1/2}$ = Constant = K, $p = \frac{K}{\sqrt{V}}$

(a) Work done for the process 1 to 2,

$$W = \int_{V_1}^{V_2} p\,dV = K\int_{V_1}^{V_2} \frac{dV}{\sqrt{V}} = K\left[\frac{\sqrt{V}}{1/2}\right]_{V_1}^{V_2} = 2K(\sqrt{V_2} - \sqrt{V_1})$$

$$= 2p_1V_1^{1/2}(\sqrt{V_2} - \sqrt{V_1}) = 2p_2V_2^{1/2}(\sqrt{V_2} - \sqrt{V_1}) \qquad [\because K = PV^{1/2}]$$

(b) From ideal gas equation,

$$pV = nRT \Rightarrow T = \frac{pV}{nR} = \frac{p\sqrt{V}\sqrt{V}}{nR}$$

$$\Rightarrow \qquad T = \frac{K\sqrt{V}}{nR} \qquad [\text{As, } p\sqrt{V} = K]$$

Hence, $T_1 = \frac{K\sqrt{V_1}}{nR}$, $T_2 = \frac{K\sqrt{V_2}}{nR}$

$$\Rightarrow \qquad \frac{T_1}{T_2} = \frac{\frac{K\sqrt{V_1}}{nR}}{\frac{K\sqrt{V_2}}{nR}} = \sqrt{\frac{V_1}{V_2}} = \sqrt{\frac{V_1}{2V_1}} = \frac{1}{\sqrt{2}} \qquad [\because V_2 = 2V_1]$$

(c) Given, internal energy of the perfect gas $= U = \left(\frac{3}{2}\right)RT$

$$\Delta U = U_2 - U_1 = \frac{3}{2} R(T_2 - T_1)$$

$$= \frac{3}{2} RT_1(\sqrt{2} - 1) \qquad [\because T_2 = \sqrt{2}\, T_1 \text{ from (b)}]$$

$$\Delta W = 2p_1V_1^{1/2}(\sqrt{V_2} - \sqrt{V_1}) \qquad \text{[From part (a)]}$$

$$= 2p_1V_1^{1/2}(\sqrt{2} \times \sqrt{V_1} - \sqrt{V_1})$$

$$= 2p_1V_1(\sqrt{2} - 1) = 2RT_1(\sqrt{2} - 1)$$

$$\because \quad \Delta Q = \Delta U + \Delta W = \frac{3}{2} RT_1(\sqrt{2} - 1) + 2RT_1(\sqrt{2} - 1)$$

$$= (\sqrt{2} - 1)RT_1(2 + 3/2)$$

$$= \left(\frac{7}{2}\right)RT_1(\sqrt{2} - 1)$$

This is the amount of heat supplied.

Q.23 A cycle followed by an engine (made of one mole of perfect gas in a cylinder with a piston) is shown in figure.

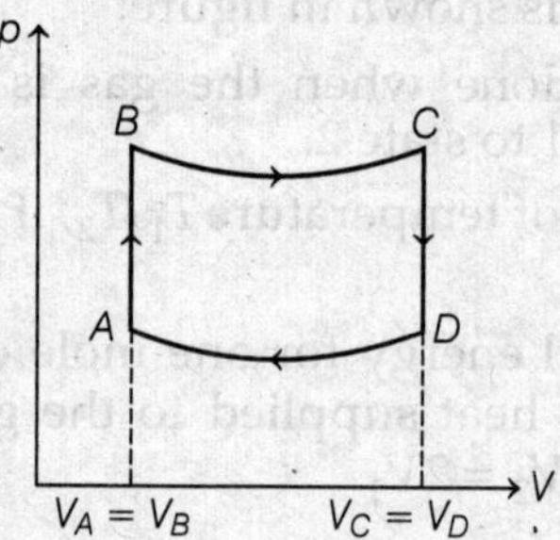

A to *B* volume constant, *B* to *C* adiabatic, *C* to *D* volume constant and *D* to *A* adiabatic

$$V_C = V_D = 2V_A = 2V_B$$

(a) In which part of the cycle heat is supplied to the engine from outside?

(b) In which part of the cycle heat is being given to the surrounding by the engine?

(c) What is the work done by the engine in one cycle? Write your answer in term of p_A, p_B, V_A?

(d) What is the efficiency of the engine?

$(\gamma = \frac{5}{3}$ for the gas), $(C_V = \frac{3}{2}R$ for one mole)

Ans. (a) For the process *AB*, (isochoric process)

$$dV = 0 \Rightarrow dW = 0 \qquad [\because \text{volume is constant}]$$

$$dQ = dU + dW = dU$$

$$\Rightarrow \quad dQ = dU = \text{Change in internal energy.}$$

Hence, in this process heat supplied is utilised to increase, internal energy of the system.

So temperature increases with increases of pressure in process AB which inturn increases internal energy of the system i.e. $dU > 0$. This imply that $dQ > 0$. So heat is supplied to the system in process AB.

(b) For the process CD, volume is constant but pressure decreases.

Hence, temperature also decreases so heat is given to surroundings.

(c) To calculate work done by the engine in one cycle, we calculate work done in each part separately.

$$W_{AB} = \int_A^B pdV = 0,\ W_{CD} = \int_{V_c}^{V_D} pdV = 0 \qquad [\because dV = 0]$$

$$W_{BC} = \int_{V_B}^{V_C} pdV = k\int_{V_B}^{V_C} \frac{dV}{V^{\gamma}} = \frac{k}{1-\gamma}[V^{1-\gamma}]_{V_B}^{V_C}$$

[In adiabatic process $PV^{\gamma} = K$ constant]

$$= \frac{1}{1-\gamma}[PV^{\gamma}\, V^{1-\gamma}]_{V_B}^{V_C}$$

$$= \frac{1}{1-\gamma}[pV]_{V_B}^{V_C} = \frac{(p_C V_C - p_B V_B)}{1-\gamma}$$

Similarly, $$W_{DA} = \frac{p_A V_A - p_D V_D}{1-\gamma} \qquad [\because\ BC \text{ is adiabatic process}]$$

$\because$ B and C lies on adiabatic curve BC.

$\therefore$ $$p_B V_B^{\gamma} = p_C V_C^{\gamma}$$

$$p_C = p_B\left(\frac{V_B}{V_C}\right)^{\gamma} = p_B\left(\frac{1}{2}\right)^{\gamma} = 2^{-\gamma}\, p_B$$

Similarly, $$p_D = 2^{-\gamma} p_A$$

Total work done by the engine in one cycle $ABCDA$.

$$W = W_{AB} + W_{BC} + W_{CD} + W_{DA} = W_{BC} + W_{DA}$$

$$= \frac{(p_C V_C - p_B V_B)}{1-\gamma} + \frac{(p_A V_A - p_D V_D)}{1-\gamma}$$

$$W = \frac{1}{1-\gamma}[2^{-\gamma} p_B(2V_B) - p_B V_B + p_A V_A - 2^{-\gamma} p_B(2V_B)]$$

$$= \frac{1}{1-\gamma}[p_B V_B(2^{-\gamma+1} - 1) - p_A V_A(2^{-\gamma+1} - 1)]$$

$$= \frac{1}{1-\gamma}(2^{1-\gamma} - 1)(p_B - p_A)V_A$$

$$= \frac{3}{2}\left[1 - \left(\frac{1}{2}\right)^{2/3}\right](p_B - p_A)V_A$$

Mistake Alert ! *Ensure that the correct formula for efficiency is being applied (based on heat supplied and work done). The derivation should involve proper handling of all processes in the cycle.*

Q.24 A cycle followed by an engine (made of one mole of an ideal gas in a cylinder with a piston) is shown in figure. Find heat exchanged by the engine, with the surroundings for each section of the cycle. $[C_V = (3/2)R]$

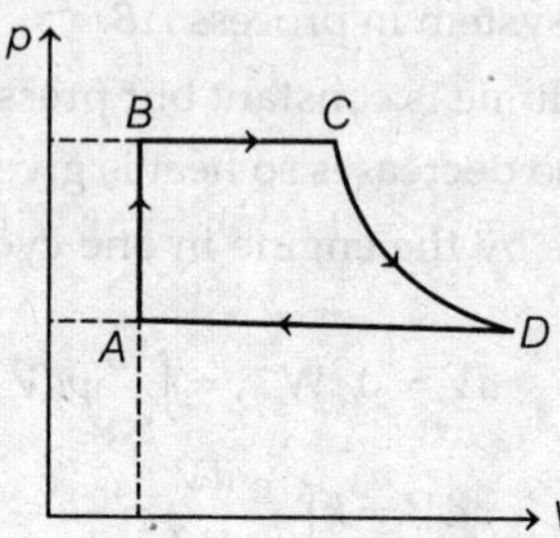

(a) AB : constant volume (b) BC : constant pressure
(c) CD : adiabatic (d) DA : constant pressure

Thinking Process Find amount of heat associated with each process by using first law of thermodynamics.

Ans. (a) For process AB,

Volume is constant, hence work done $dW = 0$

Now, by first law of thermodynamics,

$$dQ = dU + dW = dU + 0 = dU$$

$$= n\,C_v\,dT = n\,C_v\,(T_B - T_A) = \frac{3}{2}R\,(T_B - T_A) \qquad [\because n = 1]$$

$$= \frac{3}{2}(RT_B - RT_A) = \frac{3}{2}(p_BV_B - p_AV_A)$$

$$\text{Heat exchanged} = \frac{3}{2}(p_BV_B - p_AV_A)$$

(b) For process BC, $p = \text{constant}$

$$dQ = dU + dW = \frac{3}{2}R(T_C - T_B) + p_B(V_C - V_B)$$

$$= \frac{3}{2}(p_CV_C - p_BV_B) + p_B(V_C - V_B) = \frac{5}{2}p_B(V_C - V_B)$$

$$\text{Heat exchanged} = \frac{5}{2}p_B(V_C - V_A) \qquad [\because p_B = p_C \text{ and } V_B = V_A]$$

(c) For $C \rightarrow 0$, adiabatic process $dQ =$ Heat exchanged $= 0$

(d) DA involves compression of gas from V_D to V_A at constant pressure p_A.

$\therefore$ Heat exchanged can be calculated by similar way as BC

Hence, $$dQ = \frac{5}{2}p_A(V_A - V_D).$$

Q.25 Consider that an ideal gas (n moles) is expanding in a process given by $p = f(V)$, which passes through a point (V_0, p_0). Show that the gas is absorbing heat at (p_0, V_0) if the slope of the curve $p = f(V)$ is larger than the slope of the adiabatic passing through (p_0, V_0).

Ans. According to question, slope of the curve $P = f(V)$, where V is volume.

$\therefore$ Slope of $p = f(V)$, curve at $(V_0, p_0) = f(V_0)$

Slope of adiabatic at $(V_0, p_0) = k(-\gamma)\,V_0^{-1-\gamma} = -\gamma\,p_0/V_0$

Now heat absorbed in the process $p = f(V)$

$$dQ = dU + dW = nC_V\,dT + pdV \quad \text{...(i)}$$

$\because$ $$pV = nRT \Rightarrow T = \left(\frac{1}{nR}\right) pV$$

$\Rightarrow$ $$T = \left(\frac{1}{nR}\right) V\, f(V)$$

$\Rightarrow$ $$dT = \left(\frac{1}{nR}\right) [f(V) + Vf'(V)]\, dV \quad \text{...(ii)}$$

Now from Eq. (i) $$\frac{dQ}{dV} = nC_V \frac{dT}{dV} + p\frac{dV}{dV} = nC_V \frac{dT}{dV} + p$$

$$= \frac{n\,C_V}{nR} \times [f(V) + V\, f'(V)] + p \quad \text{[from Eq. (ii)]}$$

$$= \frac{C_V}{R} [f(V) + V\, f'(V)] + f(V) \quad [\because p = f(V)]$$

$\Rightarrow$ $$\left[\frac{dQ}{dV}\right]_{V=V_0} = \frac{C_V}{R} [f(V_0) + V_0\, f'(V_0)] + f(V_0)$$

$$= f(V_0)\left[\frac{C_V}{R} + 1\right] + V_0\, f'(V_0) \frac{C_V}{R}$$

$\because$ $$C_V = \frac{R}{\gamma - 1} \Rightarrow \frac{C_V}{R} = \frac{1}{\gamma - 1}$$

$\Rightarrow$ $$\left[\frac{dQ}{dV}\right]_{V=V_0} = \left[\frac{1}{\gamma - 1} + 1\right] f(V_0) + \frac{V_0\, f'(V_0)}{\gamma - 1}$$

$$= \frac{\gamma}{\gamma - 1} p_0 + \frac{V_0}{\gamma - 1} f'(V_0)$$

Heat is absorbed where $\frac{dQ}{dV} > 0$, when gas expands

Hence, $\frac{\gamma}{\gamma - 1} p_0 + \frac{V_0}{\gamma - 1} f'(V_0) > 0$ or $f'(V_0) > \left(-\gamma \frac{p_o}{V_o}\right)$

Q.26 Consider one mole of perfect gas in a cylinder of unit cross-section with a piston attached (figure). A spring (spring constant k)is attached (unstretched length L) to the piston and to the bottom of the cylinder. Initially the spring is unstretched and the gas is in equilibrium. A certain amount of heat Q is supplied to the gas causing an increase of value from V_0 to V_1.

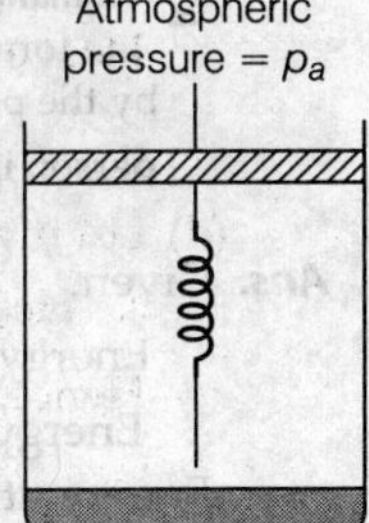

(a) What is the initial pressure of the system?

(b) What is the final pressure of the system?

(c) Using the first law of thermodynamics, write down a relation between Q, p_a, V, V_0 and k.

Thinking Process We will assume the piston is massless, hence, at equilibrium atmospheric pressure and inside pressure will be same.

Ans. (a) Initially the piston is in equilibrium hence, $p_i = p_a$

(b) On supplying heat, the gas expands from V_0 to V_1

$\therefore$ Increase in volume of the gas $= V_1 - V_0$

As the piston is of unit cross-sectional area hence, extension in the spring

$$x = \frac{V_1 - V_0}{\text{Area}} = V_1 - V_0 \quad \text{[Area=1]}$$

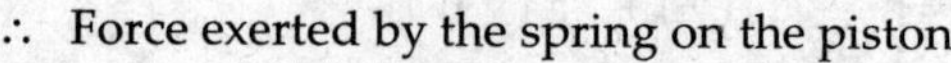

$\therefore$ Force exerted by the spring on the piston

$$= F = kx = k(V_1 - V_0)$$

Hence, final pressure $= p_f = p_a + kxA$ [As area $A = 1$]

$$= p_a + k \times (V_1 - V_0)$$

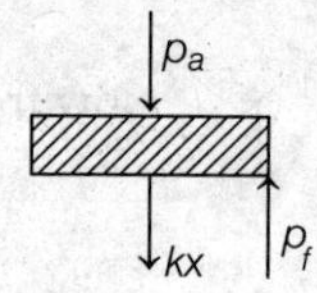

(c) From first law of thermodynamics $dQ = dU + dW$

If T is final temperature of the gas, then increase in internal energy

$$dU = C_V (T - T_o) = C_V (T - T_0)$$

We can write, $$T = \frac{p_f V_1}{R} = \left[\frac{p_a + k(V_1 - V_0)}{R}\right]\frac{V_1}{R}$$

Work done by the gas $= pdV$ + increase in PE of the spring

$$= p_a (V_1 - V_0) + \frac{1}{2} kx^2$$

Now, we can write $dQ = dU + dW = C_V (T - T_0) + p_a (V_1 - V_0) + \frac{1}{2} kx^2$

$$= C_V (T - T_0) + p_a (V_1 - V_0) + \frac{1}{2}(V_1 - V_0)^2$$

This is the required relation.

Q.27 A person of mass 60 kg wants to lose 5kg by going up and down a 10 m high stairs. Assume he burns twice as much fat while going up than coming down. If 1 kg of fat is burnt on expending 7000 k cal, how many times must he go up and down to reduce his weight by 5 kg?

Thinking Process Potential energy(PE) of an object at height (h) is mgh. The energy in the form of fat will be utilised to increase PE of the person. Thus, the calorie consumed by the person in going up is mgh, then according to problem calorie consumed by the person in coming down is $\frac{1}{2} mgh$.

Ans. Given, height of the stairs $= h = 10$ m

Energy produced by burning 1 kg of fat = 7000 kcal

$\therefore$ Energy produced by burning 5 kg of fat $= 5 \times 7000 = 35000$ kcal $= 35 \times 10^6$ cal

Energy utilised in going up and down one time

$$= mgh + \frac{1}{2} mgh = \frac{3}{2} mgh = \frac{3}{2} \times 60 \times 10 \times 10$$

$$= 9000 \text{ J} = \frac{9000}{4.2} = \frac{3000}{1.4} \text{ cal}$$

$\therefore$ Number of times, the person has to go up and down the stairs

$$= \frac{35 \times 10^6}{(3000/1.4)} = \frac{35 \times 1.4 \times 10^6}{3000} = 16.3 \times 10^3 \text{ times}$$

Chapter 12

Kinetic Theory

Multiple Choice Questions (MCQs)

Q.1 A cubic vessel (with face horizontal + vertical) contains an ideal gas at NTP. The vessel is being carried by a rocket which is moving at a speed of 500 m s^{-1} in vertical direction. The pressure of the gas inside the vessel as observed by us on the ground

(a) remains the same because 500 ms^{-1} is very much smaller than v_{rms} of the gas.

(b) remains the same because motion of the vessel as a whole does not affect the relative motion of the gas molecules and the walls.

(c) will increase by a factor equal to $(v_{rms}^2 + (500)^2) / v_{rms}^2$ where v_{rms} was the original mean square velocity of the gas.

(d) will be different on the top wall and bottom wall of the vessel.

- **Concept Insight** This phenomenon is based on the concept of relative motion that is when collision takes place, it is the relative velocity which changes.

Ans. ***(b)*** As the motion of the vessel as a whole does not effect the relative motion of the gas molecules with respect to the walls of the vessel, hence pressure of the gas inside the vessel, as observed by us, on the ground remains the same.

[$P = \dfrac{nRT}{V}$, As volume and temperature is same so 'P' also remains the same]

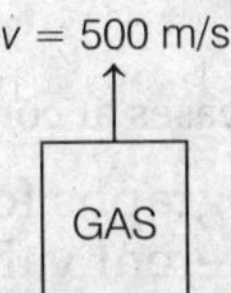

Q.2 1 mole of an ideal gas is contained in a cubical volume V, $ABCDEFGH$ at 300K (figure). One face of the cube ($EFGH$) is made up of a material which totally absorbs any gas molecule incident on it. At any given time,

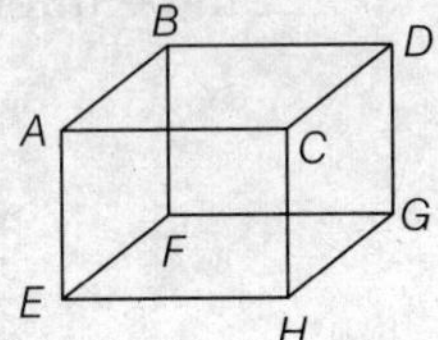

(a) the pressure on $EFGH$ would be zero

(b) the pressure on all the faces will the equal

(c) the pressure of $EFGH$ would be double the pressure on $ABCD$

(d) the pressure on $EFGH$ would be half that on $ABCD$

Ans. ***(d)*** The wall experienced pressure due to the force exerted by molecules on walls because of its rate of transfer of momentum to the wall. Due to elastic collision and magnitude of momentum transferred to the wall by each molecule is 2 mV but wall $EFGH$ absorbs those molecules which strike on it. Therefore, the rate of change in momentum to it becomes only mv so the pressure of $EFGH$ would be half of $ABCD$. Thus, option (d) is correct.

Q.3 Boyle's law is applicable for an

(a) adiabatic process
(b) isothermal process
(c) isobaric process
(d) isochoric process

Ans. *(b)* Boyle's law is applicable when temperature is constant .

i.e. For ideal gas $pV = nRT = \text{constant}$

$\Rightarrow$ $pV = \text{constant (at constant temperature)}$

i.e. $p \propto \frac{1}{V}$ [where , p = pressure, V = volume]

So, this process can be called as isothermal process.

Q.4 A cylinder containing an ideal gas is in vertical position and has a piston of mass M that is able to move up or down without friction (figure). If the temperature is increased

(a) Both p and V of the gas will change
(b) Only p will increase according to Charles' law
(c) V will change but not p
(d) p will change but not V

Ans. *(c)* Consider the diagram where an ideal gas is contained in a cylinder, having a piston of mass M. Friction is absent.

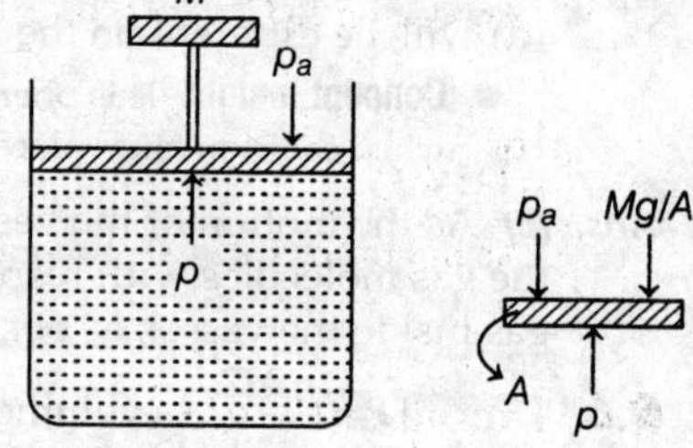

The pressure inside the gas will be

$$p = p_a + Mg/A$$

where, p_a = atmospheric pressure

A = area of cross-section of the piston.

Mg = weight of piston

Hence, p = constant.

When temperature increases

as $pV = nRT \Rightarrow$ volume (V) increases at constant pressure.

Q.5 Volume *versus* temperature graphs for a given mass of an ideal gas are shown in figure. At two different values of constant pressure. What can be inferred about relation between p_1 and p_2?

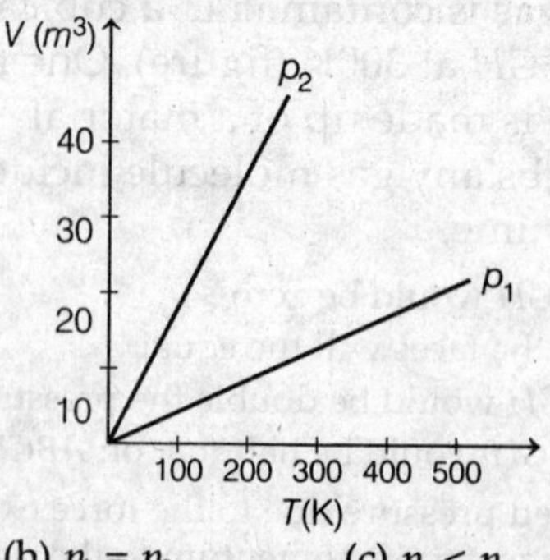

(a) $p_1 > p_2$
(b) $p_1 = p_2$
(c) $p_1 < p_2$
(d) Data is insufficient

Thinking Process To find the required relation, we have to consider slope of the $V - T$ graph. By ideal gas equation, the slope of V-T curve is V/T = nR/p. This imply that greater the slope, smaller the pressure and vice-versa.

Ans. ***(a)*** We know for an ideal gas,

$$pV = nRT \Rightarrow V = \left(\frac{nR}{p}\right) T$$

Slope of the $V - T$ graph, $m = \frac{dV}{dT} = \frac{nR}{p}$ [m = slope of $V - t$ graph]

$\Rightarrow$ $m \propto \frac{1}{p}$ [$\because nR$ = constant]

$\Rightarrow$ $p \propto \frac{1}{m}$

hence, $\frac{p_1}{p_2} = \frac{m_2}{m_1}$

P = pressure
V = volume
n = number of moles of gases
R = gas constant
T = temperature

where, m_1 is slope of the graph corresponding to p_1 and similarly m_2 is slope corresponding to p_2.

$\Rightarrow$ $m_2 > m_1$ or $p_1 > p_2$

Alternate Method

According to Charle's law

$$V \propto T$$

or $\frac{V}{T}$ = costant $= \frac{1}{p}$

As in graph, slope at P_2 is more than slope at P_1

$\therefore$ $P_1 > P_2$

Q.6 1 mole of H_2 gas is contained in a box of volume $V = 1.00\ m^3$ at $T = 300$ K. The gas is heated to a temperature of $T = 3000$ K and the gas gets converted to a gas of hydrogen atoms. The final pressure would be (considering all gases to be ideal)

(a) same as the pressure initially
(b) 2 times the pressure initially
(c) 10 times the pressure initially
(d) 20 times the pressure initially

Ans. ***(d)*** Consider the diagram, when the molecules breaks into atoms, the number of moles would become twice.

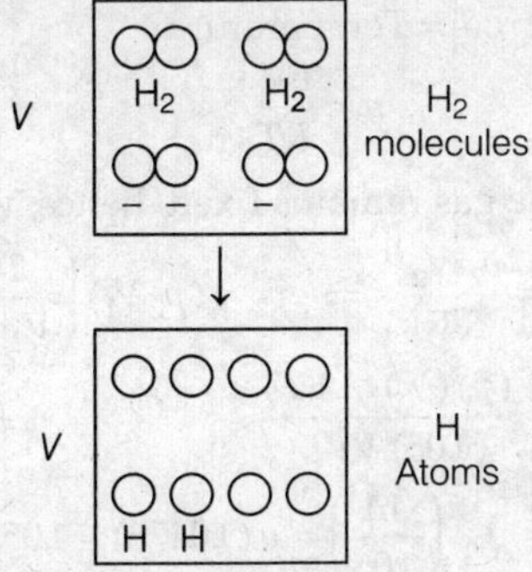

As gases breaks number of moles becomes twice of initial, so $n_2 = 2n_1$

Now, by ideal gas equation, $pV = nRT$

P = Pressure of gas, n = Number of moles, R = Gas constant, T = Temperature

As volume (V) of the container is constant.

So, $$p \propto nT$$

$$\Rightarrow \quad \frac{p_2}{p_1} = \frac{n_2 T_2}{n_1 T_1} = \frac{(2n_1)(3000)}{n_1(300)} = 20$$

$$\Rightarrow \quad p_2 = 20p_1$$

Hence, final pressure of the gas would be 20 times the pressure initially.

Mistake Alert ! *When hydrogen molecules* (H_2) *break atoms (H), then number of moles becomes twice the initial amount. If this is ignored, the pressure calculation will be incorrect.*

Q.7 A vessel of volume V contains a mixture of 1 mole of hydrogen and 1 mole oxygen (both considered as ideal). Let $f_1(v)dv$, denote the fraction of molecules with speed between v and $(v + dv)$ with $f_2(v)dv$, similarly for oxygen. Then,

(a) $f_1(v) + f_2(v) = f(v)$ obeys the Maxwell's distribution law

(b) $f_1(v)$, $f_2(v)$ will obey the Maxwell's distribution law separately

(c) neither $f_1(v)$, nor $f_2(v)$ will obey the Maxwell's distribution law

(d) $f_2(v)$ and $f_1(v)$ will be the same

Ans. ***(b)*** For a function $f(v)$, the number of molecules $n = f(v)$, which are having speeds between v and $v + dv$.

For each function $f_1(v)$ and $f_2(v)$, n will be different, hence each function $f_1(v)$ and $f_2(v)$ will obey the Maxwell's distribution law separately. $\left[\text{As } N_v = \frac{dN}{dV}\right]$

Q.8 An inflated rubber balloon contains one mole of an ideal gas, has a pressure p, volume V and temperature T. If the temperature rises to 1.1 T, and the volume is increased to 1.05 V, the final pressure will be

(a) 1.1 p (b) p

(c) less than p (d) between p and 1.1 p

Ans. ***(d)*** We know for an ideal gas, $pV = nRT$ [Ideal gas equation]

$\Rightarrow$ n = Number of moles, p = Pressure, V = Volume

R = Gas constant, T = Temperature

$$n = \frac{pV}{RT}$$

As number of moles of the gas remains fixed, hence, we can write

$$\frac{p_1 V_1}{RT_1} = \frac{p_2 V_2}{RT_2} \Rightarrow p_2 = (p_1 V_1)\left(\frac{T_2}{V_2 T_1}\right)$$

$$= \frac{(p)(V)(1.1\,T)}{(1.05)\,V(T)} \qquad \left[\begin{array}{l} p_1 = p \\ V_2 = 1.05V \text{ and } T_2 = 1.1\,T \end{array}\right]$$

$$= p \times \left(\frac{1.1}{1.05}\right) = p\,(1.0476) \approx 1.05\,p$$

Hence, final pressure p_2 lies between p and $1.1p$.

Multiple Choice Questions (More Than One Options)

Q.9 *ABCDEFGH* is a hollow cube made of an insulator (figure) face *ABCD* has positive charge on it. Inside the cube, we have ionised hydrogen. The usual kinetic theory expression for pressure

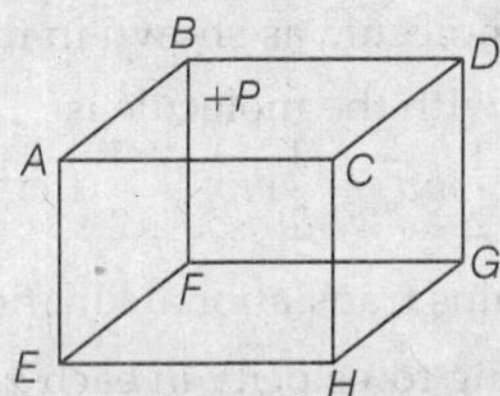

(a) will be valid

(b) will not be valid, since the ions would experience forces other than due to collisions with the walls

(c) will not be valid, since collisions with walls would not be elastic

(d) will not be valid because isotropy is lost

Thinking Process As ionised hydrogen is present inside the cube, they are having charge. Now, due to presence of positive charge on the surface ABCD hydrogen ions would experience forces of electrostatic nature.

Ans. ***(b, d)*** The usual expression for pressure on the basis of kinetic theory will not be valid as ions would also experience electrostatic forces other than the forces due to collisions with the walls of the container. Due to presence of positive charge the isotropy is also lost.

Q.10 Diatomic molecules like hydrogen have energies due to both translational as well as rotational motion. From the equation in kinetic theory $pV = \frac{2}{3}E$, E is

(a) the total energy per unit volume

(b) only the translational part of energy because rotational energy is very small compared to the translational energy

(c) only the translational part of the energy because during collisions with the wall pressure relates to change in linear momentum

(d) the translational part of the energy because rotational energies of molecules can be of either sign and its average over all the molecules is zero

Ans. ***(c)*** According to kinetic theory, we assume the walls only exert perpendicular forces on molecules. They do not exert any parallel force, hence there will not be any type of rotation present.

The wall produces only change in translational motion.

Hence, in the equation

$$pV = \frac{2}{3}E \qquad \left[\begin{array}{l}\text{where } P = \text{pressure} \\ \qquad\ \ V = \text{volume}\end{array}\right]$$

E is representing only translational part of energy.

Q.11 In a diatomic molecule, the rotational energy at a given temperature

(a) obeys Maxwell's distribution
(b) have the same value for all molecules
(c) equals the translational kinetic energy for each molecule
(d) is (2/3)rd the translational kinetic energy for each molecule

Ans. *(a, d)* Consider a diatomic molecule as shown in the diagram.

The total energy associated with the molecule is

$$E = \frac{1}{2}mv_x^2 + \frac{1}{2}mv_y^2 + \frac{1}{2}mv_z^2 + \frac{1}{2}I_x\omega_x^2 + \frac{1}{2}I_y\omega_y^2$$

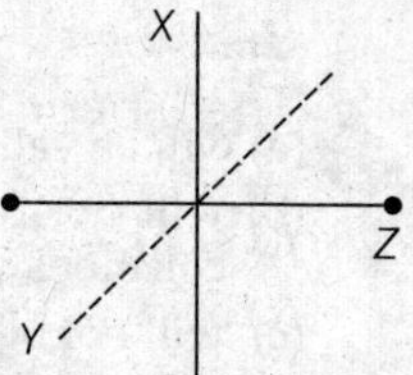

This above expression contains translational kinetic energy $\left(\frac{1}{2}mv^2\right)$ corresponding to velocity in each x, y and z-directions as well as rotational KE $\left(\frac{1}{2}I\omega^2\right)$ associated with axis of rotations x and y.

The number of independent terms i.e. the degrees of freedom the above expression is 5.

As we can predict velocities of molecules by Maxwell's distribution, hence the above expression also obeys Maxwell's distribution.

$\because$ 2 rotational and 3 translational energies are associated with each molecule.

$\therefore$ Rotational energy at a given temperature is $\left(\frac{2}{3}\right)$rd of translational KE of each molecule.

Q.12 Which of the following diagrams (figure) depicts ideal gas behaviour?

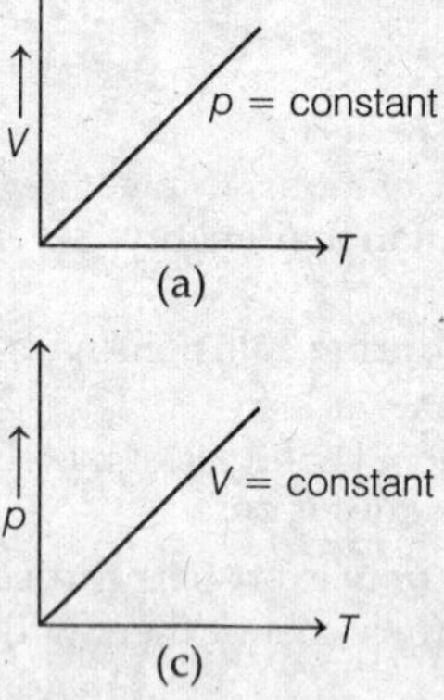

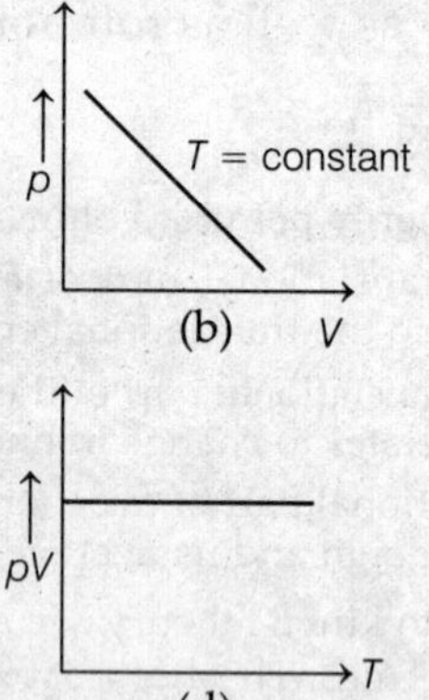

Ans. *(a, c)* We know that ideal gas equation is

$$pV = nRT \quad \text{...(i)}$$

(a) When pressure, p = constant
From (i) volume $V \propto$ Temperature T

(b) When T = constant
From (i) pV = constant
Hence, the graph will be rectangular hyperbola. So (b) is incorrect.

(c) When V = constant.

From (i) $p \propto T$

So, the graph is straight line passes through the origin.

(d) From (i) $pV \propto T$

$\Rightarrow \dfrac{pV}{T}$ = constant

$\Rightarrow$ So, the graph will be a straight line passing through origin.

So, (d) is incorrect.

Q.13 When an ideal gas is compressed adiabatically, its temperature rises the molecules on the average have more kinetic energy than before. The kinetic energy increases,

(a) because of collisions with moving parts of the wall only
(b) because of collisions with the entire wall
(c) because the molecules gets accelerated in their motion inside the volume
(d) because of redistribution of energy amongest the molecules

Thinking Process The elastic collisions of the molecules with a moving part of the system increases their energy.

Ans. ***(a)*** When the gas is compressed adiabatically, the total work done on the gas increases its internal energy which in turn increase the KE of gas molecules and hence, the collisions between molecules also increases. (Because collision of gas molecules with walls of container is treated to be elastic).

Very Short Answer Type Questions

Q.14 Calculate the number of atoms in 39.4 g gold. Molar mass of gold is 197g mole^{-1}.

Ans. We know that,

Molar mass = Mass of Avogadro's number of atoms (Molecules).

$= 6.023 \times 10^{23}$ atoms.

Given, molar mass of gold = 197 g/mol

Now,

$\therefore$ 197 g of gold contains $= 6.023 \times 10^{23}$ atoms

$\therefore$ 1 g of gold contains $= \dfrac{6.023 \times 10^{23}}{197}$ atoms

$\therefore$ 39.4 g of gold contains $= \dfrac{6.023 \times 10^{23} \times 39.4}{197} \Rightarrow 1.20 \times 10^{23}$ atoms.

Q.15 The volume of a given mass of a gas at 27°C, 1 atm is 100cc. What will be its volume at 327°C ?

Ans. We have to convert the given temperatures in kelvin.

If pressure of a given mass of the gas is kept constant, then

$$V \propto T$$

$$\Rightarrow \frac{V}{T} = \text{constant} \qquad \begin{bmatrix} V = \text{Volume of gas} \\ T = \text{Temperature of gas} \end{bmatrix}$$

$\Rightarrow \quad \dfrac{V_1}{T_1} = \dfrac{V_2}{T_2} \Rightarrow V_2 = V_1\left(\dfrac{T_2}{T_1}\right)$

$T_1 = 273 + 27 = 300\,\text{K}$

$T_2 = 273 + 327 = 600\,\text{K}$

But $\quad V_1 = 100\,\text{cc}$

$$V_2 = V_1\left(\frac{600}{300}\right)$$

$$V_2 = 2V_1$$

$\therefore \quad V_2 = 2 \times 100 = 200\,\text{cc}$

Note To apply ideal gas equation, we must convert the given temperature in kelvin.

Q.16 The molecules of a given mass of a gas have root mean square speeds of 100 ms^{-1} at 27°C and 1.00 atmospheric pressure. What will be the root mean square speeds of the molecules of the gas at 127°C and 2.0 atmospheric pressure?

Ans. We know that for a given mass of a gas

$$v_{\text{rms}} = \sqrt{\frac{3RT}{M}}$$

where, R is gas constant
T is temperature in kelvin
M is molar mass of the gas.

Clearly, $\quad v_{\text{rms}} \propto \sqrt{T} \quad$ [v_{rms} is independent of pressure]

As R, M are constants,

$$\frac{(v_{\text{rms}})_1}{(v_{\text{rms}})_2} = \sqrt{\frac{T_1}{T_2}}$$

Given, $\quad (v_{\text{rms}})_1 = 100\,\text{m/s}$

$T_1 = 27°\text{C} = 27 + 273 = 300\,\text{K}$

$T_2 = 127°\text{C} = 127 + 273 = 400\,\text{K}$

$\therefore$ From Eq. (i)

$$\frac{100}{(v_{\text{rms}})_2} = \sqrt{\frac{300}{400}} = \frac{\sqrt{3}}{2}$$

$\Rightarrow \quad (v_{\text{rms}})_2 = \dfrac{2 \times 100}{\sqrt{3}} = \dfrac{200}{\sqrt{3}}\,\text{m/s}$

Q.17 Two molecules of a gas have speeds of $9 \times 10^6\,\text{ms}^{-1}$ and $1 \times 10^6\,\text{ms}^{-1}$, respectively. What is the root mean square speed of these molecules.

Ans. For n-molecules, we know that

$$v_{\text{rms}} = \sqrt{\frac{v_1^2 + v_2^2 + v_3^2 + \ldots\ldots + v_n^2}{n}} \quad \left[v_{rms} = \text{root mean square velocity}\right]$$

where $v_1, v_2, v_3 \ldots\ldots\ldots v_n$ are individual velocities of n-molecules of the gas.
For two molecules,

$$v_{\text{rms}} = \sqrt{\frac{v_1^2 + v_2^2}{2}} \quad [v_1, v_2, v_3 \ldots\ldots\ldots v_n \text{ are individual velocity}]$$

Given, $v_1 = 9 \times 10^6 \text{m/s}$ and $v_2 = 1 \times 10^6 \text{m/s}$

$$\therefore \quad v_{rms} = \sqrt{\frac{(9 \times 10^6)^2 + (1 \times 10^6)^2}{2}}$$

$$= \sqrt{\frac{81 \times 10^{12} + 1 \times 10^{12}}{2}} = \sqrt{\frac{(81+1) \times 10^{12}}{2}}$$

$$= \sqrt{\frac{82 \times 10^{12}}{2}} = \sqrt{41} \times 10^6 \text{ m/s}$$

Q.18 A gas mixture consists of 2.0 moles of oxygen and 4.0 moles of neon at temperature T. Neglecting all vibrational modes, calculate the total internal energy of the system. (Oxygen has two rotational modes.)

Thinking Process To find exact value of total energy for a given molecule of a gas, we must know the number of degree of freedom associated with the molecules of the gas.

Ans. O_2 is a diatomic gas having 5 degrees of freedom.

Energy (total internal) per mole of the gas $= \frac{5}{2} RT$ $\left[\begin{array}{l} R = \text{Universal gas constant} \\ T = \text{temperature} \end{array}\right]$

For 2 moles of the gas total internal energy $= 2 \times \frac{5}{2} RT = 5RT$ ...(i)

Neon (Ne) is a monoatomic gas having 3 degrees of freedom.

$\therefore$ Energy per mole $= \frac{3}{2} RT$

We have 4 moles of Ne.

Hence, Energy $= 4 \times \frac{3}{2} RT = 6RT$ ...(ii) [Using Eqs. (i) and (ii)]

$\therefore$ Total energy $= 5RT + 6RT = 11RT$

Q.19 Calculate the ratio of the mean free paths of the molecules of two gases having molecular diameters 1Å and 2Å. The gases may be considered under identical conditions of temperature, pressure and volume.

Ans. Mean free path of a molecule is given by

$$\lambda = \frac{1}{\sqrt{2}\pi d^2 n}$$

where, n = number of molecules/ volume

d = diameter of the molecule

Now, we can write $\lambda \propto \frac{1}{d^2}$

Given, $d_1 = 1 \text{ Å}, d_2 = 2\text{Å}$

As $\lambda_1 \propto \frac{1}{d_1^2}$ and $\lambda_2 \propto \frac{1}{d_2^2}$

$\Rightarrow$ So, $\frac{\lambda_1}{\lambda_2} = \left(\frac{d_2}{d_1}\right)^2 = \left(\frac{2}{1}\right)^2 = \frac{4}{1}$

Hence, $\lambda_1 : \lambda_2 = 4 : 1$

Short Answer Type Questions

Q.20 The container shown in figure has two chambers, separated by a partition, of volumes $V_1 = 2.0\text{ L}$ and $V_2 = 3.0\text{ L}$. The chambers contain $\mu_1 = 4.0$ and $\mu_2 = 5.0$ mole of a gas at pressures $p_1 = 1.00$ atm and $p_2 = 2.00$ atm. Calculate the pressure after the partition is removed and the mixture attains equilibrium.

p_1, V_1 μ_1	p_2, V_2 μ_2

$V_1, \mu_1,$ p_1	V_2 $\mu_2,$ $p_2,$

Ans. Consider the diagram,

Given,
$$V_1 = 2.0\text{ L},\ V_2 = 3.0\text{ L}$$
$$\mu_1 = 4.0\text{ mol},\ \mu_2 = 5.0\text{ mol}$$
$$p_1 = 1.00\text{ atm},\ p_2 = 2.00\text{ atm}$$

For chamber 1, $p_1, V_1 = \mu_1 RT_1$

For chamber 2, $p_2, V_2 = \mu_2 RT_2$

When the partition is removed the gases get mixed without any loss of energy. The mixture now attains a common equilibrium pressure and the total volume of the system is sum of the volume of individual chambers V_1 and V_2.

So,
$$\mu = \mu_1 + \mu_2,\ V = V_1 + V_2$$

From kinetic theory of gases, pressure extertd by gas per mole is

$$P = \frac{2E}{3V} \quad \text{[where } V \text{ is volume of gas]}$$

For l mole
$$pV = \frac{2}{3}E \quad \left[E = \text{translational kinetic energy}\right]$$

For μ_1 moles,
$$p_1 V_1 = \frac{2}{3}\mu_1 E_1$$

For μ_2 moles,
$$p_2 V_2 = \frac{2}{3}\mu_2 E_2$$

Total energy is
$$(\mu_1 E_1 + \mu_2 E_2) = \frac{3}{2}(p_1 V_1 + p_2 V_2)$$

From the above relation,
$$pV = \frac{2}{3}E_{\text{total}} = \frac{2}{3}\mu E_{\text{per mole}}$$

$$p(V_1 + V_2) = \frac{2}{3} \times \frac{3}{2}(p_1 V_1 + p_2 V_2)$$

$$p = \frac{p_1 V_1 + p_2 V_2}{V_1 + V_2}$$

$$= \left(\frac{1.00 \times 2.0 + 2.00 \times 3.0}{2.0 + 3.0}\right)\text{ atm}$$

$$= \frac{8.0}{5.0} = 1.60\text{ atm}$$

Q.21 A gas mixture consists of molecules of A, B and C with masses $m_A > m_B > m_C$. Rank the three types of molecules in decreasing order of (a) average KE (b) rms speeds.

Ans. (a) $v_{av} = \bar{v} = \sqrt{\dfrac{8K_BT}{\pi m}}$

$$= \sqrt{\frac{8RT}{\pi m}} = \sqrt{\frac{8PV}{\pi m}}$$

According to the question, because temperature and pressure are same

$$v_{av} = \bar{v} \propto \frac{1}{\sqrt{m}}$$

$$v_C > v_B > v_A$$

as $\quad$ $\text{KE} \propto v^2$

and $\quad$ $\text{KE} \propto m$

Thus, KE will be affected by u more than the mass of the atom.

Thus, decreasing order of KE of molecules is

$$\text{KE}_C > \text{KE}_B > \text{KE}_A$$

Mistake Alert ! *The common mistake in this problem is confusing the relationship between mass and rms speed. while the average kinetic energy is same for all molecules at the same temperature, students often incorrectly assume that heavier molecules have higher rms speeds.*

Q.22 We have 0.5 g of hydrogen gas in a cubic chamber of size 3 cm kept at NTP. The gas in the chamber is compressed keeping the temperature constant till a final pressure of 100 atm. Is one justified in assuming the ideal gas law, in the final state? (Hydrogen molecules can be consider as spheres of radius 1 Å).

Thinking Process For justification of assuming the ideal gas law, the molecular volume and the volume occupied of the ideal gas is compared. If both matches, then law holds good otherwise not.

Ans. Hydrogen molecules as spheres of radius 1 Å.

So, $r = 1\,\text{Å} =$ radius.

The volume of hydrogen molecules $= \dfrac{4}{3}\pi r^3$

$$= \frac{4}{3}(3.14)(10^{-10})^3 \approx 4 \times 10^{-30}\ \text{m}^3$$

$$\text{Number of moles of } H_2 = \frac{\text{Mass}}{\text{Molecular mass}} = \frac{0.5}{2} = 0.25$$

Molecules of H_2 present = Number of moles of H_2 present $\times 6.023 \times 10^{23}$

$$= 0.25 \times 6.023 \times 10^{23}$$

$\therefore$ Volume of molecules present = Molecules number $\times$ volume of each molecule

$$= 0.25 \times 6.023 \times 10^{23} \times 4 \times 10^{-30}$$

$$= 6.023 \times 10^{23} \times 10^{-30} \approx 6 \times 10^{-7}\ \text{m}^3 \quad \text{...(i)}$$

Now, in ideal gas law if temperature is constant

$$p_i V_i = p_f V_f$$

$$V_f = \left(\frac{p_i}{p_f}\right) V_i = \left(\frac{1}{100}\right)(3 \times 10^{-2})^3$$

$$= \frac{27 \times 10^{-6}}{10^2} = 2.7 \times 10^{-7} \text{ m}^3 \qquad \text{...(ii)}$$

Hence, on compression the volume of the gas is of the order of the molecular volume [from Eq.(i) and Eq.(ii)]. The intermolecular forces will play role and the gas will deviate from ideal gas behaviour.

Q.23 When air is pumped into a cycle tyre the volume and pressure of the air in the tyre both are increased. What about Boyle's law in this case?

Ans. When air is pumped, more molecules are pumped and Boyle's law is stated for situation where number of molecules remains constant.

In this case, as the number of air molecules keep increasing. Hence, this is a case of variable mass. Boyle's law (and even Charle's law) is only applicable in situations, where number of gas molecules remains fixed.

Hence, in this case Boyle's law is not applicable.

Q.24 A balloon has 5.0 mole of helium at 7°C. Calculate

(a) the number of atoms of helium in the balloon.

(b) the total internal energy of the system.

Thinking Process Energy associated with a monoatomic molecule is $\frac{3}{2}kT$.

Ans. Given, number of moles of helium = 5

$$T = 7°\text{C} = 7 + 273 = 280 \text{K}$$

(a) Hence, number of atoms (He is monoatomic)

$$= \text{Number of moles} \times \text{Avogadro's number}$$
$$= 5 \times 6.023 \times 10^{23}$$
$$= 30.115 \times 10^{23}$$
$$= 3.1 \times 10^{24} \text{ atoms}$$

(b) Now, average kinetic energy per molecule $= \frac{3}{2} k_B T$

[As helium is monoatomic gas so, it has only 3 degrees of freedom]

Here, k_B = Boltzmann constant.

$\therefore$ Total energy of all the atoms

$$= \text{Total internal energy}$$
$$= \frac{3}{2} k_b T \times \text{number of atoms}$$
$$= \frac{3}{2} \times 1.38 \times 10^{-23} \times 280 \times 3.1 \times 10^{24}$$
$$= 1.79 \times 10^4 \text{ J}$$

Q. 25 Calculate the number of degrees of freedom of molecules of hydrogen in 1 cc of hydrogen gas at NTP.

Thinking Process Total number of degrees of freedom in a thermodynamical system = number of degrees of freedom associated per molecule × number of molecules.

Ans. As given molecules are of hydrogen.

$\therefore$ Volume occupied by 1 mole

$$= 1 \text{ mole of the gas at NTP}$$
$$= 22400 \text{ mL} = 22400 \text{ cc}$$

$\therefore$ Number of molecules in 1 cc of hydrogen

$$= \frac{6.023 \times 10^{23}}{22400} = 2.688 \times 10^{19}$$

H_2 is a diatomic gas, having a total of 5 degrees of freedom

(3 translational + 2 rotational)

$\therefore$ Total degrees of freedom possessed by all the molecules

$$= 5 \times 2.688 \times 10^{19} = 1.344 \times 10^{20}$$

Note Any ideal gas has a molar volume of 22400 mL (cc) at NTP.

Q.26 An insulated container containing monoatomic gas of molar mass m is moving with a velocity v_o. If the container is suddenly stopped, find the change in temperature.

Thinking Process As the container is suddenly stopped there is no time for exchange of heat in the process.

Ans. According to kinetic interpretation of temperature, absolute temperature of a given sample of a gas is proportional to the total translational kinetic energy of its molecules.

Hence, any change in absolute temperature of a gas will contribute to corresponding change in translational KE and *vice-versa.*

Assuming n = number of moles.

Given, m = molar mass of the gas.

When, the container stops, its total KE is transferred to gas molecules in the form of translational KE, thereby increasing the absolute temperature.

If ΔT = change in absolute temperature.

Then, KE of molecules due to velocity v_o, $\text{KE} = \frac{1}{2}(mn)\, v_0^2$ ...(i)

Increase in translational $\text{KE} = n\frac{3}{2} R(\Delta T)$ ...(ii)

According to kinetic theory Eqs. (i) and (ii) are equal

$$\Rightarrow \quad \frac{1}{2}(mn)\, v_0^2 = n\frac{3}{2} R(\Delta T)$$

$$(mn)\, v_0^2 = n3R(\Delta T)$$

$$\Rightarrow \quad \Delta T = \frac{(mn)\, v_0^2}{3nR}$$

$$\Rightarrow \quad \Delta T = \frac{mv_0^2}{3R}$$

Long Answer Type Questions

Q.27 Explain why

(a) there is no atmosphere on moon

(b) there is fall in temperature with altitude

Ans. (a) Acceleration due to gravity on the moon is $\frac{1}{6}$ th of g on earth. Thus, the escape velocity on moon is

$$V_{es} = 2.38\ \text{kms}^{-1}, \quad M = \text{mass of hydrogen}$$

Because H_2 is the lightest gas $m = 1.67 \times 10^{-24}$ kg

$$v_{rms} = \sqrt{\frac{3K_BT}{m}} = \sqrt{\frac{3 \times 1.38 \times 10^{-23} \times 300}{1.67 \times 10^{-24}}} = 2.72\ \text{kms}^{-1}$$

The molecule of air can escape out due to the small gravitational force and v_{rms} is greater than escape velocity.

Because the distance of the moon from the sun is roughly equal to that of earth, thus the intensity of energy of the sun reaches to the moon is larger because of the lower density of the atmosphere. Distance between the moon and sun becomes smaller than earth when the moon is towards the sun during its rotation around the earth.

Because of this, the rms speed of molecules increases and some of the molecules can speed up more than escape velocity and so the possibility of escaping out increases. Thus, over a long-time the moon has lost most of its atmosphere.

(b) As the molecules move higher; their potential energy increases and hence, kinetic energy decreases and hence, temperature reduces.

At greater height more volume is available and gas expands and hence, some cooling takes place.

Note We should not relate temperature directly with potential energy. It is directly related with kinetic energy of the molecules.

Q.28 Consider an ideal gas with following distribution of speeds.

Speed (m/s)	% of molecules
200	10
400	20
600	40
800	20
1000	10

(a) Calculate v_{rms} and hence T. $(m = 3.0 \times 10^{-26}$ kg)

(b) If all the molecules with speed 1000 m/s escape from the system, calculate new v_{rms} and hence T.

Thinking Process In this problem, it is shown that cooling takes place after evaporation.

Ans. (a) We know that $$v_{rms}^2 = \frac{\sum_i n_i v_i^2}{\sum n_i}$$

This is the rms speed for all molecules collectively.

$$\text{Now, } v_{rms} = \left(\frac{\sum_i n_i v_i^2}{\sum n_i}\right)^{\frac{1}{2}} = \sqrt{\frac{n_1v_1^2 + n_2v_2^2 + n_3v_3^2 + n_4v_4^2 + n_5v_5^2}{n_1 + n_2 + n_3 + n_4 + n_5}}$$

$$= \sqrt{\frac{10\times(200)^2 + 20\times(400)^2 + 40\times(600)^2 + 20\times(800)^2 + 10\times(1000)^2}{100}}$$

$$v_{rms} = \sqrt{\frac{4\times10^5 + 32\times10^5 + 144\times10^5 + 128\times10^5 + 1000\times10^5}{100}}$$

$$= \sqrt{1000\times(4 + 32 + 144 + 128 + 100)}$$

$$= \sqrt{408\times1000} \approx 639 \text{ m/s.}$$

Now, according to kinetic theory of gasses

$$\frac{1}{2}mv_{rms}^2 = \frac{3}{2}k_B T \qquad \left[\begin{array}{l} K_B = \text{Boltzmann constant} \\ m = \text{mass of gaseous molecules}\end{array}\right]$$

$$\therefore \qquad T = \frac{1}{3}\frac{mv_{rms}^2}{k_B} = \frac{1}{3}\times\frac{3.0\times10^{-26}\times4.08\times10^5}{1.38\times10^{-23}}$$

$$= 2.96\times10^2 \text{ K} = 296 \text{ K}$$

(b) If all the molecules with speed 1000 m/s escape, then

$$v_{rms}^2 = \frac{10\times(200)^2 + 20\times(400)^2 + 40\times(600)^2 + 20\times(800)^2}{90}$$

$$= \frac{10\times100^2\times(1\times4 + 2\times16 + 4\times36 + 2\times64)}{90}$$

$$= 10000\times\frac{308}{9} = 342\times1000 \text{ m}^2/\text{s}^2$$

$$v_{rms} = 584 \text{ m/s}$$

$$\text{Again} \qquad T = \frac{1}{3}\frac{mv_{rms}^2}{k} = \frac{1}{3}\times\frac{3\times10^{-26}\times3.42\times10^5}{1.38\times10^{-23}}$$

$$= 2.478\times10^2 = 247.8 \approx 248 \text{ K}$$

Note After escaping of molecules with speed of 1000 m/s, the temperature in part (b) is 248 K whereas in part (a) before escaping of molecules the temperature was 296 K. Thus, evaporation facilitates cooling.

Q.29 Ten small planes are flying at a speed of 150 km/h in total darkness in an air space that is $20\times20\times1.5 \text{ km}^3$ in volume. You are in one of the planes, flying at random within this space with no way of knowing where the other planes are. On the average about how long a time will elapse between near collision with your plane. Assume for this rough computation that a saftey region around the plane can be approximated by a sphere of radius 10 m.

Thinking Process To solve this problem, we have to consider the relaxation time as well as mean free path.

Ans. The situation can be considered as the time of relaxation, based on kinetic theory of gases. Mean free path is the distance between two successive collisions, which we will consider here as the distance travelled by the plane before it just avoids the collision safe radius is equivalent to radius of the atom.

Hence, the required time

$$t = \frac{\lambda}{v},\ \lambda = \text{mean free path} = \frac{1}{\sqrt{2}\pi d^2 n},\ n = \text{number density} = \frac{N}{V}$$

$$n = \frac{\text{Number of aeroplanes (N)}}{\text{Volume (V)}} = \frac{10}{20 \times 20 \times 1.5} = 0.0167\ \text{km}^{-3}$$

Now, $$\text{Time} = \frac{\text{Mean free path}}{\text{Velocity}}$$

$$t = \frac{1}{\sqrt{2}\pi d^2 (N/V)} \times \frac{1}{v}$$

By putting the given data,

$$t = \frac{1}{\sqrt{2} \times 3.14 \times (20)^2 \times 0.0167 \times 10^{-6} \times 150}$$

$$= \frac{10^6}{1776.25 \times 2.505} = \frac{10^6}{4449.5} = 224.74\ \text{h} \approx 225\ \text{h}$$

Q.30 A box of 1.00 m^3 is filled with nitrogen at 1.50 atm at 300 K. The box has a hole of an area 0.010 mm^2. How much time is required for the pressure to reduce by 0.10 atm, if the pressure outside is 1 atm.

Ans. Given, volume of the box, $V = 1.00\ \text{m}^3$

$$\text{Area} = a = 0.010\ \text{mm}^2$$
$$= 0.01 \times 10^{-6}\ \text{m}^2$$
$$= 10^{-8}\ \text{m}^2$$

N_2 gas
$p = 1.5$ atm
Hole
$p_{\text{outside}} = 1$ atm

Temperature outside = Temperature inside

Initial pressure inside the box = 1.50 atm.

Final pressure inside the box = 0.10 atm.

Assuming,

v_{ix} = Speed of nitrogen molecule inside the box along x-direction.

n_i = Number of molecules per unit volume in a time interval of ΔT, all the particles at a distance $(v_{ix}\Delta t)$ will collide the hole and the wall, the particle colliding along the hole will escape out reducing the pressure in the box.

Let area of the wall, number of particles colliding in time

$$\Delta t = \frac{1}{2} n_i (v_{ix} \Delta t)\, A$$

$\frac{1}{2}$ is the factor because all the particles along x-direction are behaving randomly.

Hence, half of these are colliding against the walls on either side.

Inside the box, $$v_{ix}^2 + v_{iy}^2 + v_{iz}^2 = v_{\text{rms}}^2$$

$\therefore$ $$v_{ix}^2 = \frac{v_{\text{rms}}^2}{3} \qquad [\because v_{ix} = v_{iy} = v_{iz}]$$

or $$\frac{1}{2} m v_{\text{rms}}^2 = \frac{3}{2} k_B T$$

$\left[\begin{array}{l} v_{\text{rms}} = \text{Root mean square velocity} \\ K_B = \text{Boltzmann constant} \\ T = \text{Temperature} \end{array}\right]$

$$\Rightarrow \quad v_{\text{rms}}^2 = \frac{3k_BT}{m} \quad \Rightarrow \quad v_{\text{rms}} = \sqrt{\frac{3k_BT}{m}}$$

[According to kinetic theory of gases]

Now, $\quad v_{ix}^2 = \frac{v_{\text{rms}}^2}{3} = \frac{1}{3} \times \frac{3k_BT}{m} \quad$ or $\quad v_{ix}^2 = \frac{k_BT}{m}$

$\therefore$ Number of particles colliding in time

$$\Delta t = \frac{1}{2} n_i \sqrt{\frac{k_BT}{m}}\ \Delta tA$$

If particles collide along hole, they move out. Similarly, outer particles colliding along hole will move in.

If a = area of hole

Then, net particle flow in time

$$\Delta t = \frac{1}{2}(n_1 - n_2)\sqrt{\frac{k_BT}{m}}\, \Delta ta$$

[Temperatures inside and outside the box are equal]

$$pV = \mu RT \Rightarrow \mu = \frac{pV}{RT}$$

Let n = number density of nitrogen $= \frac{\mu N_A}{V} = \frac{pN_A}{RT}$ $\quad \left[\because \frac{\mu}{V} = \frac{p}{RT}\right]$

Let N_A = Avogardro's number

If after time τ pressure inside changes from p to p_1'

$$\therefore \quad n_1' = \frac{vN_A}{RT}$$

Now, number of molecules gone out $= n_1V - n_1'V$

$$= \frac{1}{2}(n_1 - n_2)\sqrt{\frac{k_BT}{m}}\ \tau a$$

$$\therefore \quad \frac{p_1N_A}{RT}V - \frac{vN_A}{RT}V = \frac{1}{2}(p_1 - p_2)\frac{N_A}{RT}\sqrt{\frac{k_BT}{m}}\tau a$$

or $$\frac{p_1N_A}{RT}V - \frac{vN_A}{RT}V = \frac{1}{2}(p_1 - p_2)\frac{N_A}{RT}\sqrt{\frac{k_BT}{m}}\ \tau a$$

$$\therefore \quad \tau = 2\left(\frac{p_1 - pv_1}{p_1 - p_2}\right)\frac{V}{a}\sqrt{\frac{m}{k_BT}}$$

Putting the values from the data given,

$$\tau = 2\left(\frac{1.5 - 1.4}{1.5 - 1.0}\right)\frac{1 \times 1.00}{0.01 \times 10^{-6}}\sqrt{\frac{46.7 \times 10^{-27}}{1.38 \times 10^{-23} \times 300}}$$

$$= 2\left(\frac{0.1}{0.5}\right)\frac{1}{10^{-8}}\sqrt{\frac{4.7}{1.38 \times 3} \times 10^{-6}}$$

$$= 2\left(\frac{1}{5}\right)1 \times 10^8 \times 10^{-3} \times \sqrt{\frac{46.7}{4.14}} = \frac{2}{5} \times 10^5\sqrt{\frac{45.7}{4.14}} = \frac{2}{5} \times 10^5\sqrt{11.28}$$

$$= \frac{2}{5} \times 3.358 \times 10^5 = \frac{6.717}{5} \times 10^5 = 1.343 \times 10^5 \text{ s}$$

Q.31 Consider a rectangular block of wood moving with a velocity v_0 in a gas at temperature T and mass density ρ. Assume the velocity is along x-axis and the area of cross-section of the block perpendicular to v_0 is A. Show that the drag force on the block is $4rAv_0\sqrt{\frac{kT}{m}}$, where, m is the mass of the gas molecule.

Thinking Process If a massive body is moving with respect to a lighter body with velocity $v + v_o$, then the lighter body suffers a change in momentum $2m(v + v_o)$ which is transferred to the heavier body.

Ans. Consider the diagram

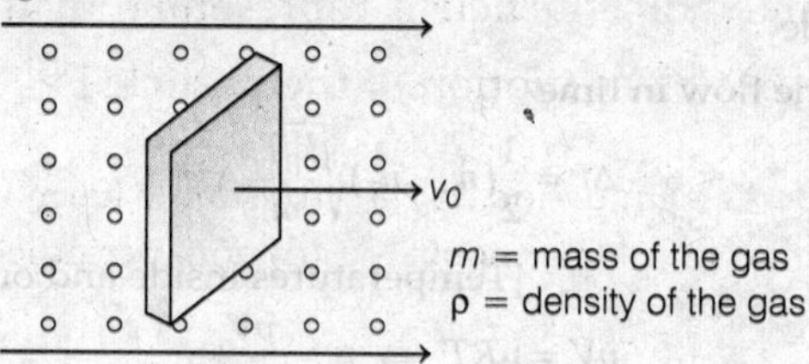

Let n = number of molecules per unit volume

v_{rms} = rms speed of the gas molecules

When block is moving with speed v_o, relative speed of molecules w.r.t. front face $= v + v_o$

Coming head on, momentum transferred to block per collision $= 2m(v + v_o)$, where, m = mass of molecule.

Number of collission in time $\Delta t = \frac{1}{2}(v + v_o)n\Delta tA$, where, A = area of cross-section of block and factor of 1/2 appears due to particles moving towards block.

∴ Momentum transferred in time $\Delta t = m(v + v_0)^2 nA\Delta t$ from front surface.

Similarly, momentum transferred in time $\Delta t = m(v - v_0)^2 nA\Delta t$ (from back surface)

∴ Net force (drag force) $= mnA[(v + v_0)^2 - (v - v_0)^2]$ [from front]

$$= mnA(4vv_0) = (4mnAv)v_0$$

$$= (4\rho Av)v_0 \quad \text{... (i)}$$

where we have assumed $\rho = \frac{mn}{V} = \frac{M}{V}$

If v = velocity along x-axis

Then, we can write $\text{KE} = \frac{1}{2}mv^2 = \frac{1}{2}k_BT$

$$\Rightarrow \quad v = \sqrt{\frac{k_BT}{m}}$$

[K_B = Boltzmann constant, KE = Kinetic energy, T = Temperature]

∴ From Eq. (i), Drag force $= (4\rho Av)v_0 = 4\rho A\sqrt{\frac{k_BT}{m}}\, v_0$.

Chapter 13

Oscillations

Multiple Choice Questions (MCQs)

Q.1 The displacement of a particle is represented by the equation $y = 3\cos\left(\frac{\pi}{4} - 2\omega t\right)$. The motion of the particle is

(a) simple harmonic with period $2\pi/\omega$
(b) simple harmonic with period π/ω
(c) periodic but not simple harmonic
(d) non- periodic

Ans. *(b)* Given, $y = 3\cos\left(\frac{\pi}{4} - 2\omega t\right)$

Velocity of the particle

$$v = \frac{dy}{dt} = \frac{d}{dt}\left[3\cos\left(\frac{\pi}{4} - 2\omega t\right)\right]$$

$$= 3(-2\omega)\left[-\sin\left(\frac{\pi}{4} - 2\omega t\right)\right] = 6\omega\sin\left(\frac{\pi}{4} - 2\omega t\right)$$

Acceleration, $$a = \frac{dv}{dt} = \frac{d}{dt}\left[6\omega\sin\left(\frac{\pi}{4} - 2\omega t\right)\right]$$

$$= 6\omega \times (-2\omega)\cos\left(\frac{\pi}{4} - 2\omega t\right) = -12\omega^2\cos\left(\frac{\pi}{4} - 2\omega t\right)$$

$$= -4\omega^2\left[3\cos\left(\frac{\pi}{4} - 2\omega t\right)\right]$$

$\Rightarrow$ $$a = -4\omega^2 y$$

$\Rightarrow$ As acceleration, $a \propto -y$

Hence, due to negative sign motion is SHM.

Clearly, from the equation

$\omega' = 2\omega$ [$\because$ Standard equation $y = a\cos(\omega t + \phi)$]

$\Rightarrow$ $\frac{2\pi}{T'} = 2\omega \Rightarrow T' = \frac{2\pi}{2\omega} = \frac{\pi}{\omega}$ [and given equation $y = 3\cos\left(-2\omega t + \frac{\pi}{4}\right)$]

So, motion is SHM with period $\frac{\pi}{\omega}$.

Alternate Method

Given $$Y = 3\cos\left(\frac{\pi}{4} - 2\omega t\right)$$

$$Y = 3\cos\left[-\left(2\omega t - \frac{\pi}{4}\right)\right] = 3\cos\left(2\omega t - \frac{\pi}{4}\right)$$

It represents simple harmonic motion with time period

$$T = \frac{2\pi}{2\omega} = \frac{\pi}{\omega}$$

Q.2 The displacement of a particle is represented by the equation $y = \sin^3 \omega t$. The motion is

(a) non-periodic (b) periodic but not simple harmonic

(c) simple harmonic with period $2\pi/\omega$ (d) simple harmonic with period π / ω

Ans. ***(b)*** Given equation of displacement of particle

$$y = \sin^3 \omega t$$

$$\sin 3\theta = 3\sin\theta - 4\sin^3\theta$$

Hence, $$y = \frac{3\sin\omega t - \sin(3\omega t)}{4}$$

$$\Rightarrow \quad 4\frac{dy}{dt} = 3\omega\cos\omega t - 3\omega\cos 3\omega t$$

$$\Rightarrow \quad 4\times\frac{d^2y}{dt^2} = -3\omega^2 \sin\omega t + 9\omega^2 \sin 3\omega t$$

$$\Rightarrow \quad \frac{d^2y}{dt^2} = \frac{-3\omega^2\sin\omega t + 9\omega^2\sin 3\omega t}{4}$$

$\Rightarrow \dfrac{d^2y}{dt^2}$ is not proportional to y.

Hence, motion is not SHM.

As the expression is involving sine function, hence it will be periodic.

Q.3 The relation between acceleration and displacement of four particles are given below

(a) $a_x = +2x$ (b) $a_x = +2x^2$ (c) $a_x = -2x^2$ (d) $a_x = -2x$

Which, one of the particle is exempting simple harmonic motion?

Ans. ***(d)*** For motion to be SHM acceleration of the particle must be proportional to negative of displacement.

i.e. $$a \propto -(y \text{ or } x)$$

We should be clear that y has to be linear.

Q.4 Motion of an oscillating liquid column in a U-tube is

(a) periodic but not simple harmonic

(b) non-periodic

(c) simple harmonic and time period is independent of the density of the liquid

(d) simple harmonic and time period is directly proportional to the density of the liquid

Ans. ***(c)*** Consider the diagram in which a liquid column oscillates. In this case, restoring force acts on the liquid due to gravity. Acceleration of the liquid column, can be calculated in terms of restoring force.

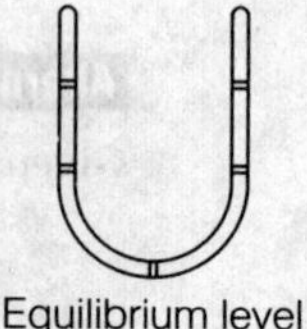
Equilibrium level

Restoring force $f =$ Weight of liquid column of height $2y$

$2y$ represents the height difference between the two arms.

$$\Rightarrow \quad f = -(A \times 2y \times \rho) \times g = -2A\rho g y$$

$\Rightarrow f \propto -y \Rightarrow$ Motion is SHM with force constant $k = 2A\rho g$.

$$\Rightarrow \text{Time period} \quad T = 2\pi\sqrt{\frac{m}{k}} = 2\pi\sqrt{\frac{A\times 2h\times\rho}{2A\rho g}} = 2\pi\sqrt{\frac{h}{g}}$$

$$T = 2\pi\sqrt{\frac{l}{g}}, \text{ where } l = h$$

Which is independent of the density of the liquid.

Q.5 A particle is acted simultaneously by mutually perpendicular simple harmonic motion $x = a\cos\omega t$ and $y = a\sin\omega t$. The trajectory of motion of the particle will be

(a) an ellipse
(b) a parabola
(c) a circle
(d) a straight line

Thinking Process We have to find resultant-displacement by adding x and y-components. According to variation of x and y, trajectory will be predicted.

Ans. *(c)* Given,

$$x = a\cos\omega t \quad \text{... (i)}$$

$$y = a\sin\omega t \quad \text{... (ii)}$$

Squaring and adding Eqs. (i) and (ii),

$$x^2 + y^2 = a^2(\cos^2\omega t + \sin^2\omega t)$$

$$\Rightarrow \quad x^2 + y^2 = a^2 \quad [\because \cos^2\omega t + \sin^2\omega t = 1]$$

This is the equation of a circle

Clearly, the locus is a circle of constant radius a.

Q.6 The displacement of a particle varies with time according to the relation $y = a\sin\omega t + b\cos\omega t$.

(a) The motion is oscillatory but not SHM.
(b) The motion is SHM with amplitude $a + b$.
(c) The motion is SHM with amplitude $a^2 + b^2$.
(d) The motion is SHM with amplitude $\sqrt{a^2 + b^2}$.

Ans. *(d)* According to the question, the displacement

$$y = a\sin\omega t + b\cos\omega t$$

Let $\quad a = A\sin\phi$ and $b = A\cos\phi$

Now, $\quad a^2 + b^2 = A^2\sin^2\phi + A^2\cos^2\phi = A^2 \Rightarrow A = \sqrt{a^2 + b^2}$

$$y = A\sin\phi\cdot\sin\omega t + A\cos\phi.\cos\omega t$$

$$= A\sin(\omega t + \phi)$$

$$\frac{dy}{dt} = A\omega\cos(\omega t + \phi)$$

$$\frac{d^2y}{dt^2} = -A\omega^2\sin(\omega t + \phi) = -Ay\omega^2 = (-A\omega^2)y$$

$$\Rightarrow \quad \frac{d^2y}{dt^2} \propto (-y)$$

Hence, it is an equation of SHM with amplitude $A = \sqrt{a^2 + b^2}$.

Q.7 Four pendulums A, B, C and D are suspended from the same elastic support as shown in figure. A and C are of the same length, while B is smaller than A and D is larger than A. If A is given a transverse displacement,

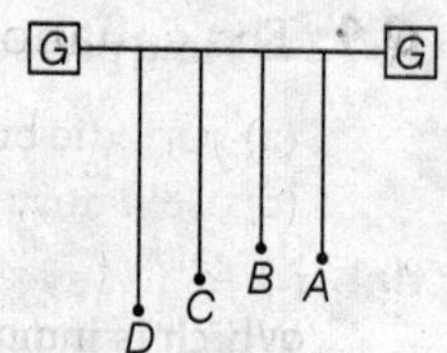

(a) D will vibrate with maximum amplitude
(b) C will vibrate with maximum amplitude
(c) B will vibrate with maximum amplitude
(d) All the four will oscillate with equal amplitude

Ans. ***(b)*** According to the question, A is given a transverse displacement.

Through the elastic support the disturbance is transferred to all the pendulums.

A and C are having same length, hence they will be in resonance, because their time period of oscillation.

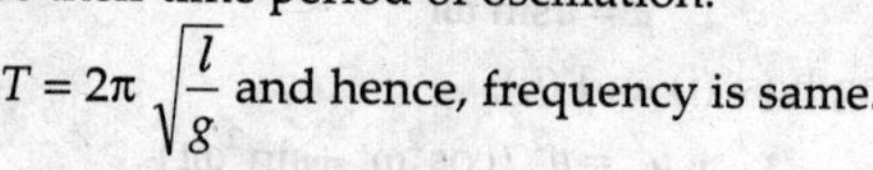

$$T = 2\pi\sqrt{\frac{l}{g}} \text{ and hence, frequency is same.}$$

So, amplitude of A and C will be maximum.

Note In this problem, we have assumed that the support is perfectly elastic and there is no damping. Hence, oscillation is considered as undamped.

Q.8 Figure shows the circular motion of a particle. The radius of the circle, the period, sense of revolution and the initial position are indicated on the figure. The simple harmonic motion of the x-projection of the radius vector of the rotating particle P is

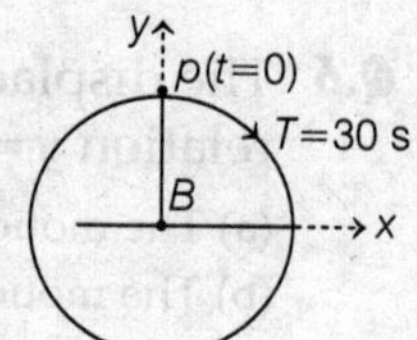

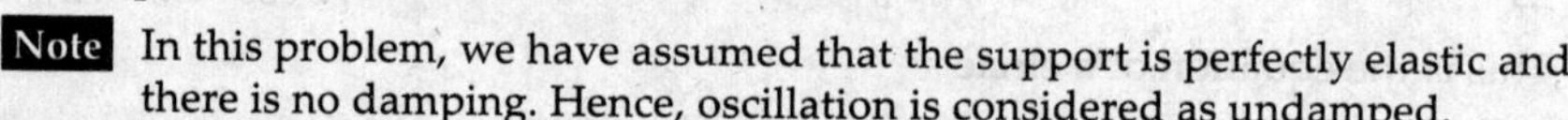

(a) $x(t) = B\sin\left(\frac{2\pi t}{30}\right)$
(b) $x(t) = B\cos\left(\frac{\pi t}{15}\right)$
(c) $x(t) = B\sin\left(\frac{\pi t}{15} + \frac{\pi}{2}\right)$
(d) $x(t) = B\cos\left(\frac{\pi t}{15} + \frac{\pi}{2}\right)$

Ans. ***(a)*** Let angular velocity of the particle executing circular motion is ω and when it is at Q makes and angle θ as shown in the diagram.

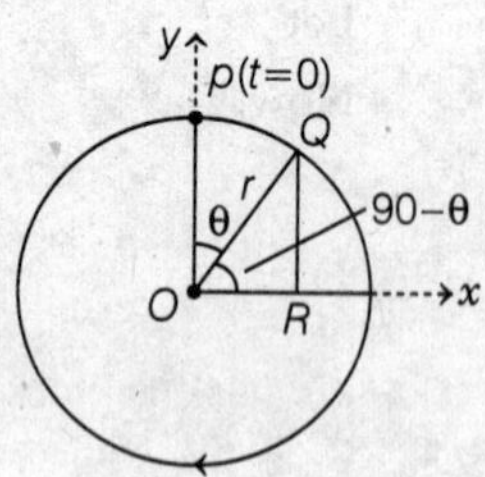

Clearly, $\theta = \omega t$

Now, we can write $OR = OQ\cos(90 - \theta)$

$$= OQ\sin\theta = OQ\sin\omega t$$

$$= r\sin\omega t$$

$[\because OQ = r]$

$\Rightarrow$ $x = r\sin\omega t = B\sin\omega t$ $[\because r = B]$

$$= B\sin\frac{2\pi}{T}t = B\sin\left(\frac{2\pi}{30}t\right)$$

Clearly, this equation represents SHM.

Q.9 The equation of motion of a particle is $x = a\cos(\alpha t)^2$. The motion is

(a) periodic but not oscillatory
(b) periodic and oscillatory
(c) oscillatory but not periodic
(d) neither periodic nor oscillatory

Ans. *(c)* As the given equation is $x = a\cos(\alpha t)^2$ is a cosine function. Hence, it is an oscillatory motion.

Now, putting $t + T$ in place of t

$$x(t+T) = a\cos[\alpha(t+T)]^2 \quad [\because x(t) = a\cos(\alpha t)^2]$$

$$= a\cos[\alpha t^2 + \alpha T^2 + 2\alpha t T] \neq x(t)$$

where, T is supposed as period of the function $\omega(t)$.

Hence, it is not periodic.

Q.10 A particle executing SHM has a maximum speed of 30 cm/s and a maximum acceleration of 60 cm/s^2. The period of oscillation is

(a) π sec
(b) $\frac{\pi}{2}$ sec
(c) 2π sec
(d) $\frac{\pi}{t}$ sec

Ans. *(a)* Let equation of an SHM is represented by $y = a\sin\omega t$

$$v = \frac{dy}{dt} = a\omega\cos\omega t$$

$$\Rightarrow \quad (v)_{max} = a\omega = 30 \quad \text{...(i)}$$

$$\text{Acceleration } (A) = \frac{d^2x}{dt^2} = -a\omega^2\sin\omega t$$

$$A_{max} = \omega^2 a = 60 \quad \text{...(ii)}$$

From Eqs. (i) and (ii), we get $\omega(\omega a) = 60 \Rightarrow \omega(30) = 60$

$$\Rightarrow \quad \omega = 2 \text{ rad/s}$$

$$\Rightarrow \quad \frac{2\pi}{T} = 2 \text{ rad/s} \Rightarrow T = \pi \text{ sec}$$

Q.11 When a mass m is connected individually to two springs S_1 and S_2, the oscillation frequencies are ν_1 and ν_2. If the same mass is attached to the two springs as shown in figure, the oscillation frequency would be

(a) $\nu_1 + \nu_2$
(b) $\sqrt{\nu_1^2 + \nu_2^2}$
(c) $\left(\frac{1}{\nu_1} + \frac{1}{\nu_2}\right)^{-1}$
(d) $\sqrt{\nu_1^2 - \nu_2^2}$

Thinking Process To solve this question, we have to find equivalent spring constant of the system when mass is connected in between.

Ans. *(b)*

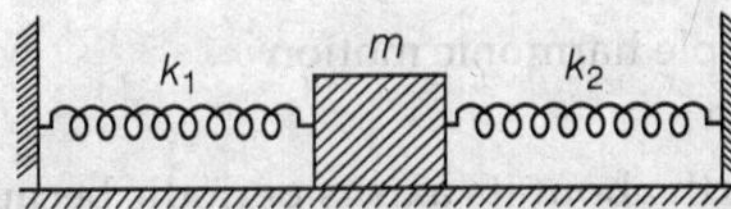

In the diagram, two springs can be considered as parallel combination.

Hence, k_{eq} = Equivalent spring constant

$$= k_1 + k_2$$

Time period of oscillation of the spring block- system

$$T = 2\pi\sqrt{\frac{m}{k_{eq}}} = 2\pi\sqrt{\frac{m}{k_1 + k_2}}$$

$$\Rightarrow \quad \nu = \frac{1}{T} = \frac{1}{2\pi} \times \sqrt{\frac{k_1 + k_2}{m}} \quad ...(i)$$

= Equivalent oscillation frequency.

When the mass is connected to the two springs individually

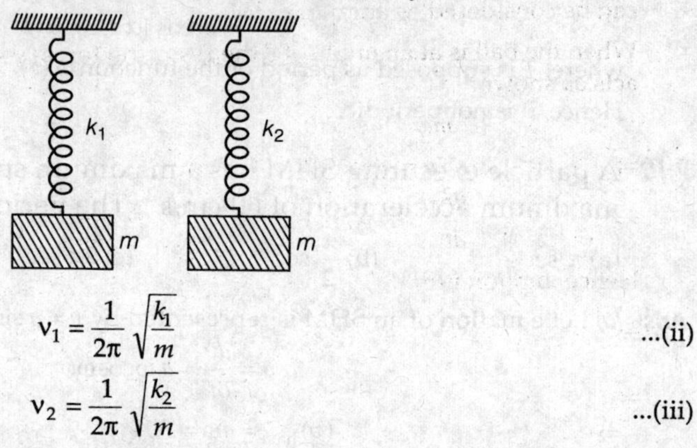

$$\nu_1 = \frac{1}{2\pi}\sqrt{\frac{k_1}{m}} \quad ...(ii)$$

$$\nu_2 = \frac{1}{2\pi}\sqrt{\frac{k_2}{m}} \quad ...(iii)$$

From Eqs. (i), (ii) and (iii),

$$\nu = \frac{1}{2\pi}\left[\frac{k_1}{m} + \frac{k_2}{m}\right]^{1/2} \quad \text{[from Eq. (i)]}$$

$$= \frac{1}{2\pi}\left[\frac{4\pi^2\nu_1^2}{1} + \frac{4\pi^2\nu_2^2}{1}\right]^{1/2}$$

$$\left[\because \text{ from Eq. (ii) } \frac{k_1}{m} = 4\pi^2\nu_1^2 \text{ and from Eq. (iii), } \frac{k_2}{m} = 4\pi^2\nu_2^2\right]$$

$$= \frac{2\pi}{2\pi}[\nu_1^2 + \nu_2^2]^{1/2} \Rightarrow \nu = \sqrt{\nu_1^2 + \nu_2^2}$$

Mistake Alert! *Do not confuse with parallel and series combinations of springs.*

Multiple Choice Questions (More Than One Options)

Q.12 The rotation of earth about its axis is

(a) periodic motion

(b) simple harmonic motion

(c) periodic but not simple harmonic motion

(d) non-periodic motion

Ans. ***(a, c)*** The rotation of earth about its axis is periodic because it repeats its path after a regular interval of time.

The rotation of earth is obviously not a to and fro type of motion about a fixed point, hence its motion is not SHM.

Q.13 Motion of a ball bearing inside a smooth curved bowl, when released from a point slightly above the lower point is

(a) simple harmonic motion (b) non-periodic motion
(c) periodic motion (d) periodic but not SHM

Ans. ***(a, c)*** Consider the motion of the ball inside a smooth curved bowl.

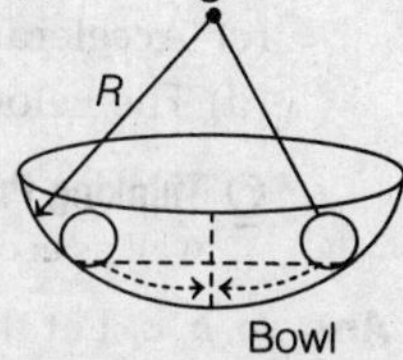

For small angular displacement or slightly released motion, it can be considered as angular SHM.

When the ball is at an angle of θ the restoring force $(g \sin \theta) m$ acts as shown.

$\because$ $ma = mg\sin\theta$

$\Rightarrow$ $a = g\sin\theta$

$\Rightarrow$ $\frac{d^2x}{dt^2} = -g\sin\theta = -g \times \frac{x}{R}$ $[\because \sin\theta \simeq \theta = x/R]$

Hence ,motion is SHM

$\Rightarrow$ $\frac{d^2x}{dt^2} \propto (-x)$ $[\because a \propto -x]$

$\Rightarrow$ $\omega = \sqrt{g/R}$

Time period $T = \frac{2\pi}{\omega} = 2\pi\sqrt{\frac{R}{g}}$.

As motion is SHM, hence it must be periodic.

Q.14 Displacement *versus* time curve for a particle executing SHM is shown in figure. Choose the correct statements.

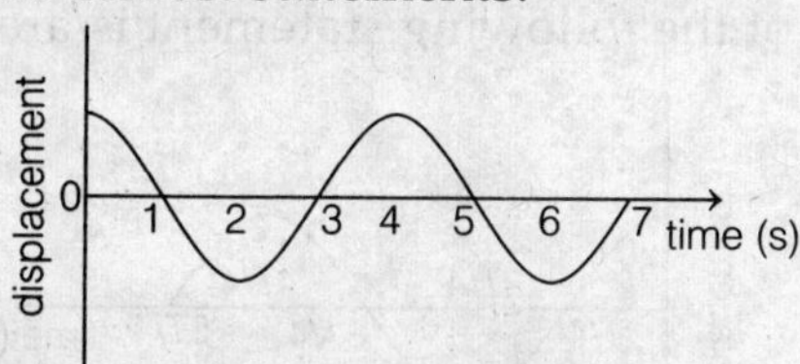

(a) Phase of the oscillator is same at $t = 0$ s and $t = 2$ s.
(b) Phase of the oscillator is same at $t = 2$ s and $t = 6$ s.
(c) Phase of the oscillator is same at $t = 1$ s and $t = 7$ s.
(d) Phase of the oscillator is same at $t = 1$ s and $t = 5$ s.

Ans. ***(b, d)*** It is clear from the curve that points corresponding to $t = 2$ s and $t = 6$ s are separated by a distance belongs to one time period. Hence, these points must be in same phase.

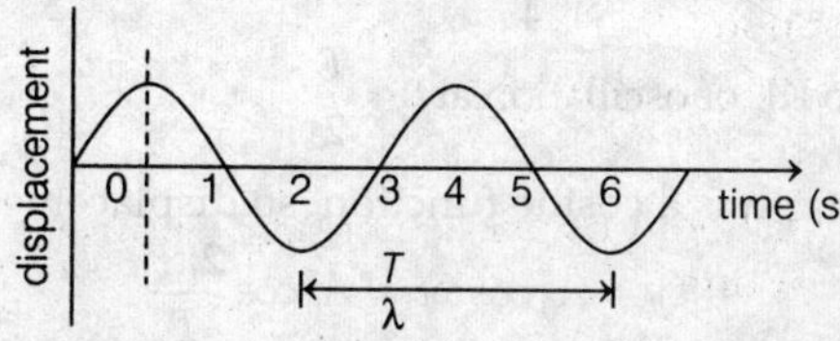

Similarly, points belong to $t = 1$ s and $t = 5$ s are at separation of one time period, hence must be in phase.

Q.15 Which of the following statements is/are true for a simple harmonic oscillator ?

(a) Force acting is directly proportional to displacement from the mean position and opposite to it
(b) Motion is periodic
(c) Acceleration of the oscillator is constant
(d) The velocity is periodic

Thinking Process We have to write equation for the SHM and then find out velocity as well as acceleration corresponding to the displacement.

Ans. *(a, b, d)* Let the equation for the SHM is $x = a \sin \omega t$.

Clearly, it is a periodic motion because it involves sine function. [i.e. option (b)]

$$\text{Velocity } v = \frac{dx}{dt} = \frac{d}{dt}(a \sin \omega t) = a\,\omega \cos \omega t$$

Velocity is also periodic because of cosine function. i.e. option (d)

Acceleration, $$A = \frac{dv}{dt} = \frac{d^2x}{dt^2} = -a\,\omega^2 \sin \omega t$$

[∵ Acceleration is a sine function, hence cannot be constant]

$$= -(\omega^2 a) \sin \omega t = -\omega^2 x$$

Force, $$F = \text{mass} \times \text{acceleration}$$
$$= mA = -m\omega^2 x$$

Hence, force acting is directly proportional to displacement from the mean position and opposite to it. [i.e. option (a)]

Q.16 The displacement-time graph of a particle executing SHM is shown in figure. Which of the following statement is/are true ?

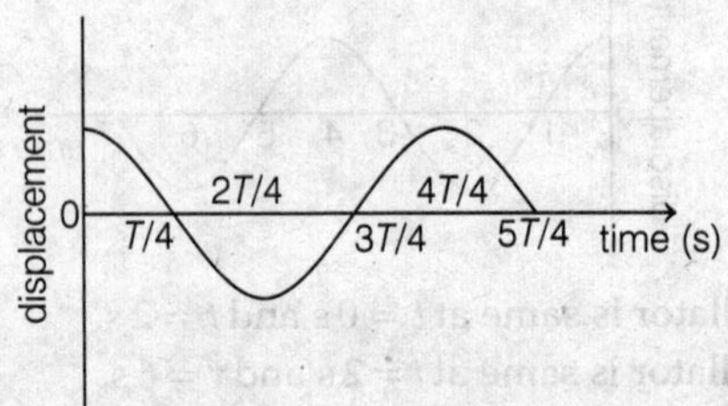

(a) The force is zero at $t = \frac{3T}{4}$

(b) The acceleration is maximum at $t = \frac{4T}{4}$

(c) The velocity is maximum at $t = \frac{T}{4}$

(d) The PE is equal to KE of oscillation at $t = \frac{T}{2}$

Ans. *(a, b, c)* The given graph is a cosine function, so displacement of particle is

$$y = A_0 \cos \omega t = A_0 \cos \frac{2\pi t}{T}$$

(a) Force $F = m\omega^2 y$

At $t = \frac{3T}{4}$ $\quad y = A_0 \cos\frac{2\pi}{T}\cdot\frac{3T}{4} = 0$

$\Rightarrow$ $\quad F = 0$

(b) $a = \omega^2 y$

At $t = \frac{4T}{4}$, $\quad y = A_0 \cos\frac{2\pi}{T}\cdot\frac{4T}{4} = A_0$

So, acceleration $a = \omega^2 A_0$ is maximum

(c) $v = \omega\sqrt{A^2 - y^2}$

At $t = \frac{T}{4}$, $\quad y = A_0 \cos 2\frac{\pi}{T}\cdot\frac{T}{4} = 0$

So, velocity $v = A\omega$ is maximum

(d) At $t = \frac{T}{2}$, $\quad y = A_0 \cos 2\frac{\pi}{T}\cdot\frac{T}{2} = -A_0$

So, displacement is maximum. Thus PE is maximum and KE is zero.

Q.17 A body is performing SHM, then its

(a) average total energy per cycle is equal to its maximum kinetic energy.

(b) average kinetic energy per cycle is equal to half of its maximum kinetic energy.

(c) mean velocity over a complete cycle is equal to $\frac{2}{\pi}$ times of its maximum velocity.

(d) root mean square velocity is $\frac{1}{\sqrt{2}}$ times of its maximum velocity.

Ans. ***(a, b, d)*** Let the equation of a SHM is represented as $x = a \sin \omega t$

Assume mass of the body is m.

(a) Total mechanical energy of the body at any time t is

$$E = \frac{1}{2} m\omega^2 a^2 \quad \text{...(i)}$$

Kinetic energy at any instant t is

$$K = \frac{1}{2} m v^2 = \frac{1}{2} m\left[\frac{dx}{dt}\right]^2 \quad \left[\because v = \frac{dx}{dt}\right]$$

$$= \frac{1}{2} m\omega^2 a^2 \cos^2 \omega t \quad [\because x = a \sin \omega t]$$

$$\Rightarrow \quad K_{max} = \frac{1}{2} m\omega^2 a^2 = E \quad [\because \text{for } K_{max}, \cos \omega t = 1] \text{ ...(ii)}$$

(b) KE at any instant t is

$$K = \frac{1}{2} m\omega^2 a^2 \cos^2 \omega t$$

$$(K_{av}) \text{ for a cycle} = \frac{1}{2} m\omega^2 a^2 [(\cos^2 \omega t)_{av}] \text{ for a cycle}$$

$$= \frac{1}{2} m\omega^2 a^2 \left[\frac{0+1}{2}\right]$$

$$= \frac{1}{4} m\omega^2 a^2 = \frac{K_{max}}{2} \quad \text{[from Eq. (ii)]}$$

(c) Velocity $= v = \dfrac{dx}{dt} = a\,\omega\cos\omega t$

$$v_{mean} = \frac{v_{max} + v_{min}}{2} = \frac{a\omega + (-a\omega)}{2} = 0 \quad \text{[For a complete cycle]}$$

$$v_{max} \neq v_{mean}$$

(d) $v_{rms} = \sqrt{\dfrac{v_1^2 + v_2^2}{2}} = \sqrt{\dfrac{0 + a^2\omega^2}{2}} = \dfrac{a\omega}{\sqrt{2}} \Rightarrow v_{rms} = \dfrac{v_{max}}{\sqrt{2}}$

Q.18 A particle is in linear simple harmonic motion between two points *A* and *B*, 10 cm apart (figure). Take the direction from *A* to *B* as the positive direction and choose the correct statements.

B O C A

$$AO = OB = 5 \text{ cm}$$
$$BC = 8 \text{ cm}$$

(a) The sign of velocity, acceleration and force on the particle when it is 3 cm away from *A* going towards *B* are positive.
(b) The sign of velocity of the particle at *C* going towards *B* is negative.
(c) The sign of velocity, acceleration and force on the particle when it is 4 cm away from *B* going towards *A* are negative.
(d) The sign of acceleration and force on the particle when it is at points *B* is negative.

Ans. *(a, c, d)* Consider the diagram.

u=0 v=positive v=0
B O C A

(a) When the particle is 3cm away from *A* going towards *B*, velocity is towards *AB* i.e. positive.
In SHM, acceleration is always towards mean position (*O*) in this case.
Hence, it is positive.
(b) When the particle is at *C*, velocity is towards *B* hence positive.
(c) When the particle is 4 cm away from *B* going towards *A* velocity is negative and acceleration is towards mean position (*O*) hence negative.
(d) Acceleration is always towards mean position (*O*). When the particle is at *B* acceleration and force are towards *BA* that is negative.

Very Short Answer Type Questions

Q.19 Displacement *versus* time curve for a particle executing SHM is shown in figure. Identify the points marked at which (i) velocity of the oscillator is zero, (ii) speed of the oscillator is maximum.

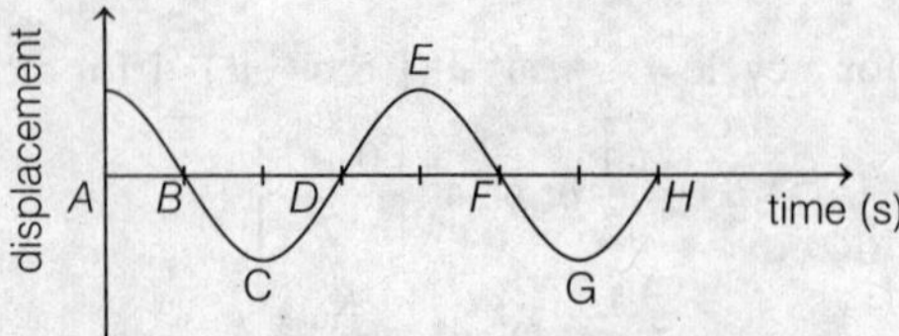

Ans. In SHM y-t graph, zero displacement values correspond to mean position; where velocity of the oscillator is maximum.

Whereas the crest and troughs represent extreme positions, where displacement is maximum and velocity of the oscillator is minimum and is zero. Hence,

(a) A, C, E, G are either crest or trough having zero velocity.

(b) speed is maximum at mean positions represented by B, D, F, H points.

Q.20 Two identical springs of spring constant k are attached to a block of mass m and to fixed supports as shown in figure. When the mass is displaced from equilibrium position by a distance x towards right, find the restoring force.

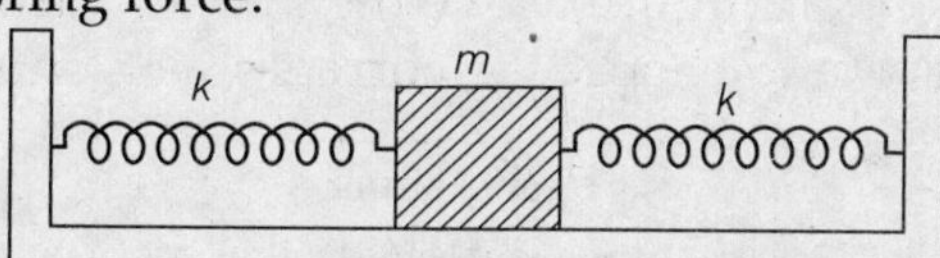

Ans. Consider the diagram in which the block is displaced right through x .

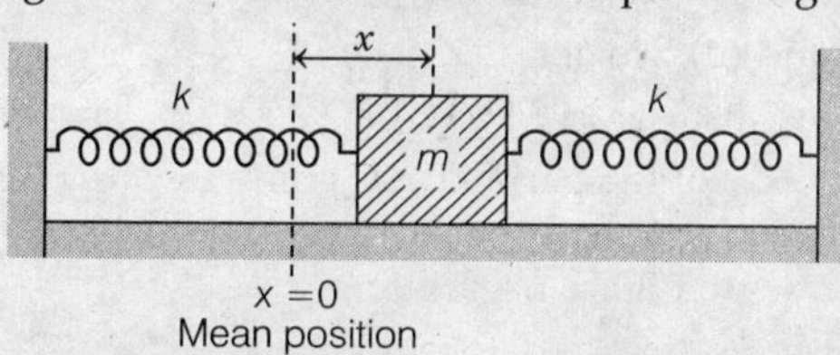

The right spring gets compressed by x developing a restoring force kx towards left on the block. The left spring is stretched by an amount x developing a restoring force kx towards left on the block as gven in the free body diagram of the block.

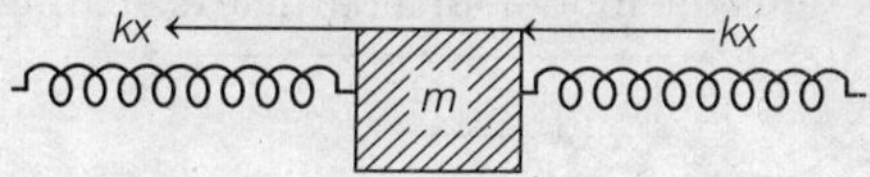

Hence, total force (restoring) $= (kx + kx)$ [$\because$ Both forces are in same direction]

$= 2kx$ towards left

Q.21 What are the two basic characteristics of a simple harmonic motion?

Ans. The two basic characteristics of a simple harmonic motion

(i) Acceleration is directly proportional to displacement.

(ii) The direction of acceleration is always towards the mean position, that is opposite to displacement.

Q.22 When will the motion of a simple pendulum be simple harmonic?

Ans. Consider the diagram of a simple pendulum.

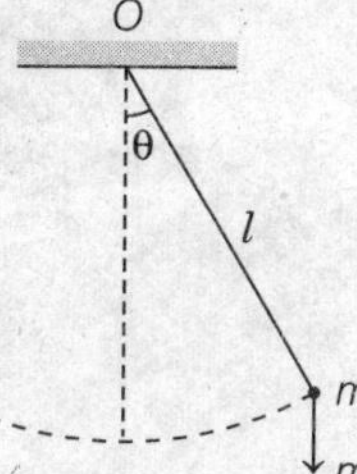

The bob is displaced through an angle θ shown.

The restoring torque about the fixed point O is

$$\tau = -mg\sin\theta$$

If θ is small angle in radians, then $\sin\theta \approx \theta$

$$\Rightarrow \qquad \tau \approx -mg\,\theta \Rightarrow \tau \propto (-\theta)$$

Hence, motion of a simple pendulum is SHM for small angle of oscillations.

Q.23 What is the ratio of maximum acceleration to the maximum velocity of a simple harmonic oscillator?

Thinking Process We have to find velocity by differentiating the equation representing displacement and acceleration by differentiating the equation relating velocity and time.

Ans. Let $x = A\sin\omega t$ is the displacement function of SHM.

Velocity, $$v = \frac{dx}{dt} = A\omega\cos\omega t$$

$$v_{max} = A\omega\,|\cos\omega t|_{max}$$

$$= A\omega \times 1 = \omega A \qquad \ldots\text{(i)} \quad [\because |\cos\omega t|_{max} = 1]$$

Acceleration, $$a = \frac{dv}{dt} = -\omega A \cdot \omega\sin\omega t$$

$$= -\omega^2 A\sin\omega t$$

$$|a_{max}| = |(-\omega^2 A)(+1)| \qquad [\because (\sin\omega t)_{max} = 1]$$

$$|a_{max}| = \omega^2 A \qquad \ldots\text{(ii)}$$

From Eqs. (i) and (ii), we get

$$\frac{v_{max}}{a_{max}} = \frac{\omega A}{\omega^2 A} = \frac{1}{\omega}$$

$$\Rightarrow \quad \frac{a_{max}}{v_{max}} = \omega$$

Q.24 What is the ratio between the distance travelled by the oscillator in one time period and amplitude?

Ans. The diagram represents the motion of a particle executing SHM between A and B.

A O B
|← A →|

Total distance travelled while it goes from A to B and returns to A is

$$= AO + OB + BO + OA$$

$$= A + A + A + A = 4A \qquad [\because OA = A]$$

Amplitude $= OA = A$

Hence, ratio of distance and amplitude $= \frac{4A}{A} = 4:1$

Alternate Method

In SHM, distance travelled by a a particle in one time period

$$= AO + DB + BO + OA = 4AO$$

A O B

SHM executing by a particle on straight line

$\therefore$ Required ratio $= \frac{4AO}{AO} = 4:1$

Q.25 In figure, what will be the sign of the velocity of the point P', which is the projection of the velocity of the reference particle P. P is moving in a circle of radius R in anti-clockwise direction.

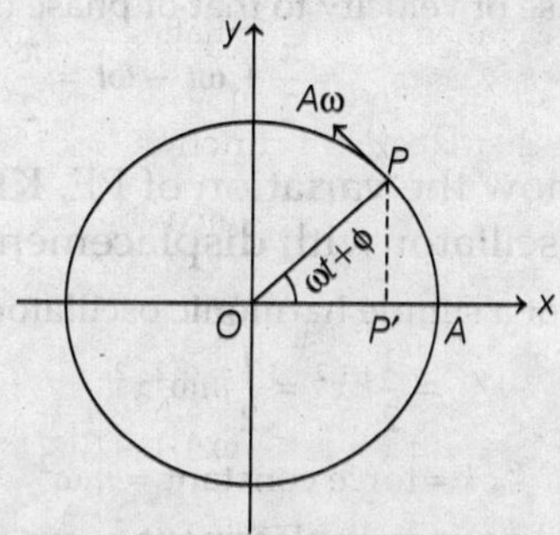

Ans. As the particle on reference circle moves in anti-clockwise direction. The projection will move from P' to O towards left.

$$\left[\text{On } x\text{-axis } x = A_0 \cos(\omega t + \phi),\ v = \frac{dx}{dt} = -A_0\, \omega t \sin(\omega t + \phi)\right]$$

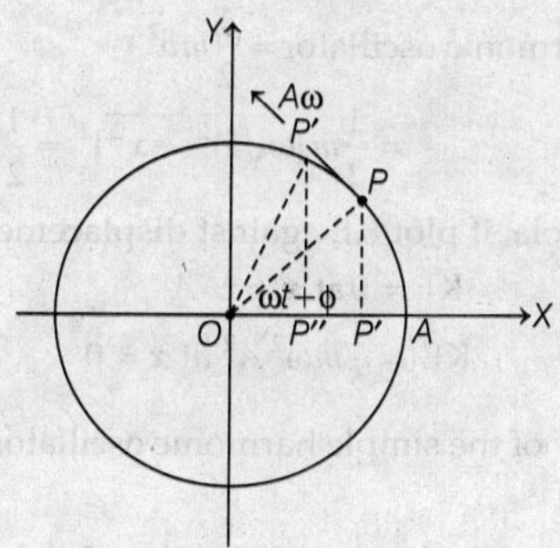

Hence, in the position shown the velocity is directed from $P' \to P''$ *i.e.*, from right to left, hence sign is negative.

Q.26 Show that for a particle executing SHM, velocity and displacement have a phase difference of $\pi/2$.

Ans. Let us assume the displacement function of SHM

$$x = a\cos\omega t$$

where, a = amplitude of motion

$$\text{velocity } v = \frac{dx}{dt}$$

or $$\frac{dx}{dt} = a(-\sin\omega t)\omega = -\omega\, a\sin\omega t$$

or $$v = -\omega\, a\sin\omega t$$

$$= \omega\, a\cos\left(\frac{\pi}{2} + \omega t\right) \qquad \left[\because \sin\omega t = -\cos\left(\frac{\pi}{2} + \omega t\right)\right]$$

Now, phase of displacement $= \omega t$

$$\text{Phase of velocity} = \frac{\pi}{2} + \omega t$$

$\therefore$ Difference in phase of velocity to that of phase of displacement

$$= \frac{\pi}{2} + \omega t - \omega t = \frac{\pi}{2}$$

Q.27 Draw a graph to show the variation of PE, KE and total energy of a simple harmonic oscillator with displacement.

Ans. Potential energy (PE) of a simple harmonic oscillator is

$$= \frac{1}{2} kx^2 = \frac{1}{2} m\omega^2 x^2 \quad \text{...(i)}$$

where, $k =$ force constant $= m\omega^2$

When, PE is plotted against displacement x, we will obtain a parabola.

When $x = 0$, PE $= 0$

When $x = \pm A$, PE = maximum

$$= \frac{1}{2} m\omega^2 A^2$$

KE of a simple harmonic oscillator $= \frac{1}{2} mv^2$ $\quad [\because v = \omega\sqrt{A^2 - x^2}]$

$$= \frac{1}{2} m [\omega\sqrt{A^2 - x^2}]^2 = \frac{1}{2} m\omega^2 (A^2 - x^2) \quad \text{...(ii)}$$

This is also parabola, if plot KE against displacement x.

i.e., KE $= 0$ at $x = \pm A$

and KE $= \frac{1}{2} m\omega^2 A^2$ at $x = 0$

Now, total energy of the simple harmonic oscillator = PE + KE

[using Eqs. (i) and (ii)]

$$= \frac{1}{2} m\omega^2 x^2 + \frac{1}{2} m\omega^2 (A^2 - x^2)$$

$$= \frac{1}{2} m\omega^2 x^2 + \frac{1}{2} m\omega^2 A^2 - \frac{1}{2} m\omega^2 x^2$$

$$\text{TE} = \frac{1}{2} m\omega^2 A^2$$

Which is constant and does not depend on x.

Plotting under the above guidelines KE, PE and TE *versus* displacement x-graph as follows

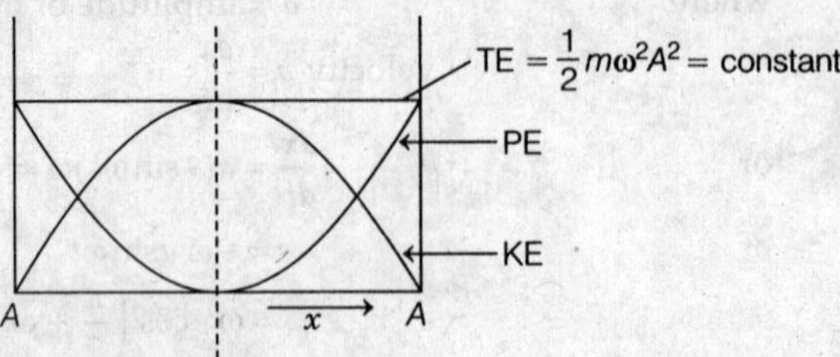

Mistake Alert ! *Believing total energy changes with displacement could result in drawing a varying TE graph instead of a constant line.*

Q.28 The length of a second's pendulum on the surface of earth is 1 m. What will be the length of a second's pendulum on the moon?

Ans. A second's pendulum means a simple pendulum having time period $T = 2$ s.

For a simple pendulum, $T = 2\pi\sqrt{\frac{l}{g}}$

where, l = length of the pendulum and

g = acceleration due to gravity on surface of the earth.

$$T_e = 2\pi\sqrt{\frac{l_e}{g_e}} \quad \text{...(i)}$$

On the surface of the moon, $T_m = 2\pi\sqrt{\frac{l_m}{g_m}}$ ...(ii)

$$\therefore \quad \frac{T_e}{T_m} = \frac{2\pi}{2\pi}\sqrt{\frac{l_e}{g_e}} \times \sqrt{\frac{g_m}{l_m}}$$

$T_e = T_m$ to maintain the second's pendulum time period.

$$\therefore \quad 1 = \sqrt{\frac{l_e}{l_m} \times \frac{g_m}{g_e}} \quad \text{...(iii)}$$

But the acceleration due to gravity at moon is 1/6 of the acceleration due to gravity at earth, i.e. $g_m = \frac{g_e}{6}$

Squaring Eq. (iii) and putting this value,

$$1 = \frac{l_e}{l_m} \times \frac{g_e / 6}{g_e} = \frac{l_e}{l_m} \times \frac{1}{6}$$

$$\Rightarrow \quad \frac{l_e}{6l_m} = 1 \Rightarrow 6l_m = l_e$$

$$\Rightarrow \quad l_m = \frac{1}{6}l_e = \frac{1}{6} \times 1 = \frac{1}{6}\text{ m}$$

Short Answer Type Questions

Q.29 Find the time period of mass M when displaced from its equilibrium position and then released for the system shown in figure.

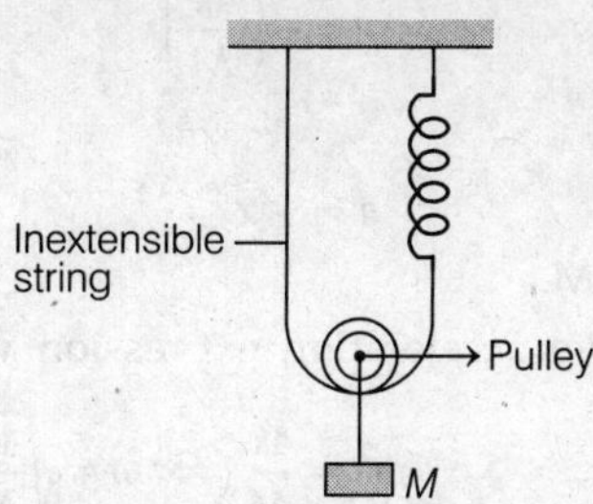

Thinking Process To predict the nature of the motion, we have to displace the mass slightly and find the acceleration due to the restoring force.

Ans. For the calculation purpose, in this situation we will neglect gravity because it is constant throughout and will not effect the net restoring force.

Let in the equilibrium position, the spring has extended by an amount x_0.

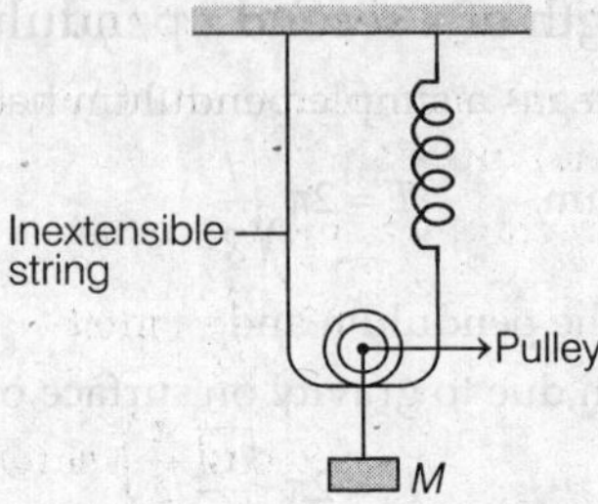

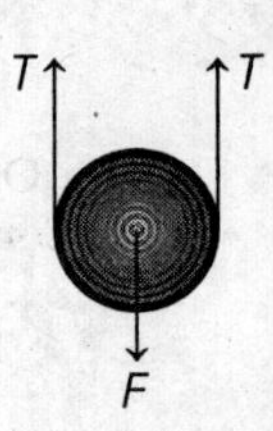

Now, if the mass is given a further displacement downwards by an amount x. The string and spring both should increase in length by x.

But, string is inextensible, hence the spring alone will contribute the total extension $x + x = 2x$, to lower the mass down by x from initial equilibrium mean position x_0. So, net extension in the spring $(= 2x + x_0)$.

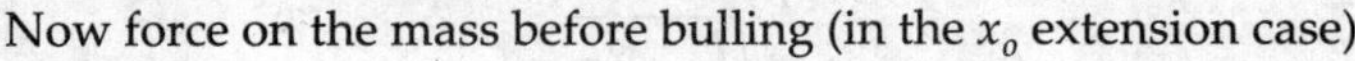

Now force on the mass before bulling (in the x_o extension case)

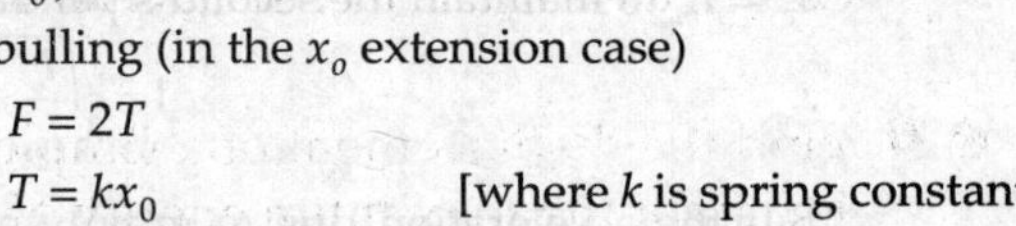

$$F = 2T$$

But $\quad T = kx_0 \quad$ [where k is spring constant]

$\therefore \quad F = 2kx_0 \quad$ ...(i)

When the mass is lowered down further by x,

$$F' = 2T'$$

But new spring length $= (2x + x_0)$

$\therefore \quad F' = 2k(2x + x_0) \quad$ ...(ii)

New restoring force on the system.

$$F_{\text{restoring}} = -[F' - F]$$

Using Eqs. (i) and (ii), we get

$$F_{\text{restoring}} = -[2k(2x + x_0) - 2kx_0]$$

$$= -[2 \times 2kx + 2kx_0 - 2kx_0]$$

$$= -4kx$$

T T F

or $\quad Ma = -4kx$

where, $\quad a =$ acceleration $\quad$ [As, $F = Ma$]

$\Rightarrow \quad a = -\left(\frac{4k}{M}\right)x$

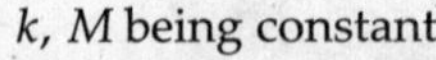

k, M being constant.

$\therefore \quad a \propto -x$

Hence, motion is SHM.

Comparing the above acceleration expression with standard SHM equation $a = -\omega^2 x$, we get

$$\omega^2 = \frac{4k}{M} \Rightarrow \omega = \sqrt{\frac{4k}{M}}$$

$\therefore \quad$ Time period $T = \frac{2\pi}{\omega} = \frac{2\pi}{\sqrt{\frac{4k}{M}}} = 2\pi\sqrt{\frac{M}{4k}} = \pi\sqrt{\frac{M}{k}}$

Q.30 **Show that the motion of a particle represented by $y = \sin \omega t - \cos \omega t$ is simple harmonic with a period of $2\pi / \omega$.**

Ans. We have to convert the given combination of two harmonic functions to a single harmonic (sine or cosine) function.

Given, displacement function $y = \sin\omega t - \cos\omega t$

$$= \sqrt{2}\left(\frac{1}{\sqrt{2}}\cdot\sin\omega t - \frac{1}{\sqrt{2}}\cdot\cos\omega t\right)$$

$$= \sqrt{2}\left[\cos\left(\frac{\pi}{4}\right)\cdot\sin\omega t - \sin\left(\frac{\pi}{4}\right)\cdot\cos\omega t\right]$$

$$= \sqrt{2}\left[\sin\left(\omega t - \frac{\pi}{4}\right)\right]$$

Comparing with standard equation

$$y = a\sin(\omega t + \phi), \text{ we get } = \omega = \frac{2\pi}{T} \Rightarrow T = \frac{2\pi}{\omega}$$

Clearly, the function represents SHM with a period $T = \frac{2\pi}{\omega}$.

Q.31 **Find the displacement of a simple harmonic oscillator at which its PE is half of the maximum energy of the oscillator.**

Ans. Let us assume that the required displacement be x.

$\therefore$ Potential energy of the simple harmonic oscillator $= \frac{1}{2}kx^2$

where, k = force constant $= m\omega^2$

$$\therefore \quad \text{PE} = \frac{1}{2}m\omega^2x^2 \quad \text{...(i)}$$

Maximum energy of the oscillator

$$\text{TE} = \frac{1}{2}m\omega^2A^2 \quad [\because x_{max} = A] \text{ ...(ii)}$$

where, A = amplitude of motion

Given, $\text{PE} = \frac{1}{2}\text{TE}$

$$\Rightarrow \quad \frac{1}{2}m\omega^2x^2 = \frac{1}{2}\left[\frac{1}{2}m\omega^2A^2\right]$$

$$\Rightarrow \quad x^2 = \frac{A^2}{2} \text{ or } x = \sqrt{\frac{A^2}{2}} = \pm\frac{A}{\sqrt{2}}$$

Sign $\pm$ indicates either side of mean position.

Q.32 **A body of mass m is situated in a potential field $U(x) = U_0\,(1 - \cos\alpha x)$ when, U_0 and α are constants. Find the time period of small oscillations.**

Ans. Given potential energy associated with the field

$$U(x) = U_0\,(1 - \cos\alpha x) \quad \text{..... (i)}$$

Now, force $F = -\frac{dU(x)}{dx}$

$[\because$ for conservative force f, we can write $f = \frac{-du}{dx}]$

[We have assumed the field to be conservative]

$$F = -\frac{d}{dx}(U_0 - U_0 \cos \alpha x) = -U_0 \alpha \sin \alpha x$$

$$F = -U_0 \alpha^2 x \quad \text{... (ii)}$$

[$\because$ for small oscillations αx is small, $\sin \alpha x \approx \alpha x$]

$$\Rightarrow \quad F \propto (-x)$$

As, U_0, α being constant.

$\therefore$ Motion is SHM for small oscillations.

Standard equation for SHM $\quad F = -m\omega^2 x \quad$ ...(iii)

Comparing Eqs. (ii) and (iii), we get

$$m\omega^2 = U_0\alpha^2$$

$$\omega^2 = \frac{U_0\alpha^2}{m} \text{ or } \omega = \sqrt{\frac{U_0\alpha^2}{m}}$$

$$\therefore \quad \text{Time period } T = \frac{2\pi}{\omega} = 2\pi\sqrt{\frac{m}{U_0\alpha^2}}$$

Note The motion is SHM only for small oscillations and hence, the time period calculation is valid only under the condition of small oscillations.

Q.33 **A mass of 2 kg is attached to the spring of spring constant 50 Nm^{-1}. The block is pulled to a distance of 5 cm from its equilibrium position at $x = 0$ on a horizontal frictionless surface from rest at $t = 0$. Write the expression for its displacement at anytime t.**

Thinking Process The spring- block system will perform SHM about the mean position with an amplitude of 5cm.

Ans. Consider the diagram of the spring block system. It is a SHM with amplitude of 5cm about the mean position shown.

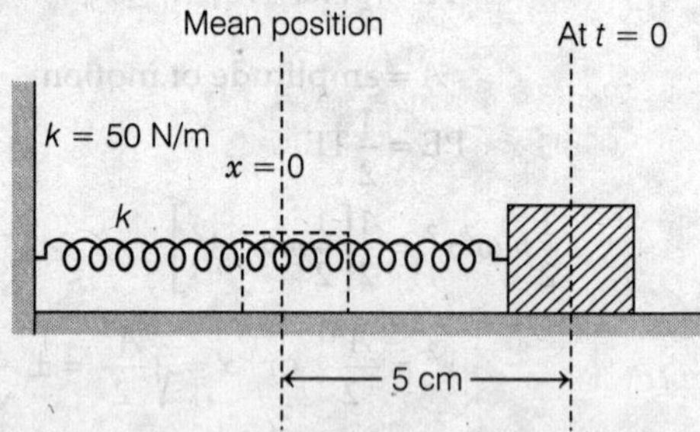

Given, spring constant $k = 50$ N/m

$$m = \text{mass attached} = 2 \text{ kg}$$

$$\therefore \quad \text{Angular frequency } \omega = \sqrt{\frac{k}{m}} = \sqrt{\frac{50}{2}} = \sqrt{25} = 5 \text{ rad/s}$$

Assuming the displacement function

$$y(t) = A\sin(\omega t + \phi)$$

where, ϕ = initial phase

But given at $t = 0$, $y(t) = +A$

$$y(0) = +A = A\sin(\omega \times 0 + \phi)$$

or $$\sin\phi = 1 \Rightarrow \phi = \frac{\pi}{2}$$

$\therefore$ The desired equation is $y(t) = A\sin\left(\omega t + \frac{\pi}{2}\right) = A\cos\omega t$

Putting $A = 5$ cm, $\omega = 5$ rad/s

we get, $y(t) = 5\sin\left(5t + \frac{\pi}{2}\right)$

where, t is in second and y is in centimetre.

Q.34 Consider a pair of identical pendulums, which oscillate with equal amplitude independently such that when one pendulum is at its extreme position making an angle of 2° to the right with the vertical, the other pendulum makes an angle of 1° to the left of the vertical. What is the phase difference between the pendulums?

Ans. Consider the situations shown in the diagram (i) and (ii)

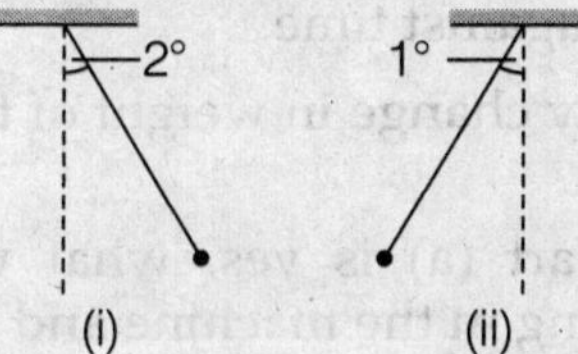

Assuming the two pendulums follow the following functions of their angular displacements

$$\theta_1 = \theta_0 \sin(\omega t + \phi_1) \quad \text{...(i)}$$

and $$\theta_2 = \theta_0 \sin(\omega t + \phi_2) \quad \text{...(ii)}$$

As it is given that amplitude and time period being equal but phases being different.

Now, for first pendulum at any time t

$$\theta_1 = +\theta_0 \quad \text{[Right extreme]}$$

From Eq. (i), we get

$$\Rightarrow \quad \theta_0 = \theta_0 \sin(\omega t + \phi_1) \text{ or } 1 = \sin(\omega t + \phi_1)$$

$$\Rightarrow \quad \sin\frac{\pi}{2} = \sin(\omega t + \phi_1)$$

or $$(\omega t + \phi_1) = \frac{\pi}{2} \quad \text{...(iii)}$$

Similarly, at the same instant t for pendulum second, we have

$$\theta_2 = -\frac{\theta_0}{2}$$

where $\theta_0 = 2°$ is the angular amplitude of first pendulum. For the second pendulum, the angular displacement is one degree ,therefore $\theta_2 = \frac{\theta_0}{2}$ and negative sign is taken to show for being left to mean position.

From Eq. (ii), then $$-\frac{\theta_0}{2} = \theta_0 \sin(\omega t + \phi_2)$$

$$\Rightarrow \quad \sin(\omega t + \phi_2) = -\frac{1}{2} \Rightarrow (\omega t + \phi_2) = -\frac{\pi}{6} \text{ or } \frac{7\pi}{6}$$

or $$(\omega t + \phi_2) = -\frac{\pi}{6} \text{ or } \frac{7\pi}{6} \quad \text{...(iv)}$$

From Eqs. (iv) and (iii), the difference in phases

$$(\omega t + \phi_2) - (\omega t + \phi_1) = \frac{7\pi}{6} - \frac{\pi}{2} = \frac{7\pi - 3\pi}{6} = \frac{4\pi}{6}$$

or $$(\phi_2 - \phi_1) = \frac{4\pi}{6} = \frac{2\pi}{3} = 120°$$

Long Answer Type Questions

Q.35 A person normally weighing 50 kg stands on a massless platform which oscillates up and down harmonically at a frequency of 2.0 s^{-1} and an amplitude 5.0 cm. A weighing machine on the platform gives the persons weight against time.

(a) Will there be any change in weight of the body, during the oscillation?

(b) If answer to part (a) is yes, what will be the maximum and minimum reading in the machine and at which position?

Ans. In this case acceleration is variable. In accelerated motion, weight of body depends on the magnitude and direction of acceleration for upward or downward motion.

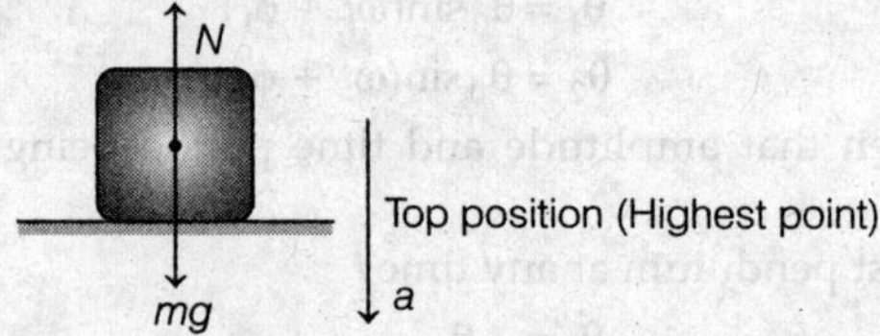

(a) Hence, the weight of the body changes during oscillations.

(b) Considering the situation in two extreme positions, as their acceleration is maximum in magnitude.

we have, $$mg - N = ma$$

∵ At the highest point, the platform is accelerating downward.

$$\Rightarrow \quad N = mg - ma$$

But $$a = \omega^2 A \quad \text{[in magnitude]}$$

$$\therefore \quad N = mg - m\omega^2 A$$

where, A = amplitude of motion.

Given, $m = 50\text{kg}$, frequency $\nu = 2\text{ s}^{-1}$

$$\therefore \quad \omega = 2\pi\nu = 4\pi \text{ rad/s}$$

$$A = 5\text{cm} = 5 \times 10^{-2}\text{ m}$$

$$\therefore \quad N = 50 \times 9.8 - 50 \times (4\pi)^2 \times 5 \times 10^{-2}$$

$$= 50[9.8 - 16\pi^2 \times 5 \times 10^{-2}] = 50[9.8 - 7.89]$$

$$= 50 \times 1.91 = 95.5\,N$$

When the platform is at the lowest position of its oscillation,

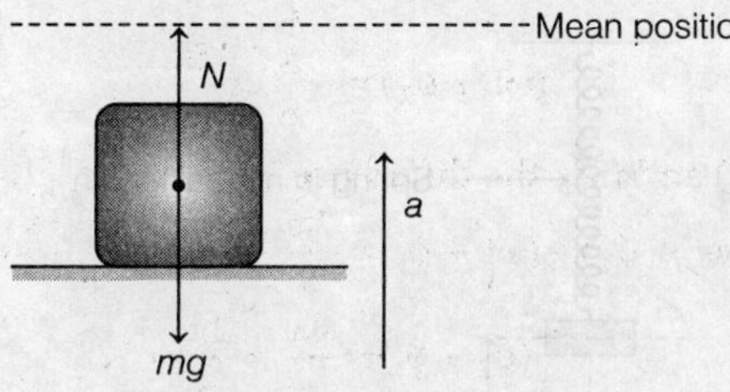

It is accelerating towards mean position that is vertically upwards.

Writing equation of motion

$$N - mg = ma = m\omega^2 A$$

or $$N = mg + m\omega^2 A = m[g + \omega^2 A]$$

Putting the data $$N = 50[9.8 + (4\pi)^2 \times 5 \times 10^{-2}]$$

$$= 50[9.8 + (12.56)^2 \times 5 \times 10^{-2}]$$

$$= 50[9.8 + 7.88]$$

$$= 50 \times 17.68$$

$$= 884\,N$$

Now, the machine reads the normal reaction. It is clear that

maximum weight = 884 N [at lowest point]

minimum weight = 95.5 N [at top point]

Alternate Method

When platform is accelerating downward

$$W_1 = N = m(g - a) = m(g - w^2 A]$$

$$= 50[9.8 - 4\pi^2 \times 2 \times 5 \times 10^{-2}]$$

$$= 95.5\,N$$ [at top point]

When platform is accelerating upwards

$$W_2 = N = m(g + a) = m(g + w^2 A]$$

on putting values, we get

$$W_2 = 884\,N$$ [at lowest point]

Q.36 A body of mass m is attached to one end of a massless spring which is suspended vertically from a fixed point. The mass is held in hand, so that the spring is neither stretched nor compressed. Suddenly, the support of the hand is removed. The lowest position attained by the mass during oscillation is 4 cm below the point, where it was held in hand.

(a) What is the amplitude of oscillation?

(b) Find the frequency of oscillation?

Thinking Process When we have given the support of hand, net force = 0 and when it is released, all of its PE will convert into KE.

Ans. (a) When the support of the hand is removed, the body oscillates about a mean position.

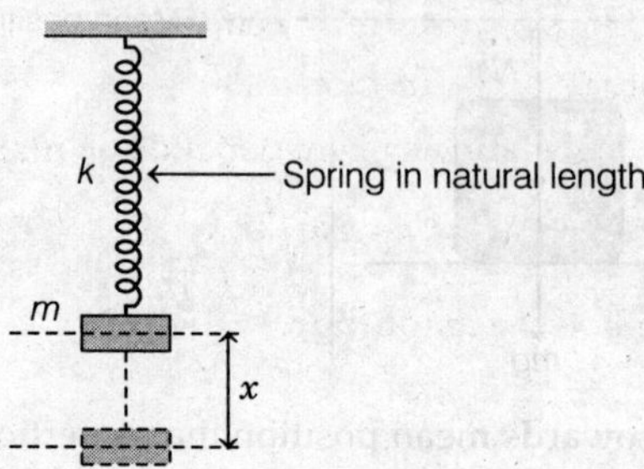

Suppose x is the maximum extension in the spring when it reaches the lowest point in oscillation.

Loss in PE of the block $= mgx$ ...(i)

where, m = mass of the block

Gain in elastic potential energy of the spring

$$= \frac{1}{2}kx^2 \quad \text{...(ii)}$$

As the two are equal, conserving the mechanical energy,

we get, $$mgx = \frac{1}{2}kx^2 \text{ or } x = \frac{2mg}{k} \quad \text{...(iii)}$$

Now, the mean position of oscillation will be, when the block is balanced by the spring.

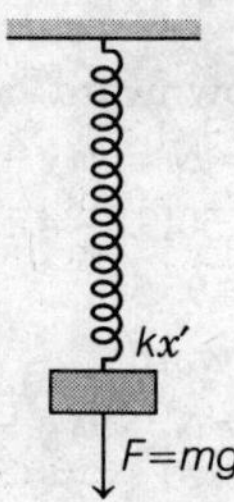

If x' is the extension in that case, then

$$F = +kx'$$

But $$F = mg$$

$\Rightarrow$ $$mg = +kx'$$

or $$x' = \frac{mg}{k} \quad \text{...(iv)}$$

Dividing Eq. (iii) by Eq. (iv),

$$\frac{x}{x'} = \frac{2mg}{k} / \frac{mg}{k} = 2$$

$\Rightarrow$ $$x = 2x'$$

But given $x = 4$ cm (maximum extension from the unstretched position)

$\therefore$ $$2x' = 4$$

$\therefore$ $$x' = \frac{4}{2} = 2\text{cm}$$

But the displacement of mass from the mean position to the position when spring attains its natural length is equal to amplitude of the oscillation.

$\therefore \qquad A = x' = 2\,\text{cm}$

where, A = amplitude of the motion.

(b) Time period of the oscillating system depends on mass spring constant given by

$$T = 2\pi\sqrt{\frac{m}{k}}$$

It does not depend on the amplitude.

But from Eq. (iii), $\frac{2mg}{k} = x$ [maximum extension]

$$\frac{2mg}{k} = 4\,\text{cm} = 4 \times 10^{-2}\ \text{m}$$

$$\therefore \qquad \frac{m}{k} = \frac{4 \times 10^{-2}}{2g} = \frac{2 \times 10^{-2}}{g}$$

$$\therefore \qquad \frac{k}{m} = \frac{g}{2 \times 10^{-2}}$$

and $\nu = \text{frequency} = \frac{1}{T} = \frac{1}{2\pi}\sqrt{\frac{k}{m}}$

$$\therefore \qquad \nu = \frac{1}{2 \times 3.14}\sqrt{\frac{g}{2 \times 10^{-2}}}$$

$$= \frac{1}{2 \times 3.14}\sqrt{\frac{4.9}{10^{-2}}} = \frac{1}{6.28} \times \sqrt{4.9 \times 100}$$

$$= \frac{10}{6.28} \times 2.21 = 3.51\,\text{Hz}.$$

Note The block during oscillation cannot go above the position it was released, as it is given that there is no velocity in the upward direction either by the system or external agent.

Q.37 A cylindrical log of wood of height h and area of cross-section A floats in water. It is pressed and then released. Show that the log would execute SHM with a time period.

$$T = 2\pi\sqrt{\frac{m}{A\rho g}}$$

where, m is mass of the body and ρ is density of the liquid.

Thinking Process To find the time period for the SHM displace the log from equilibrium position by a small displacement and then find the restoring force.

Ans. Consider the diagram.

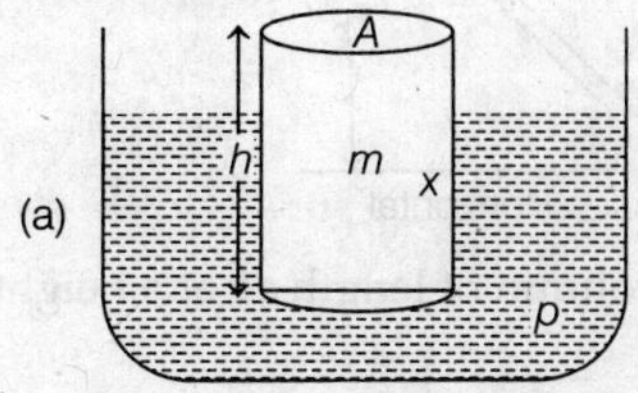

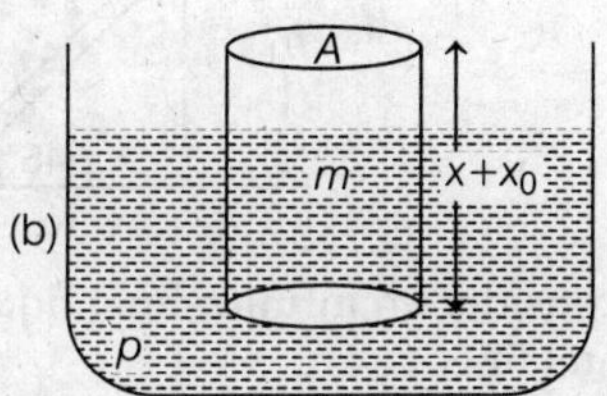

Let the log be pressed and let the vertical displacement at the equilibrium position be x_0.

At equilibrium,

$$mg = \text{buoyant force} = (\rho A x_0)g \quad [\because m = V\rho = (Ax_o)\rho]$$

When it is displaced by a further displacement x, the buoyant force is $A(x_0 + x)\rho g$

$\therefore$ Net restoring force = Buoyant force − Weight

$$= A(x_0 + x)\rho g - mg$$

$$= (A\rho g)x \quad [\because mg = \rho A x_0 g]$$

As displacement x is downward and restoring force is upward, we can write

$$F_{\text{restoring}} = -(A\rho g)x$$

$$= -kx$$

where k = constant = $A\rho g$

So, the motion is SHM $[\because F \propto -x]$

Now, Acceleration, $a = \dfrac{F_{\text{restoring}}}{m} = -\dfrac{k}{m}x$

Comparing with $a = -\omega^2 x$

$$\Rightarrow \quad \omega^2 = \frac{k}{m} \Rightarrow \omega = \sqrt{\frac{k}{m}}$$

$$\Rightarrow \quad \frac{2\pi}{T} = \sqrt{\frac{k}{m}} \Rightarrow T = 2\pi\sqrt{\frac{m}{k}}$$

$$\Rightarrow \quad T = 2\pi\sqrt{\frac{m}{A\rho g}}$$

Q.38 One end of a V-tube containing mercury is connected to a suction pump and the other end to atmosphere. The two arms of the tube are inclined to horizontal at an angle of 45° each. A small pressure difference is created between two columns when the suction pump is removed. Will the column of mercury in V-tube execute simple harmonic motion? Neglect capillary and viscous forces. Find the time period of oscillation.

Ans. Consider the diagram shown below

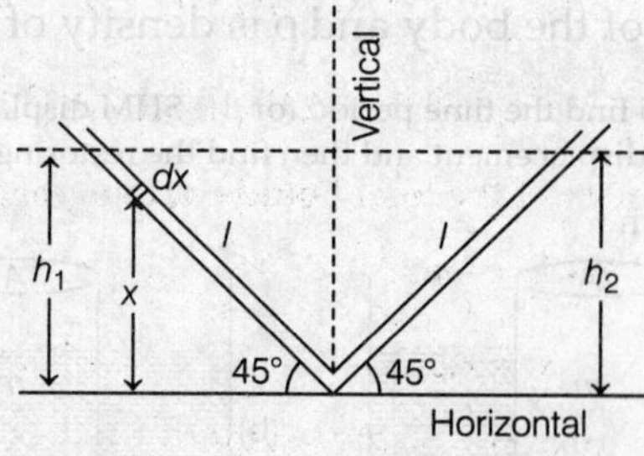

Let us consider an infinitesimal liquid column of length dx at a height x from the horizontal line.

If ρ = density of the liquid

A = cross-sectional area of V-tube

PE of element dx will be given as

$$PE = dmgx = (A\rho dx)gx \qquad [\because dm = \rho V = pAdx]$$

where $A\rho dx = dm$ = mass of element dx

$\therefore$ Total PE of the left column

$$= \int_0^{h_1} A\rho gx dx$$

$$= A\rho g \int_0^{h_1} x\, dx$$

$$= A\rho g \left|\frac{x^2}{2}\right|_0^{h_1} = A\rho g \frac{h_1^2}{2}$$

But, $h_1 = l \sin 45°$

$$\therefore \quad PE = \frac{A\rho g}{2} l^2 \sin^2 45° \qquad \text{...(i)}$$

In a similar way,

$$\text{PE of right column} = \frac{A\rho g}{2} l^2 \sin^2 45° \qquad \text{...(ii)}$$

$$\text{Total PE} = \frac{A\rho g}{2} l^2 \sin^2 45° + \frac{A\rho g}{2} l^2 \sin^2 45°$$

$$= 2 \times \frac{1}{2} A\rho g l^2 \left(\frac{1}{\sqrt{2}}\right)^2 = \frac{A\rho g l^2}{2} \qquad \text{...(iii)}$$

If due to pressure difference created y element of left side moves on the right side, then

liquid present in the left arm = $l - y$

liquid present in the right arm = $l + y$

$$\therefore \quad \text{Total PE} = A\rho g(l-y)^2 \sin^2 45° + A\rho g(l+y)^2 \sin^2 45°$$

$$= \frac{A\rho g}{2}[(l-y)^2 + (l+y)^2]$$

$$\text{Changes in PE} = (\text{PE})_{\text{final}} - (\text{PE})_{\text{initial}}$$

or

$$\Delta PE = \frac{A\rho g}{2}[(l-y)^2 + (l+y)^2 - l^2]$$

$$= \frac{A\rho g}{2}[l^2 + y^2 - 2ly + l^2 + y^2 + 2ly - l^2]$$

$$= \frac{A\rho g}{2}[2(l^2 + y^2)] = A\rho g(l^2 + y^2) \qquad \text{...(iv)}$$

If v is the change in velocity of the total liquid column, then change in KE

$$\Delta KE = \frac{1}{2} m v^2$$

But $m = A\rho(2l)$

$$\therefore \quad \Delta KE = \frac{1}{2} A\rho 2lv^2 = A\rho l v^2 \qquad \text{...(v)}$$

From Eqs. (iv) and (v),

$$\Delta PE + \Delta KE = A\rho g(l^2 + y^2) + A\rho l v^2 \qquad \text{...(vi)}$$

System being conservative.

$\therefore$ Change in total energy = 0

From Eq. (vi),

$$A\rho g(l^2 + y^2) + A\rho l v^2 = 0$$

Differentiating both sides with respect to time (t), we get

$$A\rho g\left[0 + 2y\frac{dy}{dt}\right] + A\rho l(2v)\frac{dv}{dt} = 0$$

But, $\frac{dy}{dt} = v$ and $\frac{dv}{dt} = a$ [acceleration]

$\Rightarrow$ $$A\rho g(2yv) + A\rho l(2v)a = 0$$

$\Rightarrow$ $$(gy + la)\, 2A\rho v = 0$$

$2A\rho v =$ constant and $2A\rho v \neq 0$

$\therefore$ $$la + gy = 0$$

$$a + \left(\frac{g}{l}\right)y = 0$$

or $$\frac{d^2y}{dt^2} + \left(\frac{g}{l}\right)y = 0$$

This is the standard differential equation for SHM of the form

$$\frac{d^2y}{dt^2} + \omega^2 y = 0$$

$\therefore$ $$\omega = \sqrt{\frac{g}{l}}$$

$\therefore$ $$T = \frac{2\pi}{\omega} = 2\pi\sqrt{\frac{l}{g}}$$

Q.39 A tunnel is dug through the centre of the earth. Show that a body of mass m when dropped from rest from one end of the tunnel will execute simple harmonic motion.

Ans. Consider the situation shown in the diagram.

The gravitational force on the particle at a distance r from the centre of the earth arises entirely from that portion of matter of the earth in shells internal to the position of the particle. The external shells exert no force on the particle.

More clearly,

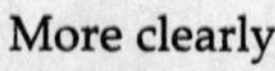

let g' be the acceleration at P.

So, $$g' = g\left(1 - \frac{d}{R}\right) = g\left(\frac{R-d}{R}\right)$$

From figure, $$R - d = y$$

$\Rightarrow$ $$g' = g\frac{y}{R},$$

Force on body at p, $$F = -mg' = \frac{-mg}{R}y \quad \text{...(i)}$$

$\Rightarrow$ $F \propto -y$ [where, y is distance from the centre]

So, motion is SHM.

For time period, we can write Eq. (i)

As $$ma = -\frac{Mg}{R}y \Rightarrow a = -\frac{g}{R}y$$

Comparing with $a = -\omega^2 y$

$$\omega^2 = \frac{g}{R} \Rightarrow \left(\frac{2\pi}{T}\right)^2 = \frac{g}{R} \Rightarrow T = 2\pi\sqrt{\frac{R}{g}}$$

Q.40 A simple pendulum of time period 1s and length l is hung from a fixed support at O. Such that the bob is at a distance H vertically above A on the ground (figure) the amplitude is θ_0 the string snaps at $\theta = \theta_0 / 2$. Find the time taken by the bob to hit the ground. Also find distance from A where bob hits the ground. Assume θ_0 to be small, so that $\sin\theta_0 \simeq \theta_0$ and $\cos\theta_0 \simeq 1$.

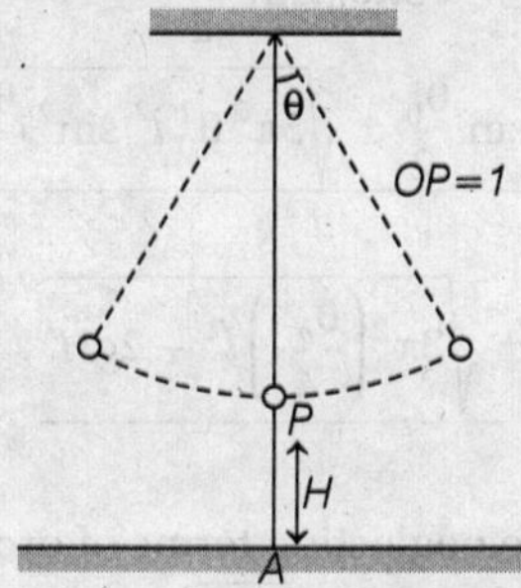

Thinking Process We have to consider $\theta = \theta_0$ as reference point that is when $\theta = \theta_0$ the time will be considered as $t = 0$. Then, equation of rectilinear motion will be applied.

Ans. Consider the diagram.

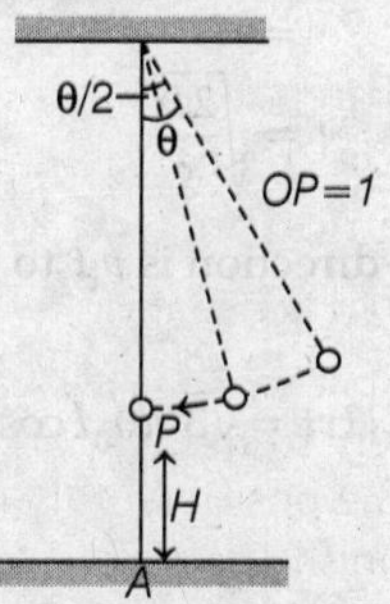

Let us assume $t = 0$ when $\theta = \theta_0$, then $\theta = \theta_0 \cos\omega t$

Given a seconds pendulum $\omega = 2\pi \Rightarrow \theta = \theta_0 \cos 2\pi t$ ......(i)

At time t_1 let $\theta = \theta_0 / 2$

$\therefore$ $$\cos 2\pi t_1 = 1/2 \Rightarrow t_1 = \frac{1}{6} \quad \left[\because \cos 2\pi t_1 = \cos\frac{\pi}{3} \Rightarrow 2\pi t_1 = \frac{\pi}{3}\right]$$

$$\frac{d\theta}{dt} = -(\theta_0\, 2\pi)\sin 2\pi t \quad \text{[from Eq. (i)]}$$

At $t = t_1 = \frac{1}{6}$

$$\frac{d\theta}{dt} = -\theta_0\, 2\pi \sin\frac{2\pi}{6} = -\sqrt{3}\,\pi\,\theta_0$$

Negative sign shows that it is going left.

Thus, the linear velocity is

$$u = -\sqrt{3}\pi\theta_0 l \text{ perpendicular to the string.}$$

The vertical component is

$$u_y = -\sqrt{3}\pi\theta_0 l \sin(\theta_0/2)$$

and the horizontal component is

$$u_x = -\sqrt{3}\pi\theta_0 l \cos(\theta_0/2)$$

At the time it snaps, the vertical height is

$$H' = H + l(1-\cos(\theta_0/2)) \quad \text{... (ii)}$$

Let the time required for fall be t, then

$$H' = u_y t + (1/2)gt^2 \quad \text{[notice } g \text{ also in the negative direction]}$$

or

$$\frac{1}{2}gt^2 + \sqrt{3}\pi\theta_0 l\sin\frac{\theta_0}{2}t - H' = 0$$

$$\therefore \quad t = \frac{-\sqrt{3}\pi\theta_0\ l\sin\frac{\theta_0}{2} \pm \sqrt{3\pi^2\theta_0^2 l^2\sin^2\frac{\theta_0}{2} + 2gH'}}{g}$$

$$= \frac{-\sqrt{3}\pi l\frac{\theta_0^2}{2} \pm \sqrt{3\pi^2\left(\frac{\theta_0{}^4}{4}\right)l^2 + 2gH'}}{g} \quad \left[\because \sin\frac{\theta_0}{2} \simeq \frac{\theta_0}{2} \text{ for small angle}\right]$$

Given that θ_0 is small, hence neglecting terms of order θ_0^2 and higher

$$t = \sqrt{\frac{2H'}{g}} \quad \text{[from Eq. (iii)]}$$

Now,

$$H' \approx H + l(1-1) \quad [\therefore \cos\theta_0/2 \approx 1]$$

$$= H \quad \text{[from Eq. (ii)]}$$

$$\Rightarrow \quad t = \sqrt{\frac{2H}{g}}$$

The distance travelled in the x-direction is $u_x t$ to the left of where the bob is snapped

$$X = Uxt = \sqrt{3}\ \pi\theta_0 l\cos\left(\frac{\theta_0}{2}\right)\sqrt{\frac{2H}{g}}$$

As θ_0 is small $\Rightarrow \cos\left(\frac{\theta_0}{2}\right) \approx 1$

$$X = \sqrt{3}\ \pi\ \theta_0 l\sqrt{\frac{2H}{g}} = \sqrt{\frac{6H}{g}}\ \theta_0 l\pi$$

At the time of snapping, the bob was at a horizontal distance of $l\sin(\theta_0/2) \approx l\frac{\theta_0}{2}$ from A.

Thus, the distance of bob from A where it meets the ground is

$$= \frac{l\theta_0}{2} - X = \frac{l\theta_0}{2} - \sqrt{\frac{6H}{g}}\ \theta_0\ l\pi = \theta_0 l\left(\frac{1}{2} - \pi\sqrt{\frac{6H}{g}}\right)$$

Chapter

14 Waves

Multiple Choice Questions (MCQs)

Q.1 Water waves produced by a motorboat sailing in water are

(a) neither longitudinal nor transverse (b) both longitudinal and transverse

(c) only longitudinal (d) only transverse

- **Concept Insight** In this problem the concept of transverse wave is used, where wave motion involves individual particle of medium executing simple harmonic motion about their mean positions in the direction of propagation of the wave.

Ans. ***(b)*** Water waves produced by a motorboat sailing in water are both longitudinal and transverse, because the waves, produce transverse as well as lateral vibrations in the particles of the medium.

Q.2 Sound waves of wavelength λ travelling in a medium with a speed of v m/s enter into another medium where its speed in $2v$ m/s. Wavelength of sound waves in the second medium is

(a) λ (b) $\frac{\lambda}{2}$ (c) 2λ (d) 4λ

Ans. ***(c)*** Let the frequency in the first medium is ν and in the second medium is ν.′

Frequency remains same in both the medium

So, $$\nu = \nu' \Rightarrow \frac{v}{\lambda} = \frac{v'}{\lambda'} \Rightarrow \lambda' = \left(\frac{v'}{v}\right)\lambda$$

λ and λ′, v and v' are wavelengths and speeds in first and second medium respectively.

So, $$\lambda' = \left(\frac{2v}{v}\right)\lambda = 2\lambda$$

Q.3 Speed of sound wave in air

(a) is independent of temperature (b) increases with pressure

(c) increases with increase in humidity (d) decreases with increase in humidity

Ans. ***(c)*** Due to presence of moisture density of air decreases.

We know that speed of sound in air is given by $v = \sqrt{\frac{\gamma p}{\rho}}$

For air γ and p are constants.

$$v \propto \frac{1}{\sqrt{\rho}}, \text{ where } \rho \text{ is density of air.}$$

$$\frac{v_2}{v_1} = \sqrt{\frac{\rho_1}{\rho_2}}$$

where ρ_1 is density of dry air and ρ_2 is density of moist air.

As $\rho_2 < \rho_1 = \frac{v_2}{v_1} > 1 \Rightarrow v_2 > v_1$

Hence, speed of sound wave in air increases with increase in humidity.

Q.4 Change in temperature of the medium changes

(a) frequency of sound waves (b) amplitude of sound waves

(c) wavelength of sound waves (d) loudness of sound waves

Ans. ***(c)*** Speed of sound in air $v = \sqrt{\frac{\gamma RT}{M}}$

Speed of sound wave in a medium $v \propto \sqrt{T}$

[where T is temperature of the medium]

Clearly, when temperature changes speed also changes.

As, $v = \nu\lambda$

where ν is frequency and λ is wavelength.

Frequency (ν) remains fixed

$\Rightarrow$ $v \propto \lambda$ or $\lambda \propto v$

As does not change, so wavelength (λ) changes.

Q.5 With propagation of longitudinal waves through a medium, the quantity transmitted is

(a) matter (b) energy

(c) energy and matter (d) energy, matter and momentum

Ans. ***(b)*** Propagation of longitudinal waves through a medium leads to transmission of energy through the medium without matter being transmitted.

There is no movement of matter (mass) and hence momentum.

Q.6 Which of the following statements are true for wave motion?

(a) Mechanical transverse waves can propagate through all mediums

(b) Longitudinal waves can propagate through solids only

(c) Mechanical transverse waves can propagate through solids only

(d) Longitudinal waves can propagate through vacuum

Ans. ***(c)*** When mechanical transverse wave propagates through a medium, the constituent of the medium oscillate perpendicular the direction of wave motion causing a change in shape. That is each, element of the medium is subjected to shearing stress. Solids and strings have shear modulus, which allow them to sustain shearing stress.

Fluids have no definite shape of, their own, they yield to shearing stress. This is why transverse waves are possible in solids and strings but not in fluids.

Q.7 A sound wave is passing through air column in the form of compression and rarefaction. In consecutive compressions and rarefactions,

(a) density remains constant (b) Boyle's law is obeyed

(c) bulk modulus of air oscillates (d) there is no transfer of heat

Ans. (d) (a) Due to compression and rarefactions density of the medium (air) changes. At compressed regions density is maximum and at rarefactions density is minimum

(b) As density is changing, so Boyle's law is not obeyed

(c) Bulk modulus remains same

(d) The time of compression and rarefaction is too small i.e., we can assume adiabatic process and hence no transfer of heat

Q.8 Equation of a plane progressive wave is given by $y = 0.6 \sin 2\pi\left(t - \frac{x}{2}\right)$. On reflection from a denser medium its amplitude becomes $\frac{2}{3}$ of the amplitude of the incident wave. The equation of the reflected wave is

(a) $y = 0.6 \sin 2\pi\left(t + \frac{x}{2}\right)$
(b) $y = -0.4 \sin 2\pi\left(t + \frac{x}{2}\right)$
(c) $y = 0.4 \sin 2\pi\left(t + \frac{x}{2}\right)$
(d) $y = -0.4 \sin 2\pi\left(t - \frac{x}{2}\right)$

Thinking Process Due to reflection from a denser medium there is a phase change of 180° in the reflected wave.

Ans. (b) Amplitude of reflected wave

$$A_r = \frac{2}{3} \times A_i = \frac{2}{3} \times 0.6 = 0.4 \text{ units}$$

Given equation of incident wave

$$y_i = 0.6 \sin 2\pi\left(t - \frac{x}{2}\right)$$

Equation of reflected wave is

$$y_r = A_r \sin 2\pi\left(t + \frac{x}{2} + \pi\right)$$

[∵ At denser medium, phase changes by π]

The positive sign is due to reversal of direction of propagation

So, $$y_r = -0.4 \sin 2\pi\left(t + \frac{x}{2}\right)$$ [∵ $\sin(\pi + \theta) = -\sin\theta$]

Q.9 A string of mass 2.5 kg is under tension of 200 N. The length of the stretched string is 20.0 m. If the transverse jerk is struck at one end of the string, the disturbance will reach the other end in

(a) 1s
(b) 0.5s
(c) 2s
(d) data given is insufficient

Ans. (b) Mass $m = 2.5$ kg

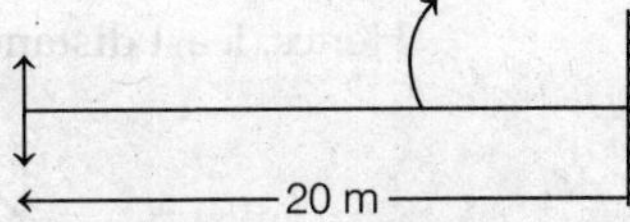

μ = mass per unit length

$$= \frac{m}{l} = \frac{2.5 \text{kg}}{20} = \frac{1.25}{10} = 0.125 \text{ kg/m}$$

Speed $v = \sqrt{\frac{T}{\mu}} = \sqrt{\frac{200}{0.125}}$ [speed of transverse waves in any string]

$$v = \sqrt{\frac{200 \times 1000}{125}} = \sqrt{1600} = 40 \text{ m/s}$$

So Time $t = \frac{\text{Distance}}{\text{Speed}} = \frac{20}{40} \Rightarrow t = 0.5$ second.

Mistake Alert ! *It* $\mu = \frac{Mass}{Length}$ *is calculated in corrected it will lead to the wrong wave speed.*

Multiple Choice Questions (More Than One Options)

Q.10 A transverse harmonic wave on a string is described by

$$y(x, t) = 3.0 \sin\left(36t + 0.018x + \frac{\pi}{4}\right)$$

where x and y are in cm and t is in sec. The positive direction of x is from left to right.

(a) the wave is travelling from right to left
(b) the speed of the wave is 20 m/s
(c) frequency of the wave is 5.7 Hz
(d) the least distance between two successive crests in the wave is 2.5 cm

Thinking Process To find the characteristic parameters associated with a wave, compare the given equation of the wave with a standard equation.

Ans. ***(a, b, c)*** Given equation is $y(x, t) = 3.0 \sin\left(36t + 0.018x + \frac{\pi}{4}\right)$ ...(i)

Compare the equation with the standard form.

$$y = a\sin(\omega t + kx + \phi) \quad \text{...(ii)}$$

(a) As the equation involves positive sign with x ,hence the wave is travelling from right to left. Hence, option (a) is correct.

(b) On comparing Eq. (i) and (ii) we have

$$\omega = 36 \Rightarrow 2\pi\nu = 36$$

$$\Rightarrow \quad \nu = \text{frequency} = \frac{36}{2\pi} = \frac{18}{\pi}$$

$$k = 0.018 \Rightarrow \frac{2\pi}{\lambda} = 0.018$$

$$v = \frac{\omega}{k} = \frac{36}{18 \times 10^3} = 2000 \text{ cm/s} = 20 \text{ m/s}$$

(c) $2\pi\nu = 36 \Rightarrow \nu = \frac{36}{2\pi}\text{Hz} = \frac{18}{\pi} = 5.7\text{Hz}$

(d) $\frac{2\pi}{\lambda} = 0.018 \Rightarrow \lambda = \frac{2\pi}{0.018} = \frac{2000\pi}{18} \text{ cm} = \frac{20\pi}{18}\text{m} = 3.48 \text{ cm}$

Hence, least distance between two successive crests = λ = 3.48 m .

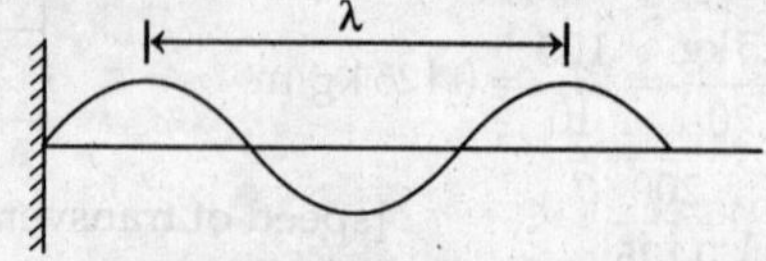

Q.11 The displacement of a string is given by

$$y(x, t) = 0.06 \sin\left(\frac{2\pi x}{3}\right)\cos(120\pi t)$$

where x and y are in metre and t in second. The length of the string is 1.5 m and its mass is 3.0×10^{-2} kg.

(a) It represents a progressive wave of frequency 60 Hz
(b) It represents a stationary wave of frequency 60 Hz
(c) It is the result superposition of two waves of wavelength 3 m, frequency 60 Hz each travelling with a speed of 180 m/s in opposite direction
(d) Amplitude of this wave is constant

Ans. *(b, c)* Given equation is $y(x,t) = 0.06 \sin\left(\frac{2\pi x}{3}\right)\cos(120\pi t)$

(a) Comparing with a standard equation of stationary wave

$$y(x,t) = a \sin(kx)\cos(\omega t)$$

Clearly, the given equation belongs to stationary wave. Hence, option (a) is not correct.

(b) By comparing, $\omega = 120\pi \Rightarrow 2\pi f = 120\pi \Rightarrow f = 60$ Hz

So option (b) is correct.

(c) $k = \frac{2\pi}{3} = \frac{2\pi}{\lambda}$

$$\Rightarrow \qquad \lambda = \text{wavelength} = 3\text{m}$$

$$\text{Frequency} = f = 60 \text{ Hz}$$

$$\text{Speed} = v = f\lambda = (60 \text{ Hz})(3\text{m}) = 180 \text{ m/s}$$

So option (c) is correct.

(d) Since in stationary wave, all particles of the medium execute SHM with varying amplitude forming nodes and antinodes. So option (d) is incorrect.

Q.12 Speed of sound wave in a fluid depends upon

(a) directly on density of the medium
(b) square of Bulk modulus of the medium
(c) inversly on the square root of density
(d) directly on the square root of bulk modulus of the medium

Ans. *(c, d)* Speed of sound waves in a fluid is given by

$v = \sqrt{\frac{B}{\rho}}$, where B is Bulk modulus and ρ is density of the medium.

Clearly, $\qquad v \propto \frac{1}{\sqrt{\rho}} \qquad$ [$\because$ for any fluid, B=constant]

and $\qquad v \propto \sqrt{B} \qquad$ [$\because$ for medium, ρ=constant]

Q.13 During propagation of a plane progressive mechanical wave,

(a) all the particles are vibrating in the same phase
(b) amplitude of all the particles is equal
(c) particles of the medium executes SHM
(d) wave velocity depends upon the nature of the medium

Ans. ***(b, c, d)*** During propagation of a plane progressive mechanical wave, like shown in the diagram, amplitude of all the particles is equal.

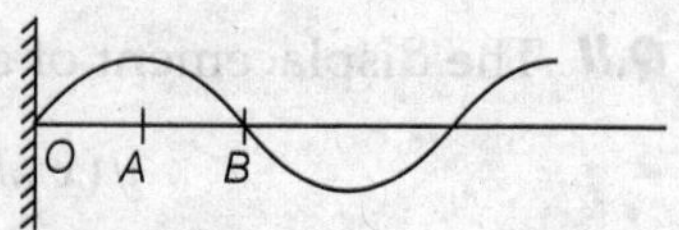

(i) Clearly, the particles O, A and B are having different phase.

(ii) Particles of the wave shown in the figure are having up and down SHM.

(iii) For a progressive wave propagating in a fluid.

$$\text{Speed} = v = \sqrt{\frac{B}{\rho}}$$

Hence, $$v \propto \sqrt{\frac{1}{\rho}} \qquad [\because B \text{ is constant}]$$

As density ρ depends upon nature of the medium, hence v also depends upon the nature of the medium.

Q.14 The transverse displacement of a string (clamped at its both ends) is given by $y(x, t) = 0.06 \sin\left(\frac{2\pi x}{3}\right)\cos(120\pi t)$.

All the points on the string between two consecutive nodes vibrate with

(a) same frequency (b) same phase (c) same energy (d) different amplitude

Ans. ***(a, b, d)*** Given equation is $y(x,t) = 0.06 \sin\left(\frac{2\pi}{3}x\right)\cos(120\pi t)$

Comparing with standard equation of stationary wave

$$y(x, t) = a\sin(kx)\cos(\omega t)$$

It is represented by diagram.

where N denotes nodes and A denotes antinodes.

(a) Clearly, frequency is common for all the points.

(b) Consider all the particles between two nodes they are having same phase of $(120\pi t)$ at a given time.

(c) and (d) are having different amplitudes of $0.06 \sin\left(\frac{2\pi}{3}x\right)$ and because of different amplitudes they are having different energies.

Q.15 A train, standing in a station yard, blows a whistle of frequency 400 Hz in still air. The wind starts blowing in the direction from the yard to the station with a speed of 10 m/s. Given that the speed of sound in still air is 340 m/s. Then

(a) the frequency of sound as heard by an observer standing on the platform is 400 Hz

(b) the speed of sound for the observer standing on the platform is 350 m/s

(c) the frequency of sound as heard by the observer standing on the platform will increase

(d) the frequency of sound as heard by the observer standing on the platform will decrease

Thinking Process When the wind is blowing in the same direction as that of sound wave then net speed of the wave is sum of speed of sound wave and speed of the wind.

Ans. ***(a, b)*** Given, $\nu_0 = 400$ Hz, $v = 340$ m / s

Speed of wind $v_w = 10$ m/ s

(a) As both source and observer are stationary, hence frequency observed will be same as natural frequency $\nu_0 = 400$ Hz

(b) The speed of sound $v = v + v_w = 340 + 10 = 350$ m / s

There will be no effect on frequency,because there is no relative motion between source and observer hence (c),(d) are incorrect.

Alternate Method

Given, Frequency of whistle, $u = 400$ Hz

Speed of sound, $V = 340 \text{ ms}^{-1}$

Speed of wind (medium), $V_w = 10 \text{ ms}^{-1}$

So, effective speed of sound for the observers i.e. $V + V_w = 340 + 10 = 350 \text{ ms}^{-1}$.

As there is relative motion between the source and observer, the frequency remains unchanged.

Q.16 Which of the following statement are true for a stationary waves?

(a) Every particle has a fixed amplitude which is different from the amplitude of its nearest particle

(b) All the particles cross their mean position at the same time.

(c) All the particles are oscillating with same amplitude.

(d) There is no net transfer of energy across any plane.

(e) There are some particles which are always at rest.

Ans. ***(a, b, d, e)*** Consider the equation of a stationary wave $y = a\sin(kx)\cos\omega t$

(a) clearly every particle at x will have amplitude $= a\sin kx =$ fixed

(b) for mean position $y = 0$

$$\Rightarrow \quad \cos\omega t = 0 \Rightarrow \omega t = (2n-1)\frac{\pi}{2}$$

Hence, for a fixed value of n, all particles are having same value of

$$\text{time}(t) = (2n-1)\frac{\pi}{2\omega} \qquad [\because \omega = \text{constant}]$$

(c) amplitude of all the particles are $a\sin(kx)$ which is different for different particles at different values of x

(d) the energy of a stationary wave oscillates between two nodes and antinodes.

(e) particles located at nodes always remain at rest because their amplitude is zero.

Very Short Answer Type Questions

Q.17 A sonometer wire is vibrating in resonance with a tuning fork. Keeping the tension applied same, the length of the wire is doubled. Under what conditions would the tuning fork still be is resonance with the wire?

Ans. Wire of twice the length vibrates in its second harmonic. Thus, if the tuning fork resonates at L, it will resonate at $2L$.

This can be explained as below

The sonometer frequency is given by

$$\nu = \frac{n}{2L}\sqrt{\frac{T}{m}} \qquad [n = \text{number of loops}]$$

Now, as it vibrates with length L, we assume $\nu = \nu_1$

[m = mass per unit length of string]

$$n = n_1$$

$$\therefore \qquad \nu_1 = \frac{n_1}{2L}\sqrt{\frac{T}{m}} \qquad \ldots(i)$$

When length is doubled, then

$$\nu_2 = \frac{n_2}{2 \times 2L}\sqrt{\frac{T}{m}} \qquad \ldots(ii)$$

Dividing Eq. (i) by Eq. (ii), we get

$$\frac{\nu_1}{\nu_2} = \frac{n_1}{n_2} \times 2$$

To keep the resonance $\quad \frac{\nu_1}{\nu_2} = 1 = \frac{n_1}{n_2} \times 2 \Rightarrow n_2 = 2n_1$

Hence, when the wire is doubled the number of loops also get doubled to produce the resonance. That is it resonates in second harmonic.

Q.18 An organ pipe of length L open at both ends is found to vibrate in its first harmonic when sounded with a tuning fork of 480 Hz. What should be the length of a pipe closed at one end, so that it also vibrates in its first harmonic with the same tuning fork?

Thinking Process We should not confuse between pressure wave and displacement wave. By considering any type of wave outcome will be same.

Ans. Consider the situation shown in the diagram

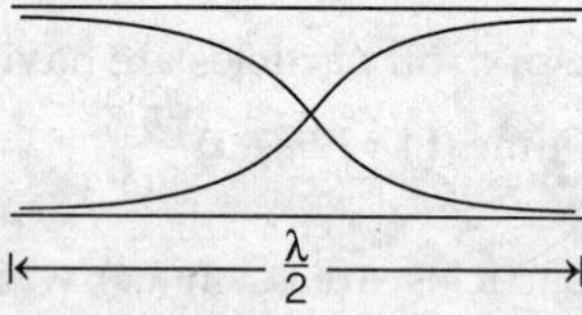

As the organ pipe is open at both ends, hence for first harmonic

$$l = \frac{\lambda}{2} \Rightarrow \lambda = 2l \Rightarrow \frac{c}{\nu} = 2l \Rightarrow \nu = \frac{c}{2l}$$

where c is speed of the sound wave in air.

For pipe closed at one end $\nu' = \frac{c}{4L'}$

c for first harmonic

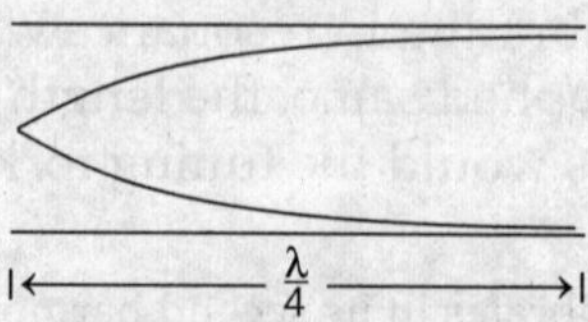

Hence, $\nu = \nu'$ [for resonance with same tuning fork]

$\Rightarrow \quad \dfrac{c}{2L} = \dfrac{c}{4L'}$ [$\because$ speed remains constant]

$\Rightarrow \quad \dfrac{L'}{L} = \dfrac{2}{4} = \dfrac{1}{2} \Rightarrow L' = \dfrac{L}{2}$

Q.19 A tuning fork A, marked 512 Hz, produces 5 beats per second, where sounded with another unmarked tuning fork B. If B is loaded with wax the number of beats is again 5 per second. What is the frequency of the tuning fork B when not loaded?

Ans. Frequency of tuning fork A, $\nu_A = 512$ Hz

Probable frequency of tuning fork B, $\nu_B = \nu_A = 5 \pm 512 \pm 5 = 517$ or 507Hz

when B is loaded, its frequency reduces.

If it is 517 Hz, it might reduced to 507 Hz given again a beat of 5 Hz.

If it is 507 Hz, reduction will always increase the beat frequency, hence $\nu_B = 517$ Hz

Note For production of beats frequencies of the two tuning forks must be nearly equal i.e. slight difference in frequencies.

Q.20 The displacement of an elastic wave is given by the function $y = 3 \sin \omega t + 4 \cos \omega t$, where y is in cm and t is in second. Calculate the resultant amplitude.

Ans. Given, displacement of an elastic wave $y = 3 \sin \omega t + 4 \cos \omega t$

Assume, $3 = a \cos \phi$ ...(i)

$4 = a \sin \phi$ ...(ii)

On dividing Eq. (ii) by Eq. (i)

$$\tan \phi = \frac{4}{3} \Rightarrow \phi = \tan^{-1}(4/3)$$

Also, $a^2 \cos^2 \phi + a^2 \sin^2 \phi = 3^2 + 4^2$

$\Rightarrow \quad a^2 (\cos^2 \phi + \sin^2 \phi) = 25$

$$a^2 \cdot 1 = 25 \Rightarrow a = 5\text{cm}$$

$$Y = 5 \cos \phi \sin \omega t + 5 \sin \phi \cos \omega t$$

$$= 5[\cos \phi \sin \omega t + \sin \phi \cos \omega t] = 5 \sin(\omega t + \phi)$$

$$Y = 5 \sin(\omega t + \phi)$$

where $\phi = \tan^{-1}(4/3)$

Q.21 A sitar wire is replaced by another wire of same length and material but of three times the earlier radius. If the tension in the wire remains the same, by what factor will the frequency change?

Thinking Process In a sitar wire, the vibration is assumed to be similar as a wire fixed at both ends.

Ans. Frequency of vibrations produced by a stretched wire

$$\nu = \frac{n}{2l}\sqrt{\frac{T}{\mu}}$$

$$\text{Mass per unit length } \mu = \frac{\text{Mass}}{\text{Length}} = \frac{\pi r^2 l\rho}{l} = \pi r^2 \rho \qquad [\because M = v\rho = Al\rho = \pi r^2 l\rho]$$

$$\therefore \qquad \nu = \frac{n}{2l}\sqrt{\frac{T}{\pi r^2 \rho}} \Rightarrow \nu \propto \sqrt{\frac{1}{r^2}}$$

$$\nu \propto \frac{1}{r}$$

Hence, when radius is tripled, v will be $\frac{1}{3}$ rd of previous value.

Q.22 At what temperatures (in °C) will the speed of sound in air be 3 times its value at 0° C?

Ans. We know that speed of sound in air $v \propto \sqrt{T}$

$$\therefore \qquad \frac{v_T}{v_0} = \sqrt{\frac{T_T}{T_0}} = \sqrt{\frac{T_T}{273}} \qquad \text{[where } T \text{ is in kelvin]}$$

But $$\frac{v_T}{v_0} = \frac{3}{1} \qquad [\because \text{ speed becomes three times}]$$

$$\therefore \qquad \frac{3}{1} = \sqrt{\frac{T_T}{T_0}} \Rightarrow \frac{T_T}{273} = 9$$

$$\therefore \qquad T_T = 273 \times 9 = 2457 \text{ K}$$

Hence, $$T_T = 2457 - 273 = 2184°\text{C}$$

Q.23 When two waves of almost equal frequencies n_1 and n_2 reach at a point simultaneously, what is the time interval between successive maxima?

Thinking Process When two waves of almost equal frequencies interfere, they are producing beats.

Ans. Let, $$n_1 > n_2$$

Beat frequency $$\nu_b = n_1 - n_2$$

$$\therefore \qquad \text{Time period of beats} = T_b = \frac{1}{\nu_b} = \frac{1}{n_1 - n_2}$$

Short Answer Type Questions

Q.24 A steel wire has a length of 12 m and a mass of 2.10 kg. What will be the speed of a transverse wave on this wire when a tension of 2.06×10^4 N is applied?

Ans. Given, length of the wire $l = 12$ m

Mass of wire $m = 2.10$ kg

Tension $T = 2.06 \times 10^4$ N

Speed of transverse wave $$v = \sqrt{\frac{T}{\mu}} \qquad [\text{where } \mu = \text{mass per unit length}]$$

$$= \sqrt{\frac{2.06 \times 10^4}{\left(\frac{2.10}{12}\right)}} = \sqrt{\frac{2.06 \times 12 \times 10^4}{2.10}} = 343 \text{ m/s}$$

Q.25 A pipe 20 cm long is closed at one end. Which harmonic mode of the pipe is resonantly excited by a source of 1237.5 Hz? (sound velocity in air $= 330\,\text{ms}^{-1}$)

Ans. Length of pipe

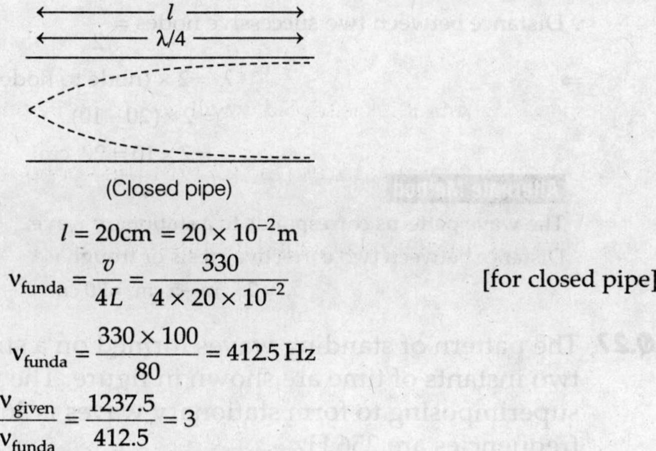

(Closed pipe)

$$l = 20\text{cm} = 20 \times 10^{-2}\text{m}$$

$$\nu_{\text{funda}} = \frac{v}{4L} = \frac{330}{4 \times 20 \times 10^{-2}} \qquad \text{[for closed pipe]}$$

$$\nu_{\text{funda}} = \frac{330 \times 100}{80} = 412.5\,\text{Hz}$$

$$\frac{\nu_{\text{given}}}{\nu_{\text{funda}}} = \frac{1237.5}{412.5} = 3$$

Hence, 3rd harmonic node of the pipe is resonantly excited by the source of given frequency.

For a pipe close at one end $\quad f = \frac{nv}{4L}$

Where n is the harmonic $\quad \frac{V}{4L} = \frac{330}{4 \times (0.2)} = 412 \cdot 5$

$$\frac{nv}{4L} = 123.75$$

$$n \times 412 \cdot 5 = 1237.5$$

$$n = 3$$

Q.26 The wave pattern on a stretched string is shown in figure. Interpret what kind of wave this is and find its wavelength.

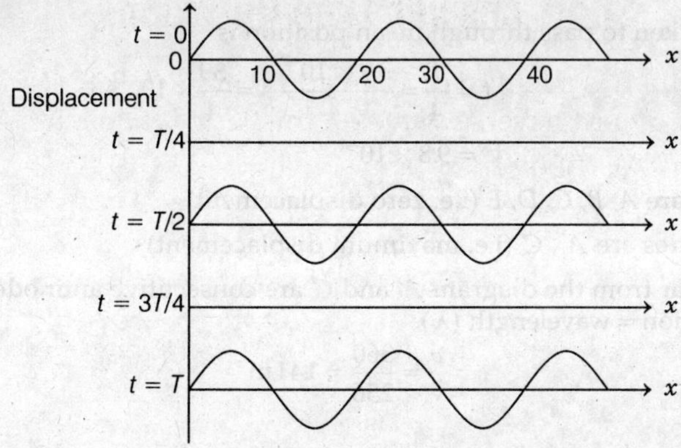

Ans. We have to observe the displacement and position of different points, then accordingly nature of two wave is decided.

Points on positions $x = 10, 20, 30, 40$ never move, always at mean position with respect to time. These are forming nodes which characterise a stationary wave.

$\because$ Distance between two successive nodes $= \dfrac{\lambda}{2}$

$$\Rightarrow \qquad \lambda = 2 \times \text{(node to node distance)}$$
$$= 2 \times (20 - 10)$$
$$= 2 \times 10 = 20 \text{ cm}$$

Alternate Method

The wave patterns corresponds to a stationary wave.

Distance between two corrective crests or trough is

$$\lambda = 25 \text{ cm} - 5 \text{ cm} = 20 \text{ cm}$$

Q.27 The pattern of standing waves formed on a stretched string at two instants of time are shown in figure. The velocity of two waves superimposing to form stationary waves is 360 ms^{-1} and their frequencies are 256 Hz.

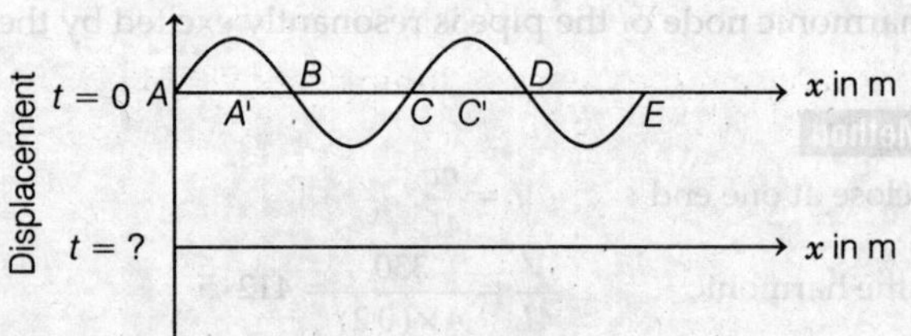

(a) Calculate the time at which the second curve is plotted.

(b) Mark nodes and antinodes on the curve.

(c) Calculate the distance between A' and C'.

Ans. Given, frequency of the wave $\nu = 256$ Hz

Time period $\qquad T = \dfrac{1}{\nu} = \dfrac{1}{256} \text{ s} = 3.9 \times 10^{-3} \text{ s}$

(a) Time taken to pass through mean position is

$$t = \frac{T}{4} = \frac{3.9 \times 10^{-3}}{4} \text{ s} = \frac{39}{4} \times 10^{-4} \text{ s}$$
$$= 9.8 \times 10^{-4}$$

(b) Nodes are A, B, C, D, E (i.e. zero displacement)

Antinodes are A', C' (i.e. maximum displacement)

(c) It is clear from the diagram A' and C' are consecutive antinodes, hence separation = wavelength (λ)

$$= \frac{v}{\nu} = \frac{360}{256} = 1.41 \text{ m} \qquad [\because v = \nu\lambda]$$

Q.28 A tuning fork vibrating with a frequency of 512 Hz is kept close to the open end of a tube filled with water (figure). The water level in the tube is gradually lowered. When the water level is 17 cm below the open end, maximum intensity of sound is heard. If the room temperature is 20°C, calculate

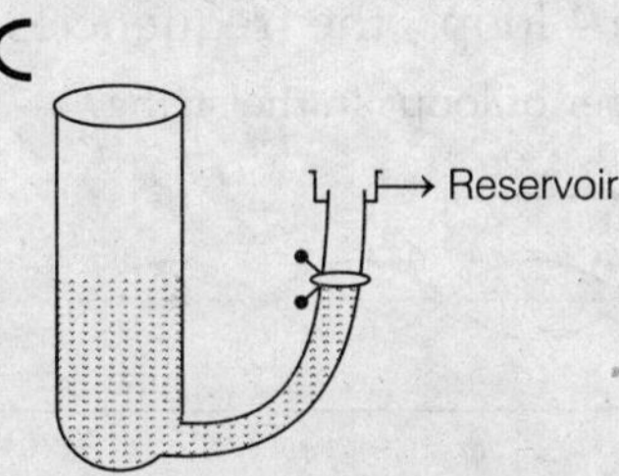

(a) speed of sound in air at room temperature.
(b) speed of sound in air at 0°C.
(c) if the water in the tube is replaced with mercury, will there be any difference in your observations?

Thinking Process The pipe partially filled with water, acts as closed organ pipe. According to this, we will find associated frequencies.

Ans. Consider the diagram frequency of tuning fork $\nu = 512\,\text{Hz}$.

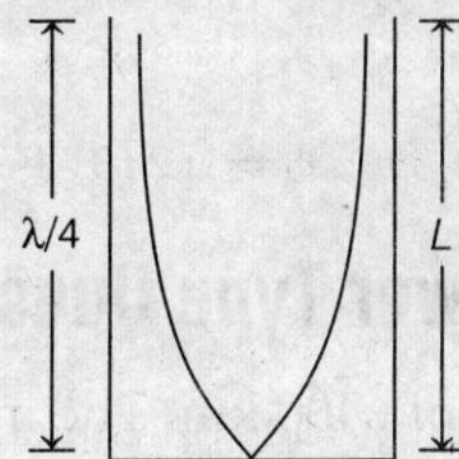

For observation of first maxima of intensity

(a) $L = \frac{\lambda}{4} \Rightarrow \lambda = 4L$ [for closed pipe]

$$v = \nu\lambda = 512 \times 4 \times 17 \times 10^{-2} = 348.16\,\text{m/s}$$

(b) We know that $V \propto \sqrt{T}$

$$\frac{V_0}{V_T} = \sqrt{\frac{T_0}{T}}$$

$$T_0 = 273\,\text{K}$$

$$V_T = V_{20} = 348.16\,\text{m/s}$$

$$T = 20 + 273 = 293\,\text{K}$$

$$V_0 = V_T\sqrt{\frac{T_0}{T_T}}$$

$$V_0 = 348.16\sqrt{\frac{273}{293}} = 348.16\sqrt{0.9317}$$

$$V_0 = 348.16 \times 0.96526$$

$$V_0 = 336\,\text{m/s}$$

(c) Resonance will be observed at 17 cm length of air column, only intensity of sound heard may be greater due to more complete reflection of the sound waves at the mercury surface because mercury is more denser than water and better reflector of sound.

Q.29 Show that when a string fixed at its two ends vibrates in 1 loop, 2 loops, 3 loops and 4 loops, the frequencies are in the ratio $1:2:3:4$.

Ans. Let, there are n number of loops in the string.

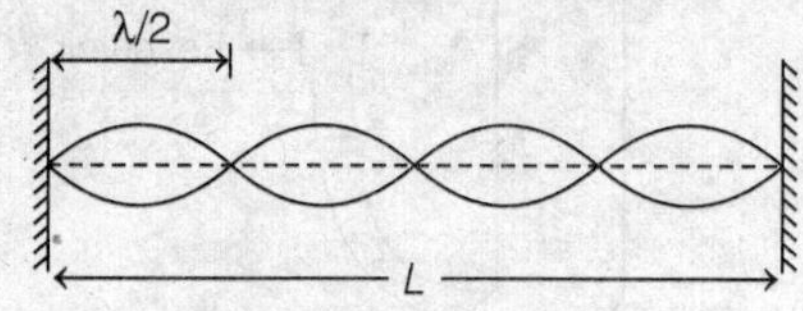

Length corresponding each loop is $\frac{\lambda}{2}$.

Now, we can write

$$L = \frac{n\lambda}{2} \Rightarrow \lambda = \frac{2L}{n} \quad \text{[for } n \text{ loops]}$$

$$\Rightarrow \quad \frac{v}{\nu} = \frac{2L}{n} \quad [\because v = \nu\lambda]$$

$$\Rightarrow \quad \nu = \frac{n}{2L} v = \frac{n}{2L}\sqrt{\frac{T}{\mu}} \quad [\because \text{velocity of transverse waves} = \sqrt{T/\mu}]$$

$$\Rightarrow \quad \nu \propto n \quad [\because \text{length and speed are constants}]$$

So, $\nu_1 : \nu_2 : \nu_3 : \nu_4 = n_1 : n_2 : n_3 : n_4 = 1:2:3:4$

Long Answer Type Questions

Q.30 The earth has a radius of 6400 km. The inner core of 1000 km radius is solid. Outside it, there is a region from 1000 km to a radius of 3500 km which is in molten state. Then again from 3500 km to 6400 km the earth is solid. Only longitudinal (P) waves can travel inside a liquid.

Assume that the P wave has a speed of 8 km s^{-1} in solid parts and of 5 km s^{-1} in liquid parts of the earth. An earthquake occurs at some place close to the surface of the earth. Calculate the time after which it will be recorded in a seismometer at a diametrically opposite point on the earth, if wave travels along diameter?

Ans. Speed of wave in solid = 8 km / s

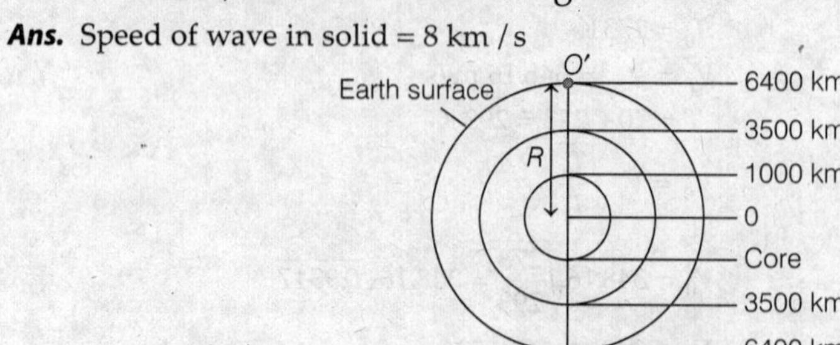

Speed of wave in liquid = 5 km / s

$$\text{Required time} = \left[\frac{1000-0}{8} + \frac{3500-1000}{5} + \frac{6400-3500}{8}\right] \times 2$$

[∵ diameter = radius × 2]

$$= \left[\frac{1000}{8} + \frac{2500}{5} + \frac{2900}{8}\right] \times 2 \qquad \left[\text{time} = \frac{\text{distance}}{\text{speed}}\right]$$

$$= [125 + 500 + 362.5] \times 2 = 1975 \text{ sec}$$

As we are considering at diametrically opposite point, hence there is a multiplication of 2.

Q.31 If c is rms speed of molecules in a gas and v is the speed of sound waves in the gas, show that c/v is constant and independent of temperature for all diatomic gases.

Ans. We know that rms speed of molecules of a gas

$$c = \sqrt{\frac{3p}{\rho}} = \sqrt{\frac{3RT}{M}} \qquad \ldots\text{(i)}$$

where M = molar mass of the gas.

$$\text{Speed of sound wave in gas } v = \sqrt{\frac{\gamma p}{\rho}} = \sqrt{\frac{\gamma RT}{M}} \qquad \ldots\text{(ii)}$$

On dividing Eq. (i) by Eq. (ii), we get

$$\frac{c}{v} = \sqrt{\frac{3RT}{M} \times \frac{M}{\gamma RT}} \Rightarrow \frac{c}{v} = \sqrt{\frac{3}{\gamma}}$$

where γ = adiabatic constant for diatomic gas

$$\gamma = \frac{7}{5} \qquad \left[\text{since } \gamma = \frac{C_p}{C_V}\right]$$

Hence, $$\frac{c}{v} = \sqrt{\frac{15}{7}} = \text{constant}$$

Q.32 Given below are some functions of x and t to represent the displacement of an elastic wave.

(i) $y = 5\cos(4x)\sin(20t)$

(ii) $y = 4\sin(5x - t/2) + 3\cos(5x - t/2)$

(iii) $y = 10\cos[(252 - 250)\pi t]\cos[(252 + 250)\pi t]$

(iv) $y = 100\cos(100\pi t + 0.5x)$

State which of these represent

(a) a travelling wave along– x-direction (b) a stationary wave

(c) beats (d) a travelling wave along– x-direction

Given reasons for your answers.

Thinking Process To predict the nature of wave we have to compare with standard equations.

Ans. (a) The equation $y = 100\cos(100\pi t + 0.5x)$ is representing a travelling wave along x-direction.

(b) The equation $y = 5\cos(4x)\sin(20t)$ represents a stationary wave, because it contains sin, cos terms i.e. combination of two progressive waves. Its amplitude is $5\cos 4x$.

(c) As the equation $y = 10\cos[(252-250)\pi t]\cdot\cos[(252+250)\pi t]$ involving sum and difference of two near by frequencies 252 and 250 have this equation represents beats formation.

(d) As the equation $y = 4\sin(5x - t/2) + 3\cos(5x - t/2)$

$$y = A\cos\theta \sin\left(5x - \frac{t}{2}\right) + A\sin\theta\left(5x - \frac{t}{2}\right)$$

$$= A\sin\left[5x - \frac{t}{2} + \theta\right] \qquad \left[\text{Here } A = \sqrt{4^2 + 3^2} = 5\text{m}\right]$$

It represents wave travelling along $+ x$ axis.

Mistake Alert! *We must not confuse with sign connected with x and direction of propagation of wave. It is just reversed, positive sign with x shown propagation of the wave in negative x-direction and vice-versa.*

Q.33 In the given progressive wave $y = 5\sin(100\pi t - 0.4\pi x)$ where y and x are in metre, t is in second. What is the

(a) amplitude? (b) wavelength?
(c) frequency? (d) wave velocity?
(e) particle velocity amplitude?

Ans. Standard equation of a progressive wave is given by

$$y = a\sin(\omega t - kx + \phi)$$

This is travelling along positive x-direction.

Given equation is $y = 5\sin(100\pi t - 0.4\pi x)$

Comparing with the standard equation

(a) Amplitude = 5m

(b) $k = \dfrac{2\pi}{\lambda} = 0.4\pi$

$\therefore$ Wavelength $\lambda = \dfrac{2\pi}{k} = \dfrac{2\pi}{0.4\pi} = \dfrac{20}{4} = 5\text{m}$

(c) $\omega = 100\pi$

$$\omega = 2\pi\nu = 100\pi$$

$\therefore$ Frequency $\nu = \dfrac{100\pi}{2\pi} = 50$ Hz

(d) Wave velocity $\nu = \dfrac{\omega}{k}$, where k is wave number and $k = \dfrac{2\pi}{\lambda}$.

$$= \frac{100\pi}{0.4\pi} = \frac{1000}{4} = 250 \text{ m/s}$$

(e) $$y = 5\sin(100\pi t - 0.4\pi x) \qquad \text{...(i)}$$

$$\frac{dy}{dt} = \text{particle velocity}$$

From Eq. (i),

$$\frac{dy}{dt} = 5(100\pi)\cos[100\pi t - 0.4\pi x]$$

For particle velocity amplitude $\left(\frac{dy}{dt}\right)_{max}$

Which will be for $\{\cos[100\pi t - 0.4\pi x]\}_{max} = 1$

$\therefore$ Particle velocity amplitude $= \left(\frac{dy}{dt}\right)_{max} = 5(100\pi) \times 1 = 500\,\pi$ m / s

Q.34 For the harmonic travelling wave $y = 2\cos 2\pi(10t - 0.0080x + 3.5)$ where x and y are in cm and t is in second. What is the phase difference between the oscillatory motion at two points separated by a distance of

(a) 4 m
(b) 0.5 m
(c) $\frac{\lambda}{2}$
(d) $\frac{3\lambda}{4}$ (at a given instant of time)

(e) What is the phase difference between the oscillation of a particle located at $x = 100$ cm, at $t = T$ sec and $t = 5$?

Ans. Given, wave functions are

$$y = 2\cos 2\pi(10t - 0.0080x + 3.5)$$
$$= 2\cos(20\pi t - 0.016\pi x + 7\pi)$$

Now, standard equation of a travelling wave can be written as

$$y = a\cos(\omega t - kx + \phi)$$

On comparing with above equation, we get

$$a = 2\text{ cm}$$
$$\omega = 20\pi \text{ rad/s}$$
$$k = 0.016\pi$$

Path difference = 4 m

(a) Phase difference $\Delta\phi = \frac{2\pi}{\lambda} \times$ Path difference

$\therefore$ $\Delta\phi = 0.016\pi \times 4 \times 100$ $\left[\because \frac{2\pi}{\lambda} = k\right]$

$= 6.4\pi$ rad

(b) $\Delta\phi = \frac{2\pi}{\lambda} \times (0.5 \times 100)$ [$\because$ Path difference = 0.5 m]

$= 0.016\pi \times 0.5 \times 100 = 0.8\pi$ rad

(c) $\Delta\phi = \frac{2\pi}{\lambda} \times \left(\frac{\lambda}{2}\right) = \pi$ rad [$\because$ Path difference $= \lambda/2$]

(d) $\Delta\phi = \frac{2\pi}{\lambda} \times \frac{3\lambda}{4} = \frac{3\pi}{2}$ rad

(e) Now phase difference

$$\phi = \omega t = \frac{2\pi}{t} . t$$

At time $t = T$, $\phi_1 = \frac{2\pi}{T} \times T = 2\pi$ radian

and at time $t = 5$ second

$$\phi_2 = \frac{2\pi}{T} \times 5 = \frac{10\pi}{0.1} = 100\pi \text{ radian}$$

$\Delta\phi$ = phase difference $= \phi_2 - \phi_1 = 98\pi$ radian

Q.35 A train whistling at constant frequency is moving towards a station at a constant speed v. The train goes past a stationary observer on the station. The frequency n' of the sound as heard by the observer is plotted as a function of time t (figure). Identify the expected curve.

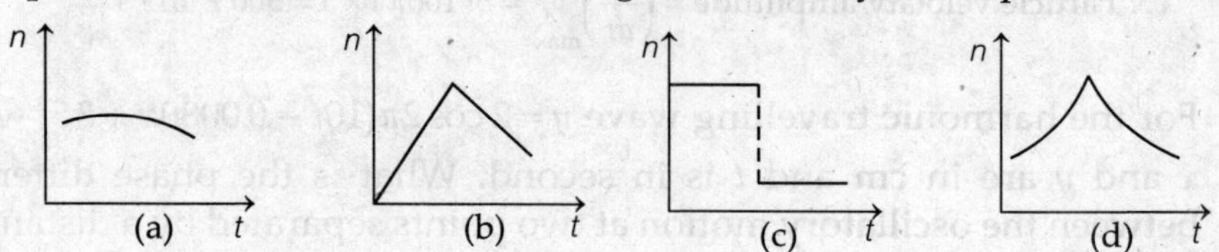

Thinking Process The observed frequency is apparent frequency due to Doppler shift.

Ans. **(c)** Let the original frequency of the source is n_0.

Let the speed of sound wave in the medium is v.
As observer is stationary

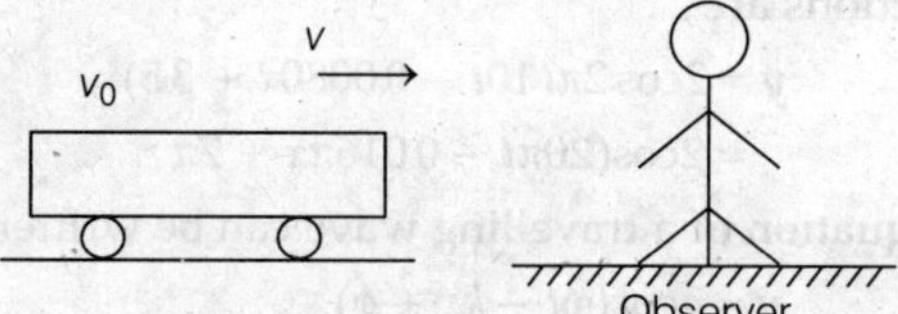

Apparent frequency $n_a = \left(\frac{v}{v - v_s}\right) n_o$ [when train is approaching]

$$= \left(\frac{v}{v - v_s}\right) n_o = n_a > n_o$$

When the train is going away from the observer

Apparent frequency $n_a = \left(\frac{v}{v + v_s}\right) n_o = n_a < n_o$

Hence, the expected curve is (c).

Q.36 A train standing at the outer signal of a railway station blows a whistle of frequency 400 Hz still air. The train begins to move with a speed of 10 ms^{-1} towards the platform. What is the frequency of the sound for an observer standing on the platform? (sound velocity in air = 330 ms^{-1})

Ans. As the source (train) is moving towards the observer (platform) hence apparent frequency observed is more than the natural frequency.

Frequency of whistle $\nu = 400$ Hz
Speed of train $v_t = 10$ m/s
Velocity of sound in air $v = 330$ m/s
Apparent frequency when source is moving towards observer is

$$\nu_{app} = \left(\frac{v}{v - v_t}\right)\nu = \left(\frac{330}{330 - 10}\right)400$$

$$\Rightarrow \quad \nu_{app} = \frac{330}{320} \times 400 = 412.5 \text{ Hz}$$

NCERT EXEMPLAR

Problems – Solutions

Science 9th

Author
Shashi Prakash Tiwari
Tarnija Midha
Hema Batra

ARIHANT PRAKASHAN (Series), MEERUT

卐 **Administrative & Production Offices**

Regd. Office

'Ramchhaya' 4577/15, Agarwal Road, Darya Ganj, New Delhi -110002
Tele: 011- 47630600, 43518550

卐 **Head Office**

Kalindi, TP Nagar, Meerut (UP) - 250002
Tel: 0121-7156203, 7156204

卐 **Sales & Support Offices**

Agra, Ahmedabad, Bengaluru, Bareilly, Chennai, Delhi, Guwahati, Hyderabad, Jaipur, Jhansi, Kolkata, Lucknow, Nagpur & Pune.

卐 **PRICE** ₹200.00

卐 **PO No. :** TXT-59-T070861-5-26

Published by Arihant Publications (India) Ltd.

For further information about the books published by Arihant, log on to www.arihantbooks.com or e-mail at info@arihantbooks.com

Follow us on   

PREFACE

NCERT Exemplar Problems, published by the NCERT, are designed to provide students with a diverse range of quality questions in formats such as Multiple Choice Questions, Short Answer Questions, and Long Answer Questions, catering to varying levels of difficulty.

These problems are essential for success in school and board exams, as well as competitive exams like engineering and medical entrances. Regular practice with these problems prepares students to tackle challenging questions effectively.

This book, **NCERT Exemplar Problems-Solutions Science 9th**, offers precise and detailed solutions to all the questions in the NCERT Exemplar Science textbook. Each solution is complemented by explanatory notes and authentic explanations, enabling students to deepen their conceptual understanding and enhance their analytical skills.

Key features

- **Thinking Process** Provides simple steps to approach and solve the question, clearing up any confusion.
- **Concept Insight** Explains the main ideas and concepts needed to answer the questions correctly.
- **Mistake Alert!** Points out common mistakes students might make and helps them avoid these errors.

We hope this book proves to be a valuable resource, aiding students in their academic journey and leading them to great success.

Authors

CONTENTS

Note (*) These Chapters have been deleted from Latest NCERT.

Chapter

01

Matter in Our Surroundings

Multiple Choice Questions (MCQs)

Choose the correct answer from the given four options in the following questions :

Q. 1 Which one of the following sets of phenomena would increase on raising the temperature?

(a) Diffusion, evaporation, compression of gases

(b) Evaporation, compression of gases, solubility

(c) Evaporation, diffusion, expansion of gases

(d) Evaporation, solubility, diffusion, compression of gases

Thinking Process Compression of gases occurs on decreasing the temperature as molecules come closer and kinetic energy decreases. Solubility of most gases in liquids decrease with increase in temperature.

Ans. *(c)* **Evaporation, diffusion** and **expansion** of gases increases on raising the temperature.

Evaporation rate increases because on increasing temperature, kinetic energy of molecules increases, so the molecules present at the surface of the liquid leave the surface quickly and go into the vapour state. Diffusion and expansion of gases also increase as the molecules move more rapidly and try to occupy more space.

Q. 2 Seema visited a Natural Gas Compressing Unit and found that the gas can be liquefied under specific conditions of temperature and pressure. While sharing her experience with friends she got confused. Help her to identify the correct set of conditions.

(a) Low temperature, low pressure

(b) High temperature, low pressure

(c) Low temperature, high pressure

(d) High temperature, high pressure

- **Concept Insight** The concept of liquefaction of gases is used in this question. It is the process of converting a gas into a liquid by applying pressure and reducing temperature.

Ans. *(c)* Low temperature and high pressure are required to liquefy gases to liquids. There is a lot of space between the particles of a gas. On applying high pressure, the particles of gas gets closer and they start attracting each other sufficiently to form a liquid.

A lots of heat is generated when a gas is compressed, so it is necessary to cool it. Cooling lowers the temperature of compressed gas and helps in liquefying it. Hence, a gas can be liquefied by applying high pressure and lowering the temperature (cooling).

Q. 3 The property to flow is unique to fluids. Which one of the following statements is correct?

(a) Only gases behave like fluids.
(b) Gases and solids behave like fluids.
(c) Gases and liquids behave like fluids.
(d) Only liquids are fluids.

Thinking Process A fluid is a substance that can flow easily and needs a container to be stored in.

Ans. *(c)* Gases and liquids behave like fluids. Both gases and liquids tend to flow due to less force of attraction between their particles. Also, they require vessel to keep them. However, solids do not flow.

Q. 4 During summer, water kept in an earthen pot becomes cool because of the phenomenon of

(a) diffusion
(b) transpiration
(c) osmosis
(d) evaporation

Thinking Process As the pot is made of a porous material, allowing some water to seep through its surface. Once water is on the surface of the pot, it is exposed to air. The heat from the pot's surface and the surrounding environment is used to convert this water into vapour which is called evaporation.

- **Concept Insight** In this question, the concept of the cooling effect of evaporation is used. It is the process where liquid water evaporates by absorbing heat from its surroundings. This results in a decrease in temperature and thus, gives a cooling effect.

Ans. *(d)* During summer, water kept in an earthen pot becomes cool because of the phenomenon of evaporation. Earthen pot has a large number of tiny pores in its walls and some of the water molecules continuously seep through these pores to outside the pot.

This water evaporates continuously and takes the latent heat required for vaporisation from the remaining water. In this way, the remaining water loses heat and gets cooled (evaporation causes cooling).

Q. 5 A few substances are arranged in the increasing order of 'forces of attraction' between their particles. Which one of the following represents a correct arrangement?

(a) Water, air, wind
(b) Air, sugar, oil
(c) Oxygen, water, sugar
(d) Salt, juice, air

Thinking Process In solids, the particles are closely packed whereas in gases the particles are very far apart and move freely. Liquids have the inter-particle distances intermediate to that present in solids and gases.

Ans. *(c)* The correct order of increasing 'forces of attraction' between their particles is :

Oxygen < Water < Sugar

It is because the force of attraction increases in the order *i.e.*, Gas < Liquid < Solid.

Q. 6 On converting 25°C, 38°C and 66°C to kelvin scale, the correct sequence of temperature will be

(a) 298 K, 311 K and 339 K
(b) 298 K, 300 K and 338 K
(c) 273 K, 278 K and 543 K
(d) 298 K, 310 K and 338 K

Thinking Process $T\,°C + 273 = T\,K$

Ans. ***(a)*** Therefore, the correct sequence of temperature will be 298 K, 311 K and 339 K.
On converting 25°C, 38°C and 66°C, to kelvin scale, we get the following temperatures :
25°C + 273 = 298 K; 38°C + 273 = 311 K; 66°C + 273 = 339 K
Therefore, the correct sequence of temperature will be 298 K, 311 K and 339 K.

Mistake Alert ! *Student can make a mistake in the inter conversion of temperature among kelvin celsius and fahrenheit scale.*

Q. 7 Choose the correct statement of the following.

(a) Conversion of solid into vapours without passing through the liquid state is called **sublimation**.

(b) Conversion of vapours into solid without passing through the liquid state is called **vaporisation**.

(c) Conversion of vapours into solid without passing through the liquid state is called **freezing**.

(d) Conversion of solid into liquid is called **sublimation**.

Ans. ***(a)*** Conversion of solid into vapours on heating without changing into liquid state is called sublimation. The other statements in their correct form are as follows :

- The conversion of gas (vapour) into solid on cooling without changing into liquid is called **deposition**.
- The conversion of liquid into gas (vapour) is called **vaporisation**.
- The conversion of liquid into solid is called **freezing**.
- The conversion of solid into liquid is called **melting**.

Q. 8 The boiling points of diethyl ether, acetone and *n*-butyl alcohol are 35°C, 56°C and 118°C, respectively. Which one of the following correctly represents their boiling points in kelvin scale?

(a) 306 K, 329 K, 391 K (b) 308 K, 329 K, 392 K

(c) 308 K, 329 K, 391 K (d) 329 K, 392 K, 308 K

Ans. ***(c)*** The correct order of boiling points of diethyl ether, acetone and *n*-butyl alcohol in kelvin scale is 308 K, 329 K and 391 K, which can be explained as ($\because T\,°C + 273 = TK$).

Boiling point of diethyl ether = 35°C + 273 = 308 K

Boiling point of acetone = 56°C + 273 = 329 K

Boiling point of *n*-butyl alcohol = 118°C + 273 = 391 K

Q. 9 Which condition out of the following will increase the evaporation of water?

(a) Increase in temperature of water (b) Decrease in temperature of water

(c) Less exposed surface area of water (d) Adding common salt to water

- **Concept Insight** The concept of how temperature, surface area and the addition of salt affects the rate of evaporation is used in this question. It is based on the idea that higher temperature and larger surface area increases evaporation, whereas adding salt can lower the rate of evaporation.

Ans. ***(a)*** Increase in temperature of water will increase the evaporation of water. It is because, on increasing the temperature, kinetic energy of water molecules increases and more particles get enough kinetic energy to go into the vapour state. This increases the rate of evaporation.

Evaporation is the surface phenomenon, so it depends upon the exposed surface area. Higher the exposed surface area of water, higher will be the evaporation.

When common salt is added to water, then interparticle space at surface of solvent is occupied by the non-volatile solute particles. So, the escaping tendency of solvent particles decreases and thus the evaporation of water decreases.

Therefore, other options (b), (c) and (d) will decrease the evaporation of water while option (a) will increase the evaporation of water.

Q.10 In which of the following conditions, the distance between the molecules of hydrogen gas would increase?

(i) Increasing pressure on hydrogen contained in a closed container.

(ii) Some hydrogen gas leaking out of the container.

(iii) Increasing the volume of the container of hydrogen gas.

(iv) Adding more hydrogen gas to the container without increasing the volume of the container.

(a) (i) and (ii) (b) (i) and (iv)

(c) (ii) and (iii) (d) (ii) and (iv)

Ans. *(c)* In option (ii), hydrogen gas leaking from the container leaves some vacant space inside the container. So, hydrogen gas molecules inside the container occupy all the space available and the distance between the molecules of hydrogen gas will increase.

In option (iii), on increasing the volume of the container of hydrogen gas, more space will be available inside the container and hydrogen gas molecules will occupy all the space available and hence, distance between the molecules will be increased.

In option (i) on increasing pressure, hydrogen molecules will come closer and the distance between them will be decreased.

In option (iv) more hydrogen gas molecules are available in less volume, so the distance between them will be decreased.

Thus, option (c) is correct.

Short Answer Type Questions

Q.11 A sample of water under study was found to boil at 102°C at normal temperature and pressure. Is the water pure? Will this water freeze at 0°C? Comment.

Thinking Process

(i) The presence of impurities increases the boiling point.

(ii) The presence of impurities decreases the freezing/melting point.

Ans. No, the water is not pure. It is because, the boiling point of pure water is 100°C but the given sample boils at 102°C. It indicates that it has some dissolved impurities. Also, the water will not freeze at 0°C. Instead it will freeze below 0°C as it has impurities dissolved in it.

Mistake Alert ! *One can make a mistake in describing how impurities affect the freezing and boiling points of water.*

Q.12 A student heats a beaker containing ice and water. He measures the temperature of the content of the beaker as a function of time. Which of the following would correctly represent the result? Justify your choice.

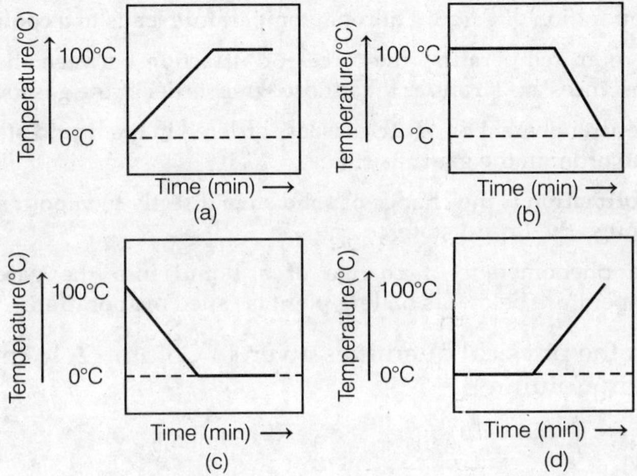

Thinking Process

(i) Latent heat is the heat hidden into the contents of the beaker.

(ii) The amount of heat energy required to change 1 kg of a solid into liquid at atmospheric pressure at its melting point is called the latent heat of fusion.

Ans. Figure (d) would correctly represent the result. Because when heat is provided to the mixture of water and ice at 0°C, the ice absorbs this heat and converts it into the water at 0°C. During this period, there is no rise in temperature. On further heating, the temperature starts rising.

This is because, in ice (solid), the particles attract one another with strong forces. The heat which we supply to ice during melting is all used up to overcome the forces of attraction between ice particles, so that they become loose and form liquid water.

This heat does not increase the kinetic energy of particles and hence no rise in temperature takes place during the melting of ice because of latent heat of fusion. When all the ice has melted forming water, further heating increases the kinetic energy of water, due to which the temperature of water starts rising sharply.

Mistake Alert! *One can make a mistake of not considering the latent heat of fusion in the question.*

Q.13 Fill in the blanks.

(a) Evaporation of a liquid at room temperature leads to a .... effect.

(b) At room temperature the forces of attraction between the particles of solid substances are ...... than those which exist in the gaseous state.

(c) The arrangement of particles is less ordered in the .... state. However, there is no order in the .... state.

(d) .... is the change of solid state directly to vapour state without going through the .... state.

(e) The phenomenon of change of a liquid into the gaseous state at any temperature below its boiling point is called ....

Ans. (a) Evaporation of a liquid at room temperature leads to a **cooling** effect.

(b) At room temperature the forces of attraction between the particles of solid substances are **stronger** than those which exist in the gaseous state.

(c) The arrangement of paritcles is less ordered in the **liquid** state. However, there is no order in the **gaseous** state.

(d) **Sublimation** is the change of solid state directly to vapour state without going through the **liquid** state.

(e) The phenomenon of change of a liquid into the gaseous state at any temperature below its boiling point is called **evaporation**.

Q.14 Match the physical quantities given in Column A to their SI units given in Column B.

	Column A		Column B
(a)	Pressure	1.	cubic metre
(b)	Temperature	2.	kilogram
(c)	Density	3.	pascal
(d)	Mass	4.	kelvin
(e)	Volume	5.	kilogram per cubic metre

Ans. The correct matching is

(a)	Pressure	3.	pascal
(b)	Temperature	4.	kelvin
(c)	Density	5.	kilogram per cubic metre
(d)	Mass	2.	kilogram
(e)	Volume	1.	cubic metre

Q.15 The non-SI and SI units of some physical quantities are given in Column A and Column B respectively. Match the units belonging to the same physical quantity.

	Column A		Column B
(a)	degree celsius	1.	kilogram
(b)	centimetre	2.	pascal
(c)	gram per centimetre cube	3.	metre
(d)	bar	4.	kelvin
(e)	milligram	5.	kilogram per metre cube

Ans. The correct matching is

(a)	degree celsius	4.	kelvin
(b)	centimetre	3.	metre
(c)	gram per centimetre cube	5.	kilogram per metre cube
(d)	bar	2.	pascal
(e)	milligram	1.	kilogram

Q.16 'Osmosis is a special kind of diffusion'. Comment.

Ans. Diffusion is the process in which molecules of a substance move from a place of their higher concentration to a place of their lower concentration.

Similarly during osmosis, the solvent (water) molecules move from the place of their higher concentration to that place of their lower concentration through a semi-permeable membrane. Thus, osmosis is termed as a special kind of diffusion.

Q.17 Classify the following into osmosis/diffusion.

(a) Swelling up of a raisin on keeping in water.
(b) Spreading of virus on sneezing.
(c) Earthworm dying on coming in contact with common salt.
(d) Shrinking of grapes kept in thick sugar syrup.
(e) Preserving pickles in salt.
(f) Spreading of smell of cake being baked throughout the house.
(g) Aquatic animals using oxygen dissolved in water during respiration.

Thinking Process

(i) Osmosis is the process in which solvent molecules move from the place of their higher concentration to the place of their lower concentration through a semi-permeable membrane.

(ii) Diffusion is the spreading out and mixing of a substance from the region of its higher concentration with another substance due to motion of its particles. It goes on until a uniform mixture is formed.

Ans. Osmosis occurs in

(a) Swelling up of a raisin on keeping in water.

(c) Earthworm dying on coming in contact with common salt.

(d) Shrinking of grapes kept in thick sugar syrup.

(e) Preserving pickles in salt.

Diffusion occurs in

(b) Spreading of virus on sneezing.

(f) Spreading of smell of cake being baked throughout the house.

(g) Aquatic animals using oxygen dissolved in water during respiration.

Mistake Alert ! *Osmosis and diffusion are not the same, infact osmosis is considered a special kind of diffusion, as in osmosis movement of solvent is across a semi-permeable membrane.*

Q.18 Water as ice has a cooling effect, whereas water as steam may cause severe burns. Explain these observations.

Thinking Process Particles in ice are at lower energy (at 0°C), whereas particles in steam higher energy (at 100°C).

Ans. When ice melts, it absorbs the energy equal to the latent heat of fusion from the surroundings, therefore causing a cooling effect. But steam releases the extra heat (equal to the latent heat of vaporisation) which it has absorbed when water was converted into steam. So, steam produces severe burn.

Q.19 Alka was making tea in a kettle. Suddenly she felt intense heat from the puff of steam gushing out of the spout of the kettle. She wondered whether the temperature of the steam was higher than that of the water boiling in the kettle. Comment.

Thinking Process Particles in steam have more energy than liquid water at 373K (or 100°C), due to latent heat of vaporisation.

Ans. The temperature of both boiling water and steam is 100°C, but steam gives out more heat (due to latent heat of vaporisation) in comparison to boiling water. It is because, when water changes into steam, it absorbs latent heat of vaporisation, but when steam condenses to form water, an equal amount of latent heat is given out without changing the temperature.

Hence, she felt intense heat from puff of steam gushing out of the spout of the kettle, as steam is hotter than boiling water.

Q.20 A glass tumbler containing hot water is kept in the freezer compartment of a refrigerator (temperature < 0° C). If you could measure the temperature of the content of the tumbler, which of the following graphs would correctly represent the change in its temperature as a function of time

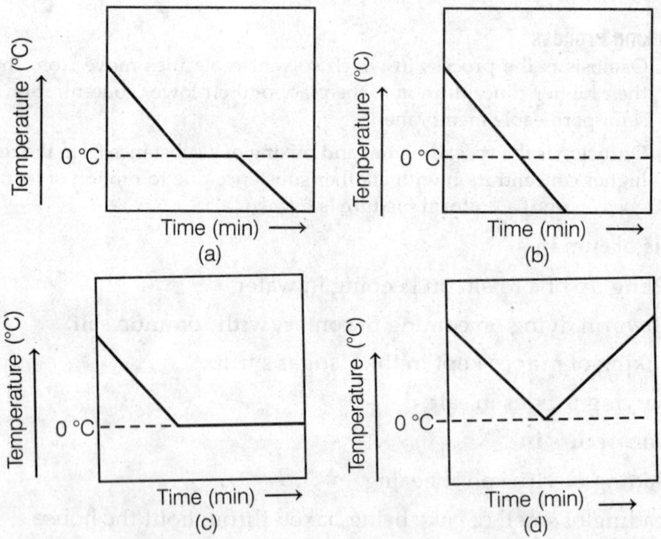

Ans. ***(a)*** Figure (a) represents the change of temperature with time correctly. The temperature of water first decreases up to zero degree celsius, then remains constant for some time (till the ice is formed), then again starts decreasing. At 0°C, water loses heat *i.e.*, latent heat of fusion, till entire water freezes into ice.

Q.21 Look at the figure and suggest in which of the vessels *A*, *B*, *C* or *D*, the rate of evaporation will be the highest? Explain.

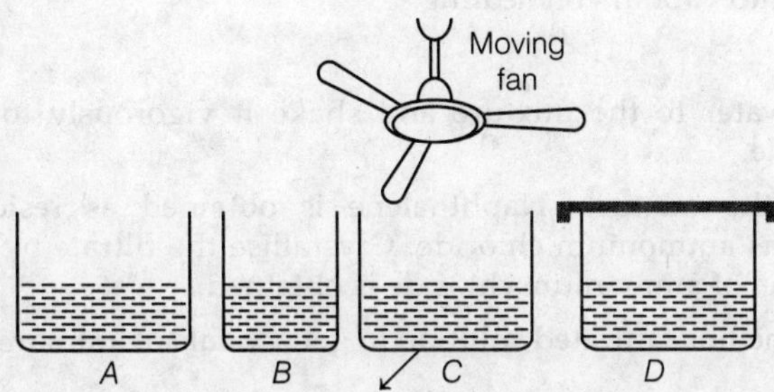

Thinking Process Rate of evaporation increases by increasing the surface area (exposed to evaporation) and by increasing wind speed.

Ans. The rate of evaporation will be highest in vessel *C* as the surface area exposed for evaporation is larger than *B* (smaller size). The moving fan increases the wind speed which also increases the rate of evaporation. Although *A* and *D* are also equal in size to that of *C* but *A* is at a greater distance from the fan and *D* is covered with a lid.

Q.22 (a) Conversion of solid to vapour is called sublimation. Name the term used to denote the conversion of vapour to solid.

(b) Conversion of solid state to liquid state is called fusion; what is meant by latent heat of fusion?

Thinking Process Sublimation is the process of converting solids to vapours which is opposite of deposition process where vapour directly changes to solid state.

Ans. (a) The direct conversion of vapour to solid without changing into liquid is called deposition.

(b) The amount of heat energy required to change 1 kg of a solid into liquid at atmospheric pressure at its melting point is known as the latent heat of fusion.

Long Answer Type Questions

Q.23 You are provided with a mixture of naphthalene and ammonium chloride by your teacher. Suggest an activity to separate them with well labelled diagram

Thinking Process

(i) First dissolve naphthalene and ammonium chloride into water.

(ii) Filter the solution. Separate the residue from filtrate.

(iii) Heat the filtrate to crystallise the crystals of ammonium chloride.

- **Concept Insight** The question is based on separating the components of a mixture of naphthalene and ammonium chloride.
  The separating is done using dissolution of a component, filtration and crystallisation method.

Ans. Naphthalene is insoluble in water, but soluble in benzene (organic solvent). Ammonium chloride is soluble in water, but insoluble in benzene. Naphthalene changes into vapours at room temperature whereas, ammonium chloride changes into vapours on heating.

Method

(a) Add water to the mixture and shake it vigorously to dissolve ammonium chloride.

(b) Filter the mixture. Naphthalene is obtained as residue whereas, filtrate contains ammonium chloride. Crystallise the filtrate by heating till saturated solution of ammonium chloride is obtained.

(c) Cool the hot saturated solution to get crystals of ammonium chloride.

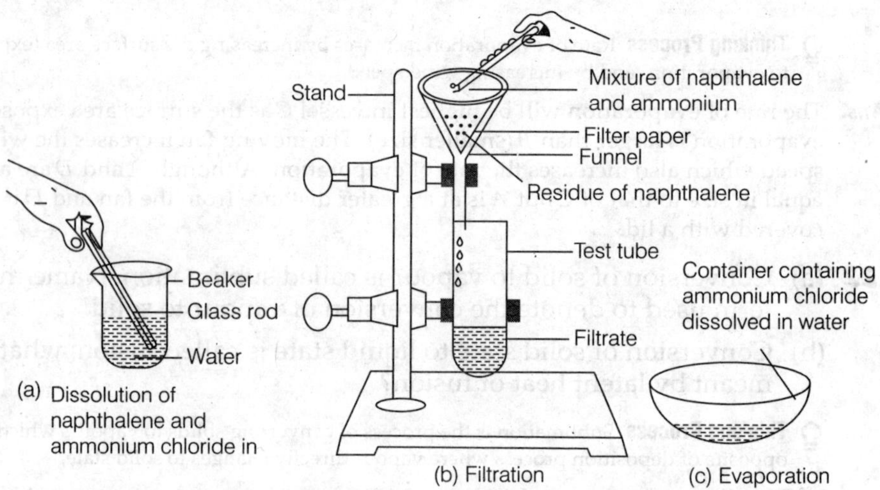

Separation of naphthalene and CH_4Cl (Ammonium Chloride)

Q.24 It is a hot summer day, Priyanshi and Ali are wearing cotton and nylon clothes respectively. Who do you think would be more comfortable and why?

Thinking Process Evaporation causes cooling.

Ans. Priyanshi would be more comfortable as cotton being a good absorber of water, absorbs sweat from the body and provides larger surface area for evaporation causing a more cooling effect. On the other hand, nylon does not absorb sweat as efficiently as cotton, so the sweat does not evaporate easily and Ali would feel uncomfortable.

Q.25 You want to wear your favourite shirt to a party, but the problem is that it is still wet after a wash. What steps would you take to dry it faster?

Thinking Process The washed wet clothes dry more quickly, if we increase the rate of evaporation.

Ans. Washed wet clothes can be dried quickly by the following (any one or more) steps

(i) **Dry it under the fan :** Under the fan when the speed of wind increases, the particles of water vapour from the shirt move away with the wind, decreasing the amount of water vapour in the surroundings. It increases the rate of evaporation of water and the washed wet shirt dries more quickly.

(ii) **Use hanger for exposing its larger surface to air :** When shirt is spread, it has large surface area. This makes the evaporation of water faster. Due to this, shirt dries up more quickly.

(iii) **Dry it in Sun :** On a sunny day, temperature of atmosphere is more, therefore, the rate of evaporation increases. It is because, on increasing temperature, more particles of water get enough kinetic energy to go into the vapour state. This increases the rate of evaporation.

(iv) **Use iron** By the use of iron, temperature increases and water converts into vapour state (steam) very quickly. Hence, rate of evaporation increases and shirt dries very quickly.

Q.26 Comment on the following statements.

(a) Evaporation produces cooling.

(b) Rate of evaporation of an aqueous solution decreases with increase in humidity.

(c) Sponge though compressible is a solid.

Ans. (a) Evaporation produces cooling. This is based on the fact that when a liquid evaporates, it takes (or draws) the latent heat of vaporisation from 'another matter' which it touches. This 'another matter' looses heat and gets cooled. Therefore, evaporation causes cooling.

(b) If humidity is high, then air is already saturated with water vapour *i.e.,* it has a lots of water vapour. Therefore, it will not take more water vapour easily produced by evaporation. Hence, rate of evaporation decreases.

(c) Sponge has minute holes in which air is trapped. The material is also not so rigid. On pressing it, air is expelled out, that is why it can be compressed, but it is a solid as it has a definite shape and volume and it does not change its shape unless compressed.

Q.27 Why does the temperature of a substance remain constant during its melting point or boiling point?

- **Concept Insight** The concept of latent heat of fusion and latent heat of vaporisation is used in this question, which causes the temperature of a substance to remain constant during its melting and boiling point.

Ans. The temperature of a substance remains constant during melting and boiling points till the completion of melting and boiling of a substance. It is because, the substance makes use of latent heat of fusion to overcome the force of attraction between particles of solid to change into liquid during melting and latent heat of vaporisation to overcome force of attraction between particles of liquid to change into vapours during boiling. Therefore, temperature remains constant.

Chapter

02

Is Matter Around us Pure

Multiple Choice Questions (MCQs)

Q. 1 Which of the following statements are true for pure substances?

(i) Pure substances contain only one kind of particles.

(ii) Pure substances may be compounds or mixtures.

(iii) Pure substances have the same composition throughout.

(iv) Pure substances can be exemplified by all elements other than nickel.

(a) (i) and (ii)
(b) (i) and (iii)
(c) (iii) and (iv)
(d) (ii) and (iii)

Thinking Process All elements (*e.g.*, hydrogen, oxygen, sulphur, iron, nickel, mercury, gold, silver, etc.) and compounds (*e.g.*, water, carbon dioxide, sodium chloride, copper sulphate, etc.) are pure substances. Mixtures are impure substances.

Ans. ***(b)*** A pure substance is one which is made up of only one kind of particles (atoms or molecules). They have the same composition throughout.

Q. 2 Rusting of an article made up of iron is called

(a) corrosion and it is a physical as well as chemical change.
(b) dissolution and it is a physical change.
(c) corrosion and it is a chemical change.
(d) dissolution and it is a chemical change.

Thinking Process Dissolution is the process in which a solute is dissolved in a solvent to form a solution, and corrosion is the process by which a material degrades.
Physical changes are those changes in which no new substances are formed. The substances do not change their identity and they can be easily returned to their original form by some physical processes. *e.g.*, melting of ice, glowing of an electric bulb, breaking of glass tumbler, etc.
Chemical change brings change in the chemical properties of a substance and we get a new substance, which cannot be returned to their original form.

Ans. ***(c)*** Rusting of an article made up of iron is called corrosion. It is a chemical change as new substance is formed in this process when iron reacts with moistures or water.

Corrosion is a chemical change because a new substance i.e., rust (hydrated iron oxide, $Fe_2O_3 \cdot xH_2O$) is formed which is totally different from elemental iron (Fe). Corrosion of iron can be seen by the reaction.

$$4Fe + 3O_2 + xH_2O \longrightarrow \underbrace{2Fe_2O_3 \cdot xH_2O}_{\text{Rust}}$$

Mistake Alert ! *One can make a mistake in writing the composition of the rust by incorrectly assuming it to be only iron oxide. But, the rust is primarily composed of hydrated iron (III) oxide, i.e.,* $Fe_2O_3 \cdot xH_2O$.

Q. 3 A mixture of sulphur and carbon disulphide is

(a) heterogeneous and shows Tyndall effect.

(b) homogeneous and shows Tyndall effect.

(c) heterogeneous and does not show Tyndall effect.

(d) homogeneous and does not show Tyndall effect.

Thinking Process

(i) Homogeneous mixtures are those mixtures in which the substances are completely mixed together and can not be distinguished from one another. They have uniform composition throughout.

(ii) Heterogeneous mixtures are those mixtures in which the substances remain separate. They do not have a uniform composition throughout.

(iii) The scattering of light by colloidal particles is known as Tyndall effect. Colloids are actually heterogeneous in nature though they appear to be homogeneous.

Ans. ***(a)*** A mixture of sulphur and carbon disulphide is a heterogeneous colloid and it shows Tyndall effect. In a colloidal solution, the particles are big enough to scatter light.

Mistake Alert ! *Tyndall effect is the property shown by colloids only, and not by homogeneous mixtures.*

Q. 4 Tincture of iodine has antiseptic properties. This solution is made by dissolving

(a) iodine in potassium iodide

(b) iodine in vaseline

(c) iodine in water

(d) iodine in alcohol

Thinking Process Tincture of iodine is also called **weak iodine solution**. It is prepared by dissolution of usually 2-7% elemental iodine, along with potassium iodide or sodium iodide, in a mixture of alcohol (ethanol) and water.

Ans. ***(d)*** Tincture of iodine is made by dissolving iodine in alcohol.

Q. 5 Which of the following are homogeneous in nature?

(i) Ice (ii) Wood (iii) Soil (iv) Air

(a) (i) and (iii)

(b) (ii) and (iv)

(c) (i) and (iv)

(d) (iii) and (iv)

- **Concept Insight** The concept of homogenous mixture is used in this question. It is based on the principle that homogeneous mixtures have a uniform composition throughout.

Ans. *(c)* Options (i) Ice and (iv) Air are homogeneous in nature as their particles are not distinctly visible. A homogeneous mixture has a uniform composition throughout its mass. It has no visible boundaries of separation between its various constituents, *e.g.*, air, sugar solution, brass, etc.

A heterogeneous mixture does not have a uniform composition throughout its mass. It has visible boundaries of separation between its various constituents. *e.g.*, soil, wood, blood, etc.

Q. 6 Which of the following are physical changes?

(i) Melting of iron metal
(ii) Rusting of iron
(iii) Bending of an iron rod
(iv) Drawing a wire of iron metal

(a) (i), (ii) and (iii)
(b) (i), (ii) and (iv)
(c) (i), (iii) and (iv)
(d) (ii), (iii) and (iv)

- **Concept Insight** The concept of physical and chemical changes is used in this question. Physical change alters the state of the substances, without changing its chemical composition whereas a chemical change results in the formation of new substances by altering the chemical composition.

Ans. *(c)* Options (i) Melting of iron metal, (iii) Bending of an iron rod and (iv) Drawing a wire of iron metal are physical changes, because in these three processes, iron changes its form, not the chemical composition. In rusting of iron (option (ii)), its chemical composition is changed. (*Also, refer to Q.* 2)

Q. 7 Which of the following are chemical changes?

(i) Decaying of wood
(ii) Burning of wood
(iii) Sawing of wood
(iv) Hammering of a nail into a piece of wood

(a) (i) and (ii)
(b) (ii) and (iii)
(c) (iii) and (iv)
(d) (i) and (iv)

Ans. *(a)* Options (i) Decaying of wood and (ii) Burning of wood are chemical changes, because in these processes, the chemical composition of wood is changed and new substances are formed, which cannot be converted back into their original form.

In (iii) Sawing of wood and (iv) Hammering of a nail into a piece of wood, chemical composition of wood is not changed, therefore, (iii) and (iv) are physical changes. (*Also, refer to Q.* 2)

Q. 8 Two substances, A and B were made to react to form a third substance, A_2B according to the following reaction $2A + B \rightarrow A_2B$. Which of the following statements concerning this reaction are incorrect?

(i) The product A_2B shows the properties of substances A and B.
(ii) The product will always have a fixed composition.
(iii) The product so formed cannot be classified as a compound.
(iv) The product so formed is an element.

(a) (i), (ii) and (iii) (b) (ii), (iii) and (iv)
(c) (i), (iii) and (iv) (d) (ii), (iii) and (iv)

Ans. ***(c)*** A_2B is a compound and not an element. It is made up of two elements A and B in a fixed ratio. The properties of a compound (*e.g.,* A_2B) are entirely different from those of its constituent elements (*e.g.,* A and B). The composition of a compound is fixed.

Mistake Alert ! *One can make a mistake of considering that a compound shows the properties of its constituent elements.*

Q. 9 Two chemical species X and Y combine together to form a product P which contains both X and Y, $X + Y \rightarrow P$, X and Y cannot be broken down into simpler substances by simple chemical reactions. Which of the following concerning the species X, Y and P are correct?

(i) P is a compound. (ii) X and Y are compounds.
(iii) X and Y are elements. (iv) P has a fixed composition.

(a) (i), (ii) and (iii) (b) (i), (ii) and (iv) (c) (ii), (iii) and (iv) (d) (i), (iii) and (iv)

Thinking Process An element is a substance which can not be broken down into two or more simpler substances by simple chemical methods of applying heat, light or electric energy. Compounds have fixed composition and they can be broken down into elements by chemical or electrochemical reactions.

Ans. ***(d)*** In this reaction, X and Y cannot be broken down into simpler substances by chemical reactions, therefore, X and Y are elements.

A compound is a substance made up of two or more elements chemically combined in a fixed proportion by mass, therefore, P is a compound, having a fixed composition.

Short Answer Type Questions

***Q. 10** Suggest separation technique(s) one would need to employ to separate the following mixtures.

(a) Mercury and water
(b) Potassium chloride and ammonium chloride
(c) Common salt, water and sand
(d) Kerosene oil, water and salt

Ans. (a) Mercury and water are separated by decantation using a separating funnel as the separation of two immiscible liquids by a separating funnel depends on the difference in their densities.

Note (*) Topics related to these question have been removed from latest NCERT.

Mercury is heavier than water therefore, forms the lower layer and can be separated from water.

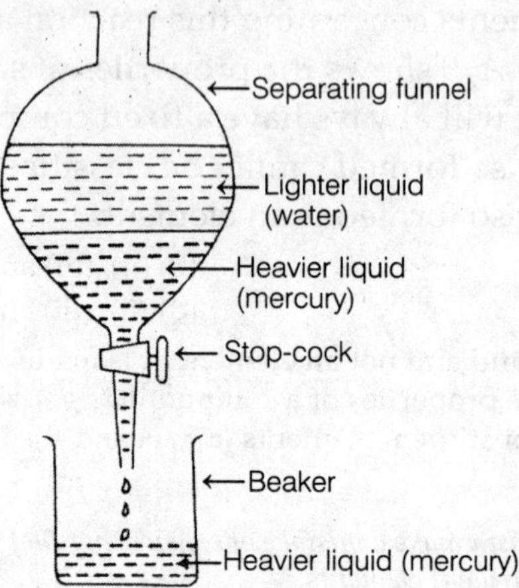

Separation of two immiscible liquids by using a separating funnel

(b) Potassium chloride and ammonium chloride are separated by **sublimation method** because ammonium chloride being a sublimate, sublimes leaving behind the potassium chloride as residue. A solid changes directly into vapours on heating by sublimation and then vapours change into solid on cooling without going in liquid state (by deposition).

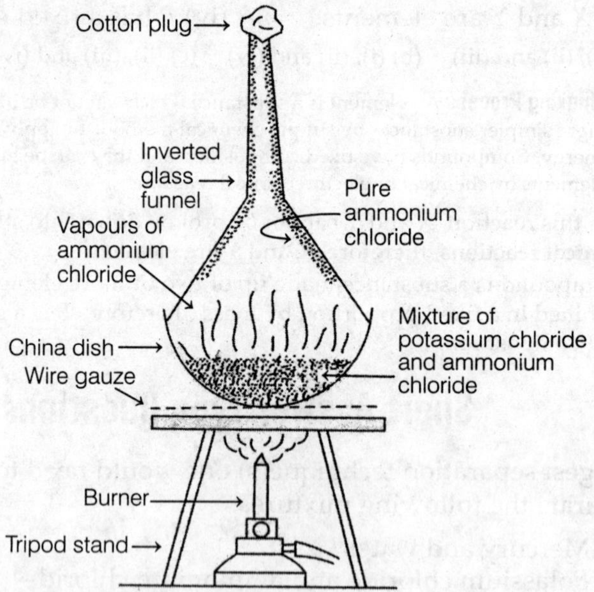

Separation of potassium chloride and ammonium chloride by sublimation

(c) Common salt, water and sand are separated by

(i) **Filtration** process is used to separate sand from common salt solution in water because common salt is soluble in water whereas sand is insoluble in water. Therefore, by filtration, sand will be separated as insoluble substance (as residue) and filtrate will be common salt solution in water.

Note Sand can be separated from common salt solution by the process of **decantation**. As it is heavier and will settle down when left undisturbed for some time. Then common salt solution can be paused separately in another container.

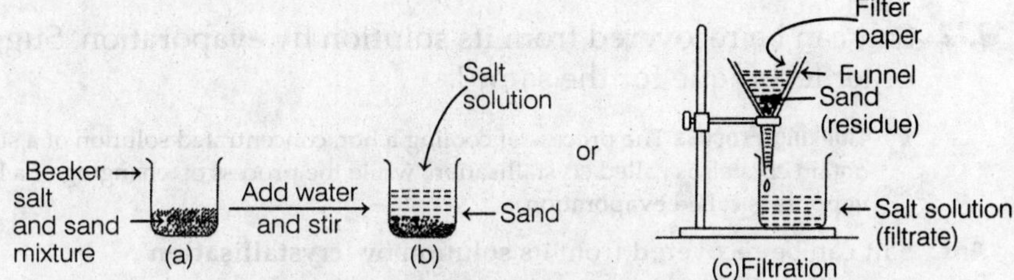

Separation of sand form common salt solution

(ii) **Evaporation** process is used to separate common salt from water. Water evaporates and common salt remains as residue.

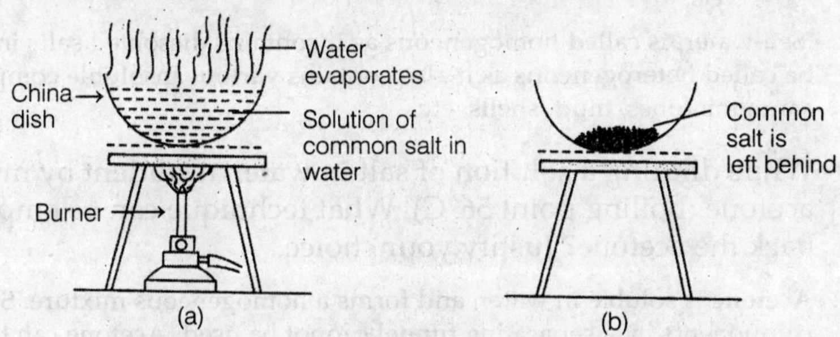

Separation of common salt dissolved in water by evaporation

(d) (i) **Decantation by using separating funnel** is used to separate kerosene oil from salt solution in water as they form separate layers (salt is soluble in water). (*Refer to ans.* 10(*a*)).

(ii) **Evaporation** is used to separate salt from water. (*Also, refer to Q.* 10 (*c*))

***Q.11** Which of the tubes in Figure. (a) and (b) will be more effective as a condenser in the distillation apparatus?

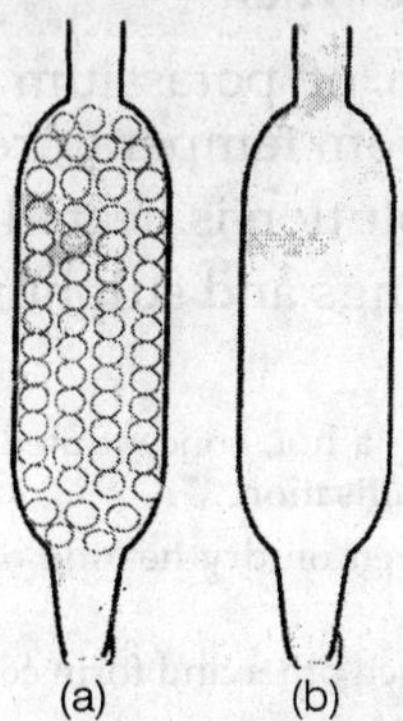

Thinking Process Condenser is an equipment which is used to condense vapours to from liquids. So, greater is the surface area, faster is the condensation.

Note (✱) Topics related to these question have been removed from latest NCERT.

Ans. Figure (a) will be a more effective condenser in the distillation apparatus because beads present will provide more surface area for cooling of the vapours passing through it.

***Q.12** Salt can be recovered from its solution by evaporation. Suggest some other technique for the same?

Thinking Process The process of cooling a hot, concentrated solution of a substance to obtain crystals is called crystallisation, while the process of changing of a liquid into vapours is called evaporation.

Ans. Salt can be recovered from its solution by **'crystallisation'**.
Crystallisation is a better technique than evaporation because it removes soluble impurities also, which do not get removed in the process of evaporation.

Q. 13 The 'sea-water' can be classified as a homogeneous as well as heterogeneous mixture. Comment.

Ans. 'Sea-water' is called homogeneous as it contains dissolved salts in it. It may also be called heterogeneous as it also contains various insoluble components like sand, microbes, mud, shells, etc.

***Q.14** While diluting a solution of salt in water, a student by mistake added acetone (boiling point 56°C). What technique can be employed to get back the acetone? Justify your choice.

Ans. Acetone is soluble in water, and forms a homogeneous mixture. So, separation of components by a separating funnel cannot be used. Acetone can be obtained by simple distillation because the difference in the boiling points of acetone and water is more than 25°C.

Boiling point of acetone — 56°C
Boiling point of water — 100°C

In distillation flask, acetone will boil at 56°C and change into vapours first and then can be collected in flask after condensation leaving behind the salt solution.

***Q.15** What would you observe when

(a) a saturated solution of potassium chloride prepared at 60°C is allowed to cool at room temperature?
(b) an aqueous sugar solution is heated to dryness?
(c) a mixture of iron filings and sulphur powder is heated strongly?

Thinking Process

(i) The process of cooling a hot, concentrated solution of a substance to obtain crystals is called crystallisation.
(ii) Evaporation occurs even on dry heating of sugar and it turns black (due to charring).
(iii) Elements react with each other and form compounds.

Ans. (a) When a saturated solution of potassium chloride prepared at 60°C is allowed to cool at room temperature, crystals of potassium chloride will be formed by crystallisation.

Note (✱) Topics related to these questions have been removed from latest NCERT.

(b) Initially, on heating sugar, water will get evaporated. But on dry heating, sugar gets charred and it turns black.

$$C_{12}H_{22}O_{11} \xrightarrow{\Delta} \underset{\text{(Black)}}{12C} + 11H_2O\uparrow.$$

(c) The black coloured compound, iron sulphide is formed when a mixture of iron filings and sulphur powder is heated strongly.

$$\underset{\text{Iron filings}}{Fe} + \underset{\text{Sulphur powder}}{S} \xrightarrow{\Delta} \underset{\text{Iron sulphide}}{FeS}$$

Q. 16 Explain why particles of a colloidal solution do not settle down when left undisturbed, while in the case of a suspension they do?

Thinking Process Recall Brownian movement and compare the size of colloidal particles and suspension particles, also the effect of gravity on them.

Ans. The colloidal particles are smaller and not heavy. They always remain in a state of *zig-zag* motion, called **Brownian movement**, which counters the force of gravity acting on colloidal particles and hence, helps in providing stability to colloidal sols by not allowing them to settle down. Apart from this, colloidal particles are charged and repel each other. This fact also do not allow the particles of colloidal solution to settle down. Whereas, particles of suspension are larger, heavy and have less movement, thus they settle down due to gravity.

Q. 17 Smoke and fog both are aerosols. In what way are they different?

Thinking Process An aerosol is a colloid in which a solid or liquid is dispersed in a gas (including air).

Ans. In smoke and fog, dispersion medium is same, *i.e.*, air but they differ in dispersed phase. In smoke, solid carbon particles are dispersed in air, while in fog, liquid water particles are dispersed in air.

Q. 18 Classify the following as physical or chemical properties.

(a) The composition of a sample of steel is 98% iron, 1.5% carbon and 0.5% other elements.

(b) Zinc dissolves in hydrochloric acid with the evolution of hydrogen gas.

(c) Metallic sodium is soft enough to be cut with a knife.

(d) Most metal oxides form alkalis on interacting with water.

Ans. (a) It is a **physical property** as no new compound is formed because steel is an alloy and it is a homogeneous mixture of two or more metals or of metallic elements with non-metallic elements.

(b) It is a **chemical property** because chemical reaction occurs between zinc and hydrochloric acid with the evolution of hydrogen gas and a compound zinc chloride is formed.

$$Zn(s) + 2HCl\ (dil) \longrightarrow ZnCl_2(aq) + H_2(g)$$

(c) It is a **physical property** because cutting sodium with knife does not form a new substance.

(d) It is a **chemical property** as new compound is being formed by the reaction of metal oxide and water.

$$\underset{\text{Metal oxide}}{M_2O\ (s)} + \underset{\text{Water}}{H_2O\ (l)} \longrightarrow \underset{\text{Metal hydroxide}}{2MOH\ (aq)}$$

Q. 19 The teacher instructed three students '*A*', '*B*' and '*C*' respectively to prepare a 50% (mass by volume) solution of sodium hydroxide (NaOH). '*A*' dissolved 50g of NaOH in 100 mL of water. '*B*' dissolved 50g of NaOH in 100g of water while '*C*' dissolved 50g of NaOH in water to make 100 mL of solution. Which one of them has made the desired solution and why?

Thinking Process The percentage concentration (w/v) of a solution is the amount of solute(*g*) present in 100 mL of its solution.

Ans. In the given question, student '*C*' has made it correctly because 50% (mass by volume) means 50 g of solute for every 100 mL of solution and not in 100 mL of solvent.

$$\text{Mass/volume per cent} = \frac{\text{mass of solute (in g)}}{\text{volume of solution (in mL)}} \times 100$$

$$= \frac{50}{100} \times 100 = 50\%$$

Student '*A*' dissolved 50 g of NaOH in 100 mL of water (solvent) which is incorrect. Student '*B*' dissolved 50 g of NaOH in 100 g of water (solvent), which is also incorrect.

Mistake Alert ! *Mass by volume per cent is the mass of solute in 100 mL of solution and not 100 mL or 100 g of solvent.*

***Q.20** Name the process associated with the following.

(a) Dry ice is kept at room temperature and at one atmospheric pressure.

(b) A drop of ink placed on the surface of water contained in a glass spreads throughout the water.

(c) A potassium permanganate crystal is in a beaker and water is poured into the beaker with stirring.

(d) A acetone bottle is left open and the bottle becomes empty.

(e) Milk is churned to separate cream from it.

(f) Settling of sand when a mixture of sand and water is left undisturbed for some time.

(g) Fine beam of light entering through a small hole in a dark room, illuminates the particles in its paths.

Ans. (a) The process is **sublimation** because when dry ice (solid CO_2) is kept at room temperature at one atmospheric pressure, it sublimes leaving no residue.

(b) This process is **diffusion** because in diffusion, mixing of one substance (ink) into another substance (water) goes on until a uniform mixture is formed.

(c) This process is **dissolution/diffusion** as potassium permanganate crystal is dissolved in water.

(d) This process is **evaporation and diffusion** as acetone evaporates and gets diffused when kept open in the bottle.

Note (*) Topics related to these question have been removed from latest NCERT.

(e) This process is **centrifugation**. Milk is put in a closed container in big centrifuge machine. When machine is switched on, milk is rotated at a very high speed.

Due to this, milk separates into 'cream' and 'skimmed milk'. The cream being lighter, floats over the skimmed milk and then can be removed.

(f) This process is **sedimentation** as sand does not dissolve completely in water and forms suspension. It settles down at the bottom when left undisturbed for some time.

(g) This shows **Tyndall effect, *i.e.*, scattering of light** by colloidal solution or by particles in a fine suspension. Dust particles are suspended in air which scatter the light coming from small hole.

Q. 21 You are given two samples of water labelled as '*A*' and '*B*'. Sample '*A*' boils at 100°C and sample '*B*' boils at 102°C. Which sample of water will not freeze at 0°C? Comment.

Thinking Process The presence of impurities increases the boiling point and decreases the freezing point/melting point of a substance.

Ans. Sample '*B*' will not freeze at 0°C as, it is impure water. It is because sample '*B*' boils at 102°C, while the boiling point of pure water is 100°C. It means this sample contains impurities.

Mistake Alert ! *One can make a mistake in considering the effect of impurity on melting freezing and boiling points.*

Q. 22 What are the favourable qualities given to gold when it is alloyed with copper or silver for the purpose of making ornaments?

- **Concept Insight** The question is based on alloys. Alloys are homogeneous mixtures of two or more metals, or a metal and a non-metal, which combine to enhance the properties of individual components, such as strength, durability, etc.,

Ans. Gold is a soft metal and can easily change its shape with a little force. Therefore, it is not suitable for making ornaments. But, when it is alloyed with copper or silver, the gold becomes harder and stronger and its brittleness decreases. Thus, it becomes suitable for making ornaments.

Q. 23 An element is sonorous and highly ductile. Under which category would you classify this element? What other characteristics do you expect the element to possess?

Thinking Process

(i) Classify the elements into metals, non-metals and metalloids and compare their properties with the given properties of the given element and then classify this element.

(ii) Write the characteristics of this category.

Ans. As the given element is sonorous and highly ductile, therefore, it is categorised as a metal.

Some other expected characteristics of the element are :

(i) It should possesses metallic lustre and can be polished.

(ii) It should be good conductor of heat and electricity.

(iii) It should be ductile.

(iv) It should be malleable.

(v) It should have high tensile strength.

(vi) It should have high density and melting point/boiling point too.

(vii) It should be hard (except sodium and potassium which are soft metals).

(viii) It should be solid at room temperature (except mercury, which is liquid at room temperature).

While the characteristics of non-metals and metalloids are:

(i) Non-metals are neither malleable nor ductile. They are poor conductors of heat and electricity. They are not lustrous and sonorous.

(ii) Metalloids show some properties intermediate to those of metals and non-metals.

***Q.24** Give an example each for the mixture having the following characteristics. Suggest a suitable method to separate the components of these mixtures.

(a) A volatile and a non-volatile component.

(b) Two volatile components with appreciable difference in boiling points.

(c) Two immiscible liquids.

(d) One of the components changes directly from solid to gaseous state.

(e) Two or more coloured constituents soluble in some solvent.

Ans. (a) **Example** Mixture of acetone and water.

Method Simple distillation or evaporation can be used to separate a mixture of volatile and non-volatile components.

(b) **Example** Mixture of kerosene and petrol.

Method Simple distillation can be used to separate two volatile components with appreciable difference in boiling points.

(c) **Example** Mixture of mustard oil and water.

Method Separating funnel is used to separate a mixture of immiscible liquids.

(d) **Example** Mixture of ammonium chloride and common salt.

Method Sublimation can be used to separate the mixture in which one component changes directly from solid to gas.

(e) **Example** A mixture of different pigments from an extract of flower petals.

Method Chromatography method can be used to separate two different substances present in the same solution.

Q. 25 Fill in the blanks.

(a) A colloid is a .... mixture and its components can be separated by the technique known as ....

(b) Ice, water and water vapour look different and display different .... properties but they are .... the same.

Note (✱) Topics related to these question have been removed from latest NCERT.

(c) A mixture of chloroform and water taken in a separating funnel is mixed and left undisturbed for some time. The upper layer in the separating funnel will be of .... and the lower layer will be that of ....

(d) A mixture of two or more miscible liquids, for which the difference in the boiling points is less than 25 K can be separated by the process called ....

(e) When light is passed through water containing a few drops of milk, it shows a bluish tinge. This is due to the .... of light by milk and the phenomenon is called .... This indicates that milk is a .... solution.

Ans. (a) A colloid is a **heterogeneous** mixture and its components can be separated by the technique known as **centrifugation**.

(b) Ice, water and water vapour look different and display different **physical** properties but they are **chemically** the same.

(c) A mixture of chloroform and water taken in a separating funnel is mixed and left undisturbed for some time. The upper layer in the separating funnel will be of **water** and the lower layer will be that of **chloroform** (It is because water is lighter than chloroform).

(d) A mixture of two or more miscible liquids, for which the difference in the boiling points is less than 25 K can be separated by the process called **fractional distillation**.

(e) When light is passed through water containing a few drops of milk, it shows a bluish tinge. This is due to the **scattering** of light by milk and the phenomenon is called **Tyndall effect**. This indicates that milk is a **colloidal solution**.

Q. 26 Sucrose (sugar) crystals obtained from sugarcane and beetroot are mixed together. Will it be a pure substance or a mixture? Give reasons for the same.

Ans. According to the law of constant composition or definite proportions; irrespective of the source of a chemical compound, it is always found to be made of the same elements combined together in the same fixed proportion by mass.

Thus, in the light of the above law, sucrose (sugar) crystals will be a pure substance. It is because sugar obtained by different sources like sugarcane and beetroot will have the same composition.

Q. 27 Give some examples of Tyndall effect observed in your surroundings.

Thinking Process The scattering of light by colloidal particles or by particles in a fine suspension is called Tyndall effect.

Ans. *Examples of Tyndall effect*

(i) When sunlight passes through the canopy of a dense forest.

(ii) When a fine beam of light enters a dark room through a small hole.

***Q.28** Can we separate alcohol dissolved in water by using a separating funnel? If yes, then describe the procedure. If not, explain.

Thinking Process Separating funnel is used to separate immiscible liquids. Miscible liquids can be separated by the process of distillation.

Ans. No, alcohol cannot be separated from water by using a separating funnel because alcohol is completely miscible in water.

Q.29 On heating, calcium carbonate gets converted into calcium oxide and carbon dioxide.

(a) is this a physical or a chemical change?

(b) can you prepare one acidic and one basic solution by using the products formed in the above process? If so, write the chemical equation involved.

Ans. (a) The phenomena given in question is a chemical change because the composition of product formed is different from the substance taken. The reaction involved is

$$\underset{\text{Calcium carbonate}}{CaCO_3(s)} \xrightarrow{\Delta} \underset{\text{Calcium oxide}}{CaO(s)} + \underset{\text{Carbon dioxide}}{CO_2(g)}$$

(b) Yes, we can prepare one acidic and one basic solution by using the products formed in the above process.

(i) When CaO dissolves in water, it forms calcium hydroxide solution which is basic in nature.

$$CaO(s) + H_2O(l) \longrightarrow \underset{\text{Calcium hydroxide}}{Ca(OH)_2(aq)}$$

(ii) When $CO_2(g)$ dissolves in water, it forms carbonic acid solution which is acidic in nature.

$$CO_2(g) + H_2O(l) \longrightarrow \underset{\text{Carbonic acid}}{H_2CO_3(aq)}$$

Q.30 Non-metals are usually poor conductors of heat and electricity. They are non-lustrous, non-sonorous, non-malleable and are coloured.

(a) Name a lustrous non-metal.

(b) Name a non-metal which exists as a liquid at room temperature.

(c) The allotropic form of a non-metal is a good conductor of electricity. Name the allotrope.

(d) Name a non-metal which is known to form the largest number of compounds.

(e) Name a non-metal other than carbon which shows allotropy.

(f) Name a non-metal which is required for combustion.

Ans. (a) Iodine is a lustrous non-metal.

(b) Bromine is a non-metal which exists as a liquid at room temperature.

(c) Graphite is the allotropic form of carbon and it is a good conductor of electricity.

Note (✱) Topics related to these question have been removed from latest NCERT.

(d) Carbon is a non-metal which is known to form the largest number of compounds.

(e) Phosphorus is a non-metal other than carbon which shows allotropy.

(f) Oxygen is a non-metal which is required for combustion.

Q.31 Classify the substances given in Figure into elements and compounds.

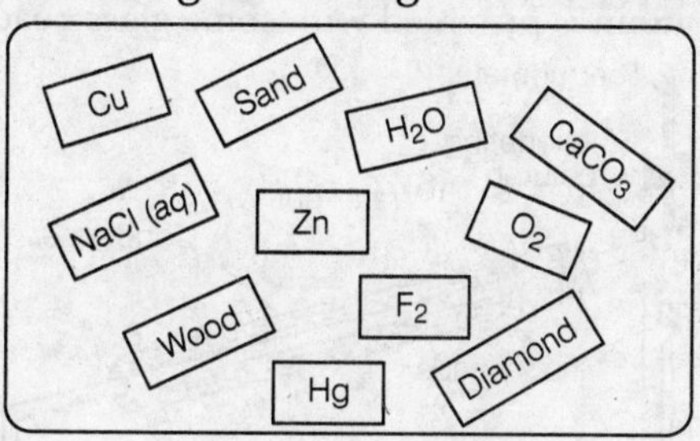

Thinking Process

(i) An element is a substance which is made of only one kind of atoms.

(ii) A compound is a substance made up of two or more elements chemically combined in a fixed proportion by mass.

Ans.

Elements	Compounds
Cu	Sand
O_2	H_2O
Zn	$CaCO_3$
F_2	NaCl (*aq*)
Hg	
Diamond (Carbon)	

Wood is neither an element nor a compound. It is a mixture.

Mistake Alert ! *One can make a mistake of considering wood as a pure substance, instead of a mixture.*

Q. 32 Which of the following are not compounds?

(a) Chlorine gas
(b) Potassium chloride
(c) Iron
(d) Iron sulphide
(e) Aluminium
(f) Iodine
(g) Carbon
(h) Carbon monoxide
(i) Sulphur powder

Thinking Process An element is a substance which is made up of only one kind of atoms, while a compound is a substance made up of two or more elements chemically combined in a fixed proportion by mass.

Ans. These are not compounds:

(a) Chlorine gas
(c) Iron
(e) Aluminium
(f) Iodine
(g) Carbon
(i) Sulphur powder

Long Answer Type Questions

***Q.33** Fractional distillation is suitable for separation of miscible liquids with a boiling point difference of about 25 K or less. What part of fractional distillation apparatus makes it efficient and possess an advantage over a simple distillation process. Explain using a diagram.

Ans. Fractionating column is the most important part of the fractional distillation apparatus. This column is provided with some glass beads in it.

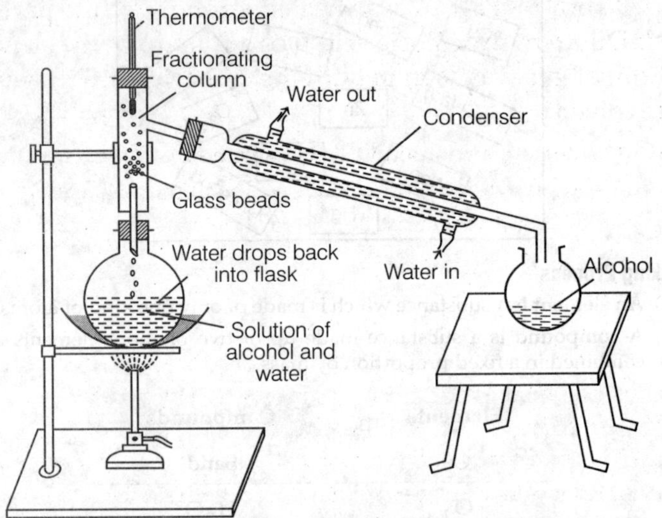

Separation of miscible liquids by fractional distillation

The beads provide more surface area for the vapours to lose energy, get cooled down and condense. The vapours of high boiling liquid gets condensed earlier (at lower level). The advantages of fractional distillation are as given below:

(i) This method can separate the liquids with a boiling point difference about or less than 25 K.

(ii) During the process, both evaporation and condensation take place simultaneously.

(iii) A mixture (like petroleum) can also be separated by fractional distillation process which contains several components.

Q. 34 (a) Under which category of mixtures will you classify alloys and why?

(b) A solution is always a liquid. Comment.

(c) Can a solution be heterogeneous?

Ans. (a) *Alloys are homogeneous mixtures of two or more metals, or a metal and a non-metal because*

(i) it shows the properties of its constituents, and

(ii) it has variable composition. *e.g.*, brass is considered a mixture, because it shows the properties of its constituents, copper and zinc, and it has a variable composition (amount of Zn in brass can vary from 20 to 35 per cent).

Note (✱) Topics related to these question have been removed from latest NCERT.

(b) A solution is generally a liquid, not always. It may involve solids and gases also, *e.g.*, alloys are solution of solid in solid. Air is a solution of gases in gases.

(c) Colloidal solutions are heterogeneous in nature, even though they appear to be homogeneous.

Q. 35 Iron filings and sulphur were mixed together and divided into two parts, '*A*' and '*B*'. Part '*A*' was heated strongly, while part '*B*' was not heated. Dilute hydrochloric acid was added to both the parts and evolution of gas was seen in both the cases. How will you identify the gases evolved?

Ans. As part '*A*' is heated, a compound FeS is formed by the reaction between iron filings and sulphur. When dilute HCl is added to part *A*, FeS will react with dil HCl to form H_2S gas which has smell of rotten eggs and will turn lead acetate paper black.

$$Fe(s) + S(s) \xrightarrow{\text{Heat}} FeS(s)$$

$$FeS(s) + 2HCl(\text{dil.}) \longrightarrow FeCl_2(aq) + H_2S(g)$$

$$\underset{\text{Lead acetate}}{(CH_3COO)_2Pb(aq)} + H_2S(g) \longrightarrow \underset{\text{Black ppt}}{PbS(s)} + \underset{\text{Acetic acid}}{2CH_3COOH}$$

As part '*B*' is not heated, so *B* is a mixture of iron filings and sulphur powder. When dil. HCl is added to it, iron filings react with dil. HCl to form $H_2(g)$ which burns with a 'pop' sound if burning match stick is brought near it.

$$Fe(s) + 2HCl(\text{dil.}) \longrightarrow FeCl_2(aq) + H_2(g)$$

Mistake Alert ! *Remember that iron, filings and sulphur powder do not react until they are heated strongly.*

***Q.36** A child wanted to separate the mixture of dyes constituting a sample of ink. He marked a line by the ink on the filter paper and placed the filter paper in a glass containing water as shown in figure. The filter paper was removed when the water moved near the top of the filter paper.

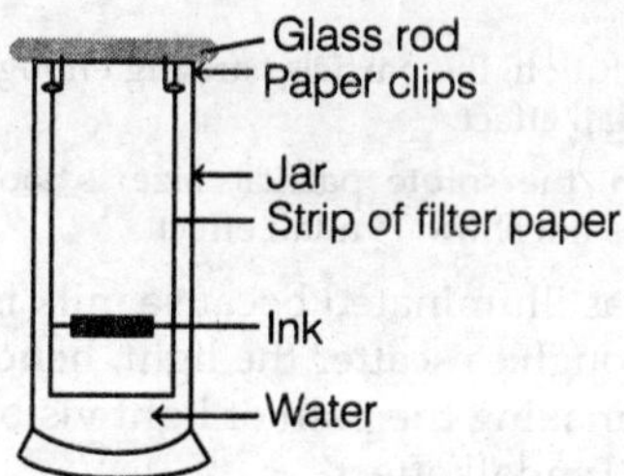

(a) What would you expect to see, if the ink contains three different coloured components?

(b) Name the technique used by the child.

(c) Suggest one more application of this technique.

Thinking Process

(i) Chromatography is a technique of separating two or more dissolved solids which are present in a solution in very small quantities.

(ii) The simplest form of chromatography is paper chromatography.

Apply the principle of chromatography, *i.e.*, it is based on the fact that though two (or more) substances are soluble in the same solvent (say water) but their solubilities may be different.

The substance that is more soluble in the solvent rises faster on the filter paper.

Ans. (a) Three different coloured spots are obtained on the strip at different heights as the components will travel with water on the filter paper.

(b) Chromatography (paper chromatography) technique is used.

(c) The chromatography method is also employed to separate drugs from the blood.

Q. 37 A group of students took an old shoe box and covered it with a black paper from all sides. They fixed a source of light (a torch) at one end of the box by making a hole in it and made another hole on the other side to view the light. They placed a milk sample contained in a beaker/tumbler in the box as shown in the Figure. They were amazed to see that milk taken in the tumbler was illuminated. They tried the same activity by taking a salt solution but found that light simply passed through it?

(a) Explain why the milk sample was illuminated? Name the phenomenon involved.

(b) Same results were not observed with a salt solution. Explain.

(c) Can you suggest two more solutions which would show the same effect as shown by the milk solution?

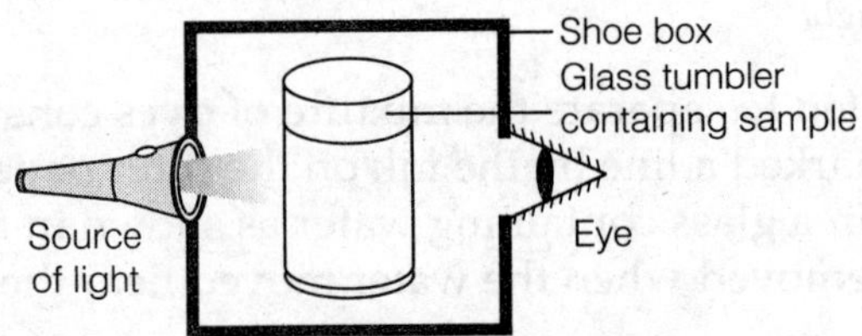

Thinking Process

(i) In a colloidal solution, the particles are big enough to scatter light. Therefore, they show Tyndall effect.

(ii) In true solution, the solute particle size is too small to scatter the light, therefore, it does not show Tyndall effect.

Ans. (a) The milk sample was illuminated because milk is a colloidal solution and its particles are big enough to scatter the light, hence, they scatter the light passing through it making the path of light visible. The phenomenon observed is called 'Tyndall effect'.

(b) As salt solution is a true solution *i.e.*, solute particle size is too small to scatter the light, hence, it does not show 'Tyndall effect'.

(c) Examples of colloid are gold sol, arsenius sulphide (As_2S_3) sol., blood, etc.

Note (✱) Topics related to these question have been removed from latest NCERT.

Q. 38 Classify each of the following, as a physical or a chemical change. Give reasons.

(a) Drying of a shirt in the Sun.

(b) Rising of hot air over a radiator.

(c) Burning of kerosene in a lantern.

(d) Change in the colour of black tea on adding lemon juice to it.

(e) Churning of milk cream to get butter.

Thinking Process In a physical change, no change occurs in the chemical composition of the substance and in chemical change, chemical composition of the substance is changed.

Ans. (a) It is a physical change because evaporation of water takes place while drying a shirt in the sun, but no change occurs in the composition of the substance.

(b) It is a physical change because it also involves only movement of air, with no change in composition of air.

(c) In this first physical change takes place when kerosene vaporises. After that, burning of kerosene is a chemical change as new products are also formed such as soot, CO_2 etc.

(d) It is a chemical change as lemon juice reacts with the ingredients of black tea to form new substances.

(e) It is a physical change as in churning of milk there is no change in its composition. Only the separation of components takes place by the physical method which is called centrifugation as

Q. 39 During an experiment the students were asked to prepare a 10% (mass/mass) solution of sugar in water. Ramesh dissolved 10 g of sugar in 100 g of water while Sarika prepared it by dissolving 10 g of sugar in water to make 100 g of the solution.

(a) Are the two solutions of the same concentration.

(b) Compare the mass % of the two solutions.

Thinking Process

(i) The concentration of a solution is the mass of solute in grams present in 100 g of the solution and not in 100 g of the *solvent*.

(ii) $\text{Concentration of solution} = \dfrac{\text{mass of solute}}{\text{mass of solution}} \times 100$

(iii) Mass of solution = mass of solute + mass of solvent.

Ans. (a) No, the two solutions do not have the same concentration.

(b) $\text{Mass percentage of solution prepared by Ramesh} = \dfrac{\text{mass of solute}}{\text{mass of solution}} \times 100$

$$= \frac{\text{mass of solute} \times 100}{\text{mass of solute} + \text{mass of solvent}}$$

$$= \frac{10\text{ g}}{(10\text{ g} + 100\text{ g})} \times 100 = \frac{100}{11} = 9.09\%$$

$\text{Mass percentage of solution prepared by Sarika} = \dfrac{10}{100} \times 100 = 10\%$

The solution prepared by Ramesh has less percentage (9.09%) by mass than that of Sarika (10%).

Q.40 **You are provided with a mixture containing sand, iron filings, ammonium chloride and sodium chloride. Describe the procedures you would use to separate these constituents from the mixture?**

Thinking Process The steps involved in separation of these constituents are

(i) Magnetic separation

(ii) Sublimation

(iii) Filtration after dissolution

(iv) Crystallisation or evaporation

Ans. (i) **Remove iron filings with the help of magnet.**

Place the mixture on a paper or petridish, move a bar magnet many times over the mixture. Iron filings get attached to the magnet and get separated.

(ii) **Remove ammonium chloride from sand and sodium chloride by sublimation.**

The remaining mixture is transferred to China dish and subjected to sublimation. Ammonium chloride will get vaporised and change into vapours and on condensation will form $NH_4Cl(s)$. Sand and sodium chloride will be left in China dish.

(iii) **Remove sand from sodium chloride by filtration after dissolution.**

Dissolve the sand and sodium chloride in water. Sodium chloride will dissolve in water. Filter the solution, sand will be left as residue and is separated by filtration.

(iv) **Get sodium chloride by evaporation or crystallisation.** In the filtrate sodium chloride is present. So, evaporate the filtrate to dryness to get sodium chloride back or use crystallisation method.

Q.41 **Arun has prepared 0.01% (by mass) solution of sodium chloride in water. Which of the following correctly represents the composition of the solutions?**

(a) 1.00 g of NaCl + 100 g of water

(b) 0.11 g of NaCl + 100 g of water

(c) 0.01 g of NaCl + 99.99 g of water

(d) 0.10 g of NaCl + 99.90 g of water

- **Concept Insight** The concept of mass percent of solution is used in this question. It is the amount of solute (in g) present in 100 g of its solution.

Ans. *(c)* Here, Mass% $= \dfrac{\text{mass of solute} \times 100}{(\text{mass of solute} + \text{mass of solvent})}$

$$= \frac{0.01\text{g} \times 100}{(0.01 + 99.99)\text{g}}$$

$$= \frac{0.01 \times 100}{100.00} = 0.01\%$$

This is equal to the percentage of sodium chloride in water prepared by Arun. So, option (c) is correct.

In option(a), mass% $= \dfrac{1.00\text{ g} \times 100}{(1.00 + 100)\text{ g}} = \dfrac{1.00 \times 100}{101.00} = 0.99\%$

In option(b), mass% $= \frac{0.11\text{g} \times 100}{(0.11 + 100)\text{ g}} = \frac{11}{100.11} = 0.11\%$

In option(d), mass% $= \frac{0.1\text{g} \times 100}{(0.1 + 99.90)\text{ g}} = \frac{10}{100} = 0.1\%$

These % are not equal to the % of sodium chloride solution in water prepared by Arun. So, these are incorrect.

Q.42 Calculate the mass of sodium sulphate required to prepare its 20% (mass per cent) solution in 100 g of water?

Ans. In the given question, mass% of sodium sulphate solution = 20%
Mass of the solvent = 100g
Let the mass of solute (sodium sulphate) = xg

Applying the formula, Mass% $= \frac{\text{mass of solute}}{\text{mass of solution}} \times 100$

$$= \frac{\text{mass of solute} \times 100}{\text{mass of solute} + \text{mass of solvent}}$$

$$20 = \frac{x\text{g}}{(x + 100)\text{g}} \times 100$$

$$\Rightarrow \quad 20(x + 100) = 100x$$

$$20x + 2000 = 100x$$

$$\Rightarrow \quad 100x - 20x = 2000$$

$$80x = 2000$$

$$\Rightarrow \quad x = \frac{2000}{80} = 25\text{ g}$$

Mass of sodium sulphate = 25 g

Chapter

03 Atoms and Molecules

Multiple Choice Questions (MCQs)

Choose the correct answer from the given four options in the following questions :

***Q. 1** Which of the following correctly represents 360 g of water?

(i) 2 moles of H_2O

(ii) 20 moles of water

(iii) 6.022×10^{23} molecules of water

(iv) 1.2044×10^{25} molecules of water

(a) only (i)
(b) (i) and (iv)
(c) (ii) and (iii)
(d) (ii) and (iv)

Thinking Process 1 mole = 6.022×10^{23} atoms/molecules/ions of a substance = gram molecular mass

Ans. ***(d)*** (ii) and (iv) correctly represents 360 g of water.

(ii) $\because$ 1 mole of water = molar mass of water = 18 g

$\therefore$ 20 moles of water = 18 g × 20 = 360 g

(iv) $\because$ 6.022×10^{23} molecules of water = 1 mole = 18g of water

$$\therefore 1.2044 \times 10^{25} \text{ molecules of water} = \frac{18\text{ g} \times 1.2044 \times 10^{25}}{6.022 \times 10^{23}} = 360\text{g}$$

Therefore, (ii) and (iv) represent 360 g of water, and option (d) is correct.

Students can check (i) and (iii) also, as

(i) 1 mole of water = molar mass of water = 18 g of water.

$\therefore$ 2 moles of water = 18 × 2 = 36 g

(iii) 6.022×10^{23} molecules of water = 1 mole of water = 18g water.

Q. 2 Which of the following statements is not true about an atom?

(a) Atoms are not able to exist independently.
(b) Atoms are the basic units from which molecules and ions are formed.
(c) Atoms are always neutral in nature.
(d) Atoms aggregate in large numbers to form the matter that we can see, feel or touch.

Ans. ***(a)*** Statement (a) is not true as atoms of inert gases exist independently as they are chemically inert and stable. Rest all the statements are true about an atom.

Note (*) Topics related to these question have been removed from latest NCERT.

Q. 3 The chemical symbol for nitrogen gas is

(a) Ni (b) N_2 (c) N^+ (d) N

Ans. ***(b)*** Nitrogen molecule is a diatomic molecule. Therefore, it exists as N_2 molecules.

Q. 4 The chemical symbol for sodium is

(a) So (b) Sd (c) NA (d) Na

Ans. ***(d)*** The chemical symbol for sodium is derived from its Latin name 'Natrium'. In a 'two letter' symbol, the first letter is the 'capital letter' but the second letter is the 'small letter'. Therefore, its symbol is 'Na'.

***Q. 5** Which of the following would weigh the highest?

(a) 0.2 mole of sucrose ($C_{12}H_{22}O_{11}$) (b) 2 moles of CO_2
(c) 2 moles of $CaCO_3$ (d) 10 moles of H_2O

Thinking Process 1 mole =gram molecular mass of the compound.

Ans. ***(c)*** 2 moles of $CaCO_3$ would weigh the highest.

$\therefore$ Mass of 1 mole of $CaCO_3 = 40 + 12 + (16 \times 3) = 100$ g

$\therefore$ Mass of 2 moles of $CaCO_3 = 100 \times 2 = 200$ g

(a) $\therefore$ Mass of 1 mole of sucrose ($C_{12}H_{22}O_{11}$)
$= (12 \times 12) + (1 \times 22) + (16 \times 11) = 342$ g

$\therefore$ Mass of 0.2 mole of sucrose $= 342 \times 0.2 = 68.4$ g

(b) $\therefore$ Mass of 1 mole of $CO_2 = 12 + (16 \times 2) = 44$ g

$\therefore$ Mass of 2 moles of $CO_2 = 44 \times 2 = 88$ g

(d) $\therefore$ Mass of 1 mole of $H_2O = 2 + 16 = 18$ g

$\therefore$ Mass of 10 moles of $H_2O = 18 \times 10 = 180$ g

Therefore, mass of 2 moles of $CaCO_3$ is the highest, *i.e.*, 200 g.

***Q. 6** Which of the following has maximum number of atoms?

(a) 18 g of H_2O (b) 18 g of O_2 (c) 18 g of CO_2 (d) 18 g of CH_4

Thinking Process Number of atoms $= \dfrac{\text{mass}}{\text{molecular mass}} \times 6.022 \times 10^{23} \times P$

where, P = number of atoms in the molecule

Ans. ***(d)*** 18 g of CH_4 contains the maximum number of atoms.

Number of atoms in 18 g of $CH_4 = \dfrac{18}{16} \times 6.022 \times 10^{23} \times 5 = 3.387 \times 10^{24}$

(a) Number of atoms in 18 g of $H_2O = \dfrac{18}{18} \times 6.022 \times 10^{23} \times 3$
$= 18.066 \times 10^{23} = 1.8066 \times 10^{24}$

(b) Number of atoms in 18 g of $O_2 = \dfrac{18}{32} \times 6.022 \times 10^{23} \times 2$
$= 3.387 \times 10^{23} \times 2 = 6.774 \times 10^{23} = 0.6774 \times 10^{24}$

(c) Number of atoms in 18 g of $CO_2 = \dfrac{18}{44} \times 6.022 \times 10^{23} \times 3 = 7.390 \times 10^{23}$
$= 0.739 \times 10^{24}$

Note (✱) Topics related to these question have been removed from latest NCERT.

***Q. 7** Which of the following contains maximum number of molecules?

(a) 1g CO_2 (b) 1g N_2 (c) 1g H_2 (d) 1g CH_4

Thinking Process In 1 mole, number of molecules = 6.022×10^{23}

Ans. ***(c)*** 1g H_2 contains the maximum number of molecules.

Number of molecules in 2g $H_2 = 6.022 \times 10^{23}$ (molar mass of H_2 = 2 g)

$\therefore$ Number of molecules in 1 g $H_2 = \frac{6.022 \times 10^{23}}{2} = 3.011 \times 10^{23} = 30.11 \times 10^{22}$

(a) Number of molecules in 44g $CO_2 = 6.022 \times 10^{23}$ (molar mass of CO_2 = 44 g)

$\therefore$ Number of molecules in 1g $CO_2 = \frac{6.022 \times 10^{23}}{44} = 1.37 \times 10^{22}$

(b) Number of molecules in 28 g $N_2 = 6.022 \times 10^{23}$ (molar mass of N_2 = 28 g)

$\therefore$ Number of molecules in 1g $N_2 = \frac{6.022 \times 10^{23}}{28} = 2.15 \times 10^{22}$

(d) Number of molecules in 16g $CH_4 = 6.022 \times 10^{23}$ (molar mass of CH_4 = 16 g)

$\therefore$ Number of molecules in 1g $CH_4 = \frac{6.022 \times 10^{23}}{16} = 3.76 \times 10^{22}$

***Q. 8** Mass of one atom of oxygen is

(a) $\frac{16}{6.023 \times 10^{23}}$ g (b) $\frac{32}{6.023 \times 10^{23}}$ g (c) $\frac{1}{6.023 \times 10^{23}}$ g (d) 8 u

Thinking Process 1 mole of oxygen = 6.023×10^{23} atoms of oxygen = gram atomic mass of oxygen

Ans. ***(a)*** $\because$ Mass of 6.023×10^{23} atoms of oxygen = gram atomic mass of oxygen

Mass of 6.023×10^{23} atoms of oxygen = 16 g

$\therefore$ Mass of 1 atom of oxygen = $\frac{16}{6.023 \times 10^{23}}$ g

Thus, option (a) is correct.

***Q. 9** 3.42 g of sucrose are dissolved in 18g of water in a beaker. The number of oxygen atoms in the solution are

(a) 6.68×10^{23} (b) 6.09×10^{22}
(c) 6.022×10^{23} (d) 6.022×10^{21}

Thinking Process

(i) First we find out the number of O-atoms in 3.42 g of sucrose.
(ii) Then, we find out the number of O-atoms in 18 g of water.
(iii) By adding these two, we will find out the total number of O-atoms in the solution.

Ans. ***(a) Step*** 1. Molar mass of sucrose, $C_{12}H_{22}O_{11} = 12 \times 12 + 1 \times 22 + 16 \times 11 = 342$ g/mol

or 342 g = 1 mole of sucrose

3.42 g = 0.01 mole of sucrose

Note (*) Topics related to these questions have been removed from latest NCERT.

$\because$ 1 mole of sucrose ($C_{12}H_{22}O_{11}$) contains O-atoms $= 11 \times 6.022 \times 10^{23}$ atoms

$\therefore$ 0.01 mole of sucrose will contain O-atoms

$$= 0.01 \times 11 \times 6.022 \times 10^{23} \text{ atoms}$$
$$= 6.6242 \times 10^{22} \text{ atoms}$$

***Step* 2.** 18 g of water (H_2O) = 1 mole of water

1 mole of water (H_2O) contains O-atoms $= 6.022 \times 10^{23}$ atoms

***Step* 3.** By adding the number of O-atoms present in 3.42 g of sucrose and 18 g of water, we get

$$6.022 \times 10^{23} + 6.6242 \times 10^{22} = 10^{22}\ (60.22 + 6.6242)$$
$$= 66.844 \times 10^{22} = 6.68 \times 10^{23} \text{ atoms}$$

Q. 10 A change in the physical state can be brought about

(a) only when energy is given to the system.

(b) only when energy is taken out from the system.

(c) when energy is either given to, or taken out from the system.

(d) without any energy change.

Thinking Process The heat energy which has to be supplied to change the state of a substance is called its **latent heat**. It does not raise the temperature. It is used up in overcoming the forces of attraction between the particles of a substance during the change of state.

Ans. ***(c)*** A change in the physical state can be brought about when energy is either given to, or taken out from the system. It is because, energy change helps in changing the magnitude of attractive forces between the particles, thus helps in changing the physical states (*i.e.,* solid, liquid, gas) of matter.

Short Answer Type Questions

Q.11 Which of the following represents a correct chemical formula? Name it.

(a) CaCl (b) $BiPO_4$

(c) $NaSO_4$ (d) NaS

Ans. ***(b)*** $BiPO_4$ is the correct formula, its name is Bismuth phosphate. Rest all are incorrect and they can be corrected as:

(i) Option (a) has correct formula — $CaCl_2$ — Calcium chloride

(ii) Option (c) has correct formula — Na_2SO_4 — Sodium sulphate

(iii) Option (d) has correct formula — Na_2S — Sodium sulphide

Q. 12 Write the molecular formulae for the following compounds

(a) Copper (II) bromide (b) Aluminium (III) nitrate

(c) Calcium (II) phosphate (d) Iron (III) sulphide

(e) Mercury (II) chloride (f) Magnesium (II) acetate

Thinking Process The combining power of an element is called its **valency**. Valency is used to find out how the atoms of an element will combine with atoms (s) of other element to form a chemical compound.

Ans. (a) $Cu^{2+} \times Br^{1-} = CuBr_2$ (b) $Al^{3+} \times NO_3^{1-} = Al(NO_3)_3$

(c) $Ca^{2+} \times PO_4^{3-} = Ca_3(PO_4)_2$ (d) $Fe^{3-} \times S^{2-} = Fe_2S_3$

(e) $Hg^{2+} \times Cl^{1+} = HgCl_2$ (f) $CH_3COO^{1-} \times Mg^{2+} = (CH_3COO)_2Mg$

Q. 13 Write the molecular formulae of all the compounds that can be formed by the combination of following ions.

$$Cu^{2+}, Na^{+}, Fe^{3+}, Cl^{-}, SO_4^{2-}, PO_4^{3-}$$

Thinking Process Remember the rules for writing the chemcial formula of compounds.

(i) The valencies or the charges on the ion must balance. (so, cross over the valencies of the combining atoms).

(ii) Write the name of the symbol of metal first (on left) and then the symbol of the non-metal.

(iii) Write the polyatomic ion in bracket (ignore if the number of such ion is 1).

Ans. **Compounds of Cu^{2+}**

(i) with $Cl^{-} \rightarrow Cu^{2+} \times Cl^{1-} = CuCl_2$

(ii) with $SO_4^{2-} \rightarrow Cu^{2+} \times SO_4^{2-} = CuSO_4$

(iii) with $PO_4^{3-} \rightarrow Cu^{2+} \times O_4^{3-} = Cu_3(PO_4)_2$

Compounds of Na^{+}

(i) with $Cl^{-} \rightarrow Na^{1+} \times Cl^{1-} = NaCl$

(ii) with $SO_4^{2-} \rightarrow Na^{1+} \times SO_4^{2-} = Na_2SO_4$

(iii) with $PO_4^{3-} \rightarrow Na^{1+} \times PO_4^{3-} = Na_3PO_4$

Compounds of Fe^{3+}

(i) with $Cl^{-} \rightarrow Fe^{3+} \times Cl^{1-} = FeCl_3$

(ii) with $SO_4^{2-} \rightarrow Fe^{3+} \times SO_4^{2-} = Fe_2(SO_4)_3$

(iii) with $PO_4^{3-} \rightarrow Fe^{3+} \times PO_4^{3-} = FePO_4$

Q. 14 Write the cations and anions present (if any) in the following compounds.

(a) CH_3COONa (b) NaCl (c) H_2 (d) NH_4NO_3

Thinking Process Positively charged ions are called cations while negatively charged ions are called anions.

Ans.

S.No.	Compounds	Cation	Anion
(a)	CH_3COONa	Na^{+}	CH_3COO^{-}
(b)	NaCl	Na^{+}	Cl^{-}
(c)	H_2	—	—
(d)	NH_4NO_3	NH_4^{+}	NO_3^{-}

Mistake Alert ! *One can make a mistake of considering H_2 as an ionic compound (made up of H^{+} and H^{-} ions), instead of a covalent compound.*

Q. 15 Give the formulae of the compounds formed from the following sets of elements.

(a) Calcium and fluorine
(b) Hydrogen and sulphur
(c) Nitrogen and hydrogen
(d) Carbon and chlorine
(e) Sodium and oxygen
(f) Carbon and oxygen

Ans.

(a)	Calcium and fluorine	$Ca^{2+} \times F^{1-} = CaF_2$
(b)	Hydrogen and sulphur	$H^{1+} \times S^{2-} = H_2S$
(c)	Nitrogen and hydrogen	$N^{3-} \times H^{1+} = NH_3$
(d)	Carbon and chlorine	$C^{4+} \times Cl^{1-} = CCl_4$
(e)	Sodium and oxygen	$Na^{1+} \times O^{2-} = Na_2O$
(f)	Carbon and oxygen	$C^{4+} \times O^{2-} = C_2O_4$ or CO_2

Q.16 Which of the following symbols of elements are incorrect? Give their correct symbols.

(a) Cobalt CO
(b) Carbon c
(c) Aluminium AL
(d) Helium He
(e) Sodium So

Ans. (a) Cobalt CO is a incorrect symbol. Its correct symbol is Co.

(b) Carbon c is a incorrect symbol. Its correct symbol is C.

(c) Aluminium AL is a incorrect symbol. Its correct symbol is Al.

(d) Helium, He is the correct symbol.

(e) Sodium So, is the incorrect symbol. Its correct symbol is Na. (It is derived from Latin name 'Natrium').

Q.17 Give the chemical formulae for the following compounds and compute the ratio by mass of the combining elements in each one of them.

(a) Ammonia
(b) Carbon monoxide
(c) Hydrogen chloride
(d) Aluminium fluoride
(e) Magnesium sulphide

Ans.

S.No.	Compounds	Chemical formula	Ratio by mass of the combining elements
(a)	Ammonia	NH_3	N : H = 14 : 3
(b)	Carbon monoxide	CO	C : O = 12 : 16 = 3 : 4
(c)	Hydrogen chloride	HCL	H : Cl = 1 : 35. 5
(d)	Aluminium fluoride	AlF_3	Al : F = 27 : 57 = 9 : 19
(e)	Magnesium sulphide	MgS	Mg : S = 24 : 32 = 3 : 4

Q.18 State the number of atoms present in each of the following chemical species

(a) CO_3^{2-} (b) PO_4^{3-} (c) P_2O_5 (d) CO

- **Concept Insight** The question is based on the concept of atomicity. It is the number of atoms present in the compounds.

Ans. (a) Number of atoms in CO_3^{2-} = number of C-atoms + number of O-atoms = 1 + 3 = 4

(b) Number of atoms in PO_4^{3-} = number of P-atoms + number of O-atoms = 1 + 4 = 5

(c) Number of atoms in P_2O_5 = number of P-atoms + number of O-atoms = 2 + 5 = 7

(d) Number of atoms in CO = number of C-atoms + number of O-atoms = 1 + 1 = 2

Q.19 What is the fraction of the mass of water due to neutrons?

Thinking Process

(i) First we will find out the total number of neutrons in water molecule (H_2O).

(ii) Then, we will find out the mass of total number of neutrons. Then the fraction of the mass of water due to neutrons.

Ans. In water molecule (H_2O), number of neutrons = [(number of neutrons in H) × 2 + (number of neutrons in O)]

$$= 0 \times 2 + 8 = 8 \text{ (as number of neutrons in H = 0)}$$

Mass of 8 neutrons = $8 \times 1.00893 = 8.07$ ($\because$ mass of one neutron = 1008934)

Molar mass of water = $1.008 \times 2 + 16.0 = 18.016$ u

$$\therefore \text{Fraction of mass due to neutrons} = \frac{\text{mass of total neutrons in water} \times 100}{\text{molar mass of water}}$$

$$= \frac{8.07}{18.016} \times 100 \simeq 44.8\%$$

Q.20 Does the solubility of a substance change with temperature? Explain with the help of an example.

Ans. Yes, the solubility of a substance changes with temperature.

The maximum amount of a solute which can be dissolved in 100 g of a solvent at a specified temperature is called its solubility.

Effect of temperature on solubility

(i) The solubility of solids in liquids usually increases on increasing the temperature and decreases on decreasing the temperature.

(ii) The solubility of gases in liquids usually decreases on increasing the temperature and increases on decreasing the temperature.

Let us take an example of copper sulphate.

The solubilities of copper sulphate in water at various temperatures are given below.

Temperature	0°C	10°C	20°C	30°C	40°C	50°C	60°C	70°C
Solubility of copper sulphate	14 g	17 g	21 g	24 g	29 g	34 g	40 g	47 g

From the above data, it is clear that, when the temperature is increased from 0°C to 70°C, the solubility of copper sulphate in water increases from 14 g to 47g. Thus, the above data shows that the solubility of a salt increases on increasing the temperature.

Mistake Alert ! *One can make a mistake in considering the effect of solubility of solids and gases in liquids to be the same, with change in temperature.*

Q. 21 Classify each of the following on the basis of their atomicity.

(a) F_2 (b) NO_2 (c) N_2O (d) C_2H_6
(e) P_4 (f) H_2O_2 (g) P_4O_{10} (h) O_3
(i) HCl (j) CH_4 (k) He (l) Ag

Thinking Process The number of atoms present in one molecule of an element is called its atomicity.
On the basis of atomicity, elements can be classified as **monoatomic** (having 1-atom molecules), **diatomic** (having 2-atoms molecules) and **polyatomic** (having more than 2-atoms molecules).

Ans. *They are classified as*

Monoatomic (k) He, (*l*) Ag

Diatomic (a) F_2, (i) HCl

Polyatomic (b) NO_2, (c) N_2O, (d) C_2H_6, (e) P_4, (f) H_2O_2, (g) P_4O_{10}, (h) O_3, (j) CH_4.

Atomicity = 3 :- (b) NO_2, (c) N_2O, (h) O_3

Atomicity = 4 :- (e) P_4, (f) H_2O_2

Atomicity = 5 :- (j) CH_4

Atomicity = 8 :- (d) C_2H_6

Atomicity = 14 :- (g) P_4O_{10}

Q.22 You are provided with a fine white coloured powder which is either sugar or salt. How would you identify it without tasting?

Ans. There are many ways by which we can differentiate between sugar and salt without tasting

(i) Dissolve the sample of this powder separately in alcohol, sugar will be dissolved in it while salt will not be dissolved (like dissolves like principle).

(ii) Heat the sample of this white powder separately, sugar will melt readily while salt will not.

(iii) Dissolve these two separately in water. Salt solution will conduct electricity due to the presence of Na^+ ion and Cl^- ion while, sugar solution will be a non-conductor (as it does not dissociate into ions).

Long Answer Type Questions

***Q.23** Calculate the number of moles of magnesium present in a magnesium ribbon weighing 12g. Molar atomic mass of magnesium is 24 g mol^{-1}.

Thinking Process 1 mole = molar mass of the substance

Ans. Given that molar atomic mass of Mg = 24 g mol^{-1}

$\because$ 24 g of Mg = 1 mol

$\therefore$ $12 \text{ g of Mg} = \frac{1 \times 12}{24} = \frac{1}{2} = 0.5 \text{ mol}$

Alternate Method

$$\text{Number of moles of Mg} = \frac{\text{given mass}}{\text{molar mass}} = \frac{12 \text{ g}}{24 \text{ g mol}^{-1}} = 0.5 \text{ mol}$$

***Q.24** Verify by calculating that

(a) 5 moles of CO_2 and 5 moles of H_2O do not have the same mass.

(b) 240 g of calcium and 240 g magnesium elements have a mole ratio of 3 : 5.

Thinking Process 1 mole = molar mass of the substance.

Ans. (a) Molar mass of $CO_2 = 12 + 2 \times 16 = 12 + 32 = 44$ g mol^{-1}

$\because$ 1 mole of CO_2 has mass = 44 g

$\therefore$ 5 moles fo CO_2 have mass = $44 \times 5 = 220$ g

Similarly, molar mass of $H_2O = 2 \times 1 + 16 = 18$ g mol^{-1}

$\because$ 1 mole of H_2O has mass = 18 g

$\therefore$ 5 moles of H_2O have mass = $18 \times 5 = 90$ g

$\therefore$ Both the values are not same.

So, it is verified.

(b) Molar mass of calcium = 40 g mol^{-1}

$\because$ 40 g of Ca has number of moles = 1 mol

$\therefore$ 240 g of Ca has number of moles $= \frac{1}{40} \times 240 = 6$ mol

Molar mass of magnesium = 24 g mol^{-1}

$\because$ 24 g of Mg has number of moles = 1 mol

$\therefore$ 240 g of Mg has number of moles $= \frac{1}{24} \times 240 = 10$ mol

$$\frac{\text{Number of moles of Ca}}{\text{Number of moles of Mg}} = \frac{6}{10} = \frac{3}{5}$$

So, it is verified.

Note (*) Topics related to these question have been removed from latest NCERT.

Q.25 Find the ratio by mass of the combining elements in the following compounds.

(a) $CaCO_3$ (b) $MgCl_2$ (c) H_2SO_4 (d) C_2H_5OH
(e) NH_3 (f) $Ca(OH)_2$

Ans. (a) $CaCO_3 \rightarrow Ca : C : O = 40 : 12 : 48 = 10 : 3 : 12$

(b) $MgCl_2 \rightarrow Mg : Cl = 24 : 2 \times 35.5 = 24 : 71$

(c) $H_2SO_4 \rightarrow H : S : O = 2 \times 1 : 32 : 4 \times 16 = 2 : 32 : 64 = 1 : 16 : 32$

(d) $C_2H_5\,OH \rightarrow C : H : O = 2 \times 12 : 6 \times 1 : 16 = 24 : 6 : 16 = 12 : 3 : 8$

(e) $NH_3 \rightarrow N : H = 14 : 3 \times 1 = 14 : 3$

(f) $Ca(OH)_2 \rightarrow Ca : O : H = 40 : 2 \times 16 : 2 \times 1 = 40 : 32 : 2 = 20 : 16 : 1$

Mistake Alert ! *One can make a mistake in writing the correct mass of combining elements of the compounds.*

***Q.26** Calcium chloride when dissolved in water dissociates into its ions according to the following equation.

$$CaCl_2(aq) \longrightarrow Ca^{2+}(aq) + 2Cl^-(aq)$$

Calculate the number of ions obtained from $CaCl_2$, when 222 g of it is dissolved in water.

Thinking Process 1 mole = 6.022×10^{23} ions

- Concept Insight mole concept is used in the question to calculate the number of ions obtained from dissolving $CaCl_2$ in water.

Ans. Molar mass of $CaCl_2 = 40 + 2 \times 35.5$
$= 40 + 71 = 111 \text{ g mol}^{-1}$

$CaCl_2$ ionises in water as

$$\underset{\substack{1\text{ mol}\\ [111\text{ g}]}}{CaCl_2\,(aq)} \longrightarrow \underbrace{\underset{1\text{ mol}}{Ca^{2+}(aq)} + \underset{2\text{ mol}}{2Cl^-(aq)}}_{3\text{ mol}}$$

$\because$ 111 g of $CaCl_2$ produces ions $= 3 \text{ mol} = 3 \times 6.022 \times 10^{23}$ ions

$\therefore$ 222 g of $CaCl_2$ produces ions $= \dfrac{3 \times 6.022 \times 10^{23}}{111} \times 222$

$= 36.132 \times 10^{23} = 3.6132 \times 10^{24}$ ions

***Q.27** The difference in the mass of 100 moles each of sodium atoms and sodium ions is 5.48002 g. Compute the mass of an electron.

Thinking Process 1 mole = 6.002×10^{23} electrons.

Ans. Sodium atom loses an electron to form sodium ion,

$$\underset{\text{Sodium atom}}{Na} \longrightarrow \underset{\text{Sodium ion}}{Na^+} + \underset{\text{Electron}}{e^-}$$

For 100 moles of each sodium atom and sodium ion there would be difference of 100 e^-.

$\because$ Mass of 100 moles of electron = 5.48002 g

Note (✱) Topics related to these question have been removed from latest NCERT.

$\therefore$ Mass of 1 mole of electron $= \dfrac{5.48002}{100}$ g

$\because$ 6.022×10^{23} electrons are present in 1 mole of electron

[as 1 mole = 6.022×10^{23} electrons]

i.e., mass of 6.022×10^{23} electrons = 5.48002 / 100g

$\therefore$ Mass of 1 electron $= \dfrac{5.48002}{100 \times 6.022 \times 10^{23}} = 9.1 \times 10^{-26}$ g

Q.28 **Cinnabar (HgS) is a prominent ore of mercury. How many grams of mercury are present in 225 g of pure HgS? Molar mass of Hg and S are 200.6 g mol^{-1} and 32g mol^{-1} respectively.**

Ans. Given that, molar mass of Hg = 200.6 g mol^{-1}
and that of S = 32 g mol^{-1}

Molar mass of HgS = molar mass of the Hg + molar mass of the S

Molar mass of HgS = 200.6 + 32 = 232.6 g

$\because$ 232.6 g of HgS contains Hg = 200.6 g (as molar mass of Hg = 206 g mol^{-1})

$\therefore$ 225 g of HgS will contains Hg $= \dfrac{200.6 \times 225}{232.6} \approx 194.05$ g

***Q.29** **The mass of one steel screw is 4.11 g. Find the mass of one mole of these steel screws. Compare this value with the mass of the earth (5.98×10^{24} kg). Which one of the two is heavier and by how many times?**

Ans. Given that, mass of one steel screw = 4.11 g

Mass of earth = 5.98×10^{24} kg = 5.98×10^{27} g

We know that, 1 mole = 6.022×10^{23} atoms/molecules/ions

Mass of 1 mole of screws = $6.022 \times 10^{23} \times 4.11$ g = 2.48×10^{24} g

$$\frac{\text{Mass of 1 mole screw}}{\text{Mass of earth}} = \frac{2.48 \times 10^{24}\ \text{g}}{5.98 \times 10^{27}\ \text{g}}$$

$$= \frac{1}{2.411 \times 10^{3}} = \frac{1}{2411}$$

$\therefore$ Ratio of 1 mole of screw and mass of earth = 1 : 2411

$\therefore$ Earth is heavier than one mole of screw by 2411 times.

***Q.30** **A sample of vitamin C is known to contain 2.58×10^{24} oxygen atoms. How many moles of oxygen atoms are present in the sample?**

Ans. Given that, number of oxygen atoms in the given sample = 2.58×10^{24}
We know that, 6.022×10^{23} oxygen atoms = 1 mol

$\therefore$ 2.58×10^{24} oxygen atoms $= \dfrac{2.58 \times 10^{24}}{6.022 \times 10^{23}}$

= 4.28 mol

Note (*) Topics related to these questions have been removed from latest NCERT.

***Q.31** Raunak took 5 moles of carbon atoms in a container and Krish also took 5 moles of sodium atoms in another container of same weight.

(a) Whose container is heavier?

(b) Whose container has more number of atoms?

Ans. (a) 1 mole = molar mass of a substance.

$\because$ 1 mole of carbon atoms weigh = 12 g

$\therefore$ 5 moles of carbon atoms will weigh = $12 \times 5 = 60$ g

Hence, Raunak's container has weigh = 60 g

In the same way,

$\because$ 1 mole of sodium atoms weigh = 23 g

$\therefore$ 5 moles of sodium atoms will weigh = $23 \times 5 = 115$ g

Hence, Krish's container has weigh = 115 g

Thus, Krish's container is heavier than Raunak's container.

As, 1 mole = 6.022×10^{23} atoms

(b) Here, both containers have 5 moles of each carbon and sodium, therefore, both containers have equal number of atoms, *i.e.*, $5 \times 6.022 \times 10^{23}$ atoms.

or 3.011×10^{24} atoms in each.

Mistake Alert ! *Remember that 1 mole of any compound contains the same number of atoms.*

***Q.32** Fill in the missing data in the following table.

Species property	H_2O	CO_2	Na-atom	$MgCl_2$
Number of moles	2	—	—	0.5
Number of particles	—	3.011×10^{23}	—	—
Mass	36 g	—	115 g	—

Thinking Process Number of moles = $\dfrac{\text{Mass}}{\text{Molar mass}} = \dfrac{\text{Number of particles}}{6.022 \times 10^{23}}$

Ans. For H_2O

Given, number of moles = 2 and mass = 36 g

$\therefore$ Number of particles = number of moles $\times 6.022 \times 10^{23}$

$$= 2 \times 6.022 \times 10^{23} = 1.2044 \times 10^{24}$$

For CO_2

Given, number of particles = 3.011×10^{23}

$\therefore$ Number of moles of CO_2 = $\dfrac{\text{number of particles}}{6.022 \times 10^{23}}$

$$= \frac{3.011 \times 10^{23}}{6.022 \times 10^{23}} = 0.5 \text{ mol}$$

Note (✱) Topics related to these questions have been removed from latest NCERT.

Mass of CO_2 = moles × molar mass = 0.5 × 44 = 22 g

(∵ molar mass of $CO_2 = 12 + 2 \times 16 = 44$)

For Na-atom

Given, mass = 115 g

$$\text{Number of moles} = \frac{\text{Mass}}{\text{Molar mass}} = \frac{115}{23} = 5 \text{ mol}$$

∴ Number of particles $= 5 \times 6.022 \times 10^{23} = 3.011 \times 10^{24}$

For $MgCl_2$

Given, number of moles = 0.5

∴ Number of particles $= 0.5 \times 6.022 \times 10^{23} = 3.011 \times 10^{23}$

Mass = number of moles × molar mass

(molar mass of $MgCl_2 = 24 + 2 \times 35.5 = 24 + 71 = 95$)

$= 0.5 \times 95 = 47.5$ g

Thus, the completed table is :

Species property	H_2O	CO_2	Na-atom	$MgCl_2$
Number of moles	2	0.5	5.0	0.5
Number of particles	1.2044×10^{24}	3.011×10^{23}	3.011×10^{24}	3.011×10^{23}
Mass	36 g	22 g	115 g	47.5 g

*** Q.33** The visible universe is estimated to contain 10^{22} stars. How many moles of stars are present in the visible universe?

Ans. 6.022×10^{23} stars = 1 mole of stars.

$$10^{22} \text{ stars} = \frac{1 \times 10^{22}}{6.022 \times 10^{23}} = 1.67 \times 10^{-2} \text{ mol}$$

Q.34 What is SI prefix for each of the following multiples and submultiples of a unit?

(a) 10^3 (b) 10^{-1}

(c) 10^{-2} (d) 10^{-6}

(e) 10^{-9} (f) 10^{-12}

Ans. (a) $10^3 \rightarrow$ kilo (b) $10^{-1} \rightarrow$ deci

(c) $10^{-2} \rightarrow$ centi (d) $10^{-6} \rightarrow$ micro

(e) $10^{-9} \rightarrow$ nano (f) $10^{-12} \rightarrow$ pico

Q.35 Express each of the following in kilograms.

(a) 5.84×10^{-3} mg

(b) 58.34 g

(c) 0.584 g

(d) 5.873×10^{-21} g

Thinking Process 1 kg = 10^3 g = 10^6 mg

Note (*) Topics related to these question have been removed from latest NCERT.

Ans. (a) $\because$ 10^6 mg = 1 kg

$$\therefore \quad 5.84 \times 10^{-3} \text{ mg} = \frac{1 \times 5.84 \times 10^{-3}}{10^6} \text{ kg} = 5.84 \times 10^{-9} \text{ kg}$$

(b) $\because$ 10^3 g = 1kg

$$\therefore \quad 58.34 \text{ g} = \frac{1 \times 58.34}{10^3} \text{ kg} = 58.34 \times 10^{-3} \text{ kg}$$

$$= 5.834 \times 10^{-2} \text{ kg}$$

(c) $0.584 \text{ g} = \frac{1 \times 0.584}{10^3} \text{ kg} = 0.584 \times 10^{-3} \text{ kg} = 5.84 \times 10^{-4} \text{ kg}$

(d) $5.873 \times 10^{-21} \text{ g} = \frac{5.873 \times 10^{-21}}{10^3} \text{ kg} = 5.873 \times 10^{-24} \text{ kg}$

Mistake Alert ! *One can make a mistake in converting the mass given in miligram or gram to kilogram.*

***Q.36** **Compute the difference in masses of 10^3 moles each of magnesium atoms and magnesium ions. (Mass of an electron = 9.1×10^{-31} kg)**

Thinking Process

(i) First we find out the number of Mg atoms and number of Mg ions in 10^3 moles of the Mg atom and Mg ions.

(ii) Then we calculate the difference in their masses.

Ans. 10^3 moles of Mg atoms = $10^3 \times 6.022 \times 10^{23} = 6.022 \times 10^{26}$ Mg atoms

10^3 moles of Mg^{2+} ions = $10^3 \times 6.022 \times 10^{23} = 6.022 \times 10^{26}$ Mg^{2+} ions

One Mg^{2+} ion is formed from one Mg atom by loss of 2 electrons, As

$Mg \rightarrow Mg^{2+} + 2e^-$

i.e., difference in the mass of 1 Mg atom and 1Mg^{2+} ion = mass of 2 electrons

$\therefore$ Difference in the mass of 6.022×10^{26} Mg atoms and Mg^{2+} ions

$= \text{mass of } 2 \times 6.022 \times 10^{26} \text{ electrons}$

$= 2 \times 6.022 \times 10^{26} \times 9.1 \times 10^{-31}$ kg.

(as mass of an electron = 9.1×10^{-31} kg)

$= 109.6004 \times 10^{-5} \text{ kg} = 1096 \times 10^{-3} \text{ kg} = 1.096 \text{ g}$

***Q.37** **Which has more number of atoms?**

100 g of N_2 or 100 g of NH_3

- **Concept Insight** Mole concept is used in this question to compare the number of atoms in two different compounds.

Ans. Molar mass of $N_2 = 2 \times 14 = 28 \text{ g mol}^{-1}$

$\because$ 28 g of N_2 has number of molecules = 6.022×10^{23}

$\therefore$ 100 g of N_2 has number of molecules $= \frac{6.022 \times 10^{23} \times 100}{28} = 2.15 \times 10^{24}$ molecules.

Atoms in 100 g of $N_2 = 2.15 \times 10^{24} \times 2$

$= 4.30 \times 10^{24}$ atoms

Similarly, molar mass of $NH_3 = 14 + 3 \times 1 = 17 \text{ g mol}^{-1}$

$\because$ 17 g NH_3 has number of molecules = 6.022×10^{23}

Note (✱) Topics related to these question have been removed from latest NCERT.

$\therefore$ 100 g NH_3 has number of molecules $= \frac{6.022 \times 10^{23} \times 100}{17} = 3.54 \times 10^{24}$ molecules

$$\text{Atoms in 100 g of } NH_3 = 3.54 \times 10^{24} \times 4 = 1.416 \times 10^{25} \text{ atoms}$$

Thus, 100 g of NH_3 has more number of atoms.

***Q.38** **Compute the number of ions present in 5.85 g of sodium chloride.**

Ans. Molar mass of sodium chloride (NaCl) = 23 + 35.5 = 58.5 g mol^{-1}

$\because$ 58.5 g of NaCl has number of ions $= 6.02 \times 10^{23} \times 2$

As,
$$\underset{\text{Sodium chloride}}{NaCl} \longrightarrow \underset{\text{Sodium ion}}{Na^+} + \underset{\text{Chloride ion}}{Cl^-}$$

$\therefore$ 5.85 g of NaCl has number of ions $= \frac{6.022 \times 10^{23} \times 2 \times 5.85}{58.5}$

$$= 12.044 \times 10^{22} = 1.2044 \times 10^{23} \text{ ions}$$

***Q.39** **A gold sample contains 90% of gold and the rest copper. How many atoms of gold are present in one gram of this sample of gold?**

Ans. Let, the mass of the sample is 100 g

$\therefore$ Mass of gold = 90 g

and mass of copper = (100 − 90) = 10 g

$\because$ 100 g of sample has gold = 90 g

$\therefore$ 1 g of this sample has gold $= \frac{90}{100} = 0.9$ g

Atomic mass of gold (Au) = 197 g

$\because$ 197 g of gold have number of atoms $= 6.022 \times 10^{23}$

$\therefore$ 0.9 g of gold will have number of atoms $= \frac{6.022 \times 10^{23} \times 0.9}{197}$

$$= 2.75 \times 10^{21} \text{ atoms}$$

Q.40 **What are ionic and molecular compounds? Give examples.**

Ans. Ionic compounds are those compounds which are made up of ions. In ionic compounds, the positively charged ions **(cations)** and negatively charged ions **(anions)** are held together by the **strong electrostatic forces of attraction**, which are known as **ionic bonds** or **electrovalent bonds.** *e.g.*, sodium chloride (NaCl), calcium oxide (CaO), etc.

Molecular compounds are those compounds in which the atoms of the elements share electrons and form covalent bonds *e.g.*, methane (CH_4), water (H_2O), etc.

***Q.41** **Compute the difference in masses of one mole each of aluminium atoms and one mole of its ions (Mass of an electron is 9.1×10^{-28} g). Which one is heavier?**

Ans. Ionisation of Al atom occurs as $Al \longrightarrow Al^{3+} + 3e^-$

Therefore, Al^{3+} ion is formed from Al atom by loss of 3 electrons. Difference in mass of 1 mole of Al atoms and 1 mole of Al^{3+} ions

Note (*) Topics related to these question have been removed from latest NCERT.

$= \text{mass of } 3 \times 6.022 \times 10^{23} \text{ electrons}$

$= (3 \times 6.022 \times 10^{23}) \times (9.1 \times 10^{-28} \text{ g})$

(as mass of an electron $= 9.1 \times 10^{-28}$ g)

$= 164.4 \times 10^{-5} \text{ g} = 1.644 \times 10^{-3} \text{ g}$

1 mole of Al atoms is heavier than 1 mole of Al^{3+} ions.

It is because 1 mole of Al atom have $e^- = 13 \times 6.022 \times 10^{23}$ electrons and 1 mole of Al ion have $e^- = 10 \times 6.022 \times 10^{23}$ electrons.

Alternate method

Molar mass of Al = 27 g mol^{-1}

Molar mass of $Al^{3+} = (27 - 0.001644) g \text{ mol}^{-1} = 26.9984 \text{ g mol}^{-1}$

Difference in molar mass of Al and $Al^{3+} = (27 - 26.9984) g = 0.0016$ g

$\therefore$ 1 mole of Al is heavier than 1 mole of Al ions.

***Q.42** **A silver ornament of mass 'm' gram is polished with gold equivalent to 1% of the mass of silver. Compute the ratio of the number of atoms of gold and silver in the ornament.**

Thinking Process 1 mole = 6.022×10^{23} atoms or molecules = molar/atomic mass of substance

Ans. Mass of silver (Ag) ornament = m g

Mass of gold used for polishing $= \dfrac{1}{100} \times m \text{ g} = 0.01 m$ g

Atomic mass of Ag = 108 u

$\therefore$ 1 mole of Ag = 108 g = 6.022×10^{23} atoms

Thus, 108 g of Ag have atoms = 6.022×10^{23}

$\therefore$ m g of Ag will have atoms $= \dfrac{6.022 \times 10^{23}}{108} \times m$

Similarly, atomic mass of gold (Au) = 197 u

1 mole of Au = 197 g = 6.022×10^{23} atoms

Thus, 197 g of Au have atoms = 6.022×10^{23}

$\therefore$ 0.01 m g of Au will have atoms $= \dfrac{6.022 \times 10^{23} \times 0.01 \text{ m}}{197}$

$\therefore$ Ratio of the number of atoms of gold and silver

$$= \frac{6.022 \times 10^{23}}{197} \times 0.01 \text{ m} : \frac{6.022 \times 10^{23}}{108} \text{ m}$$

$$= \frac{1}{19700} : \frac{1}{108} = 108 : 19700$$ (or = 1 : 182.41)

Note (*) Topics related to these question have been removed from latest NCERT.

***Q.43** A sample of ethane (C_2H_6) gas has the same mass as 1.5×10^{20} molecules of methane (CH_4). How many C_2H_6 molecules does the sample of gas contain?

Thinking Process

(i) First we will find out the mass of 1.5×10^{20} molecules of methane.

(ii) Then, we will find out the mass of ethane, which is equal to the mass of methane.

(iii) From this mass, we will then find out the number of C_2H_6 molecules.

Ans. $\because$ 6.022×10^{23} molecules of methane have mass = molar mass of methane (CH_4) $= 12 + 4 \times 1 = 16$ g

$\therefore$ 1.5×10^{20} molecules of methane have mass $= \dfrac{16 \times 1.5 \times 10^{20}}{6.022 \times 10^{23}} = 3.98 \times 10^{-3}$g

This is also the mass of ethane (C_2H_6).

Molar mass of ethane $(C_2H_6) = 2 \times 12 + 6 \times 1 = 24 + 6 = 30 \text{ g mol}^{-1}$

As 30 g of ethane has number of molecules $= 6.022 \times 10^{23}$

$\therefore$ 3.98×10^{-3} g of ethane has number of molecules $= \dfrac{6.022 \times 10^{23} \times 3.98 \times 10^{-3}}{30 \text{ g}}$ g

$= 7.99 \times 10^{19} \approx 8 \times 10^{19}$ molecules

Q.44 Fill in the blanks.

(a) In a chemical reaction, the sum of the masses of the reactants and products remains unchanged. This is called ....

(b) A group of atoms carrying a fixed charge on them is called ....

(c) The formula unit mass of $Ca_3(PO_4)_2$ is ....

(d) Formula of sodium carbonate is .... and that of ammonium sulphate is ....

Ans. (a) In a chemical reaction, the sum of the masses of the reactants and products remains unchanged. This is called **law of conservation of mass.**

(b) A group of atoms carrying a fixed charge on them is called **polyatomic ion.**

(c) The formula unit mass of $Ca_3(PO_4)_2$ is **310 u.**

(d) Formula of sodium carbonate is $\mathbf{Na_2CO_3}$ and that of ammonium sulphate is $\mathbf{(NH_4)_2SO_4}$.

Q.45 Complete the following crossword puzzle (Figure) by using the name of the chemical elements. Use the data given in the table following.

	Across		Down
2.	The element used by Rutherford during his α –scattering experiment.	1.	A white lustrous metal used for making ornaments and which tends to get tarnished black in the presence of moist air.
3.	An element which forms rust on exposure to moist air.	4.	Both brass and bronze are alloys of the element.

Note (✱) Topics related to these question have been removed from latest NCERT.

Across		Down	
5.	A very reactive non-metal stored under water.	6.	The metal which exists in the liquid state at room temperature.
7.	Zinc metal when treated with dilute hydrochloric acid produces a gas of this element which when tested with burning splinter produces a pop sound.	8.	An element with symbol Pb.

Ans.

	Across		Down
2.	Gold	1.	Silver
3.	Iron	4.	Copper
5.	Phosphorus	6.	Mercury
7.	Hydrogen	8.	Lead

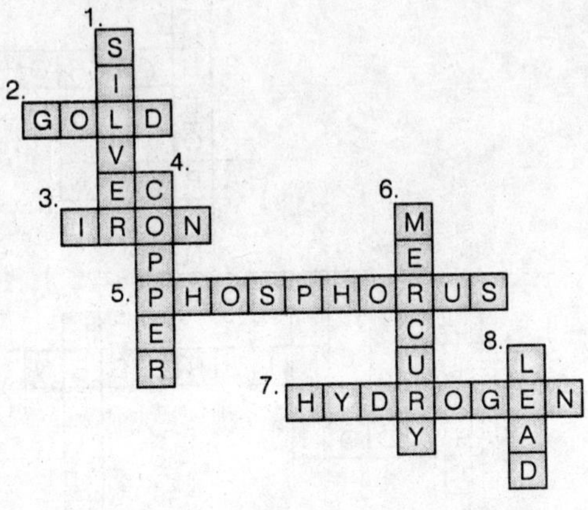

Q.46 (a) In this crossword puzzle (Figure), names of 11 elements are hidden. Symbols of these are given below. Complete the puzzle.

1. Cl	2. H	3. Ar	4. O
5. Xe	6. N	7. He	8. F
9. Kr	10. Rn	11. Ne	

(b) Identify the total number of inert gases, their names and symbols from this crossword puzzle.

Ans. (a) The names of these elements are given as follows

1. Cl - Chlorine
2. H - Hydrogen
3. Ar - Argon
4. O - Oxygen
5. Xe - Xenon
6. N - Nitrogen
7. He - Helium
8. F - Fluorine
9. Kr - Krypton
10. Rn - Radon
11. Ne - Neon

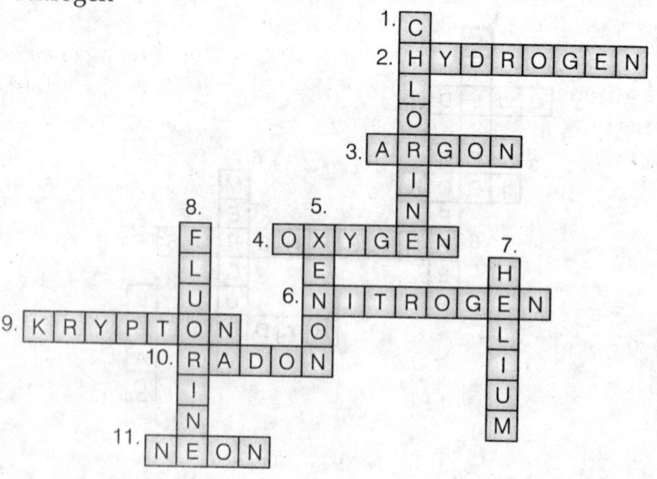

(b) Total number of inert gases in this crossword puzzle is 6. Their names and symbols are as follows

S.No.	Name of gas	Symbol
1.	Helium	He
2.	Neon	Ne
3.	Argon	Ar
4.	Krypton	Kr
5.	Xenon	Xe
6.	Radon	Rn

Q.47 Write the formulae for the following and calculate the molecular mass for each one of them.

(a) Caustic potash (b) Baking powder (c) Lime stone
(d) Caustic soda (e) Ethanol (f) Common salt

Thinking Process Baking soda is sodium hydrogen carbonate $NaHCO_3$. Baking powder is a mixture of baking soda and an acid, (which can be tartaric acid from grapes or citric acid or others)

Ans.

S.No.	Compound	Formula	Molecular mass
(a)	Caustic potash	KOH	$39+16+1=56$ u
(b)	Baking powder	$NaHCO_3$	$23+1+12+3\times16=84$ u
(c)	Lime stone	$CaCO_3$	$40+12+3\times16=100$ u
(d)	Caustic soda	NaOH	$23+16+1=40$ u
(e)	Ethanol	C_2H_5OH	$2\times12+5\times1+16+1=46$ u
(f)	Common salt	NaCl	$23+35.5=58.5$ u

Q.48 In photosynthesis, 6 molecules of carbon dioxide combine with an equal number of water molecules through a complex series of reactions to give a molecule of glucose having a molecular formula $C_6H_{12}O_6$. How many grams of water would be required to produce 18 g of glucose? Compute the volume of water so consumed assuming the density of water to be 1 g cm^{-3}.

Ans. During photosynthesis, following reaction takes place

$$6\,CO_2 + 6\,H_2O \xrightarrow[\text{Sunlight}]{\text{Chlorophyll}} C_6H_{12}O_6 + 6O_2$$

$$6(2\times1+16) = 6\times18 = 108\text{ g}$$

Molecular formula of glucose $(C_6H_{12}O_6) = 6\times12+12\times1+6\times16$

$$= 72+12+96 = 180\text{ g}$$

$\because$ 180 g of glucose require the amount of water = 108 g

$\therefore$ 18 g of glucose will require the amount of water $= \dfrac{108\text{g}\times18\text{g}}{180\text{g}} = 10.8\text{ g}$

As the amount of water consumed $(m) = 10.8$ g

Given that, density (d) of water = 1g cm^{-3}

$\therefore$ Volume (V) of water consumed $= \dfrac{m}{d} = \dfrac{10.8\text{ g}}{1\text{g cm}^{-3}} = 10.8\text{ cm}^3$ $\left[\text{As } d = \dfrac{m}{V}\right]$

Chapter

04 Structure of the Atom

Multiple Choice Questions (MCQs)

Choose the correct answer from the given four options in the following questions :

Q. 1 Which of the following correctly represent the electronic distribution in the Mg atom?

(a) 3, 8, 1 (b) 2, 8, 2 (c) 1, 8, 3 (d) 8, 2, 2

Thinking Process

(i) Atomic number of Mg = 12.

(ii) First of all, electrons will go to K shell which can take maximum of 2 electrons. After that, electrons will go to L shell, which can take maximum of 8 electrons.

(iii) Now, the remaining 2 electrons will go to M shell.

Ans. ***(b)*** Atomic number and the number of electrons in magnesium atom is 12. So, electronic configuration is 2, 8, 2 (because 12 = 2 + 8 + 2).

Q. 2 Rutherford's alpha(α) particles scattering experiment resulted in to discovery of

(a) electron (b) proton

(c) Nucleus in the atom (d) atomic mass

- **Concept Insight** This question is based on the Rutherford's model of an atoms Rutherford led to the discovery of the nucleus in atom with the help of an the gold foil experiment.

Ans. ***(c)*** Rutherford discovered the nucleus in the atom by his α-particle scattering experiment.

Q. 3 The number of electrons in an element X is 15 and the number of neutrons is 16. Which of the following is the correct representation of the element?

(a) $^{31}_{15}X$ (b) $^{31}_{16}X$ (c) $^{16}_{15}X$ (d) $^{15}_{16}X$

Thinking Process

(i) The atomic number (Z) is written on the lower left side of the symbol, while mass number (A) is written on the upper left side of the symbol; $^{A}_{Z}X$

(ii) Mass number = Number of protons + Number of neutrons.

Ans. ***(a)*** Given that, number of electrons in element X = 15 and number of neutrons = 16

Atomic number = Number of protons = Number of electrons in neutral atom = 15

$$\text{Mass number} = \text{number of protons} + \text{number of neutrons}$$
$$= 15 + 16 = 31$$

Thus, the atom is represented as $^{31}_{15}X$.

Mistake Alert! *One can make a mistake of writing the representation of the element as* $^{Z}_{A}X$, *instead of* $^{A}_{Z}X$.

Q. 4 Dalton's atomic theory successfully explained

(i) law of conservation of mass.

(ii) law of constant composition.

(iii) law of radioactivity.

(iv) law of multiple proportion.

(a) (i), (ii) and (iii) (b) (i), (iii) and (iv)

(c) (ii), (iii) and (iv) (d) (i), (ii) and (iv)

Ans. *(d)* Dalton's atomic theory successfully explained the laws of chemical combination *i.e.,* law of conservation of mass, law of constant composition and law of multiple proportion, but no point about radioactivity was mentioned by Dalton in his theory.

Q. 5 Which of the following statements about Rutherford's model of atom are correct?

(i) Considered the nucleus as positively charged.

(ii) Established that the α-particles are four times as heavy as a hydrogen atom.

(iii) Can be compared to solar system.

(iv) Was in agreement with Thomson's model.

(a) (i) and (iii) (b) (ii) and (iii) (c) (i) and (iv) (d) Only (i)

Ans. *(a)* According to Rutherford's model, a central positively charged nucleus is present in the atom and electrons revolve around it. This model is similar to solar system and it is also called planetary model. Thus, statements (i) and (iii) are correct and hence option (a) is correct.

Q. 6 Which of the following are true for an element?

(i) Atomic number = number of protons + number of electrons

(ii) Mass number = number of protons + number of neutrons

(iii) Atomic mass = number of protons = number of neutrons

(iv) Atomic number = number of protons = number of electrons

(a) (i) and (ii) (b) (i) and (iii) (c) (ii) and (iii) (d) (ii) and (iv)

Ans. *(d)* Points (ii) and (iv) are correct.

[Mass number = $p + n$, Atomic number = $p = e$]

Q. 7 In the Thomson's model of atom, which of the following statements are correct?

(i) The mass of the atom is assumed to be uniformly distributed over the atom.

(ii) The positive charge is assumed to be uniformly distributed over the atom.

(iii) The electrons are uniformly distributed in the positively charged sphere.

(iv) The electrons attract each other to stabilise the atom.

(a) (i), (ii) and (iii) (b) (i) and (iii)

(c) (i) and (iv) (d) (i), (iii) and (iv)

Ans. ***(a)*** Statements (i), (ii) and (iii) are correct. According to Thomson's model of the atom, an atom consists of a sphere of positive charge with negatively charged electrons embedded in it. The mass of the atom is uniformly distributed over the atom. The negative and positive charges in an atom are equal in magnitude, due to which an atom is electrically neutral. Also, the electrons do not attract each other to stabilise the atom (infact they repel each other).

Q. 8 Rutherford's α-particle scattering experiment showed that

(i) electrons have negative charge.

(ii) the mass and positive charge of the atom is concentrated in the nucleus.

(iii) neutron exists in the nucleus.

(iv) most of the space in atom is empty.

Which of the above statements are correct?

(a) (i) and (iii)
(b) (ii) and (iv)
(c) (i) and (iv)
(d) (iii) and (iv)

Ans. ***(b)*** Statements (ii) and (iv) are correct. An atom consists of a positively charged, dense and very small nucleus which have all the protons and neutrons. Positive charge is due to protons, as neutrons have no charge. Most of the space in an atom is empty because most of the alpha particles pass straight through the gold foil without any deflection.

Q. 9 The ion of an element has 3 positive charges. Mass number of the atom is 27 and the number of neutrons is 14. What is the number of electrons in the ion?

(a) 13
(b) 10
(c) 14
(d) 16

Thinking process Atomic number = $p = e$

Mass number = $n + p$

So, Mass number = n + Atomic number

$\Rightarrow$ Atomic number = Mass number $- n$

Ans. ***(b)*** Given that, charge = + 3, mass number = 27 and number of neutrons = 14

Number of protons = atomic number

Atomic number = mass number − number of neutrons = 27 − 14 = 13

This is the atomic number of aluminium.

Therefore, this element is aluminium (Al).

Number of electrons in the Al atom = 13

Number of electrons in the Al^{3+} ion = 13 − 3 = 10.

As it is formed from the neutral atom by loss of 3 electrons.

Mistake Alert! *One can make a mistake of not considering the charge while calculating the number of electrons.*

Q.10 **Identify the Mg^{2+} ion from the figure where, *n* and *p* represent the number of neutrons and protons respectively.**

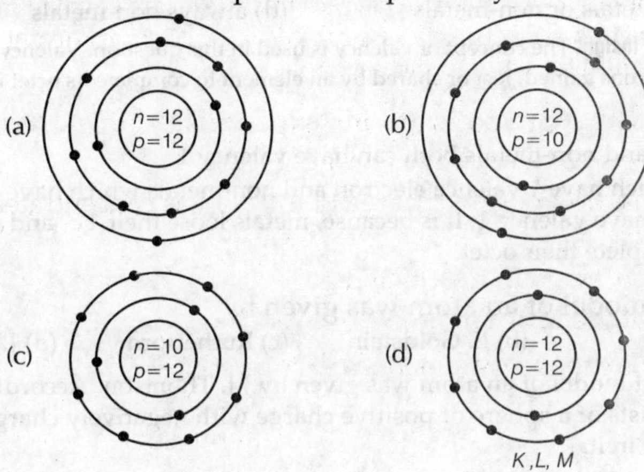

Ans. ***(d)*** Electronic configuration $_{12}Mg$ atom = 2, 8, 2 and that of

Mg^{2+} ion = 2, 8

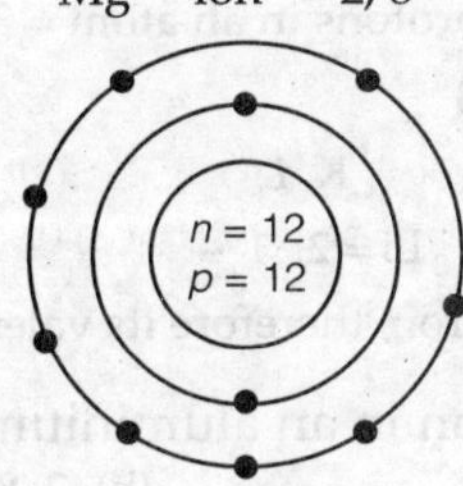

Number of protons in Mg atom = 2 + 8 + 2 = 12

Number of neutrons in Mg atom = 24 − 12 = 12

[As mass number of Mg atom = 24 and number of neutrons = mass number − number of protons]

Q. 11 **In a sample of ethyl ethanoate ($CH_3COOC_2H_5$) the two oxygen atoms have the same number of electrons but different number of neutrons. Which of the following is the correct reason for it?**

(a) One of the oxygen atoms has gained electrons.
(b) One of the oxygen atoms has gained two neutrons.
(c) The two oxygen atoms are isotopes.
(d) The two oxygen atoms are isobars.

Thinking Process Isobars of different elements have same mass number but different atomic number or number of protons (and electrons).

Ans ***(c)*** The two O-atoms in $CH_3COOC_2H_5$ can have different number of neutrons only if the two O-atoms are isotopes. It is because, isotopes of an element have same atomic number or number of protons (and electrons), but different mass number or number of neutrons.

Mistake Alert ! *One can make a mistake of confusing isotopes with isobars.*

Q. 12 Elements with valency 1 are

(a) always metals (b) always metalloids
(c) either metals or non-metals (d) always non-metals

- **Concept Insight** The concept of valency is used in this question. Valency is the number of electrons gained, lost or shared by an element to complete its octet in the outermost shell.

Ans. *(c)* Metals and non-metals both can have valency 1.
Metals which have 1 valence electron and non-metals which have 7 valence electrons, have valency 1. It is because, metals loose their 1 e^- and non-metals gain 1 e^- to complete their octet.

Q. 13 The first model of an atom was given by

(a) N. Bohr (b) E. Goldstein (c) Rutherford (d) J.J. Thomson

Ans. *(d)* The first model of an atom was given by J.J. Thomson. According to him, an atom consists of a sphere of positive charge with negatively charged electrons embedded in it.

Q. 14 An atom with 3 protons and 4 neutrons will have a valency of

(a) 3 (b) 7 (c) 1 (d) 4

Ans. *(c)* Given that, number of protons in an atom = 3 and number of neutrons = 4
So, number of electrons = 3

$$\text{Electronic configuration of } {}_{3}\text{Li} = \overset{K}{2},\ \overset{L}{1}$$

As, it has one valence electron, therefore its valency is also 1.

Q. 15 The electron distribution in an aluminium atom is

(a) 2, 8, 3 (b) 2, 8, 2
(c) 8, 2, 3 (d) 2, 3, 8

Ans. *(a)* Aluminium atom has 13 protons and 13 electrons.

$$\text{Therefore, Electronic configuration of } {}_{13}\text{Al} = \overset{K}{2},\ \overset{L}{8},\ \overset{M}{3}$$

Q. 16 Which of the following in figure do not represent Bohr's model of an atom correctly?

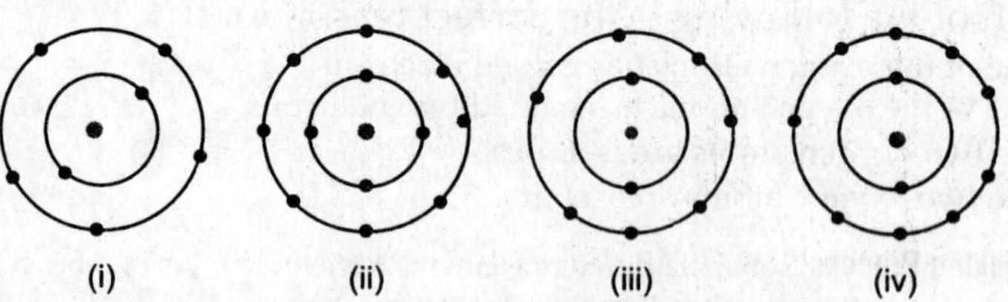

(a) (i) and (ii) (b) (ii) and (iii)
(c) (ii) and (iv) (d) (i) and (iv)

Ans. *(c)* Figures (ii) and (iv) do not correctly represent the Bohr's model of an atom. It is because maximum number of electrons in *K* shell is 2, not 4, so (ii) is wrong and maximum capacity of *L* shell is 8 electrons, not 9. So, (iv) is also wrong.

Q. 17 Which of the following statement is always correct?

(a) An atom has equal number of electrons and protons.
(b) An atom has equal number of electrons and neutrons.
(c) An atom has equal number of protons and neutrons.
(d) An atom has equal number of electrons, protons and neutrons.

Ans. *(a)* Atom is electrically neutral. It is possible only if an atom has equal number of protons and electrons.

Q. 18 Atomic models have been improved over the years. Arrange the following atomic models in the order of their chronological order.

(i) Rutherford's atomic model (ii) Thomson's atomic model
(iii) Bohr's atomic model

(a) (i), (ii) and (iii) (b) (ii), (iii) and (i) (c) (ii), (i) and (iii) (d) (iii), (ii) and (i)

Thinking Process

(i) When J. J. Thomson proposed his model, then only electrons and protons were known to be present in the atom.
(ii) After the discovery of electrons, protons and neutrons, experiments were carried out to find out how these subatomic particles were arranged in an atom. Rutherford's α-particle scattering experiment led to the discovery of nucleus in an atom containing all the protons and neutrons.
(iii) Neils Bohr gave the present concept of the structure of atom.

Ans. *(c)* The correct order of the improvements in atomic models is as Thomson's atomic model (ii), Rutherford's atomic model (i) and Bohr's atomic model (iii).

Short Answer Type Questions

Q. 19 Is it possible for the atom of an element to have one electron, one proton and no neutron. If so, name the element.

Ans. 1 proton means atomic number $(Z) = 1$
No neutron means, mass number $(A) = p + n$
$= 1 + 0 = 1$

1 electron and 1 proton means that an atom is electrically neutral.
Hence, it is possible for an atom of an element to have one electron one proton and no neutron.

The element is protium ^1_1H (an isotope of hydrogen). ^1_1H (protium) has one electron, one proton and no neutron.

Q. 20 Write any two observations which support the fact that atoms are divisible.

Ans. 'Atoms are divisible' is supported by the following facts:

(i) Formation of ionic compounds is possible due to the formation of ions which involves the transfer of electrons.

(ii) Presence of isotopes for the same element is possible due to the difference in the number of neutrons.

Above observations show that atom is formed by different particles such as electrons, protons and neutrons, *i.e.*, atom is divisible.

Q. 21 Will ^{35}Cl and ^{37}Cl have different valencies? Justify your answer.

Thinking Process Isotopes do not differ in number of electrons or protons, but they only differ in number of neutrons.

Ans. No, ^{35}Cl and ^{37}Cl have same valency. ^{35}Cl and ^{37}Cl are the isotopes. So, they have same number of protons and electrons and have the same atomic number *viz.* 17 Hence, their electronic configuration and valencies are also the same.

$$\begin{array}{rl} & K\ \ L\ \ M \\ \text{Electronic configuration} = & 2,\ 8,\ 7 \\ \text{Valency } 8 - 7 = 1 & \end{array}$$

Therefore, both of them have valency = 1

Q. 22 Why did Rutherford select a gold foil in his α-ray scattering experiment?

Ans. Gold is a heavy metal with a high mass number. A light metal cannot be used in the experiment because on being hit by fast moving α-particle, the atom of light metal will be simply pushed forward and no scattering can occur.

Moreover, gold is the best malleable metal. A very thin foil ($\approx$ 1000 atoms thick) can be made from gold easily to get the clear observations.

Q. 23 Find out the valency of the atoms represented by the Figure (a) and (b).

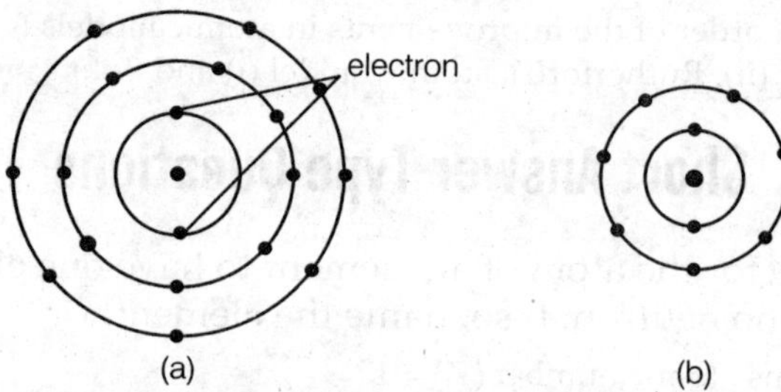

Ans. (a) It has electronic configuration

$$\begin{array}{ccc} K & L & M \\ 2 & 8 & 8 \end{array}$$

Its outer shell has complete octet.
Hence, its valency = 0

(b) It has electronic configuration

$$\begin{array}{cc} K & L \\ 2 & 7 \end{array}$$

It can easily gain one electron to complete its octet in the outermost shell.
Hence, its valency = 1.

Q.24 **One electron is present in the outermost shell of the atom of an element X. What would be the nature and value of charge on the ion formed if this electron is removed from the outermost shell?**

Thinking process Removal of electron from an atom results in the formation of a cation.

Ans. An element X is a metal because one electron is present in the outermost shell *i.e.,* 1 valence electron. When this valence electron is removed from the outermost shell, a cation (positive ion) will be formed with a charge of + 1.

Q.25 **Write down the electron distribution of chlorine atom. How many electrons are there in the *L*-shell? Atomic number of chlorine is = 17.**

Ans. Atomic number of chlorine atom = 17

So, its electronic configuration is

K	*L*	*M*
2	8	7

L shell of chlorine contains 8 electrons.

Mistake Alert ! *Remember that maximum number of electrons in a shell can only be* $2n^2$, *where n is the shell number.*

Q.26 **In the atom of an element X, 6 electrons are present in the outermost shell. If it acquires noble gas configuration by accepting requisite number of electrons, then what would be the charge on the ion so formed?**

Thinking Process Addition of electron to a neutral atom results in the formation of an anion.

Ans. Element X has 6 electrons in the outermost shell. In order to acquire noble gas configuration, element X requires 2 electrons. So, the charge on the anion (X^{2-}) so formed is –2.

Q.27 **What information do you get from the figure about the atomic number, mass number and valency of atoms *X*, *Y* and *Z*? Give your answer in a tabular form.**

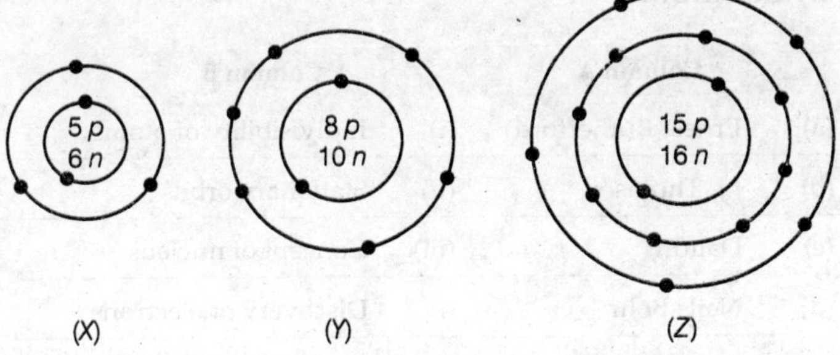

Ans. The tabular form is as given below.

Element	Atomic number (= no. of p)	Mass number = {no. of $(p+n)$}	Number of electrons (= no. of p)	Electronic configuration	Valency
X	5	5 + 6 = 11	5	2, 3	3
Y	8	8 + 10 = 18	8	2, 6	2
Z	15	15 + 16 = 31	15	2, 8, 5	3, 5

Q.28 In response to a question, a student stated that in an atom, the numbe of protons is greater than the number of neutrons, which in turn is greater than the number of electrons. Do you agree with the statement? Justify your answer.

Ans. The given statement is not correct.
According to this statement

$$p > n > e$$

But actually, the number of protons is never greater than the number of neutrons. Number of neutrons can be equal to or greater than the number of protons (as in case of isotopes).

Of course, number of neutrons can be greater than the number of electrons because number of electrons = number of protons in the neutral atom.

Q.29 Calculate the number of neutrons present in the nucleus of an element X which is represented as ${}^{31}_{15}X$.

Ans. ${}^{31}_{15}X$ represents ${}^{A}_{Z}X$, where,
Atomic number, $Z = 15$
Mass number, $A = 31$
$\therefore$ Number of neutrons $= A - Z = 31 - 15 = 16$

$[\because Z = p$ and $A = p + n \therefore n = A - p = A - Z$

Q.30 Match the names of the Scientists given in Column A with their contributions towards the understanding of the atomic structure as given in Column B.

	Column A		Column B
(a)	Ernest Rutherford	(i)	Indivisibility of atoms
(b)	J.J. Thomson	(ii)	Stationary orbits
(c)	Dalton	(iii)	Concept of nucleus
(d)	Neils Bohr	(iv)	Discovery of electrons
(e)	James Chadwick	(v)	Atomic number
(f)	E Goldstein	(vi)	Neutron
(g)	Mosley	(vii)	Canal rays

Ans.

	Column A	Column B
(a)	Ernest Rutherford	(iii) Concept of nucleus
(b)	J.J. Thomson	(iv) Discovery of electrons
(c)	Dalton	(i) Indivisibility of atoms
(d)	Neils Bohr	(ii) Stationary orbits
(e)	James Chadwick	(vi) Neutron
(f)	E. Goldstein	(vii) Canal rays
(g)	Mosley	(v) Atomic number

Q.31 **The atomic number of calcium and argon are 20 and 18 respectively, but the mass number of both these elements is 40. What is the name given to such a pair of elements?**

Ans. Atomic number and mass number of calcium are 20 and 40 *i.e.*, ${}^{40}_{20}Ca$
Atomic number and mass number of argon are 18 and 40 *i.e.*, ${}^{40}_{18}Ar$

A pair of elements having same mass number but different atomic number are called isobars.

Q.32 **Complete the table on the basis of information available in the symbols given below.**
(a) ${}^{35}_{17}Cl$ (b) ${}^{12}_{6}C$ (c) ${}^{81}_{35}Br$

Element	n_p	n_n

Thinking Process Atomic number is written on the lower left side of the symbol of element whereas mass number is written on the upper left side of the symbol of element.
Number of protons (n_p) = Atomic number of atoms and number of neutrons (n_n) = mass number – atomic number.

Ans.

	Element	n_p	n_n
(a)	${}^{35}_{17}Cl$	17	35 – 17 = 18
(b)	${}^{12}_{6}C$	6	12 – 6 = 6
(c)	${}^{81}_{35}Br$	35	81– 35 = 46

Q.33 **Helium atom has 2 electrons in its valence shell but its valency is not 2. Explain.**

Ans. Helium atom has only one shell (*K* shell) which can have maximum 2 electrons. Thus, its shell is already completely filled, called duplet. It can neither lose electrons nor gain electrons. Hence, its valency is 'zero'. It is called **noble gas** or **inert gas**.

Q.34 Fill in the blanks in the following statements.

(a) Rutherford's α-particle scattering experiment led to the discovery of the ....

(b) Isotopes have same .... but different ....

(c) Neon and chlorine have atomic numbers 10 and 17 respectively. Their valencies will be .... and .... respectively.

(d) The electronic configuration of silicon is .... and that of sulphur is ....

Ans. (a) nucleus.

(b) atomic number, mass number.

(c) zero, one.

$_{10}Ne$ – Electronic configuration 2, 8. Its outermost shell is completely filled. Hence, its valency is zero.

$_{17}Cl$ – Electronic configuration 2, 8, 7

It can complete its outermost shell by gaining 1 electron.

Hence, its valency = 1

(d) 2, 8, 4 and 2, 8, 6.

Q. 35 An element X has a mass number 4 and atomic number 2. Write the valency of this element.

Ans. Atomic number = 2

Hence, number of electrons = 2

Thus, the elements has only *K* shell containing 2 electrons *i.e.*, a complete duplet.

Hence, its valency = 0

The element X is $^{4}_{2}He$ (noble gas).

Long Answer Type Questions

Q. 36 Why do helium, neon and argon have a zero valency?

Ans. Helium (He), neon (Ne) and argon (Ar) have completely filled outermost shell,

i.e., $_2He \longrightarrow \begin{matrix} K \\ 2 \end{matrix}$ (duplet) $_{10}Ne \longrightarrow \begin{matrix} K & L \\ 2 & 8 \end{matrix}$ (octet)

$_{18}Ar \longrightarrow \begin{matrix} K & L & M \\ 2 & 8 & 8 \end{matrix}$ (octet)

Thus, they have stable electronic configuration. They neither lose electrons nor gain electrons. Hence, their valency is zero.

Q.37 The ratio of the radii of hydrogen atom and its nucleus is ~ 10^5. Assuming the atom and the nucleus to be spherical.

(a) What will be the ratio of their sizes ?

(b) If atom is represented by planet earth 'R_e' = 6.4×10^6 m, estimate the size of the nucleus.

Ans. (a) Atomic size is represented in terms of atomic radius,

$$\frac{r_H}{r_n} = 10^5 \qquad \text{[Given]}$$

Where, r_H is the radii of hydrogen atom and r_n is the radii of its nucleus.

As volume of sphere = $\frac{4}{3}\pi r^3$

Therefore, $V_H = \frac{4}{3}\pi r_H^3$ and $V_n = \frac{4}{3}\pi r_n^3$

(where, V_H = volume of H- atom V_n = volume of its nucleus)

Thus, the ratio of volumes or the ratio of size of atom to that of nucleus is:

$$\frac{V_H}{V_n} = \frac{\frac{4}{3}\pi r_H^3}{\frac{4}{3}\pi r_n^3} = \frac{r_H^3}{r_n^3} = \left(\frac{r_H}{r_n}\right)^3 = (10^5)^3 = 10^{15}$$

$$\frac{V_n}{V_H} = 10^{-15} \text{ or } V_n = 10^{-15} \times V_H$$

(b) If atom is represented by planet earth with $R_e = 6.4 \times 10^6$ m

Then, radius of the nucleus (r_n) is:

$$\frac{R_e}{r_n} = 10^5$$

$$r_n = \frac{R_e}{10^5} = \frac{6.4 \times 10^6 \text{ m}}{10^5}$$

$$r_n = 64 \text{ m}$$

Therefore, the size of the nucleus is 64 m.

Q.38 Enlist the conclusions drawn by Rutherford from his α-ray scattering experiment.

Ans. Conclusions of Rutherford's α-rays scattering experiment:

(i) Most of the space inside the atom is empty because most of the α-particles passed through the gold foil without getting deflected.

(ii) Very few particles were deflected from their path, indicating that the positive charge of the atom occupies very little space.

(iii) A very small fraction of α-particles were deflected by 180°, indicating that all the positive charge and mass of the gold atom were concentrated in very small volume within the atom.

From the data he also calculated that the radius of the nucleus is about 10^5 times less than the radius of the atom.

Q.39 In what way is the Rutherford's atomic model different from that of Thomson's atomic model?

Ans. According to Thomson's model, an atom is a positively charged sphere in which electrons were embedded which neutralise the positive charge so that, the atom as a whole is electrically neutral.

According to Rutherford's model of atom, the positive charge and mass of the atom are concentrated in the small nucleus in the centre of the atom and negatively charged electrons are distributed around the nucleus, *i.e.*, they revolve around the nucleus in circular paths.

Q.40 What were the drawbacks of Rutherford's model of an atom?

Ans. Rutherford's model could not explain the stability of the atom. This is because according to Rutherford's model, an atom consists of a small, heavy positively charged nucleus in the centre and the electrons were revolving around it.

These revolving electrons would loose energy as they are the charged particles and due to acceleration, charged particles would radiate energy.

Thus, the orbit of the revolving electron will keep on becoming smaller and smaller, following a spiral path as shown in figure and ultimately the electron should fall into the nucleus. In other words, the atom should collapse.

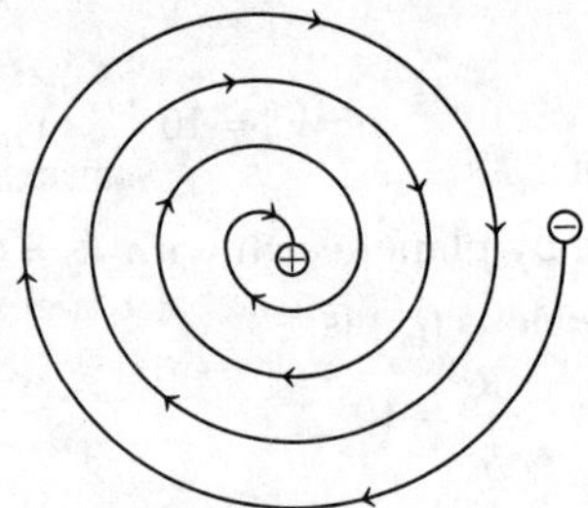

Continuous loss of energy by a revolving electron

Q.41 What are the postulates of Bohr's model of an atom?

Ans. The postulates of Bohr's model of atom are as follows:

(i) Only certain special orbits, called discrete orbits of electrons are allowed inside the atom.

(ii) These orbits are called energy levels. The orbits or shells are represented by letters *K*, *L*, *M*, *N*,...or the number $n = 1, 2, 3, 4,..$

(iii) While revolving in discrete orbits the electrons do not radiate energy.

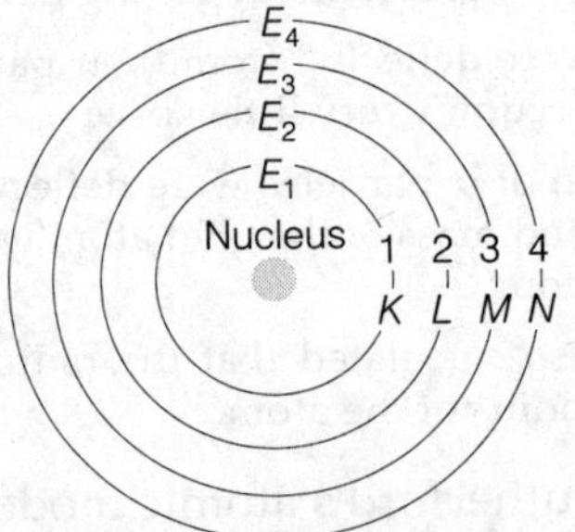

Circular orbits or energy levels or shells around the nucleus

Q.42 Show diagramatically the electron distributions in a sodium atom and a sodium ion and also give their atomic number.

Ans. Atomic number of sodium $(Z) = 11$

Mass number of sodium $(A) = 23$

$\therefore$ Number of protons in the nucleus = 11

Number of neutrons in the nucleus = 23 – 11 = 12

Number of electrons = 11

$\therefore$ Electronic configuration of Na atom = $\underset{2}{K}\ \underset{8}{L}\ \underset{1}{M}$

Na^+ ion is formed from sodium atom by loss of an electron (present in the outermost shell). Hence, its electronic configuration is $\underset{2}{K}\ \underset{8}{L}$.

However, number of protons and neutrons remains the same.

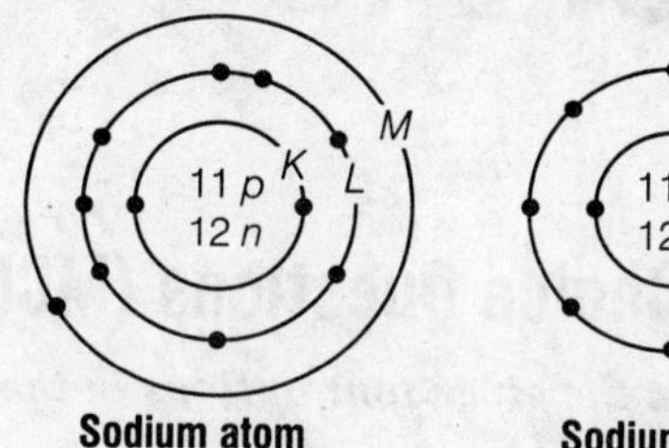

Sodium atom **Sodium ion**

Q.43 In the gold foil experiment of Geiger and Marsden, that paved the way for Rutherford's model of an atom, ~ 1.00% of the α-particles were found to deflect at angles $\geq 50°$. If one mole of α-particles were bombarded on the gold foil, compute the number of α-particles that would deflect at angles less than 50°.

- **Concept Insight** Mole concept is used in the question to calculate the number of particles that deflected at the angles less than 50°.

Ans. Total number of α-particles used for bombardment = 1 mole = 6.022×10^{23} particles.
Number of α-particles deflected at angles greater than or equal to $50°(\geq 50°) = 1\%$ (Given)

$\therefore$ Number of α-particles deflected at the angles less than $50° = 100 - 1 = 99\%$

$\therefore$ Actual number of α-particles deflected at the angles less than

$$50° = \frac{99}{100} \times 6.022 \times 10^{23}$$

$$= 5.96 \times 10^{23}$$

Chapter 05

The Fundamental Unit of Life

Multiple Choice Questions (MCQs)

Choose the correct answer from the given four options in the following questions :

Q.1 Which of the following can be made into crystal?

(a) A bacterium (b) An *Amoeba* (c) A virus (d) A sperm

Ans. ***(c)*** Viruses are considered non-living because they cannot perform life processes on their own. They consist of a protein coat (capsid) and genetic material (DNA or RNA), without the complex structure of living cells. Because of their simple structure, viruses can be purified and turned into crystals, helping scientists to study their details. This process has been crucial in understanding viruses, such as the tobacco mosaic virus, which was the first to be crystallised in the 1930s.

Q. 2 A cell will swell up if

(a) the concentration of water molecules in the cell is higher than the concentration of water molecules in surrounding medium

(b) the concentration of water molecules in surrounding medium is higher than water molecules concentration in the cell

(c) the concentration of water molecules is same in the cell and in the surrounding medium

(d) concentration of water molecules does not matter

Ans. ***(b)*** A cell swells due to osmosis, where water moves from a region of higher water concentration to lower water concentration. In a hypotonic solution, the surrounding medium has more water molecules than inside the cell, causing water to enter the cell and make it swell.

Q. 3 Chromosomes are made up of

(a) DNA

(b) protein

(c) DNA and protein

(d) RNA

Ans. ***(c)*** Chromosomes are thin, thread-like structures usually present in the nucleus which becomes visible during cell division. Each chromosome is made up of two main components *i.e.,*

(i) Deoxyribonucleic acid (DNA)

(ii) Proteins (*e.g.,* histones and acidic proteins)

Q. 4 Which of these options are not a function of ribosomes?

I. It helps in manufacture of protein molecules.
II. It helps in manufacture of enzymes.
III. In helps in manufacture of hormones.
IV. In helps in manufacture of starch molecules.

(a) I and II (b) II and III (c) III and IV (d) IV and I

Ans. *(c)* Ribosomes are responsible for synthesising proteins, including **enzymes** and **hormones** that are protein-based. However, not all hormones are proteins. Some hormones, like steroid hormones, are synthesised from lipids, not proteins, and are not made by ribosomes. Ribosomes do not play a role in the synthesis of starch, which is a carbohydrate.

Q. 5 Which of these is not related to endoplasmic reticulum?

(a) It behaves as transport channel for proteins between nucleus and cytoplasm
(b) It transports materials between various regions in cytoplasm
(c) It can be the site of energy generation
(d) It can be the site for some biochemical activities of the cell

Ans. *(c)* The **endoplasmic reticulum (ER)** is primarily involved in the synthesis, folding, modification, and transport of proteins and lipids. While it plays a role in various biochemical activities within the cell, such as lipid synthesis and protein processing, it is not a site for energy generation. Energy generation in cells occurs mainly in the mitochondria, not the ER.

Q. 6 Following are a few definitions of osmosis.
Read carefully and select the correct definition.

(a) Movement of water molecules a from a region of higher concentration to a region of lower concentration through a semipermeable membrane.
(b) Movement of solvent molecules from its higher concentration to lower concentration.
(c) Movement of solvent molecules from higher concentration to lower concentration of solution through a permeable membrane.
(d) Movement of solute molecules from lower concentration to higher concentration of solution through a semipermeable membrane.

Ans. *(a)* The movement of water molecules through selectively permeable membrane along concentration gradient is called osmosis.
It is the passage of water from a region of higher water concentration through semipermeable membrane to a region of lower water concentration (only through semi-permeable membrane).

Unicellular freshwater organisms and most plant cells tend to gain water through osmosis. Absorption of water by roots of the plants is also an example of osmosis.

Mistake Alert ! *Students should not get confused between the terms diffusion and osmosis. They should carefully learn the difference in their definitions and processes.*

Q. 7 Plasmolysis in a plant cell is defined as

(a) break down (lysis) of plasma membrane in hypotonic medium
(b) shrinkage of cytoplasm in hypertonic medium
(c) shrinkage of nucleoplasm
(d) None of the above

Ans. ***(b)*** Plasmolysis occurs when a plant cell is placed in a hypertonic solution, which has higher concentration of solutes than the fluid inside the cell.
Although, water molecules pass the cell membrane in both direction but more amount of water goes out of the cell than the amount of water which enters it. As a result of this the cell shrinks. This process is called exosmosis. If exosmosis continues in a plant cell, the cytoplasm appears to be shrunken. This is called plasmolysis and the cell is said to be plasmolysed.

Q. 8 Which of the following are covered by a single membrane?
(a) Mitochondria (b) Vacuole (c) Lysosome (d) Plastid

Ans. Both (b) and (c) are correct. Lysosomes are simple, tiny, spherical and sac-like structures that are evenly distributed in the cytoplasm. Each lysosome is surrounded by a single membrane and contains powerful enzymes capable of digesting or breaking down organic material. These enzymes are made by rough endoplasmic reticulum. Vacuoles are storage sacs for solid or liquid contents. They are also surrounded by a single membrane.

Q. 9 Find out the false sentences.
(a) Golgi apparatus is involved with the formation of lysosomes.
(b) Nucleus, mitochondria and plastid have DNA; hence they are able to make their own structural proteins.
(c) Mitochondria is said to be the power house of the cell as ATP is generated in them.
(d) Cytoplasm is called as protoplasm.

Ans. ***(d)*** Protoplasm refers to the living contents of a cell, including both the cytoplasm and the nucleus, whereas the term cytoplasm specifically refers to the material inside the cell, excluding the nucleus. Therefore, cytoplasm is not the same as protoplasm.

Mistake Alert! *Students should know that difference between the terms protoplasm and cytoplasm as this is a point of confusion always.*

Q.10 Find out the correct sentence
(a) Enzymes packed in lysosomes are made through RER (Rough Endoplasmic Reticulum)
(b) Rough endoplasmic reticulum and smooth endoplasmic reticulum produce lipid and protein respectively
(c) Endoplasmic reticulum is related with the destruction of plasma membrane
(d) Nucleoid is present inside the uncleoplasm of eukaryotic nucleus

Ans. ***(a)*** RER has ribosome present on its surface which are responsible for the synthesis of proteins and these proteins can include enzymes. Hence, the correct answer is option a.

Q. 11 Which cell organelle plays a crucial role in detoxifying many poisons and drugs in a cell?
(a) Golgi apparatus (b) Lysosomes
(c) Smooth endoplasmic reticulum (d) Vacuoles

Ans. ***(c)*** Smooth Endoplasmic Reticulum (SER) in liver cells of vertebrates helps in detoxification. It metabolises various toxic or poisonous substances such as drugs, aspirin, insecticides (DDT), petroleum products and pollutants.

Q. 12 The proteins and lipids, essential for building the cell membrane, are manufactured by
(a) endoplasmic reticulum
(b) Golgi apparatus
(c) plasma membrane
(d) mitochondria

Ans. *(a)* The rough endoplasmic reticulum (RER) is responsible for synthesising proteins. It has ribosomes attached to its surface, which are responsible for protein synthesis. Additionally, the smooth endoplasmic reticulum (SER), which lacks ribosomes, is involved in lipid synthesis.

Q. 13 The undefined nuclear region of prokaryotes are also known as
(a) nucleus
(b) nucleolus
(c) nucleic acid
(d) nucleoid

Ans. *(d)* In prokaryotic (like bacteria), the nucleoid is the region where the genetic material (DNA) is located. Unlike eukaryotic cells, prokaryotes do not have a defined nucleus, so their genetic material is not enclosed within a membrane. The nucleoid is an irregularly shaped area in the cell where the DNA is concentrated.

Q. 14 The cell organelle involved in forming complex sugars from simple sugars are
(a) endoplasmic reticulum
(b) ribosomes
(c) plastids
(d) Golgi apparatus

Ans. *(d)* The Golgi apparatus (also known as the Golgi body) plays an important role in modifying, sorting, and packaging proteins and lipids. It is also involved in carbohydrate metabolism, where it helps in forming complex sugars by modifying simple sugars.

Q. 15 Which out of the following is not a function of vacuole?
(a) Storage
(b) Providing turgidity and rigidity to the cell
(c) Waste excretion
(d) Locomotion

Ans. *(d)* Vacuoles may be small or large are filled with the liquid or sap. They are membrane-bound organelles and in some cases, they can occupy upto 90% of the cell's volume.

They may either be contractile (can contract) or non-contractile in nature.

The main functions of vacuoles include

1. **Storage** Vacuoles store various substances, including water, nutrients and waste products.
2. **Turgidity and Rigidity** In plant cells, the vacuoles help maintain turgor pressure, which keeps the cell rigid.
3. **Waste excretion** They also store and help in the excretion of waste products in the cell.

However, vacuoles do not play a role in locomotion.

Q. 16 *Amoeba* acquires its food through a process, termed

(a) exocytosis (b) endocytosis
(c) plasmolysis (d) Both exocytosis and endocytosis both

Ans. ***(b)*** Endocytosis is the process of ingestion of material by the cells through their plasma membrane. It is a collective term that describes three similar processes **phagocytosis** (cell eating), **pinocytosis** (cell drinking) and receptor-mediated endocytosis.

These processes are the pathways to specifically internalise solid particles, small molecules, ion and the macromolecules, respectively. All of them require energy, so they may be regarded as different forms of active transport.

Out of these phagocytosis is the common method of feeding among the Protozoa (*e.g.*, *Amoeba*) and lower Metazoa (*e.g.*, sponges). In *Amoeba,* the food particle is surrounded and engulf by the pseudopodia.

Q. 17 The cell wall of which out of these is not made up of cellulose ?

(a) Bacteria (b) *Hydrilla* (c) Mango tree (d) Cactus

Ans. ***(a)*** Plant cells, in addition to the plasma membrane, have another rigid outer covering called the cell wall. The cell wall lies outside the plasma membrane. The plant cell wall is mainly composed of cellulose, a complex substance that provides structural strength to plants. Out of the options given bacteria is not a plant, its cell wall is made up of peptidoglycan and not cellulose.

Q. 18 Silver nitrate solution is used to study

(a) endoplasmic reticulum (b) Golgi apparatus
(c) nucleus (d) mitochondria

Ans. ***(b)*** Camillo Golgi (1898), discovered the revolutionarily method of staining individual nerve cell and other cell structures by using weak solution of silver nitrate. This method is also called as **black reaction.** He also discovered golgi apparatus while he was examining the nerve cells of barn owl. Since, that time the solution of silver nitrate used to stain golgi apparatus. It is also valuable in tracing the processes and most delicate ramifications of cells.

Q. 19 Organelle other than nucleus, containing DNA is

(a) endoplasmic reticulum (b) Golgi apparatus
(c) mitochondria (d) lysosome

Ans. ***(c)*** Other than nucleus, mitochondria contains its own DNA and are able to synthesise their own proteins. Hence, they are regarded as semi-autonomous organelles.

Q. 20 Kitchen of the cell is

(a) mitochondria (b) endoplasmic reticulum
(c) chloroplast (d) Golgi apparatus

Ans. ***(c)*** **Chloroplasts are the green coloured plastids found in green algae and higher plants. They have a green pigment called chlorophyll and are involved in the photosynthesis of food. Therefore regarded as the 'kitchens of the cells'. Each chloroplast is bounded by two membranes (like the mitochondria).**
The chloroplasts contains their own DNA and ribosomes.

Q. 21 Lipid molecules in the cell are synthesised by

(a) smooth endoplasmic reticulum
(b) rough endoplasmic reticulum
(c) Golgi apparatus
(d) plastids

Ans. ***(a)*** Lipid molecules in the cell are synthesised by the smooth endoplasmic reticulum present in the cell. (*Also, refer to Q.* 12)

Q. 22 Cell arises from pre-existing cell was stated by

(a) Haeckel
(b) Virchow
(c) Hooke
(d) Schleiden

Ans. ***(b)*** In 1838 **Schleiden** proposed the idea that plants consist of cells. Later, in the year 1839, **Schwann** independently asserted that all animals are made up of cells. This joint finding forms the basis of cell theory.
The cell theory was refined further in 1855, when R. Virchow presented the idea that all cells arise from pre-existing cell. His amorphism was (*Omnis Cellula-e-Cellula).*

Q. 23 Cell theory was given by

(a) Schleiden and Schwann
(b) Virchow
(c) Hooke
(d) Haeckel

Ans. ***(a)*** The cell theory, that all the plant and animals are composed of cells and that the cell is the basic unit of life was presented by **Schleiden** (1838) and **Schwann** in the year (1839). The theory was later extended by **R.Virchow** (1855) with the concept that all cells arise from pe-existing cells. The main postulates of cell theory are

(i) All organisms are composed of cells and cell products.
(ii) All metabolic reactions take place in cells.
(iii) Cell are structural and functional units of life.
(iv) New cell arises from pre-existing cells only. No cell can originate spontaneously but they comes into being only by division of pre-existing cells.

Q.24 The only cell organelle seen in prokaryotic cell is
(a) mitochondria (b) ribosomes (c) plastids (d) lysosomes

Ans. ***(b)*** Unlike eukaryotic cell, a prokaryotic cell lacks membrane-bound organelles like plastids, mitochondria and endoplasmic reticulum However, they do contain, ribosomes which are not surrounded by the membrane, therefore, the small and randomly scattered ribosomes are seen in prokaryotic cells.

Q. 25 Organelle without a cell membrane is
(a) ribosome (b) Golgi apparatus (c) chloroplast (d) nucleus

Ans. ***(a)*** Ribosomes are ribonucleoprotein particles that are not surrounded by any membranes. They can either be freely suspended or remain attached to the surface of the ER. The other options are incorrect and can be corrected as.

Golgi apparatus is a set of membrane-bounded, fluid filled vesicles, vacuoles and flattened cisternae. Plastids are also membrane bound organelle. Nucleus is surrounded by double nuclear membranes both forming a nuclear envelope.

Q. 26 1 μm is
(a) 10^{-6} m (b) 10^{-9} m (c) 10^{-10} m (d) 10^{-3} m

Ans. ***(a)*** The micrometre commonly known as micron. It is standard unit of length equalling to 10^{-6} of a metre used in the field of microscopy.

Q.27 Lysosome arises from
(a) endoplasmic reticulum (b) Golgi apparatus
(c) nucleus (d) mitochondria

Ans. ***(b)*** The Golgi apparatus is involved in formation of lysosome.

Q.28 Living cells were discovered by
(a) Robert Hooke (b) Purkinje (c) Leeuwenhoek (d) Robert Brown

Ans. ***(c)*** Robert Hooke in 1665, first discovered cells. He observed the cells in a slice of a cork with the help of his primitive microscope. But he observed dead cork cell. On the other hand Anton Van Leeuwenhoek, a Dutch biologist in the year 1670, discovered the living cell when he looked at the pond water under the microscope, he made for the first time.

Q. 29 Select the odd one out
(a) The movement of water across a semi permeable membrane is affected by the amount of substances dissolved in it.
(b) Membranes are made of organic molecules like proteins and lipids
(c) Molecules soluble in organic solvents can easily pass through the membrane.
(d) Plasma membranes contain chitin sugar in plants.

Ans. ***(d)*** Each cell is bounded by an extremely delicate, thin and elastic living membrane, called the plasma membrane. The plasma membrane is made up of two layers of lipid (fat) molecules (20-79%) and protein molecules (20-70%) which is sandwiched between the lipid found either layer. It also contains carbohydrates (1 – 5%) and water (20%)
Plasma membrane does not contain chitin sugar. The structure of plasma membrane can be observed under an electron microscope only. It is a selectively permeable membrane which allows the flow of only some substances into the cell and out of the cell.

Short Answers Type Questions

Q.30 Why are lysosomes known as suicidal-bags of a cell?

Ans. Lysosomes are known as suicidal bags (or digestive bags) of cells. This is because during the breakdown of cell structure, when the cells gets damaged or due to any disturbance in the cellular metabolism, the lysosomes may burst releasing the enzymes, which are capable of digesting or breaking down organic nutrients within the cell.

Due to their ability to break down various substances digest or degrade other cell organelles leading to hampered metabolic activities and finally death of the cell.

Q.31 Do you agree that 'A cell is a building unit of on organism'. If yes, explain why?

Ans. Yes, A cell is a structural, functional and smallest unit of life which is capable of performing all living functions. A cell is composed of various organelles which perform different functions.

The number of cells varies from organism to organism. For example *Ameoba* is a single celled or unicellular structure, where all basic functions are performed in one cell only.

On the contrary, humans are multicellular having as many as 60×10^{15} cell (weight about 60 kg). In a multicellular organism, cell form tissues, which combine form organs and different functions are performed by different organs *i.e.*, they have well-developed division of labour.

Q. 32 Why does the skin of your finger shrink when you wash clothes for a long time?

Ans. Soap solution is a hypertonic solution. When the cell is immersed in a hypertonic solution, water diffuses out of the cells by osmosis (diffusion of water across semipermeable membrane), due to lower concentration of water outside the cell. As a result, the cell shrinks. This process is called exosmosis. During washing of clothes, exosmosis takes place in the skin cells. This leads to the shrinkage of skin over the fingers while washing clothes for a long time.

Q.33 Why is endocytosis found in animals only?

Ans. Endocytosis refers to the invagination of a small region of plasma membrane, forming an intracellular membrane-bound vesicle. It has been observed in many kinds of animal cells, where the plasma membrane is in direct contact with the external medium. Endocytosis is not shown by plant cells because a rigid cell wall is present over the plasma membrane in them. Thus, this process is found in animals only.

Q.34 A person takes concentrated solution of salt, after sometime, he starts vomiting. What is the phenomenon responsible for such situation? Explain.

Ans. Concentrated salt solution is a hypertonic solution (water concentration lower as compared to the cell) therefore, it causes exosmosis in stomach cells. Where outward movement of water from the cell results in irritation and excessive dehydration. This results in reverse movements and the body responds by inducing vomiting to expel the harmful substance.

Q. 35 Name any cell organelle which is non-membranous.

Ans. A non-membranous cell organelle is ribosome. The ribosomes are small, round bodies found either in the free state in the cytoplasm or attached to the surface of the endoplasmic reticulum ER. They are composed of ribonucleoprotein (ribonucleic acid and protein).

The main function of ribosomes is to serve as a platform for the synthesis of proteins.

Q.36 We eat food composed of all the nutrients like carbohydrates, proteins, fats, vitamins, minerals and water. After digestion, these are absorbed in the form of glucose, amino acids, fatty acids, glycerol, etc. What mechanisms are involved in absorption of digested food and water?

Ans. Absorption of nutrients from the alimentary canal (mainly small intestine) into the blood and lymph involved two main processes diffusion and osmosis.

(i) **Digested food**- absorb through **diffusion**, *i.e.*, the process in which the molecules move from their region of higher concentration to their region of lower concentration till they are uniformly distributed throughout the available space.

(ii) **Water**-absorb through **osmosis**, *i.e.*, the passage of water from a region of high water concentration through a semi-permeable membrane to a region of low water concentration.

Q.37 If you are provided with some vegetables to cook. You generally add salt into the vegetables during cooking process. After adding salt, vegetables release water. What mechanism is responsible for this?

Ans. On adding salt, the external medium is made hypertonic, *i.e.*, concentration of water is lowered as compared to the concentration of water inside the cell. Thus, water is released from the vegetables due to **exosmosis** (water molecules goes out of the cell resulting in shrinkage of cell).

Q.38 If cells of onion peel and RBC are separately kept in hypotonic solution, what among the following will take place? Explain the reason for your.

(a) Both the cells will swell.

(b) RBC will burst easily while cells of onion peel will resist the bursting to some extent.

(c) Both (a) and (b) are correct.

(d) RBC and onion peel cells will behave similarly.

Ans. ***(b)*** Cell of onion peel are surrounded by a cell wall whereas the RBC's (red blood cells) do not have cell wall. When the cell of onion peel and RBC's are separately kept in a hypotonic solution. RBCs will first swell up and then burst due to endosmosis. However, cell wall in the cells of onion peel exerts a counter wall pressure when the cells became fully turgid.

This stops further entry of water into the cells and thus, the cells do not burst.

Q.39 Bacteria do not have chloroplast, but some bacteria are photoautotrophic in nature and perform photosynthesis. Which part of bacterial cell performs this?

Ans. In bacteria photosynthesis occurs in specialised thylakoid membranes or photosynthetic membranes within the cells, pigment like bacterio-chlorophyll capture light energy. In photosynthetic bacteria, like cyanobacteria or purple sulfur bacteria, these thylakoids are often part of the cell membrane.

Q.40 Match the following columns

	Column I		Column II
A.	Smooth endoplasmic reticulum	1.	*Amoeba*
B.	Lysosome	2.	Nucleus
C.	Nucleoid	3.	Bacteria
D.	Food vacuoles	4.	Detoxification
E.	Chromatin material and nucleolus	5.	Suicidal bag

Ans. The correct matching is **A.** → (4) **B.** → (5) **C.** → (3) **D.** → (1) **E.** → (2)
One of the special function of smooth endoplasmic reticulum of liver in vertebrate is detoxification.

Lysosomes are called the suicidal bags of cell as they digest the organelles of their own cell. Nucleoid is the undifferentiated nuclear region of a prokaryotic cell like bacteria. Food vacuoles are present in *Amoeba* to store the food trapped by endocytosis. Nucleus is composed of nuclear membrane, nucleoplasm, nucleolus and chromatin material.

Q.41 Write the name of different plant parts in which chromoplast, chloroplast and leucoplast are present.

Ans. Plastids occur in most plant cells, but are absent in animal cells. Like mitochondria, plastids also have their own genome (*i.e.*, DNA) and ribosomes. They are self-replicating organelles like the mitochondria, *i.e.*, they have the power to divide. Plastids are of following three types

(i) **Chromoplasts** Coloured plastids (except green colour). They add colour to flowers and fruits, for attracting animals to perform pollination and fruit dispersal.

(ii) **Chloroplasts** Green-coloured plastids. These are the sites of photosynthesis and are present in the leaves of the plant.

(iii) **Leucoplasts** The colourless plastids. Leucoplasts takes part in storage of food and found in various parts such as roots and seeds.

Q.42 Name the organelles which show the analogy written as under
(a) Transporting channels of the cell
(b) Power house of the cell
(c) Packaging and dispatching unit of the cell
(d) Digestive bag of the cell
(e) Storages sacs of the cell
(f) Kitchen of the cell
(g) Control room of the cell

Ans. (a) **Endoplasmic reticulum** is the transporting channel of the cell as it connects the cell membrane to the nuclear membrane and helps in the transportation of proteins and other molecular.

(b) **Mitochondria** are called the power house of the cell because, they generate energy in the form of ATP (Adenosine Triphosphate). Which power various cellular activities.

(c) **Packaging** and dispatching unit of the cell is **golgi complex** as they store, modify, package and condense the proteins synthesised by ribosomes.

(d) **Lysosomes** are known as the digestive bags of the cell due to the presence of enzymes in them which are capable of degrading any organic material.

(e) **Vacuoles** are termed as storage sacs of the cell as they store the food, water and waste products.

(f) **Chloroplast** are termed as kitchen of cell due to their function of performing photosynthesis.

(g) **Nucleus** is the control room of the cell as it regulates almost all the activities of the cell.

Q. 43 How is bacterial cell different from onion peel cell?

Thinking Process Prokaryotic cell differs from eukaryotic cell while onion peel possess eukaryotic cell.

Ans. The bacteria is a prokaryote whereas onion peel is plant cell i.e., a eukaryotic. The major differences between bacterial cell (prokaryotic) and onion peel (eukaryotic) are tabulated below

Bacterial cell	Onion peel
1. Size of a cell is generally small (1-10 mm).	1. Size of a cell is generally large (5-100 mm).
2. Nucleus is absent (nuclear region or nucleoid is not surrounded by a nuclear membrane.)	2. Nucleus is present (nuclear material is surrounded by a nuclear membrane).
3. It contains a single chromosome.	3. It contains more than one chromosome.
4. Nucleolus is absent	4. Nucleolus is present.
5. Membrane bound cell organelles are absent.	5. Membrane bound cell organelles such as mitochondria, plastids, endoplasmic reticulum, Golgi apparatus, lysosomes, peroxisomes, etc., are present.
6. Cell division takes place by fission (no mitosis).	6. Cell division occurs by mitotic or meiotic cell division.

Q.44 How do substances like carbon dioxide (CO_2) and water (H_2O) move in and out of the cell?

Ans. When carbon dioxide (CO_2) accumulates in high concentration inside the cell, diffusion occurs. The CO_2 moves out of the cell from the region of higher concentration to a region of lower concentration.

When a cell is placed in a solution with a different solute concentration, the water tends to move either in or out of the cell according to its concentration gradient by the process of osmosis.

Q.45 How does *Amoeba* obtain its food?

Ans. *Amoeba* obtain its food by the process of **phagocytosis.** It is a common method of feeding among the protozoa and lower metazoa. *Amoeba* obtain its food by process of endocytosis, which is an invagination of small region of the plasma membrane to engulf the food particle and ultimately forming an intra cellular membrane bound vesicle.

On the basis of the type of food material, endocytosis may be

(i) Phagocytosis- intake of solid material

(ii) pinocytosis - intake of liquid material

(Also, refer to Q. 16)

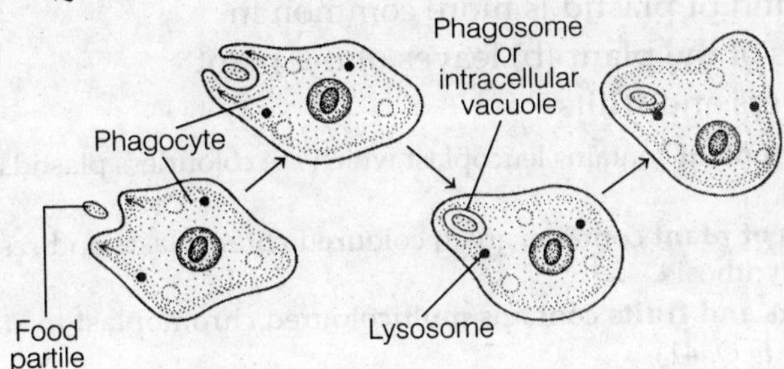

Q.46 Name the two organelles in a plant cell that contain their own genetic material and ribosome.

Ans. Mitochondria and plastids are the two cell organelles that have their own DNA and ribosome and hence, can synthesise their own protein and genetic material.

Q.47 Why are lysosomes also known as scavengers of the cells?

Ans. Lysosomes contain hydrolyic enzymes that are synthesised by endoplasmic reticulum. These enzymes removes the worn-out and malfunctioning cell organelles by digesting them so that, new cell replacements can be made. They also removes the cell debris therefore, known as **scavenger, cellular house keepers** and **demolition squads of the cell.**

Q.48 Which cell organelle controls most of the activities of the cell?

Ans. The **nucleus** is the organelle that controls most of the activities of the cell. The nucleus is a large, centrally located spherical cellular component. It is bounded by two nuclear membranes, both forming a **nuclear envelope.** The space between two nuclear membranes is called the perinuclear space and is connected to the ER (Endoplasmic Reticulum).

It possesses nucleolus, nuclear pore, chromation and nucleoplasm.

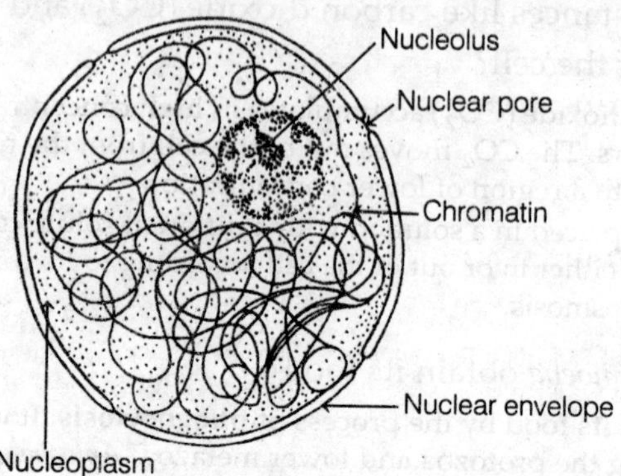

Nucleus plays some important functions as listed below

1. The nucleus controls all metabolic activities of the cell. If the nucleus is removed from a cell, the protoplasm ultimately dries up and dies.
2. It regulates the cell cycle and cell division.
3. It is concerned with the transmission of hereditary traits form the parent to offspring.

Q.49 Which kind of plastid is more common in
(a) roots of the plant (b) leaves of the plant
(c) flowers and fruits

Ans. (a) **Roots of plant** contains leucoplast which are colourless plastids and act as storage of food.

(b) **Leaves of plant** contains green coloured chloroplasts and responsible for photosynthesis

(c) **Flowers and fruits** contains multicoloured chromoplast to attract pollinators.

(Also, refer to Q. 41)

Q.50 Why do plant cells possess large sized vacuole?

Thinking Process Vacuole store food and water and act as on reservoir for the cell.

Ans. Plant cells are known to have bigger vacuoles than that of animal cells as they need to store food and water. This is because the plant don't possess the ability to move freely like that of animals. Thus, they possess large vacuoles as a reservoir in unfavourable conditions.

Q.51 How are chromatin, chromatid and chromosomes related to each other?

Ans. Inside the nucleoplasm, a tangled mass of thread-like structures is found known as chromatin. They are formed of Deoxyribonucleic Acid (DNA) and proteins.

When a cell starts to divide, the tangled mass of chromatin condense into long threads and finally, forms genetic rod-like bodies called chromosomes. The chromosomes contain stretches of DNA which carry genetic information for protein synthesis.

Chromatid
Centromere
Kinetochore
Chromatid

A gene is called the hereditary unit and DNA is called the hereditary material.

A chromatid is one copy of duplicated chromosome which is generally joined to the other copy by a centromere.

Q.52 What are the consequences of the following conditions?

(a) A cell containing higher water concentration than the surrounding medium

(b) A cell having low water concentration than the surrounding medium.

(c) A cell having equal water concentration to its surrounding medium.

Thinking Process This question is based on the concept of osmosis. Osmosis is the movement of water molecules from a region of higher concentration to region of lower concentration.

Ans. (a) When a cell possess higher water concentration than the surrounding medium then **exosmosis** occurs in the cell due to the difference in water concentration in the cell and surrounding medium and cells shrinks.

(b) When a cell has lower water concentration than surrounding medium then, **endosmosis** occurs leading to the swelling of the cell.

(c) A cell having an equal concentration to its surrounding medium will not show any changes as isotonic conditions persist in the solvent.

Long Answer Type Questions

Q.53 Draw a plant cell and label the parts which

(a) determines the function and development of the cell.

(b) packages materials coming from the endoplasmic reticulum.

(c) provides resistance to microbes to withstand hypotonic external media without bursting.

(d) is site for many biochemical reactions necessary to sustain life.

(e) is a fluid contained inside the nucleus.

Ans. A plant cell and its parts are given below

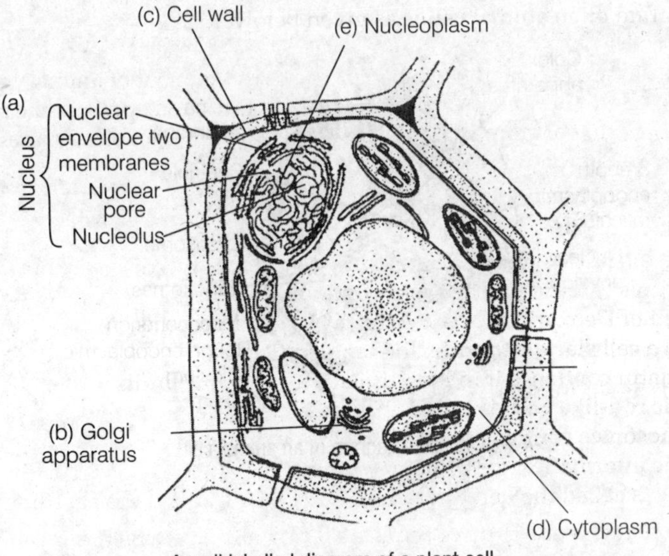

A well labelled diagram of a plant cell

Q.54 Illustrate only a plant cell as seen under electron microscope. How is it different from animal cell?

Ans. A plant cell as seen under electron microscope

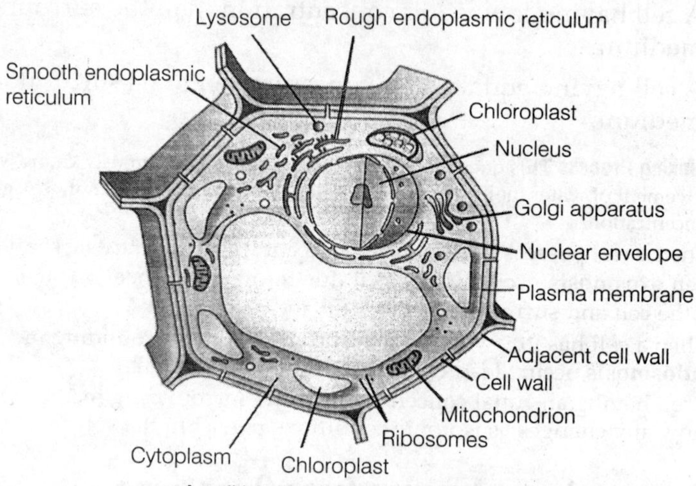

A well labelled diagram of a plant cell

Major differences between a plant cell and an animal cell are

(i) **Presence of chloroplasts** in plant cells chloroplasts are responsible for photosynthesis in plants, which animal cells lack.

(ii) **Presence of a large central vacuole** in plant cells the central vacuoles stores water and helps maintain cell turgidity, a feature generally absent in animal cells.

(iii) **Presence of cell wall** in plant cells The cell wall provides structural support and protection to plant cells, while animal cells do not have a cell wall.

Q.55 Draw a neat labelled diagram of an animal cell.

Ans. A diagram of an animal cell is as given below

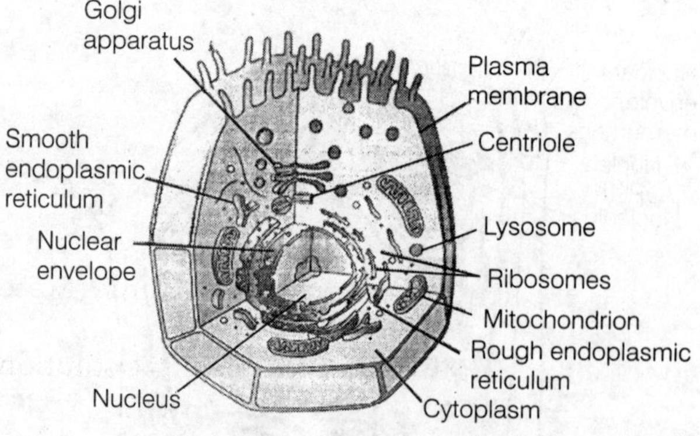

A well labelled diagram of an animal cell

Q.56 Draw a well labelled diagram of an eukaryotic nucleus. How is it different form nucleoid?

Thinking Process Nucleoid is a form of prokaryotic nucleus. It is the undifferentiated form of nucleus lying in the cytoplasm. It differs from eukaryotic nucleus in lacking many structures.

Ans.

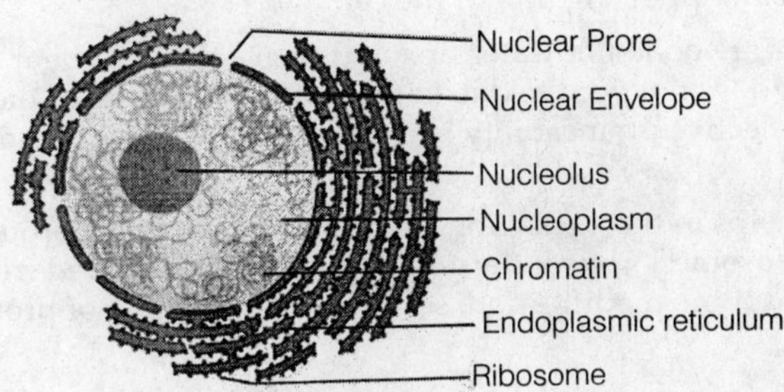

A well labelled diagram of eukaryotic nucleus

The major differences between eukaryotic and prokaryotic nucleus is that a prokaryotic nucleus (or nucleoid) is

(i) undifferentiated
(ii) not bounded by a nuclear membrane
(iii) does not possess nucleolus and nucleoplasm.

Q. 57 Differentiate between rough and smooth endoplasmic reticulum. How is endoplasmic reticulum important for membrane biogenesis?

Ans. The major differences between rough and smooth endoplasmic reticulum are

Smooth Endoplasmic Reticulum	Rough Endoplasmic Reticulum
Smooth Endoplasmic Reticulum has no ribosome on the surface, hence smooth in appearance	Rough Endoplasmic Reticulum has ribosome attached to the surface, therefore are rough in texture.
It helps in the manufacturing of lipids and fat molecules.	It acts as the sites of protein synthesis.

Endoplasmic reticulum synthesises lipids (*via* smooth endoplasmic reticulum) and proteins (*via* rough endoplasmic reticulum) which are responsible for the formation of membrane. Thus, they play a key role in membrane biogenesis.

Q. 58 In brief state what happens when

(a) Dry apricots are left for sometime in pure water and later transferred to sugar solution?
(b) A red blood cell is kept in concentrated saline solution?
(c) The plasma-membrane of a cell breaks down?
(d) Rheo leaves are boiled in water first and then a drop of sugar syrup is put on it?
(e) Golgi apparatus is removed from the cell?

Ans. (a) Dry apricots when placed in pure water swell due endosmosis (inward movement of water) and later when are transferred to a sugar solution exosmosis (outward movement of water) occurs and they shrink.

(b) When a Red Blood Cell is placed in concentrated saline solution exosmosis occurs and the RBCs shrink due to excess loss of water.

(c) Breaking of the plasma membrane leads to the scattering of the cell organelles as it forms the basic supporting unit of the cell.

(d) When Rheo leaves are boiled in water first and then a drop of sugar syrup is put on it, osmosis does not occurs, due to the death of the cells of the leaf. This shows that selective premeability is the property of living plasma membrane.

(e) Golgi apparatus helps in the packaging, storage and transfer of proteins synthesised by ribosomes. Thus if the golgi apparatus is removed from the cell, it would disrupt the modification, sorting and packaging of proteins and lipids.

Mistake Alert ! *Students should pay atttention to the concepts and logics behind the functions and phenomenon related to cell while preparing the topic.*

Q.59 Draw a neat diagram of plant cell and label any three parts which differentiate it from animal cell.

Ans.

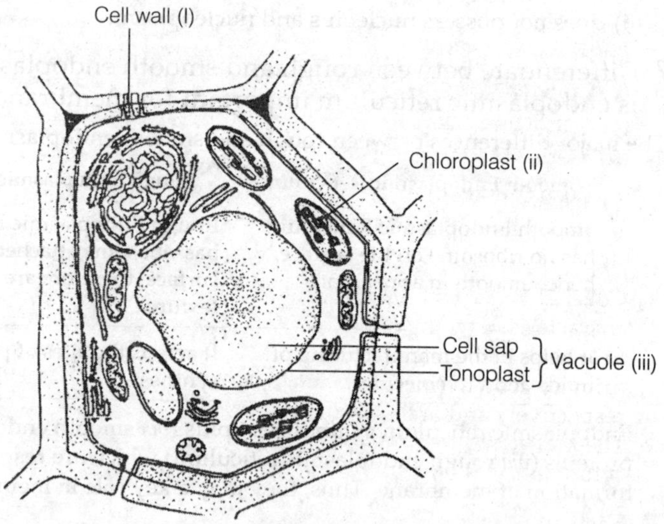

(i) Cell wall in the characteristic feature of plant cell. It provides structural support and protection.

(ii) Chloroplast is found in plant cell which helps in photosynthesis in plants. Animals cannot synthesise their own food because chloroplast is not found in the animal cell.

(iii) Large vacuoles are found in plant cell which store water and contains excretory waste of plant cell. Animal cell do not possess vacoules, if present these are of small size.

Chapter

06 Tissues

Multiple Choice Questions (MCQs)

Choose the correct answer from the given four options in the following questions :

Q. 1 Which of the following tissues has dead cells?

(a) Parenchyma
(b) Sclerenchyma
(c) Collenchyma
(d) Epithelial tissue

Ans. ***(b)*** **Sclerenchyma** cells are the simple permanent tissues present in the plants that comprised mainly of dead cells. The cells are long and narrow. They have lignified cell wall. They provide hardness and stiffness to the plant and are composed of dead cells. The sclerenchyma tissue is present in stems around vascular bundles in the veins of leaves and in hard covering of seeds and nuts, *e.g.*, the husk of coconut is made up of sclerenchymatous tissues.

Q. 2 Find out incorrect sentence.

(a) Parenchymatous tissues have intercellular spaces.
(b) Collenchymatous tissues are irregularly thickened at corners.
(c) Apical and intercalary meristems are permanent tissues.
(d) Meristematic tissues, in its early stage, lack vacuoles.

Thinking Process Apical and intercalary meristem as the name suggest cannot be a permanent tissue. They help in the growth of plants.

Ans. ***(c)*** Parenchyma tissues have large intercellular spaces which allow gas exchange. Collenchymatous tissues are mechanical tissues in the plants and are characterised by the deposition of cellulose at the corners of the cell, which leads to localised thickenings of the cell wall. Apical and intercalary meristem brings primary growth (increase in height) and secondary growth (increase in diameter) respectively and are classified under meristematic tissues, not permanent ones. The meristematic tissue are the dividing units of the plants that contains dense cytoplasm and large nucleus with few or no vacuoles at all.

Q. 3 Girth of stem increases due to

(a) apical meristem
(b) lateral meristem
(c) intercalary meristem
(d) vertical meristem

Ans. ***(b)*** Girth of the stem increases due to lateral meristematic tissues. They are found beneath the bark (called cork cambium) and in the vascular bundles of dicot roots and stems (called vascular cambium) as thin layers. This increase in the diameter and girth of the plant is called secondary growth.
The apical meristem is situated at the growing tip of stems and root. They bring about elongation, *i.e.*, increase in height (primary growth) of the plant. Intercalary meristem are located at base of leaf and internode and contribute to the growth inlength.

Q. 4 Which cell does not have perforated cell wall?

(a) Tracheids (b) Companion cells
(c) Sieve tubes (d) Vessels

Thinking Process Companion cells are associated with the sieve tubes and connected to them by numerous plasmodesmata. They help in maintaining pressure gradient in sieve tubes. These are not perforated.

Ans. *(b)* Tracheids and vessels are the xylem elements that are concerned with the transport of water. They are long tube-like structures with partially or completely dissolved walls to form water pipes (in vessels) and pits (in tracheids) for conducting water.

Sieve tubes are slender tube-like structures with their end walls perforated by numerous pores called sieve plates. They are phloem elements and are main food transporting elements. Companion cells are associated with sieve tubes and help maintain the pressure gradient within them, but they do not have perforated walls.

Q. 5 Intestine absorb the digested food materials. What type of epithelial cells are responsible for that?

(a) Stratified squamous epithelium (b) Columnar epithelium
(c) Spindle fibres (d) Cuboidal epithelium

Thinking Process Columnar epithelium are brush bordered as they contain microvilli. This increases the surface area, which is helpful for absorption processes.

Ans. *(b)* Columnar epithelium consists of pillar-like cells with their nuclei towards the base. They form the lining of stomach, small intestine and colon, forming the mucous membrane. Their main function is absorption (*e.g.*, stomach, intestine) and secretion (*e.g.*, mucous by goblet cells).

Stratified squamous epithelium, also known as pavement epithelium is covered by the help of a fibrous protein, (keratin) that covers the skin. This epithelium is waterproof and resistant to any mechanical injury. Cuboidal epithelium is found in the kidney tubules, thyroid follicles and in the glands while spindle fibres are structures involved in cell divisions, not absorption.

Q. 6 A person met with an accident in which two long bones of hand were dislocated. Which among the following may be the possible reason?

(a) Tendon break (b) Break of skeletal muscle
(c) Ligament break (d) Areolar tissue break

Thinking Process Tendons join skeletal muscles to bones and ligaments join bones to bones.

Ans. *(c)* Dislocation of joint occurs when there is an abnormal separation of bones , which are held together by ligament. A ligament is an elastic connective tissues that has great strength. Therefore, ligament break may result in the dislocation of bone.

Areolar tissues joins skin to muscles, fills spaces inside organs and are found around the muscles, blood vessels and nerves. Hence, are not concerned with bones.

Tendon break may cause inflammation and occurs due to factors including age, body weight, nutrition, sports, etc. but do not directly lead to dislocation.

Q. 7 While doing work and running, you move your organs like hands, legs, etc. Which among the following is correct?

(a) Smooth muscles contract and pull the ligament to move the bones
(b) Smooth muscles contract and pull the tendons to move the bones
(c) Skeletal muscles contract and pull the ligament to move the bones
(d) Skeletal muscles contract and pull the tendon to move the bones

Thinking Process Smooth muscles are involuntary, *i.e.*, they do not work according to our will. The ligament helps to connects bone to bone while, the tendons connects muscles to bones.

Ans. ***(d)*** Skeletal muscles are also called as striated muscles because these muscles show alternate light and dark bands or striations when stained appropriately. They are found in the body wall and the limbs (*i.e.*, both biceps and triceps of arms and legs). They are called voluntary muscles as they work according to our will. While doing work and running skeletal muscles contract and pull the tendon (which connects muscles to bones) to move the bone.

Q. 8 Which muscles act involuntarily?

(i) Striated muscles
(ii) Smooth muscles
(iii) Cardiac muscles
(iv) Skeletal muscles

(a) (i) and (ii)
(b) (ii) and (iii)
(c) (iii) and (iv)
(d) (i) and (iv)

Ans. ***(b)*** Smooth muscles are found in the walls of hollow visceral organs. They are involuntary (do not work according to our will). They are involved in peristaltic movements of gastro-intestinal tract and male genital tract. Cardiac muscles are present in the heart. They contract and relax rapidly, rhythmically and tirelessly. They help to pump the blood to various parts of the body. The working of both smooth and cardiac muscles is involuntary while skeletal or straited muscles move according to our will and are voluntary in action.

Q. 9 Meristematic tissues in plants are

(a) localised and permanent
(b) not limited to certain regions
(c) localised and dividing cells
(d) growing in volume

Ans. ***(c)*** Meristematic tissues consists of actively dividing cells and are present in the growing regions of plants, *e.g.*, the tips of roots and stems. The cells of meristematic tissue are round, oval, polygonal or rectangular. They are packed closely without intercellular spaces, have thin cellulose walls, dense cytoplasm and prominent nuclei. Vacuoles are almost absent in such cells because they are completely filled with sap.

Q.10 Which is not a function of epidermis?

(a) Protection from adverse condition
(b) Gaseous exchange
(c) Conduction of water
(d) Transpiration

Ans. ***(c)*** Epidermis is the outermost layer that covers the plant body such as leaves, flowers, stem and root. It is covered with cuticle (a waterproof a layer of waxy substance cutin).

The main function of epidermis is to protect the plant from desiccation, infection or any other plant injury. In fact, cuticle of epidermis helps to reduce the loss of water by evaporation from the plant surface and also helps in preventing the entry of pathogen (bacteria, fungi, etc.). Epidermis plays a role in transpiration, but does not conduct water, which is the function of vascular tissues like xylem.

Q.11 Select the incorrect sentence.

(a) Blood has matrix containing proteins, salts and hormones.

(b) Two bones are connected with ligament.

(c) Tendons are non-fibrous tissue and fragile.

(d) Cartilage is a form of connective tissue.

Ans. ***(c)*** Tendons are cord-like, strong, inelastic, structures that join skeletal muscles to bones. A tendon is a white fibrous tissue which has great strength but limited flexibility. It consists of parallel bundles of collagen fibres, between which rows of fibroblasts (called tendinocytes) are present.

Q.12 Cartilage is not found in

(a) nose (b) ear

(c) kidney (d) larynx

Ans. ***(c)*** Cartilage is a type of connective tissue that provides support and flexibility. It is found in several parts of the body, including the nose, ear, and larynx. In the nose, cartilage helps form its shape and structure, while in the ear, the external ear (pinna) is primarily made of cartilage. The larynx also contains cartilage, such as the thyroid cartilage, which is part of the voice box. However, cartilage is not found in the kidney. The kidney is composed of specialised tissues involved in filtration and urine production, but it does not contain cartilage.

Q. 13 Fats are stored in human body as

(a) cuboidal epithelium

(b) adipose tissue

(c) bones

(d) cartilage

Ans. ***(b)*** Adipose tissue (type of connective tissue) consists of oval and round cells which are filled with the fat globules, scattered in the matrix. This tissue is found majorly below the skin, between internal organs and in the yellow bone marrow. It stores fat and acts as an insulator.

Cuboidal epithelium help in absorption, excretion and secretion, whereas bones and cartilage are specialised connective tissue that provide support to the internal organs.

Q. 14 Bone matrix is rich in

(a) fluoride and calcium (b) calcium and phosphorus

(c) calcium and potassium (d) phosphorus and potassium

Ans. ***(b)*** Bone is a strong and a non- flexible connective tissue. The bone cells are found embedded in a hard matrix, which is strengthened by fibres, and hardened by calcium and phosphorus salts. The matrix is deposited in form of concentric layers of lamellae formed around a central Haversian canal.

Q. 15 Contractile proteins are found in

(a) bones (b) blood (c) muscles (d) cartilage

Thinking Process Bones, blood and cartilage all are different types of connective tissue and are not responsible for movement of any of the body parts.

Ans. ***(c)*** Contractile proteins are found in muscles, as they are associated with the movement of body or limbs. The contraction and relaxation of contractile proteins, present in the muscles brings about movements of limbs, internal organs, etc. The bones are the major supporting tissue which form the endoskeleton of a vertebrate body.

Blood is a fluid connective tissue responsible for the transport of the substances like oxygen, nutrients, hormones, etc., and for producing antitoxins and antibodies, etc.

On the other side, a cartilage provides both support and flexibility to the body parts and smoothens the surface at joints.

Q. 16 Voluntary muscles are found in

(a) alimentary canal (b) limbs

(c) iris of the eye (d) bronchi of lungs

Ans. ***(b)*** Voluntary muscles are the type of muscles, that are under the complete control of individual (*i.e.,* under voluntary control) . For, *e.g.,* the working and movement of limbs. On the other hand involuntary muscles are controlled by hypothalamus, *i.e.,* they are regulated rhythmically, *e.g.,* alimentary canal, iris of the eye and bronchi of lungs.

Mistakes Alert ! *Students should be clear about the meaning and difference between the terms like voluntary and involuntary.*

Q. 17 Nervous tissue is not found in

(a) brain (b) spinal cord (c) tendons (d) nerves

Ans. ***(c)*** Tendons are the connective tissue, which join skeletal muscles to bones, hence nervous tissue is absent is them. Nervous tissue is a specialised tissue that help in transmitting messages within our body. It contains highly specialised unit cells called nerve cells or neurons. They have the ability to receive stimuli and to conduct (send) impulses (signals) to different parts of the body. Brain, spinal cord are nerve are all composed of nervous tissue.

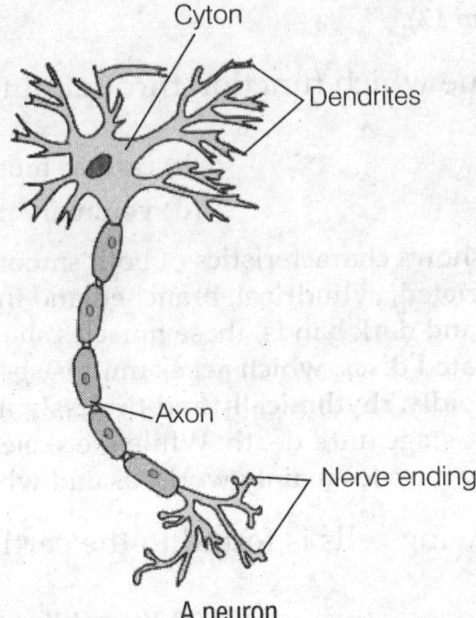

A neuron

Q. 18 Nerve cell does not contain

(a) axon (b) nerve endings (c) tendons (d) dendrites

Ans. ***(c)*** *Each nerve cell or neuron is composed of three main parts as*

(i) **Cyton or cell body** It contains central nucleus and cytoplasm with characteristic deeply stained particles called **Nissl's granules** (*i.e.*, clumps of ribosome).

(ii) **Dendron** These are short processes arising from cyton and further branching into dendrites.

(iii) **Axon** It is a single long cylindrical process of uniform diameter which forms fine branches terminally. The dendrites receives impulses and the axon transmits impulses away from the cell body.

(*Also, refer to Q.* 17)

Mistake Alert ! *Students should carefully learn about the different part of a neuron and should know the functions of each.*

Q.19 Which of the following helps in repair of tissue and fills up the space inside the organ?

(a) Tendon (b) Adipose tissue (c) Areolar (d) Cartilage

Ans. ***(c)***Areolar connective tissue is the most widely distributed connective tissue. It is a loose and cellular connective tissue, with a matrix consists of two kinds of fibres, *i.e.*, the white collagen fibres (which changes into gelatin on boiling in water) and the yellow elastic fibres or elastin. Several other kinds of irregular cells, (*e.g.*, fibroblasts), which can engulf bacteria and prevent infection (*e.g.*, macrophages) are also present in the matrix.

It is the simplest and most widely distributed connective tissue that it joins skin to muscles, fills spaces inside organs and is found around muscles, blood vessels and nerves. It acts as a supporting and packing tissue between organs lying in the body cavity. Matrix of this tissue is important in diffusion of oxygen and nutrients from small blood vessels. It helps in repairing of tissues and to combat foreign toxins.

(*Also, refer Q.* 6, 12 *and* 13).

Q.20 The muscular tissue which function throughout the life continuously without fatigue is

(a) skeletal muscle (b) cardiac muscle

(c) smooth muscle (d) voluntary muscle

Ans. ***(b)*** Cardiac muscles shows characteristics of both smooth and striated muscles. These muscles are striated, cylindrical, branched and involuntary in nature. In addition to the light and dark bands, these muscles show densely stained cross bands called intercalated discs, which act as impulse boosters. Cardiac muscles contract and relax rapidly, rhythmically and tirelessly throughout a lifetime, from early embryonic stage until death. While the skeletal muscle, smooth muscle and voluntary muscles mainly works as and when required.

Q. 21 Which of the following cells is found in the cartilaginous tissue of the body?

(a) Mast cells (b) Basophils

(c) Osteocytes (d) Chondrocytes

Ans. ***(d)*** The matrix of cartilage has a delicate network of collagen fibres and chondrocytes (living cells). These cells are present in the fluid-filled spaces called **lacunae.** Chondrocytes multiply by mitosis and help in internal growth of cartilage.

A mast cell is a resident granulocyte of several type of tissue. It contains granules rich in histamine and heparin. They play a key role in allergy and are involved in wound healing and defense against pathogens.

Basophils are granulocytes of white blood cells (WBCs) and are involved in function of body defence by engulfing bacteria and other foreign substances.

Osteocytes are the bone cells. *(Also, refer to Q.* 14)

Q. 22 The dead element present in the phloem is

(a) companion cells
(b) phloem fibres
(c) phloem parenchyma
(d) sieve tubes

Ans. ***(b)*** Phloem fibres are thick walled, elongated, spindle shaped dead cells which possess narrow lumen. They provides mechanical support to the tissue. Also, the phloem parenchyma are thin walled-living cells of parenchyma. They have two functions, storage and lateral food conduction.

(Also, refer to Q. 4)

Mistakes Alert! *Students often gets confused about the elements of xylem and phloem. So, they should especially pay attention while learning about them.*

Q.23 Which of the following does not lose their nucleus at maturity?

(a) Companion cells
(b) Red blood cells
(c) Vessel
(d) Sieve tube cells

Ans. ***(a)*** Companion cells are thin-walled, narrow, elongated living cells that have a prominent nucleus and dense cytoplasm. These are present along the sieve tube and are connected to them *via* plasmodesmata. These cells are metabolically active and sieve tube elements are dependent on these cells. They do not lose their nucleus at maturity. In contrast red blood cells (RBC) vessels xylem elements and sieve tube cells (phloem elements) lose their nuclei at maturity.

Q. 24 In desert plants, rate of water loss gets reduced due to the presence of

(a) cuticle
(b) stomata
(c) lignin
(d) suberin

Ans. ***(a)*** Cuticle is the continuous waxy layer that covers the aerial strength parts of a plant. These are protective, hydrophobic waxy covering produced by epidermal cells of leaves, young shoots and other aerial parts. It minimises the water loss through transpiration (with the help of stomata) and also reduces pathogen entry.

Lignin hardens the cell wall and provides flexibilty, tensile strength and compressional strength to the cell wall. Suberin is present in cork cells and makes the cell impermeable to water.

Q.25 A long tree has several branches. The tissue that helps in the side ways conduction of water in the branches is

(a) collenchyma
(b) xylem parenchyma
(c) parenchyma
(d) xylem vessels

Ans. ***(b)*** Xylem parenchyma is a type of living cell found in the xylem tissue, and it helps in the sideways conduction of water, particularly in the lateral movement of water between xylem vessels. Although xylem vessels are primarily responsible for the vertical transport of water from roots to leaves, xylem parenchyma aids in the lateral movement and storage of water and minerals.

Q.26 If the tip of sugarcane plant is removed from the field, even then it keeps on growing in length. It is due to the presence of

(a) cambium
(b) apical meristem
(c) lateral meristem
(d) intercalary meristem

Ans. ***(d)*** If the tip of a sugarcane plant is removed, the apical meristem is also removed as it is situated in the apices of growing roots and stem.
Intercalary meristem are located at the base of leaves or nodes and leads to the increase in the length of an organ such as leaves and internodes. It continues the growth of the plant even after the apical meristem is removed.

Q. 27 A nail is inserted in the trunk of a tree at a height of 1 metre from the ground level. After 3 years the nail will

(a) move downwards
(b) move upwards
(c) remain at the same position
(d) move sideways

Ans. ***(c)*** When a nail is inserted into the trunk of a tree at a height of 1 metre from the ground, even after 3 year the nail will remain at same level and will not move upwards. This is because the apical meristem responsible for vertical growth (length) present in the apices only while, the lateral meristem is responsible for the increase in the girth. Hence, will be no change in the vertical position of the nail.

Q. 28 Parenchyma cells are

(a) relatively unspecified and thin walled
(b) thick walled and specialised
(c) lignified
(d) None of the above

Ans. ***(a)*** Parenchyma is a living, simple permanent tissue. The parenchymatous cells form the bulk of the plant body. Its cells are living and they possess the power of division. The cells are rounded or isodiametric, *i.e.*, equally expanded in all sides. The cells are oval, round, polygonal or elongated in shape with a thin cell wall. It encloses a dense cytoplasm, which contains small nucleus and surrounds large central vacoule.

Q. 29 Flexibility in plants is due to

(a) collenchyma
(b) sclerenchyma
(c) parenchyma
(d) chlorenchyma

Ans. ***(a)*** Collenchyma is a living simple permanent tissue consist of living cells and are characterised by the presence of cellulose. Collenchyma is a mechanical tissue in young dicotyledonous stems and provides mechanical support and elasticity. It provides great tensile strength with flexibility to those organs in which it is found. It allows easy bending in various parts of a plant mainly young growing stem without breaking them.

Q. 30 Cork cells are made impervious to water and gases by the presence of

(a) cellulose (b) lipids (c) suberin (d) lignin

Ans. *(c)* Cork cells are made impervious to water and gases by the presence of suberin, a waxy substance that is deposited in the cell walls. Suberin prevent water loss and protects the plant from external environmental factors. It forms a protective barrier, making the cork layer waterproof and resistant to gas exchange.

Q.31 Survival of plants in terrestrial environment has been made possible by the presence of

(a) intercalary meristem (b) conducting tissue

(c) apical meristem (d) parenchymatous tissue

Ans. *(b)* The survival of plants in a terrestrial environment is supported by the presence of conducting tissues-xylem and phloem. These complex permanent tissues help transport water, nutrients, and food throughout the plant. Xylem conducts water from roots to the other parts of the plant, whereas phloem transports food and other material from the leaves to other parts of plants.

Q. 32 Choose the wrong statement.

(a) The nature of matrix differs according to the function of the tissue.

(b) Fats are stored below the skin and in between the internal organs.

(c) Epithelial tissues have intercellular spaces between them.

(d) Cells of striated muscles are multinucleate and unbranched.

Ans. *(c)* Epithelial tissues generally have very tight cell junctions with minimal intercellular spaces. The cells are closely packed together to form protective barriers.

Q. 33 The water conducting tissue generally present in gymnosperm is

(a) vessels (b) sieve tube (c) tracheids (d) xylem fibres

Ans. *(c)* The gymnosperms are characterised by the presence of tracheids as their major conducting tissue. These are elongated dead cells with hard lignified walls. They conduct water and do not have open ends like the vessels.

Short Answer Type Questions

Q. 34 Animals of colder regions and fishes of cold water have thicker layer of subcutaneous fat. Describe why?

Ans. The subcutaneous fat or adipose tissue lies just below the skin surface or in between internal organs. Being poor conductor of heat it acts as a good insulator. It reduces the heat loss from the body, *i.e.*, regulates the body temperature.

Q. 35 Match the Column I with the Column II.

	Column I		Column II
A.	Fluid connective tissue	1.	Subcutaneous layer
B.	Filling of space inside the organs	2.	Cartilage
C.	Striated muscle	3.	Skeletal muscle
D.	Adipose tissue	4.	Areolar tissue
E.	Surface of joints	5.	Blood
F.	Stratified squamous epithelium	6.	Skin

Ans. *The correct matching is*

	Column I	Column II
A.	Fluid connective tissue	5. Blood
B.	Filling of space inside the organs	4. Areolar tissue
C.	Striated muscle	3. Skeletal muscles
D.	Adipose tissue	1. Subcutaneous layer
E.	Surface of joints	2. Cartilage
F.	Stratified squamous epithelium	6. Skin

Q.36 Match the Column I with the Column II.

	Column I	Column II
A.	Parenchyma	1. Thin walled, packing cells
B.	Photosynthesis	2. Carbon fixation
C.	Aerenchyma	4. Localised thickenings
D.	Collenchyma	3. Buoyancy
E.	Permanent tissue	5. Sclerenchyma

Ans. *The correct matching is*

	Column I	Column II
A.	Parenchyma	1. Thin walled, packing cells
B.	Photosynthesis	2. Carbon fixation
C.	Aerenchyma	4. Buoyancy
D.	Collenchyma	3. Localised thickenings
E.	Permanent tissue	5. Sclerenchyma

Q. 37 If a potted plant is covered with a glass jar, water vapours appear on the wall of glass jar. Explain why?

Ans. Epidermis of a leaf is not continuous at all the places due to the presence of small pores, called stomata. Each stoma is bounded by a pair of specialised epidermal cells or two kidney-shaped cells called guard cells. The concave sides of these guard cells face each other and have a space forming the opening called stomatal pore.

The stomata allows gaseous exchange to occur during photosynthesis and respiration. During transpiration water vapour escapes through stomatal opening, this results in appearance of water vapour on the wall of glass jar, if a potted plant is covered with it.

Q. 38 Name the different components of xylem and draw a living component?

Ans. Xylem is made up of four different types of cells or elements

(a) tracheids

(b) xylem vessels

(c) xylem fibre

(d) xylem parenchyma

Xylem parenchyma is the living component of xylem.

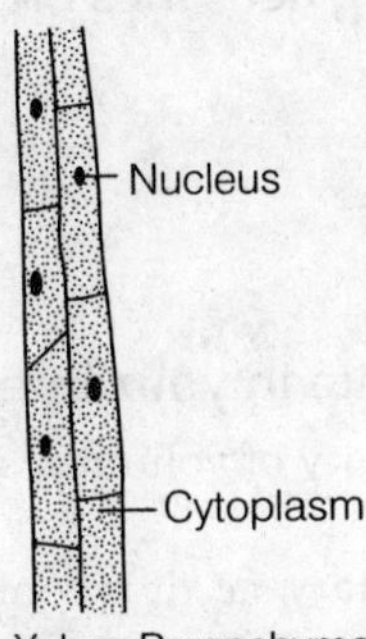

Xylem Parenchyma

Q. 39 Draw and identify different elements of phloem.

Ans. *The different elements of phloem are as below*

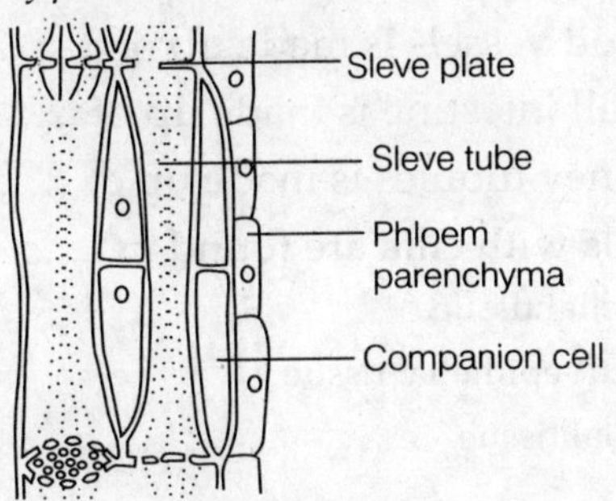

Section of phloem

Q. 40 Write True (T) or False (F).

(a) Epithelial tissue is protective tissue in animal body.

(b) The lining of blood vessels, lung alveoli and kidney tubules are all made up of epithelial tissue.

(c) Epithelial cells have a lot of intercellular spaces.

(d) Epithelial layer is permeable layer.

(e) Epithelial layer does not allow regulation of materials between body and external environment.

Ans. (a) True (b) True (c) False (d) True (e) False

Q.41 Differentiate between voluntary and involuntary muscles. Give one example of each type.

Ans. The voluntary muscles are muscles that can be regulated by our will. The functions carried by **voluntary muscle** cells is regulated by our own conscious control, *e.g.*, movement of leg or arm by striated muscles.

The involuntary muscles can not be controlled by our conscious (will). The actions of these muscles are controlled by the hypothalamus, *e.g.*, cardiac muscles regulate the beating of heart.

Q.42 Differentiate the following activities on the basis of voluntary (V) or involuntary (IV) muscles.

(a) Jumping of frog

(b) Pumping of the heart

(c) Writing with hand

(d) Movement of chocolate in your intestine

Ans. (a) Jumping of frog is the activity of voluntary muscles as it is controlled by skeletal muscles

(b) Pumping of heart involuntary, *i.e.*, it is controlled by cardiac muscles

(c) Writing with hand is voluntary muscles action.

(d) Movement of chocolate in your intestine is involuntary muscles.

Q. 43 Fill in the blanks.

(a) Lining of blood vessels is made up of ....

(b) Lining of small intestine is made up of ....

(c) Lining of kidney tubules is made up of ....

(d) Epithelial cells with cilia are found in .... of our body.

Ans. (a) Squamous epithelial tissue.

(b) Columnar (ciliated) epithelial tissue

(c) Cuboidal epithelial tissue

(d) Respiratory tract

Q.44 Water hyacinth float on water surface. Explain.

Ans. Water hyacinth floats on water surface due to presence of large air cavities in the parenchyma tissue. These specialised parenchyma tissue are called aerenchyma. It provides buoyancy by trapping air, allowing the plant to float on the water.

Q.45 Which structure protects the plant body against the invasion of parasites?

Ans. Epithelial tissue is the protective covering of our body. It provides a barrier against the invasion of pathogens and parasites, preventing damage and function. Additionally, the epidermis helps to prevent water loss and provide structural support.

Q.46 Fill in the blanks.

(a) Cork cells possesses .... on their walls that makes it impervious to gases and water.

(b) .... have tubular cells with perforated walls and are living in nature.

(c) Bone possesses a hard matrix composed of .... and ....

Ans. (a) Suberin (b) Sieve tubes

(c) Calcium and phosphorus

Q.47 Why is epidermis important for the plants?

Ans. Epidermis is the protective covering of plant body. It protects the plants from desiccation and infection. (*Also refer to Q. 10*)

Q. 48 Fill in the blanks.

(a) .... are forms of complex tissue.

(b) .... have guard cells.

(c) Cells of cork contain a chemical called ....

(d) Husk of coconut is made of .... tissue.

(e) .... gives flexibility in plants.

(f) .... and .... are both conducting tissues.

(g) Xylem transports .... and .... from soil.

(h) Phloem transport .... from .... to other parts of the plant.

Ans. (a) Xylem and phloem (b) Stomata

(c) Suberin (d) Sclerenchyma

(e) Collenchyma (f) Xylem, phloem

(g) Water, minerals (h) Food, leaves

Long Answer Type Questions

Q. 49 Differentiate between sclerenchyma and parenchyma tissues. Draw well-labelled diagram.

Ans. The major difference between sclerenchyma and parenchyma tissues are

	Parenchyma	Sclerenchyma
1.	Parenchyma tissue consist of living cells.	Sclerenchyma is composed of dead cells.
2.	It consist of thin walled cells.	Its cell walls are uniformly thickened.
3.	The cell wall is made up of cellulose.	The cell wall is made up of complex polymer lignin.
4.	Parenchyma tissue is found in soft parts of the plants such as cortex of roots, ground tissues in stems and mesophyll of leaves.	Sclerenchyma tissue is found in hard parts of the plant, such as roots, veins of leaves and hard covering of seeds and nuts.

	Parenchyma	Sclerenchyma
5.	Parenchyma function as packing tissue, serves as food storage tissue and performs photosynthesis (chlorenchyma).	Sclerenchyma is mechanical and protective in function. It gives strength, rigidity, flexibility and elasticity to the plant body.
	Parenchyma tissue (a) Transverse section Intercellular spaces	**Sclerenchyma tissue** (a) Transverse section Simple pit pair
	(b) Longitudinal section. Cytoplasm Nucleus Middle lamella Chloroplast Vacuole Intercellular space Primary cell wall	(b) Longitudinal section Narrow lumen Lignified thick wall

Q.50 Describe the structure and function of different types of epithelial tissues. Draw diagram of each type of epithelial tissue.

Ans. Epithelial tissue is the thin protective layer of cells which covers the surface of the body and lines the internal organs. The cells of this tissue are generally packed close together. The shape of the cells depends on the location and function of the tissue. Epithelial tissue originates from the ectoderm. But, epithelial tissue lining the intestine originates from the endoderm.

Epithelial tissue may be simple, *i.e.*, composed of single layer of cells or stratified, *i.e.*, made up of several layers of cells. Depending upon the shape and function of cells epithelial tissues are classified as

(i) **Squamous epithelial tissue** This tissue is composed of a single layer of thin and flat, plate-like cells. The cells fit closely, like the bricks in a wall, to form a smooth membrane. It is found in the outer layer of the skin, and covers internal cavities and ducts. Tongue, oesophagus and the lining of the mouth are made up of squamous epithelium. It is also found in blood vessels and alveoli. It protects the underlying tissues from mechanical injury, entry of germs, chemicals and drying. It also forms a selectively permeable surface through which filtration occurs.

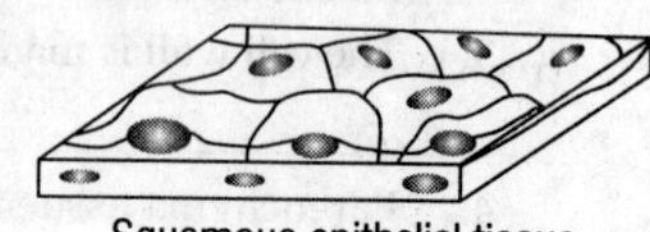

Squamous epithelial tissue

(ii) **Cuboidal epithelial tissue**

This tissue is composed of cube-like cells that fit closely. The cells look like squares in section, but the free surface appears hexagonal. This tissue lines the inside of the kidney tubules (the tubes leading from the cups of nephrons) thyroid vesicles and in glands like sweat glands, exocrine, pancreas and the salivary glands. It forms germinal epithelium of gonads (testes and ovaries). It helps in absorption, excretion and secretion. It also provides mechanical support.

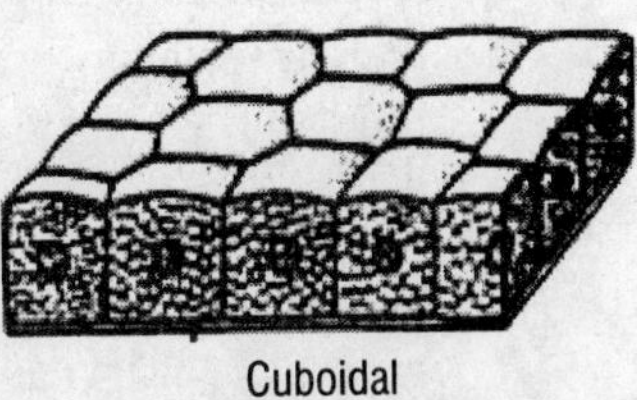
Cuboidal

(iii) **Columnar ciliated epithelial tissue** This tissue is generally composed of a single layer of column like cells. The presence of a conspicuous striated border of microvilli at the free surface end of each cell increases the surface area of the cell for absorption and secretion. It is generally found in the inner lining of the alimentary canal.

It also forms the lining of gall bladder and oviducts. The major functions of this tissue includes secretion (*e.g.*, mucus of goblet cells) and absorption (*e.g.*, stomach and intestine). In some parts of the body, columnar epithelium develops protoplasmic outgrowths called cilia. The constant lashing movements of the cilia help to move substances. It is found in the sperm ducts. It also lines trachea (wind-pipe), bronchi (lungs), kidney tubules and oviducts (Fallopian tubes). Ciliated epithelium helps the movement of ova in the fallopian tubes and the movement of mucus in the respiratory tract.

(iv) **Stratified squamous epithelial tissue** This tissue is found in the skin and covers the external dry surface of the skin. Cells of this tissue are arranged in many layers, but the cells forming different layers of this epithelium are not similar. Deeper layers of the tissue have cuboidal cells which become polygonal and finally flattened (squamous) towards the free surface.

The flattened cells of superficial layer may contain a fibrous protein, the **keratin** and become dead cells and are called keratinised stratified squamous epithelium. This epithelium is water proof and highly resistant to mechanical injury.

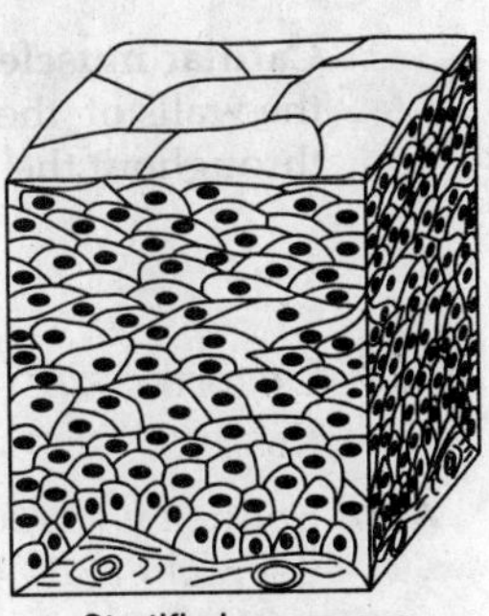
Stratified squamous epithelial tissue

(v) **Glandular epithelial tissue** Epithelial tissue often acquire additional specialisation as gland cells, which can secrete substances at the epithelial surface. Sometimes, a portion of epithelial tissue folds in wards and a multicellular gland is formed. This is called glandular epithelium. These glands can secrete substances such as enzymes, hormones and mucus.

Q. 51 Draw well-labelled diagrams of various types of muscles found in human body.

Ans. Human body consist of three types of muscles

Skeletal muscle It has striated, tubular, multinucleated fibres and is usually attached to skeleton. These are voluntary (under the control of our will muscles) in nature.

Often called striated muscles due to presence of alternate dark and light bands (straitions).

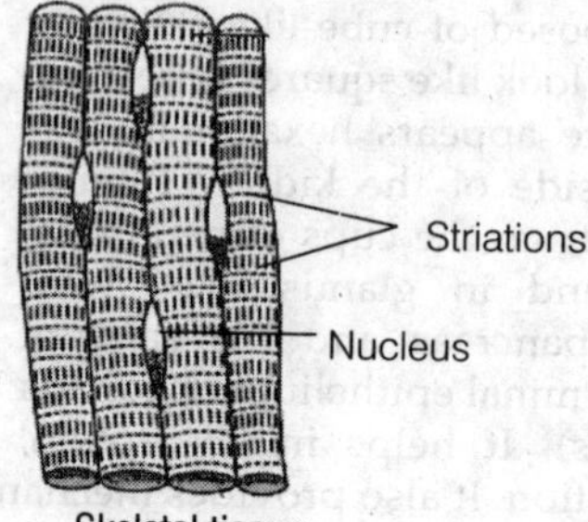

Skeletal tissue

Smooth muscle It has spindle-shaped, non-striated uninucleated fibres and occurs in walls of internal organs. It is involuntary in action.

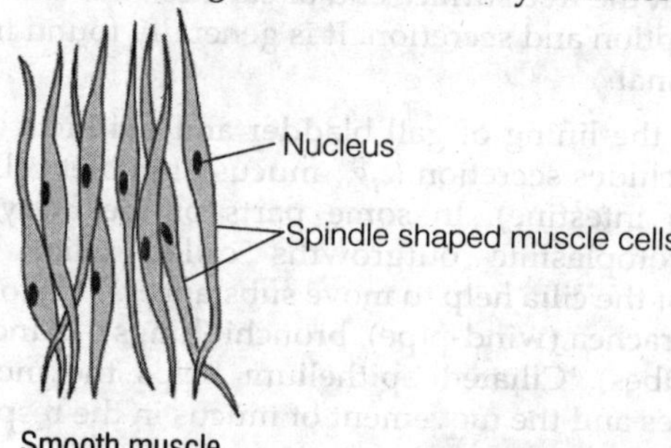

Smooth muscle

Cardiac muscle It has striated, branched, uninucleated fibres and occurs only in the walls of the heart. It is involuntary in action and its function is to pump blood throughout the body.

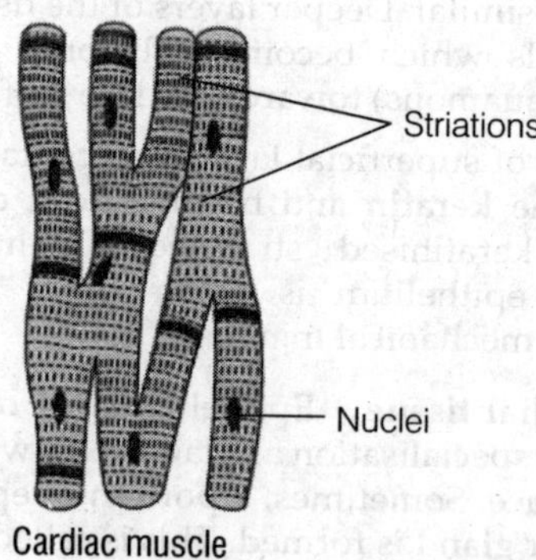

Cardiac muscle

Q. 52 Give reasons for

(a) Meristematic cells have a prominent nucleus and dense cytoplasm but they lack vacuole.

(b) Intercellular spaces are absent in sclerenchymatous tissues.

(c) We get a crunchy and granular feeling, when we chew pear fruit.

(d) Branches of a tree move and bend freely in high wind velocity.

(e) It is difficult to pull out the husk of a coconut tree.

Thinking Process Learning of different types of simple and permanent tissue.

Ans. (a) **Meristematic** cells are the continously dividing cells of the plant body, *i.e.*, they remain metabolically active and as we know that vacuoles serve the purpose of storage in plant cells. Therefore, meristematic cells do not require vacuole. while, the prominent nucleus and dense cytoplasm are necessary for their metabolic activity and cell division.

(b) **Sclerenchyma** tissue are the dead simple permanent tissue of the plant. The cells of sclerenchyma are closely packed without intercellular spaces, like tiles in mosaic floor so that, it can provide the strength, rigidity, flexibility and elasticity to the plant to withstand various strains.

(c) We get a crunchy and granular feeling when we chew pear fruit due to the presence of **sclerenchyma tissue.** The cell walls of sclerenchyma are greatly thickened due to the presence of lignin. Lignin is a complex polymer with high tensile strength, *i.e.*, it does not breaks easily on stretching and a high compressional strength, it does not buckle easily.

(d) **Collenchyma** cells are characterised by the deposition of extra cellulose at corners of the cell. In collenchyma intercellular spaces are absent and cells are elongated. It is a mechanical tissue which provides support and elasticity to the branches of a tree so that, they move and bend freely in high wind velocity.

(e) It is difficult to pull out the **husk of a coconut** tree due to the presence of **sclerenchyma tissue.** The cells of sclerenchyma tissue are closely packed without intercellular spaces, a middle lamella exists between them. Middle lamella is a thin layer of connecting substance containing pectin, lignin and protein, which contribute to the strength and resistance to separation.

Q. 53 List the characteristics of cork. How are they formed? Mention their role.

Ans. As the plants grow older, the outer protective tissue (*i.e.*, epidermis) undergoes certain changes. A strip of secondary meristem, called **phellogen** or **cork cambium** replaces the epidermis of the stem.

Cork cambium is a simple tissue, the cells are rectangular. Their protoplast are vacuolated and contain tannins and chloroplasts. Cork cambium gives off new cells on its both sides, thus, forming **cork** (phellem) on the outer side and the **secondary cortex or phelloderm** on the inner side.

The layer of cells which is cut by cork cambium on the outer side ultimately becomes several layered thick cork (bark) of trees. Cells of cork are dead and compactly arranged without intercellular spaces. The walls of cork cells are heavily thickened with an organic substance (a fatty substance), called suberin, which makes these cells impermeable to water and gases.

Cork is protective in function. It's cells prevent desiccation (loss of water from plant body), infection and mechanical injury. It is light and does not catch fire easily.

Due to these properties, cork is used as insulators, shock-absorbers, linoleum (used as flooring) and sports goods (in making of shuttle cocks, cricket balls, wooden paddles of table tennis, etc.). Commercial cork is obtained from the of cork oak tree (*Quercus suber*) found in Southern Europe and North Africa.

Q.54 Why are xylem and phloem called complex tissues? How are they different from one other?

Ans. A complex tissue consist of more than one type of cells having a common origin which coordinate to perform a common function. Xylem and phloem are the types of complex tissues because, they are made up of different types of cells.

Xylem is composed of four different types of cells (elements), namely

(i) tracheids (ii) vessels
(iii) xylem parenchyma (iv) xylem sclerenchyma (or fibre)

Phloem is also composed of four different types of elements, namely

(i) sieve tubes (ii) companion cells
(iii) phloem parenchyma (iv) phloem fibre

The basic difference between xylem and phloem is listed below

Xylem	Phloem
It conduct water and minerals.	It conducts organic solutes or food materials.
Conduction is mostly unidirectional, *i.e.,* from roots to apical parts of the plant.	Conduction may be bidirectional, *i.e.,* from leaves to storage organs or growing parts or vice-versa
Conducting channels or elements are tracheids and vessels.	Conducting channels are sieve tubes.
Three of the four elements of xylem are dead (*i.e.,* tracheids, vessels and fibre). Only xylem parenchyma is the living element.	Three of four elements are living, *i.e.,* sieve tubes, companion cells and phloem parenchyma while phloem fibre are dead elements.
In addition to conduction, xylem provides mechanical strength to the plant.	Phloem performs no mechanical function for the plants.

Q.55 (a) Differentiate between meristematic and permanent tissues in plants.
(b) Define the process of differentiation.
(c) Name any two simple and two complex permanent tissues in plants.

Ans. (a) The basic differences between meristematic and permanent tissues of plants are tabulated below

Meristematic tissue	Permanent tissue
Its component cells are living, small, spherical or polygonal and undifferentiated	Its components cells may be living or dead. They are large, differentiated with different shapes.
Cytoplasm is dense and vacuoles are nearly absent as they are metabolically active.	Large central vacuole occurs in living permanent cells as, they are less metabolically active.

Meristematic tissue	Permanent tissue
Intercellular spaces are absent.	Intercellular spaces are often present.
Cell wall of its cells is thin and elastic.	Cell wall of its cells may either thin or thick.
Nucleus of each cell of this tissue is large and prominent.	Nucleus of each cell of this tissue is less conspicuous.
Its cells grow and divide regularly.	Its cells do not divide regularly.
It is a simple tissue.	It can be simple, complex or specialised.
Cell organelles of its cells are simple.	Cell organelles of its cells are well-developed.
Cells of this tissue do not contain crystals and other inclusions.	Cells of this tissue possess crystals and other inclusions.
It provides growth to the plant.	It provides protection, support, conduction photosynthesis, storage, etc.

(b) Differetiation is the process by which meristematic cells undergo changes in shape, size and function to become specialised cells, gradually losing their ability to divide. These differentiated cells form the permanent tissues of the plant.

(c) Two simple permanent tissue in plants are **parenchyma** and **collenchyma** while two complex permanent tissue in plants are **xylem** and **phloem**.

Chapter 07

Diversity in Living Organisms*

Multiple Choice Questions (MCQs)

Q. 1 Find out incorrect sentence

(a) Protista includes unicellular eukaryotic organisms

(b) Whittaker considered cell structure, mode and source of nutrition for classifying the organisms in five kingdoms

(c) Both Monera and Protista may be autotrophic and heterotrophic

(d) Monerans have well-defined nucleus

Ans. *(d)* Sentence (d) is incorrect and can be corrected as Monera comprises of single celled prokaryotic bacteria therefore they do not have membrane bound cell organelles and a well-defined nucleus. The undefined nuclear region is termed as nucleoid.

Q. 2 Which among the following has specialised tissue for conduction of water?

(i) Thallophyta (ii) Bryophyta

(iii) Pteridophyta (iv) Gymnosperms

(a) (i) and (ii) (b) (ii) and (iii) (c) (iii) and (iv) (d) (i) and (iv)

Ans. *(c)* Pteridophyta and gymnosperms have specialised tissue for conduction of water. Pteridophyta are the oldest vascular plants and their body is differentiated into an aerial shoot system and an underground root system. All ferns fall under this group.

Gymnosperms are naked seed bearing vascular plants. They have xylem and phloem present for their conduction.

Q. 3 Which among the following produce seeds?

(a) Thallophyta (b) Bryophyta (c) Pteridophyta (d) Gymnosperms

Ans. *(d)* Gymnosperms are seed producing plants and they produce naked seeds. In thallophyta, bryophyta and pteridophyta, the reproductive organs are inconspicuous and they are known as cryptograms. They do not produce seeds.

Q. 4 Which one is a true fish?

(a) Jellyfish (b) Starfish (c) Dogfish (d) Silverfish

Ans. *(c)* Dogfish are referred as true fish as they belong to a group of vertebrates called pisces (class-chondrichthyes). They have a stream lined body, gills for breathing and fins for swimming. Whereas jellyfish is cnidarians, starfish is echinoderm and silverfish belongs to Arthropoda.

Note (*) This chapter has been deleted from latest NCERT.

Q. 5 Which among the following is exclusively marine?

(a) Porifera (b) Echinodermata
(c) Mollusca (d) Pisces

Ans. ***(b)*** Echinodermata are spiny skinned animals found only in marine environments. They have a vascular water system, example starfish.

Whereas **porifera** consist of sponges which are aquatic animals and remain fixed to the bottom of the sea. Most sponges are marine but few freshwater forms are also found like *Spongilla*.

Molluscs are marine as well as terrestrial forms.

Pisces are found in both marine water, (*e.g.*, dog fish) and freshwater (*e.g.*, rohu).

Q. 6 Which among the following have open circulatory system?

(i) Arthropoda (ii) Mollusca
(iii) Annelida (iv) Coelenterata

(a) (i) and (ii) (b) (iii) and (iv) (c) (i) and (iii) (d) (ii) and (iv)

Ans. ***(a)*** Arthropoda and mollusca have open circulatory system where the blood is not fully contained within the blood vessels and flows freely in body cavities.

Annelida has closed circulatory system where blood circulates within vessels.

Coelenterata do no have circulatory system as their body is composed of a two layer structure.

Q. 7 In which group of animals, coelom is filled with blood?

(a) Arthropoda (b) Annelida
(c) Nematoda (d) Echinodermata

Ans. ***(a)*** In Arthropoda, the coelom is filled with blood as they have an open circulatory system. This coelom is known as haemocoel.

Q. 8 Elephantiasis is caused by

(a) *Wuchereria* (b) Pinworm (c) Planarians (d) Liver flukes

Ans. ***(a)*** *Wuchereria* is a human parasite that causes elephantiasis and is spread through mosquito (vector)

Pinworm belongs to the phylum–Nematoda. It is also known as threadworm or seatworm. It is a common intestinal parasite and causes enterobiasis.

Planarians is non-parasitic flatworms. While liver flukes are flat worms that cause liver rot.

Q.9 Which one is the most striking or (common) character of the vertebrates?

(a) Presence of notochord (b) Presence of triploblastic condition
(c) Presence of gill pouches (d) Presence of coelom

Ans. ***(a)*** The presence of notochord is the most striking character of vertebrates during their embryonic development. It provides support to the body and is present in all chordates.

Notochord is a long, rod-like structure that runs along the back of the animal seperating nervous tissue from gut.

Q. 10 Which among the following have scales?

(i) Amphibians (ii) Pisces
(iii) Reptiles (iv) Mammals

(a) (i) and (iii) (b) (iii) and (iv)
(c) (ii) and (iii) (d) (i) and (ii)

Ans. ***(c)*** Pisces, along with reptiles, have hard protective scales on their skin for protection. The outer body of many fish is covered with scales, which are the part of the fish's integumentary system. The scales originates from the mesoderm (skin).

Similarily reptiles have scales on their skin which helps in protecting their bodies and reduce water loss.

Q. 11 Find out the false statement.

(a) Aves are warm blooded, egg laying and have four-chambered heart
(b) Aves have feather covered body, forelimbs are modified as wing and breathe through lungs
(c) Most of the mammals are viviparous
(d) Fishes, amphibians and reptiles are oviparous

Ans. ***(d)*** Statements (d) is incorrect and can be correct as many fishes, amphibians and reptiles are oviparous but some species of these groups are viviparous as well for example shark are viviporous.

Q. 12 Pteridophyta do not have

(a) root (b) stem
(c) flowers (d) leaves

Ans. ***(c)*** Pteridophytes are the oldest vascular plants. Their bodies are differentiated into an aerial shoot system and an underground root system. The reproductive organs are multicellular. These plants do not produce seeds but produce spores and are seedless plants that have no flowers.

Q. 13 Identify a member of Porifera

(a) *Spongilla* (b) *Euglena*
(c) *Penicillium* (d) *Hydra*

Ans. ***(a)*** *Spongilla* belongs to the phylum–Porifera. Poriferans are commonly known as sponges that are simple, multicellular organisms with pores bodies. They live in aquatic environments and filter feed through pores

Euglena is a protist, *Penicillium* belongs to kingdom Fungi and *Hydra* is a coelenterate.

Q. 14 Which is not an aquatic animal?

(a) *Hydra* (b) Jelly fish
(c) Corals (d) *Filaria*

Ans. ***(d)*** *Filaria* is not an aquatic animal, but is a worm that belong to nematoda whereas, *Hydra* is a coelenterate and is a freshwater organism. Jelly fish is a marine animal. While, corals are cnidarians and marine invertebrates.

Q. 15 Amphibians do not have the following.

(a) Three-chambered heart
(b) Gills or lungs
(c) Scales
(d) Mucus glands

Thinking Process Amphibians use their skin as secondary respiratory organs, therefore scales cannot be present.

Ans. ***(c)*** Amphibians do not have scales, instead their skin has mucus secreting glands, which helps them in respiration by the means of diffusion.
(Also, refer to Q. 10)

Q. 16 Organisms without nucleus and cell organelles belongs to

(i) fungi
(ii) Protista
(iii) cyanobacteria
(iv) Archaebacteria

(a) (i) and (ii)
(b) (iii) and (iv)
(c) (i) and (iv)
(c) (ii) and (iii)

Ans. ***(b)*** Cyanobacteria and Archaebacteria belongs to kingdom–Monera. Monerans are organisms that lack nucleus and cell organelles and are called prokaryotes.
(Also, refer to Q. 1)

Q. 17 Which of the following is not a criterian for classification of living organisms?

(a) Body design of the organism
(b) Ability to produce one's own food
(c) Membrane bound nucleus and cell organelles
(d) Height of the plant

Ans. ***(d)*** Classification deals with the arrangement of organisms or groups of organisms into categories. The living form vary in shape, size, structure, function etc. The variation in their appearance, body design and behaviours form basis of classification.

Other criterias are

(i) If the organism is prokaryotic or eukaryotic.
(ii) Mode of nutrition (animals).
(iii) Levels of organisation (animals).
(iv) Presence or absence of vascular tissue (plants).
(v) Seed bearing or not bearing (plant).
(vi) Naked seed or covered seed (plants).
(vii) Symmetry (animals).

Q. 18 The feature that is not a characteristic of Protochordata?

(a) Presence of notochord
(b) Bilateral symmetry and coelom
(c) Jointed legs
(d) Presence of circulatory system

Ans. ***(c)*** Jointed legs are the characteristics of arthropods so it is not a characteristic of protochordates The feature of protochordates are

They are triploblastic, have bilaterally symmetrical body and a coelom.

They show **notochord** at larval stages of their lives.

These are mostly marine animals, *e.g., Balanoglossus, Herdmania, Amphioxus* (or *Branchiostoma*) and *Doliolum*.

Q. 19 The locomotory organs of Echinodermata are

(a) tube feet (b) muscular feet (c) jointed legs (d) parapodia

Ans. ***(a)*** Tube feets are locomotary organs of echinoderms. They are spiny-skinned marine animals. They have an exoskeleton of calcareous plates from which the spines arise. The adults are radially symmetrical, whereas larvae are bilaterally symmetrical.

Q.20 Corals are

(a) poriferans attached to some solid support
(b) cnidarians, that are solitary living
(c) poriferans present at the sea bed
(d) cnidarians that live in colonies

Ans. ***(d)*** Corals are marine invertebrates of phylum-Cnidaria. They live in compact colonies of many identical individual 'polyps'. The group includes the important reef builders that inhabit tropical oceans and secrete calcium carbonate to form a hard skeleton.

Although some corals can trap small fish and plankton, using stinging cells on their tentacles (like those in sea anemone and jellyfish) but most corals obtain the majority of their energy and nutrients from photosynthetic unicellular algae that live within their tissue.

Q. 21 Who introduced the system of scientific nomenclature of organisms

(a) Robert Whittaker (b) Carolus Linnaeus
(c) Robert Hooke (d) Ernst Haeckel

Ans. ***(b)*** Carolus Linnaeus is considered the father of Taxonomy. He formulated the scientific method of naming organisms called **the binomial system of nomenclature**. In this system, each organism has two Latin names *i.e.*, one for its genus and the other for its species, *e.g.*, all frogs have the genus name *Rana* and the Indian bull frog has the species name *tigrina*, so the Indian bull frog is called *Rana tigrina.*

Linnaeus also introduced a hierarchial system for classifying organisms into groups. All organisms were divided into kingdoms. The kingdoms were divided into phyla (singular: phylum), the phyla into classes and the classes into **orders**. Then came family, followed by genus and species. Individuals of a species bear the closest resemblance to each other.

Organism are classified into Super kingdoms → Kingdoms → Phyla → Classes → Orders → Families → Genera → Species.

Q. 22 Two-chambered heart occurs in

(a) crocodiles (b) fish (c) Aves (d) amphibians

Ans. ***(b)*** Two-chambered heart occurs in fishes. Crocodiles have four-chambered heart whereas aves and amphibians have three-chambered heart.

Q. 23 Skeleton is made entirely of cartilage in

(a) sharks (b) tuna (c) rohu (d) None of these

Ans. ***(a)*** Cartilaginous fishes have endoskeleton made up of cartilage. *e.g., Scoliodon* (dog fish) shark, *Torpedo*, sting ray etc.

Q. 24 One of the following is not an Annelida

(a) *Nereis* (b) Earthworm (c) Leech (d) Sea urchins

Ans. ***(d)*** Sea urchins are not annelids. They belong to phylum Echinodermata and are marine organisms. They have different body structure and are characterised by a hard exoskeleton, made of calcium carbonate. They have radial symmetry.

Annelids are triploblastic animals having bilaterally symmetrical body. They exhibit metameric segmentation and are the first coelomates. *e.g.*, Nereis, earthworm and leech.

Q. 25 The book *Systema Naturae* was written by

(a) Linnaeus (b) Haeckel (c) Whittaker (d) Robert Brown

Ans. ***(a)*** *Systema Naturae* was written by Carolus Linnaeus. He described his binomial system of classification in this book.

(Also, refer to Q. 21)

Ernst Haeckel was a German biologist who gave three kingdom classification (1866).

Whittaker gave the five kingdom classification and Robert Brown discovered the cells nucleus.

Q. 26 Carl von Linnaeus was involved with which branch of science?

(a) Morphology (b) Taxonomy (c) Physiology (d) Medicine

Ans. ***(b)*** Carl von Linnaeus is known as Father of Taxonomy.

(Also, refer to Q. 21)

Q. 27 Real organs are absent in

(a) Mollusca (b) Coelenterata (c) Arthropoda (d) Echinodermata

Ans. ***(b)*** Coelenterata lack true organs as they are multicellular, diploblastic and acoelomate animals having **tissue level of organisation** (*i.e.*, they lack true organs).

Mollusca, Arthropoda and Echinodermata have organ level of organisation.

Q. 28 Hard calcium carbonate structures are used as skeleton by

(a) Echinodermata (b) Protochordata (c) Arthropoda (d) Nematoda

Ans. ***(a)*** Body wall of Echinodermata is covered with a spiny, hard, calcium carbonate plates (ossicles) that forms a rigid or flexible endoskeleton.

(Also, refer to Q. 19).

Q. 29 Differentiation in segmental fashion occurs in

(a) Leech (b) Starfish (c) Snails (d) *Ascaris*

Ans. ***(a)*** Leech (Annelida) have metameric segmentation *i.e.*, their body is divided into segments which are identical to each other and bear a set of organs in each segment.

Q.30 In taxonomic hierarchy family comes between

(a) class and order (b) order and genus

(c) genus and species (d) division and class

Ans. ***(b)*** In taxonomic hierarchy family comes between order and genus. Family is a taxonomic category that includes a group of related genera, sharing common characteristics. The taxonomical hierarchy is

Kingdom $\rightarrow$ Phylum $\rightarrow$ Class $\rightarrow$ Order $\rightarrow$ Family $\rightarrow$ Genus $\rightarrow$ Species.

Phylum The classes having same specific characters which are common to all of them are placed under same phylum. *e.g.*, Phylum–Angiospermae.

Kingdom Highest category of taxonomic studies, consisting of set of distinguishing common characters. The organisms having same fundamental characteristics are grouped together. *e.g.*, Kingdom–Plantae and Animalia.

Q.31 Five kingdom classification has given by
(a) Morgan (b) R H Whittaker (c) Linnaeus (d) Haeckel

Ans. ***(b)*** Five kingdom classification was given by R H Whittaker, whereas TH Morgan gives the chromosomal theory of inheritance.
(*Also, refer to 21 and 25*)

Q. 32 Well-defined nucleus is absent in
(a) blue-green algae (b) diatoms (c) algae (d) yeast

Ans. ***(a)*** Blue-green algae or cyanobacteria is a prokaryotic organism, that lacks well defined nucleus, whereas diatoms, algae and yeast all are eukaryotic organism, that shows the presence of true nucleus and cell membrane bound organelles.

Q. 33 The 'Origin of Species' is written by
(a) Linnaeus (b) Darwin (c) Haeckel (d) Whittaker

Ans. ***(b)*** Charles Darwin, an English naturalist, first described the theory of evolution in his book **'The Origin of Species'**, published in 1859. According to him, most of the life forms present today have developed by an accumulation of changes in body design over a period of time through natural selection and are more complex than their ancestral forms.

Q. 34 Meena and Hari observed an animal in their garden. Hari called it an insect-while Meena said it was an earthworm. Choose the character from the following which confirms that it is an insect.
(a) Bilateral symmetrical body (b) Body with jointed legs
(c) Cylindrical body (d) Body with little segmentation

Ans. ***(b)*** The most striking feature of arthropods (including insects) is the presence of jointed appendages or presence of jointed legs.

Short Answer Type Questions

Q. 35 Write true (T) or false (F).
(a) Whittaker proposed five kingdom classification.
(b) Monera is divided into Archaebacteria and Eubacteria.
(c) Starting from class species comes before the genus.
(d) *Anabaena* belongs to the kingdom–Monera.
(e) Blue-green algae belongs to the kingdom–Protista.
(f) All prokaryotes are classified under Monera.

Ans. (a) True (b) True (c) False

In linnaeus's biological hierarchical system genus comes before species.

(d) True

(e) False

Blue–green algae is prokaryotic and according to five-kingdom classification, prokaryotic unicellular organism are placed under kingdom Monera.

(f) True

Q.36 Fill in the blanks.

(a) Fungi shows .... mode of nutrition.

(b) Cell wall of fungi is made up of ....

(c) Association between blue-green algae and fungi is called as ....

(d) Chemical nature of chitin is ....

(e) .... has smallest number of organisms with maximum number of similar characters.

(f) Plants without well differentiated stem, root and leaf are kept in ....

(g) .... are called as amphibians of the plant kingdom.

Ans. (a) Saprophytic (b) Chitin

(c) Lichens (d) Carbohydrate

(e) Species (f) Thallophyta

(g) Bryophytes

Q. 37 You are provided with the seeds of gram, wheat, rice, pumpkin, maize and pea. Classify them whether they are monocot or dicot.

Ans. On the basis of number of cotyledons, the angiosperms are divided into monocots and dicots.

(a) **Gram, Pumpkin and Peas are Dicots (Dicotyledonae)**

(i) The seeds produced by these plants have embryos with two fleshy **cotyledons.**

(ii) Their leaves have reticulate venation, with a network of veins and veinlets.

(iii) The root system has a prominent tap root.

(iv) The flowers have five or multiple of five petals.

(v) The vascular bundles are arranged in a ring. They are open (*i.e.,* have cambium) between xylem and phloem and undergo secondary growth.

(b) **Wheat, Rice and Maize are Monocots (Monocotyledonae)**

(i) The seeds of these plants have only one cotyledon.

(ii) Their leaves have parallel venation.

(iii) The root system consists of fibrous roots.

(iv) The flowers have three or multiple of three petals.

(v) The vascular bundles are scattered and closed, (*i.e.,* lack cambium). Secondary growth does not occur.

Q. 38 Match items of column I with items of column II.

Column I	Column II
A. Naked seed	1. Angiosperms
B. Covered seed	2. Gymnosperms
C. Flagella	3. Bryophyta
D. *Marchantia*	4. Euglena
E. *Marsilea*	5. Thallophyta
F. *Cladophora*	6. Pteridophyta
G. *Penicillium*	7. Fungi

Ans. The correct matching is A-2, B-1, C-4, D-3, E-6, F-5, G-7

Q. 39 Match items of Column I with items of Column II.

Column I	Column II
A. Pore bearing animals	1. Arthropoda
B. Diploblastic	2. Coelenterata
C. Metameric segmentation	3. Porifera
D. Jointed legs	4. Echinodermata
E. Soft bodied animals	5. Mollusca
F. Spiny skinned animals	6. Annelida

Ans. The correct matching is A-3, B-2, C-6, D-1, E-5, F-4.

Mistake Alert! *Student should not confuse themselves in a hurry while solving the matching type Question.*

Q. 40 Classify the following organisms based on the absence/presence of true coelom, (*i.e.*, acoelomate, pseudocoelomate and coelomate)

Spongilla	Sea anemone	*Planaria*	Liver fluke
Wuchereria	*Ascaris*	*Nereis*	Earthworm
Scorpion	Birds	Fishes	Horse

Ans. Coelom is the main body cavity in most multicellular animals and it contains digestive tract and other organs. Organisms in which coelom is absent are *Spongilla*, sea anemone, *Planaria* and liverfluke, hence are, called acoelomates. Pseudocoelomates are animals without true coelom *e.g., Wuchreria bancrofti and Ascaris.*

Animals in which coelom is present are, *Nereis* (Annelida), earthworm (Annelida), scorpion (Arthropoda), birds (Aves), fishes (Pisces) and horse (Mammalia).

Q. 41 Endoskeleton of fishes are made up of cartilage and bone, classify the following fishes as cartilaginous or bony

Torpedo, Sting ray, Dog fish,

Rohu, Angler fish, *Exocoetus*.

Ans. Cartilaginous fishes are *Torpedo*, Sting ray, Dog fish. Bony fishes are Rohu, Angler fish, *Exocoetus*

	Bony fishes	Cartilaginous fishes
1.	Endoskeleton is bony	Endoskeleton is cartilaginous
2.	Four pairs of gill slits are present which are covered by an operculum.	5-7 pairs of gill slits are present and an operculum is absent.
3.	Mouth is terminal is position.	Mouth is ventral in position.
4.	Caudal fin is homocercal.	Caudal fin is heterocercal.
5.	Air or swim bladder is usually present.	Air or swim bladder is absent.
6.	Marine and freshwater	Exclusively marine fishes
7.	Mostly oviparous.	Most of them are viviparous

Q. 42 Classify the following based on number of chambers in their heart, rohu, *Scoliodon*, frog, salamander, flying lizard, king, cobra, crocodile, ostrich, pigeon, bat, whale.

Ans. Pisces (fishes) have only two-chambered hearts. *e.g.*, Rohu, *Scoliodon*.

Amphibians have three-chambered hearts *e.g.*, frog, salamander.

Reptiles also have three-chambered heart. *e.g.*, flying lizard, king cobra.

Crocodiles have four chambered heart (an exception among reptiles).

Aves are warm blooded animals having four-chambered heart. *e.g.*, ostrich, pigeon, bat, whale, etc.

Q. 43 Classify Rohu, *Scoliodon*, flying lizard, king kobra, frog, salamander, ostrich, pigeon, bat, crocodile and whale into the cold blooded/warm blooded animals.

Ans. Cold blooded animals (ectothermic) cannot regulate their body temperature and rely on external environment temperatures to maintain their body heat. Rohu, *Scoliodon*, Flying lizard, King Cobra, Frog, Salamander and crocodile are cold blooded animals. Warm blooded animals can regulate their body temperatures regardless of external conditions.

To generate heat warm blooded animals convert food into energy.

Ostrich, Pigeon, Bat and whale are warm blooded.

Q. 44 Name two egg laying mammals.

Ans. Two egg laying mammals are platypus and *Echidna* (spiny anteater)

Q. 45 Fill in the blanks

(a) Five kingdom classification of living organisms is given by ....

(b) Basic smallest unit of classification is ....

(c) Prokaryotes are grouped in kingdom ....

(d) *Paramecium* is a Protista because of its ....

(e) Fungi do not contain ....

(f) A fungus .... can be seen without microscope.

(g) Common fungi used in preparing the bread is ....

(h) Algae and fungi form symbiotic association called ....

Ans. (a) Robert Whittaker (b) Species
(c) Monera (d) Eukaryotic unicellular Organisms
(e) Chlorophyll (f) Mushroom
(g) Yeast (h) Lichens

Q. 46 Give True (T) and False (F).

(a) Gymnosperms differ from angiosperms in having covered seed.
(b) Non-flowering plants are called cryptogamae.
(c) Bryophytes have conducting tissue.
(d) *Funaria* is a moss.
(e) Compound leaves are found in many ferns.
(f) Seeds contain embryo.

Ans. (a) False. Gymnosperms differ from angiosperms in having naked seeds
(b) True
(c) False. Bryophytes lack true conducting tissues and rely on diffusion for water treatment.
(d) True (e) True (f) True

Q.47 Give examples for the following.

(a) Bilateral, dorsiventral symmetry is found in ....
(b) Worms causing disease elephantiasis is ....
(c) Open circulatory system is found in .... where coelomic cavity is filled with blood
(d) .... are known to have pseudocoelom.

Ans. (a) Liver fluke (b) Filarial worm
(c) Arthropods (d) Nematodes

Q.48 Label *a*, *b*, *c* and *d*. Given in figure. Give the function of (*b*)

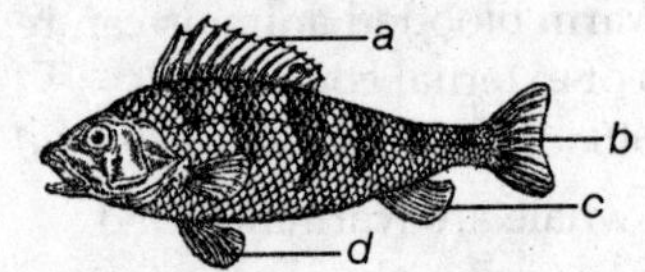

Ans.

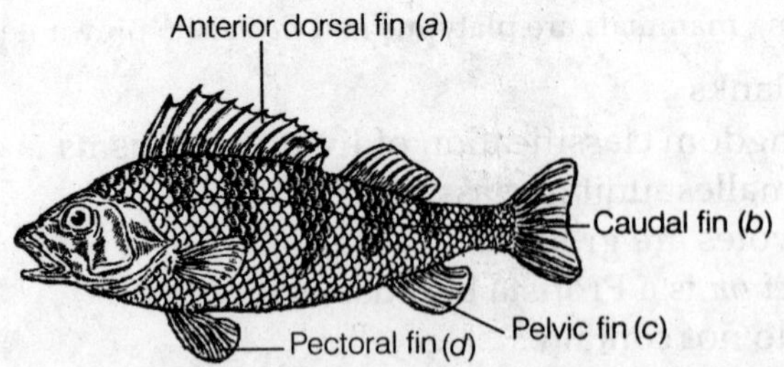

Caudal fins (b) or tail fins are responsible for forward motion in bony fishes.

Q. 49 Fill in the boxes given in figure with appropriate characteristics/plant group (s).

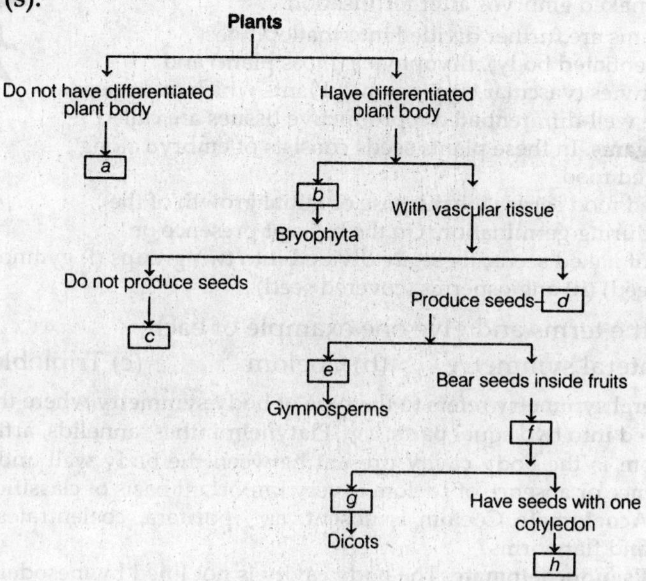

Ans.

(a) Thallophyta
(b) Without specialised vascular tissue
(c) Pteridophyta
(d) Phanerogams
(e) Bear naked seeds
(f) Angiosperms
(g) Have seeds with two cotyledon.
(h) Monocots.

Long Answer Type Questions

Q.50 Write names of few thallophytes. Draw a well-labelled diagram of *Spirogyra*.

Ans. *Few examples of thallophytes are as follows*

Spirogyra *Ulva* *Chara* *Polysiphonia*
Ulothrix *Cladophora* *Laminaria*

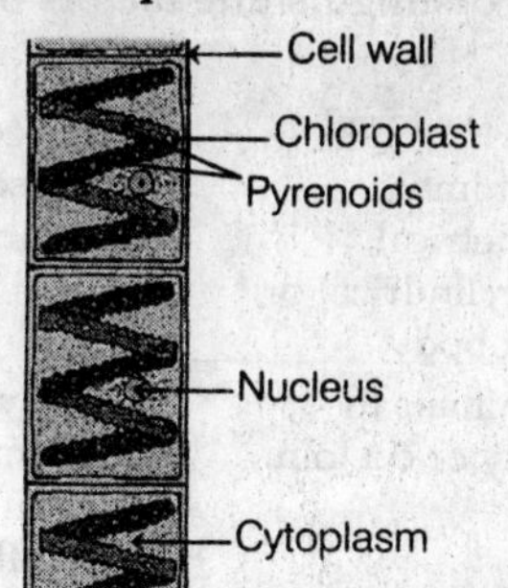

A well labelled diagram of *Spirogyra*

Q.51 Thallophyta, Bryophyta and Pteridophyta are called as 'cryptogams'. Gymnosperms and angiosperms are called as 'phanerogams'. Discus why? Draw one example of gymnosperm.

Ans. Cryptogams are seedless plants. The reproductive organs of members of cryptogams are inconspicuous or hidden. They produce naked embryos after fertilisation.

Cryptogams are further divided into thallophytes (undifferentiated body), Bryophytes (moss plant) and pteridophytes (vascular cryptogams). Plants which make seeds and have well-differentiated reproductive tissues are called **phanerogams**. In these plants seeds consists of embryo along with stored food.

The stored food serves the purpose of initial growth of the embryo during germination. On the basis of presence or absence of naked seeds, these are divided into two groups (i) gymnosperms (naked seed) (ii) angiosperms (covered seed).

Cycas
(A gymnosperm)

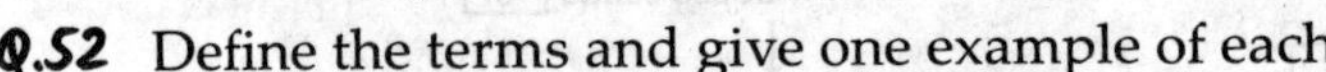

Q.52 Define the terms and give one example of each

(a) Bilateral symmetry (b) Coelom (c) Triploblastic

Ans. (a) Bilateral symmetry refers to the type of body symmetry where the body can be divided into two equal parts. *e.g.*, Platyhelminthes, annelids, arthropods, etc.

(b) Coelom is the body cavity present between the body wall and the gut wall. Presence or absence of coelom is very important basis of classification.

(i) **Acoelomate** Coelom is absent. *e.g.*, porifera, coelentrates, ctenophores and flatworms.

(ii) **Pseudocoelomate** The body cavity is not lined by mesoderm instead it is present as scattered pouches in between mesoderm and endoderm. *e.g.*, round worms.

(iii) **Eucoelomate** Presence of true coelom. True coelom is of two types

- Schizocoelom develops by splitting up of mesoderm.
- **Enterocoelom** The mesoderm arises from the wall of embryonic gut.

(c) **Triploblastic** Body wall of animals is made up of three germ layers *i.e.*, ectoderm, mesoderm and endoderm *e.g.*, Platyhelminthes to chordates.

Q.53 You are given leech, *Nereis*, *Scolopendra*, prawn and scorpion; and all have segmented body organisation. Will you classify them in one group? If no, give the important characters based on which you will separate these organisms into different groups.

Ans. The organisms here do not belong to the same group. Leech and *Nereis* belong to phylum–Annelida while, *Scolopendra*, prawn and scorpion belong to phylum–Arthropoda. The distinguishing factors of both are given below

Annelids (*Latin, annulus*-ring; *idos*-form)	Arthropods (Greek, *arthro*-jointed; *podos*-foot)
1. These are triploblastic animals having bilaterally symmetrical, elongated, vermiform, cylindrical or dorsoventrally flattened body.	1. These are triploblastic, bilaterally symmetrical and segmented animals.
2. Annelids are the first animals to develop true body cavity or coelom.	2. Body cavity is filled with blood, *i.e.*, haemocoelic and have open circulatory system, so the blood does not flow in blood vessels. Excretion takes place by Malpighian tubules (insects) and green glands (crab and prawn). In many arthropods, compound eyes are present with mosaic vision.

Annelids (*Latin, annulus*-ring; *idos*-form)	Arthropods (Greek, *arthro*-jointed; *podos*-foot)
3. The differentiation occurs in a segmental fashion, with the segments lined up one after another from head to tail (metameric segmentation).	3. Body segments are grouped into two regions, *i.e.*, **cephalothorax** (head and thorax together) and **abdomen** or three region, *i.e.*, head, thorax and abdomen. Body segment somite of these animals usually bears paired lateral and jointed legs or appendages. Muscular system along with exoskeleton for attachment is present. Gilia are absent.
4. Their sexes may be either hermaphroditic or separate.	4. Fertilisation is usually internal. They can be oviparous or ovoviviparous. Sexes are usually separate.
5. They respire through their skin.	5. Respiration occur through general body surface, gills, **air tubes** (trachea) or **book lungs**.

Q.54 Which organism is more complex and evolved among bacteria, mushroom and mango tree? Give reasons.

Ans. Mango tree is the most evolved and complex organism. It is an eukaryotic, multicellular, autotrophic, terrestrial, plant. It is an angiosperm (seeds are covered). Its reproductive organs are aggregated in a flower and therefore it is called a flowering plant.

Bacteria are prokaryotic, unicellular organism and mushroom (fungi) are heterotrophic, simple thallophyte with no body differentiation. Therefore, both of these are simple organism.

Q.55 Differentiate between flying lizard and bird. Draw the diagram.

Ans. Flying lizard is a reptile while bird belongs to class–Aves.

Class–Reptilia (L., *repre*-to crawl; creeping vertebrates)	Class-Aves (L., *avis*-bird)
1. Ectothermic (cold-blooded), terrestrial or aquatic vertebrates.	1. Endothermic (warm-blooded), tetrapodous vertebrates with various flight adaptations. Size ranges from smallest humming bird to largest ostrich.
2. The body is covered with dry water-proof skin, having horny epidermal scales or dermal scute plates.	2. Horny scales persist on the feet and **feathers** cover most of the body. Cutaneous glands are absent.
3. Body varies in form and is usually divided into head, neck, trunk and tail.	3. Spindle or boat-shaped body is divisible into head, neck, trunk and tail.

Class–Reptilia (L., *repre*-to crawl; creeping vertebrates)	Class-Aves (L., *avis*-bird)
4. Limbs are tetrapodous pentadacytle (five-toed) type; with clawed digits (limbs are absent in snakes and some lizards).	4. Forelimbs modified into wings for flight. Hind-limbs bear four clawed digits and are adapted for walking, perching, or swimming.
5. Heart is three-chambered and is divided into two auricles and an incompletely divided ventricle. Only crocodiles have four-chambered heart.	5. Four-chambered heart with two auricles and two ventricles.
6. Fertilisation is internal. Most reptiles are oviparous and lay their eggs with tough covering and do not need to lay their eggs in water. A few reptiles are viviparous, (*e.g.*, lizards and snakes). No aquatic larval stage.	6. Fertilisation is internal. They are oviparous and lay large, yolk-laden eggs having hard shell.
7. A flying Lizard	7. A bird

Q. 56 List out some common features in cat, rat and bat.

Ans. Cat, bat and rat belong to the class–Mammalia and have following common features

(i) All have notochord at some stage of their life cycle.
(ii) All are warm-blooded
(iii) All have four-chambered heart.
(iv) All have skin covered with hair and have sweat and oil glands.
(v) Body is divisible into head, neck, trunk and tail.
(vi) Females have milk producing mammary glands.
(vii) Fleshy external ear (pinna) is present.
(viii) Respiration occurs through lungs.
(ix) Excrete urea (ureotelic animals)
(x) Fertilisation is internal.

Q.57 Why do we keep both snake and turtle in the same class?

Ans. Snake and turtle belong to same class–Reptilia. They are kept in same class because both

(i) are cold-blooded.
(ii) have scales as outer covering.
(iii) have lungs for breathing.
(iv) have three-chambered heart.
(v) lay eggs with tough outer covering.
(vi) Fertilisation is internal.

Chapter

08 Motion

Multiple Choice Questions (MCQs)

Choose the correct answer from the given four options in the following questions

Q. 1 A particle is moving in a circular path of radius r. The displacement after covering half a circle would be

(a) zero (b) πr (c) $2r$ (d) $2\pi r$

Ans. ***(c)*** Given, after covering half the circle, the particle will reach the diametrically opposite point *i.e.*, from point A to point B. And we know that displacement is shortest path between initial and final point.

$\therefore$ Displacement after half circle = $AB = OA + OB$ [$\because$ Given, OA and $OB = r$]

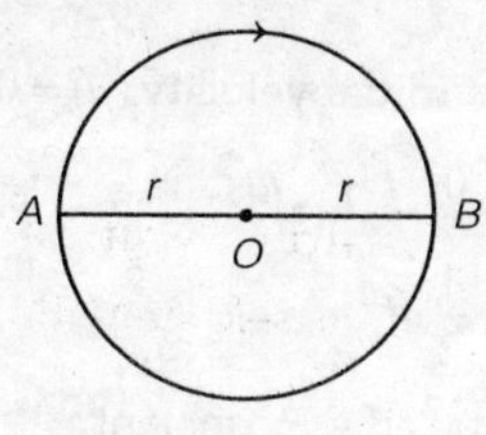

$= r + r = 2r$

Hence, the displacement after half circle is $2r$.

Q. 2 A body is thrown vertically upward with velocity u, the greatest height h to which it will rise is

(a) u/g (b) $u^2/2g$ (c) u^2/g (d) $u/2g$

Ans. ***(b)*** Given, initial velocity = u, height = h and $a = g$ (acceleration due to gravity)

At the highest point, final velocity becomes zero *i.e.*, $v = 0$

From, third equation of motion, $v^2 = u^2 - 2gh$

Where, $s = h$ and $a = -g$ [negative sign show retardation]

$$0 = u^2 - 2gh$$

$$2gh = u^2$$

$$\Rightarrow \quad h = \frac{u^2}{2g}$$

Here, we have used negative sign because the body is moving against the gravity.

Mistake Alert ! *Sometimes students forget to use the proper equation and end up using wrong height formula like* $\frac{4}{2g}$ *or* $\frac{u}{g}$.

Q. 3 The numerical ratio of displacement to distance for a moving object is

(a) always less than 1 (b) always equal to 1
(c) always more than 1 (d) equal or less than 1

Ans. **(d)** Displacement of an object can be less than or equal to the distance covered by the object, because the magnitude of displacement is not equal to distance. However, it can be, so if the motion is along a straight line without any change in direction.

So, the ratio of displacement to distance is always equal to or less than 1.

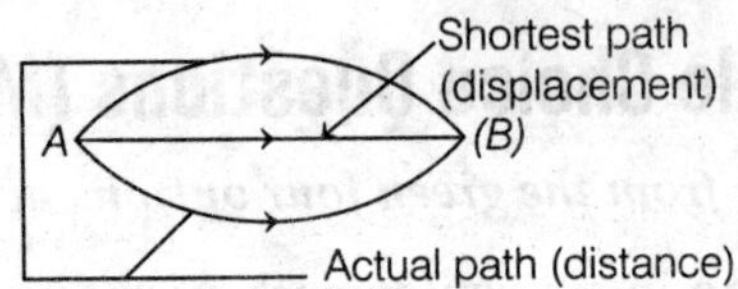

Q. 4 If the displacement of an object is proportional to square of time, then the object moves with

(a) uniform velocity (b) uniform acceleration
(c) increasing acceleration (d) decreasing acceleration

Ans. **(b)** From second equation of motion, $s = ut + \frac{1}{2}at^2$

If object starts from rest *i.e.*, initial velocity $(u) = 0$ and acceleration (a) in time (t)

Then,
$$s = 0 \times t + \frac{1}{2}at^2$$
$$s = \frac{1}{2}at^2$$
$$s \propto t^2, \text{ if } a = \text{constant}$$

So, the object moves with constant or uniform acceleration.

Q. 5 From the given v-t graph (see figure), it can be inferred that the object is

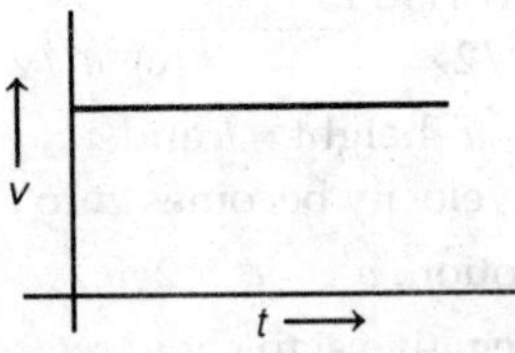

(a) in uniform motion (b) at rest
(c) in non-uniform motion (d) moving with uniform acceleration

Ans. **(a)** From the given v-t graph, it is clear that the velocity of the object is not changing with time *i.e.*, the object is in uniform motion.

Q. 6 Suppose a boy is enjoying a ride on a *merry-go-round* which is moving with a constant speed of 10 ms^{-1}. It implies that the boy is

(a) at rest (b) moving with no acceleration
(c) in accelerated motion (d) moving with uniform velocity

Ans. ***(c)*** In merry-go-round, the speed is constant but velocity is not constant, because its direction goes on changing at every point *i.e.*, there is acceleration in the motion. So, we can say that the boy is in accelerated motion.

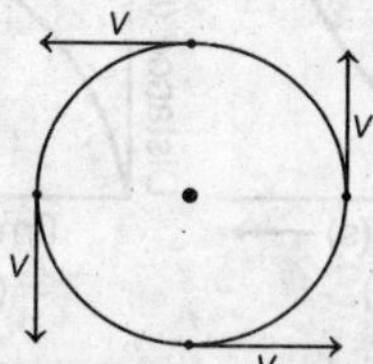

Q. 7 Area under a v-t graph represents a physical quantity which has the unit

(a) m^2 (b) m (c) m^3 (d) ms^{-1}

Ans. ***(b)*** Area under v-t graph represent displacement whose unit is metre or (m). Because, unit of velocity v = m/s and unit of time (T) = s.

$\therefore$ Unit of displacement under (v-t) graph $= \frac{m}{s} \times s = m$.

Hence, the unit of displacement under (v-t) graph is metre (m).

Q. 8 Four cars A, B, C and D are moving on a levelled road. Their distance *versus* time graphs are shown in figure. Choose the correct statement.

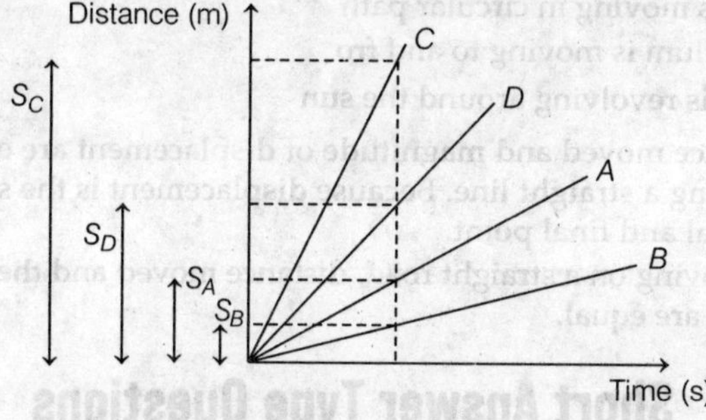

(a) Car A is faster than car D
(b) Car B is the slowest
(c) Car D is faster than car C
(d) Car C is the slowest

Ans. ***(b)*** The slope of distance- time graph represents the speed.

As speed, $v = \frac{S_2 - S_1}{t_2 - t_1}$

From the graph, it is clear that the slope of distance-time graph for car B is less than all other cars. So, the slope is minimum for car B. Hence, car B is the slowest.

Q. 9 Which of the following figures represents uniform motion of a moving object correctly?

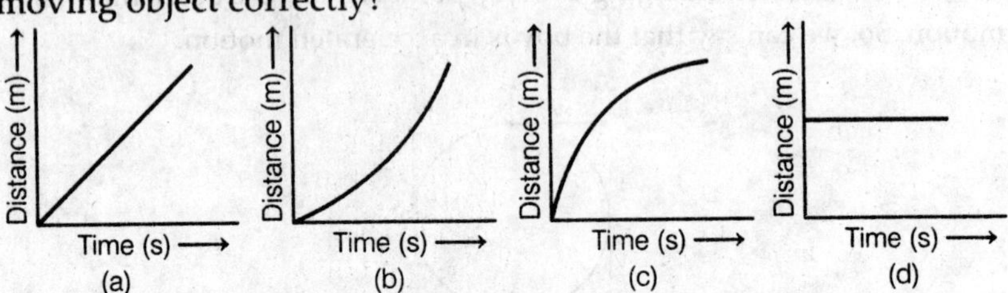

Ans. *(a)* For uniform motion, the distance-time graph is a straight line (because in uniform motion object covers equal distanced in equal interval of time).

Q.10 Slope of a velocity-time graph gives

(a) the distance (b) the displacement
(c) the acceleration (d) the speed

Ans. *(c)* Slope of velocity-time graph gives acceleration.

Because slope of the curve is $= \frac{v_2 - v_1}{t_2 - t_1}$, where , $\frac{v_2 - v_1}{t_2 - t_1}$ = acceleration.

Q.11 In which of the following cases of motions, the distance moved and the magnitude of displacement are equal?

(a) If the car is moving on straight road
(b) If the car is moving in circular path
(c) The pendulum is moving to and fro
(d) The earth is revolving around the sun

Ans. *(a)* The distance moved and magnitude of displacement are equal only in the case of motion along a straight line. Because displacement is the shortest path between initial and final point.

So, for car moving on a straight road, distance moved and the magnitude of displacement are equal.

Short Answer Type Questions

Q.12 The displacement of a moving object in a given interval of a time is zero. Would the distance travelled by the object also be zero? Justify your answer?

Ans. The displacement of a moving object in a given interval of a time is zero *i.e.,* the object comes back to its initial position in the given time (displacement is the shortest distance between the initial and final position of an object).

The distance in this case will not be zero because distance is the total path covered by the body. If the object comes back to its initial position, the displacement will be zero but not distance.

Q.13 How will the equations of motion for an object moving with a uniform velocity change?

Ans. We know that, the equations of uniformly accelerated motion are

(i) $v = u + at$

(ii) $s = ut + \frac{1}{2}at^2$

(iii) $v^2 = u^2 + 2as$

where, u = Initial velocity
v = Final velocity
a = Acceleration
t = Time
and s = Distance

For an object moving with uniform velocity (velocity which is not changing with time), then acceleration $a = 0$.

So, equations of motion will become (putting $a = 0$ in above equations)

(i) $v = u$ (ii) $s = ut$ (iii) $v^2 = u^2$

Q.14 A girl walks along a straight path to drop a letter in the letter box and comes back to her initial position. Her displacement-time graph is shown in figure. Plot a velocity-time graph for the same.

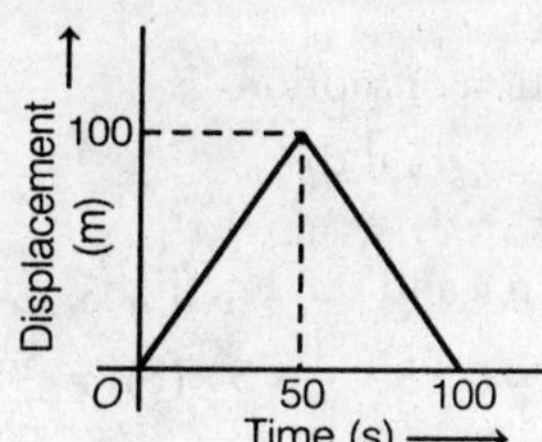

Ans. From the graph,

(i) Initial velocity, $u = 0$ [Since, displacement and time is zero]

(ii) Velocity after 50 s, $v = \frac{\text{Displacement}}{\text{Time}}$ [∵ Given, displacement = 100 m]

$\Rightarrow$ $v = \frac{100}{50} = 2\ \text{ms}^{-1}$

(iii) Velocity after 100 s, $v = \frac{\text{Displacement}}{\text{Time}}$

[Here, displacement = zero and time = 100 s]

$\Rightarrow$ $v = \frac{0}{100} = 0$

Therefore,

v	0	2	0
t	0	50	100

Velocity-time graph plotted from the above data is shown below

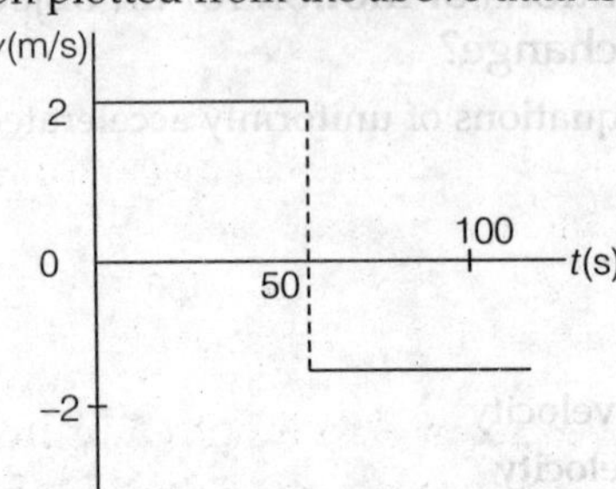

Q.15 **A car starts from rest and moves along the *x*-axis with constant acceleration 5 ms^{-2} for 8 s. If it then continues with constant velocity. What distance will the car cover in 12 s, since it started from rest?**

Ans. Given, the car starts from rest, so its initial velocity $u = 0$ m/s.

Acceleration, $(a) = 5\ ms^{-2}$ and time $(t) = 8$ s

From first equation of motion,

$$v = u + at \quad \ldots(i)$$

Putting the value of *u*, *a* and *t* in Eq. (i), we get

$$v = 0 + 5 \times 8 = 40\ ms^{-1}$$

So, final velocity v is 40 ms^{-1}.

Again, from second equation of motion,

$$s = ut + \frac{1}{2}at^2 \quad \ldots(ii)$$

Also putting the value of *u*, *a* and *t* in Eq. (ii),

$$s = 0 \times 8 + \frac{1}{2} \times 5 \times (8)^2 = \frac{1}{2} \times 5 \times 64 = 5 \times 32 = 160\text{ m}$$

So, the distance covered in 8 s is 160 m.

Given, total time $t = 12$ s.

After 8 s, the car continues with constant velocity *i.e.*, the car will move with a velocity of 40 ms^{-1}.

So, remaining time $t = 12\text{ s} - 8\text{ s} = 4$ s

The distance covered in the last 4s (s') = Velocity × Time

[∵ Distance = Velocity × Time]

$$S' = 40 \times 4 = 160\text{ m}$$

∴ Total distance travelled in 12 s from the start

$$D = s + s' = 160 + 160 = 320\text{ m}$$

Alternate Method

Here, $u = 0$, $a = 5\text{m/s}^2$, $t = 8$ s

$$\therefore \quad s = ut + \frac{1}{2}at^2$$

$$= 0 \times 8 + \frac{1}{2} \cdot 5 \times (8)^2 = 160\text{ m}$$

This is the distance moved by the car in first sec. velocity at the end of 8s is

$$v = u + at = 0 + 5 \times 8 = 40 \text{ m/s}$$

So, remaining time,

$$t^1 = 12 - 8 = 4\text{s}$$
$$S^1 = v \times t = 40 \times 4 = 160 \text{ m}$$

Total distance covered by the car in 12s

$$\Rightarrow \quad S + S^1 = 160 + 160 = 320 \text{ m}$$

Q.16 A motorcyclist drives from A to B with a uniform speed of 30 kmh^{-1} and returns back with a speed of 20 kmh^{-1}. Find its average speed.

Thinking Process To find the t_1 and t_2 by using formula, time $= \frac{\text{distance}}{\text{speed}}$ and then put this values in formula, average speed $= \frac{\text{Total distance}}{\text{Total time}}$ and further simplify it, to get the required average speed.

Ans. Let the distance between A and B be x km.

Time taken in driving from A to B

$$t_1 = \frac{\text{Distance}}{\text{Speed}} = \frac{x}{30} \text{ h} \qquad \left[\because \text{Time} = \frac{\text{Distance}}{\text{Speed}}\right]$$

Similarly, time taken in returning from B to A.

$$t_2 = \frac{\text{Distance}}{\text{Speed}} = \frac{x}{20} \text{ h}$$

$$\text{Average speed} = \frac{\text{Total distance}}{\text{Total time}} = \frac{x + x}{t_1 + t_2}$$

$$= \frac{x + x}{\frac{x}{30} + \frac{x}{20}} = \frac{2x}{\frac{2x + 3x}{60}}$$

$$= \frac{2x \times 60}{5x} = 2 \times 12 = 24 \text{ kmh}^{-1}$$

Hence, average speed of a motorcyclist is 24 kmh^{-1}.

Q.17 The velocity-time graph (see figure) shows the motion of a cyclist. Find (i) its acceleration (ii) its velocity and (iii) the distance covered by the cyclist in 15 s.

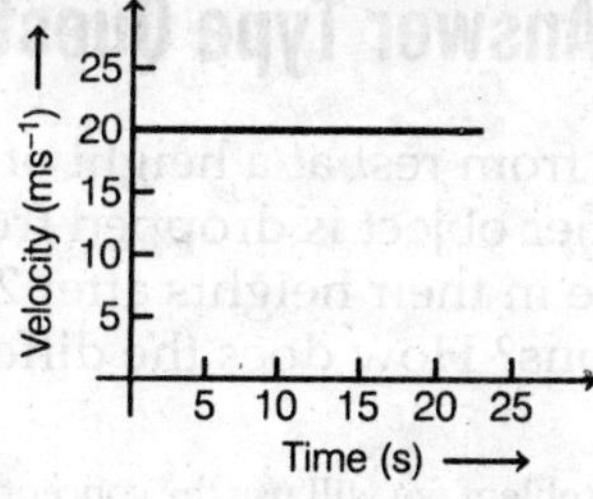

Ans. (i) From the graph, it is clear that velocity is not changing with time *i.e.*, acceleration is zero. (as $a = \frac{dv}{dt} = 0$)

(ii) Again from the graph, we can see that there is no change in the velocity with time, so velocity after 15 s will remain same as 20 ms^{-1}.

(iii) Distance covered in 15 s = Velocity × Time = 20 × 15 = 300 m

$$\left[\because \text{Time} = \frac{\text{Distance}}{\text{Speed}}\right]$$

Q.18 Draw a velocity *versus* time graph of a stone thrown vertically upwards and then coming downwards after attaining the maximum height.

Ans. When a stone is thrown vertically upwards, it has some initial velocity (let *u*). As the stone goes upwards its velocity goes on decreasing (∵ it is moving against the gravity) and at the highest point *i.e.*, maximum height) its velocity become zero. Let the stone takes time '*t*' second to reach at the highest point.

After that stone begins to fall (with zero initial velocity) and its velocity goes on increasing (since it is moving with the gravity) and it reaches its initial point of projection with the velocity *v* in the same time (with which it was thrown).

So, the velocity-time graph will look like

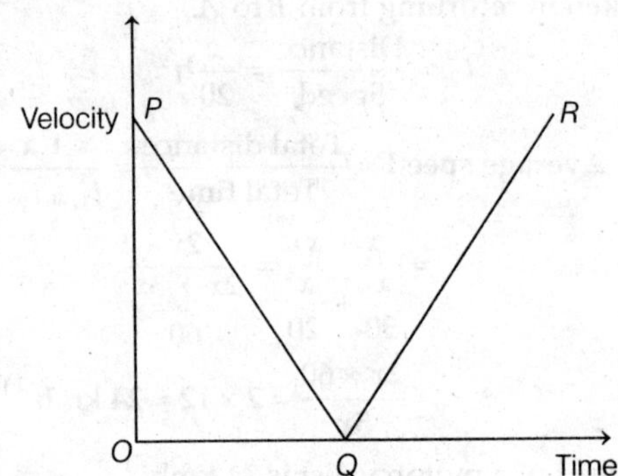

Here, PQ = Upward motion and

QR = Downward motion of stone.

Long Answer Type Questions

Q. 19 An object is dropped from rest at a height of 150 m and simultaneously another object is dropped from rest at a height 100 m. What is the difference in their heights after 2 s, if both the objects drop with same accelerations? How does the difference in heights vary with time?

- **Concept Insight** In this problem we will use the concept of second equation of motion *i.e.*, $s = ut + \frac{1}{2}at^2$, relates the displacement of an object moving under uniform acceleration, initial velocity and time.

Ans. For first object given, $u = 0$ (because object dropped from rest) and time $(t) = 2\text{s}$.
From second equation of motion, the distance covered by first object in 2 s is

$$h = ut + \frac{1}{2}gt^2$$

$$h = 0 \times 2 + \frac{1}{2} \times 10 \times (2)^2 \qquad [\because g = 10\,\text{m/s}^2]$$

$$h = 0 + \frac{1}{2} \times 10 \times 4 = 20\,\text{m}$$

A Ist object
B IInd object
150 m
100 m
ground

Height of first object from the ground after 2 s, $(h_1) = 150\,\text{m} - 20\,\text{m} = 130\,\text{m}$
For second object given, $u = 0$ and time $(t) = 2\,\text{s}$
From second equation of motion, the distance covered by second object in 2 s is

$$h = ut + \frac{1}{2}gt^2 = 0 \times 2 + \frac{1}{2} \times 10 \times (2)^2 \qquad [\because g = 10\,\text{m/s}^2]$$

$$= 0 + \frac{1}{2} \times 10 \times 4 = 20\,\text{m}$$

Height of second object from the ground after 2s then $h_2 = 100\,\text{m} - 20\,\text{m} = 80\,\text{m}$
Now, difference in the height after 2 s $= h_1 - h_2 = 130 - 80 = 50$ m
The difference in heights of the objects will remain same with time as both the objects have been dropped from rest and are falling with same acceleration *i.e.*, (acceleration due to gravity).

Q.20 An object starting from rest travels 20 m in first 2 s and 160 m in next 4 s. What will be the velocity after 7s from the start?

Thinking Process Firstly, we find the acceleration by using the second equation of motion *i.e.*, $h = ut + \frac{1}{2}at^2$ and then put this value in Newton's first equation of motion *i.e.*, $v = u + at$ to get required final velocity.

Ans. Given, object starts from rest, $u = 0, t = 2\text{s}$ and $s = 20\,\text{m}$
From second equation of motion, $s = ut + \frac{1}{2}at^2$
On putting $u = 0$ in above equation, $20 = 0 \times 2 + \frac{1}{2} \times a\,(2)^2 = 0 + \frac{1}{2} \times a \times 4$

$$20 = 2a \Rightarrow a = \frac{20}{2} \Rightarrow a = 10\,\text{m/s}^2$$

For next 4s, jouney of object;

$$t' = 4\text{s},\ u' = 20\,\text{m/s},\ s' = 160\,\text{m}$$

$$s' = u't' + \frac{1}{2}a't'^2$$

$$160 = 20 \times 4 + \frac{1}{2} \times a' \times 4^2$$

$$a' = 10\,\text{m/s}^2$$

i.e., the acceleration is constant throughtout the jouney.

Now, from first equation of motion, velocity after 7 s from the start

$$v = u + at \qquad \text{[put } a = 10 \text{ m/s}^2\text{]}$$

$$= 0 + 10 \times 7 = 70 \text{ m/s}$$

Q.21 Using following data, draw time-displacement graph for a moving object.

Time (s)	0	2	4	6	8	10	12	14	16
Displacement (m)	0	2	4	4	4	6	4	2	0

Use this graph to find average velocity for first 4 s, for next 4 s and for last 6 s.

Thinking Process Firstly, consider the time is on X -axis and displacement is on Y-axis. Now, plot all the points (0, 0), (2, 2), (4, 4), (6, 4), (8, 4), (10, 6), (12, 4), (14, 2) and (16, 0) on a graph paper and join by line segment.

Ans. Therefore, displacement-time graph is shown in figure.

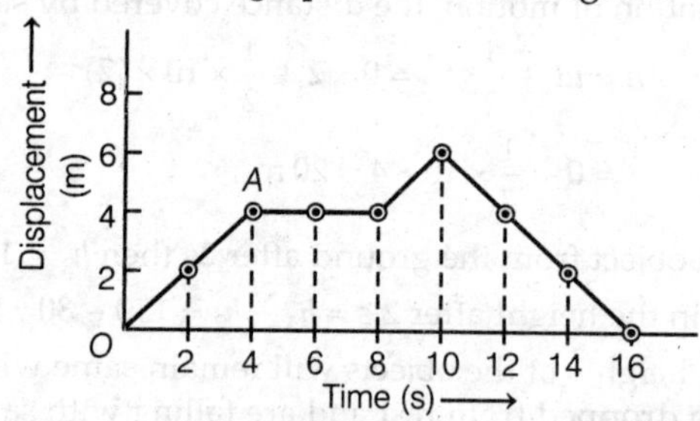

$$\text{Average velocity for first 4s} = \frac{\text{Change in displacement}}{\text{Total time taken}}$$

$$v = \frac{4-0}{4-0} = \frac{4 \text{ m}}{4 \text{ s}} = 1 \text{ ms}^{-1}$$

Average velocity for next 4 s (*i.e.*, in the interval of 4 s to 8 s), $v = \frac{4-4}{8-4} = \frac{0}{4} = 0$ m/s.

$$\text{Average velocity for last 6 s} = \frac{(0-6) \text{ m}}{(16-10) \text{ s}} = \left(\frac{-6}{6}\right) = -1 \text{ ms}^{-1}$$

Q.22 An electron moving with a velocity of $5 \times 10^4 \text{ ms}^{-1}$ enters into a uniform electric field and acquires a uniform acceleration of 10^4 ms^{-2} in the direction of its initial motion.

(i) Calculate the time in which the electron would acquire a velocity double of its initial velocity.

(ii) How much distance the electron would cover in this time?

Thinking Process Firstly, we find the time by using Newton's first equation of motion *i.e.*, $v = u + at$, and then put this value in Newton's second equation of motion *i.e.*, $s = ut + \frac{1}{2}at^2$ to get required distance.

Ans. Given, initial velocity, $u = 5 \times 10^4\ ms^{-1}$
and acceleration, $a = 10^4\ ms^{-2}$

(i) According to the question, final velocity, $v = 2u, t = ?$
From first equation of motion, $v = u + at$

$$2u = u + 10^4 \times t \quad [\because \text{put } v = 2u, a = 10^4 ms^{-2}]$$
$$2u - u = 10^4 \times t$$
$$10^4 \times t = u$$
$$\Rightarrow \quad t = \frac{(u)}{10^4} = \frac{5 \times 10^4}{10^4} = 5\text{ s} \quad [\because u = 5 \times 10^4 \text{ m/s}]$$

i.e., after 5 s electron will acquire a velocity double of its initial velocity.

(ii) From second equation of motion,
Distance covered in t second, $s = ut + \frac{1}{2}at^2$

$$= 5 \times 10^4 \times 5 + \frac{1}{2} \times 10^4 (5)^2$$
$$[\text{put, } u = 5 \times 10^4 \text{ m/s}, t = 5\text{ s and } a = 10^4 \text{ m/s}^2]$$
$$= 25 \times 10^4 + \frac{1}{2} \times 10^4 \times 25$$
$$= 25 \times 10^4 + 12.5 \times 10^4$$
$$= 10^4 (25 + 12.5)$$
$$= 37.5 \times 10^4 \text{ m} = 37.5 \times 10 \times 10^3 \text{ m} = 375 \times 10^3 \text{ m}$$
$$= 375 \text{ km} \quad [\because 1000 \text{ m} = 1 \text{ km}]$$

Q.23 Obtain a relation for the distance travelled by an object moving with a uniform acceleration in the interval between 4th and 5th second.

Thinking Process Firstly, we use the Newton's second equation of motion *i.e.*, $s = ut + \frac{1}{2}at^2$ and then find the difference between s_5 and s_4.

Ans. From second equation of motion,
Distance travelled in t s

$$s = ut + \frac{1}{2}at^2$$

Distance travelled in 4 s

$$s_4 = u \times 4 + \frac{1}{2}a(4)^2 \quad [\because \text{put } t = 4\text{ s}]$$
$$= 4u + \frac{1}{2} \times a \times 16 = 4u + 8a \quad (S_4 = \text{distance travelled in 4th sec})$$

Again, distance travelled in 5 s

$$s_5 = ut + \frac{1}{2}at^2 \quad [\because \text{put } t = 5\text{ s}]$$
$$= u \times 5 + \frac{1}{2}a(5)^2 = 5u + \frac{25}{2}a \quad (S_5 = \text{distance travelled in 5th sec})$$

So, distance travelled in the interval between 4th and 5th second.

$$s = s_5 - s_4 = \left(5u + \frac{25}{2}a\right) - (4u + 8a)$$

$$= 5u + \frac{25}{2}a - 4u - 8a$$

$$= 5u - 4u + \frac{25}{2}a - 8a$$

$$= u + \frac{25a - 16a}{2} = \left(u + \frac{9}{2}a\right) \text{m}$$

So, the relation will be $(u + 9/2a)$ m.

Q.24 Two stones are thrown vertically upwards simultaneously with their initial velocities u_1 and u_2 respectively. Prove that the heights reached by them would be in the ratio of $u_1^2 : u_2^2$ (assume upward acceleration is $-g$ and downward acceleration to be $+g$).

- **Concept Insight** In this problem, firstly we find the h_1 and h_2 by using newton's third equation of motion i.e., $v^2 = u^2 + 2\,gh$ used when dealing with objects under free fall or vertical motion influenced by gravity and then find the ratio of h_1 and h_2.

Ans. For Ist stone, given initial velocity $u = u_1$

Let height attained by it be h_1.

From third equation of motion, $v^2 = u^2 - 2gh$ for upward motion

Here, we have used negative sign, because as given upward acceleration is taken to be $-g$

At the highest point the velocity becomes zero *i.e.*, $v = 0$

$$0 = u_1^2 - 2gh_1$$

$$\Rightarrow \quad 2gh_1 = u_1^2 \Rightarrow h_1 = \frac{u_1^2}{2g}$$

Similarly,

For IInd stone, given initial velocity, $u = u_2$

Let the height attained by it be h_2.

From third equation of motion, $v^2 = u^2 - 2gh$

[at the highest point the velocity becomes zero *i.e.*, $v = 0$]

$$0 = u_2^2 - 2gh_2$$

$$\therefore \quad 2gh_2 = u_2^2$$

$$\Rightarrow \quad h_2 = \frac{u_2^2}{2g}$$

Now, ratio of heights reached by the two stones

$$h_1 : h_2 = \frac{u_1^2}{2g} : \frac{u_2^2}{2g}$$

Therefore, $$h_1 : h_2 = u_1^2 : u_2^2$$

Chapter

09

Force and Laws of Motion

Multiple Choice Questions (MCQs)

Choose the correct answer from the given four options in the following questions :

Q. 1 Which of the following statement is not correct for an object moving along a straight path in an accelerated motion?

(a) Its speed keeps changing
(b) Its velocity always changes
(c) It always goes away from the earth
(d) A force is always acting on it

Ans. ***(c)*** For an object moving along a straight path in an accelerated motion, it is not necessary that it always goes away from the earth.

Q. 2 According to the third law of motion, action and reaction

(a) always act on the same body
(b) always act on different bodies in opposite directions
(c) have same magnitude and direction
(d) act on either body at normal to each other

Ans. ***(b)*** According to third law of motion, action and reaction always act on different bodies in opposite directions.

Q. 3 A goalkeeper in a game of football pulls his hands backwards after holding the ball shot at the goal. This enables the goalkeeper to

(a) exert larger force on the ball
(b) reduce the force exerted by the ball on hands
(c) increase the rate of change of momentum
(d) decrease the rate of change of momentum

Ans. ***(d)*** The goalkeeper pulls his hands backwards after holding the ball to decrease the rate of change of momentum by increasing the time. By doing this, less force is exerted on his hands ($\because$ Force is directly proportional to the rate of change of momentum).

Q. 4 The inertia of an object tends to cause the object

(a) to increase its speed
(b) to decrease its speed
(c) to resist any change in its state of motion
(d) to decelerate due to friction

Ans. ***(c)*** The inertia of an object tends to cause the object to resist any change in its state of rest or motion.

Q. 5 A passenger in a moving train tosses a coin which falls behind him. It means that motion of the train is

(a) accelerated (b) uniform
(c) retarded (d) along circular tracks

Ans. ***(a)*** If the coin falls behind the passenger that means the train is accelerated. When the coin is tossed it has same velocity as that of train but during the time it is in air its velocity becomes less than that of train (because the train is accelerated), so it falls behind the passenger.

Q. 6 An object of mass 2 kg is sliding with a constant velocity of 4 ms^{-1} on a frictionless horizontal table. The force required to keep the object moving with the same velocity is

(a) 32 N (b) 0 N (c) 2 N (d) 8 N

Ans. ***(b)*** Given, mass $m = 2$ kg, velocity $v = 4\ ms^{-1}$

As the object is moving with a constant velocity *i.e.*, 4 ms^{-1}, So the acceleration of the object is zero *i.e.*, $a = 0$ and according to the property of inertia if there is no external force acting on the body, then body remains as it is *i.e.*, if the body is at rest, remains in rest and if it is in motion remains in motion.

Alternate Method

(b) Given,

Mass, $m = 2$ kg

Velocity, $v = 4\ ms^{-1}$

As the object is moving with a constant velocity *i.e.*, 4 ms^{-1}, so the acceleration of the object is zero. *i,e.*, $a = 0$

We know that,

Force $= ma$

By substituting the given values in the expression, we get

Force $= 2 \times 0 = 0$ N

Q. 7 Rocket works on the principle of conservation of

(a) mass (b) energy (c) momentum (d) velocity

Ans. ***(c)*** Rocket works on the principle of conservation of momentum. In a rocket, the fuel burns and produces gas at high temperature. These gases are ejected out of the rocket from a nozzle at the back side of the rocket. The ejecting gas exerts a forward force on the rocket which help in accelerating.

Through the mass of gases escaping per second is very small and their momentum is very large due to their tremendous velocity of escape. An equal and opposite momentum is imparted to the rocket which despite its large mass builds up a high velocity.

Q. 8 A water tanker filled upto $\frac{2}{3}$ of its height is moving with a uniform speed. On sudden application of the brake, the water in the tank would

(a) move backward (b) move forward
(c) be unaffected (d) rise upwards

Ans. ***(b)*** On the sudden application of brake, the tanker will come in the state of rest but the water remains in the state of motion, so the water will move forward.

Short Answer Type Questions

Q. 9 There are three solids made up of aluminium, steel and wood of the same shape and same volume. Which of them would have highest inertia?

Ans. As the mass is a measure of inertia, the solid of same shape and size, having more mass than other solids will have highest inertia. Since , the steel has greatest density and greatest mass therefore it has highest inertia.

Q.10 Two balls of the same size but of different materials, rubber and iron, are kept on the smooth floor of a moving train. The brakes are applied suddenly to stop the train. Will the balls start rolling? If so, in which direction? Will they move with the same speed? Give reasons for your answer.

Ans. When the train is stopped suddenly, then it comes in the state of rest but the balls remain in the state of motion. So, due to inertia of motion, the balls move in the forward direction.

As the balls are of same size but of different materials that means their mass will be different. So, both the balls will move with different speeds. An iron ball that is heavier than the rubber ball will move with a lower speed.

Q.11 Two identical bullets are fired one by a light rifle and another by a heavy rifle with the same force. Which rifle will hurt the shoulder more and why?

Ans. As both the bullets are identical and are fired with the same force. So, to reduce recoil velocity, we use, heavy rifle, so that its heavy mass compensate the large momentum. But for light rifle, recoil velocity will be large due to small mass thus light rifle will hurt more to the shoulder.

Q.12 A horse continues to apply a force in order to move a cart with a constant speed. Explain why?

Ans. When the cart starts moving, frictional force starts working on the wheel of cart in opposite to the motion. So, horse need to apply continuous force in forward direction to maintain constant speed.

Q.13 Suppose a ball of mass m is thrown vertically upward with an initial speed v, its speed decreases continuously till it becomes zero. Thereafter, the ball begins to fall downward and attain the speed v again before striking the ground. It implies that the magnitude of initial and final momentums of the ball are same. Yet, it is not an example of conservation of momentum. Explain why?

Ans. Momentum of a system remains conserved if no external force acts on the system. In the given example, there is gravitational force acting on the ball which is an external force, so it is not an example of conservation of momentum.

Q.14 Velocity *versus* time graph of a ball of mass 50 g rolling on a concrete floor is shown in figure. Calculate the acceleration and frictional force of the floor on the ball.

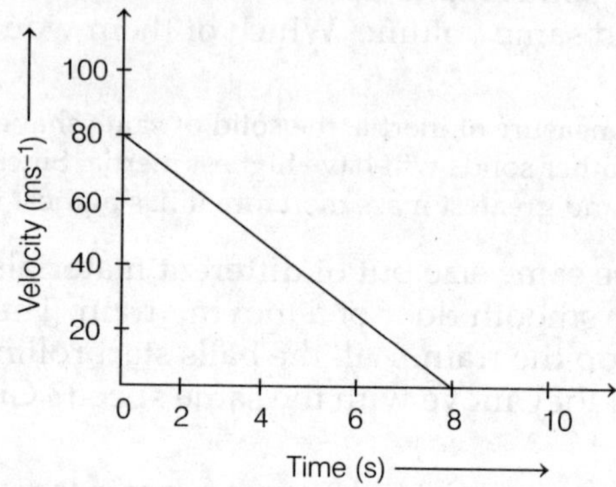

Thinking Process Firstly, we find the acceleration by using first equation of motion *i.e.*, $v = u + at$ and then put this value in Newton's second law *i.e.*, $F = ma$ to get required frictional force.

Ans. Given, mass, $m = 50\text{ g} = \dfrac{50}{1000} = 0.05\text{ kg}$ [$\because$ 1 kg = 1000 g]

Initial velocity, $u = 80\text{ ms}^{-1}$

Final velocity, $v = 0\text{ ms}^{-1}$

Time taken, $t = 8\text{ s}$

From first equation of motion $v = u + at$

$$\Rightarrow \quad at = v - u$$

$$\text{Acceleration, } a = \frac{v-u}{t} = \frac{0-80}{8} = \frac{-80}{8} = -10\text{ ms}^{-2}$$

[Negative sign shows retardation]

Now, frictional force of the floor on the ball

$$F = ma = 0.05 \times -10 = -0.5\text{ N}$$

[Negative sign shows against the direction of motion]

Alternate Method

From the graph, we find that

$$u = 80\text{ m/s},\ v = 0,\ t = 8\text{s}$$

From $v = u + at$,

$$0 = 80 + a \times 8$$

$$\Rightarrow \quad a = \frac{0-80}{8}$$

$$\Rightarrow \quad a = -\frac{80}{8} = -10\text{ m/s}$$

As,

$$m = 50\text{ g} = \frac{50}{1000}\text{ kg} = \frac{1}{20}\text{ kg}$$

$$\therefore \quad F = ma = \frac{1}{20} \times (-10) = -0.5\text{ N}$$

Negative sign is for opposing frictional force of the floor on the ball.

Q. 15 A truck of mass M is moved under a force F. If the truck is then loaded with an object equal to the mass of the truck and the driving force is halved, then how does the acceleration change?

Ans. Let, initial mass, $m_1 = M$

Initial force, $F_1 = F$

According to the question, new mass, $m_2 = M + M = 2M$

and new force, $F_2 = \frac{F}{2}$

From Newton's second law, $F = ma$

$\Rightarrow a = \frac{F}{m}$

Change in acceleration

$$\frac{a_1}{a_2} = \frac{F_1}{F_2} \times \frac{m_2}{m_1} = \frac{F}{F/2} \times \frac{2M}{M} = \frac{2F}{F} \times \frac{2M}{M} = 4$$

$$\Rightarrow \frac{a_1}{a_2} = 4 \Rightarrow 4a_2 = a_1 \Rightarrow a_2 = \frac{a_1}{4} = \frac{1}{4} \times a_1$$

Hence, the new acceleration will be one-fourth of previous acceleration.

Q.16 Two friends on roller skates are standing 5 m apart facing each other. One of them throws a ball of 2 kg towards the other, who catches it. How will this activity affect the position of the two? Explain your answer.

Ans. Separation between them will increase. Initially the momentum of both of them are zero as they are at rest. In order to conserve the momentum the one who throws the ball would move backward.

The second will experience a net force after catching the ball and therefore will move backward that is in the direction of the force.

Q.17 Water sprinkler used for grass lawn begins to rotate as soon as the water is supplied. Explain the principle on which it works.

Ans. Water sprinkler works on Newton's third law of motion. When the water supplied, it exerts an equal and opposite force on the sprinkler due to which it rotates.

Long Answer Type Questions

Q.18 Using second law of motion, derive the relation between force and acceleration. A bullet of 10 g strikes a sand-bag at speed of 10^3 ms^{-1} and gets embedded after travelling 5 cm. Calculate

(i) the resistive force exerted by the sand on the bullet.

(ii) the time taken by the bullet to come to rest.

Thinking Process

(i) Firstly, to prove the Newton's second law *i.e.*, $F = ma$ and further we will find acceleration by using third equation of motion i.e., $v^2 = u^2 + 2as$ as determine the value of 'a' and put this value in Newton's second law *i.e.*, $F = ma$ to get required force.

(ii) Again, find the value of t by using the first equation of motion *i.e.*, $v = u + at$.

Ans. If a body of mass (m), moving at velocity (u) accelerates uniformly at (a) for time 't', so that its velocity changes to v, then

$$\text{initial momentum } p_1 = mu$$

$$\text{and final momentum } p_2 = mv$$

$\therefore$ Change in momentum $= p_2 - p_1 = mv - mu = m(v-u)$

According to the second law of motion, force $F \propto \dfrac{\text{Change in momentum}}{\text{Time}}$

$$F \propto \frac{p_2 - p_1}{t}$$

$$\Rightarrow \quad F \propto \frac{m(v-u)}{t}$$

$$\Rightarrow \quad F \propto ma \qquad \left[\text{where, } \frac{v-u}{t} = a\right]$$

$$F = kma$$

Here, $k = 1$

$\therefore$ $F = ma$

Given, $m = 10\text{g} = \dfrac{10}{1000}\text{ kg} = 0.01\text{ kg}, \text{u} = 10^3\text{ m/s}, v = 0$ $[\because 1\text{ kg} = 1000\text{ g}]$

and $s = 5\text{ cm} = \dfrac{5}{100}\text{ m} = 0.05\text{ m}$ $[\because 1\text{ m} = 100\text{ cm}]$

(i) From third equation of motion, $v^2 = u^2 + 2as$

$$\Rightarrow \quad v^2 - u^2 = 2as$$

$$\Rightarrow \quad a = \frac{v^2 - u^2}{2s} = \frac{(0)^2 - (10^3)^2}{2 \times 0.05}$$

$$a = \frac{-10^6}{0.1} = -10^7\text{ m/s}^2$$

Now, force applied by the bullet,

$$F = ma$$

$$= 0.01 \times -10^7 = -10^5\text{ N}$$

[negative sign shown against the direction of motion]

The resistive force exerted by the sand on the bullet $= 10^5$ N

(ii) From first equation of motion,

$$v = u + at$$

$$\Rightarrow \quad at = v - u$$

Now, time taken by bullet to come to rest, $t = \dfrac{v-u}{a}$

$$\Rightarrow \quad t = \frac{0 - 10^3}{-10^7}$$

$$\Rightarrow \quad t = \frac{-10^3}{-10^7} = 10^3 \times 10^{-7}$$

$$\Rightarrow \quad t = 10^{-4}\text{ s}$$

Hence, force $(F) = 10^5$ N and time $(t) = 10^{-4}$ s.

Q.19 Derive the unit of force using the second law of motion. A force of 5 N produces an acceleration of 8 ms^{-2} on a mass m_1 and an acceleration of 24 ms^{-2} on a mass m_2. What acceleration would the same force provide, if both the masses are tied together?

Ans. We know that, SI unit of mass, is kg

SI unit of acceleration, is ms^{-2}

Now, from Newton's second law, $F = ma$

$\therefore$ SI unit of force, F is kg-ms^{-2}

1 kg-ms^{-2} is known as 1 newton (N)

$\therefore$ 1 newton (N) = 1 kg-ms^{-2}

$\therefore$ 1 newton can be defined as, "the force is said to be 1 newton if it produces 1 ms^{-2} acceleration in a body of 1 kg mass".

Condition I Given, $F_1 = 5$ N, $a_1 = 8$ ms^{-2} and m_1 = mass of first body

$F_2 = 5$ N, $a_2 = 24$ ms^{-2} and m_2 = mass of second body

From Newton's second law, $F = ma$ or $5 = m_1 \times 8$

$$\Rightarrow \quad m_1 = \frac{5}{8} \text{ kg}$$

Condition II Again, using Newton's second law $F = ma$, $5 = m_2 \times 24$

$$\Rightarrow \quad m_2 = \frac{5}{24} \text{ kg}$$

Sum of two masses $m_1 + m_2 = \frac{5}{8} + \frac{5}{24} = \frac{15+5}{24} = \frac{20}{24} = \frac{10}{12} = \frac{5}{6}$

Acceleration produced by the same force provided if both the masses are tied together.

i.e., $\Rightarrow$ F = same force

$\Rightarrow$ $M = m_1 + m_2$, M = combined mass

$$a = \frac{F}{(m_1 + m_2)}$$

$$= \frac{5}{5/6} = \frac{5 \times 6}{5} = 6 \text{ ms}^{-2}$$

Hence, the acceleration is 6 ms^{-2}.

Mistake Alert ! *Students can misunderstand or forget to convert units properly, like using grams instead of kilograms or not converting acceleration into m/s^2.*

Q.20 What is momentum? Write its SI unit. Interpret force in terms of momentum. Represent the following graphically

(i) momentum *versus* velocity when mass is fixed.

(ii) momentum *versus* mass when velocity is constant.

Ans. Momentum The quantity of motion possessed by a moving body is known as momentum of the body.

Momentum of an object of mass m moving with a velocity v is the product of its mass and velocity.

It is denoted by p and its SI unit is kg- ms^{-1}.

As from Newton's IInd law, rate of change of momentum is equal to force applied. So,

$$F \propto \frac{\Delta p}{\Delta t} \qquad [\because \Delta p = m \times \Delta v]$$

$$= m\frac{\Delta v}{\Delta t} = ma \quad \left[\because \text{ Acceleration} = \text{rate of change of velocity} = \frac{\Delta v}{\Delta t}\right]$$

Hence, force applied on an produces acceleration,

(i) Momentum *versus* velocity when mass is fixed.

$$p = mv$$

If m is fixed, then $p \propto v$

∴ Momentum *versus* velocity graph will be a straight line passing through the origin (if $v = 0$, then $p = 0$).

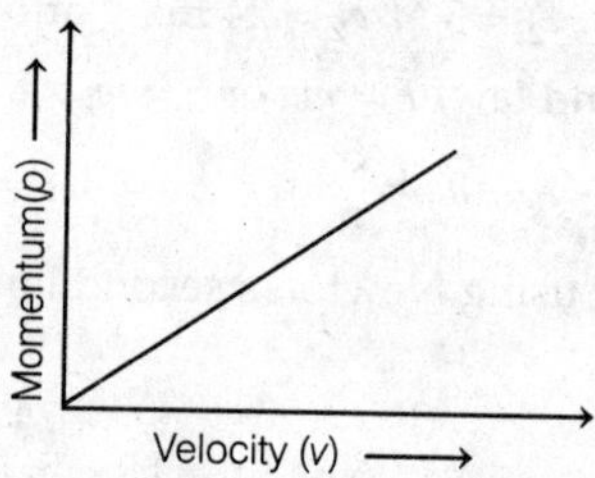

(ii) Momentum *versus* mass graph when velocity is constant for different body

$$p = mv$$

If velocity is constant for different masses, then

$$p \propto m$$

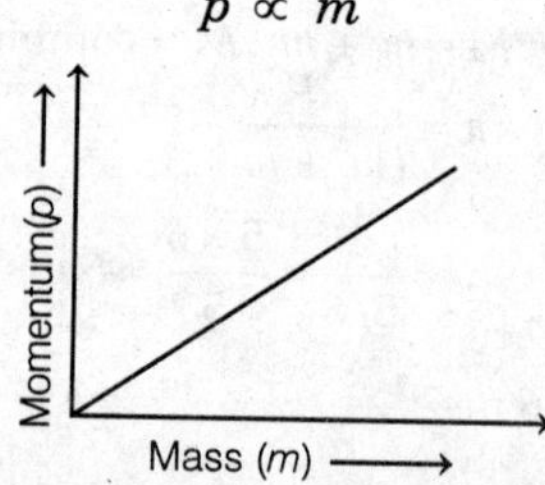

So, the momentum *versus* mass graph will be a straight line passing through the origin (if $m = 0$, then $p = 0$).

Chapter

10 Gravitation

Multiple Choice Questions (MCQs)

Choose the correct answer from the given four options in the following questions :

Q. 1 Two objects of different masses falling freely near the surface of moon would

(a) have same velocities at any instant (b) have different accelerations

(c) experience forces of same magnitude (d) undergo a change in their inertia

Ans. ***(a)*** Objects of different masses falling freely near the surface of the moon would have the same velocities at any instant because they will have same acceleration due to gravity.

Q. 2 The value of acceleration due to gravity

(a) is same on equator and poles (b) is least on poles

(c) is least on equator (d) increases from pole to equator

Ans. ***(c)*** It is least at the equator and maximum at the poles due to rotation of earth *i.e.,* it is given by

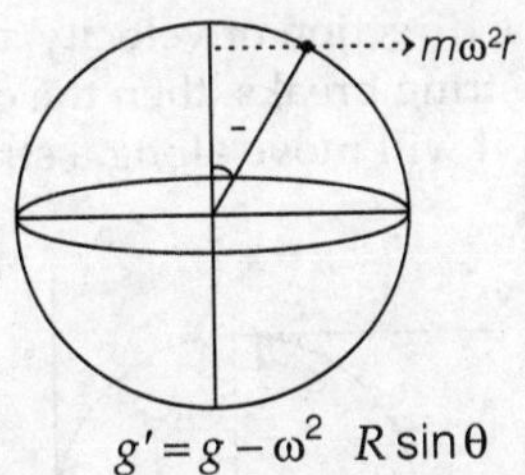

$$g' = g - \omega^2 \ R \sin\theta$$

At poles $\theta = 0$, So g maximum

At equator $\theta = 90°$, So g minimum

Q. 3 The gravitational force between two objects is F. If masses of both objects are halved without changing distance between them, then the gravitational force would become

(a) $F/4$ (b) $F/2$ (c) F (d) $2F$

Thinking Process Firstly, we use the Newton's universal law of gravitation *i.e.,* $F = \frac{G m_1 m_2}{r^2}$, further we put given condition *i.e.,* $m_1' = \frac{m_1}{2}$ and $m_2' = \frac{m_2}{2}$ in gravitational formula to get required new force.

Ans. **(a)** We know that, according to force of gravitation

$$F = \frac{Gm_1 m_2}{r^2} \text{ (G = Gravitational constant)}$$

where m_1 and m_2 are the masses of two objects respectively. And r is the distance between the two masses

Now, according to the question, if masses of both objects are halved,

i.e., $$m_1' = \frac{m_1}{2} \text{ and } m_2' = \frac{m_2}{2}$$

New force $$F = \frac{Gm_1' m_2'}{r^2} = \frac{G\left(\frac{m_1}{2}\right)\left(\frac{m_2}{2}\right)}{r^2}$$

$$= \frac{1}{4}\frac{Gm_1 m_2}{r^2} = \frac{F}{4}, \text{ where } \frac{Gm_1 m_2}{r^2} = F$$

So, new force $$F' = \frac{F}{4}$$

Thus, the new gravitational force will become $\frac{1}{4}$ times of its original gravitational force.

Q. 4 **A boy is whirling a stone tied with a string in an horizontal circular path. If the string breaks, the stone**

(a) will continue to move in the circular path

(b) will move along a straight line towards the centre of the circular path

(c) will move along a straight line tangential to the circular path

(d) will move along a straight line perpendicular to the circular path away from the boy

Ans. **(c)** In circular motion, the direction of velocity at a point is always along the tangent at that point. If string breaks, then the centripetal force acting on the stone becomes zero and it will move along a straight line tangential to the circular path.

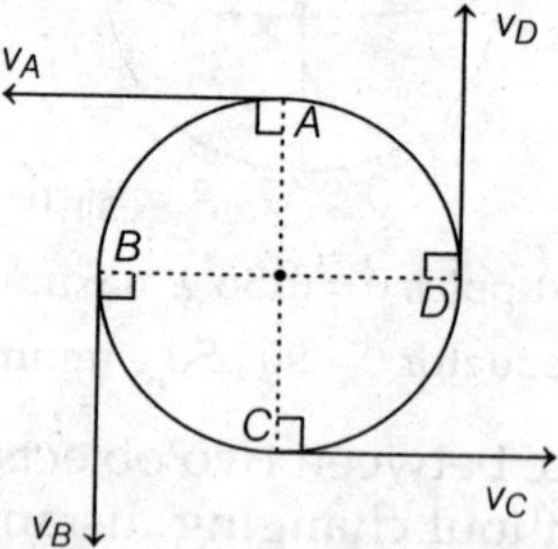

where v_A, v_B, v_C, v_D are the velocities point A, B, C, D in circular path.

Q. 5 **An object is put one by one in three liquids having different densities. The object floats with $\frac{1}{9}$, $\frac{2}{11}$ and $\frac{3}{7}$ parts of their volumes outside the liquid surface in liquids of densities d_1, d_2 and d_3, respectively. Which of the following statement is correct?**

(a) $d_1 > d_2 > d_3$

(b) $d_1 > d_2 < d_3$

(c) $d_1 < d_2 > d_3$

(d) $d_1 < d_2 < d_3$

Ans. ***(d)*** In a liquid of higher density more part of the object remains outside the liquid. Since, the order of part of their volume outside the liquid is given by (part of the body out side the liquid) $\propto$ densities of liquid

$$\frac{1}{9} < \frac{2}{11} < \frac{3}{7}$$

Thus, the order of densities in increasing order is

$$d_1 < d_2 < d_3$$

Q. 6 In the relation $F = GMm/d^2$, the quantity G

(a) depends on the value of g at the place of observation
(b) is used only when the earth is one of the two masses
(c) is greatest at the surface of the earth
(d) is universal constant of nature

Ans. ***(d)*** The quantity G is universal constant of nature. It is applied to all the body present in universe It is constant of proportionality in Newton's universal law of gravitation.

The accepted value of G is 6.67×10^{-11} Nm^2 kg^{-2}.

Q. 7 Law of gravitation gives the gravitational force between

(a) the earth and a point mass only
(b) the earth and the sun only
(c) any two bodies having some mass
(d) two charged bodies only

Ans. ***(c)*** Law of gravitation is applicable to all bodies having some mass. And is given by $\quad F = \frac{Gm_1 m_2}{r^2}$

where, F = Force of attraction between the two bodies
m_1, m_2 = Mass of two bodies
G = Gravitational constant
r = Distance between the two bodies.

Q. 8 The value of quantity G in the law of gravitation

(a) depends on mass of the earth only
(b) depends on radius of earth only
(c) depends on both mass and radius of the earth
(d) is independent of mass and radius of the earth

Ans. ***(d)*** G is the constant of proportionality and is called the universal gravitational constant. It is independent of mass and radius of the earth.

Q. 9 Two particles are placed at some distance. If the mass of each of the two particle is doubled, keeping the distance between them unchanged, the value of gravitational force between them will be

(a) $\frac{1}{4}$ times (b) 4 times
(c) $\frac{1}{2}$ times (d) unchanged

Thinking Process Firstly, we use the Newton's universal law of gravitation *i.e.*, $F = \frac{GMm}{r^2}$, further we put given condition *i.e.*, $M = 2M$ and $m = 2m$ in Newton's gravitational formula to get required new force.

Ans. ***(b)*** We know that, according to gravitational force

$$F = G\frac{Mm}{r^2} \quad \ldots(i)$$

where, F = Force between two mass
M = First mass
m = Second mass
G = Gravitational constart
r = Distant between two mass

According to the question,

F' = New force when mass is doubled

If mass of each particle is doubled

i.e., $M = 2M$

and $m = 2m$

These value put in Eq. (i), we get

$$\therefore \quad F' = G\frac{(2M)(2m)}{r^2}$$

$$F' = 4G\frac{Mm}{r^2}$$

From Eq. (i), $F' = 4F$

Q. 10 The atmosphere is held to the earth by
(a) gravity
(b) wind
(c) clouds
(d) earth's magnetic field

Ans. ***(a)*** The atmosphere is held to the earth by gravity.

Q. 11 The force of attraction between two unit point masses separated by a unit distance is called
(a) gravitational potential
(b) acceleration due to gravity
(c) gravitational field
(d) universal gravitational constant

Ans. ***(d)*** We know that, the gravitational force,

$$F = G\frac{Mm}{r^2}$$

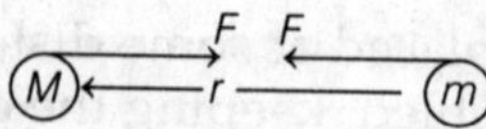

Where, F = Force between mass
m = Mass of the body
M = Gravitational Constant
r = Distance between two mass

Given, $M = 1$ unit, $m = 1$ unit and $r = 1$ unit, we get

$$F = G\frac{1 \times 1}{(1)^2} \Rightarrow F = G$$

Therefore, the force of attraction between two unit point masses separated by a unit distance is called universal gravitational constant.

Q. 12 The weight of an object at the centre of the earth of radius R, is

(a) zero

(b) infinite

(c) R times the weight at the surface of the earth

(d) $1/R^2$ times the weight at the surface of the earth

Ans. ***(a)*** The weight of an object, $w = mg$

At the centre of the earth, acceleration due to gravity g is zero. And is given by $g' = g\left(1 - \frac{h}{R}\right)$, where h = distance from surface of the earth to centre of the earth

and at centre ($h = R$) *i.e.*, $g' = 0$.

So, $w = m \times 0 = 0$

Q. 13 An object weighs 10 N in air. When immersed fully in water, it weighs only 8 N. The weight of the liquid displaced by the object will be

(a) 2N (b) 8N

(c) 10N (d) 12N

Thinking Process Loss in weight of the object when dipped in a liquid is equal to the buoancy force.

Ans. ***(a)*** Given, Weight of an object in air = 10N

Weight of an object in water = 8N

So, the weight of the liquid displaced by the object $F = 10 - 8 = 2$N and we know that according to Archimedes' Principle,

buoyancy force = weight of the liquid displaced by the body.

Q. 14 A girl stands on a box having 60 cm length, 40 cm breadth and 20 cm width in three ways. In which of the following cases, pressure exerted by the brick will be

(a) maximum when length and breadth form the base

(b) maximum when breadth and width form the base

(c) maximum when width and length form the base

(d) the same in all the above three cases

Thinking Process As we know that Pressure $= \frac{\text{Thrust}}{\text{Area}} = \frac{\text{Force}}{\text{Area}}$. Pressure exerted by the brick will be maximum when area is small.

Ans. ***(b)*** Now, according to question, when base is formed by breadth and width. Area will be minimum. And so, pressure will be maximum.

Q. 15 An apple falls from a tree because of gravitational attraction between the earth and apple. If F_1 is the magnitude of force exerted by the earth on the apple and F_2 is the magnitude of force exerted by apple on earth, then

(a) F_1 is very much greater than F_2 (b) F_2 is very much greater than F_1
(c) F_1 is only a little greater than F_2 (d) F_1 and F_2 are equal

Ans. (d) According to Newton's universal law of gravitation, force exerted by the one body to other body is equal in magnitude and given by $\left(F = \frac{Gm_1m_2}{r^2}\right)$ and opposite in direction.

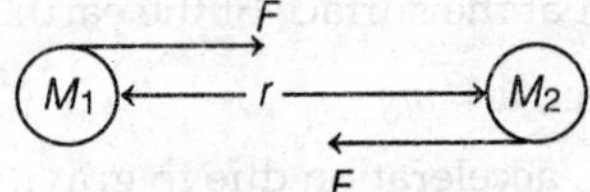

Short Answer Type Questions

Q. 16 What is the source of centripetal force that a planet requires to revolve around the sun? On what factors does that force depend?

Ans. The motion of the planet around the earth is due to the centripetal force. This centripetal force is provided by the gravitational force between the planet and the sun.

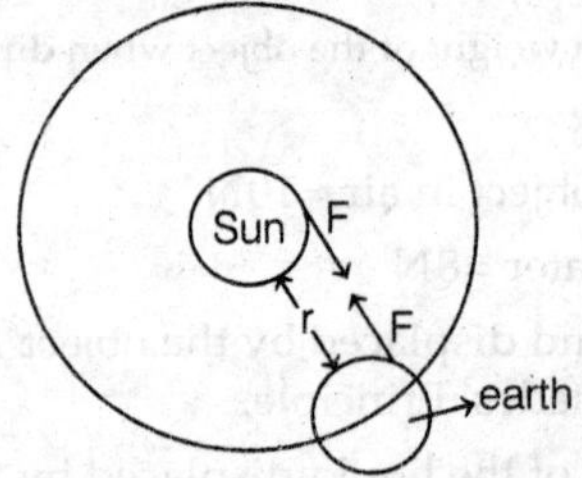

As, $F = \frac{GM_sM_p}{r^2}$ the force depends on the mass of the sun and mass of the planet, and on the distance between sun and planet.

Q. 17 On the earth, a stone is thrown from a height in a direction parallel to the earth's surface while another stone is simultaneously dropped from the same height. Which stone would reach the ground first and why?

Ans. Time taken by both stone is given by second equation of motion $s = ut + 1/2at^2$

As, $u_y = 0$, so, $s = 1/2at^2$

and here $s = h$

Where, m = Initial velocity in Y-axis

a = g acceleration due to gravity

t = time displacement to time

So, $$h = 1/2gt^2$$

$$t = \sqrt{\frac{2h}{g}}$$

Therefore, if we drop down a stone from a height (h) and at same time we throw another stone in horizontal direction, then both the stone strike the earth simultaneously at different places.

Q. 18 Suppose gravity of the earth suddenly becomes zero, then in which direction will the moon begin to move if no other celestial body affects it?

Ans. In the absence of gravity of earth, the moon flies off along a straight line. This straight line will be a tangent to the circular path.

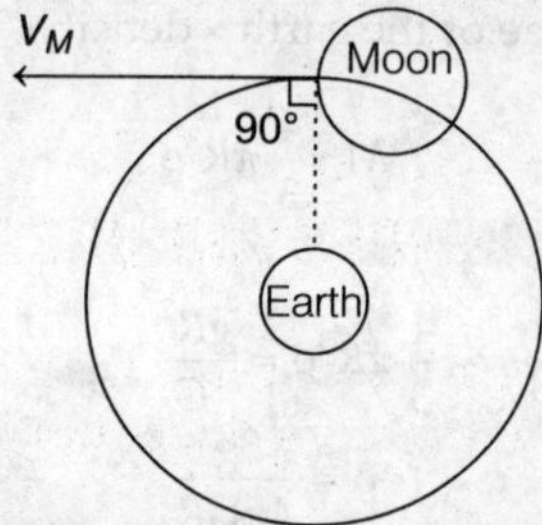

Q. 19 Identical packets are dropped from two aeroplanes, one above the equator and the other above the north pole, both at height h. Assuming all conditions are identical, will those packets take same time to reach the surface of earth. Justify your answer.

Ans. No, those packets do not take same time to reach the surface of the earth. Because the value of g (*i.e.,* acceleration due to gravity) is different at poles and equator due to rotation of the earth and is given by $g' = g - \omega^2 r \sin\theta$ and at poles $\theta = 0$ whereas at equator $\theta = 90°$. So, value of g at equator is less than value of g at poles and we know that, $t = \sqrt{\frac{2h}{g}}$ *i.e.,* $t \propto \frac{1}{\sqrt{g}}$.

Since, g is greatest at the poles than at the equator. So, packet dropped above the north pole will reach first at the surface of the earth.

Q. 20 The weight of any person on the moon is about 1/6 times that on the earth. He can lift a mass of 15 kg on the earth. What will be the maximum mass, which can be lifted by the same force applied by the person on the moon?

Ans. On Moon $W_M = \frac{1}{6} W_E$

$$g_M = \frac{1}{6} g_E \quad \text{...(i)}$$

$$m' = \frac{F}{g_M} = \frac{15 g_E}{g_M} \quad [F = m g_E = 15 g_E\, N]$$

$$\Rightarrow \quad m' = \frac{15 g_E}{\frac{g_E}{6}} = 15 \times 6 = 90\,\text{kg} \quad \text{[using Eq. (i)]}$$

As mass does not change at every place. It is a concerned quantity. So, 15 kg will be maximum mass which can be lifted by the same force applied by the person on the moon.

Q. 21 Calculate the average density of the earth in terms of g, G and R.

Ans. We know that, $\left(g = \frac{GM}{R^2}\right)$, where M = Mass of the earth, R = Radius of the earth.

So, mass of the earth, $M = \frac{gR^2}{G}$ ...(i)

If the earth is considered as a uniform sphere of radius R and of material of density ρ, then

Mass of the earth = volume of the earth × density [$\because$ volume of sphere $= \frac{4}{3}\pi r^3$]

$$M = \frac{4}{3}\pi R^3 \rho$$

From Eq. (i), we get

$$\therefore \quad \frac{4}{3}\pi R^3 \rho = \frac{gR^2}{G}$$

$$\rho = \frac{3g}{4\pi GR}$$

Mistake Alert ! *Confusing units of G, g or R can lead to incorrect calculations. Failing to correctly derive the volume of the Earth can affect the density calculation.*

Q.22 The earth is acted upon by gravitation of the sun, even though it does not fall into the sun. Why?

Ans. The earth revolves around the sun. The centripetal force is needed by the earth to revolve around the sun. This centripetal force is provided by the gravitational force between the sun and the earth and this gravitational force restricts the earth to fall into the sun.

Long Answer Type Questions

Q.23 How does the weight of an object vary with respect to mass and radius of the earth? In a hypothetical case, if the diameter of the earth becomes half of its present value and its mass becomes four times of its present value, then how would the weight of any object on the surface of the earth be affected?

Ans. Let radius and mass of the earth be R, M respectively and mass of an object be m.

Weight of the object,

$$w = mg = \frac{GMm}{R^2} \quad \text{...(i)} \quad \left[\because g = \frac{GM}{R^2}\right]$$

According to the question, the diameter of the earth becomes half of its present value. So, radius also becomes half of its initial values

So, $R' = \frac{R}{2}$

Again, mass of earth becomes four times of its present value.

So, $M' = 4M$

Now, weight of the object

$$w' = \frac{G M'm}{R'}$$

Put $R' = \frac{R}{2}$ and $M' = 4m$ in above formula, we get

$$w' = \frac{G4Mm}{(R/2)^2}$$

$$= \frac{4GMm}{\frac{R^2}{4}} = \frac{16\,GMm}{R^2}$$

From Eq. (i), we get $w' = 16\,w$

Thus, weight of the object will become 16 times of its original weight.

Alternate Method

Weight of an object of mass m,

$$W = mg = G\frac{Mm}{R^2} \quad \text{...(i)}$$

When the diameter of the Earth becomes half, the radius of the Earth also becomes half and mass becomes 4 times its initial value then.

$$W' = \frac{G(4M)m}{\left(\frac{R}{2}\right)^2} = \frac{16GMm}{R^2}$$

$$W' = 16\,W, \quad \text{[using Eq. (i)]}$$

Therefore, the weight will become 16 times its initial value.

Q.24 How does the force of attraction between the two bodies depend upon their masses and distance between them? A student thought that two bricks tied together would fall faster than a single one under the action of gravity. Do you agree with his hypothesis or not? Comment.

Ans. The force of attraction between two bodies of masses m_1 and m_2 and separated by distance r is given by Newton's universal law of gravitation

i.e., $F = \frac{G m_1 m_2}{r^2}$ where, G is the universal constant in nature.

This force is known as gravitational force. The gravitational force is directly proportional to the product of the masses of two bodies and inversely proportional to the square of the distance between them.

All bodies fall with the same acceleration due to gravity whatever their masses have.

i.e., $$g = \frac{GM}{R^2}$$

(where M = Mass of the earth, R = Radius of the earth)

And from the equation it is clear that, acceleration due to gravity (*i.e.*, g) depends only on mass of the earth, the radius of the earth. So, two bricks tied together will not fall faster than a single bricks under the action of gravity. Hence, the hypothesis is not correct.

Q.25 Two objects of masses m_1 and m_2 having the same size are dropped simultaneously from heights h_1 and h_2 respectively. Find out the ratio of time they would take in reaching the ground. Will this ratio remain the same if (i) one of the objects is hollow and the other one is solid and (ii) both of them are hollow, size remaining the same in each case. Give reason.

- **Concept Insight** In this problem, we find t_1 and t_2 by using newton's II equation of motion *i.e.*, $h = ut + \frac{1}{2}at^2$, relates displacement, initial velocity acceleration and time. After that find the ratio of $t_1$and t_2.

Ans. From second equation of motion, $h = ut + \frac{1}{2}gt^2$ [for I object $u=0$]

So, $$h = \frac{1}{2}gt^2$$

where, h = Displacement, u = Initial velocity, t = Time and g= Acceleration due to gravity

$\Rightarrow$ $$gt^2 = 2h$$

$\Rightarrow$ $$t^2 = \frac{2h}{g}$$

i.e., $$t = \sqrt{\frac{2h}{g}}$$

$\therefore$ Time taken by first object of mass, m_1

$$t_1 = \sqrt{\frac{2h_1}{g}}$$ [for II object $u=0$]

Similarly, time taken by object of mass m_2

$$t_2 = \sqrt{\frac{2h_2}{g}}$$

$\Rightarrow$ $$\frac{t_1}{t_2} = \sqrt{\frac{h_1}{h_2}}$$

(i) Acceleration due to gravity is independent of mass of falling body. So, the ratio remains the same.

(ii) If bodies are hollow, then also ratio remains the same *i.e.*, $t_1 : t_2 = \sqrt{h_1} : \sqrt{h_2}$.

Q. 26 (i) A cube of side 5 cm is immersed in water and then in saturated salt solution. In which case will it experience a greater buoyant force. If each side of the cube is reduced to 4 cm and then immersed in water, what will be the effect on the buoyant force experienced by the cube as compared to the first case for water. Give reason for each case.

(ii) A ball weighing 4 kg of density 4000 kgm^{-3} is completely immersed in water of density 10^3 kgm^{-3}. Find the force of buoyancy on it. (Given, $g = 10$ ms^{-2})

Ans. (i) Buoyant force, $F = V\rho g$

(where, ρ = Density of water, V = Volume of water displaced by the body)

Buoyant force depends upon volume and density, since, saturated salt solution have higher density than the water. So, in saturated solution, cube will experience a greater buoyant force.

If each side of the cube is reduced to 4 cm, then the volume of cube become less. As buoyant force is directly proportional to the volume. So, buoyant force will be less than as compared to the first case for water.

(ii) The magnitude of the buoyant force given by $F = V\rho g$

where V = Volume of body immersed in water or volume of water displaced, ρ = Density of liquid. [$\because$ Given, mass of a ball = 4 kg, density = 4000 kgm^{-3}]

$$\therefore \quad \text{Volume of solid} = \frac{\text{Mass}}{\text{Density}}$$

$$= \frac{4}{4000} = \frac{1}{1000} \, m^3$$

$$\text{Buoyancy,} \quad F = V\rho g$$

$$= \frac{1}{1000} \times 1000 \times 10$$

$$= 10 \text{ N}$$

Chapter 11

Work and Energy

Multiple Choice Questions (MCQs)

Choose the correct answer from the given four options in the following questions :

Q. 1 When a body falls freely towards the earth, then its total energy

(a) increases
(b) decreases
(c) remains constant
(d) first increases and then decreases

Ans. *(c)* Since, total energy of the system is always conserved, so when a body falls freely towards the earth, then its total energy remains constant *i.e.*, the sum of the potential energy and kinetic energy of the body would be same at all points.

Q. 2 A car is accelerated on a lavelled road and attains a velocity 4 times of its initial velocity. In this process, the potential energy of the car

(a) does not change
(b) becomes twice to that of initial
(c) becomes 4 times that of initial
(d) becomes 16 times that of initial

Ans. *(a)* Potential energy of the car doesn't change as it does not depend on velocity. and kinetic energy changes by as follows

Let, initial velocity = u

$\therefore$ $$\text{Kinetic energy } K_1 = \frac{1}{2} mu^2 \quad \text{...(i}$$

Given, after sometime velocity become 4 times of its initial velocity

i.e., final velocity (v) = $4u$

Now, put $v = 4u$, in Eq. (i), we get

$\therefore$ $$\text{Kinetic energy} = \frac{1}{2} m(4u)^2 = \frac{1}{2} m\, 16u^2$$

$$K_2 = 16 \frac{1}{2} mu^2$$

From Eq. (i), $$K_2 = 16\, K_1$$

So, in this process, the kinetic energy of car becomes 16 times that of initial energy

Q. 3 In case of negative work, the angle between the force and displacement is

(a) 0
(b) 45°
(c) 90°
(d) 180°

Ans. *(d)* (a) Work done $W = F.d \cos\theta$

$\therefore$ Work done at $\theta = 0°$, $W = F.d \cos 0°$ $\quad (\because \cos 0° = 1$

$\Rightarrow$ $$W = F.d$$

For angle $\theta = 0°$,

Work done is positive, so it is not true.

(b) We know that work done, $W = F \cdot d \cos \theta$

$\therefore$ Work done at $\theta = 45°$

$$W = F \cdot d \cos 45° \qquad \left(\because \cos 45° = \frac{1}{\sqrt{2}}\right)$$

$$W = \frac{F \cdot d}{\sqrt{2}}$$

For angle $\theta = 45°$,

work done is positive, so it is not true.

(c) We know that work done, $W = F \cdot d \cos \theta$

$\therefore$ Work done at $\theta = 90°$, $W = F \cdot d \cos 90°$ $(\because \cos 90° = 0)$

$$W = 0$$

So, it is not true.

(d) Work done at $\theta = 180°$, $W = F \cdot d \cos \theta$ $(\because \cos 180° = -1)$

$$W = -F \cdot d$$

For negative work, the angle between the force and displacement should be 180°. (*i.e.*, force and displacement are antiparallel to each other) So, it is true.

Alternate Method

Work done is negative when force and displacement act in opposite directions i.e., at an angle of 180°.

Q. 4 An iron sphere of mass 10 kg has the same diameter as an aluminium sphere of mass is 3.5 kg. Both spheres are dropped simultaneously from a tower. When they are 10 m above the ground, they have the same

(a) acceleration
(b) momenta
(c) potential energy
(d) kinetic energy

Ans. *(a)* When both spheres are dropped simultaneously from a tower, they have same acceleration. Because, during free fall acceleration of body becomes equals to ($g = 9.8 \text{ m/s}^2$) and 'g' depends on mass of earth and radius of earth $\left(i.e., g = \frac{GM_e}{R_e^2}\right)$.

Q. 5 A girl is carrying a school bag of 3 kg mass on her back and moves 200 m on a leveled road. The work done against the gravitational force will be ($g = 10 \text{ ms}^{-2}$)

(a) 6×10^3 J
(b) 6 J
(c) 0.6 J
(d) zero

Ans. *(d)* We know that, work done $= F \cdot d \cos \theta$

Force on school bag makes an angle 90° from the road.

Displacement
90°
Force

i.e., $\theta = 90°$

$$W = F \cdot d \cos 90° \qquad (\because \cos 90° = 0°)$$

$$W = 0$$

Hence, work done against the gravitational force is zero.

Q. 6 Which one of the following is not the unit of energy?
(a) Joule (b) Newton metre (c) Kilowatt (d) Kilowatt hour

Ans. *(c)* We know that, joule, newton metre and kilowatt hour are the units of energy and the kilowatt is the unit of power.

Q. 7 The work done on an object does not depend upon the
(a) displacement
(b) force applied
(c) angle between force and displacement
(d) initial velocity of the object

Ans. *(d)* We know that, $W = F.d \cos \theta$
Here, F = force applied on the object, d = displacement and θ is angle between force and displacement. So, the work done on an object does not depend upon the initial velocity of the object.

Q. 8 Water stored in a dam possesses
(a) no energy (b) electrical energy
(c) kinetic energy (d) potential energy

Ans. *(d)* Potential energy is stored energy or the energy of position, so water stored in a dam possesses potential energy.

Q. 9 A body is falling from a height h. After it has fallen a height $\frac{h}{2}$, it will possess
(a) only potential energy
(b) only kinetic energy
(c) half potential and half kinetic energy
(d) more kinetic and less potential energy

Ans. *(c)* As we know that when a body is at height h, it has total energy = KE + PE
and at height 'h', velocity of body is zero.

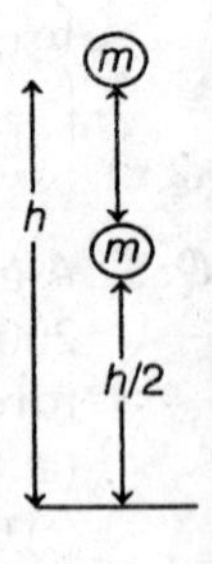

So, $\text{KE} = 0$ and $\text{PE} = mgh$

So, total energy $= mgh + 0 = mgh$

Now, at height $\frac{h}{2}$

its, $$\text{PE} = mg\frac{h}{2} = \frac{mgh}{2} \quad \text{...(i)}$$

And $$\text{KE} = \frac{1}{2}mv^2$$

Where, velocity can be determined by equation of motion

$$v^2 = u^2 + 2gh \quad (\because \text{All } v, g, h \text{ are in same direction}$$

So, $$v^2 = \frac{2gh}{2} \Rightarrow v = \sqrt{gh} \quad [\text{As } u = 0 \text{ at highest point}$$

So, $$\text{KE} = \frac{1}{2} m \times (\sqrt{gh})^2 = \frac{mgh}{2} \quad \text{...(ii}$$

So, from Eqs. (i) and (ii) body at $\left(\frac{h}{2}\right)$ possesses half potential energy and half kinetic energy.

Short Answer Type Questions

Q. 10 A rocket is moving up with a velocity v. If the velocity of this rocket is suddenly tripled, what will be the ratio of two kinetic energies?

Thinking Process Firstly, we use the formula of kinetic energy *i.e.*, $K = \frac{1}{2}mv^2$, and further use the given condition $v_1 = v$ and $v_2 = 3v$ to find kinetic energy and to get the required ratio.

Ans. Given, $v_1 = v$ and $v_2 = 3v$

$\because$ Kinetic energy of rocket $(K) = \frac{1}{2}mv^2$

The ratio of two kinetic energies, $\frac{K_1}{K_2} = \frac{\frac{1}{2}mv_1^2}{\frac{1}{2}mv_2^2}$

$$\frac{K_1}{K_2} = \frac{v_1^2}{v_2^2} \quad (\text{put } v_2 = 3v \text{ and } v_1 = v)$$

we get $= \frac{v^2}{(3v)^2} = \frac{v^2}{9v^2} \Rightarrow \frac{K_1}{K_2} = \frac{1}{9}$

Thus, the ratio of two kinetic energies $K_1 : K_2 = 1:9$

Alternate Method

We know, kinetic energy $k = \frac{1}{2}mv^2$

If the velocity is tripled K.E, $K' = \frac{1}{2}m(3v)^2$

$= \frac{9}{2}mv^2$

Now, $\frac{K'}{K} = \frac{\frac{9}{2}mv^2}{\frac{1}{2}mv^2} = 9$. So, the ratio of two kinetic energy is 9 : 1.

Q. 11 Avinash can run with a speed of 8 ms^{-1} against the frictional force of 10 N and Kapil can move with a speed of 3 ms^{-1} against the frictional force of 25 N. Who is more powerful and why?

Ans. Given, force applied by Avinash = 10 N

Speed of Avinash = 8 m s^{-1}

$\therefore$ Power of Avinash = $F \cdot v = 10 \times 8 = 80$ W

Now, force applied by Kapil = 25 N

Speed of Kapil = 3 m s^{-1}

$\therefore$ Power of Kapil = $F \cdot v = 25 \times 3 = 75$ W

Since, Avinash has more power $(80 - 75) = 5$ W than Kapil. So, Avinash is more powerful.

Q. 12 A boy is moving on a straight road against a frictional force of 5 N. After travelling a distance of 1.5 km, he forgot the correct path at a round about of radius 100 m as shown in figure. However, he moves on the circular path for one and half cycle and then he moves forward upto 2.0 km. Calculate the work done by him.

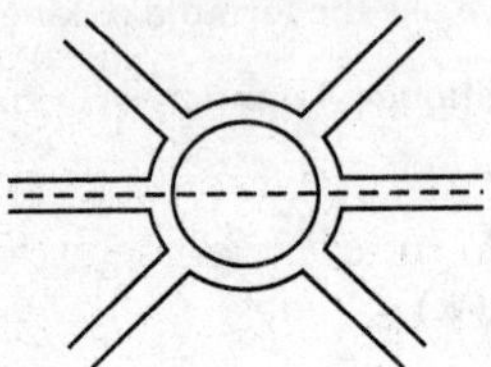

Ans. Given, force applied by boy against friction = 5 N

Displacement on the circular path = One cycle + Half cycled = 0 + Half cycle

= 0 + Diameter of circular path

(∴ Displacement depends on initial and final point)

$= 0 + 2r = 0 + 2 \times 100$ $[\because r = 100 \text{ m}]$

$= 0 + 200 = 200$ m

∴ Total displacements = 1.5 km + 200 m + 2.0 km

$= 1.5 \times 1000 + 200 + 2 \times 1000$ km (1 km = 1000 m)

= 3700 m

Work done by boy $= F \cdot s \cos \theta$

$= 5 \times 3700 \times \cos 0° = 18500$ J $\left[\begin{array}{l}\because \theta = 0° \\ \therefore \cos 0° = 1\end{array}\right]$

Q. 13 Can any object have mechanical energy even if its momentum is zero? Explain.

Ans. Since, mechanical energy is the sum of kinetic energy and potential energy. And as given that, momentum of the body is zero, it means velocity of the body is zero, so it has kinetic energy equals to zero. But it may have potential energy.

So, even if the momentum of the body is zero, it may have mechanical energy.

Q. 14 Can any object have momentum even if its mechanical energy is zero? Explain.

Ans. Since, mechanical energy = potential energy + kinetic energy

If mechanical energy = 0

So, $PE + KE = 0$

So, mechanical energy is zero, there is no potential energy and no kinetic energy. Kinetic energy being zero, velocity is zero.

Hence, there will be no momentum.

Q. 15 The power of a motor pump is 2 kW. How much water per minute, the pump can raise to a height of 10 m? [given, $g = 10 \text{ ms}^{-2}$]

Ans. Given, power of a motor = 2 kW $= 2 \times 1000$ W = 2000 W $[\because 1 \text{ kW} = 1000 \text{ W}]$

$$\text{Power, } P = \frac{\text{Energy}}{\text{Time}}$$

By putting the values, $P = \frac{mgh}{t}$ [m = mass of water]

$$2000 = \frac{m \times 10 \times 10}{60} \quad \text{[Here, } h = 10\,\text{m and } t = 1\,\text{min} = 60\,\text{s]}$$

$$\Rightarrow \quad m = \frac{2000 \times 60}{10 \times 10}$$

$$m = 1200\,\text{kg}$$

Q. 16 **The weight of a person on a planet A is about half that on the earth. He can jump upto 0.4 m height on the surface of the earth. How high he can jump on the planet A?**

Ans. It is given that weight of person on the earth = w (*i.e.*, $w = mg$)

And as he can jump upto height ($h_1 = 0.4\,\text{m}$)

So, potential energy at this point = $mgh = mg \times .04$ ...(i)

And it is given that

weight of the person on the other planet = $\frac{w}{2}$

Its potential energy height $h_2 = \frac{w}{2} h_2 = \frac{mg}{2} h_2$ ...(ii)

Since, he applied same amount of effort in both the cases to lift his body, so its potential energy will be same.

And from Eqs. (i) and (ii)

$$mg \times 0.4 = \frac{mg}{2} h_2$$

$$\Rightarrow \quad h_2 = 0.4 \times 2 = 0.8\,\text{m}$$

Q. 17 **The velocity of a body moving in a straight line is increased by applying a constant force F, for some distance in the direction of the motion. Prove that the increase in the kinetic energy of the body is equal to the work done by the force on the body.**

Ans. Consider an object of mass m moving with a uniform velocity u.

Let, it now be displaced through a distance s, when a constant force F acts on it in the direction of its displacement.

From the third equation of motion,

$$v^2 = u^2 + 2as$$

$$\Rightarrow \quad v^2 - u^2 = 2as$$

$$\Rightarrow \quad s = \frac{v^2 - u^2}{2a} \quad \text{...(i)}$$

We know that, work done by F is

$W = Fs\cos\theta$ (since, force and displacement are in same direction, so ($\theta = 0°$)

$$= ma \cdot s \quad [\because F = ma]$$

$$= ma \times \left(\frac{v^2 - u^2}{2a}\right) \quad \text{[from Eq. (i)]}$$

$$W = \frac{1}{2} m (v^2 - u^2) \quad \text{...(ii)}$$

If the object is starting from its stationary position *i.e.*, $u = 0$, from Eq. (ii), we get

$$W = \frac{1}{2} mv^2$$

It is clear that the work done is equal to the change in the kinetic energy of an object.

Q. 18 **Is it possible that an object is in the state of accelerated motion due to external force acting on it, but no work is being done by the force? Explain it with an example.**

Ans. Yes, when force acts in a direction perpendicular to the direction of displacement.

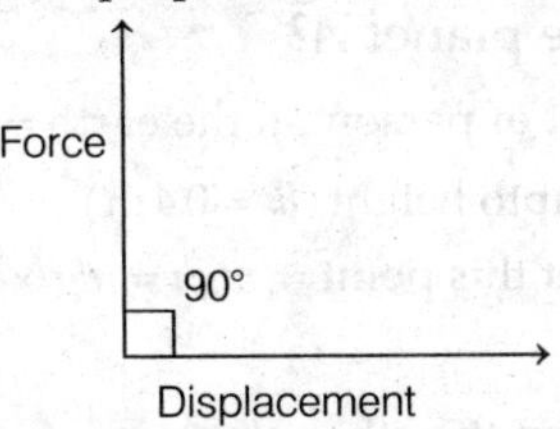

e.g., earth revolves around the sun under gravitational force of sun on earth, but no work is done by the sun, though earth has centripetal acceleration.

Q. 19 **A ball is dropped from a height of 10 m. If the energy of the ball reduces by 40% after striking the ground, how much high can the ball bounce back? [$g = 10 \text{ ms}^{-2}$]**

Ans. If the energy of the ball reduces by 40% after striking the ground, then remaining energy of the ball will be 60% of initial energy.

Let initial energy of the body of mass (m) at height(h) is (mgh).

According to the question, $mgh' = 60\% \text{ of } mgh$ [given, $h = 10$ m and $g = 10 \text{ ms}^{-2}$]

$$h' = 60\% \times h = \frac{60}{100} \times 10 = 6 \text{ m}$$

Q. 20 **If an electric iron of 1200 W is used for 30 min everyday, find electric energy consumed in the month of April.**

Thinking Process Here, for finding the energy of 30 days, firstly find the energy of one day by using the formula,
Energy = Power × Time and then multiply that energy by 30, to get required energy.

Ans. Given, power of electric iron = 1200 W

$$\text{Time } (t) = 30 \text{ min} = 30 \times 60 \text{ s} = 1800 \text{ s}$$

We know that, $\text{power} = \dfrac{\text{energy}}{\text{time}} \Rightarrow 1200 = \dfrac{E}{30 \times 60}$

$$E = 1200 \times 30 \times 60 = 21.6 \times 10^5 \text{ J}$$

Energy used in one day $= 21.6 \times 10^5$ J

$\therefore$ Energy used in 30 days $= 21.6 \times 10^5 \times 30 = 6.48 \times 10^7$ J

Long Answer Type Questions

Q. 21 A light and a heavy object have the same momentum. Find out the ratio of their kinetic energies. Which one has a larger kinetic energy?

Ans. Suppose m_1 and m_2 are masses of a light and a heavy objects, respectively.

As we know

$$\text{kinetic energy } (K) = \frac{1}{2}mv^2 \qquad [v = \text{velocity of objects}] \ldots\text{(i)}$$

and $$\text{movementum } (p) = mv \qquad \ldots\text{(ii)}$$

Multiplying and dividing with m in Eqs. (i)

So, $$K = \frac{1}{2}\frac{mv^2 \times m}{m} \Rightarrow K = \frac{1}{2}\frac{(mv)^2}{m} \text{ as from Eqs. (ii)} \qquad (p = mv)$$

So, $$K = \frac{p^2}{2m}$$

We have, $$\text{kinetic energy, } K = \frac{p^2}{2m}$$

$\because$ Momentum is same for light and heavy body

So, $$\text{kinetic energy, } K \propto \frac{1}{m}$$

Thus, kinetic energy is inversely proportional to the mass.

So, lighter body has larger kinetic energy.

Q.22 An automobile engine propels a 1000 kg car (A) along a lavelled road at a speed of 36 kmh^{-1}. Find the power if the opposing frictional force is 100 N. Now, suppose after travelling a distance of 200 m, this car collides with another stationary car B of same mass and comes to rest. Let its engine also stop at the same time. Now car B starts moving on the same level road without getting its engine started. Find the speed of the car B just after the collision.

Ans. Given, mass of car (A) = 1000 kg

Mass of car B = 1000 kg

Force applied by car A = 100 N

$$(v_A) \text{ Speed of car } (A) = 36 \text{ km h}^{-1} = 36 \times \frac{5}{18} = 10 \text{ m s}^{-1} \qquad \left[\because 1 \text{ km/h} = \frac{5}{18} \text{ m/s}\right]$$

$\therefore$ Power of car (A), $P_A = F \cdot v_A = 100 \times 10 = 1000$ W

[F= force exerted by the car $\underline{A}$ against friction]

Again, for car (A) Newton's law, $F = ma$

$$100 = 1000 \times a$$

$$\Rightarrow \qquad a = \frac{100}{1000} \Rightarrow a = \frac{1}{10} \text{ m s}^{-2}$$

Velocity of car A after travelling 200 m is given by

From third equation of motion, $v^2 = u^2 + 2as$

[for car A here, u = 10 ms^{-1}, s = 200 m]

$$v^2 = (10)^2 + 2 \times \frac{1}{10} \times 200$$

$$v^2 = 100 + 40 = 140 \Rightarrow v = \sqrt{140} = 11.8 \text{ ms}^{-1}$$

According to the question, after moving of 200 m, the speed of car A, $v_1 = 11.8\ \text{ms}^{-1}$
Just after the collision, the final speed of car A, $v_1 = 0$
before collision, the initial speed of car B, $u_2 = 0$
From conservation of linear momentum,

$$m_1 u_1 + m_2 u_2 = m_1 v_1 + m_2 v_2$$

[Let just after the collision, the speed of the car B is v_2]

$$m_1 \times 10 + m_2 \times 0 = m_1 \times 0 + m_2 \times v_2$$

$$1000 \times 10 + 1000 \times 0 = 1000 \times 0 + 1000 \times v_2$$

$$\Rightarrow \quad 1000 \times 10 = 1000 \times v_2$$

$$\Rightarrow \quad v_2 = 10\ \text{ms}^{-1}$$

Q.23 A girl having mass of 35 kg sits on a trolley of mass 5 kg. The trolley is given an initial velocity of $4\ \text{ms}^{-1}$ by appling a force. The trolley comes to rest after traversing a distance of 16 m. (a) How much work is done on the trolley? (b) How much work is done by the girl?

- **Concept Insight** In this problem, to find the acceleration(a) by using third equation of motion *i.e.*, $v^2 = u^2 + 2as$ relates the final velocity, initial velocity, acceleration and displacement of an object moving with uniform acceleration and then putting this value in $w = ma \cdot s$ to get required work.

Ans. Given, $u = 4\ \text{m/s}$, $v = 0$ and $s = 16\ \text{m}$

From the third equation of motion,[$\because$ for retardation, the acceleration is negative *i.e.*, $a = -a$]

$$v^2 = u^2 - 2as$$

$$(0)^2 = (4)^2 - 2a \times 16$$

$$0 = 16 - 32a$$

$$a = \frac{16}{32} = 0.5\ \text{ms}^{-2}$$

u = inital velocity, v = final velocity, a = acceleration and s = displacement

(a) Total mass = 35 + 5 = 40 kg

Work is done on the trolley $W = F \cdot d = ma \cdot s$ [$\because F = ma$]

$$= 40 \times 0.5 \times 16 = 320\ \text{J}$$

(b) Work done by the girl is zero as she is stationary with respect to the cart there is no displacement in her position with respect to trolley; so no work is done by the girl.

Q.24 Four men lift a 250 kg box to a height of 1 m and hold it without raising or lowering it. (a) How much work is done by the men in lifting the box? (b) How much work do they do in just holding it? (c) Why do they get tired while holding it? [given = $10\ \text{ms}^{-2}$].

Ans. Given, $m = 250$ kg, height $(h) = 1$ m and acceleration due to gravity $g = 10\ \text{m s}^{-2}$

(a) Work done by the man in lifting the box

$$W = \text{Potential energy of box}$$

$$W = mgh$$

$$W = 250 \times 1 \times 10 = 2500\ \text{J}$$

(b) Work done is zero in holding a box, because displacement is zero.

(c) The keep the box at certain height, the men exert a force that is equal and opposite to the gravitational force acting on the box. while doing, so their muscles are engaged, leading to physical effort, which causes them to feel tired even though the box is not moving.

Q.25 What is power? How do you differentiate kilowatt from kilowatt hour? The Jog Falls in Karnataka state are nearly 20 m high. 2000 tonnes of water falls from it in a minute. Calculate the equivalent power if all this energy can be utilised? $[g = 10\ ms^{-2}]$

Ans. (i) Power is defined as the rate of doing work or the rate of transfer of energy. The unit of power is watt or kilowatt. [1 kW = 1000W]

(ii) Kilowatt is the unit of power while kilowatt hour is bigger unit of energy

$$1\ kWh = 1000 \times 3600 \Rightarrow 1\ \text{kilowatt hour} = 3.6 \times 10^6\ J$$

(iii) Given, mass of water = 2000 tonnes [∵ 1 tonne = 1000 kg]

∴ Mass of water $= 2000 \times 1000 = 2 \times 10^6$ kg

We know that, $\text{power} = \dfrac{\text{energy}}{\text{time}}$

$$P = \frac{mgh}{t} \quad [\because \text{energy} = mgh]$$

$$P = \frac{2 \times 10^6 \times 10 \times 20}{60} \quad [\text{given, } h = 20\ m \text{ and } g = 10\ ms^{-2}]$$

$$P = \frac{2}{3} \times 10^7\ W \quad \left[\because \frac{2}{3} = 6.6 \times 10^6\ W\right]$$

This power can be utilised.

Q.26 How is the power related to the speed at which a body can be lifted? How many kilograms will a man working at the power of 100 W, be able to lift at constant speed of $1\ ms^{-1}$ vertically? $[g = 10\ ms^{-2}]$

Ans. (i) The power delivered to a body can also expressed in term of the force F applied to the body and the velocity v of the body

$$\text{Power}\ (P) = \frac{\text{work}}{\text{time}} \Rightarrow P = \frac{F \cdot s}{t}$$

where F = Force, S = displacement and t = time

$$P = F \cdot v \quad [\because W = F \cdot s]$$

$$\left(\because v = \frac{s}{t}\right) \quad [v = \text{velocity of the body}]$$

Given, power $(P) = 100$ W, $v = 1\ ms^{-2}$ and $g = 10\ ms^{-2}$

We know that, power $(P) = F.v$

$\Rightarrow \quad P = mg.v \quad [\because F = mg]$

$100 = mg \cdot v$

$100 = m \times 10 \times 1 \Rightarrow m = \dfrac{100}{10}$

$\Rightarrow \quad m = 10$ kg

Therefore, man working at the power of 100 W can lift 10 kg.

Q.27 Define watt. Express kilowatt in terms of joule per second. A 150 kg car engine develops 500 W for each kg. What force does it exert in moving the car at speed of 20 ms^{-1}?

Ans. (i) One watt is the power of a body which does work at the rate of 1 J/s.

$$1 \text{ watt} = 1 \frac{\text{joule}}{\text{second}}$$

(ii) 1 kilowatt = 1000 watt = 1000 J/s

(iii) Given, $m = 150$ kg, $P = 500$ W and $v = 20 \text{ ms}^{-1}$

A car engine 150 kg develops 500 watt for each kg.

So, total power = 150 × 500 = 75000 W

We have, Power = Force × speed

$$75000 = \text{Force} \times 20$$

$$\text{Force, } F = \frac{75000}{20} = 3750 \text{ N}$$

Mistake Alert! *Students can get confused between units of power like watt and kilowatt, or may forget to convert them correctly.*

Q.28 Compare the power at which each of the following is moving upwards against the force of gravity? [given, $g = 10 \text{ ms}^{-2}$]

(i) A butterfly of mass 1.0 g that flies upward at a rate of 0.5 ms^{-1}.

(ii) A 250 g squirrel climbing upon a tree at a rate of 0.5 ms^{-1}.

Thinking Process Firstly we find the power by using the formula $P = mg \cdot v$ in both parts and then comparing both powers.

Ans. (i) Given, mass of butterfly = 1.0 g = $\frac{1}{1000}$ kg, [∵ 1 kg = 1000 g]

$g = 10 \text{ ms}^{-2}$ and speed = 0.5 ms^{-1}

∴ Power = Force × Speed [∵ Force $(F) = mg$]

$$P = mgv$$

$$P = \frac{1}{1000} \times 10 \times 0.5$$

$$\Rightarrow P = \frac{10.5}{100} W = 0.005W = 5 \times 10^{-3} \text{ W}$$

(ii) Given, mass of squirrel = 250 g = $\frac{250}{1000}$ kg [∵ 1 kg = 1000 g]

and speed = 0.5 ms^{-1}

∴ Power = Force × speed [Force, $F = mg$]

$$P = mg \times v$$

$$P = \frac{250}{1000} \times 10 \times 0.5 = \frac{250}{200} \text{ W}$$

$$\therefore P = \frac{250}{200} \text{ W}$$

$$P = 1.25 \text{ W}$$

Therefore, squirrel has more power than butterfly.

Chapter 12

Sound

Multiple Choice Questions (MCQs)

Choose the correct answer from the given four options in the following questions :

Q. 1 Note is a sound

(a) of mixture of several frequencies
(b) of mixture of two frequencies only
(c) of a single frequency
(d) always unpleasant to listen

Ans. *(a)* The sound which is produced due to a mixture of several frequencies is called a note and it is pleasant to listen. An octave consists of eight different note, ranging from 256 Hz to 512 Hz.

Q. 2 A key of a mechanical piano struck gently and then struck again but much harder this time. In the second case

(a) sound will be louder but pitch will not be different
(b) sound will be louder and pitch will also be higher
(c) sound will be louder but pitch will be lower
(d) both loudness and pitch will remain unaffected

Ans. *(a)* When a key on a mechanical piano is struck with more force, the sound becomes louder because the vibrations have a greater amplitude. However, the pitch remains unchanged, as it does not depend on the force with which the key is struck.

Q. 3 In SONAR, we use

(a) ultrasonic waves
(b) infrasonic waves
(c) radio waves
(d) audible sound waves

Ans. *(a)* SONAR is a device that uses ultrasonic waves to measure the distance, direction and speed of under water objects.

Q. 4 Sound travels in air, if

(a) particles of medium travel from one place to another
(b) there is no moisture in the atmosphere
(c) disturbance moves
(d) both particles as well as disturbance travel from one place to another

Ans. *(c)* Sound travels in air if disturbance moves. As during the propagation of sound waves, particles only vibrates in its own position and disturbances created by the vibration of particle moves from one place to other.

Q. 5 When we change feeble sound to loud sound we increase its

(a) frequency
(b) amplitude
(c) velocity
(d) wavelength

Ans. *(b)* The loudness or softness of a sound is determined basically by its amplitude. Loudness or softness of sound in directly proportional to the square of amplitude of sound wave, therefore feeble sound can be changed by increasing its amplitude.

Q. 6 In the given curve, half the wavelength is

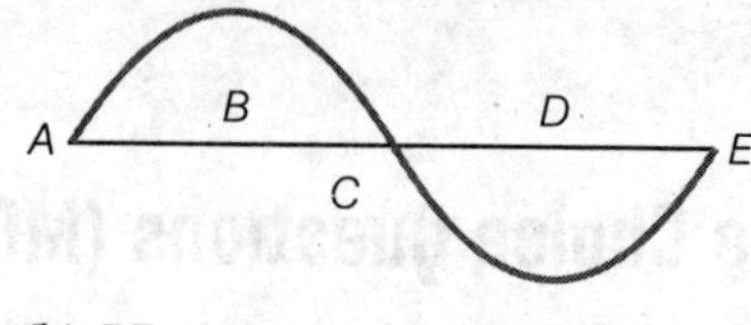

(a) *AB* (b) *BD* (c) *DE* (d) *AE*

Ans. *(b)* In this curve, half the wavelength is *BD*. Because it is half the length of one complete cycle.

Q. 7 Earthquake produces which kind of sound before the main shock wave begins

(a) ultrasound
(b) infrasound
(c) audible sound
(d) None of these

Ans. *(b)* Earthquakes produces low frequency (*i.e.*, 5 Hz) infrasound before the main shock waves begin which possibly alert the animals and they get disturbed.

Q. 8 Infrasound can be heard by

(a) dog
(b) bat
(c) rhinocerose
(d) human beings

Ans. *(c)* Infrasound are the waves whose frequency is less than 20 Hz. Rhinoceroses communicate using infrasound of frequency as low as 5 Hz.

Q. 9 Before playing the orchestra in a musical concert, a sitarist tries to adjust the tension and pluck the string suitably. By doing so, he is adjusting

(a) intensity of sound only
(b) amplitude of sound only
(c) frequency of the sitar string with the frequency of other musical instruments
(d) loudness of sounds

Ans. *(c)* Sitarist is adjusting frequency of the sitar string with the frequency of other musical instruments. Because if it is not done so, the sound will be unpleasent to listen.

Short Answer Type Questions

Q. 10 The given graph shows the displacement versus time relation for a disturbance travelling with velocity of 1500 ms^{-1}. Calculate the wavelength of the disturbance.

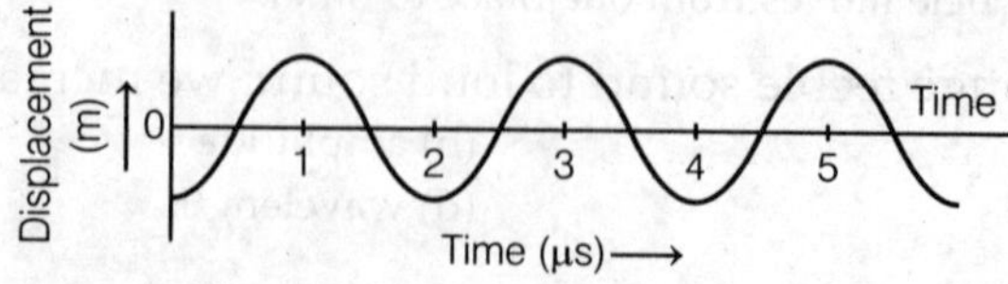

Ans. Given, velocity $(v) = 1500 \text{ ms}^{-1}$

Time taken in one complete cycle is $2\,\mu$s.

Time, $t = 2\,\mu s = 2 \times 10^{-6}$ s $(\because 1\,\mu s = 10^{-6} s)$

We know that, $v = \nu\lambda$ $\left(\because \nu = \frac{1}{T}\right)$

So, $v = \frac{\lambda}{T} \Rightarrow \lambda = vT$

where, λ = wavelength, ν = frequency

and T = time period

So, $\lambda = 1500 \times 2 \times 10^{-6} = 3000 \times 10^{-6}$

$= 3 \times 10^{+3} \times 10^{-6} = 3 \times 10^{-3}$ m

Q. 11 Which of the two graphs (i) and (ii) representing the human voice is likely to be the male voice? Give reason for your answer.

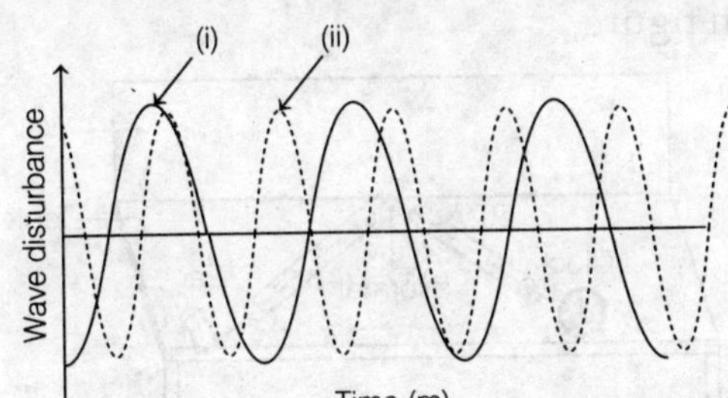

Ans. Graph (i) represents the male voice. Since the pitch and frequency of male voice is lower than the pitch of female voice and vibration of graph (ii) represents higher frequency and higher pitch.

Q.12 A girl is sitting in the middle of a park of dimension 12 m × 12 m. On the left side of it there is a building adjoining the park and on right side of the park, there is a road adjoining the park. A sound is produced on the road by a cracker. Is it possible for the girl to hear the echo of this sound? Explain your answer.

Ans. No, it is not possible for the girl to hear the echo of this sound, because the distance between girl and obstacle (building) is only 6m approx but echo is heard only if the minimum distance between the observer at the source of sound and the obstacle is 11.3 m.

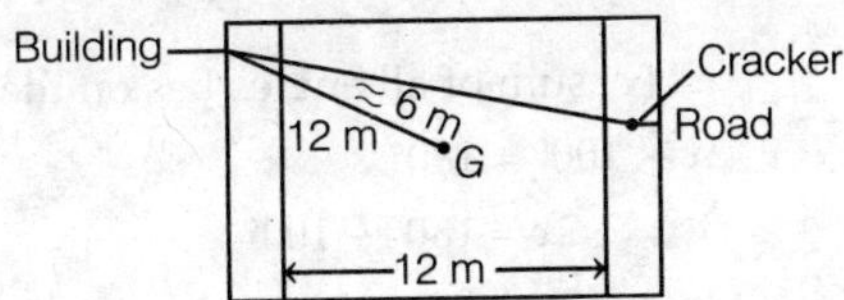

Q. 13 Why do we hear the sound produced by the humming bees while the sound of vibrations of pendulum is not heard?

Ans. The frequency of vibrations of pendulum is below 20 Hz (infrasound). We cannot hear infrasound but humming produce audible sound which can be heard by human beings.

Q. 14 **If any explosion takes place at the bottom of a lake, what type of shock waves in water will take place?**

Ans. If any explosion takes place at the bottom of a lake, longitudinal shock waves will propagate through the water. It means that particles of the medium vibrate parallel to the direction of wave propagation.

Q. 15 **Sound produced by a thunderstorm is heard 10 s after the lightning is seen. Calculate the approximate distance of the thunder cloud (Given, speed of sound = 340 ms^{-1}).**

Ans. Given, time $(t) = 10$ s and speed $(v) = 340$ m / s

We know that, distance = speed × time = $340 \times 10 = 3400$ m

$$= \frac{3400}{1000} \text{ km} = 3.4 \text{ km} \qquad [\because 1 \text{ km} = 1000 \text{ m}]$$

Q. 16 **For hearing the loudest ticking sound heard by the ear, find the angle x in the given figure.**

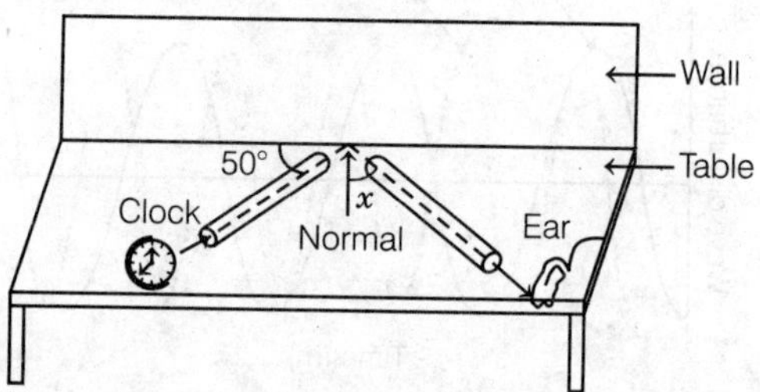

Thinking Process Firstly, we use the law of reflection, *i.e.*, angle of incidence = angle of reflection and use the property of linear pair axiom, then find the value of x.

Ans. We know that, in laws of reflection, the angle of incidence (x) is always equal to the angle of reflection (x).

Since, AOB is a straight line.

$$\therefore \quad \angle AOB = 180°$$

$$\therefore \quad 50° + x + x + 50° = 180°$$

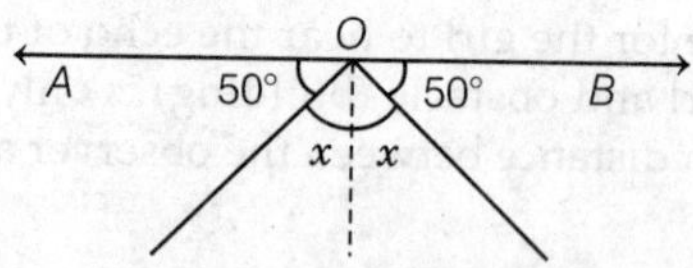

($\because$ sum of all angles lies on the same side of aline is 180°)

$$2x + 100° = 180°$$

$$2x = 180° - 100°$$

$$2x = 80°$$

$$x = \frac{80°}{2}$$

$$x = 40°$$

Hence, the value of x is 40°.

Q. 17 Why is the ceiling and wall behind the stage of good conference halls or concert halls made curved?

Ans. The ceiling of concert halls, conference halls and cinema halls are curved so that sound after reflection reaches all corners of the hall uniformly.

Long Answer Type Questions

Q. 18 Represent graphically by two separate diagrams in each case.

(i) Two sound waves having the same amplitude but different frequencies.

(ii) Two sound waves having the same frequency but different amplitudes.

(iii) Two sound waves having different amplitudes and also different wavelengths.

Ans. (i)

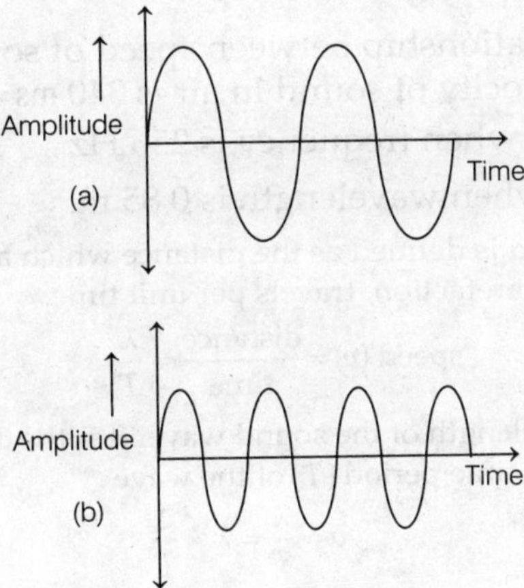

In both cases (a) and (b), same amplitude ($A_1 = A_2$) but different frequencies.

(ii)

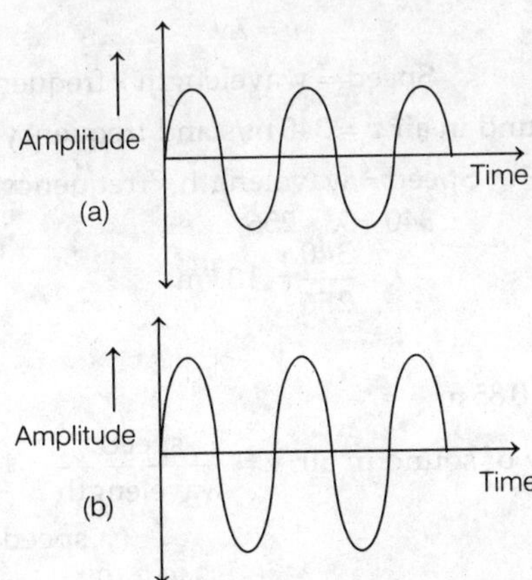

In both cases (a) and (b) same frequency and different amplitudes. *i.e.*, ($A_1 \neq A_2$)

(iii)

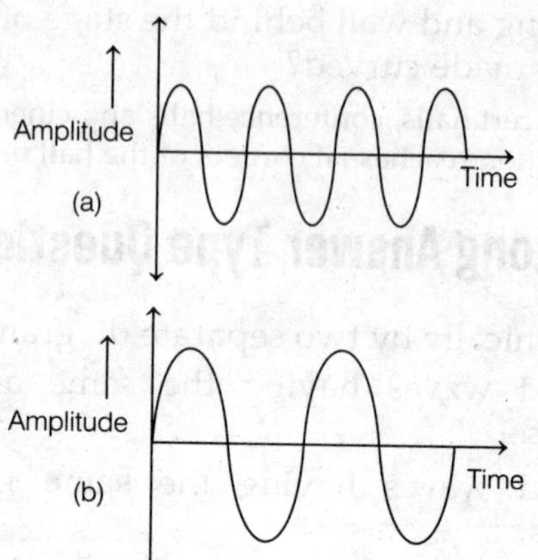

In both cases (a) and (b), different amplitudes and different wavelengths

i.e., $A_1 \neq A_2, \lambda_1 \neq \lambda_2$.

Q. 19 Establish the relationship between speed of sound, its wavelength and frequency. If velocity of sound in air is 340 ms^{-1}. Calculate

(i) wavelength when frequency is 256 Hz.

(ii) frequency when wavelength is 0.85 m.

Ans. The speed of sound is defined as the distance which a point on a wave, such as a compression or a rarefaction, travels per unit time.

We know that, $$\text{speed } (v) = \frac{\text{distance}}{\text{time}} = \frac{\lambda}{T}$$

Here, λ is the wavelength of the sound wave. It is the distance travelled by the sound wave in one time period (T) of the wave

$$v = \frac{\lambda}{T} = \lambda \times \frac{1}{T}$$

We know that, $$\nu = \frac{1}{T} \quad \text{(where } \nu = \text{frequency)}$$

$$v = \lambda\nu$$

i.e., Speed = wavelength × frequency

Given, speed of sound in air $v = 340$ m/s and frequency $\nu = 256$ Hz.

(i) ∴ Speed = wavelength × frequency

$$\Rightarrow \quad 340 = \lambda \times 256$$

$$\Rightarrow \quad \lambda = \frac{340}{256} = 1.33 \text{ m}$$

(ii) Again, given

wavelength $\lambda = 0.85$ m

Then, frequency of sound in air, $\nu = \dfrac{\text{speed}}{\text{wavelength}}$

(∵ speed = wavelength × frequency)

$$\Rightarrow \quad \nu = \frac{340}{0.85} = \frac{340 \times 100}{85} = 400 \text{ Hz}$$

Thus, frequency of sound is 400 Hz.

Alternate Method

The relationship between th speed of sound, its wavelength and frequency is given by the formula

As we know, $v = \frac{\lambda}{T}$ $\quad\therefore\ v = \nu\lambda$

where v = speed of sound

ν = frequency λ = wavelength

(i) Given, $\nu = 256$ Hz

$340 = 256\lambda \therefore \lambda = 1.33$ m

(ii) Given $\lambda = 0.85$ m

$340 = \nu(0.85) \Rightarrow \nu = 400$ Hz

Q.20 Draw a curve showing density or pressure variations with respect to distance for a disturbance produced by sound. Mark the position of compression and rarefaction on this curve. Also define wavelengths and time period using this curve.

Ans. We have a curve showing density or pressure variations with respect to distance for a disturbance produced by sound.

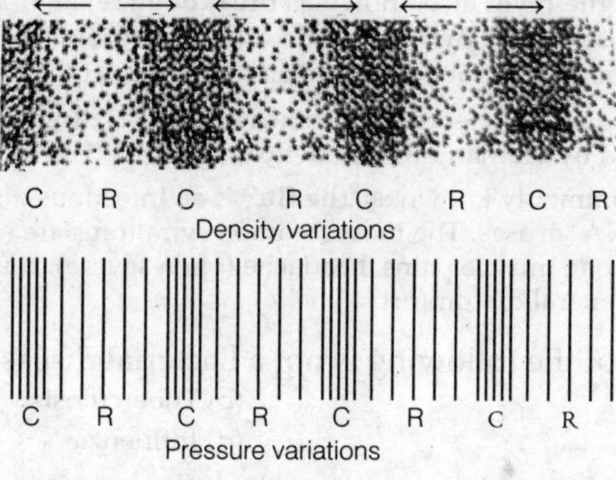

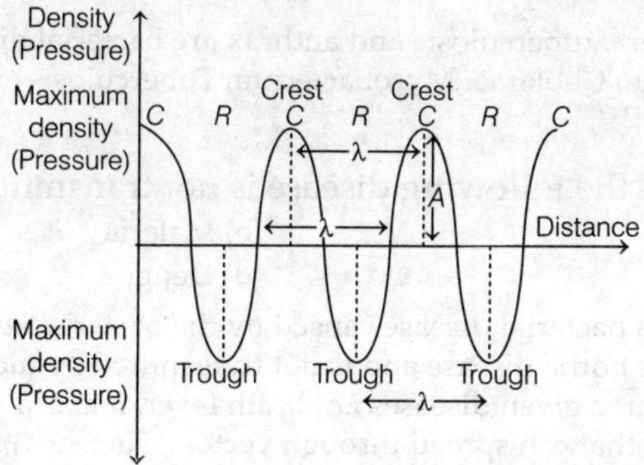

Wavelength can be defined as the distance between two successive compresion or rarefaction. It is denoted by λ.

Time taken by the waves to complete one full cycle, so that its particles are in same phase is called time period. It is denoted by T.

Chapter 13

Why Do We Fall Ill?*

Multiple Choice Questions (MCQs)

Choose the correct answer from the given four options in the following questions :

Q. 1 Which one of the following is not a viral disease?

(a) Dengue (b) AIDS

(c) Typhoid (d) Influenza

Ans. *(c)* Typhoid is not a viral disease. It is a common bacterial disease transmitted by the ingestion of food or water contaminated with the faeces of an infected person.

Whereas **dengue fever** also known as **breakbone fever**. It is a mosquito-borne tropical disease caused by the dengue virus. Symptoms include fever, headache, muscle and joint pains, and a characteristic skin rash that is similar to measles.

Acquired Immunodeficiency Syndrome (AIDS) is a disease of the human immune system caused by Human Immunodeficiency Virus (HIV).

Influenza, commonly known as **'the flu'**, is an infectious disease of mammals caused by RNA viruses. The most common symptoms are chills, fever, runny nose, sore throat, muscle pains, headache (often severe), coughing, weakness fatigue and general discomfort.

Q. 2 Which one of the following is not a bacterial disease?

(a) Cholera (b) Tuberculosis

(c) Anthrax (d) Influenza

Ans. *(d)* **Influenza is** a viral disease caused by **influenza virus.**

Where as cholera, tuberculosis and anthrax are bacterial diseases which are caused by Vibrio Cholerae, Mycobacterium Tuberculosis and Bacillus anthracis respectively.

Q. 3 Which one of the following disease is not transmitted by mosquito?

(a) Brain fever (b) Malaria

(c) Typhoid (d) Dengue

Ans. *(c)* **Typhoid** is a bacterial disease caused by the bacteria *Salmonella typhi*. It is a food and water borne disease and is not transmitted by mosquito.

All the other three given diseases *i.e.*, brain fever, malaria and dengue are communicable that can spread through vectors, such as *Anopheles* transmits malaria, *Culex* transmits filariasis and *Aedes* transmits dengue.

Mistake Alert ! *Students should carefully learn the names of the causative agents of the diseases.*

Note (*) This chapter has been deleted from latest NCERT.

Q. 4 Which one of the following disease is not caused by bacteria?

(a) Typhoid (b) Anthrax (c) Tuberculosis (d) Malaria

Ans. ***(d)*** Malaria is a mosquito borne infectious disease caused by *Plasmodium* (a protozoan). It is characterised by periodic attacks of shivering followed by high fever, headache and muscular pains. Anaemia and enlarged spleen are some other symptoms of malaria.

(*Also, refer to Q.*1 *and Q.*2)

Q. 5 Which one of the following disease is caused by protozoans?

(a) Malaria (b) Influenza

(c) AIDS (d) Cholera

Thinking Process Different types of *Plasmodium sp.* causes different forms of malaria.

Ans. ***(a)*** Malaria is caused by a protozoan called *Plasmodium*. While influenza is caused by RNA virus, **AIDS** is caused by HIV and **cholera** is caused by the bacterium *Vibrio cholerae*.

Q. 6 Which of the following has long term effect on the health of an individual?

(a) Common cold (b) Chickenpox

(c) Chewing tobacco (d) Stress

Ans. ***(c)*** Chewing tobacco may cause long term effect on the health of an individual. A chewing tobacco has been known to cause cancer, particularly of mouth and throat.

Q. 7 Which of the following can make you ill if you come in contact with an infected person?

(a) High blood pressure (b) Genetic abnormalities

(c) Sneezing (d) Blood cancer

Thinking Process *Remember communicable disease can be spread coming in contact with the infected person.*

Ans. ***(c)*** Sneezing can make a person ill as the transmission of microbes occurs through the little droplets that are sneezed out by an infected person. A person living in close proximity of an infected person can inhale these disease causing microbes and may become infected.

Mistakes Alert! *Students should not be confused with the symptoms of the disease.*

Q. 8 AIDS cannot be transmitted by

(a) sexual contact (b) hugs

(c) breast feeding (d) blood transfusion

Ans. ***(b)*** AIDS can not be transmitted through hugs. It is transmitted by body fluids, sexual contact, blood transfusions, sharing of needles, and from infected mother to child.

Mistake Alert! *Because HIV can be transmitted only through blood, semen and breast milk. Thus, a person can get infected through HIV transfusion of infected blood, sharing of needle with an infected person or having sexual intercourse with an infected person. Thus, HIV is not spread by touching an infected person, nor can it be spread by breathing in the virus when the patient coughs or sneezes.*

Q. 9 Making anti-viral drugs is more difficult than making anti-bacterial medicines because

(a) viruses make use of host machinery

(b) viruses are on the border line of living and non-living

(c) viruses have very few biochemical mechanisms of their own

(d) viruses have a protein coat

Ans. *(c)* Making anti-viral drugs is more difficult than making anti-bacterial medicines because any anti bacterial medicines works commonly by blocking the biochemical pathways important for bacteria. *e.g.*, penicillin blocks the process that builds cell wall in bacteria. As viruses have very few biochemical pathway of their own unlike bacteria, thus it is difficult to make anti-viral drugs. Both options (a) and (c) are correct.

Q. 10 Which one of the following causes kala-azar?

(a) *Ascaris* (b) *Trypanosoma* (c) *Leishmania* (d) Bacteria

Ans. *(c) Leishmania,* a protozoa causes kala-azar or black fever. The signs and symptoms of the disease includes, fever, weight loss, fatigue, anaemia and swelling of liver and spleen.

Q. 11 If you live in an over crowded and poorly ventilated house, it is possible that you may suffer from which of the following diseases?

(a) Cancer (b) AIDS

(c) Air borne diseases (d) Cholera

Ans. *(c)* In closed areas, the droplets nuclei recirculate and pose a risk to everybody. Thus, over crowded and poorly ventilated houses is a major factor in spread of airborne diseases.

Q. 12 Which disease is not transmitted by mosquitoes?

(a) Dengue (b) Malaria

(c) Brain fever or encephalitis (d) Pneumonia

Thinking Process Remember all the diseases that are spread through mosquitoes

Ans. *(d)* Pneumonia is an inflammatory condition of lung and is not caused by mosquitoes. It is caused by a virus, fungi or bacteria. Symptoms include cough, chest pain, fever and difficulty in breathing. Pneumonia is an airborne disease whereas dengue, malaria and brain fever are vector (mosquito) borne diseases.

Q. 13. Which one of the following is not important for individual health?

(a) Living in clean space

(b) Good economic condition

(c) Social equality and harmony

(d) Living in a large and well furnished house

Ans. *(d)* The conditions essential for good health are clean surrounding because they have

(i) Availability of clean drinking water.

(ii) Availability of clean adequate, nutritious food.

(iii) Social equality and harmony.

Q. 14 Choose the wrong statement.

(a) High blood pressure is caused by excessive weight and lack of exercise.
(b) Cancer can be caused by genetic abnormalities
(c) Peptic ulcers are caused by eating acidic food
(d) Acne in not caused by staphylococci

Ans. ***(c)*** The incorrect statement is (c) and it can be corrected as. Peptic ulcers are caused by the bacterium *Helicobacter pylori*, which is found in stomach.

Q. 15 We should not allow mosquitoes to breed in our surroundings because they

(a) multiply very fast and cause pollution (b) are vectors for many diseases
(c) bite and cause skin diseases (d) are not important insects

Ans. ***(b)*** Mosquitoes serve as vectors for various infectious diseases, such as malaria (*Anopheles*), Filariasis (*Culex*), Yellow fever, dengue (*Aedes*). Thus, it should not be allowed for the mosquitoes to breed in populated surroundings.

Q. 16 You are aware of Polio Eradication Programme in your city. Children are vaccinated because

(a) vaccination kills the polio causing microorganisms
(b) prevents the entry of polio causing organism
(c) it creates immunity in the body
(d) All of the above

Thinking Process Vaccination is a process of developing immunity in individual artificially.

Ans. ***(c)*** Children are vaccinated to improve immunity against a particular disease. It contains an agent that resembles a disease causing microorganism and are made from weakened or killed microbe etc.

The polio programme is an immunization drive against polio. Polio is a disease of the muscles and nerves which can even cause paralysis. To prevent this disease, oral vaccines are given periodically to all children under 5 years of age in our country.

Q. 17 Viruses, which cause hepatitis, are transmitted through

(a) air (b) water (c) food (d) personal contact

Ans. ***(b)*** Hepatitis is an infectious disease and can be transmitted through contaminated food and water. The symptoms of the disease includes yellowing of skin and whitening of eyes etc.

Mistake Alert ! *Students should know about the various modes of transmission of a disease.*

Q. 18. Vectors can be defined as

(a) animals carry the infecting agents from sick person to another healthy person
(b) microorganisms which cause many diseases
(c) infected person
(d) diseased plants

Ans. ***(a)*** Vectors are carriers that transmit infecting agents from sick person to another healthy person. The vectors includes mosquitoes (for malaria, filariasis, yellow fever and dengue), flies (for typhoid, kala-azar, sleeping sickness), and rat (for plague).

Short Answer Type Questions

Q. 19 Give two examples for each of the following.

(a) Acute disease (b) Chronic diseases

(c) Infectious diseases (d) Non-infectious diseases

Ans. (a) Acute disease last for a short period of time and do not cause long term effect, *e.g.*, cold and cough.

(b) Chronic disease last for a long period of time, sometimes for a lifetime and cause long term effects on human health. *e.g.*, tuberculosis and arthritis.

(c) Infectious diseases are caused by attack of pathogens and can pass from one person to another. *e.g.*, malaria and chickenpox.

(d) Non-infectious diseases are caused by factors other than living pathogens and are not transmitted from one person to another. *e.g.*, diabetes and goitre.

Q.20 Name two diseases caused by protozoans. What are their causal organisms?

Ans. There are many disease caused by protozoans. Two of them are :

(i) Sleeping sickness caused by *Trypanosoma*.

(ii) Kala-azar caused by *Leishmania*.

Q. 21 Which bacterium causes peptic ulcers? Who discovered the above pathogen for the first time?

Ans. Peptic ulcers are caused by a bacterium called *Helicobacter pylori*, earlier named as *Compylobacter pylori*. It is found in stomach. It was first identified in 1982 by Australian scientists Barry Marshall and Robin Warren.

Q.22 What is an antibiotic? Give two examples.

Ans. Antibiotics are the drugs that are used to cure diseases caused by bacteria.There are different kinds of antibiotics that attacks different processes and structures in bacteria to kill them or to stop their growth.

Examples : Penicillin and Streptomycin.

Q.23 Fill in the blanks.

(a) Pneumonia is an example of .... disease.

(b) Many skin diseases are caused by ....

(c) Antibiotics commonly block biochemical pathways important for the growth of ....

(d) Living organisms carrying the infecting agents from one person to another are called ....

Ans. (a) Pneumonia is an example of **communicable** disease.

(b) Many skin diseases are caused by **fungi**.

(c) Antibiotics commonly blocks the biochemical pathways important for the growth of **bacteria**.

(d) Living organisms carrying the infecting agents from one person to another are called **vectors**.

Q.24 Name the target organs for the following diseases

(a) Hepatitis targets ....

(b) Fits or unconsciousness targets ....

(c) Pneumonia targets ....

(d) Fungal disease targets ....

Ans. (a) liver (b) brain

(c) lungs (d) skin

Q.25 Who discovered 'vaccine' for the first time?
Name two diseases which can be prevented by using vaccines.

Ans. A 'vaccine' is a biological preparation that improves immunity to a particular disease. An English physician, Edward Jenner discovered vaccine for the first time. He developed the vaccine for smallpox.

Two examples of disease that can be presented by using vaccines are : Small pox and polio.

Q.26 Fill in the blanks.

(a) .... disease continues for many days and causes .... on body.

(b) .... disease continue for a few days and causes no longer term effect on body.

(c) .... is defined as physical, mental and social well-being and comfort.

(d) Common cold is .... disease.

(e) Many skin diseases are caused by ....

Ans. (a) Chronic, long term effect (b) Acute

(c) Health (d) Infectious

(e) Fungi

Q.27 Classify the following diseases as infections or non-infectious.

(a) AIDS (b) Tuberculosis

(c) Cholera (d) High blood pressure

(e) Heart disease (f) Pneumonia

(g) Cancer

Ans. AIDS, Tuberculosis, cholera and pneumonia are infectious disease whereas, high blood pressure, heart disease and cancer are non-infectious disease.

Q.28 Name any two groups of microorganisms from which antibiotics could be extracted.

Ans. Fungi (*Penicillium notatum*) and bacteria (*Streptomyces cerevisae*) are the two groups of microorganisms from which the antibiotics could be extracted.
(Also refer to Q. 22)

Q.29 Name any three disease transmitted through vectors.

Ans. Disease caused by vectors are (*Also, refer to Q.* 18)

	Insect Vector	Disease Transmitted
1.	Mosquitoes	
	(i) *Anopheles* (female)	Malaria
	(ii) *Culex*	Filariasis
	(iii) *Aedes*	Yellow fewer (jaundice), dengue, filariasis
2.	Flies	
	(i) House fly	Typhoid, diarrhoea, dysentery, cholera, tuberculosis, conjunctivitis (an eye disease)
	(ii) Sandfly	Kala-azar,
	(iii) Tse-tse fly	Sleeping sickness
3.	Rat flea	Plague

Long Answer Type Questions

Q.30 Explain giving reasons

(a) Balanced diet is necessary for maintaining healthy body.

(b) Health of an organism depends upon the surrounding environmental conditions.

(c) Our surrounding area should be free of stagnant water.

(d) Social harmony and good economic conditions are necessary for good health.

Ans. (a) A balanced diet is necessary for the good health. A balanced diet provides all the nutrients *e.g.*, proteins, carbohydrates, fats, vitamins and minerals required by the body in correct proportions. When our diet lacks one or more of these nutrients, we get deficiency diseases or nutritional disorders.

Excessive or inadequate intake of food and nutrients leads to condition such as obesity, kwashiorkor and rickets. For example if our diet, lacks the mineral iron, we may get a disease called anaemia. A balanced diet also increases our ability to fight against infections . Thus, balanced diet is necessary for maintaing healthy body.

(b) Health depends on the cleanliness of the surroundings.

Health of an individuals depends upon various factors like physical, social, mental, economic condition etc. A clean environment is one of these factor. If there is dirty environment like garbage on the streets, open drainage etc then it would serve as breeding ground for various infection carrying vectors like mosquitoes, flies etc. Thus, it is important that surrounding environment conditions are clean and hygienic to avoid the risk of infection.

People tend to fall ill quite often if the area in which they live or work has uncleaned garbage, stagnant water or open drains. Clean air is also a part of our surrounding and a basic requirement for good health.

(c) Stagnant water becomes a breeding ground for mosquitoes and other microbes which cause many health diseases. As water-borne diseases flourish in stagnant water. Therefore, our surrounding area should be free of stagnant water.

(d) Health in not just the well being of physical body it also involves the good mental health of individuals as well. For both the physical and mental health, social harmony and good economic conditions are important factors. For ex. when societies are harmonious they tend to have better access to healthcare, improved social support system, lower stress, all of which contribute to overall better health.

Q.31 What is a disease? How many types of diseases have you studied? Give examples.

Ans. **Disease** can be defined as an impairment (malfunctioning) of the normal state of the living organism that disturbs or modifies the performance of the vital organs and hampers their function. Disease may be a response to

(i) Environmental factors (as industrial hazards or climate).

(ii) Specific infective agents (as worms, protozoans, fungi, bacteria or viruses).

(iii) Inherent defects of the organism (as genetic anomalies).

(iv) Combination of these factors. (*Also, refer to Q.* 19)

A table listing various type of diseases, their causes and examples is given below.

Different Type of Disease	Causes of Diseases	Examples
1. Physical	Temporary or permanent damage to any body part	Bone fracture, strain or sprain.
2. Infectious	Invasion of the body by microorganisms (viruses, bacteria, fungi, protozoans, nematodes, insects, etc.)	Typhoid, diarrhoea, malaria, hepatitis, AIDS, TB, polio, influenza, cholera
3. Deficiency	Inadequate diet or lack of balanced diet.	Kwashiorkor, marasmus, scurvy, rickets, anaemia, goitre, beri-beri.
4. Inherited	Defective genes are passed from parents to their offspring.	Haemophilia, sickle-cell anaemia, .
5. Degenerative	Organs and tissues wear away and do not work well with the age	Arthritis, hearing and sight defects, gout.
6. Mental	Brain damage or psychological illness	Depression.

Q. 32 What do you mean by disease symptoms? Explain giving two examples?

Ans. Symptoms are the signs or evidences that indicates the presence of a disease. They are visible in the form of either structural or functional changes in the body or any of its parts. On the basis of these symptoms doctors look for definite clues or sings for a particular disease. Examples : (i) Lesion on the skin are symptoms of chickenpox. (ii) Cough is the symptom of lung infection.

Q. 33 Why is immune system essential for our health?

Ans. Immune system acts as defence system of the body and helps in combating the action of pathogens that may harm our body. Immune system possess specialised cells that can kill microbes. The entry of microbes activates the immune system which eliminate these microbes. Thus, the immune system is essential for our health.

Q. 34 What precautions will you take to justify "prevention is better than cure"?

Ans. When someone gets a disease

(i) Their body function may get damaged and may never recover completely.

(ii) They may become bedridden of sometime.

Preventon is always better than cure as a disease causes damage to the body, loss of working days, and expenditure on medicine.

Thus its always better to take preventive measures against diseases.

The important precautions for preventing diseases are

(i) Avoid exposure to airborne microbes.

(ii) Adopt living conditions that are not overcrowded and have proper ventilation system.

(iii) Safe drinking water should be used.

(iv) Establish hygienic and clean environment to avoid vector-borne disease.

Q.35 Why do some children fall ill more frequently than others living in the same locality?

Thinking Process Immunity is ability of the body to protect itself from the disease causing arganism

Ans. Some children fall ill more frequently than other living in a same area due to their weak immunity, or slow immune response. (*Also, refer Q.* 33)

Q.36 Why are antibiotics not effective for viral disease?

Ans. Antibiotics are not effective for viral diseases because virus uses the host organisms machinery to grow and divide. Therefore, it becomes difficult to aim the virus without affecting the host. (*Also, refer to Q.* 9 *and Q.* 22)

Q.37 Becoming exposed to or infected with an infectious microbe does not necessarily mean developing noticeable disease. Explain.

Ans. The strong immune system of a healthy person normally fights against microbes. The body has specialised cells to kill the pathogenic microbes. These cells are active when infectious microbes enter the body and if they are successful in removing the pathogen, body remains disease-free. So, even exposure to infectious microbes may not cause disease to a person having strong immune system. (*Also, refer to Q.* 33)

Q.38 Give any four factors necessary for a healthy person.

Ans. Four factors necessary for a healthy person are as follows

(i) Balanced diet

(ii) Clean surrounding environment

(iii) Social harmony

(iv) Good economic conditions (*Also, refer to Q.* 30)

(v) Personal hygiene

(vi) Immunisation against various disease (Any four)

Q.39 Why is AIDS considered to be a 'Syndrome' and not a disease?

Ans. HIV causes a syndrome, because it does not directly cause a specific illness. Instead it weakens the immune system, which in turn makes the body vulnerable to a wide range of infections, cancers and other health issues. These conditions are not directly caused by HIV itself but by the body's inability to fight off pathogens due to damaged immune system. This collection of symptoms and diseases is referred to as AIDS. Therefore HIV leads to a syndrome, which is group of related symptoms and illness, rather than one specific diseases.

Chapter

14 Natural Resources*

Multiple Choice Questions (MCQs)

Choose the correct answer from the given four options in the following questions :

Q. 1 The atmosphere of the earth is heated by radiations which are mainly

(a) radiated by the sun
(b) re-radiated by land
(c) re-radiated by water
(d) re-radiated by land and water

Ans. ***(d)*** When solar radiations fall on earth, some are absorbed by the land but majority of them get reflected back or re-radiated by land and water bodies. These re-radiated or reflected solar radiation, heat up the atmosphere. This results in convection currents.

Q. 2 If there were no atmosphere around the earth, the temperature of the earth will

(a) increase
(b) go on decreasing
(c) increase during day and decrease during night
(d) be unaffected

Ans. ***(c)*** If there was no atmosphere around the earth, the temperature will increase during the day and decrease during the night. This will lead to extreme variations in temperature.

This is because atmosphere helps to prevent sudden increase in temperature during the day. At night, it also slows down the escape of heat into outer space.

Q. 3 What would happen, if all the oxygen present in the environment is converted to ozone?

(a) We will be protected more
(b) It will become poisonous and kill living forms
(c) Ozone is not stable, hence it will be toxic
(d) It will help harmful sun radiations to reach earth and damage many life forms

Ans. ***(b)*** If all oxygen present in the environment is converted into ozone, the atmosphere will become poisonous. This will further kill living forms as ozone is toxic in nature and will lead to respiratory diseases, damaging the lungs.

Q. 4 One of the following factors does not lead to soil formation in nature

(a) the sun
(b) water
(c) wind
(d) polythene bags

Thinking Process Water and wind are the climatic factors that breakdown bigger rock into smaller parts *i.e.,* weathering and sun helps the living organisms to grow and multiply causing paedogenesis and biological weathering.

Note (*) This chapter has been deleted from latest NCERT.

Ans. *(d)* Soil is formed from the rocks undergoing various physical, chemical and biological processes. They include
Weathering of rocks, climate conditions, microbial activities and physical agents like sun, water and wind. On the contrary polythene bags are non-biodegradable substances. These cannot be broken down by paedogenesis or weathering (physical, chemical or biological), Therefore they do not contribute in soil formation and are considered to be degradable pollutants of the soil.

Q. 5 The two forms of oxygen found in the atmosphere are
(a) water and ozone
(b) water and oxygen
(c) ozone and oxygen
(d) water and carbon-dioxide

Thinking Process Along with oxygen atom, water and carbon-dioxide are made up of hydrogen and carbon respectively.

Ans. *(c)* Two forms of oxygen present in the atmosphere are oxygen and ozone. Oxygen is present in our atmosphere in the form of a diatomic molecule. It is required by all living beings for respiration and combustion (burning)of materials. Its percentage in air is balanced by the process of photosynthesis. Ozone is an allotrope of oxygen present in a significant amount in the stratosphere. It is a triatomic blue gas with pungent odour. The ozone is highly essential as it absorbs high energy UV radiations from the sun. These radiations split ozone into molecular and atomic oxygen.

$$\underset{\text{Ozone}}{O_3} \xrightarrow{[UV]} \underset{\text{Molecular oxygen}}{O_2} + \underset{\text{Atomic oxygen}}{[O]} + \text{Heat}$$

Q. 6 The process of nitrogen fixation by bacteria does not take place in the presence of
(a) molecular form of hydrogen
(b) elemental form of oxygen
(c) water
(d) elemental form of nitrogen

Ans. *(b)* The process of nitrogen fixation by bacteria does not take place in the presence of elemental form of oxygen because nitrogenase enzymes which are present in bacteria (like *Rhizobium*) grow in anaerobic conditions.
Hence making them susceptible to oxygen.

Q. 7 Rainfall patterns depends on
(a) the underground water table
(b) the number of water bodies in an area
(c) the density pattern of human population in an area
(d) the prevailing season in an area

Ans. *(b)* The rainfall pattern and the amount of rainfall is directly dependent on the number of water bodies in an area. As more number of water bodies like sea, lakes etc . in an area lead to more evaporation, resulting in increased amount of moisture in the atmosphere, leading to rainfall.

Q. 8 Among the given options, which one is not correct for the use of large amount of fertilisers and pesticides?

(a) They are eco-friendly

(b) They turn the fields barren after some time

(c) They adversally affect the useful component from the soil

(d) They destroy the soil fertility

Thinking Process Fertilisers and pesticides are the synthetic chemicals used in modern agricultural practices.

Ans. ***(a)*** Statements (a) is not correct and can be corrected as. Use of pesticides and fertilisers over long period of time can destroy the fertility and structure of the soil by killing the soil microorganism that recycle nutrients in the soil. It also kills earthworms which are instrumental in making rich humus.

Q. 9 The nitrogen molecules present in air can be converted into nitrates and nitrites by

(a) a biological process of nitrogen fixing bacteria present in soil

(b) a biological process of carbon fixing factor present in soil

(c) any of the industries manufacturing nitrogenous compounds

(d) the plants used as cereal crops in field

Ans. ***(a)*** Nitrogen fixation is a process by which atmospheric nitrogen (N_2) is converted into usable nitrates and nitrites, which can be used by plants. It is achieved with the help of nitrogen-fixing bacteria like *Azotobacter* and *Rhizobium* present in the soil.

Q. 10 One of the following processes is not a step involved in the water cycle operating in nature

(a) evaporation (b) transpiration (c) precipitation (d) photosynthesis

Thinking Process Photosynthesis is a process by which plants synthesis their food in the presence of light energy of sun and chlorophyll.

Ans. ***(d)*** Photosynthesis is not a part water cycle, as it is not directly involved in the movement of water in the environment. While, various process involved in water cycle are evaporation, transpiration and precipitation are directly involved in movement of water.

Q. 11 The term 'water pollution' can be defined in several ways. Which of the following statements does not give the correct definition?

(a) The addition of undesirable substances to water-bodies

(b) The removal of desirable substances from water-bodies

(c) A change in pressure of the water-bodies

(d) A change in temperature of the water-bodies

Ans. ***(c)*** Statement (c) is incorrect and can be corrected. Change in pressure of water bodies does no effect on water's pollution level. As water pollution is an undesirable change in the physical, biological or chemical qualities of water that adversely affects the aquatic life and makes the water unfit for use. It is one of the most serious environmental problems of the world.

The contaminants leading to pollution in water include a wide spectrum of chemicals, pathogens and physical or sensory changes such as elevated temperature and discolouration, leading to waterborne diseases.

Q. 12 Which of the following is not a green house gas?

(a) Methane (b) Carbon dioxide
(c) Carbon monoxide (d) Ammonia

Thinking Process Ammonia contributes to the nutritional needs of terrestrial organism by serving as precursor of food, and building blocks of pharmaceuticals.

Ans. *(d)* Some gases like methane, carbon monoxide and carbon dioxide prevents the heat to escape from earth which will lead to an average in crease in the temperature of earth. This phenomenon is called greenhouse effect. Ammonia, however, is not considered a greenhouse gas.

Q. 13 Which step is not involved in the carbon-cycle?

(a) Photosynthesis
(b) Transpiration
(c) Respiration
(d) Burning of fossil fuels

Thinking Process Transpiration is the loss of water from the aerial parts of the plants.

Ans. *(b)* Transpiration is the process by which water evaporates from plants into the atmosphere. It is a part of water cycle. Whereas photosynthesis, respiration and burning of fossil fuels are part of carbon cycle, which involves the movement of carbon through different ecosystem.

Q. 14 'Ozonehole' means

(a) a large sized hole in the ozone layer
(b) thinning of the ozone layer
(c) small holes scattered in the ozone layer
(d) thickening of ozone in the ozone layer

Ans. *(b)* Ozone hole refers to thinning of ozone layer above the Earth.

The depletion of ozone layer is due to various man made compounds like CFC's (carbon compounds having chlorine and fluorine) which are not degraded by any biological processes. This resulted in the reduction of ozone layer leading to formation of a ozone hole.

Q. 15 Ozone layer is getting depleted because of

(a) excessive use of automobiles
(b) excessive formation of industrial units
(c) excessive use of manmade compounds containing both fluorine and chlorine
(d) excessive deforestation

Ans. *(c)* Reduction in the concentration of ozone layer is called **ozone depletion**. It is caused by certain chemicals which are generally rich in some of the man made compounds containing chlorine, fluorine and carbon called **Ozone Depleting Substances** (ODS). Some of the important ODSs are **Chlorofluorocarbons** (CFCs),**nitrogen oxides.**

CFCs are commonly used as aerosol propellants, refrigerants, shaving foams, spray agent in scents, etc. Some ODS are released in the stratosphere by jets flying at height.

Q. 16 Which of the following is a recently originated problem of environment?

(a) Ozone layer depletion (b) Greenhouse effect
(c) Global warming (d) All of these

Ans. ***(d)*** Ozone layer depletion, greenhouse effect and global warming are recently originated problems of environment due to human activities such as the extensive use of vehicles and thermoelectric plants, gaseous emission from industries, use of aerosol propellants, refrigerants, shaving foams, spray agents etc. leading to the emission of various harmful gases like sulphur dioxide, carbon dioxide, CO, chloroflorocarbons etc. in the atmosphere.

These gases are the major constituents of air pollution and are inter-linked in causing the depletion, of ozone layer, greenhouse effect and global warming.

Q. 17 When we breathe in air, nitrogen also goes inside along with oxygen. What is the fate of this nitrogen?

(a) It moves along with oxygen into the cells
(b) It comes out with the CO_2 during exhalation
(c) It is absorbed only by the nasal cells
(d) Nitrogen concentration is already more in the cells so it is not at all absorbed.

Ans. ***(b)*** During inhalation of air, nitrogen also goes inside with oxygen as it is a major component of air. But nitrogen is an inert gas and does not participate in respiration or any other processes and gets expelled from the body during exhalation.

Q. 18 Top-soil contains the following.

(a) humus and living organisms only
(b) humus and soil particles only
(c) Humus, living organisms and plants
(d) Humus, living organisms and soil particles

Ans. ***(d)*** Top soil is a mixture of bits of dead decaying living organisms called humus, microscopic live forms and small particles of rocks, which help in maintaing the structure of soil. Presence of humus enhances the fertility of soil and helps retain moisture, while presence of microorganisms help in nutrient recycling. They aid in plant growth and agricultural practices as well.

Q. 19 Choose the correct sequences

(a) CO_2 in atmosphere → Decomposers → Organic carbon in animals → Organic carbon in plants
(b) CO_2 in atmosphere → Organic carbon in plants → Organic carbon in animals → Inorganic carbon in soil
(c) Inorganic carbonates in water → Organic carbon in plants → Organic carbon in animals → scavengers
(d) Organic carbon in animals → Decomposers → CO_2 in atmosphere → Organic carbon in plants

Ans. *(b)* The correct sequence is
CO_2 in atomsphere → organic carbon in plants → organic carbon in animals. → inorganic carbon in soil, which can be explained with the help of the diagram given below.

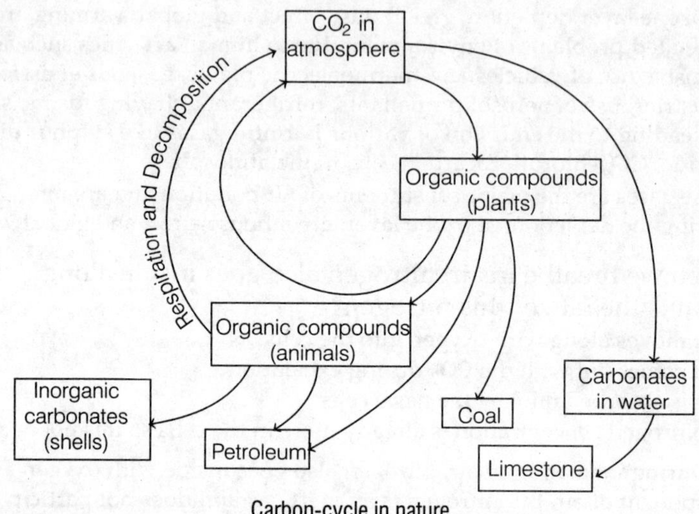

Carbon-cycle in nature.

Q. 20 Major source of mineral in soil is the
(a) parent rock from which soil is formed
(b) plants
(c) animals
(d) bacteria

Ans. *(a)* The physical and chemical weathering of rocks is the process involved in the formation of soil. Rocks are the naturally occurring soil aggregates of one or more minerals or mineraloids. For example, common granite is combination of quartz, feldspar and biotite minerals.

Q. 21 Total Earth's surface covered by water is
(a) 75% (b) 60% (c) 85% (d) 50%

Ans. *(a)* Water covers approximately 75% of the Earth's surface and is vital for all known forms of life. On Earth 96.5% of planets water is found in seas and oceans, 1.7% in glaciers and ice caps and 0.001% in air as water vapour, clouds and precipitation.
Only 2.5% of Earth's water is freshwater and 98.8% of that water is in ice and groundwater. The remaining occurs as surface water (rivers, lakes and ponds) and soil water.

Mistake Alert ! *Students fails to correctly learn about the amount of percentage coverage by water on Earth's surface*

Q. 22 Biotic component of biosphere is not constituted by
(a) producers (b) consumers (c) decomposer (d) air

Thinking Process Biosphere contained all abiotic and biotic components of the ecosystem

Ans. ***(d)*** Biosphere is the global sum of all ecosystems, integrating all living beings and their relationship including their interaction with the elements of lithosphere (land), hydrosphere (water) and atmosphere (air).

Biosphere is composed of

(i) **Biotic Components** are the living things that shape an ecosystem. Biotic components usually includes producers, consumers and decomposers.

(ii) **Abiotic Components** are the non-living chemical and physical part of the ecosystem like air, water, soil, temperature and sunlight.

Q. 23 An increase in carbon-dioxide content in the atmosphere would not cause

(a) more heat to be retained by the environment
(b) increase in photosynthesis in plants
(c) global warming
(d) abundance of desert plants

Thinking Process The ability of a plant to take up carbon dioxide depends upon the temperature of atmosphere. A rise in temperature may adversely affect the CO_2 taking up capaity and vice-versa.

Ans. ***(d)*** An increase in carbon dioxide content in the atmosphere may lead to global warming but it would not cause abundance of desert plants as, when the temperature rises (due to excessive carbon dioxide emission) their ability to take up carbon dioxide reduces which is not conductive to their growth.

Q.24 Oxygen is returned to the atmosphere mainly by

(a) burning of fossil fuel
(b) respiration
(c) photosynthesis
(d) fungi

Ans. ***(c)*** Oxygen is primarily returned to the atmosphere through photosynthesis, a process by which plants make their food in the presence of carbon dioxide and sunlight, by releasing oxygen in the atmosphere. Respiration, on the other hand, releases carbon dioxide and burning of fossil fuels results in the emmission of CO_2 in the atmosphere.

Q. 25 Low visibility during cold weather is due to

(a) formation of fossil fuel
(b) unburnt carbon particles or hydrocarbons suspended in air
(c) lack of adequate power supply
(d) None of the above

Ans. ***(b)*** The combustion of fossil fuels increases the amount of suspended particles in the air. These suspended particles could be unburnt carbon particles (*i.e.,* hydrocarbons). Presence of high levels of these pollutants causes low visibility especially in the cold weather when water also condenses out of air. This is known as **smog** and it is a visible indication of air pollution.

Q.26 Growth of lichens on barren rocks is followed by the growth of

(a) moss (b) ferns

(c) gymnosperms (d) algae

Ans. *(a)* Lichens are the pioneer of primary succession as they produce acid and erodes the barren rocks etc. Most lichens grows on stable rock surfaces or the bark of the old trees. They also acts as an important part of soil stabilisation and help to retain water in the soil. This enables the mosses to grow on the soil after lichen.

Q.27 Marked temperature changes in aquatic environment can affect

(a) breeding of animals

(b) more growth of aquatic plants

(c) process of digestion in animals

(d) availability of nutrients

Ans. *(a)* Marked temperature changes in aquatic enviornment can affect breeding of animals. Most of the aquatic animals are cold blooded and they required optimum temperature to lay eggs for breeding.

Q.28 Soil erosion can be prevented by

(a) raising forests (b) deforestation

(c) excessive use of fertiliser (d) overgrasing by animals

Ans. *(a)* Soil erosion is the process of removal of top layer of the soil. Trees in the forests help to hold on the soil due to the ability of the roots to anchor into the soil deeply. Hence growing forest or preventing deforestation can help to prevent soil erosion.

Q.29 What happens when rain falls on soil without vegetational cover?

(a) Rain water percolates in soil efficiently

(b) Rain water causes loss of surface soil

(c) Rain water leads to fertility of the soil

(d) Rain water does not cause any change in soil

Ans. *(b)* In the absence of vegetative cover, rainwater can lead to soil erosion, washing away the surface of soil. Vegetation helps in water absorption and prevents the loss of top soil.

Q. 30 Oxygen is harmful for

(a) ferns

(b) nitrogen fixing bacteria

(c) chara

(d) mango tree

Ans. *(b)* Nitrogen fixing bacteria are found in anaerobic conditions, *i.e.,* absence of oxygen. Thus they, get killed when exposed to oxygen. Hence, oxygen is considered to be harmful to them.

Short Answer Type Questions

Q.31 Rivers from land, add minerals to sea water. Discuss how?

Ans. Water is able to dissolve a large number of substances. When water flows over different types of rock containing soluble minerals, some amount of these minerals get dissolved in the water. This mineral containing water reaches the rivers, which flows to sea. Therefore, the rivers from land add minerals to sea water.

Q. 32 How can we prevent the loss of top soil?

Ans. Top soil is composed of humus, earthworm and other living organisms.It is mainly lost due to excessive winds, floods, rainfall, etc. The major causes of soil erosion (loss of top soil) are deforestation, desertification etc.

It can be prevented by various methods like.

(i) Afforestation (ii) contour farming

(iii) Crop-rotation (v) Proper irrigation methods

(*Also, refer to Q. 28*)

Mistake Alert ! *Students, should not gets confused between the causes and preventive methods related to soil erosion.*

Q. 33 How is the life of organisms living in water affected when water gets polluted ?

Ans. Addition of pollutants like pesticides, fertilisers, industrial waste and domestic wastes affect the life forms living in the water. These pollutants encourage the growth of some life forms and can harm the growth of other life forms. This affects the balance between various organisms in the water.

With the increase in the amount of organic wastes in water, bacteria multiply very rapidly thus consuming the available oxygen. The lack of oxygen kills the fish and other aquatic animals.

Q.34 During summer, if you go near the lake, you feel relief from the heat, why?

Ans. During summer, the air near lake feels cooler and provides relief from the heat because the flow of high pressure air present over the lake blows towards the low pressure air present over land. The air present over lake is comparatively cooler due to evaporation as compared to the air present over the land.

Q. 35 In coastal area, wind current moves from the sea towards the land during day; but during night it moves from land to the sea. Discuss the reason.

Ans. In coastal areas, during day time, there is a regular flow of cool air from the sea towards the land. While, during the night time, there is a reverse flow of air from land to the sea. This happens because during the daytime, land gets heated faster than water and heats the air above it. The hot air rises and creates an area of low pressure. Sea water does not get heated so rapidly, so air above the sea is comparatively cool. A high pressure area forms above sea water as compared to air over land.

Therefore, cooler air over the sea, flows towards the land (region of low pressure) area . The movement of air from one region to the other creates winds.

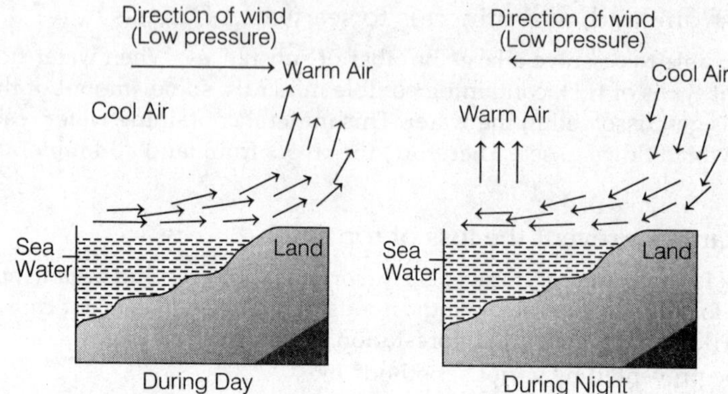

Movement of wind from sea to land during day and from land to sea during night

Q. 36 Following are a few orgaisms

(a) lichen (b) mosses (c) mango tree (d) cactus

Which among the above can grow on stones; and also help in formation of soil? Write the mode of their action from making soil.

Ans. Out of the above given organisms, lichens (a) and mosses (b) can grow on rocks. During growth, they release certain substances that cause the rock surface to powder down and form a thin layer of soil. Lichens grow on the rock surface, extract minerals from them and creates small crevices at places where a thin layer of soil builds up.

Mosses grow over these crevices and causes deepening of the crevices that results in building up of more soil inside them. Deeper crevices form cracks and cracks becomes wider and deeper when the roots of short lived herbs pass into them.

With the passage of time, the roots of bigger plants, (*e.g.*, peepal, banyan tree) pass into the cracks. Cracks gradually widen and cause slow fragmentation and eventually pulverisation of rocks leading to formation of soil.

Q. 37 Soil formation is done by both abiotic and biotic factors. List the names of these factors by classifying them as abiotic and biotic ?

Thinking Process Abiotic includes are the physical or environmental factors while, biotic includes the biological factors.

Ans. Abiotic factors involved in soil formation are

(a) Rocks (b) Water

(c) Sun (d) Wind

Biotic factors involved in soil formation are

(a) Lichens (b) Bryophytes

(c) Bacteria (d) Fungi

(e) Nematodes (f) Earthworm

(g) Arthropods *e.g.*, ants.

Q.38 All the living organisms are basically made up of C, N, S, P, H and O. How do they enter the living forms? Discuss.

Ans. The elements like carbon, nitrogen, sulphur, phosphorus, hydrogen and oxygen enter into living forms through plants. Most of these elements are taken up by plants and become components of their organic material during the process of photosynthesis. From plants, these elements pass on to other organisms through the food chain.

e.g., Plant (grasses) is eaten by goats which are further consumed by humans. Thus, the organic materials are transferred from grass to goat and then to humans

Q. 39 Why does the percentage of gases like oxygen, nitrogen and carbon dioxide remain almost the same in the atmosphere?

Ans. In the environment the percentage of the gases like oxygen, nitrogen and carbon dioxide is maintained by their cyclic flow.

The oxygen cycle, nitrogen cycle and carbon cycle operate continuously in the nature by the constant interaction between the biotic and abiotic components of the biosphere. These interactions consist of a transfer of matter and energy between the different components of the biosphere.

Thus, their levels in the atmosphere is maintained constantly up to the required limit.

Q. 40 Why does moon have very cold and very hot temperature variations *e.g.*, from - 190°C to 110°C even though it is at the same distance from the sun as the Earth is?

Ans. The moon is at the same distance from the sun as the earth but it experiences extreme temperature variations, ranging from –190°C to 110°C. The main reason behind this huge variation in temperature of moon is that it has no atmosphere.

The atmosphere plays very important role in the temperature control. Air is a bad conductor of heat thus, it acts as temperature buffer and checks excessive rise of temperature during the day and excessive cooling during the night. Since, the moon lacks this atmosphere, it cannot maintain a stable temperature, leading to a significant fluctuations.

Q. 41 Why do people love to fly kites near the seashore ?

Ans. Near the seashore or coastal regions, during the day, the air above the land gets heated faster and starts rising. As this air rises, a region of low pressure is created and air over the sea moves to this area of low pressure.

This movement of air from one region to the other creates winds. During the day, the direction of wind is from the sea to the land. So, flying kites near sea shore is easy as compared to anywhere else.

(*Also, refer to Q.* 35)

Q. 42 Why does Mathura refinery pose problems to the Taj Mahal ?

Ans. Mathura refinery releases many air pollutants such as sulphur dioxide (SO_2), which reacts with water in the atmosphere to forms sulphuric acid. This sulphuric acid is washed away into the soil by rain (acid rain). This acid also erodes the stone, surface of buildings, brick works, etc.

This poses a great threat to Taj Mahal as they can destroy the marble quality and its colour, etc.

Q. 43 Why do not lichens occur in Delhi whereas they commonly grow in Manali or Darjeeling?

Ans. Lichens are bio-indicators of air pollution. They are highly sensitive to sulphur dioxide (SO_2) pollution in air from automobiles and other factories.

Delhi has maximum level of air pollution due to a large number of vehicles compared to Manali and Darjeeling. Therefore, the growth of lichens does not occur in Delhi or any place, where air pollution is high.

Q. 44 Why does water need conservation even though large oceans surround the land masses?

Ans. Water is one of the most unusual natural resource on Earth and it is also very important constituent of life. It exists as snow, water and water vapour. Terrestrial life forms require fresh water for their existence and the fresh water is not available easily. (*Also, refer to Q.* 21)

Q. 45 There is mass mortality of fishes in a pond. What may be the reasons?

Ans. The reason of mass mortality of fishes in a pond are.

(i) Thermal pollution
(ii) Addition of mercuric compounds and other toxic chemicals
(iii) Blockage of gills by pollutants

Q. 46 Lichens are called pioneer colonisers of bare rock. How can they help in formation of soil ?

Ans. Lichens grow on the rock surface releasing chemical substances that extract minerals from rocks and creates small crevices at places where a thin layer of soil builds up.

(*Also refer to Q.* 36)

Q. 47 'Soil is formed by water.' If you agree to this statement then give reasons.

Ans. Water helps in the breakdown of bigger rocks into smaller mineral particles. It gets into cracks in the rocks formed due to uneven heating by the sun. When this water freezes, it cause the cracks to widen resulting in formation of smaller pieces.

Flowing water wears away hard rock over long periods of time. Fast flowing water often carries big and small particles of rocks downstream. These rocks rub against other rocks causing the rocks to break down into smaller particles. The water then takes these particles alongwith it and deposit them further.

Q. 48 Fertile soil has lots of humus. Why?

Ans. Fertile soil has lots of humus because it contains microorganisms that decompose dead organic matter present in soil and help in the formation of humus. Humus is a source of minerals, absorbs water and makes the soil porous for easy passage of plant roots.

Q.49 Why step farming is common in hills?

Ans. Step farming is commonly practiced in hilly areas as a preventive measure against soil erosion caused due to rain water and strong winds.

(*Also, refer to Q.* 28)

Q. 50 Why are root nodules useful for the plants?

Ans. Root nodules are specialised structures found on the roots of the plants where nitrogen fixing bacteria are present. These bacteria converts inert nitrogen into nitrates for the use of plants. The process of biofixation of nitrogen by nitrogen fixing bacteria like *Rhizobium*, etc., is called nitrogen fixation. It is crucial for enhancing the nitrogen content in soil.
(*Also, refer to* Q. 6)

Long Answer Type Questions

Q. 51 How do fossil fuels cause air pollution?

Ans. Fossil fuels like coal and petroleum contains small amount of gases like nitrogen and sulphur.

When these fossil fuels are burnt in industries, they release oxides of sulphur and nitrogen. The release of these toxic gases cause respiratory problems. Also when these gases come in contact with rain water they form sulphuric acid and nitric acid which falls on ground as acid rain.

Burning of fossil fuels also increases amount of supended particles in air causing low visibility and more air pollution.

Q.52 What are the causes of water pollution? Discuss how you can contribute in reducing water pollution.

Ans. Different causes of water pollution are

(i) **Industrial wastes** Effluents of mills and industries such as paper mills, petroleum refineries, etc., contain large quantities of harmful chemicals including acids, alkalis and heavy metals, (*e.g.*, mercury salts from paper industries). These chemicals are discharge into water bodies (rivers and lakes).

(ii) **Synthetic soaps and detergents** Water containing soaps and detergents is discharged into rivers from houses and certain factories and pollute water.

(iii) **Fertilisers and pesticides** Fertilisers and pesticides are being used excessively in the fields to increase crop production. These are washed by rainwater into water bodies and pollute them.

(iv) **Petroleum oil** Drilling and shipping operations are common in the oceans. Leakage of petroleum oil during such operations or due to accidents (*i.e.*, oil spill) cause water pollution.

(v) **Thermal pollution** Discharge of hot water from industries and thermal plants into water body changes the normal temperature of the water. The content of oxygen decrease. Reduced oxygen content kills aquatic animals and reduces the rate of decomposition of organic matter which, therefore, accumulates.

(vi) **Sewage** Organic wastes are contributed as domestic and commercial sewage by food processing plants, dairy, farms, piggeries, poultry farms, slaughter houses, breweries, tanneries, etc. Animal excreta discharged into fields or dumped in to pits reaches water bodies through run off and leaching, particularly during the rainy season and cause water pollution.

Ways to reduce water pollution are

(i) If sewage and garbage generated by homes and industries is treated properly before discharging into water sources, it will reduce water pollution and cause less harm to the aquatic life.

(ii) If hot water generated by the industries is collected at common place, allowed to cool and then discharged in water-bodies, it will not affect the breeding capacity of aquatic organisms.

(iii) If commercial areas, factories and industries are shifted to the isolated area far away from residential areas, it can reduce the effect of air pollution on people.

Q.53 A motor car, with its glass totally closed, is parked directly under the sun. The inside temperature of the car rises very high. Explain why?

Ans. Sunlight emits ultraviolet radiations which pass through the glass and heat the interior of the car. The radiations emitted by inner parts of the car cannot pass through the glass, so the heat trapped inside raises the temperature of the car. This is because glass is transparent to infrared radiations released from the sun, having smaller wavelength than that emitted by the interior of the car which have longer wavelength to which the glass of the car is opaque.

Q.54 Justify 'Dust is a Pollutant'. Dust is a fine powder of tiny earth particles and waste matter It is carried to the atmosphere by wind dust.

Ans. Dust is considered as a pollutant because

(i) Dust consists of suspended particles. Inhalation of dust causes lots of discomfort and health issues including asthma, bronchitis, cold or cough.

(ii) It reduces intensity of light.

(iii) Dust particles settle over leaf and can block stomata and reduce gaseous exchange in plants reducing photosynthetic activities.

(iv) It causes irritation of eyes.

(v) It contains harmful substances like smoke, fly ash, particle of silica, lead, etc., which pollute environment.

Q.55 Explain the role of the sun in the formation of soil.

Ans. The sun heats up the rocks during the day, resulting in the expansion of rock. At night, these rocks cool down and contract. Since, different part of rock expand and contract at the different rate, (ultimately huge rocks break into smaller pieces). This results in the formation of soil.

(*Also, refer to* Q. 47)

Q. 56 Carbon dioxide is necessary for plants. Why do we consider it as a pollutant?

Ans. Carbon dioxide is necessary for plants to performs photosynthesis. It is also a greenhouse gas. Upto certain concentration in atmosphere, it is beneficial for both plants and the environment. But, when concentration of carbon dioxide form certain level rises it becomes a pollutant because it, contributes to greenhouse effect, causing global warming It may also cause various respiratory disorders and helps in the formation of smog.

Chapter

15 Improvement in Food Resources

Multiple Choice Questions (MCQs)

Choose the correct answer from the given four options in the following questions :

Q. 1 Which one is an oil yielding plant among the following?

(a) Lentil (b) Sunflower (c) Cauliflower (d) *Hibiscus*

Ans. ***(b)*** Sunflower is an oil yeilding plant. Oil seed crops include cottonseed, niger (Ramtil), soyabean, linseed, rapeseed, groundnut, sesame, mustard, sunflower, olive, etc. These are the sources of oil, fats and fatty acids and are typically high in unsaturated fats. When these seeds are consumed in moderation these are regarded as healthy foods.

Lentil is used as pulses, cauliflower is an inflorescence which is used as vegetable and *Hibiscus* is an ornamental flowering plant.

Q. 2 Which one is not a source of carbohydrate?

(a) Rice (b) Millets (c) Sorghum (d) Gram

Ans. ***(d)*** Gram is not a source of carbohydrate but a rich source of protein. It falls under the category of pulses. Pulses include legumes such as chick pea, gram, pea, etc that are rich sources of protein.

Rice, millets and sorghum are rich sources of carbohydrates.

Q. 3 Find out the wrong statement from the following.

(a) White revolution is meant for increase in milk production.

(b) Blue revolution is meant for increase in fish production.

(c) Increasing food production without compromising with environmental quality is called as sustainable agriculture.

(d) None of the above

Ans. ***(d)*** All the statements are true. Operation flood is a project of the National Dairy Development Board (NDDB). This was the world's biggest dairy development program, which made India, a milk-sufficient nation and the largest milk producer in the world. The father of the white revolution in India was Verghese Kurien. The white revolution mentioned is used for milk production. Verghese kurien was able to implement programs that took India from a country with very little dairy production to the world's largest producer.

The blue revolution is similar to the green revolution only that it deals with aquaculture and water preservation for human use. In India the Blue Revolution has been used for several years for fish production. In 1930's, India produced 600,000 tonnes of fish due to blue revolution. It has assisted India to produce more fresh water fish.

Sustainable agriculture can be defined as adoption of various farming and production management technique to maximise agricultural need without compromising the environment.

Q. 4 To solve the food problem of the country, which among the following is necessary?

(a) Increased production and storage of food grains

(b) Easy access of people to the food grain

(c) People should have money to purchase the grains

(d) All of the above

Ans. ***(d)*** To effectively solve the food problem of a country all the above factors are crucial because-

(i) Increased production and storage of food grains ensures that there is enough food available for everyone. This leads to prevention of starvation during any crises a well.

(ii) Easy access of food grains ensures food distribution systems are efficient and food reaches remote or unreserved regions as well.

(iii) People should have money to purchase the grains ensuring socio-economic balance. Therefore every person in an economy will be able to meet their basic needs instead of being subjected to poverty and starvation.

Q. 5 Find out the correct sentence.

(i) Hybridisation means crossing between genetically dissimilar plants.

(ii) Cross between two varieties is called as inter specific hybridisation

(iii) Introducing genes of desired character into a plant gives genetically modified crop

(iv) Cross between plants of two species is called as inter varietal hybridisation

(a) (i) and (iii) (b) (ii) and (iv) (c) (ii) and (iii) (d) (iii) and (iv)

Ans. ***(a)*** Statements (i) and (iii) are correct about hybridisation as The crossing between genetically unidentical plants to produce a new variety, *i.e.*, hybrid is called hybridisation. Genetically, modified crops can be produced by the insertion of genes with desired traits through techniques such as hybridisation. Statements (ii) and (iv) are incorrect and can be corrected as a cross between two varieties known as intervarietal hybridisation whereas cross between plants of two species is known as interspecific hybridisation.

Q. 6 Weeds affect the crop plants by

(a) killing of plants in field before they grow

(b) dominating the plants to grow

(c) competing for various resources of crops (plants) causing low availability of nutrients

(d) All of the above

Ans. ***(c)*** Weeds are the unwanted plants that grow spontaneously in the cultivated fields. They compete with the main crop plants for nutrients and reduce the growth of crops. The reasons behind their spontaneous growth is easy germination of seeds their seedlings grow faster, they flower early, their seed production begins after a very short growth period and produce many seeds.

Q. 7 Which one of the following species of honey bee is an Italian species?

(a) *Apis dorsata* (b) *Apis florae* (c) *Apis cerana indica* (d) *Apis mellifera*

Ans. ***(d)*** *Apis mellifera* is an italian species of honey bee. They have high honey production and helps in pollination.

A. The indigenous varieties are

Apis cerona indica (Indian honey bee)
Apis dorsata (Rock bee)
Apis florae (Little bee)

B. Exotic varieties

Apis mellifera (European or Italian bee)
Apis adamsoni (South African bee)

Q. 8 Find out the correct sentence about manure.

(i) Manure contains large quantities of organic matter and small quantities of nutrients.
(ii) It increases the water holding capacity of sandy soil.
(iii) It helps in draining out of excess of water from clayey soil.
(iv) Its excessive use pollutes environment because it is made of animal excretory waste.

(a) (i) and (iii) (b) (i) and (ii) (c) (ii) and (iii) (d) (iii) and (iv)

Ans. ***(b)*** Statements (i) and (ii) are correct about manure as manures are the natural fertilisers. They are bulky sources of organic matter which supply nutrients in small quantities, and organic matter in large quantities to the soil. Manures are prepared by the decomposition of animal excreta and plant waste. Manures includes Farm Yard Manure (FYM), compost, green manures, vermicompost etc. The organic matter in manures provides food for the soil organisms, (decomposers such as bacteria, fungi, etc), which help in providing nutrients to plants.

Statements (iii) and (iv) are incorrect and can be corrected as manure does not aid in draining out excess water from clayey soil, but improves the structure of clayey soil by adding nutrients to it.

Excessive use of manure does not pollute the environment as they are biodegradeable.

Q. 9 Cattle husbandry is done for the following purposes

(i) Milk production (ii) Agricultural work
(iii) Meat production (iv) Egg production

(a) (i), (ii) and (iii) (b) (ii), (iii) and (iv) (c) (iii) and (iv) (d) (i) and (iv)

Ans. ***(a)*** The branch of agriculture that deals with the feeding, caring and breeding of domestic animals is called animal husbandry (done carefully and without any waste). Human beings domesticate cattle for milk production, agricultural work, meat production, transportation and leather, etc.

Q. 10 Which of the following are Indian cattle?

(i) *Bos indicus* (ii) *Bos domestica*
(iii) *Bos bubalis* (iv) *Bos vulgaris*

(a) (i) and (iii) (b) (i) and (ii) (c) (ii) and (iii) (d) (iii) and (iv)

Ans. ***(a)*** *Bos indicus* (or zebu or humped cattle) is an Indian breed adapted to drier regions.
Bos bubalis (or wild water buffalo) is an Indian breed as well. It is also found in Nepal, Bhutan, Thailand and Cambodia. Whereas *Bos domestica* is found in Africa, Asia, and Western Europe

Q. 11 Which of the following are exotic breeds?
(i) Brawn (ii) Jersey
(iii) Brown Swiss (iv) Jersey Swiss
(a) (i) and (iii) (b) (ii) and (iii) (c) (i) and (iv) (d) (ii) and (iv)

Ans. ***(b)*** Exotic breeds are the type of breeds that are not native to that place. Brown Swiss and Jersey are the exotic breeds of cow. Brown swiss cow has a high protien ratio in their milk, whereas Jersey cow produces larger quantity of milk with higher milk fat.

Q. 12 Poultry farming is undertaken to raise following
(i) Egg production (ii) Feather production
(iii) Chicken meat (iv) Milk production
(a) (i) and (iii) (b) (i) and (ii) (c) (ii) and (iii) (d) (iii) and (iv)

Thinking Process Poultry farming is the raising of domesticated birds such as chickens, turkeys, ducks and geese, for the purpose of egg production and meat.

Ans. ***(a)*** The poultry industry with its production in the form of eggs and meat farm birds such as domestic fowl, chickens, geese, ducks etc. is of particular importance in providing a balanced diet for human population. They are not only efficient converters of agricultural by products but also provide egg, feathers and rich manure.

Q. 13 Poultry fowl are susceptible to the following pathogens
(a) viruses (b) bacteria (c) fungi (d) All of these

Ans. ***(d)*** Common diseases caused by different pathogen of fowl are

	Name of Disease	Causative Organism
1.	Dermatitis	Bacteria
2.	Fowl pox	Virus
3.	Fowl cholera	Bacteria
4.	Aspergillosis	Fungus

Q. 14 Which one of the following fishes is a surface feeder?
(a) Rohus (b) Mrigals (c) Common carps (d) Catlas

Ans. ***(d)*** Catla is a surface feeder fish. Surface feeder fishes have a back that is perfectly straight, this allows their upturned mouths to easily get right on the surface and scoop up the food. In their natural habitat they eat insects present on the water surface.

Q. 15 Animal husbandry is the scientific management of
(i) animal breeding (ii) culture of animals
(iii) animal livestock (iv) rearing of animals
(a) (i), (ii) and (iii) (b) (ii). (iii) and (iv)
(c) (i), (ii) and (iv) (d) (i), (iii) and (iv)

Ans. ***(d)*** Animal husbandry is a scientific management of animal breeding, animal livestock and rearing of animals. (*Also, refer to Q.*9)

Q. 16 Which one of the following nutrients is not available in fertilisers?

(a) Nitrogen (b) Phosphorus (c) Iron (d) Potassium

Ans. ***(c)*** Iron is not available in fertilisers. Fertiliser are inorganic compound that contains neccessary plant nutrients. These are manufactured by using chemicals and supply nutrients such as nitrogen, phosphorus and potassium (NPK). They are used for good vegetative growth, (*i.e.*, growth of leaves, branches and flowers).

Fertilisers contain much higher amount of nutrients in comparison to the manures and are, therefore, used in very small quantities.

Q. 17 Preventive and control measures adopted for the storage of grains include

(a) strict cleaning (b) proper disjoining

(c) fumigation (d) All of these

Ans. ***(d)*** The biotic as well as abiotic factors which causes destruction of grains during storage can be prevented by the methods given below.

(i) **Cleaning** The grains and other agricultural produce should be properly cleanded and dried under the sun before storing them.

(ii) **Safe and proper storage :** The godowns, warehouses and stores should also be cleaned, dried and repaired properly. Also, the bags of grains should be stacked carefully to allow aeration and they should be checked that they are not cluttered at a place.

(iii) **Fumigation** - This is the method of preventive storage in which the chemical pesticides are used as fumigants. The farmes produced by these fumigants to kills the insects, pests and other pathogens that can cause harm to the grains.

Short Answer Type Questions

Q. 18 Match the column I with the column II.

Column I		Column II	
A.	Catla	1.	Bottom feeders
B.	Rohu	2.	Surface feeders
C.	Mrigal	3.	Middle-zone feeders
D.	Fish farming	4.	Culture fishery

Ans. The correct matching is

Column I		Column II
A.	Catla	2. Surface feeders
B.	Rohu	3. Middle-zone feeders
C.	Mrigal	1. Bottom feeders
D.	Fish farming	4. Culture fishery

Q. 19 Fill in the blanks.

(a) Pigeon pea is a good source of ....
(b) Berseem is an important .... crop.
(c) The crops which are grown in rainy season are called .... crops.
(d) .... are rich in vitamins.
(e) .... crop grows in winter season.

Ans.

(a) Protein (b) Fodder
(c) Kharif crops (d) Fruits and vegetables
(e) Rabi

Q. 20 What is a GM crop? Name any one such crop which is grown in India.

Ans. Crops which are developed by introducing a new gene from any other source, *e.g.*, bacteria or any other organism to obtain the desired character are called Genetically Modified (GM) crops. Bt cotton is a well known example of GM crop which is made insect-resistant by introducing a new gene from a bacteria.

Q. 21 List out some useful traits in improved crop.

Ans. Some useful traits in improved crop are

(i) **Higher yield** The main aim of crop improvement is to improve the productivity of the crop *e.g.*, grain, vegetables and fodder.

(ii) **Improved quality** Quality considerations of crop products varies from crop to crop, *e.g.*, baking quality in wheat, protein quality in pulses, oil quality in oil seeds and preserving quality of fruits and vegetables.

(iii) **Biotic and abiotic resistance** Under varied situations crop suffers from different stresses, such as biotic stresses (diseases, insects and nematodes) or **abiotic stresses** (such as drought, salinity, water logging, heat, cold and frost). Crop varieties should be resistant to these stresses, to significantly improve the crop production. *e.g.*, **MUW 318** is a HYV (High Yielding Variety) of wheat which is released for cultivation in non-traditional areas as **Nilgiri** and **Palini hills** that are resistant to all types of rusts.

(iv) **Changes in maturity duration** Early maturing varieties in short-duration crops can make the crop fit into double and multiple cropping system. This will also reduce the crop's cost of production.

(v) **Desirable agronomic traits** If we develop those varieties of crops which contain desired agronomic traits then it will help in higher production of crops. *e.g.*, breeding for resistance to **red rot** has led to sugarcane varieties such as **Co 975** and **Co 62399** which increase cane production in affected areas.

(vi) **Wider adaptability** If we develop those varieties of crops which have wider adaptability, then it will help in stabilising the crop production under different environmental conditions. *e.g.*, **ICPH 8** is a hybrid pigeon pea plant which takes a short duration to mature, escapes diseases such as **fusarium wilt** and **sterility mosaic** and yields 30 to 40 per cent more than the popular breed.

Q.22 Why is organic matter important for crop production?

Ans. Organic matter is important for crop production because it improves soil structure, increases water retention, and provides nutrients for plants. Organic matter helps soil structure by following ways

(i) **Soil structure improvement** helps roots to grow into a more permeable soil so that nutrients move easily and get absorbed by roots.

(ii) **Increased** water retention because organic matter increases the water holding capacity of soil especially in sandy soil.

(iii) Organic matter **provides nutrients** like nitrogen, phosphorous potassium, calcium etc required by plants.

(iv) It also helps **maintain pH of the soil** for microbial action.

Q. 23 Why is excess use of fertilisers detrimental for environment?

Ans. Fertilisers should be applied scientifically, in terms of proper dose, time, pre-and post-application precautions for their complete utilisation.

Excess fertilisers usually get washed away through irrigation, rainfall, etc. and pollute rivers, lakes, streams, causing algal bloom, toxicity and eutrophiciation.

Q. 24 Give one word for the following.

(a) Farming without the use of chemicals as fertilisers, herbicides and pesticides is known as ....

(b) Growing of wheat and groundnut on the same field is called as ....

(c) Planting soyabean and maize in alternate rows in the same field is called as ....

(d) Growing different crops on a piece of land in pre-planned succession is known as ....

(e) *Xanthium* and *Parthenium* are commonly known as ....

(f) Causal organism of any disease is called as ....

Ans. (a) Organic farming (b) Mixed cropping
(c) Inter cropping (d) Crop rotation
(e) Weeds (f) Pathogen

Q. 25 Match the following column I and II

	Column I		Column II
A.	Cattle used for tilling and carting	1.	Milk producing female
B.	Indian breed of chicken	2.	Broiler
C.	Sahiwal, Red sindhi	3.	Drought animals
D.	Milch	4.	Local breed of cattle
E.	Chicken better fed for obtaining meat	5.	Aseel

Ans. The correct matching is

	Column I	Column II
A.	Cattle used for tilling and carting	3. Drought animals
B.	Indian breed of chicken	5. Aseel
C.	Sahiwal, Red sindhi	1. Local breed of cattle
D.	Milch	4. Milk productng female
E.	Chicken better Fed for obtaining meat	2. Broiler

Q. 26 If there is low rainfall in a village throughout the year. What measures will you suggest to the farmers for better cropping?

Ans. Suggestion for farmers for better cropping practices are:

(i) Practice farming with drought resistant and early maturing varieties of crops.
(ii) To enrich the soil with more humus content as it increases the water-holding capacity and retains water for longer duration.
(iii) Adopting different kinds of irrigation systems to supply water to agricultural lands. For *e.g.*, wells, canals, river left systems, tanks, etc.

Q. 27 Group the following and tabulate them as energy yielding, protein yielding, oil yielding and fodder crop.
Wheat, rice, berseem, maize, gram, oat, pigeon gram, sudan grass, lentil, soyabean, groundnut, castor and mustard.

Ans. These are as given

Energy yielding	Protein yielding	Oil yielding	Fodder crops
Wheat	Gram	Groundnut	Sudan grass
Rice	Pigeon gram	Castor	Barseem
Maize	Lentil	Mustard	Oat
Oat	—	Soyabean	—

Q.28 Define the term hybridisation and photoperiod.

Ans. **Hybridisation** The cross between two genetically distinct plant to give rise to a new variety with desired trait is called hybridisation. (*Also, refer to Q.* 5)

Photoperiodism The effect of light duration and daily exposure of light on the flowering of plant is called photoperiodism. On the basis of light or dark exposure, plants are classified as short day plant (requires short photoperiods) or long day plants (requires long exposure of light).

Q. 29 Fill in the blanks

(a) Photoperiod affect the ....
(b) Kharif crops are cultivated from .... to ....
(c) Rabi crops are cultivated from .... to ....
(d) Paddy, maize, green gram and black gram are .... crops.
(e) Wheat, gram, pea, mustard are .... crops.

Ans. (a) Growth of plant and flowering
(b) June to October (c) November to April
(d) Kharif crops (e) Rabi crops

Q.30 Cultivation practices and crop yield are related to environmental condition. Explain.

Ans. Cultivation, refers to the preperation and processes of raising crops, rearing livestock and cultivating soil. All crops do not grow under same environmental conditions. Thus, their cultivation practices and yield, are related to the condition of the environment such as high humidity, duration of sunlight, high temperature, low temperature, etc. For *e.g.*, Apple cannot be grown in plains because it requires several days of low temperature exposure.

On the basis of the seasonal variations, crops in India can be classified into three major categories as

(i) **Rabi crops** These crops are sown during winters and harvested by the end of either March or April. *e.g.*, gram, pea, almond, etc.

(ii) **Kharif crops** These crops are sown during monsoons and are harvested at the end of monsoon season. *e.g.*, sugar cane, cotton, groundnut etc

(iii) **Zaid crops** These crops are summer season crops that are sown from March to April. They are grown between Rabi and Kharif season *e.g.*, cucumber, water melon, etc

Q. 31 Fill in the blanks.

(a) A total of .... nutrients are essential to plants.
(b) .... and .... are supplied by air to plants.
(c) .... is supplied by water to plants.
(d) Soil supply .... nutrients to plants.
(e) .... nutrients are required in large quantity and called as ....
(f) .... nutrients are needed in small quantity for plants and are called ....

Ans. (a) 16 (b) Carbon and oxygen (c) Hydrogen
(d) 13 (e) 6, macronutrients (f) 7, micronutrients

Q. 32 Differentiate between compost and vermicompost?

Ans. Difference between compost and vermicompost are

	Compost	Vermicompost
1.	It is prepared from all type of organic wastes like sewage, animal refuse, farm waste, etc., and takes 3-6 months to prepare.	It is prepared from domestic waste, vegetable waste and takes 1-2 months to prepare.
2.	Organic remains are decomposed by microbes.	Organic remains are pulverised by earthworms.

Q. 33 Arrange these statements in correct sequence of preparation of green manure.

(a) Green plants are decomposed in soil.
(b) Green plants are cultivated for preparing manure or crop plants parts are used.
(c) Plants are ploughed and mixed into the soil.
(d) After decomposition it becomes green manure.

Ans. (b) Green plants are cultivated for preparing manure or crop plants are used.
(c) Plants are ploughed and mixed into the soil.
(a) Green plants are decomposed in soil.
(d) After decomposition it becomes green manure.

Q. 34 An Italian bee variety *A. mellifera* has been introduced in India for honey production. Write about its merits over other varieties.

Ans. Merits of Italian bee variety A. mellifera are

(i) It is sting less.
(ii) It has high honey collection capacity and produces large quantity of honey.
(iii) It stays in given beehive for long periods and breeds very well.

Q.35 In agricultural practices, higher input gives higher yield. Discuss how?

Ans. In agricultural practices, higher inputs gives higher yield. This means higher money inputs to raise the yield.

(i) Improved financial conditions of the farmers allow them to adopt differen[t] farming practices and technologies.
(ii) The farmer's increased purchasing capacity can help the farmer to provid[e] right nutrients to their crops.
(ii) Farmers can invest in research to improve their farming practices. This wil[l] help them decide their cropping system and production practices.

Long Answer Type Questions

Q.36 Discuss the role of hydridisation in crop improvement.

Ans. The **crossing** between genetically dissimilar plants to produce a new variety known as hybrid is called **hybridisation**. The crossing may be done either between two different varieties **(inter-varietal cross-breeding)**, between two different species of the same genus **(interspecific cross-breeding)** and between different genera **(intergeneric cross-breeding)**. The most common type of breeding is **inter-varietal.**

In India, the crops are grown in diverse types of soil and different climatic conditions by poor or progressive, farmers. Keeping climatic factor, input application, disease and pest resistance, quality and adaptability etc., in mind, a large number of varieties have been developed in India. These varieties are high yielding and resistant to diseases and pests. They have better quality and early to late maturing time.

Q. 37 Define

(i) Vermicompost (ii) Greenmanure (iii) Biofertiliser

Ans. (i) **Vermicompost** is a nutrient-rich manure made from decomposed organic matter. Vermicompost is prepared by using earthworms to hasten the process of decomposition of plants and animals refuses. Earthworm act as aerator, crusher and mixer, chemically a degrader and biological stimulator of decomposition.

(ii) **Green manure** is prepared by decomposition of green plants in the field itself. It helps in enriching the soil in nitrogen and phosphorus and used for improving hydration, aeration and structure of soil. It is the also provides protection against erosion and leaching.

e.g., sunhemp is grown in fields, mulched by ploughing and allowed to decompose in the field for the preparation of green manure.

(iii) **Biofertiliser** Living organisms used as fertiliser to supply the nutrients to the crop plants and called as biofertilisers *e.g.*, nitrogen fixing blue green algae, nitrogen fixing bacteria, which fix atmospheric nitrogen in soil, rice fields, are act as biofertiliser.

Q. 38 Discuss various methods for weed control.

Ans. Methods of weed control are

(i) **Mechanical Methods** The process of removing weeds from crop fields is called **weeding**. It is done by the following methods.

(a) Weeds may be pulled out by hand.

(b) **Ploughing** helps in removing large number of the weeds.

(c) Before sowing or transplanting, weeds are removed by using a big comb called **harrow**. Harrow cannot be used in standing crops because it will also uproot the crop plants.

The weeds which appear during the growth of crop plants are removed manually by using a **trowel** (Khurpa).

(ii) **Cultural Methods** They include proper bed preparation, timely sowing of crops, inter cropping and crop rotation.

(iii) **Chemical Methods** Chemical weed killers, called **herbicides** or **weedicides**, are sprayed on weeds to destroy (kill) them. This is called **chemical control of weeds**. Some common examples of weedicides are (i) 24-D (2, 4-Dichlorophenoxyacetic acid) (ii) atraxine (iii) fluchloralin (iv) isoproturon.

(iv) **Biological Control** Biological control of weed involves deliberate use of insects or some other organism which consume and specifically destroy the weed plants.

The best Indian example of biological control is eradication of prickly pear cactus (*Opuntia*) by using the cochineal insects in Maharashtra and Tamil Nadu. Generally, a combination of one or more of these weed control methods are employed to get good results. Aquatic weeds are controlled by the fish grass carp.

Mistake Alert! *Students should carefully pay attention towards the names of different methods of weed control.*

Q. 39 Differentiate between the following
(i) capture fishery and culture fishery
(ii) mixed cropping and intercropping
(iii) bee keeping and poultry farming

Ans.
(i) Differences between capture fishery and culture fishery are as follows

Capture Fishery	Culture Fishery
It is a way of obtaining fish from natural resources.	It is a way of obtaining fish from fish farms.
There is no seeding and raising of fish.	The fish is reared in controlled environment
It is undertaken in marine waters.	It is undertaken mostly near sea shore.

(ii) Differences between intercropping and mixed copping are as follows

Intercropping	Mixed Cropping
It's main aim is to increase productivity per unit.	It's main aim is to reduce chances of crop failue.
The crops are grown in a specific pattern of rows.	There is no set pattern of rows for crops.
Pesticides can be sprayed easily on individual crops.	Pesticides cannot be sprayed easily to individual plants.
Harvesting and threshing of crops can be done separately and easily.	Harvesting and threshing of individual crops cannot be done so easily or separately.

(iii) Differences between bee keeping and poultry farming are as follows

Bee keeping	Poultry Farming
It is a practice of rearing and management of honey bees.	It is the practice of raising domestic fowl.
Bees obtain food (nectar) from flower.	Poultry birds are provided food by the rearers.
It provides honey and wax.	It provides eggs and meat (flesh).

Q. 40 Give the merits and demerits of fish culture?

Ans. Merits of fish culture
(i) Quality and quantity of desired fishes can be increased.
(ii) Fishes are cheap source of animal protein, thus increases the quality of food.
(iii) Export of fishes brings foreign currency.

Demerits of fish culture
(i) It is a threat to biodiversity.
(ii) Only economically important and valued fishes will be cultured.

Q. 41 What do you understand by composite fish culture?

Ans. Composite fish culture system is adopted for intensive fishing. Some characteristics of composite fish culture are

(i) Both local as well as imported fish species can be used in such systems.
(ii) A combination of five or six fish species is used in a single fish pond.
(iii) These species have different feeding habits.
(iv) These species having different food habits are selected so that they do not compete for food among them.

e.g., Catla surface feeders.
Rohu feed in middle zone of the pond.
Mrigals bottom feeders.
Common carps bottom feeders.
Grass carps weed feeders.

Advantages of Composite Fish Culture are as follows

(i) All the food available in the pond is utilised.
(ii) There is no competition for food.
(iii) There is increase in the fish yield from the pond.

Disadvantage of Composite Fish Culture

(i) Lack of availability of good quality fish seeds.
(ii) Many fish species breed during monsoon season therefore, hormonal stimulation may be required.

Q. 42 Why bee keeping should be done in good pasturage?

Ans. Apiculture or bee keeping is known as an important aspect of agriculture and is concerned with the commercial production of honey and wax. The quality and taste of honey depends upon the type of flora available. Hence, availability of flowering plants in the vicinity is considered to be the major factor in bee keeping .

The term pasturage refers to the area land that is covered with the flowering plants that bee can use for the collection of pollen and nectar. Thus, the bee keeping should be done in good pasturage.

The pasturage flora of honey bees include a variety of flowering plants such as mango (Aam), coconut (Narial), almond (Badam) tamarind (Imli), ber, berseem, litchi, cotton, shisham, apple, mahua, coriander, cashew, coffee, rubber plants, guava, sunflower, *neem*, etc.

Q. 43 Write the modes by which insects affect the crop yield.

Ans. Some common insect pests of stored grain and their mode of infection are

(i) **Gram dhora** or **Pulse beetle** (*Callosobruchus maculatus*) Its grubs damage the stored gram
(ii) **Rice weevil** (*Sitophilus oryzae*) Both grub and beetle (adult) damage rice.
(iii) **Khapra** or **Wheat weevil** (*Trogoderma granarium*) Infests stored wheat.
(iv) **Grain and flour moth** (*Sitotroga cerealella*) Its caterpillars bore into grains of rice, wheat, barley, maize and jowar.
(v) **Rust red flour beetle** (*Tribolium castaneum*) Both larvae and adult damage flour and flour products.
(vi) **Rice moth** (*Corcyra cephalonica*) Larvae damage rice and maize.
(vii) **Lesser grain borer** (*Rhizopertha dominica*) Both grub and adult (beetle) damage the grains, reducing them into perforated shells.

Q. 44 Discuss why pesticides are used in very accurate concentration and in very appropriate manner?

Ans. Pesticides are the chemicals that removes or eliminates the pests that infects crops. They majorly include, weedicides (kill weeds), insecticides (killes insects), rodenticides (kills rats), fungicides (kills fungus). These pesticides should be used in a very accurate concentration as they are very harmful to the environment. Pesticides are non-biodegradable and can get accumulated at higher trophic level. The environmental impact of **pesticides** consists of the effects of pesticides on non-target species such as animals or humans.

Over 98% of sprayed insecticides and 95% of herbicides reach a destination other than their target species, because they are sprayed or spread across entire agricultural fields. Runoff water can carry pesticides into aquatic environments while wind can carry them to other fields, grazing areas, human settlements and undeveloped areas, potentially affecting other species. Other problems emerge from poor production, transport and storage practices.

Q.45 Name two types of animal feed and write their functions.

Ans. The dairy cattle is given a **balanced ration**, which contains all nutrients in proportionate amounts. A **ration** is the amount of food which is given to the animal during a twenty-four hour period.
The animal feed includes two types of substances

(i) **Roughage** It largely contains fibres such as green fodder, silage, hay (straw of cereals) and legumes, (*e.g.*, berseem, lucerne, cow pea and agathi)

(ii) **Concentrates** The concentrates used in feed of cattle and bufaloes are a mixture of substances which are rich in one or more of the nutrients, *e.g.*, cotton seeds, oil seeds, grains of maize, oats, barley jowar, bajra, gram as well as their byproducts such as wheat bran, rice bran (polish), gram husk, oil seed cakes and molasses.

1. Green fodder and dry grasses (roughage) = 15 to 20 kg
2. Grain mixture (concentrates) = 4 to 5 kg
3. Water 30 to 35 litres.

Besides above mentioned nutritious food material, dairy animals require certain additive feed to promote the growth of the animals which contain **antibiotics, minerals**, and **hormones**. They facilitate good yield of milk and protect them from diseases.

Q. 46 What would happen if poultry birds are larger in size and have no summer adaptation capacity? In order to get small sized poultry birds, having summer in adaptibility, what method will be employed?

Ans. If poultry birds are large in size, it will become very difficult to manage them during summers. Some difficulties include.
Larger birds have a larger surface area of body which will make it difficult for the birds to maintain their body temperature. This will lead to decline in egg production.
To get small sized poultry birds with summer adceptibility following method can be employed.

(i) Introduction of exotic breeds with desired qualities.
(ii) Cross breeding of poultry birds with high heat tolerance and smaller sizes.
(iii) small size is also needed for better housing and low feed.

Q.47 Suggest some preventive measures for the diseases of poultry birds.

Thinking Process The poultry birds suffers from various diseases caused by viruses (like flu, dermatitis, fowl pox, ranikhet disease) bacteria (tuberculosis, chlolera diarrhoea) fungi (aspergillosis) and parasites (worms, mites lice) etc
These diseases reduces the bird growth decrease egg production, decrease fertility and may even cause death.

Ans. Some of the preventive measures for poultry bird diseases are

(i) Proper hygiene and cleanliness of the poultry form to prevent infections.
(ii) Regular disinfections of poultry houses, equipments and tools.
(iii) Providing regular vaccinations to poultry birds against diseases.
(iv) Proper ventilation in poultry houses to maintain healthy air quality and prevent respiratory diseases.
(v) Providing proper nutrition and a balanced diet to the birds to boost their immunity.
(vi) Selection of disease free and healthy breeds.

Q. 48 Figure shows the two crop fields [Plots A and B] have been treated by manures and chemical fertilisers respectively, keeping other environmental factors same. Observe the graph and answer the following questions.

(i) Why does plot B show sudden increase and then gradual decrease in yield?
(ii) Why is the highest peak in plot A graph slightly delayed ?
(iii) What is the reason for the different pattern of the two graphs?

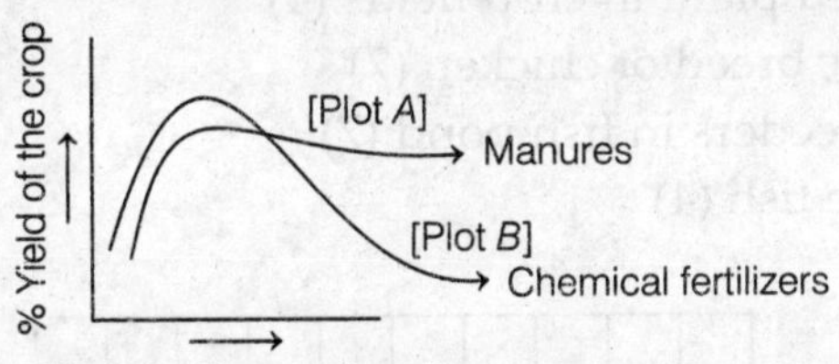

Ans. (i) Plot *B* refers to the use of chemical fertilisers which gives short-term benefits because they are nutrient specific (release of N,P,K nutrients in soil). The continuous use of fertilisers in an area decreases soil fertility so there is gradual decrease in yield after sometime.

(ii) Manures have large quantity of organic matter and comparatively small amount of nutrients. Hence, addition of manures enriches the soil with nutrients slowly and increases the decreases soil fertility continuously. Consequently by the addition of manures the rise in the peak in plot A is slightly lower than that of the plot B and it is also delayed.

(iii) Manures are the natural ways of enriching the soil whereas fertilisers are commercially produced plant nutrients. They do not have organic matter like in manure to replenish the soil with useful microbes. Therefore, in plot A manures give high yield while plot *B* gives high yield for a short time and then it decreases.

Q. 49 Complete the crossword puzzle figure.

		10							
	1			2			6		
8									7
				3		4			
9									
		5							

Across

1. Oil yielding plant (9)
3. Crop grown in winter season (4)
5. Fixed by *Rhizobium* (8)
9. Common honey bee (4)

Downward

2. Animal feed (6)
4. A micronutrient (5)
6. Unwanted plant in crop fields (4)
7. An exotic breed of chicken (7)
8. Bottom feeders in fish pond (7)
10. A marine fish (4)

Ans.

		T[10]							
	[1]S	U	N	[2]F	L	O	[6]W	E	R
		N		O			E		
[8]M		A		D			E		L[7]
R				D			D		E
I				E					G
G				[3]R	A	B[4]	I		H
[9]A	P	I	S			O			O
L						R			R
S		[5]N	I	T	R	O	G	E	N
						N			